The Durrell

THE DURRELL-MILLER LETTERS 1935-80

Edited by Ian S. MacNiven

A NEW DIRECTIONS BOOK

Published in cooperation with Faber and Faber Limited, London, in
association with Michael Haag Limited, London, and manufactured
in Great Britain
First published clothbound by New Directions in 1988
First Published as New Directions Paperbook 1095 in 2007
Library of Congress Cataloging-in-Publication Data

Durrell, Lawrence.
    The Durrell-Miller letters, 1935–1980.
    (A New Directions Book)
    "Published in cooperation with Faber & Faber
Limited, London" – T.p. verso.
    1. Durrell, Lawrence – Correspondence.   2. Miller,
Henry, 1891–1980 – Correspondence.   3. Authors,
English – 20th century – Correspondence.   4. Authors,
American – 20th century – Correspondence.   1. Miller,
Henry, 1891–1980.   II. MacNiven, Ian S.   III. Title.
PR6007.U76Z485   1988   828'.91209 [B]   88-9847

ISBN 978-0-8112-1730-9

New Directions Books are published for James Laughlin
by New Directions Publishing Corporation,
80 Eighth Avenue, New York 10011

Contents

List of illustrations

Preface

There are more letters being written today than ever before in the history of man. I daresay the Royal Mail in this country, the PTT in France, and the United States Post Office are annually handling billions of letters. But how many specimens of genuine epistolary worth can be found in this veritable Everest of mail? Perhaps an infinitesimally small handful. Trying to pick them out is like looking for a few earmarked snowflakes in an Alpine avalanche. The present carefully selected correspondence between Henry Miller and Lawrence Durrell belongs to that infinitesimal handful.

What about the correspondence between Miller and Durrell? First let me talk a little about the correspondents – Henry and Larry. My friendship with Henry, now dead although not for me, dates from the first day we met, which was in the rue Delambre more than half a century ago. Larry appeared on the scene a few years later, in 1937 if I can rely on my dwindling memory. As with Henry, the enduring friendship that unites us was sealed on the first day of our meeting.

My friendship with Henry Miller was based less on an identity of mind than an identity of temperament. For over ten years we saw each other nearly every day. For two or three years we even shared a flat in Clichy, a rather leftish-oriented suburb of Paris, where Céline also had his boutique of medical surgery. Every morning we met at breakfast we had something to laugh about. Our long friendship was impregnated with laughter and irrepressible gaiety. We were always gay, even when we didn't have the price of a bottle of wine between us. Joyous, buoyant, light-hearted and gay are the adjectives that best describe our life together. I thought it inconceivable that that special brand of gaiety that bound us together could ever be enhanced.

And yet, the inconceivable happened! It coincided with the arrival of

Lawrence Durrell in Paris. That was a veritable event. Larry had been in correspondence with Henry ever since a copy of *Tropic of Cancer* had fallen into his hands. His early letters were infused with admiration for his American *confrère*. He felt drawn to him like a chela to his guru, but at their first meeting the chela–guru relationship came to an abrupt end. Or, to be more precise, they came to be, turn by turn, both chela and guru. The relationship was interchangeable. Larry's brilliant conversation, his sense of humour and sparkling wit made blood brothers of the two at first sight.

I was lucky enough to be present on the very day Larry showed up in Villa Seurat. I described this meeting years ago in *My Friend Lawrence Durrell*:

> ... I climbed up the stairs to Henry's studio, and there was—
>
> Lawrence Durrell, fresh from Corfu, with the Ionian tan still on his face and hands. Of him, I first perceived the laughter, which kept reverberating through the high-ceilinged studio: an almost continuous laughter, loud and persistent: from the guts. He and Henry were gay. They were having a party that must have been going on for the better part of the day, and which was to go on, intermittently, for over a year. The place was littered with bottles and glasses, books, remnants of food and manuscript pages, the smoke of their cigarettes spiralling up to the ceiling, curling along the ceiling, like clouds of incense.

No introduction was needed, we were on Christian name terms before we actually started talking. But when the talk began it never ended and is now prolonged in the present volume of letters exchanged between the two protagonists. Larry was just a boy compared to Henry, who was already approaching middle age, and yet the two were on the same wavelength, so to speak; from the moment of Larry's entry into Villa Seurat our gaiety reached a new high that cannot be expressed in figures like the Dow Jones averages. There was war in the offing – we laughed it off. Larry was good at laughing; he laughed so loudly that he was sometimes turned out of a cinema. Something about his temperament aroused immediate partisanship between us. We promptly became partisans, partisans in laughter.

The letters you are about to read have lost none of their pristine freshness, originality, humour and wit. This is true for the whole of the correspondence, covering nearly half a century.

Alfred Perlès
Wells, England
1988

Introduction

Miller and Durrell began life a generation and a world apart. Born on 26 December 1891 to an impoverished German-descended tailor, Henry Valentine Miller grew up in Brooklyn ('Orpheus in Brooklyn', in Bertrand Mathieu's phrase) and worked in New York City at countless menial jobs until he fled America and his alimony payments during 1928 to live and write in Paris. Lawrence George Durrell was born in Jullundur, India, on 27 February 1912 into a family with colonial roots in the civil service. At eleven he was sent to England for further schooling, destined, so his engineer father hoped, for a solid career in the land of his birth. By the time he was eighteen Durrell had asserted his independence by steadfastly refusing to study subjects he disliked or to pass university entrance examinations: he wanted to become a writer! Early in 1935 he decoyed his widowed mother to Corfu and soon he initiated the correspondence with Miller in Paris.

The early meetings between Durrell and Miller occurred from 1937 through 1939, when the Second World War drove Miller back to the USA and Durrell, a year and a half later, to Egypt. Thereafter, Durrell lived as close as he could manage to the Mediterranean – the one exception was the year he spent being miserable in Argentina – while Miller established himself in California, first at Big Sur, later in Pacific Palisades near Los Angeles. Reunions were infrequent but the friendship flourished by post.

We are lucky in the preservation of such an extensive collection of correspondence. Both principals took great risks, and suffered more than their share of those disasters of war and personal upheavals which separate many of us from our files. Miller stored a trunk of his belongings in Paris during the Second World War, and got almost everything back after the Liberation. Durrell left most of his effects on Corfu when he fled Kalamata three days ahead of the German tanks and learned years later that Axis soldiers had used his manuscripts and letters for lighting fires. Fortunately, when he was lightening his kit for possible flight, he had sent those documents he valued most, including his file of Paris letters from Miller, to his friend Alan G. Thomas in Bournemouth, and Thomas, with the meticulous habits of an antiquarian bookseller, had faithfully preserved them in his loft. Some letters disappeared during Durrell's wartime shifts, and Miller was able to save little during his 1940–1 travels around the USA while he was gathering impressions for *The Air-Conditioned Nightmare*. Three of Durrell's letters to Miller, written while Durrell was living in Greece under the threat of Italian bombing raids and German invasion, were long thought lost. These turned up recently in a California book-dealer's catalogue and are included in this collection through the courtesy of Southern Illinois University at Carbondale.

One factor favoured the survival of the letters: both writers sensed at the outset that they were engaged in a significant enchange, and each made considerable efforts to save the other's letters. This conviction that the correspondence was in itself important led Durrell and Miller to take extra pains in the writing of the letters, so that even the prodigious and almost pathological letter-writer Miller – who estimated that by the 1970s he had written between 100,000 and 200,000 of them – wrote not merely prosaic communications to Durrell but crafted essays, keeping carbons of those he thought most worthwhile. These pages are, then, more than the raw material of biography: they are the testing ground for ideas, the refined thoughts of men writing to complementary spirits, at times almost *alter egos*.

When *Lawrence Durrell–Henry Miller: A Private Correspondence* was published in 1963 it was justly acclaimed as a spirited exchange between two geniuses. But it was to be only slightly over half the exchange chronologically (the last letter in the book is dated 31 October 1959). Miller survived, against all medical odds, until June 1980, and he and Durrell remained in frequent contact. Miller's last letter, printed in full in this volume, was dictated only weeks before his death. The correspondence began in 1935, when Durrell was a worldly twenty-three and Miller a boyish forty-three. It continued, virtually unabated, through Durrell's sixty-eighth year and Miller's eighty-eighth. What we have, therefore, is an intellectual and personal record of both men throughout a good part of their creative lives.

To avoid giving offence, many passages were omitted from the letters included in the 1963 edition of the correspondence, and most of these omissions can now be restored. Every effort has been made to publish genuinely important material and to print, whenever space permitted, the complete texts of letters. The reader should understand that what is given in the present book is a distillation: 210,000 words out of a million-word correspondence. Many of the excised letters and passages involve merely topical references and discussion of subsequently aborted projects. The researcher into minutiae is directed to the special collections of Southern Illinois University, UCLA, and the other repositories. Readers should approach this record as a double life in letters: Lawrence Durrell as he presented himself to Henry Miller, and vice versa. It has all the candour of an eavesdropped conversation between intimates.

Editorial apparatus has been kept to a minimum to preserve as much as possible the spontaneous nature of this 'conversation'. The letterhead information is reproduced as found, which means that many of Miller's dates must be read following the American convention: thus, 5/2/53 means 2 May 1953. I have supplied within square brackets conjectural readings for letterhead places and dates, have given family names on the first appearances of some individuals, and have appended a few endnotes to letters where an explanation would aid understanding. Most supplied dates are based on postmarks or internal information; the most questionable are preceded by '*c.*' (circa). Authorial annotations and emendations are set within angle brackets: <. . .>. The punctuation, particularly Durrell's, is often idiosyncratic. Aside from silently correcting obvious typographical errors and mistakes, I have chosen to follow each writer's capitalization, punctuation and spelling. Thus, the reader will find predominantly British practice for Durrell, American for Miller.

It is time that the full chronological sweep of the Durrell–Miller correspondence be seen. Miller has been dead for eight years, and a revaluation of his place in American and indeed in world literature is due. Durrell, seventy-six at the time of writing, has recently completed *The Avignon Quintet*, his longest sustained effort in fiction, and his readers should have the opportunity of examining the friendship that, more than any other, encouraged and informed his art and Miller's as well. Most important, this exchange, valuable in itself, should turn the reader back to the major writings of both men.

Ian S. MacNiven
New York
February 1988

First Contact

As Lawrence Durrell likes to tell it, he first came across *Tropic of Cancer* discarded, presumably by a disgusted or shocked American tourist, in a public toilet on Corfu. The account he gave Henry Miller is that a common friend, Barclay Hudson, had tossed *Tropic* in his direction during one of their literary discussions on the Greek island during mid-1935. Those who enter Durrell's world soon discover the meaning of 'heraldic': the visible phenomena of the world are not stable, but take on mantic significance, coloured by contexts, emotions, language. The discovery of the first *Tropic* by Durrell was in fact an heraldic event: neither he nor Henry was ever to be the same thereafter.

Until 1935 neither Durrell nor Miller had achieved, at least in public, anything approaching heraldic stature. If they existed for anyone beyond their immediate families and circles of friends, it was as promissory notes or question marks on the pages of literary history. True, Miller had been spinning like a dervish for nearly forty-four years, collecting that vast catalogue of failures and emotional disasters which would eventually surface as his life's work, and had turned his studio at 18 Villa Seurat into a virtual sweatshop of literature. Durrell had only published a booklet of competent but derivative poems, *Quaint Fragment*, and *Bromo Bombastes*, a satire on the formidable G. B. Shaw, prudently signed with the pseudonym 'Gaffer Peeslake'.

Durrell and Miller had both found models – Durrell had discovered the Elizabethans and had met the London poet, bibliophile and bohemian John Gawsworth, while Miller had laid claim to an array of heroes from Knut Hamsun to Walt Whitman. And both could muster a crew of supporters. Durrell had the friendship of antiquarian bookseller Alan G. Thomas and actor Peter Bull, while Miller's cohorts included some impressive names – Herbert Read, Count Keyserling – and he had acquired in Anaïs Nin and Alfred Perlès literary allies who would be loyal to him throughout his life. But neither Durrell nor Miller had found exactly that colleague of complementary affinities who could be at once mirror and rebounding surface for his art. When Durrell wrote his first letter to Miller – 'Tropic turns the corner into a new life which has regained its bowels' – the American realized he had hooked his ideal reader and replied, 'You're the first Britisher who's written me an intelligent letter about the book.'

*C/o The British Consul, Villa Agazini, Perama, Corfu   [August 1935]

Dear Mr. Miller:

I have just read Tropic of Cancer again and feel I'd like to write you a line about it. It strikes me as being the only really man-size piece of work which this century can really boast of. It's a howling triumph from the word go; and not only is it a literary and artistic smack on the bell for everyone, but it really gets down on paper the blood and bowels of our time. I have never read anything like it. I did not imagine anything like it could be written; and yet, curiously, reading it I seemed to recognise it as something which I knew we were all ready for. The space was all cleared for it. Tropic turns the corner into a new life which has regained its bowels. In the face of it eulogy becomes platitude; so for Godsake don't blame me if this sounds like the bleat of an antique reviewer, or a cold-cream ad. God knows, I weigh the words as well as I am able, but the damn book has rocked the scales like a quake and muddled up all my normal weights and measures. I love its guts. I love to see the canons of oblique and pretty emotion mopped up; to see every whim-wham and bagatelle of your contemporaries from Eliot to Joyce dunged under. God give us young men the guts to plant the daisies on top and finish the job.

Tropic is something they've been trying to do since the war. It's the final copy of all those feeble, smudgy rough drafts – Chatterley, Ulysses, Tarr etc. It not only goes back, but (which none of them have done) goes forward as well.

It finds the way out of the latrines at last. Funny that no one should have thought of slipping out via the pan during a flush, instead of crowding the door. I salute Tropic as the copy-book for my generation. It's man-size, and goes straight up among those books (and they are precious few) which men have built out of their own guts. God save me, that sounds pompous, but what can one say? Perish the Rahuists! Skoal to the stanchless flux!

Yours Sincerely,
Lawrence Durrell

Rahu, a tribal god in northern India, is supposed to become incarnate in priests who then walk on hot embers and cure diseases and barrenness. Perhaps Durrell sees them as hidebound traditionalists.

*18 Villa Seurat, Paris (xiv)   Sept. 1st, 1935

Dear Mr. Durrell:

Your letter rocks me a bit too. You're the first Britisher who's written me an intelligent letter about the book. For that matter, you're the first anybody who's hit the nail on the head. I particularly prize your letter because it's the kind of letter I would have written myself had I not been the author of the book. That isn't just sheer vanity and egotism, believe me. It's curious how few people know *what* to admire in the book.

The phrase that struck me particularly, in your letter, was – "I seem to recognize it as something we were all ready for." That's just it. The world *is* ready for something different, something new, but it seems that it requires a war or some colossal calamity to make people realize it.

Your letter is so vivid, so keen, that I am curious to know if you are not a writer yourself. How did you come by the book – through Barclay Hudson?

I don't know if I read your name correctly – Durrell or Duvvell?

Cordially yours,
Henry Miller

*C/o Ionian Bank, Corfu, Greece   [September? 1935]

Dear Mr. Miller:

Thank you for the letter which I got yesterday when the boat went to town. I was pleased. Yes, it was Barclay Hudson all right who gave me *Tropic* to read. His hot gospel work will be putting the book into a new edition before long. He and Jane, his wife, live in the old Venetian

3

house up the hill from us. We eat together, bathe together, and have a number of good times. Barclay read me bits from a letter you wrote him, and I am as glad as hell that those sons of bitches in literary England are rallying to the standards already. They keep up such a whine for great men that one almost expects them to ignore them when they do show up. I bet the book makes every writer in England and America feel a sort of cheese-mite. Every writer with a sense of conscience, that is. I wish D.H. Lawrence were alive to give a great bloody whoop of joy over it.

I suppose you can imagine how flattering your curiosity was? Yes, a writer, save the mark. Vague premonitions of facility, mediocrity, and, perhaps later, prosperity. When I read *Tropic* I wished to hell I was an established literary gent so that I could do a fat essay on it. Alas!

I was surprised at people going for the "Elizabethan prose" in the book. That sounded crooked to me. The Elizabethans had all the balls, but none of the freedom from literary canons of style which was necessary to write the *Tropic* of their age. Literary sauria, somehow, weighed down by the grand manner. Ben Jonson would have said you lack'd art, or some such damn silly thing. I have a curious feeling that the one man who would have acknowledged *Tropic* as something he was trying to write in his own age, and his own style, is François Villon. But as I read French with difficulty, and whenever possible with a literal English text, I'm not really fit to judge. But I get the same feeling from him. It's rather curious. A state of being beyond damage somehow. A bright, hard immunity to life. However, this is all rather presumptuous.

For the time being I can get news of your activities from Barclay; but to our sorrow they will be going south when the weather breaks. I would be very grateful if you could give your publisher my name and address and tell him to keep me in touch with everything you write.

Yours sincerely,
Lawrence Durrell

Dear Lawrence Durrell:

Well, I thought you were a writer! Why don't you send me something
of yours so that I can return some of the audacious compliments you
pay me? I had a letter from Barclay Hudson just the other day and if
you see him soon please thank him for the subscriptions he enclosed.
The letter – *Aller Retour New York* should be out this week some time
and his copies will be forwarded immediately. You might also say
that I ran across his friends the Nixons last night and had quite a
conversation with them in a café. Also had a big blow-out at Roberts'
place – he and his wife seem like damned swell people. Anyhow I'm
writing Barclay Hudson in a few days – just now frightfully harassed
with work. It's only in the last two months that the book has gotten
properly under weigh – and the result is a steady stream of letters and
visitors and invitations and what not – which is beginning to bore the
shit out of me, though at first it seemed wonderful. This doesn't apply
to you people – I'm talking about the regular shits who come down
on you like a ton of bricks and clog the drains. I guess you know what
I mean!

To answer a remark of yours in the letter – curious thing is that in
the review by Montgomery Belgion (last issue of *Criterion*) I come
under the French Chronicle and am tagged with a guy named Fer-
nandez, author of *Les Violents*. I think it was a rather weak, silly
review, and much beside the mark. Would like to have your opinion,
should you ever see it. I am rather intrigued by your reference to
Villon, the Elizabethans, etc. It seems that my book was turned down
(for translation) by the N.R.F., not because of the obscenity, but on
"literary" grounds! You're absolutely right about it lacking "Art".
But that's what makes "art". I wish I had the time to explain more
fully. I'm going into some detail about this question in my work on
D.H. Lawrence – which again will be lacking as a "critical" work. I'm
talking about a new attitude towards art which the writer needs to-day.
I think this is revealed even better by my second book – *Black Spring* –
which breaks all the canons, and which I myself like much better than
Tropic, though few will agree with me perhaps. (The Obelisk Press
may put this out some time this Winter – it seems quite definite.)

Meanwhile there's a guy named Cyril Connolly wants to meet me
and write a review of *Tropic* for *The New Statesman*. I don't

understand it. If they understood what I'm driving at I don't think they would want very much to review my book. I think they're all fog-eyed . . . .

Well, more later. Keep in touch with me, as I say, and let's see some of *your* stuff. And regards to the Hudsons.

Cordially yours,
Henry Miller

N.R.F.: *Nouvelle Revue Française.*

Dear Lawrence Durrell:
Your letters take a hell of a while to reach here. Your last one arrived a few days ago and I want you to know that I am far from being bored and hope you will continue to keep in touch with me. It may interest you to know that I regard your letters about *Tropic* and Barclay's as the best testimonials received thus far (barring the letter and review of Blaise Cendrars which I esteem because of its downright humanness!). You guys got right down into the sub-cellar. Naturally I don't expect too much of the critics, especially the *English* critics – and still less, to be sure, of the *American* critics. All the more reason, therefore, that your reviews should see the light. But how? I really wish you would make an effort, between you, to get something in somewhere – something with dynamite in it. And don't just praise the shit out of me! Keep to that general line about the fundamental purpose of the book, about its significance in connection with the usual drift-wood. That's the best note. Barclay's idea of destroying the "comparative" method I like extremely. It's just what I believe myself – and of course, it's almost impossible ever to obtain from the critics, because their primary function is to display their erudition, or their book-tasting acquirements.

Anyway, here's what I plan to do myself about it. I am going to make a reprint, at my own expense, of all the important letters and reviews (some of the letters are knock-outs – and come, as you might well expect, from obscure sources, mais tant mieux!). I will send this brochure out to every fucking magazine, revue, and newspaper in the world of any consequence – particularly to "foreign" organs, particularly to the Orient and to South America. It's a colossal job and is

6

going to cost me a pretty penny – and for the moment I don't even know where the dough is going to come from – but I'll do it nevertheless. I am thoroughly disgusted with the general inertia. *Action at any cost!* that's my motto.

I had to wait over two years for the publication of *Tropic* and when it appeared I had damned well lost all interest in it, as a book. I am waiting now almost a year for something to be done about *Black Spring*. I have a contract and a promise – but if the world situation gets worse I know my publisher will fuck me up on it. (In which case it will devolve upon me to do it myself.)

But the brochure, with its reprints, may have the advantage of securing me a little publicity, whether favorable or unfavorable I don't care. I won't have the book die in its second printing! And I'll make it damned clear, that in spite of its value, it is almost unobtainable. Let those who are interested in this sort of phenomenon do something about it then!

The "World of Lawrence" is going along slowly. I am doing too many things to make much headway with it. Probably I told you already that I have begun, in collaboration with Perlès and Fraenkel, a thousand page book to be called *Hamlet*. This will definitely be published by the Carrefour Press, in Belgium, as my collaborator, Fraenkel, *is* Carrefour! He also plans to bring out shortly a volume of Three Essays by three Americans – himself, Walter Lowenfels and myself. This book we can sell anywhere: it's a serious work about our ideology – about the "spiritual weather", I might say.

I am also going ahead with the publication of Siana Series Nos. 2 & 3 which will appear simultaneously. No. 2 is the *Scenario* I may have told you about before. These will be limited editions, *assez cher*, for subscribers only.

Was introduced to Jonathan Cape by my publisher the other day – and found him an idiotic old fart of the worst sort. Practically walked out on him. My publisher thought he could interest Cape in a volume of short stories from my hand – but one look at that old blowser and I knew it was useless.

There was another review of *Tropic* recently in *The New English Weekly* (Nov. 14th) – by George Orwell. Talks about "the vilification of human nature" (sic!). Oh well . . . . . .

I hope you still see Barclay and that you will show him this letter. I am rather expecting him to come to Paris. Hope he does – we can surely find a suitable place for him. If you birds decide to write anything, whether separately or jointly, and if you want to send a carbon of the review to America I give you herewith the address of an enterprising young man at Harvard who will certainly bestir himself about it. James Laughlin IV, Eliot House, E–31, Cambridge, Mass. Laughlin is the chap who tried to reprint my *Aller Retour New York* (under the title "Glittering Pie"). He had the first ten pages published in the Harvard *Advocate* and then the Boston police descended upon the paper, destroyed the existent copies and locked up the editorial staff over night, threatening them with a severe jail sentence. Mine wasn't the only offending contribution. Seems a story by Laughlin himself was also responsible for the mess. Anyway it's all blown over sweetly and the boys have promised "to behave". Laughlin is now co-editor, with Gorham Munson, of a magazine called *The New Democracy*, headquarters in New York. You can write him directly, if you choose. He's a good egg. (And he has connections!)

Well, that's about enough for the present. Why don't you tell me the name of your novel which I understand is to appear shortly? I certainly want to read it.

Cordially yours,
HVM.

Alfred Perlès is referred to in the correspondence variously as Fred, Alf, Joe or Joey – the last a name Miller and Perlès applied indiscriminately to one another.

The Siana Series was a publishing venture underwritten by Anaïs Nin and controlled by Miller. The name is 'Anais' spelled backwards.

Durrell's first novel, *Pied Piper of Lovers* (London, Cassell, 1935) appeared on 17 October. His second, *Panic Spring*, was published under the pseudonym 'Charles Norden' by Faber and Faber in 1937.

*C/O IONIAN BANK, CORFU   [early 1936]

Dear Henry Miller:
What news? Why no news, except local news, and god knows what with wars and the yapping of dictators, it's comforting enough. A week of hellish storms. Two children struck by lightning and burnt to toffee. A tree stripped. The olives safely gathered. From that horrid world outside nothing except a statement from a publisher showing heavy losses, and a raving postcard from New York asking for news. A new and facile novel being castrated by the big-wigs. First they agreed

to let the word fuck stay in if it went thus: & f—k: then f—: now the libraries might get touchy so they want —. Or something milder. What with feeling ashamed and angry with myself for writing cheaply, and knowing the book isn't worth a — either way, I don't know what to do. It's so disheartening when you sweat and sweat and sweat and then something sheerly puerile comes on the paper. As *Tropic* is your first book, you can't know that feeling. Myself I am going to take to carpentry or something soothing where facility and a fine smell of glue are all one need worry about. And when you're finished for the day you just wipe your hands magnificently in a fistful of shavings and let it go at that.

This book business is a washout. I see that a twenty-four year old reviewer – one of these horn-rimmed advanced birds – has just written a filthy attack on Lawrence. I don't know why it should hurt so much to see the swine trample on him. Thus: "And there the poor little wretch sat, half-tight and consumptive as hell, cursing them for not following him." I've written a letter so angry and so rhetorical to his paper, *Time & Tide*, that the editor wrote back thanking me for it, and saying it would be bad taste to print it. So now I'm depressed coz I have no copy of the letter to print [with?] my collected poems. I suppose one has to get tough enough to stand the racket, but it does make me wince. And that slimy little Jesus, Middleton Murry, croaking among the marshes. The same's going to happen to my poor *Tropic*. I beg your pardon, your *Tropic*. Several times I've sat down to try and write a little thing on it, and each time I give up. First I'm afraid of misinterpreting it: and second I know that [there] will be a powerful faction sitting in judgement against it. Thirdly of course that no one will print the fruit of my brain. Fourthly I wonder whether I really appreciate it. Not with my mind, I mean. But sort of corroborate it with myself. The me. Sounds queer but no matter. Yes, Pat Evans is on its trail among others in Oxford. Again my hopes will be dashed. People don't seem to *feel* it, even if they agree intellectually and all that crap . . . I suppose though young men without much experience can't be expected to get at it. God damn my loftiness, they're mostly all about my age. Perhaps then I'm a precocious exception. That's a nice thought. Yes, let's say that provisionally. O by the way, you haven't put me on your black books, have you? No *Aller Retour* turned up, though Barclay swore he was mailing me one from Paris. And I wait patiently with my hands in my lap for *Black Spring*. And the *Hamlet*. Believe me I am so furious that people haven't simply burst in on your privacy and carried you off to found American literature at home: as it is I suppose you've burst in on theirs. Agents and people have been very ladylike since my enthusiastic letters telling them to go over to Paris and buy every stitch of MS in your Villa Seurat. And of course the would-be great ones will pat you on the head and try to keep you down as much as possible, for fear of their own mediocrity. I do hate them for their lack of generosity as well as for their deadness. Still, it must have cost Eliot a lot of agony wondering whether to sanction certain pages of *Tropic*. Maybe this is spite, but I can just see him (I've never seen him). Wondering whether to admit the book and get ticked off by the catholic arch-pontiff in Lambeth, or to ignore it and sacrifice his reputation as a great critic of discernment. My wife and I had great fun. When the storm was on and we could hardly think, and the thunder walked with great thumps up and down the house, we sat on the floor, had the window locked, and thought of all the great critics and their thoughts and public utterances when *Tropic* appeared. Middleton Murry, Eliot, Leavis etc.

We miss Barclay very much. We used to quarrel so dreadfully about his beastly science and statistics that I miss the quietness now. And the gramophone's bust, and Beethoven rots in the cupboard. But today comes a whole pile of magazines and papers with your card. What a blessing journalism is after all. I take back my lofty trumpetings.

Have you printed your collection of letters yet? Is there any advance as yet – I always imagine that book scorching through apathy like a hot knife in butter. But then I always get excited and enthusiastic about things and blind myself to the obvious consequences. In a month or two I am going to buy another copy and send it to the Bishop of London. He is the biggest shit in England: and once a quarter I send him a little abusive postcard from down here. It sort of helps me to keep going, abusing him at intervals. At present the big stiff is trying to lessen immorality on the stage, and get a law passed for the lengthening of chorus girls' practice knickers. Photos in every paper of the dear Bishop surrounded by another chorus. I think he ought to get you a wide Sunday paper public if nothing else. He and James Douglas first made the public conscious of Lawrence. A couple of grade A shits. They know not what they do, but are useful indirectly.

I was sorry I couldn't send Alf any money. I'd have liked to. I'm not absolutely starving. But we spend a good bit on clothes (and never seem to have any) and on paints and a few books to read. But if I get a fat advance on this new novel I might send in a little, on condition that he drinks the damnation of all scientific world-reformers, censors, philistines, queer-cuffins, and (the health I mean what else?) Rabelais, Villon, Shax and all those wise birds who didn't just write books but *were* books. At present any healths drunk down this way are strictly in sea-water.

Well, it seems I'm running to news after all. Never mind. We see so few people living up here in the stony north end of this island, that I take any chance I can to spread myself. ￭

A friend writes that *Tropic* "cheapens dirt". How long O god, how long. I lent it to a Britisher of the old flag-waving type here. He worried me like hell to read it. He's quite nice but thick in the attic. And all his words end in ah. Puzzled him did *Tropic*. It wasn't just smut as he'd hoped. He's read Cecil Barr in the same press and got the idea you were even hotter than *Daffodil*. It made him uncomfortable a bit as well as puzzled. Finally he blurted out: "I don't mind ah the fellah consorting with buggahs, and all that. But ah I do draw the line at him PINCHING things from whores ah."

But wait till you hear what the Bishop says. It'll give you an idea of what criticism can be. Please will you tell me if any of the following people showed any interest in *Tropic*. I think they're the men with real balls. Roy Campbell, Aldington, Wyndham Lewis. I hope they do some sort of thumping. They're the only people the children of light and the literary poor in spirit are really scared of coz they take such a high line in blasphemy, and are apt with their satire. Particularly Lewis, tho I don't like his positive work too much. I'm a bit frightened of it.

Please bear with my youthfulness and write me a short p.c. from time to time telling me what's going on in Paris. I've always wanted to be in on a movement of some kind, but I've never found the kind of writing and people I could whole-heartedly back. *Tropic* makes me feel great things are happening over there in Paris, and I want to lift my eyes unto the hills. I am slowly learning French so I can start reading it easily soon. I want to read *Sentiments limitrophes* etc but as yet am a babe in the language.

There's a faction of my old friends started a paper called *Janus* in London. I thought they might take an essay on you, but their first number showed me how wrong I was. They fairly lashed into my poor wretched sniveling 1st novel, so I see that they don't want me in on the little game. If you pass through London buy *Janus*, it's cheap and pretty

6d. But what crap what crap in the first number. If only I could find a backer I could write the whole first number of a paper myself and make a better show. But this is spite, because they took the dust out of my pants. And what is more I am angry that the book deserved it, so I can't retaliate. Brodzky is art editor, and seems to have some of Gaudier's stuff up his sleeve which they print attractively. But I am impatient of this endless parade of mere intellects. The war cry ringing across this bay from morn to night is: people with bowels and tripes and spirit. It sounds a little like St. John Ervine, but I can't help it. That's how I feel. Or St. John the Baptist perhaps.

When I said movement up above I didn't mean movement, but a sort of unharnessed free association of spirits. Not a sort of Marinettiesque parade. By the way, what is this schizophrenic age you've ushered in. I haven't noticed anything. Perhaps it was in the air. And what does it mean. I look about me with eager eyes but notice nothing.

If you see Barclay in New York will you give him my star-chiming greetings and tell him he's WRONG. UTTERLY WRONG. And I'll write him a letter big and fat with rhetoric in a few days to PROVE he's wrong.

But now I'm guilty a bit about this vast wad of paper. We toy from time to time with the idea of a paper here in the island, distributed in London Paris & New York. But the initial money question ("monetary motivations" EZ. Pound) hangs us up. Also a feeling of distrust among the potential writers coz we're all so different in taste and ideas. Some bright youth from England suggested a juvenile anthology, by some thirty young men, entitled MY FIRST FUCK. But the boredom of correcting the proofs and getting reader's eye over it: not to mention the eternal repetitions: prevents me from encouraging it. He wants it printed here and distributed in Paris & London. Nothing doing.

Well the sun's come up today and we're going to lie outside in pyjamas and eat lunch. Forgive this huge letter. There did seem to be some news after all. And don't swear and feel you've got to answer it or anything. But you're not likely to. And above all, if you ever do strike south Italy or Greece, do drop in on us and stay a while. I'd love to meet you, and hear about all the amazing things that people have said and done and thought and written about *Tropic*. It seems this is the age of wonders after all. Who is it talks of the decline of the west?

Yours Sincerely,
Lawrence Durrell

Tropic of Cancer was indeed Miller's first published novel, but he was very familiar with failed attempts: previously he had written, among other works, 'Clipped Wings', 'Moloch', and 'Crazy Cock', manuscripts that he knew were not very good, and that were rejected by publishers.

Miller had sent a copy of *Tropic of Cancer* to Eliot who replied that it 'seems to me a very remarkable book . . . . Without drawing any general comparisons, your own book is a great deal better both in depth of insight and of course in the actual writing than *Lady Chatterley's Lover.*' When Miller requested permission to quote, Eliot qualified his comments to one sentence, omitting the Lawrence comparison and terming *Cancer* 'a very remarkable book . . . a rather magnificent piece of work'.

Miller had sent Durrell and many others copies of his pamphlet *What Are You Going to Do About Alf?* (1935), ostensibly a plea to fund Perlès so he could write, but in fact an exposé on the plight of the artist. The few contributions received went into the operating expenses of 18 Villa Seurat.

Jack Kahane, owner of the Obelisk Press, wrote (and published) *Daffodil* under the pseudonym 'Cecil Barr'. In 1938 he was to bring out Durrell's *Black Book*.

Henri Gaudier-Brzeska, sculptor and friend of Horace Brodzky, Wyndham Lewis and Ezra Pound, was killed during 1915 while serving in the French army.

F. T. Marinetti: Italian author of the 'Futurist Manifesto' and passionate crusader for modernism.

*Barbizon Plaza Hotel, Central Park South,
New York   March 3rd [1936]

Dear Durrell –

Your card just reached me here via Paris. I had dropped you a card myself only a day or two before getting yours.

No, there's nothing on the Obelisk list that I could truly recommend. Neagoe is feeble shit. I know him – he doesn't even write his own books (*entre nous*). My friend Fraenkel, for whose new book (*Bastard Death*, to be out any day now) I wrote a long prefatory letter, would like me to have you buy a copy of his book – but I can't be sure you'd relish it and I wouldn't want you to be disappointed.

If you read French, as I suppose you do, I'd recommend Fred Perlès' book (*Sentiments limitrophes*) and one by Henri Calet called *La Belle Lurette* (N.R.F.) and Francis Carco's latest – *Brumes*. I can't think of anything truly important at the moment. (Myself I'm just about to read Augustine's *City of God*.)

About the Obelisk Press – don't have any illusions. I don't know how long my relations will last with Kahane. I rather feel like doing it all myself. I'm sick of dealing with publishers and agents – and I'll never make a cent anyway. Barclay & Jane are here and we've met. You probably are hearing from them. I'm clearing out about the end of March – back to the Villa Seurat – #18. So write me there, won't you?

Had a *long* letter from Patrick Evans. Yes, I guess Oxford's gonna hear about the book at last. Thanks for doing so much. Is the review impossible to get printed anywhere? Am going up to Harvard very soon to see the "boys". More anon. Greetings. HVM.

P.S. Give me all the good names you can for my list – I'll have a little dough on returning & things are going to happen.

P.P.S. About that symposium – are you in earnest or are you just kidding me?

*18 Villa Seurat, Paris (xiv)   Tuesday [*c.* June 1936]

Dear Lawrence Durrell:

Got your two letters and the poems in short succession. Am returning the poems herewith, having made carbon copies for myself. Think they are splendid, though the fact is I know nothing about verse. However, I certainly prefer them to Eliot's or Fraenkel's verse. Have you a book of them? It seems to me they ought to be publishable. What you say about the new book sounds good to me – as though you had broken the ice at last. Perhaps it will be a sort of English Surréalisme, eh wot? I got somewhat surrealistic myself in *Black Spring*, as you will see. By the way, it ought to be out in about two weeks; have just handed in the second proofs. Yesterday Curtis Brown, the agents, notified my publisher that Cerf, of Random House, N.Y., was on his way over to Paris, to look up my book and Connolly's – to see if there was any possibility of doing an American edition. (I'm not pissing in my pants about it, however. I know these birds . . . .)

About Fred and the missing geniuses hereabouts. Listen, to be quite honest with you, I really don't know any geniuses at all. That Ibiza pamphlet, or letter, was a bit of a blague, intended solely to retrieve some dough – which it did not, generally speaking. Ibiza, me lad, is one of the Balearic islands, one of the least, but the cheapest, they say. Fraenkel is on his way there now, stopping off at Barcelona first.

As to why Fred writes French. Well, he's a Viennese, you know, and his mother was French and his father something else. When he came to Paris twelve years or so ago, he already spoke French fluently. Since then he has become thoroughly French and finds his own language clumsy – in fact, he's forgetting it rapidly. His English is a third language – I've seen him write some excellent things in English, but he can't push it far enough. It's too damned bad you will have to use a dictionary with his book. I should use one myself now and then, but I don't. Anyway, I believe you'll get the drift – there are a few fine salacious bits about some English cunts which will make your mouth water.

Was just invited to make a trip to Budapest – all expenses paid – but the guy is a homo and I thought it better to turn it down. Just the same it hurts. I know Budapest a bit, and like it. Like Vienna too. By the way, it's useless to quote Greek to me – I don't know a fucking word. I'm almost an illiterate, you know. No classics, except what was rammed down my throat at school – and that was quickly forgotten. But I envy you – that sail-boat! Sure, call it the *Van Norden* . . . why not? Some time, when we meet, I'll tell you all about him. He was a rum bird, and I only gave a profile, a line drawing, as it were.

HVM.

[P.S.] My regards to your wife – how do you call her, par exemple?
P.P.S. Father Eliot is in town. Gave a reading of his "poems" at Sylvia Beach's recently. Understand he is a total failure – as an individual. A sort of lean-faced Calvinist. Is that right?

The 'Ibiza pamphlet': *What Are You Going to Do About Alf?*
Van Norden appears in *Tropic of Cancer*, Durrell not only borrowed the name for his sailboat, but also published *Panic Spring* (1937) under the pseudonym 'Charles Norden'.

* 18 Villa Seurat, Paris (xiv)   [*c.* August 1936]

Dear Durrell:

Thanks a lot for the book which as yet I haven't had time to read – but I will soon. Your friend Evans hasn't shown up yet. I am looking forward to his visit and will give him a few copies of a little French revue called *Orbes* for you – something to while away the time with. [. . .] About *Capricorn*, that's a long way from being finished – maybe I'll have the first volume done the end of this year. There ought to be three. About Surréalisme. Maybe you're one yourself. I agree that the leaders of the movement are highly conscious and deliberate and that's of course destructive. But what constitutes Surréalisme is a permanent thing in art, more especially in literature. Swift was a good one, and so was Lewis Carroll, in my opinion – and Shakespeare too now and then.

And what about Rabelais? The French, because they are so lucid and so cerebral, sort of scare one off, but then the peculiar emphasis they give to it is inevitable, considering how rigorous and formal is their style of thought. In the films, the burlesque ones, the Americans achieve a pure and unadulterated Surréalisme now and then – always unconsciously. I hope some time to send you a few back numbers of the French reviews, so that you can judge for yourself. It's only an effort, at bottom, to return to the original vital source, which is in the solar plexus, or in the Unconscious, or in the stars, if you like. I have used the method here and there, when it came naturally and spontaneously. At least, I hope so. I don't start out by trying to be Surrealistic. Sometimes it comes at the beginning and sometimes at the end – it's always an effort to plough through, to say what can't or won't be said. Did I tell you of a book by an English Surréaliste, Hugh Sykes Davies? It's called *Petron*, and I recommend it to you fervidly, as a most excellent piece of work. If you don't like that then you don't like Surréalisme, that's all. And that's your privilege. But I think you will. Try and get hold of it – I don't own a copy, or I would lend you it.

The head of the Obelisk Press is Jack Kahane – 338 Rue St. Honoré (1), Paris. He knows of you through me. I'll tell you about him. He won't publish a thing unless it has a sensational quality, unless it might be banned in England or America. That's his strategy for the present. He is trying to hook up with the Albatross (*confidential*) and may succeed, whereupon he may change his policy. No use sending him a manuscript unless it is sure to be rejected by the English and Americans. He hasn't much taste either, I can tell you. My relationship with him is in the nature of a pure accident. The other two presses are out of commission. Beach still has the bookshop, but does no printing.

Queer that you mention Lao Tse. Some one just handed me the book the other day. I was up till four A.M. the other night discussing it with Perlès. And did we laugh! To me the Chinese humor is marvellous. I don't mean that I laughed *at* him, but *with* him. To my mind he was one of *the* very great guys. I wish there were more of it – it seems to be a very small testament. You know, I'm nuts about China. I always think that that is the place I will eventually wind up in. I *feel* like a Chinaman very often.

Listen, Durrell, don't despair yet. (Ne faut pas désespérer.) If you have the guts for it the thing to do is to go to the bitter end, in your writing, I mean. If you can possibly hold out, and I imagine you can, write only what you please. There is nothing else to do, unless you want to become famous. They will shit on you anyway, so have your say first. I'm not recommending obscenity necessarily. Each man has his own way of being himself and of saying it so ultimately that he can't be denied. Compromise is futile and unsatisfactory. You will always have a hundred readers and, if they have taste and discernment, what more can you ask? Even when you elect to be absolutely honest it is difficult. Expression seems such a natural, God-given thing – and yet it's not either. It's a lifelong struggle to find yourself. Think of Cézanne, Van Gogh, Gauguin, Lawrence. Think of Dostoievsky – or Titian, if you will. I like the autobiographical documents: they teach you more than anything. Well, enuf . . . . . Fred is grateful for the coming subscriptions and wants me to thank you. He is living across the way, like a prince – at NO. 7, Villa Seurat. HVM.

*[Corfu]   [c. August 1936]

Dear Miller: Come let us sit upon the ground and tell strange stories of the death of kings. Thanks for the pamphlet. Good old London. We're late, as usual, but for sheer doggedness you can't beat us. But where are the jaded dowagers of art who usually sit at the head of these chic movements? Ezra, answer. Nina Hamnett, answer, Vanessa Bell, speak up, Virginia Woolf, take that cigar out of your mouth and get busy. Come, Leonardo, an essay on the surreal. However, we have all the jaded failures of the second rank to back us up. Nash has been such a flop that he's decided to try a new racket. Rupert Lee has forsaken Taoism for thermometers. As for Henry Moore, he's just finding himself. But let me be serious. My first impression is yes, definitely yes. I have always wanted to be in with people, feel myself part of a band of people. It's chilly work sitting all by yourself in the dark. Good. Let's look at the manifestoes. Begins a political discussion. The artist's place in society. A definite lean leftward. Well, what's wrong with that? Nothing, provided politics are not going to be confused with art. I'm tired of political people. They have confused the inner struggle with the outer one. They want to bread-poultice a primary chancre. Politics is an art that deals in averages. Art is a man that deals in people. If the people are wrong then no system is foolproof enough to stop them cutting each other's throats. And the artist finds that the people are wrong. The driving force behind him is his self isolation, the dislocation of the societal instinct. Vide Lawrence, Gauguin, etc.

This manifesto would be a lot clearer if these brave young revolutionaries started by defining what they mean by art. To begin with they seem to mean Marx. They want art to become easier for the artist. Well, that won't affect the genius any, he always gets through. It will increase the ease of production for average art. A good thing perhaps. But they do not state that they are founding a trade union for artists, just like the Royal Academy. There is yet talk of art. Proceed. A definition of the word surrealism, please. There are some good remarks about it. Breton etc. Very true, but surely as ancient as Oedipus? Or am I wrong? Henry Miller wrote to me, "Swift was a good surrealist, so was Lewis Carroll." I believe firmly in the ideal of cementing reality with the dream, but I do not believe the rest of this stuff. That the artist must be a socialist for example. That he wants to transform the world (He wants to transform *men*). That he can work anyhow except alone.

Listen, Miller, what I feel about it is this. To have art you've first got to have a big personality, pass it through the social mincer, get it ready for misery. Art nowadays is going to be real art, as before the flood. IT IS GOING TO BE PROPHECY, in the biblical sense. What I propose to do, with all deadly solemnity, is to create my HERALDIC UNIVERSE quite alone. The foundation is being quietly laid. I AM SLOWLY BUT VERY CAREFULLY AND WITHOUT ANY CONSCIOUS THOUGHT DESTROYING TIME.

You never tell me what you think. I'm sure you can't be in with these people because they are so wretched and hopeless. Tell me what you think some time will you?

I am editing my poems for printing. My God, some of them are so natural and easy that no one will take any notice. I enclose a copy of my advance notice which I'll have printed. By the way, have you heard the Beethoven Violin Concerto? There's something of the same kind of terrifying pathology about the themes that there is in *Hamlet*. The fusion of the dream with reality that you like so much. But how disciplined by the person. How personal in fact. I think I don't know what I mean. I have a horrible feeling that I mean what you do, but don't express it very well. Tell me if you think this is, in the words of

Barclay, one hundred percent bullshit.

Yours sincerely,
Lawrence Durrell.

P.S. Fuck Herbert Read, don't you think, really, on the whole? I can't help feeling that quietly.
[P.P.S.] This is the beginning of a new poem. It makes you dizzy if you repeat it over and over.

IF I SAY WHAT I HONESTLY MEAN
IT IS ONLY BECAUSE
I HONESTLY MEAN WHAT I SAY.

[P.P.P.S.] I have discovered that the idea of duration is false. We have invented it as a philosophic jack-up to the idea of physical disintegration. THERE IS ONLY SPACE. A solid object has only three dimensions. Time, that old appendix, I've lopped off. So it needs a new attitude. An attitude without memory. A spatial existence in terms of the paper I'm writing on now at this moment. I'm using the old proof of determinism: "Whether I am going to be knighted tomorrow is either true or false NOW. Therefore whether I am going to be knighted or not tomorrow is decided beforehand." You can see what a pure confusion of terms the idea of time has led to in this.

Well, I am coming to believe that art is that pure selfless action (as a flower growing etc) that your pal Lao Tse mentions. This is the big lust of the artist. To be spatialised. TO BE WITHOUT MEMORY. To flow from the original spring of living – not writing. I consider writing no use except that it's old tissue sloughed off the man. What the man is is important. The bigger the writing etc Q.E.D. Now what I don't like about the surrealists is that they consist only of memory. Their present is always limited by their past, in spite of all that cock about leaving the ancient works of art where they are etc. They haven't realised that the greatest art is timeless. What it is is the man. Art is merely the chart of his diseases. You examine it as a doctor examines stools. And another thing. As far as I can make out the quibble about surrealism is a quibble over a technique – as you might say Huxley is too ladylike, or Eliot uses too many reflexive clauses. For everyone uses naturalism, cubism, surrealism etc AS HE WANTS IT. But to make such a stink about it is like me starting a league for more conditional clauses in poetry. I wonder if this is clear. Don't think it is. I'm too excited. There is some truth in it, but it is not all truth. Being grounded in Freud frinstance. This memory trick again. Yes, yes, it's all true. But they don't seem to make anything of it. You do yourself. Because *Tropic* and *B.S.* are of your bone, not of your critical faculty.

Hudson was always saying to me genuinely: "What can Villon have to say to me? He never went through the great war." But what great war are we talking about, but the personal war, I used to bay. Art is not politics, i.e. averages. It is men. It is not the outer struggle but the inner. My dear Henry Miller, unless I completely misunderstand your books, or unless you simply don't know what you're doing, this is what I mean. There is no one to shout at except my wife who is drawing, so I'll ask you. Is *Black Spring* more Surrealist than it is Miller? If it were I should burst into tears. BUT IS *ULYSSES* MORE SURREALIST THAN IT IS JOYCE? I think yes.

But by now you will be bored with me. But I tell you seriously, is this comic, that the heraldic universe when I get through with it, will be the only habitable place. It will be full of creators of real calibre because it sets out [to] cater for the social jackal. It will never be chic because it is my personal property and I don't want any movements made up of people who agree with each other even on first principles.

ARE YOU A WRITER – OR MERELY A LITERARY GENT?

IN fact, vegetable or mineral? Fish or fruit? The question being whether to write what you bloody well like and try to get it privately subscribed; or give in and turn out (supposing you could) the kind of stuff that would entitle a literary clique to take some interest in you? The question is finely epitomised above. Seriously, fish or fruit?

Did someone mention the modern reviews? Sweet reader, what would you do if you were too traditional for one half of the world, and too advanced for the other half? You would? Very well, then. THIS HAS BEEN ALREADY DONE. Enquire therefore into your most inward psyche as to what you are, and either fill in the forms below or else ring the chain on them. Remember Shakespeare lack'd art. And anything written from the waist downwards must face a world thick with honest, greasy Bens. Adieu.

Dear H.M: In a hell of a mess packing to move into town for the winter. I have just finished *Hamlet*, sitting among the wreckage. Let me try and tell you what I feel. Seems it's a perfect picture of the inner struggle, done in terms of the outer one – as all great books are – at least for me. Why everyone is so puzzled by poor Hamlet is because they always try to see a relation between the external battle (the murder, Ophelia etc) and the internal one. A failure, because the inner and the outer reality move along separate planes, and only seldom meet. There's your dialectical interplay, but through the reality always the magic is seen. Naturally the people who try to equate the moods with the external events never hit the mark. There are two Hamlets. We are presented with the Prince of Denmark, and it's only through the chinks in his armour that we can see the inner man, the worm turning in the bowels of compassion etc. But as the play goes on, the inner Hamlet, no longer Prince, grows and begins to strip his fellow characters of their masks. The great shock is to find himself alone in life – with no contact – not even with that sweet but silly little wretch Ophelia. Horatio a heart-of-oak dumbbell. Laertes a boring soldier. Polonius a blow-fly. The Queen a toad. Then, realising that he should really turn away from these fakes to his real self, he feels the pressure of society suddenly on him. He is forced to be the Prince, however much his private Hamlet suffers. It is a marvellous picture of psychic & social disorganisation in an individual and Shax was not the only one who found himself trying to write it. The tragedy of Hamlet was the tragedy of the Elizabethan Age. The age which poisoned its young men with the humanities and then showed them none. It is the tragedy of England now, but more advanced, more grey and carious than ever. But for those birds it was do or die. A lot died. Webster & Shakespeare came thro'. Marston found God, and Donne and Hall. Tourneur was starved. Southwell tortured 13 times and then burned. And out of all this muck the bright ideal of chivalry was eating their livers. They were recoiling from the real the whole time. *Hamlet* is a local effort. An epitome of what England's madness means. In Lawrence you see the same thing in a new version. Idealism in the bud eating eating eating ..... All the questions posed in literature since Marlowe mean the same thing.

In my opinion *Tropic* is the answer to them. The wheel turned right back to the pre-glacial ice age when dung was dung and angels were angels. In *Tropic* the borderline has been passed. Those of us who realise what it means rejoice because the whole pattern has been put back into proportion by it. This may amaze you but it's true. And an Englishman could never have done it. Somehow you have to be a real exile to do things on that scale. But for you, I shouldn't bother to read *Hamlet* except for the poetry. Its doubts and grimaces you have already solved for yourself. But by God, Shakespeare was on the point of solving it more than once. But he failed, so Hamlet failed. There was nothing left but the stagnant end, the conventional Elizabethan pogrom, and a brief but witty epitaph. Shakespeare went home and buried the guts under his cherry tree. The same question comes up all over the place, though less than in *Hamlet* and no nearer a solution. *Lear*, *Timon* and the marvellous heart breaking Sonnets show his madness. But chained. Englishmen have always, in spite of the national anthem, been slaves. Only Chaucer, Skelton and perhaps a few others, authentic barbarians, broke away or were born free.

But no writer as great as Shax or of his age escaped. In *Hamlet* the biggest evidences of the inner feud are in the Ophelia bits. Society – the fact that he had a penis – forced him to consider her. But she was uncomprehending, and his inner Hamlet soon made him negligent of her. Contemptuous. Nay, he even wanted to destroy her.

The terrible irony of his ravings at the grave has never been experienced except by me. To assure himself? No. Simply because he was so far beyond anything like her death, living in his own chronology, he engaged in a word-duel with her too-protesting brother. Irony beyond anything ever seen. Two minutes after, he picks himself up like a drunk and goes off with Horatio, chattering away. Ophelia is the external tragedy – SHE DOES NOT COUNT.

Well, I don't know whether you follow this crazy idea of mine, if you don't please say and I'll send you the essay I'm going to write on our dear Hamlet. A fellow of infinite jest. Irony like iron. And could you please keep this note? In a little while I want to start making notes for the essay and it might help me a bit. I have not yet written anything at all about it and my ideas are a bit tangled. This would help me finally to get them clear.

I say, *Hamlet must* be a great play. T.S. Eliot says it's an 'artistic failure'. That makes me dead certain. Eliot's struggle is so feeble he can't have any idea what it's all about. *Waste Land* reminds me of those

little printed exhortations to muscular development students on how
not to masturbate – Cheero.

Lawrence Durrell

[P.S.] What does Stein say about American Literature? I'm interested.
But hate her tone of voice like a multiplication table. Have you read
Lewis' attack on Joyce, Pound, Stein and that crowd?
I'm writing such poetry these days. Such poetry!

Manuscript Exchanges

Among the refrains of the early correspondence are Miller's requests for work from Durrell, with Durrell parrying because he is embarrassed at the quality of his early writing and his alleged small current output. He is being unnecessarily modest: most twenty-four-year-olds with a novel published by Cassell and another accepted by Faber and Faber would not feel the need to protest so much. Durrell even omits mentioning to Miller the existence of *Pied Piper of Lovers*.

Then in November 1936 Durrell writes, in red ink on graph-lined oversized paper, a letter on Hamlet (the text immediately precedes this note), later published in expanded form in the *New English Weekly*. Durrell had already written about his theory of heraldry – akin to Keats's concept of the power of the imagination – and about Hamlet, but this letter Miller excitedly calls a 'note for an essay'. Other work from Durrell soon follows: 'A Christmas Carol' (published as 'Asylum in the Snow' in *Seven*) and, with a reverberating impact, *The Black Book*: Durrell recklessly posts his unique typescript to Miller, telling him to 'pitch it into the Seine' if he does not approve. It is Miller's turn to salute Durrell, and the roles of helper and helped are henceforth to alternate throughout their friendship. The Hamlet letters have given Durrell the chance to cut in as a creative equal.

Miller remains Durrell's mentor, however, and this section ends with ruthlessly honest letters on artistic integrity. Durrell had been working out schemes to promote Miller: now Miller is circulating the 'Hamlet' essay to publishers, foreshadowing the enormous task he and Anaïs Nin, primarily, will assume in typing out copies of *The Black Book* and negotiating its publication.

Dear Durrell:

Just a hasty squirt to let you know that I read your Hamlet essay, or note for an essay, and was quite wrought up about it. Took the liberty of making copies and sending them to Fraenkel and to Philip Mairet, editor of the N.E.W., with suggestion that he get in touch with you and find out if you would like to have it printed in his sheet. He answered immediately that he was extremely interested and was writing you at once about it. Here's Fraenkel's quick response. I think, with your kind permission, that we should incorporate this into our *Hamlet* book – or perhaps that would be running counter to your own plans? Let me know, anyway.

Here's a typed copy for you, as you wanted to have it back again. May I keep the original in red ink? I rather prize it. Have it tacked up on the wall for all and sundry to read as they go out the door.

Mairet seems rather decent. Took a little article of mine – which I had to cut in half for him – on Schizophrenia, the Nov. 5th issue. Says he will take more stuff, if I like. *But doesn't pay*! However, if you can enter England by the back-door, I suppose it's something.

Herbert Read sent me the new book, *Surrealism*, which I am answering immediately with a broadside, in the hope that his gang of English and French surrealists will have the guts to publish it in one of their forthcoming manifestoes or what not. I'll try to send you the carbon copy when I'm through with it. Finished the *Money* pamphlet (50 pages of hilarious farce meaning absolutely nothing) and think my publisher will bring it out as a cheap pamphlet. More of this anon. Hastily,

HVM.

P.S. Is *Corfu* still the right address? Is Evans still down there? My regards to him. Ask him, please, if the editors of those Oxford magazines are still alive and kicking?

Money and How It Gets That Way, a burlesque of Ezra Pound's economic theories, appeared in 1936.

*[Corfu]   [20? November (not 13 as Durrell states) 1936]

Dear H.M. This is Friday the thirteenth, my lucky day. First a letter from Mairet enclosing my letter to you, and asking for a finished article on Ham. Then a letter from Henry Miller enclosing ANOTHER copy of my by this time famous essay to him, with praises. Hurrah. I'm delighted by your delight. And very many thanks for the N.E.W. scoop. Payment, I said to Mairet, was the least of one's considerations. WHAT ONE NEEDS IS A PULPIT. Onward, onward. I am trying to write out the article a bit more explicitly for him. I want to send it you first to see if you think it poorer than the letter. Literary journalism; but then I've got something iron-clear to say, and I mustn't miss this, my first, perhaps my last chance of saying it. The inner battle. I'VE GOT PROOF. Something that even the dons have missed. When Shakespeare cut down the long *Hamlet* for the stage he CUT OUT NEARLY ALL THE INNER BATTLE BECAUSE HE KNEW THEY WOULD NEVER UNDERSTAND IT. By a miracle this cut version was pirated and printed, and we have the first Quarto which is all OUTER STRUGGLE. Have you read it? I'd like to know what you think of the idea. You see this is not just another poetic and intuitive interpretation of *Hamlet*, with wine and flowers à la Swinburne. It's cast iron, based on the observations of the pathology of genius and madness, and on the two quartos. S. was called upon to put on a show which wouldn't look too crazy. In order to clean it up, to *simplify*, he even altered a part of the plot. Now this is a discovery which even the critics can't help admitting. I tell you it's not fanciful. I was saving it for the book about the heraldic universe called THE PRINCE AND HAMLET: A Pathology of Genius, but I'm so avid for print I'll spill it now. It was only a sideline on the main theme anyway, which dealt (will deal) with the two parallel realities, inner and outer. All great art of every kind and degree is this struggle to impose the inner on the outer, to transform the material, the social, to the psychic. The Heraldic Universe is just a name for that element in which that queer fish the artist swims. THE PRECISE ~~NATURE~~ <Position> OF THIS REALITY, WHICH DEMANDS AS YET A REAL PHILO-SOPHIC PLACE IN THOUGHT, I WANT TO TRY AND FIX. !!!!!! <Each writer establishes the *nature* for himself. But I want a *philosophic admission of this reality*.> Now don't chuckle. Have you read Rank's *The Trauma of Birth*? Would you like a 1st Quarto? Unfortunately I'm using my copy. It costs 2/6d, published by John Lane, The Bodley Head. Number VII in The Bodley Head Quartos. Send you mine with the article if you want.

As soon as I'm through I'll post you the article. See what you think. If you prefer the letter I'll tell Mairet he can print that or nothing. Of course all the extraneous stuff, which is related in general to art, comes out. The nice things about you frinstance.

AND PRINT THE THING WHEREVER AND WHENEVER YOU WANT. What is the real fame is you pinning it to the wall. I'm glad Fraenkel liked it. He's got a beautiful soul, as they say. And I loved Anonymous. What a pity he is so hemmed inside himself, seeking the whole time, but really acquiescent in his death, his inner death. But to produce surely the struggle is to keep on converting one's dying into some sort of permanent coin, the whole time, the spiritual bullion being saved and sifted and put on one side. I must read [*Bastard*] *Death* again.

Evans and Zarian and I are planning an international anthology of poetry here. God knows if it will come to anything. Faber have my poems (all gold) in one hand and a romantic novel (all dross) in the other, and they don't know what the fuck to do or think. I've grown up so suddenly that I'm in danger of striking the ceiling, and there's NO COMPARISON between the stuff I wrote even six months ago, and what I'm trying now. Very queer. It's all due to TROPIC I think. And my wife, who is divinely mad.

How does your *Hamlet* go? My wife is writing this mail to the bank to send ten pounds to you for Perlès. Good wishes to him, and wish it were more but we are never very stable in money. In income we only have twelve pounds a month, and a few odd pounds here and there from advances on books (very rare). But if one is given a little money for bad work, why not send a mite of conscience money to the people who produce good? Explain it's good for the Durrell soul.

Well, I must go back to the ditch and see the *Van Norden* hoisted out of the water! Summer is going, but in a kind of peaceful damp quiet. Soon snow and then we will go into Albania to shoot. My brother says you must be a very curious person. I don't know what he means.

Yours etc.
Lawrence Durrell

[P.S.] Yes. Same address. Living in the hotel just opposite the Ionian Bank.
[P.P.S.] Yes, send me the Titus please. Enclose a Surrealist young man [David Gascoyne?] I like very much in parts. But it's all poem of course.

Durrell's 'romantic novel' is *Panic Spring*.

Dear H.M.

We had a fine night with the bottles last night and decided, Zarian and I, that it is time to write the NEW BIBLE. What we mean by this is very vague but most exciting. Zarian's idea was to get three, seven, or nine writers (any cabbalistic number): all to meet one year and have great festivities and discuss the architecture of this tome. Each take his share of the work and go away, farther the better with it. Then, when each section was complete and entire, we should all meet in a big city, Paris or Rome or Constantinople, and publish the book – *ANONYMOUSLY.* What a gesture in the face of the world! Well now, Zarian was all for making a printed pact etc on the spot and circulating it among ALL the writers, but I was just drunk enough to say: "Suppose Ethel M. Dell or Babbitt said YES." "To hell," said he. "I know Bragaglia, Unamuno, Saroyan," and I forget who else. "AND," says he, "YOU WRITE TO HENRY MILLER TO ASK HIM IF HE FEELS AS PROPHETIC AS WE DO, AND IF HE KNOWS ANY CHINESE PROPHET WHO WOULD SWALLOW THE IDEA. BECAUSE HE IS, AFTER ALL, A REAL WRITER." MY DEAR MILLER, WHAT THE HELL THIS MEANS I DON'T KNOW BUT IT SOUNDS A LARGE, FRUITY, RICH, MANTIC, AND MILKY IDEA.

I like best the idea of printing anonymously. This would be a break for me, coz I could give out discreetly that I was a contributor, and be mistaken either for you or Unamuno, which is one quick road to fame. Also I like the idea of meeting and discussing the architecture of the book. What enormous cloudy ideas. A NEW SONG OF SOLOMON, sans peur and sans reproche, sans vin, sans clothes. A NEW REVELATION. A new PROVERBS. AND A NEW SET OF BEATITUDES. HURRAH FOR PROGRESS. And above all, three, seven or nine separate agonies in the garden instead of one. THE NEW CRUCIFICTION. Not fiction but fact. Have spent the morning composing subtitles and psalms to be played on the loudest of loud sacbuts, psalters, cymbals, and whimbrels. THE NEW BIBLE. THE NEW WORLD. THE HERALDIC BOOK OF JOB. What delirious sores one could expose for the world. Three seven or nine mutilated bodies instead of one.

Hope you got the quarto. Many thanks for the good work. Very depressed. My proofs of the shit novel have just come. WHY DOES ONE WRITE LIKE THIS?

Sincerely.   Lawrence Durrell.

[P.S.] Will rustle up something for you I HOPE. Have nothing.

I enclose a photograph to prove
that I am NOT a Greek, but a
pure Anglo-Irish-Indian ASH BLOND.
In the second one I am congratulating
my youngest brother. He has written
the following poem. And I am still envious.

death

On a mound a boy lay
While a stream went tinkling by.
Mauve irises stood round him as if to
Shield him from the eye of death
Which was always taking people unawares
And making them till his ground.

Rhododendrons peeped
At the boy counting sheep.
The horror is spread.
The boy is dead.

But death himself is not seen.

Gerald Durrell was eleven when he wrote this poem, subsequently published in *The Booster*, 3ᵉ Année, No. 9 (November 1937).

*C/o Ionian Bank: Corfu.   [*c.* 19 December 1936]

Dear H.M.: I am so struck dumb by your generosity that I don't know
what to say or how to make a polite bow to you. Villa Seurat I always
imagine as an immense factory – rather like the Walt Disney studio –
with you in the centre, surrounded by a few hundred active typewriters
all making copies of the *Hamlet* essay. It's splendid of you to send me
about like this. It's more than Curtis Brown can do for me in years. But
I chuckle slightly when I see that you are writing to one of these people
about me, because, SHOULD you interest one of them in me, they will,
AT THE WORST, demand to see some work of mine which justifies your
enthusiasm. MY DEAR H.V.M. I HAVE NONE!!!! I have no work, and no
typist, and no dictionary. So I always keep what I write in my pocket
for fear of losing it. I have no copy of the *Hamlet* essay for instance. As

for Eliot, well, Faber & Faber have put me on a three novel contract, starting with a cheap romance called *Panic Spring* which is a leprous distilment: BUT REFUSED THE POEMS which are not at all bad for a small boy like me. Actually I am up against the wall properly now, just finishing a Black Book which Fabers will reject and rupture the contract, because it is good – (I AM TERRIFIED OF IT IT IS SO GOOD IN LITTLE FLASHES) – BUT NOT POPULAR. I need a few months revision on it. But there again I am shy of sending it to anyone because I have no copy. I really must grow up and buy carbons. But as I write straight onto the machine and am lazy, I have chosen as my motto: EVERY COPY A FAIR COPY. Needless to say this only works once in every five pages. As for work. Why, I have only grown up in the last year or so, and so have hardly anything to show. But I'll send you a little prose-song called "Ionian Profile" when I rewrite it in a day or two. Maybe it will interest Laughlin enough to print it. Go easy on me, will you, because I don't want to let down your golden opinions of me, which I value above everything else? I am going quietly mad in this book and feel very sore and strained. So far no one has seen it, I am so jealous of it. The curse is that I must submit it to Faber for rejection. They have been very decent to me and are editing the romance, parts of which I must rewrite, wince I never so much. It's a filthy trick to publish a writer before he's grown up. Am starting to realise that. I WANT TO BE IN YOUR HAMLET BOOK LIKE HELL. ARE YOU JOKING OR SERIOUS? A nice letter from Fraenkel from Bruges. Is he in N. Y. now? Have planned the heraldic book, but lack reference books on psychology, the pathology of childhood, cretinism, genius etc . . . . LET US KILL THE LITERARY MEN ONCE AND FOR ALL AND *FORCE* THEM TO A PHILOSOPHIC ADMISSION OF THE *MYSTERY*. ONWARD. ONWARD. HAVE YOU READ CYRIL TOURNEUR?

Did I tell you about Zarian? All yesterday he kept rushing into my room with *Bastard Death* in his hands, his silver mane flying, his glasses on his forehead, saying: "How is possible this? HOW IS POSSIBLE? I wrote all these things in Armenian and here . . . the same phrases . . . same words . . . Meeler writes of the Middle Ages . . . and I wrote it." He is immensely thrilled with the letter. "It's in the air," he says, "in the air these ideas." He is a great friend of Saroyan and wants to write you a letter about God, so I said Go ahead. *Tropic* worried him a bit, and he said it was destructive, but *Black Spring* has him by the sash. Is writing an immense trilogy in Armenian and apparently well thought of by Saroyan. We were on the point of starting a quarterly calendar called EOS, for which we were going to ask you & Fraenkel and Saroyan and others for material, but the Fascists intervened with a comic economic law which doesn't permit you to send books outside the country unless you receive them back!!! The Greeks are amazing in this way. Pity, we had the best poets and writers of everywhere, including Greece, Palamas and Co. Owing to this law I can't even print the bloody poems which are festering on my shelf.

I am delighted at the breaks which are coming your way, but I knew it was only a question of time. By the way, talking of Bibliographies, tell your publisher to see that you are represented in the British Museum Reading Room. It'll be very useful in any cases of piracy, or copyright troubles in England. Apart from the fact that your readers will increase. It's the mistake D.H.L. made when printing abroad, and got pirated. I say, don't bother about payment if you ever land anything of mine. I'd be delirious with just a copy of it. As for French I don't care myself. Dislike the literary set-up of that nation, so it wouldn't shake me to be translated. BUT congratulations on the Chinese translations. God knows how it will sound, but congrats anyway. There's a kind of evocative surrealism in the idea of a mandarin dozing under the plantains, fanned by eunuchs, and reading *Tropic* quietly and inscrutably. I must ask my wife to make a picture of it for you.

We were going to America when I found that [we had?] mistaken the bank balance of ten for a hundred pounds. But sooner or later. About the Perlès money, if you don't think he ought to have it, or if he has enough to go on with, well send it back. I'll buy my girl something really good with it, a rocking horse, or a set of good paints, or a model. Send it to my account ('account'? that would sound ironic) at Messrs Grindlay & Co. Bankers. 54 Parliament Street. S.W. London. I've sent the quarto on. Am interested in the HOUSE OF INCEST. Like the review *very much*. Lend me a copy will you. Maybe it'll be useful for the Heraldic Book. Soon I'll send "Ionian Profile" and see what you think. A million Chinese salutations and thanks. I'm delighted by your delight.

Sincerely.
L. Durrell.

[P.S.] Moving out of this damn hotel today: going to stay with my mother for a while. How about a trip down south for a month or two next summer? If you are interested, if the idea is at all near the bone, let me know and I'll make enquiries etc.

Fête day for me. I've finished *The Black Book*. I'm in love with it. Hurrah!

*[Paris]   Tuesday [22? December 1936]

Dear Durrell,

Your letter this morning interests me profoundly. Especially about the magazine which you have abandoned.[. . .]

About yourself. First of all, *order!* Why not put in a carbon when you write? What's to prevent it? You will find that you save time and energy. Another little thing – if you don't mind. Why should *you* compromise? You have a little income. You can afford to speak your mind, do as you please. You will save ten years of sweat and anguish if you do it now, and not later. Of course, doing as you please also involves a certain kind of anguish, but it's different, and more tolerable. The other eats you out and leaves you dry. Doing as you please either kills you or strengthens you. Naturally I surmised that you hadn't a great deal to show. How could you, at your age? *But* – just assume that people are going to ask you for something. Start now and give it from the guts. No matter what you do to please the editors it will never please them. Better please yourself and trust in God! So many good men had to print their books themselves first. Walt Whitman peddled his own book from door to door! Believe it or not!

Sure I intend putting you in the *Hamlet* book. I am suggesting to Fraenkel that we put your essay in the Appendix. Just sent a copy off to the *Southern Review*, Baton Rouge, La. You may hear from them direct. Am expecting a reply from Levesque, of *Orbes*, any day now. And something more definite from Lundkvist. Don't be too grateful. I did what I did because it was worth doing. I never do anything that is not worth while.

You speak of the factory. Yes, this is a sort of factory, but *without* assistants. I do everything myself, and I'm half dead. I have had to retype over 200 pages of stuff in the last few weeks, besides doing fresh things, and carrying on my Gargantuan correspondence. And reading the books that are sent me! But I'm in the plenitude of my powers now and one has to make hay while the sun shines. I can hardly sleep at night for the ideas that are surging in my brain. A little more dough, a little assistance, and I would be another Victor Hugo or a Balzac, so far as output goes.

And now about the dough. Yes, I will send it to the people you mention – but that will be three or four days hence, when I receive my Christmas present. Is that O.K.? I hope so. I used up four pounds while waiting.

To-day I see Stuart Gilbert who has the copies of the ten *Hamlet* letters I sent to Eliot recently. Perhaps I will forward them to you to give you an idea of the substance of the book – especially now that I realize you are going to stay in Corfu.

And about a trip. Yes, I think it might be possible early in the spring. I am going to be fagged out. Pooped out, I might say. Going at a terrific pace the last few months. And no sunshine ever. Sleep between moist cold sheets, the walls wet, the heat almost nil, etc. Beastly climate, Paris. My dream has always been to see Constantinople and Stamboul. You will laugh, but I got that way reading Pierre Loti years ago. Never forget *Disenchantment*, even though it's old hat and senti-mental now. As for the Greeks, as for Athens, I am no great admirer of that venerable civilization. But just the same – the sun, the water, the resined wine, the little blue islands. Listen, could we possibly see the isle of Lesbos, or Corinth, or *Crete*? I would give a lot to see the labyrinth at Knossos. Read all about Sir Arthur Evans' work years ago. Am crazy about that stuff. But I know no Greek and I know nothing of the classics – practically nothing. I am ignorant. Even about English literature. But I want to read *The White Devil* some time. John Ford, is it? I saw his '*Tis Pity She's a Whore* in French. Made a great impression upon me.

Sending you a copy of *House of Incest*, to keep. Must let me know what your "wife" thinks. So long.

HVM.

[P.S.] And Merry Christmas to you all! You ought at least give me your wife's name!

*C/o IONIAN BANK. KERKERA. GREECE.   [c. 25 December 1936]

dear henry miller:

With a merry christmas I enclose this carol which happened to me last night. I don't want to look at it any more so I send it to you. Perhaps you might think it promising. Anyway, I know that you will not hesitate to say what you feel. If you like it and contemplate sending it to the anthology you mentioned, let me put a small "To Henry Miller" on it. As after all you are doing for me I feel I want to dedicate some little thing to you. Punctilio, don't you know. A salute of one toy cannon passing your enormous broadsides. Or a squib to celebrate your victories over the infidel.

If you don't like it, then send it back coz I have no copy: and I'll offer you better food at a slightly later date. I feel I'm very near now.

Am reading Rivers' *Conflict & Dream*. And a study of genius by Ernst Kretschmer. It's all dove-tailing into my heraldry. But the old meaningless phrase 'universal experience' haunts these people. I don't think there is such a thing: just degrees of faith with which you give yourself to the people with manna.

> I like Rivers though.
> Much good wishes: and a verry
> merry christmas, if the damned
> event means anything to you.
> Heraldically yours.
> Lawrence Durrell.

Durrell is apparently referring above to Kretschmer's *The Psychology of Men of Genius* (1931).

*CORFU GREECE ETC.   [end December? 1936]

Dear H.M.

Very many thanks. You can't stop me. I'm delirious about that essay: particularly the *Hamlet* book which is *my* private piece of fame. When I do it in the long version I shall offer it to you on a platter if any one wants to print it. [. . .] *The Black Book* by the way is not bad, unless you're extra fastidious. I've revived it. Just rewriting it: trying to demillerise as I go along. Unhealthy influence you are, whatever positive virtues you have. Sticks like fluff. As for Evans, he's lost. He's worn out my copies of the two tomes so that I've had to have them bound. From now on nothing but Jeremy Taylor for me with interludes of George Moore to settle my literary stomach. Otherwise this book will never get done. Zarian leaves for Vienna on Friday. He is waiting to begin the 3rd vol of a trilogy before sending out some messages in the form of letters. One to you, one to Unamuno, possibly (hush) one to wretched me, and so on. Signal and countersignal printed in the book. As for the Bible it seems misty. One can never get any real allies. Or are all good writers mad?

O the book has come for which many many thanks. This is becoming sort of inevitable. As for the plangent mysterious stuff, where do you get it from? " "MY WIFE" ". She is Nancy only in name. Nancy Isobel DURRELL. And she makes a pretty bow of thanks for the book. It's beautiful. Also is making a drawing of herself in the mirror to try and live up to a few of her adjectives. [. . .]

About the journal: we were set with the writers: we were set with the manifestoes etc, from you and other prophets. And what better than an island as a centre? But the latest greek fascist law is this: books sent out of the country are the same as MONEY. One has to make it good to the bank of greece whether one gets the returns or not: or face jail. Unhealthy position for an editor? So one has in effect to issue the book and buy up the whole issue oneself before you can send it into the world. Even with the cheap printing and free contributions we couldn't do *that*. I think Bruges is a good idea, but the printing rates are enormous: and we wanted (as we had here) a printer under our thumb, a fount of our own type, and a feeling of personalness about the business. Also CHEAP GOOD PRINTING. And here the quotations were a third of english or french or italian quotes. Alas for Lycidas. Zarian was going to carry thru from Vienna where he goes in a week, but again the printing costs a lot. I'm no business man either. By the way Z. is also a friend of Saroyan so you are on common ground there.

About ORDER: yes. And again yes. And a third time . . . Of course it's a kind of pregnancy tic my loathing for carbons, their foul soft blurred print: and the soapy feel of the type-heads against them. I lack faith, that's all. But I will be good. And it's only decent to offer to pay the typing fees on the article: because a hell of a number of copies and you probably didn't do them yourself with all your other work. Couldn't have been sweller if I'd sent you the original *Hamlet* instead of just a note about it. Skoal. Yes, Ford is fine. You would like the

36

Elizabethans, I know you would. If you haven't struck Webster and Tourneur there's a treat in store. Best seen or read aloud. And Nashe's prose is one long dysentery of delight. Middleton, Dekker, Greville, Marlowe. Very rich age.

As for compromise. You are perfectly right if you think you are addressing St. Lawrence. But if you are talking to me I say: yes, but I'm going to have my cake and eat it. I have no hesitation about what to write any more. I am discovering what I am. Only it's a bit painful because I started in another direction, and being forced to write what I'm going to will estrange me dreadfully. It's inevitable, but I shed a few pious tears now, at the beginning of the trip, so that I can be dry as cork and controlled when we put out to sea. Sometimes I wonder whether it wouldn't be better to leave both trails and enter a bank. I'm writing about all that now with great charity. It's good in spite of the drops. Send you *The Black Book* on its way through to Fabers for a rejection. It's an ave atque vale for me. Maybe a laugh or two or a good image for you: or an action for plagiarism.

Hope you're serious about the spring. If you keep me posted I'll get the new house finished in time and you can live here for a month or so and go quietly blind. We could be a spring-board for any trip you want to make. Don't need greek except a few phrases like "You are a liar" and "Give me that wallet back, it's mine" and "Fetch a policeman". Also any invitation here extends to any of your mysterious plangent etc wives: unless you're a travelling Bluebeard which would strain the exchequer beyond repair. (Evans is puzzled by the number of them in your books. Not to mention children.) Sends greetings. Myself I'm going to see Crete properly as soon as I've consolidated my home base. I'm not a nomad at heart. I must have a landing somewhere to be happy. Hudsons say they're coming back next year, so if you're gregarious you couldn't wish for more agitated unbalanced enthusiastic charming people. Even if B. is a comic behaviorist. I must get an engine for the *Van Norden* so we can take trips into the wilderness etc.

As for Constantinople. Why destroy your illusions by going there? You'll get those unspotted memories mixed up with spit and scrofula and mosaic and pellagra and offal etc. As for scholarship, we'll try not to show erudition. It doesn't exist. Shall I send you a nice piece of the Tiberius summer villa ruin above Cassiope? Or the date of the battle of Salamis? The Kosters have taken a house on the west point of the island for a year, and seem to love it. Quite quite remote and cut off and sunken and done-for. Paleocastrizza. Ancient fort, that is, translated.

post-prandial.

Going on a snipe-shoot tomorrow at dawn. Chorissa. Big lake to the south. Mairet very charming to me. What do you do to these editors? Sent me his essay on *Hamlet* which is after Freud. Good observation. Seems a nice generous person. If you place the tract anywhere, will you let me agitate for a free copy of each printing as payment? A trophy to hang among the mouldering boars' heads at the baronial hearth.

Knossos now that's a dream: with the blue hills and the saffron and the women's clothes. If Evans was there it would be easy to call on him. I believe Knossos is on his own private property. He bought it. I met Dawkins last year on his way through to Athos to finish a book about it.

Have discovered two good men. Blondel of *Conscience morbide* and Crookshank, an english M.D. IT IS WE WHO ARE INSANE AFTER ALL. Hurrah.

I have finished *House of Incest* at last. What a silly title, but I like it, in spite of the technique. It's the first book in this mode that I've read that is alive. In spite of the method. Dream minus reality etc. It's really alive god help my soul with a queer kind of poignance about it. Like sudden dazzling tears. Who is Anaïs Nin? I remember Barclay saying something about her. And the introduction to *Tropic* of course. What else has she written? It's a queer name: has a sort of oriental flavour. But this wasn't written by a sleek soot-black Cleo with a vermilion cigarette-holder I'm sure. Nancy (my wife) is reading it and seems to like it. Those first two poems are grand. Choked in its sails etc. *House of Incest* is a bad title. It sounds stale and a bit wormy, whereas the book is fresh and sweet and squeezes itself into sudden malleable shapes and colours. Nice. I think your review didn't do it justice quite. Or is this where I get a smack in the neck?

For the time addio. Don't write. I know how busy you are and am glad. Onwards into a new season. Capricornus, Capricornus; for you this must be where even the dream ends and the spirit comes through the rind, clean as bone. I'm eager to see it. Up Capricorn!

Sincerely.
Lawrence Durrell.

*[Paris]   Jan. 3, 1936 [i.e., 1937]

Dear Durrell,

The Christmas Carol flabbergasts me! It's so damned perfect that it makes me green with jealousy. You will begin to think I have lost my critical faculties altogether. But not so! Whether you realize it or not you have done a masterpiece, the most perfect thing of its kind that I have ever read. Not only that, I should like to add that it is the sort of thing I have always wanted to do myself – and never could. This puts you in a class with Léon-Paul Fargue. It's far superior to Breton or to Dylan Thomas. I read it in the dentist's office, waiting for him to go to work on me. Almost got hysterical over it.

This is just an acknowledgment. I will have more to say about it later, after I read it over a few times. [...]

What am I going to do about it? Well, I have already written Laughlin about it, asking him if he wants it for the next issue of his anthology. Haven't sent him a copy of it as I am perplexed. It's this. I have a little scheme of my own – another! – which I want to propose to you. Perhaps we can do both – adopt my plan and have Laughlin take it also. Anaïs and I are thinking of investing in a machine, a sort of mimeograph machine (not exactly that), which enables one to make innumerable copies from an original typewritten sheet in any colored ink one wants. We have been wondering if, instead of a magazine, with all the difficulties it entails, we could not do better by bringing out one thing at a time, after this process. We would put a thin paper cover around it with the title printed on it – by the same process – or else each one separately, in Chinese ink or something like that. We would send the thing to a select list of people whom we think might be interested. Put no price on it, but suggest that they pay what they like towards the expense, if it appeals to them. We haven't solved all the technical problems involved yet, nor have we the dough immediately. But all that can be solved all right, in a little time.

Now I thought, if the idea appealed to you, that we might bring out your Christmas Carol first. You would still have the right, I believe, to sell it to a magazine or publisher, if you could get one. (In this instance I frankly think it to be difficult – because it's too damned good and too unusual and too uncategorizable.) Laughlin, however, ought to fall for it, unless I am greatly mistaken.

If you have any ideas, practical ones, shoot them! I am the most

39

impracticable, unhandy fellow in the world. The idea is, as I see it, to do the thing as simply as possible, and yet not have it look commercial. The postage stamps is a big item – depending, of course, on the list. The rest is labor, that's all. And the advantage lies in *placing* them where one wants!

I am sending you to-morrow the ten letters from the *Hamlet* which I sent Eliot and which of course he has just turned down, with a mildly sarcastic letter about it being more suitable for my "admirers" and not calculated to "widen my public". Blasted idiot! That's my last effort in that direction. I can do better with the French. May I suggest that when you return these letters please put them in a strong envelope. Your Carol came open, the envelope in shreds. Not the first time either. The mail from Greece must get rough handling! Perhaps soon I'll be able to send you a carbon of "The Universe of Death" thing. The woman who translated "The Crown" (of Lawrence) is now reading it, likes it very much, and intends showing it to Louis Gillet here who in turn may present it to the *Revue des Deux Mondes* (sic). I am about to get another review – in the *Cahiers du Sud*. That means I have made every important French revue now, excepting the *Mercure de France* (which is about on a par with the *Criterion*). And did I say that Kahane got a letter from the translator of *Ulysses*, asking for the translation rights to both books *in German*? That doesn't mean it will be published immediately, but it's a step in the right direction. 1936 was not a bad year for me at all!

Of course, I am going to see what I can do about the Carol with the French – and possibly the Scandinavians. By the way, was the "Hamlet" printed in the *New English Weekly*? I haven't heard a word from Mairet recently.

And now here's a little excerpt from my Lawrence book which I think applies to you, to your work . . . .

> "The poem is the dream made flesh, in a two-fold sense: as work of art, and as life itself, which is a work of art. When man becomes fully conscious of his powers, his role, his destiny, he is an artist and he ceases his struggle with reality. *He becomes a traitor to the human race.* He creates war because he has become permanently out of step with the rest of humanity. He sits on the doorstep of his mother's womb with his race memories and his incestuous longings and he refuses to budge. He lives out his dream of Paradise. He

transmutes his real experience of life into spiritual equations. He scorns the ordinary alphabet which yields at most only a grammar of thought, and adopts the symbol, the metaphor, the ideograph. *He writes Chinese.* He creates an impossible world out of an incomprehensible language, a lie that enchants and enslaves men . . . ."

Chinese! That reminds me. In the last issue of *Life and Letters Today* there is a notice about a Chinese journal, review, which is printed in English, at Shanghai. Appears there was an article in the last number concerning *Shakespeare as a Taoist!* I have written for a copy of it. Also to inquire if they take contributions from Europeans. Must be a queer assortment of fish.

You asked me about Cyril Tourneur. The same day I saw Stuart Gilbert and he asked me the same question! No, I never even heard of him. I'm ignorant, I tell you. Know scarcely anything of the Elizabethan literature. Practically nothing, I should say. Alors, inform me. And who wrote that White Devil or White Whale? Now I am trying to get hold of an English version of Calderon's *Life is a Dream.* Anaïs just read it in Spanish and told me the story of it. Sounds quite marvellous to me. I am also on the trail of Léon Bloy's *Le Désespéré* and Roussel's *Comment j'ai écrit la plupart de mes livres.* (Ça doit être quelque chose!)

Fraenkel writes he may come back – or go to Mexico. Can't stand New York another minute! Well, greetings and profound thanks. More anon. You're a stinking genius!

HVM.

P.S. Want to make a suggestion. Would you mind changing the title, if it's to be printed? Something about "the five of us", or the snow. *Anything* – but not "A Christmas Carol".
P.P.S. Didn't send the balance (300 frs.) 3 Lbs. – to Grindlay yet – but will in a few more days. Hope it doesn't inconvenience you too much.

The World of Lawrence: A Passionate Appreciation (1980) was begun in 1932 at Kahane's suggestion, but was not published until a month after Miller's death.
Raymond Roussel's title is *Comment j'ai écrit certains de mes livres* (1935).

Dear H.M.   No one will print them. I'll tell you why. You choose a title with the word Hamlet, and ring an old psychic chord (vide 'letters') in the cranium. You excite the critics (damn the critics) in your first letter by some real death-rays on the subject, immensely profound: then you begin rough-necking and capering the theme round in your second: AND THEN SUDDENLY the whole arena shifts round, and empties for a duel between you and Fraenkel. Your last letter is magnificent. MAGNIFICENT. It's all magnificent, but why kill the book by calling it *Hamlet?* Because somehow it's so unexpected this tissue of mirth and magnificence. It's all Henry Miller, PRINCE OF DENMARK. When I said in that letter that Hamlet's major problems you had solved for yourself, I was nearer the mark than I realised. You cannot write anything about *Hamlet* because the place it occupies in the Heraldic pattern is below you. There is only going up not down. This peculiar English death which is epitomised in the play is foreign to you. I say foreign, and I mean by that China. The stratosphere. It was a stratosphere that Shakespeare inhabited, but only *wrote* about BY ACCIDENT. Your whole propensity is set towards the recording of the flora and fauna of that stratosphere. You have penetrated it further, and at a higher level. This is not Shakespeare's fault. It was the fault of the damning literary formulae of his age. If he had faced the world as it is now, in which canon is no longer balanced on anything, he would have written things greater than you can IMAGINE. But poor fellow, he didn't realise for a moment that what was the important thing was the description of his inner heraldic territory. Only sometimes the malaise shook him, tied him up, and presto, out of the folds fell a genuine bit of heraldry. When I say this I am not patting you on the back for being a better writer than Shakespeare, QUA WRITER. I am saying that you have realised yourself as a man more fully: also this IMPORTANT THING. In our age we have reached a point in writing when it is possible for the writer to BE HIMSELF on paper. It's more than possible. It's inevitable and necessary. But for the Elizabethan writing was separated entirely from living. The self you put on paper then might have a HALL MARK: that is to say it was recognisable by a few mannerisms, a style of moral thought etc. But it no more corresponded to the author than Hamlet corresponds to you. The virtue of the Elizabethan was this: their exuberance was so enormous, so volatile, so pest-ridden, so aching and vile and repentant and spew-stuck, that here and there, by glorious mistakes, they transcended the canon. But their critical apparatus was interested only in the NARR-ATION. Was it good Seneca or wasn't it? If you look at the state of criticism now, you will find a whole terminology OF MYSTICISM has entered it. Even the critic has been trying to accustom himself to the disturbing factor, which all this new ego-writing has brought to light. Lawrence is bad Seneca, Ben Jonson would have said, and meant it. The man can write, but having opinions about oneself is not enough. He lacks art. Off with his head. Now we have the timely recognition that each man is entitled to his own reality, interpret it as he wants. THE HERALDIC REALITY. To the Elizabethan all types of experience were easily alloyed, epitomised, and REDUCED TO THE COMMON DENOMINATOR OF THE INTELLIGENCE. Even now, there are traces of that heresy about among writers – the flotsam left over from the cheap scientific hog-wash of the last century. Fraenkel seems also to be one of these crows. But what you say clearly enough (damn it), a thing I have been trying to say myself in private, is that there is only one canon: FAITH. Have you the faith to deliver yourself to the inner world of Gauguin, or haven't you? The critics will get there on about five p.m. next Tuesday. It'll be the death of criticism, but their terminology is so full of VOICES OF EXPERIENCES, and SPIRITUAL TERRITORIES, that they'll have to do something about it.

Frankly I don't like what Fraenkel has to say, or rather hasn't got to say. He is one of the whole crowd of writers who out of fear, and a deceit, gives experience the lie. I am meeting people every day like him. Mostly Jews. [When] I try to explain to them that the reality of each artist deserves to receive the philosophic admission of the audience they yell: "But this isn't life. The artist isn't scientific, he isn't rational." They will not admit the claim of the artist's experience to be as valid as any so called rational truth. They have no faith. THAT IS THE JEWISH NATIONAL DISEASE, LACK OF FAITH. (By the way, I hope Fraenkel isn't a Jew.)

O shit. They won't realise that the artist is really the artificer, the pioneer. Leave them their bloody little systems and terminologies. It keeps them embalmed and out of reach of life. More later.

Yes. I like what he says about you being at a critical pass in your writing. I feel that too. The next few years will show me whether you can support the theory of the ego-protagonist indefinitely. I rather think you can't. I was surprised by *Hamlet*, because I thought that it was going to be a sort of opus: but ~~that ass~~ <Fraenkel> has reduced it a little by introducing personalities. Its value therefore will be documentary. I'm amazed at the pacific ocean which you keep in your nib. The fertility. The immensely fructuous energy. The paper seems quite used up when once you have written something on it. That is why I'm impatient. These are letters from high altitudes, but the drama that's coming as yet . . . the drama that you have up your sleeve – it scares me a bit. But it's coming. I have an idea that if any man can bust open the void and figure it out in a new dazzling mythology you can. And I have another idea, probably a bit repellent to you, that when you do give us this thing, it will be full of a divine *externality*. IT will be a synthesis not only of the self you have explored so devastatingly in your two books – and of which these letters are a pendant – but also of the Chinese figures which you find in the stratosphere: AND THEIR STRUGGLE. It is that titanic war which I feel you are going to offer us: I don't think the others understand properly. Fraenkel accuses you of such trivialities and frills that I don't understand what you are doing in such poor literary company. After all, this is the behaviorist attitude, cutely inverted, and cut into a red hunting-coat – with a few pretty tassels like mystery, and TRUTH! (I hope you don't mind me talking like this, but it alarms me when I see how little your own friends and contemporaries understand you. Or is this the way to the asylum?) But his letters are such poor stuff, really. Their only purpose is to goad you into some of the most magnificent pieces of prose you've ever written. But *Hamlet*? *Hamlet* is going to be the title of this drama of yours. *Hamlet* squared, *Hamlet* cubed: *Hamlet* in an atmosphere which gives trigonometry cold fingers, and logic blunt thumbs.

I wonder if I am right. It seems clear. Walking about this dead town among the flies etc I had a long and fruitful think about that letter of Fraenkel's. Poor fellow, he wants you to end inside a system. Perhaps even the Catholic system. He cannot bear to see such a high trapeze act without safety nets. He identifies himself so closely with your acrobatics that he vomits at each flutter of your tropical parasol. His only act of bravery is to do a clever trick with death. Death, after all, that is simple. It is here on the ground. But a trapeze . . . . . . Well, this is impertinent and neither here nor there.

What I thought was this: you have been beating forward into this territory alone, quite alone. In order not to go mad, you had to keep yourself with you as company. That self, the basis of your ego-protagonist work, you raised to a square root. It had to be or else you would have gone crazy. But there is a more terrible time coming. I can't imagine what the work will be like. I can't imagine you writing anything GREATER than you have and are: but there is some intelligence in my bones that now you are getting a grip on the stratosphere: the self, which you used as a defence against the novel terrors of this heraldic universe (as one might use a smoked glass to look at the sun) is diffusing itself: it is less necessary. You are looking round and beginning to see the shapes of things. That ultimate battle, which I tremble when I think about, is almost announced. IN IT ALL THAT IS YOU WILL BE SUBJECTED TO THE DRAMA. YOU WILL LOOSE YOUR POWER OVER THE ARMIES, and the result will be those immense mythical figures which will fertilise all our books for centuries and our minds. I tell you this in confidence. It may be nonsense but it's what I feel. No artist as yet has reached the peak you have without being exhausted. Reading these letters I can see clearly that far from being exhausted you are refreshed by each new battle. This is because you travel so light, with such little baggage. AND THIS BRINGS ME BACK TO HAMLET. Shakespeare & Lawrence, and Co, have been crippled from the start by being unable to realise themselves. Consequently the final drama, THE HAMLET, when they wrote it was entangled in their diseases, held down by them. But you it seems to me are going into this final contortion with the purest mind we have yet had, by what propitious circumstances, social, literary, and personal, God only knows. I said PURE. That is why when you begin this *Hamlet* the veil of the temple will be rent in twain, and it's no good asking people like Fraenkel to hand you the meat-axe for the job. My quarrel with your title is this. THIS BOOK IS NOT YOUR *HAMLET*. And it's a pity to waste the title on it, and have to call the real *Hamlet* Ophelia or something. It will never be your *Hamlet* because your correspondent finds the axe too heavy to lift. And even if he could lift it it wouldn't be your *Hamlet* because that is something you can only do alone, in your own unorganised privacy.

What I say is this: YOU CAN WRITE *HAMLET*, but in this book so far you have only written ABOUT *Hamlet*. Incidentally I should read *Hamlet* again: because you have the idea that it is purely a drama of the ideal. But there is more to it. Subtract the ideal, and you have the framework of your own struggle, every great artist's struggle, stated terribly. <Damned cheek.> The ideal is secondary – though it is the main thing that disfigures Shaxpeer, all Englishmen really. (Englishmen have always been, in spite of the national anthem, slaves.) It is this lie which I want to tackle myself in England. Shax made a complete statement of it, but died from it. You, for your part, are going into it as blind as a hooded falcon, and undiseased in this particular way. *There is no chance of a stillbirth.*

If I am rude, rap me. If I am wrong, tell me. If I am worth an attack, attack me. If I am right . . . . Salut in the name of the UR-HAMLET, and the *Hamlet* to come. There!

I'm tired. Your praise of Carol has set me working so hard that it hurts. *The Black Book* is shaping for a minor eclipse. I wish I could grow up a bit. Proofs of the *Hamlet* essay today. No news. Lovely weather, but I've got a dour Cornish mist in my belly and the hump generally. Why does one bother? If only the summer would come. *Destroy this letter please.* I wouldn't like to hurt Fraenkel's feelings, because he has been nice and friendly to me: and because he suffers as we all suffer, and that's a bond, even if one is poles apart. Well, yours ever, as this machine is to you Hamlet. I must reread the letters in bed. By the way I've only been through them once. What gems lie hidden [in] them! Maybe tomorrow I'll write the opposite of all I've said to you. Bear with me. In the name of faith, hope and hilarity.

Sincerely.   Lawrence Durrell.

[P.S.] Leave the title: when you do your own opus I hope you call it:
Hamlet, *Prince of China*!!!!
[P.P.S.] I suppose you haven't a full face photograph of yourself? Reading Kretschmer and would like to see whether you resemble the pycniks or the leptosomes.

This letter was published as 'Hamlet, Prince of China', in *Delta*, 2me Année, No. 3 (Christmas 1938).

*[Paris]   Jan. 20, 1937

Dear Durrell,

Your last letter about *Hamlet* is, as I told you, the finest letter I ever received in my life. I hope that means something to you. Heretofore I have been on the sending end; for the first time in my life someone bobs up who is more than a match for me. My letter-writing days are almost over, I fear. I am harassed. It is a great pity because you deserve the fullest response. Unfortunately I gave in the past of my best to my old friends in America who never really understood me, not deep down anyway, and now I am so possessed by the work in hand that I haven't the energy to give myself in letters. But I want you to know that even if I deal out a meagre response I am deeply appreciative – not only that, but touched, almost overwhelmed. I say *almost* because, *entre nous*, I can honestly say I deserve it. (Without egotism or vanity.) We get back in the measure that we give. That's the sort of poetic justice which rules the world and there is no other I recognize. Now the tide is turning for me. I have definitely gotten a foothold, a grip on the world. I have made them stop and listen, I feel, and perhaps a little later it will be a terrible avalanche. I am almost afraid of it – of what the future holds.

<Sent you the "Max" MS. yesterday – for Evans.> Not long ago, as you will surmise when you read the "Max" story, I read the correspondence between Georg Brandes and Nietzsche. It was Fraenkel who lent it to me. I came to a startling conclusion about his insanity. Something like this. That he, Nietzsche, was all right so long as he took a fighting stance, so long as he was fighting the world. What took the pins from under him was Brandes' whole-hearted acceptance and admiration. Against that he was powerless. He fell over backwards. It's an amazing correspondence and worth reading. I think you will see what I mean if you ever get to it.

I mention this because you say something about madness. There was a time in my life when it seemed as though I might go mad. That was between 20 and 25 years of age. I hadn't written anything, *couldn't* write anything, and yet felt myself all-powerful, able to cope with anything, able to do anything. I was in a ridiculous position, as regards everything. I was that "failure" which Papini writes about. I had to do something desperate, something active in the world of men, or go nuts. I did it. Every move I made I burned my bridges behind me. Despair, desperation, megalomania. I rolled up such an experience of life that if I live to be a hundred years old it will never be fully told. I know literally thousands of people. I know hundreds intimately. I saw what few men have seen without losing their faith or their balance. (All this, by the way, I discovered recently from my astrologic acquaintances, is decreed in the horoscope. And further, that I would either go mad or accomplish something tremendous.) I have had innumerable crises. Well, I am alive, gay, energetic, optimistic in a crazy unoptimistic way. I have taken the world in and now I am spewing it out. Mairet writes me an incredible letter the other day, anent *Tropic*, which he just read, to the effect that it is a chaos and incredible and so on and so forth. But if I ever told him the truth, the whole story, what would he say? He would call me a monster, no doubt.

This is a prelude. What amazes me in you is your intuition, your very genuine and vital understanding. May I say that I honestly believe that there is not a man in England who is thinking as you are thinking? I believe that absolutely. I believe that if in your creative work you will show anything like the penetration and insight which you reveal in your letters – and the fragments you have shown me of your work – you will be the foremost writer in England. (You said you had some Indian blood – and that seems to explain a great deal to me. Tell me more about it, more about yourself, your upbringing, your ancestry, etc. I believe in stock. In race, in blood, in the ancestral horde.)

What strikes me again is your quick evaluation of Fraenkel, which is quite just. No need to feel sorry. We are not dealing with personalities, but with the fact, the written record. Naturally he is more complex, more variegated, more interesting perhaps than you imagine. But the paralysis, the feebleness of the death motif, all that is only too true. But, as regards the *Hamlet* book, I have no regrets. Whom else could I have found? One must take whatever comes to hand. First come, first served. There is still a good spot to do, and perhaps before we reach the thousandth page I shall have wrung the very guts out of him. The letter which he so slyly talks about, the one you refer to, was a piece of brutality on my part, but superb. I gave it to him straight and cold. He was ill for several days thereafter. It was about the Jews, about their role in life – as "microbe". I retract nothing I said therein. But it's tough to get a jolt like that – especially from your bosom friend who lives right above you.

What you say about "realizing yourself as an artist, i.e., God", struck me as one of the most profound things you've written. The very core of the matter. No, I do realize it all. I came to the most tremendous decision in New York, the voyage before last. Shattering realizations. Above all, the determination to be absolutely responsible myself for everything. I really have no fight any longer with the world. I accept the world, in the ultimate sense. Yes, I fight and I bellyache now, but it's rather old habit-patterns than anything real in me. The fight is over – I mean that fight which sunk Lawrence, and maybe Shakespeare too, as you infer. And that is how I interpret your Chinese allusions. Am I right? One enters a new dimension, certainly non-English, non-American, non-European. *That* world belongs to the past, to infancy – it gets sloughed off, like a snake's skin. So how talk to Eliot, Mairet, Orwell, Connolly – all these bloody, bleeding blokes with their navel-strings uncut.

Oddly enough, I too have felt that the great opus lies ahead, and in somewhat the manner indicated. Not *Capricorn*, which will be tremendous enough, I can assure you. No, something of a wholly different order. Something to put beside *Quixote, Gargantua, Satyricon*, etc. A classic for the 21st or 22nd century. First all this Brobdingnagian experience must be vomited forth. I must clear the decks of vital experience. It bumps around inside like huge stones. When I have turned completely inside out the new work will shine forth of itself. I fear nothing. I will simply show my new skin. And, if you won't laugh, I think that is what the astrologers are trying to say, though they haven't invented a language for it yet. They need a flesh and blood language instead of this stratospheric algebra or logarithmic junk which they spout. That is why I listen to them. I don't give a fuck about what they predict. I do my own predicting. Or rather, I act and let the predictions take care of themselves. But, in another way – crudely – it's something like this, I think . . . . that we are all working towards the realization of the potential. The man who realizes it most – in no matter what field – floors the world. Has the world by the balls. *Just as man.* I'm trying to say that over again in the Lawrence book. That is why I can make absurd cracks about the man 20,000 years hence. I see man passing in long waves like that. Pithecanthropus erectus . . . . Neanderthal . . . . Cro-Magnon . . . . . Maybe we are about 10,000 years or so along in our cycle of development. Maybe it will take 15,000 more years for us to show all we've got. Then out! Out like a flash! And another brand new race, new ideas, new taboos, etc. Not higher necessarily. No, but totally different. Totally. Gloriously different. That's always in the back of my head – the new man to come who won't even know how to read our relics. [. . .]

Anyway, I'm tired, done in. I'm going to Copenhagen for a short stay about the middle of February. Will see Lundkvist, the Swedish poet, there. Have a swell letter from him about the books and mss. I sent him. He's doing things for me up there. And for you too, I believe. Said so, anyway. (Your essay got published, you know – Jan. 14th issue.) I'll come back and work some more, and then, towards late spring, try to get down to Corfu, and to Crete. *Must see the labyrinth!* An obsession since the last fifteen years. Read Evans years and years ago it seems. Knocked cold. Same for Schliemann or whatever his name is – about Troy.

Well, more later. Going to bed. Fagged.

HVM.

*C/o Ionian Bank, *Corfu*: *Greece*   [*c.* 27 January 1937]

Dear H.M.

I was born 27th February. 1912. at one o'clock of the morning. The Indian Blood must have been a mistake. I'm Irish mother English father. God-fearing, lusty, chapel-going Mutiny stock. (My grandma sat up on the veranda of her house with a shot-gun across her knee waiting for the mutiny gang: but when they saw her face they went another way. Hence the family face.) I may have a touch of Indian in me – who knows? I'm one of the world's expatriates anyhow. It's lonely being cut off from one's race. So much of England I loved – and hated so much – I try and wipe it off my tongue but it clings. O what the hell. I was born to be Hamlet's little godchild. The horoscopes can't touch me – I'm already *mad*!

Yours Sinc.
Larry Durrell

[P.S.] I daren't answer your letter because what I might write (all that [I] could write in fact) would ultimately concern neither of us. I have moments of complete authority when I see clearly, act purely, laugh. And then a mood settles on me like [a] flap and I'm in a convulsion again: fragments get shaken out of my clothes without my knowing it. Believe me what I write to you when I'm serious seems under compulsion. I always have the sneaking hope you won't understand – won't implicate me in the process by showing that you understand. This is because at bottom I feel one must accept it. No option. Even if the horoscope says tumour of the parietal lobe at the coronal suture ONE MUST ACCEPT IT. It's cold comfort, Brother etc etc in the words of the old song.

50

However, we connect.

Goodnight.

The Chinese allusions were *right* – need I say?

Corfu: [next day]

This morning I feel better. Much better. I shall take a stroll with the gun later on and shoot a couple of snipe to give my courage a flip. I read "Max" today in bed, before breakfast. It's terrifying – and the Eyes of Paris too. Are these recent? How can you stay there in the ant-heap? Myself I shall go lonelier and lonelier ultimately – to some white Parian little island – with nothing but a set of clean togas and a few brainless flute-girls for company. I shall not teach or heal or anything. Just eat watermelons and fondle the second from the left – and learn the flute maybe. Please H.M. *Don't* crack up *The Black Book* until you see it yourself – will you? Because I don't want to let you down – and the book mightn't be so good after all: one is so familiar with the story of the young author no great man will help, that when you are so damn generous I feel an obligation to live up to your opinion of me – that's all. You shall have it the second it's done.

My birth and upbringing?

I was born in India. Went to school there – under the Himalayas. The most wonderful memories – a brief dream of Tibet until I was eleven. Then that mean, shabby little island up there wrung my guts out of me and tried to destroy anything singular and unique in me. My so called up-bringing was quite an uproar. I have always broken stable when I was unhappy. The list of schools I've been to would be a yard long. I failed every known civil service exam. I hymned and whored in London – playing jazz in a nightclub, composing jazz songs, working in real estate. Never really starved – but I wonder whether thin rations are not another degree of starvation – I met Nancy in an equally precarious position and we struck up an incongruous partnership: a dream of broken bottles, sputum, tinned food, rancid meat, urinals, the smell of the lock-hospitals. And so – well we did a bit of drinking and dying. The second lesson according to St. Paul. Ran a photographic studio together. It crashed. Tried posters, short stories, journalism – everything short of selling our bottoms to a clergyman. I wrote a cheap novel. Sold it – well that altered things.

Here was a stable profession for me to follow. Art for money's sake. I began. My second I finished when we reached here. After that – the deluge. All this epic Iliad of course took about three or four years. Feels like a million.

Well there it is. My life is like a chopped worm. Until eleven marvellous memories – white, white the Himalayas from the dormitory windows. The gentle black Jesuits praying to our lady and outside on the frontier roads the Chinese walking stiffly and Tibetans playing cards on the ground: the blue fissures in the hills. God what a dream, the *passes* into Lhasa – blue with ice and thawing softly towards the holy forbidden city. I think Tibet is for me what China is to you. I lived on the edge of it with a kind of nursery-rhyme happiness. I wanted to go one summer into the passes. They promised to take me. But I left without going – alamort – it is a kind of unreasoning disease when I think of it. I am illogical again like a child. I whimper. I pant. And so on.

And now, illustrious, came the day when *Tropic* opened a pit in my brain. It freed me immediately. I had such a marvellous sense of absolution – freedom from guilt – I thought I'd drop you a note.

Tropic taught me one valuable thing. To write about people I knew something about. Imagine it! I had this collection of grotesques sitting inside and I hadn't written a line about them – only about heroic Englishmen and dove-like girls etc (7/6^d a volume). The whole collection of men and women opened up for me like a razor. I borrowed the historic present and sat down to it. You mustn't judge this book from very high standards. It's only a beginning – but I can feel it all beginning to unroll inside me at last. I am entering into my tuistic self without responsibility. The rest should follow. I tell you – two years ago – God couldn't have prophesied more than a Hugh Walpole income for me: now I don't know – Rimbaud's solution is always in the air. If there's a war now . . . . I suppose I'll be among the killers – ENUF

I send you a few pamphlets that might amuse you. One brilliant satire on Eliot by *Aldington*: did you get the 'carbon'? One poem about the night-club I worked in. I send you another: also a copy of an early volume of poems – with good will and apologies for poor quality. I have atoned since by one or two real poems.

Don't bother to write. I know how fagged you must be. Just a p.c. if any thing crops up.

Sincerely.
Lawrence Durrell

Dear Durrell:

A few more words about the Hamlet letter you wrote me recently. To repeat, for one thing – after letting it lie cold a few days – that it is the best and the most important letter I ever received in all my life. I have just been typing it off – *instead of destroying it,* as you so naïvely suggested. And while so doing – while thinking of the people to whom I intend to show it (not out of arrant egotism, believe me, but rather in *your* interests) – I was laughing aloud. Because in that part where you talk about consulting the books (Jung, etc.) I was thinking what a face you'd make if you knew how "the sin-guilt-idealism" trinity gets served up in these parts, how we mop it up for breakfast and dinner or over the coffee at the cafés, etc. You said a marvellous thing there about the artist becoming God – I marvelled the more because I have written about that precisely, elaborately, and in my very best vein in the Lawrence book. (The little squirt about the Tree of Life and Death was just a fillip – I had to redo it recently and thought the theme – the Dionysian theme – would interest you. But wait till you see some of the developed parts. We're going to give each other the accolade all over again!) Everything lately is revision – because of that book Kahane promises to bring out. That sets me back in one way, but advances me in another, because as I retype and revise I do a lot of peripheral thinking. About the things I am not writing. I have explained the value of that to Anaïs time and again because she writes every day from scratch – in the voluminous diary. Not holding a thing in, letting it harden and become gem-like and twisted and poisonous robs one's writing of some precious qualities – at least, so I think. All the time in rereading your explanations of my method or my terrain, if you like, I say to myself that a great deal of it has to do with this – with the holding it in, holding it in your guts until it almost kills you. In *Capricorn* there are passages relating to experiences, ideas, even shreds, vague, vague shreds of ideas or emotions, which I have held in for fifteen years and more, some much more. These erupt now in explosive crystallizations which, despite the tenuous surface quality are hard as steel and as durable, I believe. Writing, if I may venture a pronunciamento, is what you are every day, no? Writing fools nobody, no more than the man fools his neighbor with his lies and grimaces. People see right through you, disguise yourself as you may. The disguise, or mask, is inevitable, *soit.* But my aim is to rip it off more and more, to stand naked and so to glow that neither the stethoscope nor the X Ray will be necessary. The admiration for what all of us regard as superior writing is always falsely accented. The discrepancy between what we do and what we admire in others is finally a discrepancy in *living.* The goad which art furnishes men is only the result of a blind recognition that we have not lived enough. Living, to be sure, can be on all sorts of planes. But living is always living – the test, or the optimum, if you like, of proved faith.

(to be continued when I get more time.)

HVM.

[. . .]

Durrell's Hamlet essay had appeared as 'The Prince and Hamlet' in the *New English Weekly*, 10 (14 January 1937), and is distinct from his 'Hamlet letter' of mid January 1937, given above.

*C/o Ionian Bank: Corfu: Greece.   [February? 1937]

Honoured and illustrious:

Firstly it's your output that staggers me. Evans is so damned grateful he's left his novel off for a bit. That for "Max". As for the way you crack me up to these people, gratitude is a poor word. I should say FRIGHT. Supposing I ain't? And as for *The Black Book*, poor thing, the position with regard to it is, to say the least, anagogic. Like this: I am a proud father of a cheap romance, wishy-washy stuff. Sheer lochia. But Faber and Faber, on the strength of it, gave me a 3-vol contract: not realising, poor people, what a phoenix lurked under the lamb's evening-clothes. I wrote them recently and said: I am writing one of the most amazing books ever completed outside an asylum. It is, though mild, unprintable in England. What will you do? THEY HAVE THE OPTION ON IT, you see. They replied decently enough, that it was o.k. with them, so long as they got the first offer, where it was printed. Accordingly I am bound to them firmly, until they give *The Black Book* the K.O. I don't think they could do anything but refuse. It is so short

(70,000 words) that it won't stand castration. Myself I don't know. I like it, frankly. It's a good little chronicle of the english death, done in a sort of hamstrung tempo, with bursts of applause here and there. I think it's a book Huxley could have written if he were a mixture of Lawrence and Shakespeare. It dates from that insomniac day when I felt a sort of malaise, and began to wonder if I would really be content as a best-selling novelist (once my ideal). Very little is censorable in the ego of the book. Nothing in fact. I had to go easy on the ego because a twenty-four year old ego is a dull thing to contemplate. But there is an irrepressible dying diarist called Gregory, and a quite unprintable person called Tarquin. These two are slightly libellous. Very, in fact. I am going to send it to you to read first when it's done, because technically it's very influenced by you: but after millions of anxious nights Nancy says she sees a distinct personality in it which is not Miller. This must be a comfort to you. In order to destroy time I use the historic present a great deal – not to mention the gnomic aorist. It is not too risky, but here and there it was necessary, when dealing with Tarquin, who is (if he lives yet) something of a frontal sarcoma, a fairly wide excavation, not to mention a spot of oblique traction. And once the foetus is really manhandled in a sort of Church of England fashion. For the rest, you might like passages. [. . .]

Sincerely.   Lawrence Durrell.

*[Paris]   March 8, 1937

Dear Durrell,

The Black Book came and I have opened it and I read goggle-eyed, with terror, admiration and amazement. I am still reading it – slowing up because I want to savor each morsel, each line, each word. You are the master of the English language – stupendous reaches, too grand almost for any book. Breaks the boundaries of books, spills over and creates a deluge which is no longer a book but a river of language, the Verb broken into its component elements and running amok. You have written things in this book which nobody has dared to write. It's brutal, obsessive, cruel, devastating, appalling. I'm bewildered still. So this is no criticism – and did you want criticism? No, this is a salute to the master! I will tell you more calmly, when I get finished, when I reread and sponge it up more thoroughly. Now it's an onslaught.

Of course I don't expect to see Faber & Faber publishing it. Did you? No English or American publisher would dare print it. We must find *the* man for it! I am pondering over it already. And right here a problem presents itself. You say this is the only copy there is. You frighten the life out of me. I can, of course, send it on to Faber registered and all that, but even so – I wouldn't rest easy putting it into the mails. Before I do anything, tell me if you don't think I had better have a copy made, several, in fact? I could arrange it, if you like, with someone I know and can trust. It's a big job – I don't know how many pages, because you didn't number your pages. But, if you deem it advisable, I will go ahead with it and defray all expenses. You could square that off – if you so wished – against my indebtedness to you. On the other hand, you may wish to get it to Faber's in a hurry. So let me know pronto what to do.

My dear Durrell, you'll never do something more to their liking, as you put it in your note. You've crossed the Equator. Your commercial career is finished. From now on you're an outlaw, and I congratulate you with all the breath in my body. I seriously think – and didn't I hint of all this in the letter to the Conference Press – that you truly are "the first Englishman!" This is way beyond Lawrence and the whole tribe. You are out among the asteroids – for good and all, I hope.

The whole thing is a poem, a colossal poem. Why you should ever want to write little finished poems I don't know. Anything you write as poem can only be a whiff, after this. *This is the poem.* It's like the black death, by Jesus. I'm stunned. My only adverse reaction is that it's too colossally colossal. You have to be Gargantua himself to take it all in.

It seems to me, at the moment, that Kahane would be the only man to do it. Possibly Fraenkel. That's why I'd like to have extra copies of it. No commercial, legitimate publisher can possibly bring it out. I can see them fainting as they read it. Unfortunately Kahane, my publisher, is rather set against you. Very unfortunately, and partly my fault. Seems he doesn't like anyone who admires me too much. Curious thing that, but a fact. Sort of professional jealousy. (He writes too you know, under the name of Cecil Barr – vile vile crap, the vilest of the vile – and he admits it, but with that English insouciance that makes my blood creep.) But, if you assent, I will try him. I will wheedle and cajole and jig for him, if necessary – because I believe in it wholeheartedly. And I see no one else on the horizon. Only Fraenkel. Again we will be up against the professional problem. Fraenkel however is more capable of being objective, capable of admiring something he could not do himself. He *is* Carrefour you know. He has the money and the press. Has he the courage, the initiative? Perhaps it could be brought out in a deluxe edition, through subscription. All this I must think about.

Anyway, now I understand the Himalayan background. You should thank your lucky stars you were born there at the gateway to Thibet. There's a new dimension in your book which could only have come from such a place. It's like we're out among new constellations. How long, for Christ's sake, did it take you to write this? I can understand that you must be exhausted. It's a tour de force.

Well, more when I finish. And salute!

HVM.

*[Paris]   March 13, 1937

Dear Durrell:

One of the best evidences of the great merit of your book is this, that I haven't yet finished it! This is not flippant paradox. I mean sincerely that your book has caused such an upheaval, has had such a fecundating power, that the discussion of it outstrips the reading. I myself am deliberately prolonging the achievement. Even I, voracious and gluttonous as I am, find it too rich and savory to gulp down quickly. I don't even feel like saying much about it until I have read it several times. And part of my desire to have copies made is to keep one on hand for ready reference, to bite into it now and again or show it to others.

This evening, suffering from a bit of a hangover, I was in bed when my friend Edgar knocked at the door. I told him to glance at the part about the womb. That's all I permitted him to read. Came another knock and Anaïs arrived. We sat on the bed and dived right into the schizophrenic zone. Time to eat. Walking down the Villa Seurat towards the restaurant we were still discussing the book. Now it is after midnight. We have been talking Durrell for five hours, and yesterday it was almost the same. In the midst of the discussion we were going to send you a telegram. We were going to ask you a vital question. What the question was I forbear to tell you, as it would take too long to explain what led up to it. But anyway I felt constrained to remark that it was a great pity you weren't here to listen to what we had to say. That would have been a real reward.[. . .]

Myself I think that there are whole blocks in your book which are nothing short of miraculous. Gracie, Miss Smith, the Womb, for example, to mention just a few. You seem to have expressed the ultimate. The demonic quality of the writing comes from a super-consciousness which is simply a mystery. How you attained it God only knows. You are absolutely one with the writing. Edgar thinks you must be living on this plane of significance. I myself can't believe it. You would almost be God if you were. At any rate, you're an apocalyptic writer.

March 15th

The reading of your book was an event in my life. I had the impression of having finished a simply "colossal" work, something of two or three thousand pages! Partly due to the form in which you cast it, a form rigidly imposed upon you by the very nature of the book, and partly by the poetic significance, the *symbolic* nature of the work. It is a modern poem of the first dimension, something that not only frees you from the Ego and the Id but the reader also. The *few* readers there will be! For this is a book for the initiated only – and how many are there at present in the world? It is a surgical operation, a self-birth: the navel string is definitely cut. No going back from this point. You are now out in the wide world, the world of your own creation in which you will be very much alone. A terrorizing prospect if it were not for the fact that you know what it is all about, that you reveal a supreme awareness, a super-consciousness. The theme is death and rebirth, the Dionysian theme which I predicted, in the Lawrence book, must be the theme for the writers to come – the only theme permissible, or possible. Your rebirth is the most violent act of destruction. A positive one, just the opposite to the Surrealist movement. Superficially there are analogies between your technique and theirs; but only superficially! The real difference is vast, a chasm veritably. And that is precisely because of your "wisdom", your ability, after terrific struggle, to effect a synthesis. (It happens that when your book came I was in the midst of a long article on Surrealism, which goes into the new book. I was writing about the stress they put on "the marvellous", though not realizing themselves what this means in any profound way.) Your book makes the bridge. It means to me, at least, that you realize that the marvellous is a not a separate, static, untapped realm towards which we yearn and by means of which we will destroy an ever-present present, sordid, ugly and untenable, but that in the here and now (which was exactly my thesis) we always have the marvellous, simply through the transforming power of the spirit. The book, though outwardly chaotic and confused, a sort of monotonous avalanche, is really structurally solid and formal as a diamond. It happens that instead of using the mineralogical material of the form-worshippers you were employing the live, plastic material of the womb. Edgar would have it that you have performed the astounding feat of following the schizophrenic trend to its logical, consummate solution, that instead of the retrogressive neurotic swing back to the womb – womb being the unattainable, the Paradise of the Ideal, the Godhood business – you have expanded the womb-feeling until it includes the whole universe. All is womb, hence you are constantly with God. Hence, like God, a thorough out and out schizoid, able to move creatively, easily, freely in all directions and all dimensions. In my charts, when trying to solve the problem of the Lawrence book, I was obsessed with a similar idea. I felt that the return to the womb feeling was a right one, but untenable simply because impossible (only the insane achieve it!); but the process of transformation, metamorphosis, symbolization, if you will, *is* this same return to the womb tendency, only in reverse. You die out utterly, as you did in your book, in order to achieve a life on a thoroughly new plane of reality. This is so clear in your book, so exhaustively and definitively written out, that it makes one dance inside to follow you. [. . .]

I blush a bit for seeming to expound back to you the meaning of your own work. If I assume more than is meet it is only because, what with a few random remarks you drop in your letters, what with the tremendous reach of your book, I feel that a great, great deal remains to be said and written about the meaning of your book. In another sense, there is not a word to be said. In the sense, I mean, that you have so thoroughly welded the meaning and the expression that to explain would be to diminish your work. It has the perfection of the poem, which is not poetry, if you get what I mean. Here, in *The Black Book*, you are no longer poetizing, no longer writing or making verse. *You do a poem.* (If I could only say it in Chinese, with the plastic, concrete, all-sufficient ideogram!) A work like yours shows up the absurdity and futility of writing "poetry" in our age. With poetry gone there is left only the poem to be achieved – and here I mean to emphasize that poetry in life and action quality which the artist is always stressing but never quite reaching, since he himself is not sufficiently aware usually of the meaning of art. You can grasp it again when you think of history as being quite meaningless – as a repetition ad infinitum of the wrong way of living, which is never overcome on the historical plane, by new ideologies, new wars and revolutions, new conversions, etc. Which is accomplished only at one fell swoop, by the pure act of revelation. Yesterday, as it were, and all the yesterdays before, *failure*. Tomorrow, utter clarity, utter, ripe wisdom, utter perfection – through realization. And towards this all art has tended, but never stated it. It is this I feel you have been grappling with and have expressed magnificently. And perhaps, as a result, that feeling of utter isolation – which leads to the remarkable obsessive use of the word "loneliness" in your book, a word you constantly mis-spell, by the way! And from icy clear loneliness a fear of madness – but not truly, not real, only a pose unconsciously assumed in order to re-provoke the marvellous feeling of sheer loneliness, of your rightness.

There is, in a profound way, *sense* to everything that is going on in the world. The *poetic* justice that we hear about now and then. The realization that nothing is to be accomplished – in the way that everything heretofore has been accomplished. Realization, through complete acceptance and understanding, of a completely new way of life, *for the individual* who is ready for it. Everything pivoted back to the solid nucleus of the individual life. A new stance which permits you to function with the perfection of automatism in the world of reality, leaving you free to explore the stratospheric regions where your real problems commence. A fourth-dimensional sort of jump, then, into the a-historical realities. A work such as yours thoroughly impossible to ignore. Because it is of this future condition and hence fecundating. A little drop of colored ink which will stain the whole body of life; a work which will accomplish by silent osmosis what revolutions are powerless to bring about. A chemical metamorphosis because the little drop of ink comes directly from God's fountain pen. Because the chemical here is the divine. And so we are no longer dealing with chemistry, so-called, nor with physics, nor with astronomy, nor with meteorology. We make a musical resolution into a new and strange key. We keep alive the old by breaking it down in a full death process. Everything is made alive, because first dead, by process of white-hot incinerating poetry. This accords, laugh if you will, with the often meaningless language of the astrologers: the appearance on the zodiacal horizon of a new planet which brings about a musico-metaphysical resolution into a new way of life. Not a new way in the old ideological merry-go-round sense, but *the* way, the way which makes art (crucifixion) unnecessary. We are definitely entering this sign, and your book, to use one of your own phrases, is "an organ note" in the new dimensional field.

O High and Mighty Llama [sic], how did you come by your great wisdom? Give us a tangible, personal statement of the condition of your soul to-day! Are you still standing there on the topmost tip of Mt. Everest? Does the snow still dazzle you? Have you passed out of *snow* and into the blue? What is the favorite color now? What is the password?

In replying send a new and unabridged volume of Funk & Wagnall's Dictionary. I am beginning to re-learn the English language. *Aboulia, masma, floccus.* . . . . *Lonliness!* [sic] When you finally felt the Ark grounding on Mt. Ararat what a consolation it must have been to find that all your marvellous words were also rescued from the Flood! The Picassos on the wall! Yes, and with it floccus, masma, aboulia, alexia, aphasia, amusia, anoia, and Miss Smith's red coon slit, her conk, her poll, her carnivorous ant-eating laughter, her Chaucerian Africa with Freudian fauna and flora, with Chamberlain's agraphia, Chamberlain hanging on a hook by his own navel-string, listening with dead mastoid to the Ninth Symphony of fluked-fin futility. I must read it all again a hundred times. I sit here with a bag of dynamite and fear to mail it out. I wait for the command. It must be retyped. More carbons, more personal readers, more alexia, more aboulia, more iconography, more snow, more coon slits and coon-slatted laughter. Immense. Colossal. *Kolossal!* Alors, zero hour! God the Illogical lost in the schizophrenic rush. Alors, up with the womb and hail to the divine osmosis! [. . .]

In answer to your questions however, about the Banned Book. No, I don't know Aldington, Campbell, Lewis – you mean Wyndham Lewis? Wrote the first and last named, care of their publishers – but never heard from them. Shaw I deemed hopeless, as I would H.G. Wells. You have in the enclosures letters from Pound, Stein and Williams – the first two absolutely imbecilic, as also are Dos Passos, Dreiser and Max Eastman. I like Lowenfels' long essay and your own – nothing much outside of that.

"Zero" came and I gave it to Anaïs. She will write you. Read it, but during a hang-over. Can't properly judge it now. I'm going to send you another water-color separately which should remind you of the Himalayan thema. Fine frozen colors. Hope it appeals to you. If not, return it – it's my favorite for the time being.

Anaïs wants to know, and so do I, where you got the linen paper – and how expensive is it? And who bound the book so beautifully? You? Marvellous presentation. Needs only a few missals.

I shall probably have more to say about *The Black Book*. The most stimulating thing I have read in years and years. Leaves me wide open. Nothing pre-natal about it. The pre- is finished. *Now it IS.* And so, once again, salute, and a round salvo of 59 guns!

> Yours,
> HVM.

The typescript on linen paper of *The Black Book*, identified by Durrell as 'the one and only', is protected by a stitched binding with black boards, produced by a Corfiot bookbinder.

*C/o Ionian Bank: [Corfu, March 1937]

Dear Miller:

I'm dumb of course. Don't know what the hell to say. I knew it was good, of course – but the extravagance of your praise frightened me. In bed. Grippe. 103° and all that stuff. Had a nice letter from the reader at Fabers who has heard whispers of the book and wrote to ask after its health. Very nice people. I told them you were holding it to make copies and would send it on post-haste when you had made them. Much thanks for the idea. I know no typist who would do it for me in England, that was why it was alone. As for Kahane, tell me, where do I compete with *Daffodil*? And as your publisher isn't he happy to find his taste corroborated? Sounds a bit of a shit to me. However, no hurry. Slowly slowly. Let me get back on my feet again and I'll let you know further. In the meantime your praise rings in my ear like the silver hammers of quinine, and I'm covered in sweat and glory.

Evans and Nan and Co reading Anaïs Nin out loud and going crazy over those passages in *House of Incest*. Wow, motile silk! Now I know. It was written during the grippe.

> Best wishes, and pray god you still like
> the bloody tome when you shut it up.

Personally I find a lot wrong with it.
I'll do better. May even rewrite here and there.

Alors.

Lawrence Durrell.

*C/o Ionian Bank: Corfu: Greece.   [late March 1937]

Dear H.M.

The magnitude of my achievement deafens me. At least your letters
anent it do. Well, if we are not to bluff or become mock-modest, I
knew it was a good book, I felt that virtue had passsed out of me. But
so good . . .? This is a discovery which has illuminated today, yesterday
and the day before. I am inclined to say: "Good. Destroy it. If YOU like
it, and Edgar and Anaïs Nin do too – then hardly anyone else will
understand it." The exclusiveness is a hangover after reading your
fan-mail, which has arrived safely here. Are these the REALLY GREAT?
My god what mucus some of these people are. Mostly the names. I
doubt we can assemble any kind of anthology from the kind of anile
drivel most of these people write. The best are the least known – the
most perfect and touching is Francis Dodo (?) to me: about Paris. If you
can let me hold them until June early, I'll assemble them in an approxi-
mate design and show them to Alan Thomas when he comes (confidence). On his return to London he will carry the idea to Pringle of Faber
& Faber. In the meantime I'm sounding Gawsworth. Curtis Brown no
good it seems. The only trouble is that it's more gristle than meat.
Huxley is so charming – you'd've thought he'd write a little about the
book and less about himself; as for Gertrude – what a punctured
umbrella she is. Don't like Pound's middle english, but he seems
willing to help. E.E. Cummings? I didn't see him, but maybe I missed
him in my hurry. Orwell is a nice chap, but ignorant. MacCarthy is
charming for an old literary lion.
    BUT I am slightly deflected from my target by a letter of yours
among them all, in which you say that the censor PROMISED TO LIFT
THE BAN ON YOU IF YOU COULD PRODUCE ENOUGH EVIDENCE THAT
YOU WERE AN ARTIST. My dear H.M., here is the tangible and solid
bull we must hit. [. . .]
    AS FOR THE GRAND LAMA I'M IN A SLIGHT COMA, SOMA, OR
TRAUMA ABOUT YOUR LETTER. I'm tremendously grateful you find

so much meat in the book. By all means let us have copies since you think it worth while – tread lightly however, because I'm broke as hell at the second of writing. It is rather a mystery I suppose. I don't pretend to solve it. I look at myself in the mirror from time to time – no clue whatever. A short fat Obelisk with the features of a good-natured cattle driver. I am 25 but I feel much older. Zarian has just sent me a huge Viennese briar pipe and I have been making Nancy photograph me at all angles, with it in me. Perhaps some clue will emerge from the subsequent photographs. I'll send you one. The state of my soul is shaky just now. I've come down several thousand feet, below snow-line, and intend to stay as long as I can. Buoyancy does me no good. I get over emotional and shaky and liable to rages and fears and psychological tics – all due to this damned writing. I used to be so healthy and full of a sort of gawkish je m'en foutisme. The summer inaction will bring it back. Am planning a monastic summer. Boxing at dawn with Capt McGibbon. Diving. Swimming. No smoking. Actually the thing which will heal me is a visit to Calypso's grotto on the lonely island north of us. As soon as the boat's ready we go. No more books, no more writers, no more anything. I WANT A GOOD STEADY JOB WITH A LITTLE HOUSE LOTS OF CHILDREN A LAWN MOWER A BANK ACCOUNT A LITTLE CAR AND THE RESPECT OF THE MAN NEXT DOOR.

The Black Book took about 18 months to write: 4 rewrites: altogether in quantity I wrote about four times the amount: but it's a very short book. I'm afraid it's over-packed with lard. Well, that's a technical problem. I admire the effortless way you butter your bread, not too much, not too little. Myself I'm so scared of the butter not showing,.or of it being mistaken for mere margarine, that I over-cloy the works. A sense of proportion will come, however.

Tell Edgar that I love his guts for that criticism of his: it drove a nail into me it was so acute: helped me to realise more clearly what I am – a thing which always puzzles me. By God, there are some nice people left in the world. I'm grateful to you three more than I can say. By the way, I hope you won't be annoyed. I had a letter from Pringle of Fabers the other day. He had got wind of *The Black Book* and was asking for news. So help me your first note had just come, and as I was telling him what a wonderful book it was, I quoted a few of your outrageous praises and gloated over them. I might add that I had the good grace to tell him I was writing personally, not a business letter, and quoting without permission. So no harm can result. But I want to apologise. It's a thing

I'm not in the habit of doing. You will see, of course, that with the others I'm not modest. I tell them how wonderful the book is, and what shits they are. It is when I face the author of the original deluge that my real modesty begins. Anything positive I have as a writer I owe to your books – my stance, a new emotional attitude, the way I hold my gloves up at the world. As for the wisdom – my God – it is all a question of induction, convection, you might say contagion. I shall do better yet I hope. Don't lose sight of the ardent disciple in me, and mistake a fledgling for a full-grown phoenix. It's a point I labour because the influence is there, rather more than I would care to admit to a jury! What affects me most is the complete selfless generosity which you all shower on me. I fatten on it. Gratitude is no reply. You shall have a book, if possible, a bigger book – dedicated to Miller, Edgar, and Nin Inc., Paris. Specialists in plasm, germ-plasm, mind-plasm, ectoplasm, soul-plasm. I have planned AN AGON, A PATHOS, AN ANAGNORISIS? If I write them they should be: The Black Book, The Book of Miracles, The Book of the Dead. Perhaps I shan't write them. If I do and they are what they might be, well, as I say, one will be an answer to you all.

As for my vocabulary, mea culpa etc. Words I carry in my pocket where they breed like white mice. But there isn't a single neologism in the whole book. Every word IS. Aboulia and Co are from brain-surgery manuals. Words belonging to trades stick to my tongue. I'm a fiendish reader for mere syllables. Anoia, alexia and Co. I'm afraid you can't talk, because you have the same assimilative power. One of your best phrases is incomprehensible to most people because it's technical: "giving the womb the curette with every line". I'm afraid the average reader doesn't know the technique of abortion as intimately as this. I keep explaining in my quiet cherubic pious way what it means. Perhaps Eliot found out, hence the rejection! Similarly I suffer. Evans didn't know what the pneumatic gifts were until I told him to look them up in the encyc britt. The Greek word for breath is *pnevma* – a lovely sound. From which pneumatic etc.

More anon. [. . .]

Yours Sincerely and excitedly.
Larry Durrell.

Francis Dodo's letter moves me enormously. I want you later to let me keep a copy of it if you will. What a wonderful man. You know there are some good people left in the world with Balls to them. Enough to make the new heaven and earth I trow. It continually amazes me. I suppose I shouldn't distrust humanity so, but I do, it scares me with its dirt and its machinery for killing God.

Well, sun today. I've moved my machine out on to the terrace under the vine-leaves. Uneasy blue sea. Lizards sucking in warmth on the wall. Spring opening quietly. It is impossible to think of writing – my writing that is. Been reading you again lately without so much fear of contamination. Growing up I suppose. Feel a bit jaded, but pleased as hell you like that little book of mine. Nancy is as proud as punch, it being her book. I carry the letters around with me chewing them over slowly and smiling to myself. Fabers will wet themselves – perhaps brother Eliot will put on his striped bathing drawers and tell me what the august directors think of it all. Weep for Lycidas, dead ere his prime. I've been explaining to Alan Pringle the difference between myself and Joyce – what bloody cheek! But it makes me chuckle, I feel so exclusive about that book, no one will understand a word of it. One thing I've hammered home is that there is no word-coining in it. The vocabulary may be Elizabethan, middle-english, dutch etc, but EVERY-THING MEANS SOMETHING. I don't like neologism except used as an occasional hand-grenade. That is why Laughlin's 'dream-writing' contributors bore me stiff with their "wingle wangle obfuscating inspissate hunger-marching shitshat". Come, we demand more than chewing-gum. WE ARE HUNGRY. [. . .]

Perhaps this fall we can meet and arrange some sort of campaign to take the skin off the public's behind. Another thought struck me: you see, it must be water-tight – like those ads you read. An eminent doctor says: "I always take *Tropic of Cancer* in a glass of water before going to bed. A marked tonic effect." A famous divine writes: "Sir, I have used *Black Spring* now for a number of years and find it good for swollen joints. My wife's arthritis, for many years crippling, has vanished after a single application." In my quiet, annoying, knowing, pious little way I have been doing some quiet crusading. The one livid paradox which starts up from your writing I have been at great pains to express to my correspondents. None of them see it. Religion, I mean. *Tropic of Cancer* and *B.S.* as the most religious books written since the authorized bible. Your young 'client' Knight has been bombarding me with questions which I have taken great pains to answer. Must keep these people red hot. [. . .]

Leave for Athens Saturday to buy a tent etc. Then the black sleek douce *Van Norden* will be launched and off we go. First to get really healed, and nulled and purified, to the island north, and camp by the grotto of Calypso. In June Alan Thomas comes down here. I'll send your MSS back to you by hand with him. Safer. New Fascist restrictions open everything up and scatter it about, and you can't afford to lose originals. Send you photos of our trips this summer. Plan to leave for England in the fall, stop off a day or two in Paris and meet you and have a meeting of soul-shareholders. Maybe you won't hear from me very regularly this summer, but I'm leaving a machine on the north point with Koster, and strict instructions about mail. Return each week and see what the drag-nets bring in. Just got the egyptian BOOK OF THE DEAD. Tremendously moved by the hymns to Ra as he comes forth. That's how I feel. I want to swallow the sun and feel it in my navel this summer. That is something so far from words and works that I expect you have difficulty in understanding it. Next early spring perhaps you will come south with us when we come and experience the wakening of the old pre-diluvial world. Like a lion yawning and stretching. And then majesty – Ra the great disc spinning and roaring into summer. Sheer fantasy!

For the present I salute you in the name of Nut, the mother of Tchem-Tschek the gourmandizing son of Thoth, who is really Bennu, the sacred bird, which is in Heliopolis. There is no more solemn greeting.

L.D.

Francis *Dobo*, not Dodo, was a Hungarian friend of Miller and Brassaï.

*C/o Ionian Bank, Korfou, Greece   [late March 1937]

Dear H.M.

[. . .] Anaïs Nin's review of *Black Spring* the finest piece of writing I've ever read. Bang! Made me go right back and read *House of Incest* again: confirmed my opinion. She's curious – and you are wrong. The flow *is* outwards towards life – not the Egoismus and womb-neurosis you hint at. That is a sort of funny 'attitude' she has adopted – God knows why. It doesn't fit her shape and size of mind. Yet she has, for some reason, adopted the 'technique' of the wombers – that's what beats me. Why?

Put her beside a genuine neurotic like Fraenkel and the real colour shines out. What is she doing in the wrong camp – with neuroses that write themselves out like hot wax and creosote, and absolute mills bombs for images. It's a paradox. Seems there's a solution pending. But when it resolves (perhaps the diary has resolved it – has it?) the real colours will give the world eye-ache. I haven't seen a woman write this high ever. It's *novel* in the best sense of the word. A new woman. Well, damn it, I'll write it to her more clearly when I see it. Some curious problem somewhere. Give me the dope on that diary will you?

Thank Edgar and convey my admiration. I'm rather scared [to] write – he knows such a lot about me already – don't want to disappoint him.

Enclose some puzzle pictures of a new pipe Zarian sent me. The thing attached to it is me. Queer an't it? Also Potocki – how do you like him – distingué eh?

Brother can you spare a dime?

More *anon.*

By the way – among the words you mentioned was *masma?* Now did you mean miasma? Or MAGMA? Which – I didn't know masma existed. Full of spelling errors. It's a distinction I share with Shakespeare – about the only one I might add.

> Your
> Lawrence Durrell
> Tibet
> Greece

*[Paris]   April 5, 1937

Dear Durrell:

There's so much to answer in your last two letters that I am tackling it piecemeal, as I reread them.

Most of the people you mention I don't know. I wrote Aldington (who is a good friend of Lowenfels) and Wyndham Lewis immediately after *Tropic* came out, care of their publishers, but never had a reply from them. (I don't like Aldington's work at all – *Death of a Hero*, etc.) Lewis I do very much like, but I understand he is snorting fire all the time and suspicious as hell of every one. He could pan the shit out of me, if he wanted to, it would at least sound more intelligent to me than most of the English drivel (for instance, this latest review I enclose from the *Criterion*). [. . .] Cummings I know slightly – also a good friend of my friends Hiler and Lowenfels. But he is hellishly neurotic, askeerd and afeerd of every one and everything. Said he never read anybody else's work. Lowenfels gave him a copy of *Tropic*. Dead silence. Met him subsequently in N.Y. No word – just a friendly duel apropos of nothing at all. I like him as an individual – he is really a clown, you know. The face of a comedian, absolutely. Ezra Pound has also learned through my friend Laughlin that I don't give a hoot about currying his favor. He sent word through Laughlin that I could be "taken care of " – *if* I would sort of swing the bat for his crazy Social Credit ideas. You can imagine what I said. (All this is extremely confidential.) However, he seems to have a soft spot for me, quand même. But when he reads that *Money* article, which I have dedicated to him as a joke on him, he will likely be quite furious. Santayana is a very old man and I can't see of what use. Unreadable too. Never understood his having a reputation – except for the long beard. Havelock Ellis is the man I would most like to have a reaction from. I truly admire him, and I have told him so in my letters. He's a great old man and even in his doddering old age what he might say would be interesting. But I fear very much that he *won't* like my work.

Listen, my friend Lowenfels is an interesting but very eccentric guy – who gets things all bollixed up. Now a Communist. We are old friends – good dinners, free meals, and all that in the good days here. Lowenfels, Fraenkel, Hiler, myself. But he is undependable, erratic, has bad judgment, loud-mouthed, pushing, vulgar, thoroughly Jewish, commercial instincts, does the wrong thing always. His pencil notes were swell, I think, and I'd like to see them brought out. They do say something after all – and there's verve. He *can* write. I know his whole library of MSS. He asked me to do the editing of all his work for him, but I neatly refused. But there is something in him, and in his critical work. He knew everybody in Paris and London, and now in N.Y. But nobody has really a good word for him. He's "Jabberwhorl Cronstadt", you know. And a ringer for him too. [. . .]

You mention Joyce and Yeats. The latter no, never thought of him even – thought he was dead already. Joyce is a pseudo friend of Kahane, the publisher. And of Stuart Gilbert (who, by the way, would certainly write enthusiastically for me at a moment's notice). But by this time Joyce must know what I think of him, which is not very flattering – or haven't you yet seen my "Universe of Death" chapter from the

Lawrence book? Anyway I've just flattened him out. I've made a shit-heel of him. So that's that again.

As for the financial end – don't worry about that. If you can write the letters I can dig up the books always. Kahane is rather stingy in his Manchester way, but can always be persuaded over the bar where I usually get him. I've already hinted to him that you have a scheme up your sleeve. If he resents things it's only because he wants to do everything and be everything himself. A really impossible fellow, stupid as they make 'em, and yet "sharp", I suppose, in a business way. But gets everything wrong at the start. Suspicious. And really hating himself deep down for having failed to be an "artist". You see what a set-up I have. If it were any other man alive I would already have sold your book – with him I have to proceed like a tortoise. I have to get other people to back up my opinion – for he is like a weathercock and has no opinion of his own at all. I don't give him the least bit of credit for having published me. He was forced into it!! But he's forgotten that already. So mull it over – there's time – and let me know what you propose. Count on me for little, except the books and moral support. Maybe later I'll swing into it – but it's embarrassing, to say the least. And time is working in my favor always. I have no inner doubts about things. It seems clear as a bell, what will happen eventually. And now I am eating every day – occasional lapses which don't count any more – and so things are quite quite rosy. I have only had one serious problem all my life, you know, since I came of age: FOOD. And I'm very glad it was only that.

If I seem to ignore a lot of things you ask about forgive me, it's only because of the hectic every day living. About coming down there now . . . You've asked me so magnificently and so many times. What can I say? Honestly? *I don't know.* Why I don't know is probably because I hate to separate myself from my daily activities. My life has become a very smooth machine-like affair – in the good sense – in which writing, eating, drinking, etc. all move naturally on one level. Sort of earthly rotation. And this is quite a big thing for me to have achieved, because it wasn't always thus. So in a real way I never have need of vacations. I get a little off now and then, but just a good sleep puts things right again. Just plain loafing, in bed. I see no reason to move from this very spot. Yes, I'd like to see the world. Sure. Who wouldn't? But if I don't nothing much is lost. I've got the world inside me, so to speak. I am a man who is really content, really happy to be doing what he's doing and not doing something else. Does that explain it somewhat? As for you, to meet you would be quite an event – I'd like nothing better. [. . .]

Glad to know it took you 18 months to write *The Black Book*. I was a little worried – for fear you'd say, Oh, about six or eight weeks! That would have given me a real anxiety. Because you *are* capable almost of doing such a thing. You have genius, there's no doubt about it. You *are* a genius. And I don't say that easily. There is a strange French counterpart to your book in the way of a volume called *La Procession enchaînée*, by Carlo Suarès, which I am now reading. [. . .]

Have peace! (And throw in a good Westphalian ham from Jerusalem!)

Yours,
HVM.

P.S. And don't think about expense of typing *The Black Book*! I'm paying for it all. Part of it I owe you and the other part is a little testimonial of my *genuine* interest in this truly great work. It's *colossal*!

Walter Lowenfels is caricatured in *Black Spring* as 'JABBERWHORL CRONSTADT, poet, musician, herbologist, weather man, linguist, oceanographer, old clothes, colloids'.

*C/O IONIAN BANK. CORFU. GREECE.   [early April 1937]

DEAR H. M.

YOU MAKE ME LAUGH like hell. Of course the English are arsey versey. But what a difficult man you are to help, with your flattening of writers BEFORE you've got their help. And there's poor old Huxley, the most charming and generous of men, and all of a sudden WHACK on the neckband in B.S.! I get quite weak with laughter. You need an english manager, because you are much too human to do anything but make them feel uncomfortable. The idea is to take a self-deprecating stance, somewhere between faith hope and charity, and speak in loud treacly tones. If you cover your head with a tea-cosy so much the better. The voice is muffled, and the indeterminate buzzing MIGHT be an author speaking – and it might be just gnats. That's what the english like. A compromise. Neither here nor there, shilly-shally, niminy-piminy . . . all this I can do almost as well as a Jew. I part my hair in the middle, adjust the horn-rimmed lenses and settle like a Catholic homosexual at the master's feet. [. . .]

And I am resting, really. I am assembling the pieces slowly in this spring. It is a very hallowed process. Soon the sunshine. No, the only struggle is to write. AT PRESENT I AM WRITING EXCLUSIVELY FOR THE FUNNY PAPERS. NIGHT AND DAY it's called. STARTING JUNE. They pay like hell. Hope they like me. When you say genius it has a funny ring, exciting me. I feel a fraud really, I don't know why. Here for example, without ANY EFFORT I have begun a novel for Fabers which will best sell I'm sure. It's called ISIS BRINGING GIFTS! No strain, no worry, just humour and quietness. This is a new me, an independent person. *The Black Book* is epileptic: a fit. I pick myself up and go on where I left off, waiting for the next fit. WHY? Was I a monster? I tried to say what I was: but of course with my talent for covering myself in confetti made out a hell of an epic. I wanted to write myself so miserable and wormy and frightened as I was: NUMB, really – that terrible english provincial numbness: the english death infecting my poor little colonial soul and so on. Instead you say monster! I wish it were true: but I have yet to find which is the theatre, which the mask: time, I tell myself, give it time. I'm too young to go fucking about with a typewriter in this dangerous way. For the present I'm wrung out. Yet there is another book THERE! a 7 millimetre fetus waiting to overshadow me. I let it form on its own before I scotch it. O well. And thanks for the word about the miraculous. You are deadly right. It does. Perhaps I shall grow into it. At present I care too much to do my real best. [. . .]

> Salute O world, Salute.
> Larry Durrell.

In *Black Spring* Miller lashes out at many famous writers: 'Aldous Huxley, Gertrude Stein, Sinclair Lewis, Hemingway, Dos Passos [. . .] I hear no bell ringing inside me when I bring these birds to the water closet. I pull the chain and down the sewer they go.'

*[Paris]   May 3, 1937

Dear Durrell –

It's very hard to know what to answer you about this business of campaigning for *Tropic*. Letters perhaps would be better than petitions. I hate all the cheap publicity that goes with these things. I really don't want to have anything to do with the matter. I leave it to you. And I think too that if you decide on anything you might better write the censor yourself. Write him formally and he will answer you officially. But don't play any tricks on him, please! Shoot straight wherever possible, that's my motto. Especially when a man is friendlily disposed, as he is. His address is:

Huntington Cairns
Baltimore Trust Bldg.
Baltimore, Md. U.S.A.

If I had been able to raise the money for printing I would have done this – simply publish the letters *as is*, and not a blooming word about censorship or obscenity. No brief, no petition, no appeal. Just see that the book of letters and reviews was widely disseminated – *and gratis*. I may be a poor business man, but I think with that method I should achieve the result I wanted – *attention*.

My books, oddly enough, are not creating mortal antagonisms! Even the old farts seem to admit enjoying them. And *Black Spring* has not been officially barred from the States yet. Perhaps because the Customs have not yet seized a copy. Very very few have been mailed to America. The joke is that the censor has asked me to get him some extra copies of the books so that he can show them around to the critics – *but I daren't mail them to him!*

I have already written him about your intentions. To date I have heard nothing. Answering you *officially*, as he will, he will doubtless be cagey – naturally. You will have to read between the lines. I can only repeat that so far as the law goes there is nothing to prevent my books being *admitted* into America. The republishing of them there, the circulation through the mails, the passing of them from one state to another – these are all separate matters. There's the whole situation. And add to that the fact that no publisher over there seems sufficiently interested in me to risk starting a hullabaloo. *Entre nous* – time will solve everything. The books *will* gradually make their own way, there is no doubt of that. Brentano's here in Paris now displays them openly in the shop window. That in itself is a big step forward – for they are still very conservative.

(By the way, I am getting another review – from Bernard Fay, a French critic, in the *Franco-American Review*, which I know nothing of, have never heard of.) And the translation of fragments of *Aller Retour N.Y.* has now appeared in the April 15th issue of the revue *Europe*.

I sent Fraenkel your letter. You have hit the nail on the head. Don't have any fears, qualms or scruples – always write just what you think. Everybody enjoys it – even Fraenkel will. And I never try to protect my friends. What you do or say is up to you. You have carte blanche, always. [. . .]

As for *The Black Book* I am in the act of proof-reading the typed copies preparatory to distributing them according to your instructions. I would suggest now, when you receive your copy, that you reread with an eye to reducing the verbiage. Having read it over three times I feel sure that it would be improved by pruning. Your elaboration is excellent in the vital places, but there are passages of minor importance where you elaborate for no good reason – perhaps because the machine was geared up and you couldn't apply the brakes. Throw a cold searchlight on it! You will lose nothing by cutting. If you find that you agree with my opinion, let me know and I shall hold up the copy I intended giving to Kahane until you have altered it. But the copy to [Alan] Thomas I shall send "irregardless", as they say in N.Y. now. (Also, if it means anything to you, the opinion of several of my friends, whose judgment I respect, is pretty much d'accord. They complain of fatigue, of preciosity, while admitting to the power and beauty of your language. But *language* – a little too much of it!) This is a common enough phenomenon, so don't let it worry you. You have simply overshot your wad. Hitting the right stride is always a matter of getting "beyond" language – don't you think? Of being immediate. You sometimes talk too much about and around. *Move in closer* and deliver good body blows. Aim for the solar plexus, always. If you deliver a foul now and then you will be forgiven – because your intentions were good. But don't pull your punches – that's unforgivable.

So, mind you, I don't say rewrite the book – simply prune and trim, as the guy says in his letter to the Park Commissioner. "More light, more air, more natural light, more beauty, more safety to the pedestrians and to the general surroundings along by all parts of Queens County, etc. etc."

I may have to leave the Villa Seurat for a week or two. My friend Osborn (*Fillmore* of *Tropic*) has come to Paris and is absolutely mad. Throws himself on me. I am nurse, cook, adviser and treasurer. Can't stand it. Ten days of it and I feel a bit cuckoo myself.

The girl you spoke of in your last letter hasn't shown up as yet. But I met *Ingrid*, who lives in the same hotel as Fred. She was here one night for dinner when Osborn was here. Ask her to tell you about "my trip to

Denmark". (But she's a dull oaf – absolute blubber. Hopeless.)
I must also add that I was tremendously impressed by the photo of
Nancy. She looks like "a person".
And about the pull-over, etc. Why no, nothing. I'm quite O.K.
Always glad to get suits & overcoats – and thought, seeing as you are
from England, you might have a fine old tweed – *or a Barathea weave*!!
(Ha-ho!) How about a nice *Vicuna* for the summertime?? Anyway,
cheerio!

HVM.

Miller is referring here to the 'authentic' 'Letter to The Park Commissioner', allegedly
written by Phineas Flapdoodle, published in *The Booster*, 2, No. 7 (September 1937).

*[Paris]   Monday. [10 May 1937]
       Dear Durrell:
Just got your latest letter and latest water color. [. . .] Glad you really
liked the Tibet water color. It was a bit faked, as you see, but that doesn't
matter vitally. Not in my eyes, anyway. Give it a generous mat, and cut
it down close so that you have nothing but a solid body of color. Listen,
about these damned things. Do you realize something? You must go
slowly with them – not fast, as people ordinarily imagine. I wish you
could see my friend Reichel's work. If Thomas comes remind him to
remind me to take him there, so that he can explain it all to you. Reichel is
a genius – the poet of the water colors! And how slowly and lovingly and
patiently he works. It's [enough] to make you weep. At any rate, I am
certain you never saw anything like them in your life. He's the man I
should love to help materially. Some one told me Trevelyan, in London,
might be of service. Is he dependable, Trevelyan? Do you know anything about him? I wouldn't want him to take Reichel's work to London
and then accidentally lose a few, as is so often done. I ask because he too is
coming to Paris soon and I am to meet him.
       Anyway, do this next time . . . . Sit before the paper, ponder long,
put a little spot down on the big white sheet. Think about it. Move on
to another area, slowly, quietly, very quietly – like a mouse. Get up and
talk to yourself a bit. Look out the window. Go back. Let it dry a
while. Put it away until the morrow. Take it out, look at it at breakfast
table. Think what it is you want to paint. Don't try to paint that, but
what you are thinking and feeling only. For instance, that landscape –

was it the landscape, or was it a color in the sky you wanted? Or were you thinking of spring coming on? Or of the "mallards". Or perhaps it is aboulia and amusia and anoia you would like to serve up. Get that "about" feeling and fuck the what-is-it business. And a good paper and brush is important. But it's like chess, me lad. Once you go at it earnestly, you're hipped for good. Don't dabble in it. A good water color is like precious ointment . . . . . However, I am putting them up – your things – in my bedroom where the light comes in under the black curtains and makes them glow. That's Corfu, is it? I ask myself. Well, O.K. Corfu, then, and here's to a good sound nap!

I must write you a whole special letter about things Tibetan: the film *Lost Horizon*, your magic book on Tibet, the book *I Ging*, which I am still burrowing for – "the most extraordinary book in the history of world literature", says Keyserling. And more, please, about the first twelve years of your life there in the passes. It drives me nuts. If I go anywhere from here it will be *there*. Maybe I shall be the next Dalai Lama – from America sent! This is one of my quiet megalomaniac days. I believe anything is possible.

Listen, where did you get that "KONX OMPAX"??? Marvellous. That and Miss Smith's conk and poll! And Hilda and the Womb. I sent you and Thomas by registered mail the copies of *Black Book* the other day. Now I shall send my copy, the third one, and ask you to be kind enough to correct it against yours, as it was inconvenient for me to correct three at once. Will you mail it back soon as possible? A half dozen people are clamoring to read it. Remember, I wait to show it to Kahane until hearing whether you will make emendations or not.

Let me add another word or two on the subject. You see, writing you don't need to worry about. You *are* a writer – at present, almost too much of a one. You need only to become more and more yourself, in life and on paper. That will alter the writing radically, but very naturally. Don't make any effort. I feel you make too tremendous an effort always. Not in a bad sense, mind you – but wrongly, from any standpoint of automatic perfection, which lies at the basis of all writing . . . no? And don't shoot your bolt all at once – never. Hold it in, on the contrary. Give out just enough milk so that you feel happy and re-freshed and like doing another lick the morrow and so on perpetually. There's no single thing to get out and done with – but rather an attitude to perfect, an attitude towards life, of which the writing is only and at the best but a reflection and evidence. This is my own private opinion, at any rate, and you just take it for what it's worth, no more.

I'm impressed by your "double" nature. The man you reveal in *The Black Book* is not the same man who writes me from Corfu. Perhaps Corfu is nearer to your *climatic source*, as A.N. puts it. Anyway, had you remained in England you would have been done for. There was one curious touch I omitted to mention. A most strange use of the impersonal "one said to her while fucking her", or something like that, it went. Was that deliberately done – for some caromed irony, or what? Or was it an English locution, a relapse? I enjoyed the strangeness of it, but did you mean it to be so strange? Almost like the speech of a Hounyhymnynym!

The most terrible, damning line in the whole book is that remark of Chamberlain's – "Look, do you think it would damage our relationship if I sucked you off?" That almost tells the whole story of England! (*Since* Drake and Frobisher!) And there are, as in the womb passages, marvellous crazy things which beat all the French Surrealists stiff. "With that knowing look I always imagine the spermatozoa . . . . . etc." Or "send out to the clitoris for an ice".

I wish you would make a copy of the five or six pages on the womb. I can't find them now in my haste. But it comes about where you have made a footnote on the "return to the womb complex". Send it to Laughlin, please. I feel certain he will use it. That is to my mind magnificent, incomparable. Well, enuf.

> Yours in the "gnomic aorist",
> HVM.

P.S. I also sent the other day the big water color "The Ego and his Yid".

Durrell defended his locution to Miller: 'When I wrote "one says this" – "one says that" it was the sort of ironic impersonal fish-like tone which the clever, superior Englishman uses to belittle himself and his experiences.' However, the 'remark' Miller attributes to Chamberlain was in fact spoken in *The Black Book* by Tarquin, a homosexual recently gone public.

*Korfu: [May 1937]

Dear H.M: Just written the Censor as per instructions. Also just read the "Dieppe–Newhaven" thing – wonderful and moving simplicity: a kind of lucid quality like painless weeping. You are such a very great man I'm continually surprised at you. Forgive me! "Ego and its Yid" is lovely – framing it. [. . .] Sending *Time and Western Man*. Hate Lewis: he is so much the English blackbeetle squashed into the form of a gingerbread Nashe. Fuck his metaphysical Swedish quill say I!

Writing Thomas to call on you but I doubt if he will have time on his way out: when returning, however, he will certainly do so and give you the MSS you sent. Having a battle with him at present over Τροπικ οφ Καντσερ [tropic of cancer] – he will come round the young bugger –

Been out sailing all day: *Van Norden* going like a bird: photos soon: boats have 'souls' – did you know? I used to think it was just a Conradian hoax – but it's true – think of the Greek ψῡχή [psyche] – probably spelt wrong; and πνεῦμα [pneuma] – they're very close together always. The soul and the divine breath. Tho' what the hell this has to do with the *Van Norden* I *don't* know. Anyway . . . .

You say 4 people broke down proofing the Durrell masterpiece? I am sorry. Do you mean you set out to correct my errors in spelling typing etc? What a noble thing – I am grateful. I never correct – because the printer's devil is paid to edit the book afterwards anyway. But what nobility! Thank the other chaps for me will you for the nobility?

Just read *The Sun Also Rises*: I missed the whole point by reading fast and carelessly – Nancy tells me the hero *had no balls*: can you beat it? I thought there was a gloom over everything – but put it down to that arid steel and footrule style of his. Takes a girl with an eye for detail to put me wise I'm so simple. No balls! Well well.

Having great fun with the press cuttings of the shit novel!

Congratulate Anaïs Nin ceaselessly will you, on herself – that birth scene rocked my velure basin. What a woman! Some biographical details please. Is she young IN SPITE of the 63 vols? Really, I think she's what you say. The first woman artist. "The female ego etc." Have you read Djuna Barnes' NIGHTWOOD? I reread it and was quite moved. Try it if you get a chance will you?

All the best –
Larry Durrell

Dear Miller:

Bombardment from the directors of Fabers. Enthusiastic letter from Morley and Pringle and a typical "kind letter" from Eliot which I'm sure he thinks is terribly generous from the author of *The Waste Land* to a mere unknown young writer.

In short they want an altered English Edition; I have replied that provided it does not stand in the way of the Paris unexpurgated I don't mind. It will be advertisement I suppose. Will you, however, immediately ask Kahane whether he would like to do the book in its full dress uniform regardless of Faber? An English and American ed. would contain enough jewelry to give the Paris edition réclame and movement. On the other hand if Kahane wanted exclusive rights I could fob off Fabers. I feel the unexpurgated version is more important. Let me know what you think, will you? If you care to, hand Kahane the MSS and explain that I am not free as yet to offer it to him – but ask him how he feels about it all? Will he take it? If not I'd better castrate for Faber and wait until I have money enough to do the full version myself. It's rather a fix. If I refuse Faber and then this "weathercock" refuses me . . . . I'll be left with my first real book on my hands. No money. No edition. Nowt.

Lawrence Durrell

Continued: Been run down and depressed of late – I don't know why. Written Shaw, Muir, Ellis and am starting on the Americans tomorrow. In the meantime skoal. Sent "Paris–Dieppe" to Lehmann. Seen *New Writing* – not a chance for us – Communist Etonians. You are not classy enough for them – they want good gentlemanly prose of the vanguard quality. But no art by request. Fuck the English. Anyway good luck with them:

*[Paris] July 15, 1937

Dear Durrell:

Just got the red ink letter about Faber and Kahane. I am getting in touch with him at once, Kahane, and will let him have my copy to read if he wants. (I also will write you in the next few days about the corrections you made – I haven't had a chance to tell you about that. Some ought not to have been made, I feel. However . . .)

Frankly, I am not in accord with you about accepting Faber's plan, just because it is a pis aller. No, with that logic, that attitude, you'll always be fucked good and proper. Don't you see, according to *their* logic, you *must* conform – because they control the situation. But the moment you say to hell with that and decide to do as you damn please *you find the man* to sponsor you. Yes, as you say, our fancy weathercock may turn down your book – it will be Greek to him, that I can tell you in advance. But, canny bugger that he is, he may decide to publish and blow you to the skies, because a few *others* have seen merit in your work. One never knows with such guys. But, anyway, whether he refuses or rejects, whether you lose out permanently with Faber or not, all that is beside the point – that is *their* affair. Yours is with your own conscience. On that grain of faith on which you built your book you must rest. You stand firm and let the world come round. No, it won't be the Fabers and so on, but always some one, something unexpected, something from the blue. It may even be me! In other words, forgive my advice, but I would say you can't look two ways. You've got to accept the responsibility for your actions.

Notice that one always thinks he must do something because he must earn that money which was involved. But that is nearly always a clever excuse we make to ourselves. We usually can do very well – even better – without that money. The only thing that truly nourishes is the doing what one wants to do. I tell you, everything else is crap, and futility, and waste. Let the angel be your water-mark. If no publisher exists for you we will have to create one!

More soon.
HVM.

*C/O IONIAN BANK.
CORFUGREECE.   JULY TWENTYfirst [1937]

Dear H.M. AND ANAÏS NIN:
Another portmanteau letter. First about *The Black Book*. I think you are the most diabolically honest man I have ever met. And of course I should take the stand on my own dunghill; I am always making a brave face and then diving down the nearest manhole. As for looking both ways at once yes. It can't be done; but I'll tell you one reason – the only one which made me want to deal with Faber, apart from their extreme

niceness. (Both Morley and Pringle are real people: and even Eliot if he could come down off his gingerbread pedestal for a second would be tolerable.) It was not that I cared a fuck either way ULTIMATELY: whether the BB was cut in England. I KNOW THAT SOONER OR LATER IT WILL COME INTO ITS LITTLE OWN UNEXPURGATED. But there's another thing. My double Amicus Nordensis. He is a double I need – not for money or any of the fake reasons I'm always giving – but simply for a contact with the human world. I am so alone really that I'm a bit scared of going crazy; Norden would keep me in touch with the commonplace world which will never understand my personal struggle. Very well. When I submitted BB to Faber I was prepared to have it rejected without favour: but when they showed they were keen and willing to fly as near the wind as possible, I suddenly thought: if they print the BB in whatever form, it will destroy Amicus Nordensis and keep all my work together under one banner. This was sheer weakness: but the spectacle of going on splitting like an amoeba, each new book a new name, never getting anywhere, was a bit terrifying. I am a little more sober now. You see, I CAN'T WRITE REAL BOOKS ALL THE TIME. It's like an electric current: increase the dose very gradually. Already the BB has played havoc with me. What I want is this, frankly. Once every three years or more I shall try to compose for full orchestra. The rest of the time I shall do essays, travel-books, perhaps one more novel under Charles Norden. I shall naturally not try to write badly or things I don't want to: but there are a lot of things I want to write which don't come into the same class as *The Black Book* at all. I consider that resting. Travel essay about Greece. Literary essays, Hamletry, and all that. This kind of literary gardening will soothe me and stop me fretting myself. In the meantime my BB will come out, and be followed by the Book of the Dead, the Book of Miracles etc. Under my own sweet name. I think you will probably feel this is traitorous or something: but you must understand that I need my friend Norden in order to keep my peace of mind and be happy a little and love. It is not good to fly so violently. I am too young to cut myself off altogether, and not strong enough as yet. The carapace will come. In the meantime I have asked Faber, in curiosity, to post me the specimen cuts of the Book. I think it's useless in England really. Whether Kahane wants it or not. The book is an act in itself and I would be glad to put it in a drawer. No one can alter my having WRITTEN it. On the other hand there was only the question of réclame for a Paris edition if there was one. You think it's bad to expurgate? Perhaps you're right. But you know, for an artist of your calibre it is rather different. Nietzsche COULD stand aside and let the world come to him; so can you because you HAVE a world to offer. But as yet I have no great positive body of work and thought to offer. The BB is a goodish beginning. But it is not quite adult yet. I can do better if I lose my fear. For you there is this powerful TOTAL world unrolling itself; you are so deep in it that there is not time for anything else. With me it is different. The little world, the heraldic universe, is a cyclic, periodic thing in me: like a bout of drinking. I am not a permanent inhabitant: only on Wednesdays by invitation. I enter and leave – and presto, the ordinary individual is born, the Jekyll. In the bottom of my soul where I have some faith in myself I always know it doesn't matter; why all this agony over paper and ink and words, when life is running away like a greyhound, and everything is felt much too poignantly and passionately to try and write it down? Then I take the *Van Norden*, run up wings, and swerve off from myself. I wonder if you understand. But of course you do. You understand everything, otherwise you wouldn't be the giant you are.

Anyway: let us see what Kahane thinks: tell him there has been point blank refusal to print the book in England in its present form. Always feel apologetic for the amount *of my irons you put* in the fire. 1,000,000 thanks.

Dear anais: I was delighted with the letter. What anaïs person you are, and so unformidable too! Thank god. I know when you wrote you said 'novels': but their form was so unconventional – they were not total in the sense of novels – that I took them for diary after all. They are not good *novels*, thank god: but they are wonderful documents. No, I think in this objective form the 'father' one is better than the other, tho' the other one has much better writing in it. Somehow you've just impaled him with that feminine dagger: presented him very deftly: as artificial as wedding-cake. What a murderous thing to the male ego this queer off-beat female consciousness is! As for H.M. of course I recognised him: we all did at once. I had a chuckle over the bits where you blandly took him in tierce and tore the buttons off his chest. But he was less skilfully *presented* – because presentation is the essence of the objective form. I felt you wrote a lot ABOUT him rather than just letting himself write his own portrait through your medium. But this doesn't detract one whit from the lovely foamy quality of your prose, and the withering brilliance of your female self. I suppose you are too near to H.M. really to do him justice. You cannot write *objectively* (in the sense of novel) about someone who is very near to you I suppose. H.M's place proper must be the diary, an ego alongside your own. But in the meantime salute upon salute.

I got the Rimbaud gai letter and answered it too. I have just found the answer lying in my file. I shall destroy it. I quoted a page and a half of Middleton for no reason whatsoever – except that it had such queer colours in it, all rather like your letters. I am delighted with the way you like *The Black Book*: I have got to hate it sort of these days. You didn't agree to some of the cuts? Well, you must help me: wherever I saw the emotion going soft and hysterical I struck blindly, loathing myself. Perhaps there are other cuts you would like to make or H.M. Do so in your own good time.

Here is an answer to my letter to Shaw: not promising: however if you like to post *Tropic* to him right away there might be some sign of life. I've written telling him to expect books from Paris.

Expecting answers from one or two more in a day or so. The wheel begins to turn, however slowly. Your faith up there in Paris gives me courage. I can't thank you enuf for it. We must meet soon.

If you COULD find us a place to live in we would be grateful as hell. This is Anaïs I'm calling. Just having a fearful row with *Night and Day*: they have rewritten one of my articles and printed it under the name of another man. Nancy has just lifted five quid for a comic drawing and is quite unbearably aloof today. And I have found a goddess in the flesh. Nausicaa. I feel I want to buy her and keep her with me, framed: but nothing doing: she is 17 and going to be an archeologist, and I am dying of old age in my twenty-fifth year. Eheu! I think the innocence afflicts me: not a single stain of experience on her: so fresh and waiting for life – like a clean knife. Her hands are in her lap and she looks at men with the impersonal mindless way that cattle look at trees. I adore her for that. I hate to think of such a mindless world being smudged afterwards. What a shame!

> Love's not so pure and abstract as they use
> To say who have no mistress but their Muse!

Pity me.

Larry Durrell.

Dear Durrell:

Sent you MSS of *Black Spring* the other day, to be bound, and to-day another instalment which I just ran across. Will send others in a day or so, I mean for other volumes, so if this second batch (marked "Self-Portrait", and which belongs with *Black Spring*) arrives too late you can hold it and I will tell you what to do with it later. But please send me a card when you get them, will you, as I am always uneasy about the post. (And what is 70 drachmas? in francs?)

(Note: Don't forget to send me the name and address of the London bookstore where I may be able to get a cheap edition of the *I Ching*, will you?)

No, don't send me the other MSS you mention. If you did them already, why please keep them for yourself. Excellent. You are going to have a feast, going through these old papers. Especially the coming one – "The Brochure". And then I think I'll also send you the original Dream Book. If it's so damned cheap I'm going to bind everything I have that I want to keep.

I am returning the letters herewith. You didn't send me your answer to the Shaw letter. Is it worth while fiddling around with an old codger like that, I wonder? He's nearly 90 now. How can we expect anything of him? He's done his stroke!

Kahane is now reading *The Black Book* and promises to tell me soon what he thinks – maybe to-morrow before he leaves for the country. At any rate, I visit him in the country next week end – Aug. 6th – and then I'll surely know. The letters from Brown and from Harold Strauss are masterpieces of idiocy, no? Though it is marvellous the esteem you are in – already. That is a good omen. I think you are born under a lucky star. The American letter is typical – really nauseating, what? But listen, *Panic Spring* can't be such a damned bad book as you would have me believe. Why don't you send me a copy? I'll risk it! Your reply to Curtis [Brown] is wonderful! I am saving it. Endorsing it and passing it through the bank – for lost souls.

Alors, "I want to begin here and now to talk about your future work!" . . . . (Ahem)

Don't, my good Durrell, take the schizophrenic route! If there are just a half dozen people in the world, like myself, who believe in you, that should more than outweigh the other considerations. The danger is to the psyche – believe it or not! Fraenkel is the perfect example of the split-soul! What a mess it is. You are young, happily married, full of encouragement, praised to the skies, healthy, not hungry, not penniless, befriended, surrounded with congratulations, with what not, a boat to boot, be Jesus!, the Ionian skies, isolation (which I would give my shirt to have!), and so on. Now don't, my dear good Durrell, ask me to weep with you – because you are *alone!* You ought to be proud of that. That's in your favor. You can't be alone and be with the herd too. You can't write good *and* bad books. Not for long. (Show me examples, if you know any.) The toll is "disintegration". You must stand or fall either as Charles Norden or as Lawrence Durrell. I would choose Lawrence Durrell, if I were you. And what is the penalty, after all? What can they do to you – THEY? Nothing, really. You will soon have them hog-tied. The man who sticks to his guns has the world at his feet. That's why I prefer Mussolini a thousand times, much as I despise his program, to the whole British Empire. Mussolini's politics is Realpolitik. That's something – in a world of cagey bastards, of pussy-footers, and stinking hypocrites. For me it's simple. None of this stuff for me. Tao, me lad, and more and more of it. I'm wallowing in it. It's exactly my philosophy – every inch of it – even to the contradictions – precisely the contradictions. It's in my blood – and I am scouting about now to discover if I haven't really some Tibetan, some Mongolian blood somewhere in the line.

If, as you say, you can't write REAL books all the time, then don't write. Don't write anything, I mean. Lie fallow. Hold it in. Let it accumulate. Let it explode inside you. I can understand the phrase – Homer nodding. But that is different from Homer pseudonyming, what? A man can fall down, can underdo himself, can go haywire – but he ought not to deliberately incarnate a lesser self, a ghost, a substitute. The whole thing is a question of responsibility and willingness to accept one's fate, one's punishment, as well as one's reward. I think that is only too painfully clear, if you ask yourself. You want Charles Norden to be the scapegoat – but in the end it will be L.D. who will be obliged to kill Charles Norden! That's the "double" theme. (By the way, do read Dostoievsky's *The Double*, if you have never done so. And even *Aaron's Rod* is a good book, on this score. Lawrence suffered from it too. And he knew it. It was a little different, but fundamentally the same problem. Not accepting oneself in toto. Not integrating.)

And why couldn't you write all the other books you wish as L.D.?

Why can't L.D. be the author of travel books, etc.? What's to hinder it? And it's wrong to think you are cutting yourself off. On the contrary, you are muscling in. The other way is the way to cut yourself off. Soon enough you are found out and the smell is a bad one. The rotting part of you will stink to high heaven – believe me. Better to let that rotten part, if it *is* rotten, die off naturally. Better to acknowledge your weaknesses. You can't put perfection in one scale and imperfection in the other that way. We are imperfect through and through – thank heaven! I hate perfect books and perfect beings. Where are they, d'ailleurs? The letters from Brown and Strauss ought to convince you of the odiousness of that tack. You will be cutting their throats soon enough. You'll get vindictive, vengeful, irritable, whimsical, unreliable, etc. You'll see. They'll throw you out damned quick – just as soon as you show your claws.

No, everything is there in the Tao business. Clear as a bell, says I. If you see the truth you cannot help but obey it. There are no two ways. It's always the straight and narrow path – and a damned jolly path it is, when you hit it full on. Why people balk I never could understand. It's all gravy, once you embark in earnest. It's really gay – the other is sad, dismal, wretched. (Think of Fraenkel again!) Think of the muck around you. Think of poor, desolate Aldous Huxley. Think of Charlie Chaplin – another failure.

Note, too, how you write to me and how you write to *them*! With them you're strong – with me you're weak. Well, drive the center-board down a little deeper. An even keel, me lad. You're a sailor wot ought to know! An even keel. And no catamarans! No life-saving belts! Believe me, it's the only solution. I don't elect for the cross, and I think it's largely poppy-cock, the cross business (it's only self-pity, weakness). But if it must be the cross, then let it be the cross! Shit, that's an honorable way out. It brings relief – besides the gall and vinegar. But really, the cross is a myth. If you develop your powers you will find that it is, when all is said and done, *a gay life*! I think you're a gay bird, despite all the raving, despite *The Black Book*. Of course it's a fine jolly book, *The Black Book*. I allus said so – and everybody agrees with me too. Sling it over the counter and make no bones about it. Do your damndest and take what's coming to you.

Well, enuf of that. Think it over. And remember I'm with you to the last ditch . . . . .

My friend Fred (Perlès) is just being given a sort of white elephant in the way of a lousy magazine, owned by the American Country Club, and called *The Booster*. He has been a failure as editor and business man, and the magazine is folding up. The owner (President of the Club) wants to make him a present of the magazine – if he wants it. There is good advertising, enough to pay all expenses – for the moment at least. Fred is thinking of running it – has to keep the same name and also devote two pages to the activities of the Club – that's the price! But he will make it gradually into a literary magazine. I am going to aid him, of course, and sink some of my drivel into it. We may draw up a list of "contributing editors" and make a drive for subscriptions – and more ads. It would be a means for Fred to live. He has none at present – his job is finished. He is down to his last cent, as usual. Would you like to be a "contributing editor" – contributing gratis? Do you think, if we got it into some decent shape, that we could sell it here and there – in England? About five francs a copy – 50 francs for a year's subscription. 500 francs would buy a life's subscription! How does it sound? Now it looks like bloody hell – the worst imaginable shit – and it will look like that for a month or two to come. We have only twenty pages, of which nearly half is advertising. We think to put some of the crazy ads (like Johnny Walker, Hanan Shoes, etc.) right in the middle of a page of serious writing. And we are going to boost the shit out of everybody and everything. We are going to take an optimistic turn – for the sheer devil of it. Alors, your advice, doctor . . . . .

Signing off.
HVM.

[P.S.] Fraenkel is still in N.Y. care of Lowenfels. Just had a good Hamlet letter from him on the death of Robin – how Robin liked to fuck!!
[P.P.S.] I have now *The Musings of a Chinese Mystic* – marvellous! True, profound – and gay! That's the "joyous wisdom", all right, that Nietzsche was always begging for.

Paris
London
Corfu
Athens

In mid-August, 1937, Lawrence Durrell appears in Paris, 'with the Ionian tan still on his face and hands', as Alfred Perlès described him. It is a Sunday, and Perlès returns to 18 Villa Seurat from his part-time job at the American Golf and Country Club to find a party in progress – Larry and Henry talking, Nancy in the kitchenette grilling steaks. The party is to continue, with interruptions, until Miller parts from the Durrells at Tripolis in the Peloponnesus on 26 December 1939.

Durrell radiates tireless energy, even when seated 'Confucius-fashion' and listening to Miller. A few days in Paris, and he dashes off with Nancy to London for meetings with Havelock Ellis, T.S. Eliot, Dylan Thomas. Back in Paris, he rents a flat at 21 rue Gazan, near his friends, and the projects begin to sprout like dragons' teeth: with Miller and Perlès he takes over editorship of *The Booster*, magazine of the American Golf and Country Club; Anaïs Nin had fallen in love with Larry as quickly as had Henry and Fred, and soon the Villa Seurat Series is launched (on Nancy's money) to publish *The Black Book*, Miller's *Max and the White Phagocytes* and Nin's *Winter of Artifice*. Miller's life in Paris, at the hub of what Larry termed his 'factory', could best be described as hectic before the summer of 1937; now, the activity increases. Then the Durrells dash back to Corfu. Though the time Larry and Henry spend together means they need not rely entirely on letters, the correspondence is more prolific this year than any other.

With the Durrells back in Greece, Miller and Nin in Paris continue to labour on Larry's behalf, seeing *The Black Book* through the Obelisk Press. Next winter Larry races about Europe again: Paris, London, Stratford. But he finally manages to lure Henry to Greece, and on about 22 July he and Nancy drive up to the Corfu dock just as Henry's ship slides up to the pier. With the principals in almost daily contact, the correspondence lapses. For Miller the trip is a revelation: a confirmed city-dweller who once claimed that his soul thrived on garbage cans, he basks naked in the Greek sun and becomes a close friend of every native in sight. Later in Athens he is adopted by George Katsimbalis, Theodore Stephanides, and George Seferis – raconteur, doctor and biologist, and future Nobel laureate respectively – who were to appear in the writings of both Durrell and Miller. Miller tells the story of his trip in the book many consider his finest, *The Colossus of Maroussi*.

*[18 Villa Seurat, Paris]   [mid-August 1937]

    Dear Miller:
    Two questions:
(1) What do you do with the garbage?

AND (TWO)

(2) When you say "to be with God" do you identify yourself with God: or do you regard the God-stuff reality as something *extraneous* towards which we yearn?

    Durrell

*d'en haut! [18 Villa Seurat, Paris]   [mid-August 1937]

    My dear Durrell –
The first question is easier to answer than the second. The garbage you put in a little can (under the sink) and about sundown, or thereafter, you deposit it in front of your door, in the street. The noise you hear about 7:30 in the morning is the noise made by Madame the Garbage Collector who rolls her little truck out of the little hut at the end of the street (illuminated by a cross at night).
    As for the second question, being rather pressed for time, and slightly jocund at the moment, I should say blithely – sometimes you approach and sometimes you become! Gottfried Benn answers it nicely (via Storch) in an issue of *transition* which I will dig up for you and show you. I could discuss it better over the table. When do I eat with you downstairs? I am free for dinner this evening, if that says

anything. May have to do a stitch of work after dinner, but no great hurry about it.

How are you? Did you find clean sheets, etc.?

HVM.

*18 Villa Seurat (XIV)   Saturday [late August 1937]

Dear Durrell –

Beginning to wonder if you are ill – or is it that you are discouraged and disgusted with England? Seems strange not to hear from you. Ominous. As for us, things are going forward. *The Booster* is progressing. We are getting subscriptions in driblets – but from fairly good sources.

Betty [Ryan] returned from Belgrade with three subscriptions – Jugoslavian – and expects to round up a half dozen more, including Consuelo de St. Exupéry?! And Ludmila Pitoëff.

We landed, thru Edgar, the Princess di San Faustino, of Rapallo – and expect she will do things for us. *The Booster* will be out by the end of next week – everything quite well done.

This morning I got a letter from Curtis Brown, inspired by you. I will answer later. How did you find him? He sounds so stupid in his letters! I suppose you missed Eliot – no? Isn't he going on vacation? Write us, anyway. We are dying for news of you. And Nancy? What is *she* doing in London? It must be quite horrible.

Betty was delighted to know you had been living in her place – and looks forward with great pleasure to meeting you all. When will that be – have you any idea?

And don't worry about the money. I have explained it all. Let it come only when you are ready. "Remember, we are *boosters* first & foremost!"

We need subscriptions. But really, I see now that we are getting them, and that we will get more. I think it's a go.

Fred asks me to send you both his warmest regards. He misses you both. We all do. You left a vacuum behind you.

Henry.

[Enclosed]

Booster Placard

THE BOOSTER

is a non-successful, non-political, non-cultural review published in English and French from Paris once a month under the direction of the celebrated literary quartet:

First Violin	Alfred Perlès
Also First Violin	William Saroyan
Viola	Lawrence Durrell
'Cello and Traps	Henry Miller

18 Villa Seurat, Paris (xiv)

ON SALE HERE

5 francs   1 shilling   25 cents

———— + ————

WE ARE

For	*Against*
Food	Peace
Pocket Battleships	Poison Gas
Depressions	Fair Play
Plagues	Hygiene
Token Payments	Moderation
Epilepsy	Rheumatism and Arthritis
Taking the lead	All isms
Shangri-la	Schizophrenia

*c/o J.A. Allen, Bookseller, 53 Woburn Place,
Russell Square [London]   [1 September? 1937]

Henry I'm sorry I haven't written. Fuck the English eh? Henry the English are everywhere, all around me – like mutilated black beetles. Curtis Brown: not very nice: more later: wrote you because I told him what a mug he was missing you. Eliot and Pringle are away but met Frank Morley – a man after your own heart. Huge great slow brigand with a sense of humour. Admires you greatly. Hopes to be able to do *Max*: if it's humanly possible I know he will. Meeting Eliot and Pringle on Thursday. More talk then. Listen, I went down and bearded Havelock. I should say rather that he bearded me. Magnificent beard. He is covered with hair like a wild boar – likes your work and promises to write you in detail about the books. Hasn't finished them yet – disagrees with you about *urination*!!! Lovely old man. As yet haven't rung up Rebecca West. Will do so if I have time. Thank Anaïs a million for the letter she sent. I hate England. Hope to leave next Sunday for somewhere civilized. Will telegraph. I've got you two coats: a light velveteen and a Scotch tweed. Everything very expensive. So far no pink shirts. Listen, I met Anand and Potocki of Montalk. I hope to get a poem in *Hindi* from [Anand] (he's famous) and have got an insane document from the Count for *The Booster*, which *proves* (I said PROVES) that Bach was a Potocki!! It's if anything better than the Park Commissioner.

Two more subs for *The Booster*. One I have from Knight (I met him, rather dull) and Orwell promised one.

Henry that stuff egg Bjerre hasn't yet given in the *Black Book* copy he brought. Can you find his address, I'll kill him.

Been to the Café Royal a lot and confirmed the opinion I always had of English writers. Henry fuck the English. Listen, don't get angry if I don't write as I'm snowed under with things – proofs, engagements, work in the British Museum. Money was sent today.

Bless you all. See you as soon as I can. Love to Anaïs – we have her photo on the shelf.

Ah well!

Things are beginning – only just beginning. Why not come over for the afternoon. Choose a Sunday afternoon. See London at its best. PFUI!

Larry Durrell

*[Paris]   *Thursday* [2? September 1937]

Dear Durrell –

This in haste! Got your letter! Fine! Bjerre is away & can't find his address. Kahane just back – expect news soon. *Booster* going fine!!!

Ads & subscriptions. Saroyan is with us too. *Out to-morrow*! Where are you? Not sure I understand the address – Wolver*in* Place? Sending this to Curtis Brown. Regards from Reichel. More later.

Henry.

[P.S.] Mrs. Knopf also subscribed.

*c/o J.A. Allen, 53 Woburn Place
Russell Square, London   [early September 1937]

Dear Henry: Wonderful *The Booster* is going so very well. [. . .]

I have met Eliot who is a very charming person believe it or not! Had an impertinent note from Shaw saying that *Tropic* must wait it's turn – which may be months. Alors I wrote and asked him to return the one copy to me – the old bugger. Trevelyan out of town – damn him. Seeing MacCarthy on Wednesday, about *Tropic* – hasn't yet read it by the way. Pringle reading *Max*.

Ellis and Eliot said they thought it a little premature to fight a test-case for another 5 years over *Tropic* – in case you lost.

More later.
Larry

STOP PRESS

Dear Henry: Plan to return next Friday. Good for *Night and Day*!!! Also apropos *The Black Book* – but I want it out by January – or thereabouts. Marvellous.

Sending Potocki MSS today to you. Will bring other stuff with me. Everyone keen on *The Booster* here. More subs will follow.

Perhaps I'd better rest up for the 2nd number eh? Leave some room for contributors!

Cheers for Alfred! More power to the elbow, Alf!! Ya! Ya! F O O D!!

No, I haven't forgotten the Chinese book. Cheap American ed. 5/–. I've ordered it for you!

Eliot offers me his help. Hurrah! Love to Anaïs – we are all opening fire now on different fronts. Boom Boom. Great puffs of prose. The battle is on.

*HOTEL "GOLDENER ADLER",
INNSBRUCK   [after 25 December 1937]

Dear Henry:

A squirt to let you know the news; from Edgar you probably got all the
dirt about the English, and us being made dukes and Christ knows
what; also my crazy catapult jump across Europe to join Nancy. Snow
and ice, my dear sir, snow and ice. I reached her on Christmas eve,
right up on the Italian border, by the Brenner Pass. A hell of a time. Car
skidded into a torrent, walked for ages by crazy tracks, luggage
dragging behind on a sledge. I tell you Conway made no more violent
attempts to reach Shangri-La than I did to deliver my little Christmas
present appropriate to time. I DID IT. Climbed into bed just as she woke
up. Talk about detective-work. I did not know her address, town,
anything. Went on the hearsay of porters, hoteliers etc. Ran to earth
about four, with God's blessing, Christmas day, 1937, covered in
snow, snotty-nosed, up to the hips in thaw, hurrah! Now we sit in
Innsbruck and wait for a train to Gris where we are to ski for a week or
so, regardless of international obligations!

Now we tear each other's hair out in the very room where the poet
Goethe made his celebrated stay in this pearl of a town. The Goethe-
Stube, the Goethe-Stube, where burning Goethe loved and sung.
Myself I am all for Heine. Innsbruck, he said, is a bloody place, and the
Austrians are to be accused of IMMEASURABLE IMBECILITY! I salute.
[. . .]

Will you please reserve a copy of *Tropic* and *B.S.* for Anna Wickham,
the most amazing woman I have yet met in England. Our scheme is
fattening, my dear Henry. DYLAN THOMAS will have a book for us,
probably Honor Wyatt, but I didn't contact DJUNA BARNES. Curtis
Brown is frightfully enthusiastic, and Fabers are mumbling the dry end
of the crust and soothing down their gaiters. What can you do? They
are frightfully nice, really intend to do nothing but VALID WORK, but
are so sewn up in a fishing net of board meetings and sub-committees
that you can hardly get an answer out of them one way or another.
Well, WE WILL GET ON WITH THE JOB OURSELVES. [. . .]

George Reavey is one of the finest little men I have ever met; a really
integral and nutty little chap. He will do UNCLE in March he says. Also
he has a painter called VAN VELDE, who bowls me over; I think he is
worth a serious appreciation by you or someone of your calibre. BY

THE WAY ANAND is doing an anthology, wants something from you and Anaïs: Anaïs' womb piece I suggested and Butchart is getting on to you for something suitable. He never got his copies of *B.S.* and *Tropic*, NOR *The Booster* in which he appeared; could you find out what happened and send him another *Booster*. Likes you like hell!

I will write this evening from Gris adding anything that is missing. In the meantime letters to this address, and let me know how the flag flies, my dear Conway.

> Shangri-La for ever!
> Larry Durrell.

[Addendum:]

HENRY:

Here is an attempt at a prospectus. Play about with it will you and add a whisker here and there; let me know about the dummy. Do you think it would make the V.S.L. distinctive if one just had a frontispiece of the author in each volume; ask Kahane how much it would cost, would you? It would be good, and it would give artists a leg up also. I would love to see you in front of MAX, and dear Anaïs' gnome's skull peeping out from the diary: eh? See what you think.

Bloody snow. O bloody.

Coming back soon to Paris on my way to Tahiti. Henry this Library is going to be a huge bundle of petrol sodden firewood in Paris: one spark and you have a conflagration in which the true meaning of Revolution is discovered, WHOOPS!

> Ld

Durrell was created 'Don Cervantes Pequeña de Redonda' by John Gawsworth, eventual successor to Matthew Phipps Shiel (1865-1947) on the throne of Redonda, a tiny island in the West Indies.

*CARE OF HOTEL GOLDENER ADLER.
[i.e., Gris?, Austria]   [after 25 December 1937]

DEAR GOOD HENRY:
addenda to my last, while we are poised here on a fucking Alp with acute tonsillitis and swollen gums. [. . .]

The general opinion about *The Booster* in London is that it has fallen between two stools; the clowning is regarded with distaste, and the serious part of it is so snowballed in mysteries that people excuse themselves hurriedly and make a wry mouth; I made myself the sheathed sword of the outfit, and pictured you and Alf as a couple of insane and incorrigible cherubims running everything into the ground as hard and fast as possible; WILL the next number appear? I wasn't sure so I lay mum and said we had run it off the rails.

Shall I draft a little bit of spurious advertising for the Villa Seurat Library; not a ripple of a smile on the face of the pond; the bland and lidless protozoic eye of the commercial man dealing with Art. This of course is our Big Bertha; if it doesn't go off nothing will. Let me know what new schemes hatch; you know, it's good to be able to take twenty paces away from you people and take a good look at you all in perspective; I see that from now on you will have to rely on me a great deal as PUBLIC OPINION! Because you have created such a bubble around yourselves there in Villa Seurat, talk such a personal and strange language, that you cannot even conceive the bewilderment of people who sit outside in London for example, and listen!

The people I met I liked awfully; specially REAVEY, BUTCHART, BLAKESTON, PORTEUS.

We must widen out and print everybody, good or bad. Then in exchange they will print us for better or for worse; then we shall get into all the anthologies and finally into Westminster Abbey, so help us.

Cheers chaps. L.G.D.

*ionian bank corfu   [postmarked 3 June 1938]

Henry yes come. You'll find us on one leg but will find a corner for you where the workmen are not busy. If we are not at the dock to meet you look out for a stout middle height man in a chauffeur's cap who answers to the name SPIRO (pronounced speer-o) AMERICANO. He speaks extraordinary english but will take all responsibilities out of your hands, ring me up and make you drunk while you wait for us to come and fetch you in the *Van Norden*. I wonder if this will get you in time: yr letter took 7 days I see. Please bring package and any books you want bound here: and Henry, are you wise to go south into that inferno just now? It is the wrong month. You'll be fried alive. O.K. as far as Ithaca, Lesbos and such latitudes but Crete will be an oven. More when we meet.

Whoopee. L&N

*18 villa seurat paris XIVe   Saturday [early June 1938]

Dear Larry –

Just rereading for 6th & final time the B.B. Pages had to be re-set & so I had to read every line – like a new book. I write you this, first to assure you it is progressing, second, to reassure you that the book is magnificent. After so many readings one gets tired of even a good book. But yours improves with each reading – and that speaks wonders for it. Alors – send out to the clitoris for an ice! Or empty the womb like a bucket of mush – into the silence!

And the *kingcups shining*! I can't get this image out of my head – marvellous. The whole thing glows. It's the fucking "hypaethral" universe all right all right! I salute you, O Son of Jupiter! You will soon be crowned. Anyway – now the book should be out in July some time! There may be errors here & there, but I think they will be microscopic. It won't be my fault anyway – I've done everything possible. You had the worst printer, unfortunately . . . .

I won't be leaving for a couple of weeks – that's certain. I fell from the top of the ladder (in studio) in the dark a few nights ago. Had to be taken to hospital to be stitched up here & there. Full of glass. But recovering nicely now. No broken bones – just cuts & bruises. So I am resting on my oars a bit for the moment. Naturally I have the best of attention. It's like a vacation with all expenses paid for. I always enjoy these little mishaps.

Anaïs is doing well with her book – nearly thru now. I have just been over it. It is rather a "Neptune-Uranus" book, if that means anything to you! Anyway – Konx Ompax!

How is the climate in Summer on the island of Lesbos? What do you know about Lesbos – *physiognomically*? Love to Nancy!

Henry.

Henry: it's so quiet today, and the sea so blue, and now the garden wall is built and the floors a little polished: and the Lockharts have left so we are getting a little settled.

I was thinking: you must come about the tenth of September: it will be very quiet and quite new to you. Drop everything and leave someone in charge of your mail. Just wrap *Capricorn* in a red wool shawl and bring your portable along with you. I can give you a deep cool room with two windows over the sea; bright rugs on the floor; a desk and some books; an encyclopaedia and dictionary. Bring a woman too with you; that would make it an even keel for the days which come and go quite silently. We could sail and bathe in the mornings; have a fine sunny lunch with wine; then a long afternoon siesta: bathe before tea and then four hours' work in a slow rich evening. Even if you did not touch *Capricorn* I think you would profit; the thing would be there and the invisible chisel would be jockeying it about as you slept. Get well set on an even base, and come to terms with the scenery. Then in the middle of October you could start lashing out for Crete, Lesbos and so on.

It is perhaps not so primitive – there is a lavatory for example, and we might have a bath put in by that time; anyway we could motor into town every week and have a bath at the hotel there. No mosquitos, or any vermin; your work-room would be as flyless as villa seurat; bathing in the sea; trips into prehistory. And I think all this – a lull in your streamlined life – might just provide the shifting of the stance that *Capricorn* demands; because after all one only lets people and things impose if one wants them to; and if things intervene it really means that the Roman Road to *Capricorn*, your biggest and most dazzling child, runs not so straight.

After contemplating the circle for a week I have evolved one or two new speculative ideas on the nature of classical art; as – DETACHMENT not being synonymous with objectivity; as – in writers every new effort being vitiated by rationalisation – whereas in sculpture you will find your way sensually through your fingertips and leave the critical debris to Herb Read. As – the next phase is a CLASSICAL phase, a form of diathermy; a writing on the womb-plasm with the curette. You see today all writing is pretending to be Classical (Eliot, Hemingway, 'style', Stein) whereas the origins of it are really ROMANTIC; compare waste land with baudelaire, stein with alfred de musset. Never mind. Cut it all out. It's too hot. But in *Capricorn* your new attitude will be definable (surely not) as CLASSICAL, in the sense that a circle is classical.

Listen, the British fleet is in; two huge grey monsters, really beautiful to look [at]. War is really a fine art I feel when you think of THIS flawlessness of ingenuity spent on steel to twist and rivet and smooth it; guns like great pricks, sliding in and out and coiling on themselves. And little men like lice running about in groups by arithmetic. It's wonderful. One side of us responds to the aggregates: when you see these flawless dummies you feel it. No responsibility. The idiots dream of an ant world where giant pricks slide in and out and vomit steel semen, and a regiment could be lick[ed] off the walls of this tower and leave not even a blob of pus behind.

How is the new *Delta* and when? I enclose the canons of the unknown god whom you must visit and worship when you come here; he is the unknown, the unhonoured, undiscovered god in each of us. We will give him no name. Unless IT. I want you and Anaïs to write a prayer each to him; not long; about three pages of typescript or slightly more. I will do one too. And print it. I send you the litany tomorrow.

Now Henry: no more dilly-dallying. Tell me: shall it be definitely in September? I don't think you'll regret it for a second.

Skoal to *Capricorn*.
Larry.

*Hôtel Majestic, 2, Rue de Condé,
Bordeaux
Sunday –   25th September [1938]

Dear Larry & Nancy –
I left Paris a few days ago to take a vacation after finishing *Capricorn* and having my teeth fixed. Found the country too dull and came on here just as things began to look really bad. Before leaving Paris I packed all my belongings carefully – Anaïs will take them to storage, unless war is declared so suddenly that she hasn't time. I have been in a very bad state up until last night when things looked so bad that I could begin to think of *action*. Sending you this by air mail – hope it will reach you before declaration of war. I am stuck here – no use returning to Paris because city will be evacuated. Can't go anywhere from here as I haven't the

money. (If an American gun boat comes along I may have to take it!)

I'd like to know what you intend doing – stay in Corfu or return to England to be drafted *et cetera*. Could you send me a telegram to the above address? Anaïs is still in Paris and Hugo is in London. Communications are already poor, interrupted. I am here with just enough to last about a week. I won't budge from here, if I can help it. There's no place to go to! Have written Kahane for an advance on royalties due, but doubt if he'll come across, he's such a tight bugger. I may be stranded here in this bloody awful place where I don't know a soul and never intended to be. No doubt I shall pull out all right – Jupiter always looks after me – but I'd like a word or two from you. Maybe I might find a way to get to Corfu – *if it's safe there*? If you don't reach me here try Kahane. I have two valises with me, a cane (bequeathed by Moricand) and a typewriter. If necessary I'll throw it all overboard and swim for it.

Everything would be O.K. if Anaïs could depend on receiving money from London regularly – but who can say what will happen to communications, banks, etc.? If I need some dough in an emergency – if I have to make a break for it somewhere – can I depend on you for anything? I won't ask unless I'm absolutely up against the wall. I'm already on a war basis, ferreting about like an animal, not a thought in my head except to keep alive by hook or crook. The worse it gets the keener I will be. It's the tension, the inaction, the pourparlers, that gets me. Five minutes alone with Hitler and I could have solved the whole damned problem. They don't know how to deal with the guy. He's temperamental – and terribly earnest. Somebody has to make him laugh, or we're all lost! Haven't spoken to a soul since I left Paris. Just walk around, eat, drink, smoke, rest, shave, read papers. I'm an automaton. Fred was still at the Impasse Rouet – not called for yet. And without a cent as usual. Love to Veronica *Tester* – what a wonderful name!

Henry.

[P.S.] If you lose track of me, if Paris is bombed & Obelisk wiped out, write to my friend Emil Schnellock – c/o Mrs. L.B. Gray, Orange, Va., *U.S.A.* Anaïs is at the Acropolis Hotel – 160 Blvd. St. Germain, Paris (6ᵉ). She may come here. Everything depends on that boyo Hitler!
P.P.S. I gave Kahane MS. of *Capricorn* to put in vault of his bank. Have carbon copy with me – also *Hamlet* MS.

Dear Larry & Nancy,

After dispatching you a post-card this noon I received the package (*registered letter*) from London. It must be the money! I am not opening it. I don't want to be tempted. I write you this to ask what shall I do – send it to you at Corfou by registered mail or return it to London? If the latter, tell me exact name and address of your bank there.

Need I tell you how touched I am by your readiness to aid me, even though in such bad straits? I have other money now and shall not need to touch this – you may be sure of it. I would have sent it immediately to you at Corfou but wondered if that would be wise, for various reasons.

You can imagine what might have happened if there really had been war. I mean, as regards communications. Everything has come a week or so too late. It was my intention, just as you propose, to get together enough money in Paris to be able to jump a boat any time. I believe I shall have all the money that is necessary – feel quite certain of it.

I still feel lousy, depressed. Change my mind a dozen times a day. You see, if they would let one stay at the Villa Seurat, I wouldn't mind so much. But evacuating the whole population – that pushing and shoving, that insect life they plan for the civilians – no, I can't see it. And of course I shan't fight! I feel paralyzed because it all seems so inevitable. You have only to look at people, watch their behavior, to see that there is no solution possible.

Well – the hell with all this for awhile. Did you ever receive copies of the *B.B.*? And any other reviews? It's marvellous to hear that you are working. Keep on! The moment you draw near the arteries of "civilization" you will be paralyzed. Stay away as long as possible. Some men have gone on about their tasks right thru a war. I think I could too – if I were permitted to stay put.

Don't let your countrymen play on your emotions. England hasn't a bloody chance. Nor France. They are still "shocked" by the Germans – their talk, their behavior etc. No one takes it at par – or thinks to go them one better. I would say – don't go to war! don't waste a man! Play the devil's own dirtiest game with them! make them eat their cannons! But no, they are preparing for honorable battle. They want to go down with colors flying. *I* would use microbes – *now*, in peace time, while cordially shaking hands, while lauding them to the skies, while signing new peace treaties. Brother, be wary as the fox! Be wise as the serpent! Don't get entangled and ensnared. More from Paris. I am going to finish the "Hamlet" now, *with a vengeance*.

Henry

[P.S.] Don't forget! Let me know *immediately* what to do with this wonderful package of money. And did I say thank you? Alors, je vous remercie de tout coeur. I never expected, really, to hop the boat for America. I wanted to see whom I could count on in a pinch. From Fraenkel nary a word. It cost *me* a small fortune to find out!!!

Ionian Bank Corfu   [mid-October 1938]

Dear Henry: just got the second letter saying that the money hadn't arrived; I think it antedated the other one in which the money had. But it's sad to see you so black and grum. Myself when I look outside this house to Europe I can't help feeling that all you say is right. The cataclysm looms. It is only that this bay settles every night into black silk so that one's panic can ride at anchor. You can see deep fungus and the cypresses turned upside down like paint brushes in it; and a surface which would record the scratching of a fingernail on it.

I am alone for the time. Nancy has gone to Athens. I speak nothing but Greek, so I don't even read or write for breaking the spell of being a foreigner, a complete foreigner for once. Somehow nice tight para- graphs seem null when the bottomless pit is opening to swallow. I wish I could mail you over a bit of the hallowed sangfroid I have felt today sailing the boat over to town and back. I am not a person who can usually stay alone but for the last two days I have been happier than ever before in my life; like a bright web of sunlight drawn over everything. At night sliding into sleep like the water sliding over the pebbles. This is a period in my life, like a milestone: and no bombs can stop it. Hurrah. Now tonight I have an even more crazy idea. In another two hours we shall have the ravaged horn of the moon; I have filled the engine and stowed some blankets in the boat. I am going to set out for the Bay of Fauns, just this side of the Albanian frontier, and sleep the night there. Tomorrow? Gumanitsa or Meurte. I am taking with me an *Odyssey*, rewritten in simple Greek for schoolchildren, which I can follow easily. The language tastes sweet and sinewy. Also a dictionary and some food; my revolver in case Albanians stray over into the bay. And my new mood; it is like a keen knife which I want to try on the weather. Perhaps even a fountain pen. I may write you a little poem in the very bay, what?

Nancy and V[eronica Tester] are somewhere in Athens bless them, probably celebrating their escape from the tyrant. My writing is altered; I am acquiring formal virtues. Not just a spate of symbols converted into pure sensation; because the deepest meaning of Logos or Tao is not in a dynamic, fretful SENSATION as that crop-headed politician Spengler would have it, but in a sudden huge calm – an underground lake inside oneself. Typing bad. Light wonky. Spengler is WRONG, you know; terribly wrong; but the journey was worth it, he scores terrific truths. Like a man who continually aims at elephants which are not there, and finds that he has brought down humming-birds; brilliant occasional sparks. On Christ and Dostoievsky particularly. MARVELLOUS. But the scheme of history: life as power politics, or spate politics. That I don't like. Still each man must have his frame of thought, his inward form, without which he cannot make himself intelligible. It is a mere firing position for him; and he does fire, my god. Well, it's not the target ever. It's what you hit.

Cheer up Henry; keep the little raft of hope floating. The worse it gets the more keenly we'll store the seconds. A shaky future makes the present radiant. I taste each second believe me like a fine drop of Grecian oil, matured and pressed. And damn the Germans.

> Well, Cheero what: and do keep
> the ensign waving; you know we are
> cherishing you and sending waves of
> comfort in spite of the distance.

Love,
Larry

*[Paris]   October 25, 1938

Dear Larry –

Just got your air mail letter addressed to Obelisk. The money, both remittances, I have returned now for the second time to Grindlay & Co. – they were in doubt as to whose account it belonged in. I told them Nancy's most likely. O.K.? [. . .]

I don't feel so black any more, because I can work again, and because I am determined in advance to beat it at the first sign of trouble. I *would* like to go to America this winter – to the Southern States and to the desert! I'm afraid of the Mediterranean. It all seemed so degenerate to me. I don't like olive trees, cypresses, figs, grapes, etc. I want to see Oriental people, ultra-civilized people, decadent, rotten through and through. On the other hand, if I could scrape up the money for an easy trip – and that's the only way I will travel henceforth – I would come down there, and from there to Constantinople and Persia, which I long to see. I even wonder if we shouldn't try to establish a sort of Hindenburg Line for ourselves at Corfu? We need to have some place of retreat when the storm breaks. I wouldn't stay in America during a war. I want only to *visit* certain places there to complete my American picture, do you see?

There's another thing: both Fred and Moricand are rather a burden, financially. Can't shake them off – it's hopeless. I discussed with Fred the idea of trying to buy or rent a small house in the south of France – perhaps even Ibiza or even Corfu – where they could live dirt cheap, at our expense, and where we others might go for a rest or in case of necessity. If I found a spot I really liked I would leave Paris for good – I no longer feel obliged to stay here at the Villa Seurat. But when I see the country, peasants, degenerates, the desert of the mind, when I see cows, sheep, trees, all that which means nothing to me, I get panicky. I could live with rocks and mountains or sand, but not with Nature which is cultivated. It makes me feel like a cow myself. I don't need much space or environment. I only need to feel that I don't positively dislike a place. Naturally, if I could get to that Tibetan frontier, either side, if I could live somewhere there in the Himalayas, I haven't the slightest doubt but that I would be content for the rest of my life. Arizona would be excellent – if only it was peopled with another race. Do you get me?

I'm damned glad to know you are doing so well yourself. It sounds wonderful, all you write. You *must be* a genius! And I think, incidentally, that as I predicted originally, *The Black Book* is going to be recognized and is going to make your reputation. I hope you believe that I did my utmost to make it a decent job. It's heart-breaking to work with an insensitive bastard like Kahane. I can't stomach him . . . . .
Do you think of going to England still? We sort of look for you all the

time. Yesterday I thought I saw you on the street. And give my love to Nancy. Thank her personally for all the trouble she went to. I'm ashamed of myself begging for help all the time. But maybe the tide will turn soon. More shortly. Did Kahane send you a copy of the *Max* book??????

Do get hold of Balzac's *Seraphita* in English – it's usually included in a volume called *Etudes philosophiques*, often with his autobiographical volume called *Louis Lambert*. It is something phenomenal – and it was written with *Louis Lambert* in one month, amidst the most sordid worries, financial and otherwise.

Henry

*ionian bank corfu greece   [end] october nineteen thirty eight

henry: this is bad news you going to America all of a sudden; war? Why not go to england, it would be an easy stepping off place for USA? Listen have you got a great package of Mss and letters belonging to me, in a brown paper folder? Could you leave them somewhere where we could pick them up on our way north this winter? I need my British Museum ticket which is in among them.

[Nicholas] Moore is thrilled with "Zero" and *Seven* and will print them in "Asylum" [sic] – what do I mean? Someone is attacking the BB in this number. I've told them to open a correspondence column so I can defend myself at length. Lawrence Durrell and his art etc. What is good about it. And so on. Also lots of poems. They are doing me proud. Eliot refuses the BB excerpt as I said he would long ago unless he got proofs before publication. It's sad. I was counting on the money. Damn Kahane: and after all the delay the book wasn't perfect. However. Better luck. How is Anaïs' Inferno going along? And *Max*? Not a word. Writing stopped again. It's like April showers with me at the moment. A mere momentary moisture; and then nothing. Not even drip drip drip.

Send me some *Phoenixes*, will you? I want a good laugh to cheer me up in this stinking tomb of civilization, also a bit of the body mystical. Greece is beautiful and impoverished. Going to england soon to take a hand for a week or two in literary LIFE/Death?

Bored to death by uncertainty: now, of course, nancy wants to have a

106

child the slut. A little red general with fat legs, to ride into Czecho-Slovakia on a white horse? What sort of animal vegetable mineral is a woman's mind?

love to anais ever: IS she happier: please she must be tell her because we are all caught in the rat-trap and smiles are at a premium. We are no good if after all we have professed in talk and writing, we cannot laugh NOW: AT THIS MOMENT.

    love. larry

*18 villa seurat paris XIVᵉ   Nov 5. [1938]

    Dear Larry –

A quick note to say I will be here yet awhile and hope to see you passing through. I am asking Kahane to make copies of another review you got in *The Nation*, N.Y. – by Paul Rosenfeld – a good one too! Will send you the printed article soon as he is thru with it.

    Listen – did you send that water color, "The Ego and his Yid", to the censor? Can you, will you? I would appreciate it. Just for the show, which is definite and soon – he just writes me again to send everything I can. Put your name and address – or care of me, if you like, on the back – and the title too. (There will be a lot of them from "The Collection of So-and-So".)

    Eve Adams is just beginning to *sell* my water colors!! I might earn a little dough in this most pleasant way. Ho ho! What a joke!

    About that package you speak of – yes, I have it here safely. Should I leave suddenly I would give it to Kahane's keeping.

    A letter from Dylan Thomas – I like him more and more. A queer chap. More reviews – *N.E.W.*

    Anaïs is having Fred retype the MS. of "Chaotica" – a book of 3 novelettes in good form & style now. We will send you copy to pass judgment on – if O.K. for the Villa Seurat Series – if O.K. with *you*! Let us know, will you, if the money is still available for this book? Hope you are not bankrupt yet.

    I think all our books will sell slowly – may take a year to liquidate – unless we get an unexpected break. But I think we are making a solid foundation with them – which is more important. Eve says *The Black*

Book is *too deep* for most people – but you see that the critics are highly impressed. From early reports the *Max* book finds favor with the readers. We need not despair.

Think about Balzac's *Seraphita* for the Series – in English, with preface by all of us. It's an idea I have which might not be so impracticable. I want you to know this book – it's important. Hope you can manage to lay hands on a translation – usually it's included with other works in a volume called *Etudes philosophiques*. It's not part of the Comédie Humaine. It's far *beyond*!! Do look into it. I am eager to get your opinion.

Anyway, Larry me lad, things are going forward – slowly, but definitely – inevitably. We have only to sit tight like Hitler and play our hand, what! I predict once again that *you* will be famous in no time. I know what I'm talking about. Wish I could speak as confidently for myself.

Love from Fred and Anaïs – and from all of us more soon – substantially – the evidence and thing made manifest. Go on with all your encyclopaedic efforts. The world hasn't cracked yet.

Love to Nancy in Athens.   Henry.

P.S. Still no letter from Laughlin but I feel something radical is happening. If the breach is opened we will rush in like the Gadarene swine. It will be a clean-up. But shit, I am happy anyway. I am again writing and painting and meditating. I'll tell you some big things soon – of my private investigations.

P.P.S. Made copies of review myself – enclose clipping. Giving copy to Kahane.

*[Paris]   Friday 9⁰⁰ PM [early December? 1938]

Dropped in on chance of finding you – didn't go to meeting after all. Want to tell you, Larry me boy, that that Rank essay I find most excellent – especially the Yang-Yin womb dichotomy. Congratulations.

Also finished your Ms. It seems to go well forward – with murderous characterization – *murderous*, I tell you.

And whence did you get these prototypical creatures? What lovely monsters! *English* monsters! Sometimes this stuff seems to me to outdo

Dostoievsky. The drama takes place in the neurones somewhere, like corner rue de la Gaîté and twelve midnight, full stink ahead! One criticism I have to make. It occurs even in essays. [...] You adopt a sort of apologetic pose now & then. You smirk and bow just before saying something tremendous. Don't do it – you cheapen it. Say it, with or without the beard. No perorations, no bows, no prefaces. Give them the cold steel and the Ionian dawn. No parentheses. No coughing. You are a very old man in a boy's skin. You are really Buddha or John of the Cross – not Death Gregory or Quarles or Winston Churchill. You get me? Come around at noon, if you can – I have a list of good movies for you to see.

P.S. Maybe you'd like to winter in the Villa Seurat? I'm going to America *very soon* – soon as I raise the passage money. This is definite. [P.P.S.] An excellent remedy to intestinal catarrh, drowsiness, lumbago etc. is *one* big meal of fruit at noon, with tea and pain seigle. Try it. I am a new *man*.

[unsigned]

Durrell's 'Rank essay' was apparently never published.

---

*[Paris]   *Tuesday* [mid-December 1938]
    Dear Larry, Nancy & Fred –
At the present writing it looks dubious about my coming to London for Xmas. Still no dough in sight. To-day Anaïs had to pawn the crown jewels – for 125 frs.! To-morrow it will be O.K. again. But my fare back & forth, a visa, *pissgeld und trinkgeld*, all that would come to over a thousand francs. However, it may be that in the last Xmas mail from America I will find a check, whereupon I rush to the train & come. I would like to see Veronica & Dorothy – and go to the roller skating rink and the casinos and Covent Garden & the Café Royal. Fuck Messrs. Eliot, Symons & Co.! But thus far in my life I have never passed a jolly Xmas. Every Xmas has found me broke, balked and frustrated. And usually alone. This one promises to be the same.
    Anaïs got word that the brief-case was returned; so perhaps you will recover your things. I am now going over her book. She has taken out all the 3rd book and put it separately at the end. *Three parts.* Do send me your notes, will you?

It is freezing here – sub-glacial weather. Never saw it like this before. Slept under 6 blankets last night, with sweater & bath-robe on, and just about felt cozy. In 2100 A.D. the earth's "abstract" axis will be pointed towards the star Polaris in Ursa Minor – this will be the end of another 25,000 year epoch – beginning of the real Aquarian Age. Fire, floods, cataclysms, as usual. Perhaps another Ice Age to usher it in.

Sent you a batch of mail & Nancy's horoscope. Tell Fred if I don't come I hope anyway to have enough to pay *Delta* money end of December. That'd be something anyway. I'll write again soon as there's news. Doing some jolly fierce water colors now to keep warm. How is it in London? Freezing too?

And a very merry Xmas to you, Mister Scrooge! Next year I will receive the Nobel Prize. Patience. Patience. And regards from Betty Ryan. Henry.

Moved by this letter, Larry and Nancy scraped together enough money to bring Henry to London for Christmas.

*one hundred and forty campden hill road,
notting hill gate.   [late January 1939]

     henry:
I'm glad all is spry and dandy including nightmares etc. This is a shot at random. You talk about people respecting one's solitude? Wow, you should see mine. There is none of it left.

Barker is doing a book of my verse; Symons is allowing me a three thousand word space to write about Howe; Joe is dejected and pointless these days full of fun and dismay. It is now snowing like it will never stop; huge drifts, icy air, hairy coats – like a swan song from my hairy five-year-dead youth. Horrible.

Have I your permission to get on and do a new poetry number? I have now the best support a man could want in England; the last one (which was well noticed here) is nothing compared to what I could get together now. Barker has an unpublished 300 line poem which is marvellous; Dylan can write; Eliot will help. If you do, and you can refrain from putting in Osborn or Wambly Bald or anyone else you like, I think I can build our reputation 12 cubits higher in 1939???? <All this due to Henry Miller – ALL OF IT!!>

No humour in me these days much; the times are pressing inexorably in and people want the strong, tender words: and the ordinary thought. They are too busy to care about how one feels; and I get the feeling that the biggest joke falls flat – like a dud bomb in this damn white, murky, soft gelatine frabjous valetitshambulunucated England where the swans fuck by the lake and the ham is served icecold with snow outside in the street.

Tell anais to choose her own jacketpaper since one can make mistakes by post; as we did over the *BB*. I don't want the same to happen. Go with her, girded in all yr might, and drive a six inch nail into Kahane's tin can from me. Tell him we're all proud to be published by the obelisk, and we hope for better business in 1939. And we will write bigger and better books for him and sell them at lower prices; so that he can suck out blood as well as our brains. Tell him to be as merry as hell, because we are all here just to nourish him; he can batten, and settle like the rambunculated, swollen, gorged, panting, uncircumcised leech that he is.

And that, brother, is all for the moment. Must go to the bank.
eduardo and hugo are converts to howe. I have met a strange woman who is in touch with all the psychologists and occultists combined. Listen, why not come and live a month here: you would have a string of contacts as long as your arm.

I FORGOT TO THANK YOU FOR THE CHEQUE WHICH ELIOT DARKLY SENT ME. AWFULLY SORRY. I LEFT IT IN MY FILE AND YOUR LETTER REMINDS ME. DO YOU MIND IF WE KEEP IT? WE ARE IN A BAD WAY. I THINK NO YACHT SOON. PERHAPS A ROCKING HORSE INSTEAD?

And so on.
Larr   y.

Durrell wrote 'The Simple Art of Truth: A First Study in Doctor Graham Howe' (a review of Howe's *Time and the Child*) for W.T. Symons's magazine, *Purpose* (April–June 1939).

Dear Larry,

Enclosed find letter from *Time* which came in an opened envelope.
May have answered you meagerly by post card regarding *Delta*. Meant
simply to say that you have full rights to do as you please, Fred willing
– *he's* the editor, don't forget. I realize more and more that I must
withdraw from all this kind of activity. I don't have the least qualms
any more about not being known or recognized. I think I have already
done much more in the way of self-advertising than I had any business
to do. I'm going to write more and meditate more. This is not meant as
an indirect criticism of your enthusiasm – not at all. What's good for
you may not be good for me. I have just received a letter from
Goodland, asking me if I wish to cooperate in a grandiose scheme of
publications which he and his cronies are contemplating – without any
financial responsibility. I am answering No. Not contemptuously or
disdainfully, but because I feel it a waste of time. My time is getting
short. I have to utilize my energies in the best possible way. I see very
clearly what lies ahead of me to do – and there are many things I don't
see, in addition, which I shall probably have to do too. I am getting
more and more stripped, travelling with less and less baggage. When I
get to the dead centre (strange we should say "dead" instead of "live"!)
I will just BE!

In reading proofs of *Capricorn* I am more and more struck by the
metaphysical implications with which the book is sewn. In reading
Balzac's life I am struck by the futile detour he made of his life after
adolescence. (Innumerable analogies between his secret life – and
known life too, for that matter – and my own. Really startling, and
that's why I shall write about him with certitude.) Every time I pick up
a mystical book I am struck again, shuttled back, as it were, to some
fundamental truthful realm of my self which has been so much denied
in life. A hundred years from now the phrases I let drop here and there,
in the books and in the letters, will be studied to prove this and that
about me, I know it. But now, even now, I am struck by the prophetic
element which is an essential part of me. For example, I haven't the
slightest idea what that book I announced for 1942 – Draco and the
Ecliptic – will be about, but I am absolutely certain that it will create
itself in the interim, and that it will be vastly significant, not just for me
but for the world to come. I will add just another detail – that I am in

that period of grace wherein all my wishes are answered. I have merely to ask and it is given, to knock and the door is opened. From all sides things are mysteriously conjoining and contributing to my development and enrichment. To-night I pick up a book and take it with me to the café to read. A thin book, in French, on the Rosicrucians. The cardinal idea is so stark and simple, so thoroughly in accord with my own belief as to the way of life, that I am amazed how men can miss it. It is the doctrine of the heart, to be brief. Howe states it in an esoteric fashion in his books. (I have just finished my article on him, but will do it again. His ideas are for the rare few, but these few count heavily, and everything rests with them. He cannot possibly be understood yet.)

Well, the purport of this was merely to inform you that you have my blessing and full support, should you decide to take over all this activity which I am now dropping. Cheerio! Henry.

*140 campden hill road. Notting Hill Gate   [c. 28 January 1939]

It was strange the way your letter curled through the letter-box, so solemn and valedictory; so extra solemn and measured, as if you had written it with great deliberation and care on the wagon-lit en route for Tibet. Dear Henry: I think I know how you feel; a sudden new change of internal form, a sort of anaesthetic progression into a new key. It is so uncanny to see these grave rhythms in your letter, but I rejoice, and unpack the machine to salute you forthwith. But don't write these days: just sit and read and smile and unbrace the enthusiasm a little. In *Capricorn* you have marked the latest and largest milestone – in prose that has no more to do with paper and ink than the new Picasso has to do with paint. It is like following the rhythm of flesh with a finger in the dark; tenuous but truly knitted. So take a good deep breath, warrior, and sit under the laurel until the spring days.

We are keeping little Joe afloat truly on his keel; and are waiting for you to come back and see us. Don't let our opinionated machinery stand in the way of anything; rest on the support you have a little now. I feel you have never used your supports in your life; you have thrown up a few reserve trenches here and there, but they are always empty, and you are too much in action. Rest on us a little bit: we are all here, five or six of us, making cradles out of our fingers for you. So don't spur into action EXCEPT WHEN YOU WANT. (This is exactly what you say you are doing in yr letter so these notes by the way are late to the post.) But if there are these fucking Dover cliffs and the Channel between us, just the same I want you to feel the rhythm of a support and a purpose here that answers yours!

I am collecting a slow but strong poetry number; will you PLEASE FOR ONCE IN YOUR LIFE CONTRIBUTE. Not poems, but little sayings, three or four lines long, taken from your books, notebooks, or written new. Open TROPIC again at the first few pages and you will see the short poems in there; that type but dealing with you now. I WANT YOU IN.

It's funny you say you are desisting from 'these activities'; meaning what . . . Delta? It's funny because yesterday I told Joe that I felt bad about fooling along any more, and wanted a rest from myself – the show-off clever boy self which always appears in the circus. There is so much more in me that my tenderness will never let me bring out. And I too am in a vortex BUT WITH A COMPASS THIS TIME AND NO PANIC. Consequently the writing must change. I need a new technique to suit my world now. And the little flutter of semi-recognition I got here has scared the life out of me; people like leeches to suck a smile and sad phrase out of one. Life is like a truck that has fallen on one, and each day, if the strength keeps up, you ease a little morsel more of the body clear, very soft and very slow and almighty painful. And there it is with people asking you to collaborate on a play about a chorine and a gangster. And the horde moving around in these streets as if it were a jungle, wild and merely mad.

Today we stood around in a pub and suddenly drank to the death of Yeats; so funny, the shabby-intelligenced young with all the gut beaten out of them by social credit and monetary yields and worker's rights: so funny to see them shabbily drinking the toast, as if such a gesture of simple homage was foreign to them. And this is england with its bitter beer. By God a frenchman can still salute; but we do it like shop-walkers and cretins. Anyhow the old silver-haired giant would have been pleased I think if he could have been.

I have written nothing but grown in humanity half a cubit. This fen of adders – you should hear the poets talk. Some good cool poems, like little cold pebbles still tasting of the sea. Inside I pine for the island really, the weird premonition of the landscape down there; I would like to see it if the war doesn't intervene. I suppose you had the other war barring your life at about my age last time. It's a sad feeling but makes you give the final ounce to what you do. It sharpens the minute, so that each tick of time going through is time tasted; unbearably sweet even if trivial things and idiots intervene.

A man just passed in the street shouting ENGLAND FACING WAR: am going to get a paper.

all our love.
larry

*[Paris]   [mid-February 1939]

Henry: just a quick shot to send the best greetings and everything. The essay on Howe, like mine, was a complete misinterpretation. He came to dinner the other night and explained. His stance, believe it or not, is a pragmatic one. He says that the concept Tao gives him a pragmatic and operable system which he works the whole time. It is connected to the Einstein theory of relativity WHICH UP TO NOW HE SAYS HAS NEVER BEEN USED AS IT SHOULD HAVE BEEN IN METAPHYSICS: merely considered as a contribution to mechanics. He has never divulged the key to his system, which he claims to possess. I can't tell you what a strange demonic person he is; as if there was an inhabitant inside him giving him weird changes of voice and accent. So far, he says, all that he has said has been connected with the DERIVATIVES of his system, not the central key itself, because he has yet to forge his means of expression. It is rather strange. He is up against a creative problem; and talks about art the whole time as an inferior medium for inferior apparatuses. One of the most considerable conceptual minds I have ever struck. He is really like Pythagoras or Paracelsus or someone like that. But the essay of mine he didn't like; too resilient and too good in another sense for him. He would have liked a mechanical interpretation which [is] the strangest paradox of all. What do you think about it? I'm thrilled. He said nothing about your essay, except that it had arrived; mine he didn't like at all. I will send it on to you. It is very much like yours, but not as good.

What a strange creature; more than half evil in the best sense of the word. I would say a real demoniac. "I have prayed", he says over fish, casting those terrible eyes down like a girl, "to have this cup taken from me. But the day is coming slowly." Terrific egotism; nervous system screwed into a knot behind his eyes; almost depersonalised; but the mark of the beast on him. Surely a great and terrifying European. Wow!

Nothing much doing here; cold; stinking – getting together a new poetry number. Joe and Goodland dickering. Reading like a steam engine.

ALSO: Howe is building a machine to demonstrate the mechanical theory of Tao.

Eduardo was knocked over like a ninepin; HE HAS FOUND HIS PLUTO-NEPTUNIAN!

love to all hands,   larry

*[Paris]   3/4/39

Dear Larry –
A word or two ("and then comes night. . . ." James Russell Lowell!) regarding all the queries etc. [. . .]
No, I'm not overburdened with MSS. for V.S. Series! None at all – except West's. And I think you're a bit hard on him, *personally*. I can yawp like that too on occasion. You're harder than I am on the young'uns. But about my attitude – momentarily I feel discouraged about it. 1.) No response to our broadsides. 2.) *Are there any neglected geniuses* about? 3.) To work with Kahane is just impossible. It gripes me. I prefer to withdraw than to waste my substance fighting a losing fight. The power of inertia is overwhelming. I think if we sit back & practise "non-resistance" with him he'll topple over of his own feeble weight. I have written & talked to him so much – made so many propositions, and everything spiked or ignored – that out of sheer pride *as a human being* I refuse to move an inch further in his direction. Henceforth no more suggestions from me, no sign of life or interest in any form, no enthusiasms. Just notify him by curt letter when I have another book ready and wait for his response. He guarantees doing *my* part of *Hamlet* when I wish. I am still arguing the case with Fraenkel – but [have] given him an ultimatum. After a "reasonable" time I go to press, ethical or non-ethical. I wish he'd start a law-suit. I wouldn't defend myself – I'd give him so much rope he'd hang himself. If you write him I am supposed to be en route for Greece! My last letter to him

was posted from Marseilles. He would like to come & *argue* it out. Fuck that! I'm a monomaniac. *Me no argue.*

Aside from all this, I am getting inwardly strong as a bull from solitude & meditation. I'd like to concentrate entirely on writing. You are in a different position. You can afford to be active. I can't. The least waste of energy – that's my idea now. I've got such an iron grip on what's to come out of me, I won't relinquish it. I see now with a diamond inside me. Why should I fight with the world? Why should I push things? Anything I do will eventually be published. I wasted much too much time fighting windmills. I am reconciled now to handing my MSS. in to a National Library or Museum – if Kahane isn't ready to do them. He wants me to "space" them out more! And I want to unload them rapid-fire. It's a struggle and whatever is my destiny will decide it. I stand by destiny.

So please don't get the idea that I do not appreciate or understand your efforts. Nobody, excepting Anaïs, ever gave me such support & encouragement. Just the other day, rereading your review of *Max*, I realized all over again how generous you really are. Well, that's sufficient. To *know* these things is in itself all that is necessary. I don't demand outward proofs. I am only trying to point out that whatever involves me in fight or defense is waste motion. Now that I am sure of myself I can bide my time.

A check for the B.B. came via Colette Roberts from Jane *Hudson* Rule – she heard about it in America – wants to send it to Barclay, I think. I'm tending to it. Extracting my little commission, to be sure. (Stamps, carfare, cigarettes, laundry, income taxes.) Orders are coming in more & more now for all our books. Kahane is furious about putting Anaïs' book over on him. (Really incomprehensible rage.) I haven't told Anaïs. But that too rankles me. You know what I am about to do? He gave me a dummy once, for me to write for him. *I am.* But it is for after death – whoever kicks off first. I will deposit it with Cairns. I am going to *incinerate* him! No man will ever be flayed as I will flay him. I'll put him down in the lowest rung of evolution – and pin him there for eternity. I'm waiting for the day when he will ask me – "Are you getting on with it?" My answer will worry him till the grave. Meanwhile I will insidiously drop a word here & there that I am writing a "posthumous" book about my publisher. Ho ho! I will do something fiendish.

The list of works you have in progress sounds incredible! Jesus, you must be full of ants. Whence this dynamics? On what meat, O Caesar? Not beer & skittles? Next I expect you to tell me you will *play* in your own play. You are becoming a Shakspur! [. . .]

Nancy: I am just finishing a dummy for my friend Emil – all about the Water Color! And I have done some new ones – an improvement too, I think. One turned out to be Napoleon – dripping with gore & quite mad in the eye. And then a couple of lake scenes – without ducks. One has a green bench – one you could really sit on.

So I went to see Rouault's show the other day. Stupendous. He's a *feeling* butcher! A Seraphitus with an axe. I liked his show, disjointed as it was, infinitely better than Picasso's. The last Picassos would make chocolate box covers. *Very pretty*. They stink. He's feathering his oars – but not in the timeless flux this time. I got myself a pad & some new greasy crayons. Marvellous! And a tube of burnt umber and one of hot sepia. Still more marvellous. And I discovered the color *green*. Green as Ireland's sunny dells. Now concentrating on eyes, noses, lips & ears. Especially ears. To transmute the original cauliflower breed I use. Get me a show in London when you work up one for yourself. Let's hang together, b'Jasus! Erin Go Bragh!

Coda: When Balzac goes to visit Louis he finds him standing at the mantelpiece gazing into space like a shot horse. Alors, Louis suddenly ceases to rub one leg against the other, and breaking the spell, says: – THE ANGELS ARE WHITE. C'est inoubliable. La chose la plus folle que j'ai jamais lu. Ça colle, quoi? Henry.

[P.S.] Nancy – did you ever use Chinese white for the pupils of the eye? Try it! It makes "them" mad! *Why?* Why should *white pupils* create insanity? Ask the medicos!

French Writing Paper – *Merde!*
Second Post-Prandial *Discours*.

Informed last night that copy of *Seraphita* does not belong to Symons. Must surrender it soon. A great malheur! Must have another copy *in English* (in which there must also be *Louis Lambert* and "The Exiles" – which last is an episode in Dante's life). So, Larry, me fine bucko, you will go out northward along Campden Road and search high & low for a replica, whereupon you will proceed to devour it rapaciously and then hold it under Edgar's nose for him to sniff it and criticize it from Rudolf [Steiner's] higher view-point. After which tie a red ribbon around it and mail to me with congratulations. Then you start southward from the Kensington Gate and you search for *The Crocodile* of Saint-Martin, also for Eliphas Levi's magical tome and for all the "Correspondences", including the latest Pluto-Neptune conjunction or conjunctivitis. I have the proofs of A's book now and will probably go over it with her, doing my best to weed out dinosaurian errata.

Enjoying a life of complete solitude. Every night I mount the guillotine and have my head chopped off. And next day I grow a new head – like that! I live *among* my ideas, not with them or in them. We are friends, for the time being. The machinery roars in my ears, but I am not a "hickey", i.e. immune to the jitterbug shag. I do not feign catalepsy or psycho-pompernalia. I eat well and drink lightly. For lunch to-day – 3 dozen oysters, a goose, a filet de sole, a maatjes herring, striped & salted, some fancy olives, a grape or two, and a tarte alsacienne. All flip and no proletarian indigestion. Am looking forward to walking the streets of Lhasa, unknown, unheralded – searching for a cheap cinema or a 5 & 10 cent store. The life of a stoat is one thing – the life of a poet is another. Let us gather in His name and eat pretzels. Solitude is the paradise of the over-driven scribes who write their way into Purgatory. Hallelujah! Peace, it's wonderful. *What valises?* Henry.

*140 campden hill road, notting hill gate W8   [after 4 March 1939]

Dear Henry: I owe you more than this hasty scrawl, but am as usual wasting my time doing all sorts of meaningless things for other people. First I invite them to ask my help, then I do their work for them; then I grumble about time wasted. A ceaseless round of imbecility! I feel very much as you do about Kahane, who is a class A worm, a white slug covered with fine fluff. But I would take a strong line with him if we continued the series; or else break with him! I seem to get less and less patient instead of more – what a life. And you know I am not really hard on the young men; I help *practically* as much as I can. But I'm through with being father confessor to every young English blurb who wants to be told how to grow up in four simple lessons.

In West I feel you have another nice young Englishman like Evans. At bottom they don't want their novels corrected and placed; they want to pour out their traveled Irish hearts and be patted on the head. "I want a mother" is the prevailing cry on the literary wind. I did it myself and received no support; not because people weren't kind but simply because there *is* no solution to adolescence, except a lethal chamber. I wish they'd put me in one; feel damned low at the moment, groggy and painful and sterile! It's hard to be patient with oneself! Helping Joe to write for *Picture Post* all afternoon; he is angelic and hopeless. Joe in his little white cherubim's shirts, his paws raised, his eyes buttered, saying "You do it for me eh?! I will never learn; I don't intend to!"

Poetry number of *Delta* is made up and sent off to the printer – I think it a very good one. Am so glad you are cashing in on *The Modern Mystic*; they all look like Jewish gangsters there. Have you a copy of Fraenkel's "Weather Paper" you can give me? I admire it very much. I never saw it before. Cooney just sent his last issues – my what crap he writes that half-arsed Lawrentian. We will most definitely be out of England again by June; Corfu again thank God. This weather is a lid on my coffin of unrest, opaque, muzzy, kindly, dead. England like a fine tree arrested in its growth, and somewhere dead at the heart of oak. What are you writing now – another seven or eight Capricorns? When does she blow?

The *Max* review was considered quite a shameless blurb over here; I have spent my time trying to explain that I mean every word of it.

In the meantime the wheel goes round, birth death rebirth – I think you follow the idea. Love to Anaïs who is well again I hope poor dear. Nancy sends covers today less anaemic than K's.

> Love from us both
> Larry

*140 Campden Hill Road, Notting Hill Gate. W8   [after 21 March 1939]

Dear Henry: I have been away for the last week staying in Surrey, hence the delay in writing to tell you that the Jupiter book is wonderful; a little essay on luck and destiny – and concerning me very closely, and some great things you have said in it. At present it is being eagerly devoured by Nancy.

We have been staying with Desmond Tester and touring the coastal towns in search of boats, so far without much luck. Have not found exactly what we want. I am beginning to wonder when we will. [. . .]

Things have been very quiet over here and I am doing no work at all on my own; only an occasional poem like a sheep-dropping. Everything is so grey and shut in that there is no inducement to wake up and observe, let alone work.

I was taken to the first night of Eliot's new play and was much impressed by it; it is, of course, a flop, but I think it is his most personal and painful thing to date.

The censor [Cairns] didn't show up. I waited the first day for him, and left connections behind. Now that I am back some lousy paper wants me to become dramatic critic and sends me free seats to theatres and offers a guinea per five hundred words once a week. I suppose it will last about a week; run by highly intelligent fairies I hear.

This morning I ran into Fred Carter in a pub, who spoke highly of you; but on the whole talked some annoying rubbish, saying that the tarot was a pointless idiocy when everyone knows that it is a metaphysical system to which the key has been lost; and saying that you put him on to the Tao Teh King which he found rather surprising. Why rather surprising? And of some use with his puzzle game. Why game?

I hear that Kahane's memoirs are out; if I find just cause against Joseph the publisher, will you let me take a libel action in your name. We could get about 500 pounds over some tiny point, and incinerate Kahane as well! The cash would hurt him more than the curses.

Apart from this phantom letter there is no news; we plan to leave for Corfu, boat or not, in a month or two.

More soon,
love,
Larry

Miller wrote the 'Jupiter' book in longhand for Durrell in a printer's dummy.
Eliot's *Family Reunion* opened on 21 March.
Jack Kahane, *Memoirs of a Booklegger* (Michael Joseph, 1939).

*[Paris]   Saturday [late March? 1939]
Dear Larry,
Glad to have your letter this morning. What I hated to lose, or see lost, I mean, above all, were the two miniature water colors I pasted in your book. I thought they were gems, especially the one with the

mythological head and flower made in India ink and eaten out by a quick bath. This morning too several packages of the Easter *Delta* arrived. I glanced the poems over at breakfast, and some I found very good indeed, to my surprise. (Fred's no, terrible, sheer drivel – but don't say so to him.) I notice too how the Frenchman's poem, Jouve's, even in translation, stands out head and shoulders above the rest – your own excepted. This I mean – about your own – I read it with amazement, and though I don't "get" it, I see it's marvellous. You sound like "the" poet of the age. The others seem so *English!* No advance, I mean. Standing still, like the English countryside – always lovable, peaceful, pleasant to look at – but from a dead center. You work with the acid and the axe: you're very much like a Tarot figure, do you know it? And your poems are out of the Tarot, though no one knows it yet. (And the Tarot, my dear fellow, if it represents a metaphysical system, as you say, represents above and beyond that the philosophy of the stars. The connection is intimate and indubitable. I think you catch Carter by the wrong lapel. The "game" *is* a game, nothing more – I saw it! But it is the most wonderful game I ever looked at. You shouldn't let him get trivial with you – probe and probe, and he will yield the divine waters, you'll see. Be patient with him. He is not "occult" – he is an Apocalyptic man. Only he is confused and lacks faith.)

I was going to write and tell you by all means not to miss the three articles which have already appeared in *The Modern Mystic* by Bernard Bromage – on "Tibetan Yoga". The third one just out, in current number. I wrote him a letter and received this response I enclose just this morning. Wonder, after you read his stuff, if you would care to look him up for me, and for yourself? His leaflet sounds bad, I admit. But he seems to have the full dope on Tibetan practices. It drives me wild, delirious with joy. Read especially, in third instalment, about "Marpa" [Milarepa], the poet-saint – wonderful egg! All these great birds of Tibet remind me of the Zen masters, who are up my street. Zen is my idea of life absolutely – the closest thing to what I am unable to formulate in words. I am a Zen addict through and through. Except for the "monastic regime", which I don't believe in at all and see no necessity for. But if you want to penetrate Buddhism, read Zen. No intelligent person, no sensitive person, can help but be a Buddhist. It's clear as a bell to me. And of course all these modern mystikers, Edgar, Steiner, Merry, Kolisko and the whole Austro-Czech outfit of muckers, are stinking caricatures of the doctrine. First there is no evil in them, second no humor, third no magic, fourth no poetry, fifth no life! What is left is moth dust, the furbelows of the mind rotting in the dead sunshine of the dead.

(I liked Audrey's poems and Gervase Stewart's – and especially Dylan Thomas'. He I relish always, whether in prose or poem; he seems authentically poetic to me, blast his drunken soul! Heppenstall is thin. But Dorian Cooke I like too – young, wild-eyed, but honest and murderous. Jouve leaps right out of the page and greets you warmly with the polished gleam of another tradition of poetry, which is French, and which Fred has not at all and never will have. I think yours should create wide attention. I salute you, O Jupiterian poet of the Styx and the Aurora Borealis! If you did nothing but this all winter, it's enough.)

Down to earth . . . . *Capricorn* is due out 20th of April, as I say. Another error on printer's part – printed book without my final O.K. Only one proof-reading. We are waiting to see how many errors we will have to list in the "Errata". Anaïs' will follow a month later. Yes, accounts are due Monday or Tuesday. Kahane will send you a statement. You will get nothing – you will still owe him money. This, in spite of the 5 pounds I paid in, on Anaïs' book. Seems the printing came to more than the stipulated sum. I don't doubt it, and I hope you won't, but if you want to see the books he will doubtless show them to you. Naturally the sales weren't very high, neither for *The Black Book* nor for *Max*. But they are selling slowly all the time. I myself have bought out of my own pocket a number of your books, which friends asked for. And now that the ban is off them, in America, we may get somewhere – through the Gotham Book Mart, at least. The next ten days or so I ought to have some interesting news from them, as I have written them all about the state of affairs. Cairns may not have had time to see you, his boat left the day after he arrived. But he has a high opinion of you and all of us – a staunch fellow, full of integrity, somewhat naif, but on the right side. I count him a good friend and perhaps my best critic in America.

No, Larry, no use trying to reorganize things at present. Business is quite at a standstill now – naturally. People are not buying, nor living – just holding their breath for the expected catastrophe – which I believe will not come off for a long while yet. There is no other man whom we can appeal to, I am sure of it. I am accepting Kahane as one accepts the cross, and trying to understand it, see its meaning. He symbolizes the world for me, and in a way, I think it is better it is concentrated thus in one individual. When the "world at large" gets their grappling hooks into us it's going to be hell to pay. We are tolerated now, because we are unknown. But when the publicity gets under way, good-bye. I have just been informed by the *N.R.F.* here that they "dare not" publish my books, *Black Spring* excepted. That's France, the supposedly most liberal country in the world. Perhaps the only translation I shall ever see, during my lifetime, is that Czech edition, which fortunately nobody can read. I have had many a talk with Kahane, good and bad ones, and I see into the whole situation quite realistically, I think. *You* couldn't do much better yourself. His way, which is the cunning English way of watching and waiting and nibbling off a piece here and there – is perhaps the *only* way in these times. Nobody wants a *man* to take over the affairs of the world. Nobody will let a *man* run the affairs of the world. While things are going to pots the jackals must reign. Hitler is no worse, nay better, in my opinion, than the other lugs. He makes the German mistake of being tactless, that's all. But he has not caused *more* suffering than other conquerors before him – probably much less. He is sincere, but deluded. Whereas the English, French and Americans are downright stupid, mean, tenacious, selfish. What right have they to hog things? A handful of French, a less handful of British, a stationary population in America, with all the resources of the universe at her command. Sterilization going on, the lethal chamber in full swing, gangsterism rampant in every walk of life, a bloated, misguided idealism – what do you say? And France? Shit for France! She is narrow, petty, selfish, indifferent, cruel. She's got more than enough land right here in France, if she had any sense of management, any generosity of spirit. After reading Balzac I get the full import of it – because what he described as of 1819 is even more true as of 1939! Wait till you see my essay on *Louis Lambert*! It's done, and it's magnificent, I think. And it ends with a peroration against the French, as it should. I made a fine parallelism between Whitman's utterances and prophecies, in "Democratic Vistas", and Balzac's utterances, in the famous letter to the uncle which Louis writes. Amazing, and nobody would ever have suspected the rapport, the close rapport between these two views of the world – one in 1833, the other in 1870 – Old and New Worlds – same thing, same mess, same death. Whitman makes a plea for the poet to arise who will give us "a great poem of death"! It's magnificent.

Well, here I am, enjoying full solitude. I am a Zen right here in Paris, and never felt so well, so lucid, so right, so centered. Only a war will drive me out of it.

And here Edgar arrives and we have a lunch on "wheat and gold", the mystic deliverance. Excellent. Like Kahane, Edgar is another of my world problems. I will knock off here, hoping you received everything I sent you all – valises, books, mss. and what not. If Nancy would like her paint box now, perhaps Edgar could bring it over. Just let me know. And how *is* Nancy? the old girl never writes me. But I think of her always, and wonder how to make her more of a success than she already is. If you get a yacht buy a mine-sweeper along with it. But the war seems distant yet – nobody can afford to make war now. And who will protect the bankers this time? Where will they hide? Even the politicians are not safe any more – thanks to the high-class bombers. That leaves room for hope. When war comes right home to every one it becomes more and more dubious.

I wish I could say that I would see you in Greece soon, but I turn towards America, towards the desert particularly. I want so much to see it again, the waste places, the grandiose, the empty spots, where man is nil and where silence reigns. I think I will make it eventually – I must, damn it, before I am drafted in here as "un ami de France". Bastards! Fuck these amis! When they destroy their Maginot lines, physical and cerebral, I will become the real "ami" de France. Not before. And they must publish me too, damn their bloody quaking souls.

Anyway, read Zen – Suzuki's *Introduction to Zen Buddhism* and Alan Watts' *The Spirit of Zen*. I send you a printed slip shortly telling what to read! A little operation for haemorrhoids and payment of back taxes, and perhaps a pair of socks – from the coming royalties.

[unsigned]

P.S. Just finishing an essay on *Raimu*. Did you see *The Hero of the Marne? Great!*

*[London]   [April 1939]

Dear Henry:

I meant to write you before but have been away in Warwickshire covering the Stratford Festival for the paper I told you of, *International Post*. I have never been into the county of Warwick before and am COMPLETELY AMAZED. It is beyond words perfect and greener than this paper; the hedges and trees are all curved in a kind of sculptural balance – in fact the whole county is a piece of garden planning by a divinely Palladian architect. I made the pilgrimage I have always been planning, to Shakespeare's places, and contrary to custom was delighted by the publicity and fame that has grown round this fine industry: his county. Trinity Church, where he is buried, is lovely, facing on to the smoothest river in Christendom, on which lucid white swans go suavely up and down with not so much as a ruffled feather. We saw *Othello* and *The Comedy of Errors* by a first class cast in the new red theatre they have built him. I got up early and sneaked up the tiny Church Street to the site of the house where he lived the last few *silent* years; they have made a trim English garden where the house stood, with green lawns, and shining little trees. HERE IS THE KEY TO EVERY-THING HE WROTE. I don't think you can understand the old boy until you sit in this garden, and reflect how for those five years THE REST WAS SILENCE with him, living his small-town burgess life, cut off from the court and the London joys. With the river going like a clock at the end of the road, and the marvellous Warwickshire woods curving up towards Snitterfield where his family lived two generations before him. I tell you, you don't have to *read* him; just visit New Place sometime when you can be alone in it, and sit on a bench in the sunlight, and you get the whole meaning coming through with a radiance and clarity that his verse could never give you. I am still a little blinded by it. They laugh at me because Shakespeare is now an American industry, and 100,000 people come to Stratford every year; but somehow that only added to the charm for me. Everyone was there for the Festival, boys and girls wandering over the green lawns and ferrying the river. And the Americans, I never felt such a kinship with them before; everybody drawn by the dim alarm in their own lives, to try and find a meaning in the life of a great unknown national man. And in the hunt New Place gets overlooked; you see, there is no house standing there. It was pulled down. Only the little garden and the commemoration stone. But the real key to the secret lies here. I smelled it out at once, and pried the meaning out all in half an hour, fresh and early one morning, when the sun shone bravely and the birds played. YOU MUST GO TO STRATFORD. Mark it en route for Tibet if you must, but you must see it.

Your letter was disturbing; Henry afloat? It sounds queer to me; but I've no doubt you mean it. Listen, when you are at sea in a storm and you don't want to spring a leak dashing the boat forward against the waves you let yourself out a SEA-ANCHOR: a canvas bell shaped like a French letter but six-foot across the mouth. This holds the nose up to the wind and keeps her dead still. [. . .]

The sum in francs you mentioned is roughly 500 pounds is it not? For that you could get a fine little singlehanded boat to live on for the summer. We are held up frankly; because at the moment there is such a restriction on travel by yacht. We figured on spending a year in cheap ports, as Spain, Greece, Turkey. At the moment things look so bad I simply don't know what to do. Return to Corfu with the Italians outside our house? Spend the summer in Cornwall? OR GO TO AMERICA. It would mean a big uprooting, a big turn in the meridian: but I have a sort of feeling that sooner or later I shall take the jump: whether to do so now I don't know. Working fitfully, in gusts; but no real impetus; little squalls of wind which send me skittering along for twenty yards over the flat surface of a poem or the verse play. Nothing else. Doldrum. I am sorry you are being doctored with a glass ass; next time you invite the world to kiss your ass you will have an uncomfy feeling! What news of the books? And listen, is it any use enticing you to England, if we get a place of our own and have room? Or do you definitely feel NO? I want you to see the cathedral towns, and smiling Stratford. What do you feel?

Love to anais, Larry

P.S. I HAVE DISCOVERED ROZANOV.

*[Paris]   4/27/39

Dear Larry,

A beautiful letter that, about Shakespeare, the river like a clock, the single white swan (his double is now at Montsouris!) etc. makes my mouth water. I don't want to urge you to do anything whereby you "count on me". You know me – a temperamental guy, moody underneath and a tyrant at heart. But – if you do get a place and if, as you say, there'd be room for a passing guest, I think it's fairly probable I'd turn up by Summer.

I am looking forward to to-morrow's speech by "our" dictator, Hitler. He will tell us what we may or may not do this year. I am still going on with my treatments – rather painful and depressing now, but I shall be a new man afterwards. It's bad for literature; makes one sober and lucid in a discouraging way. The writer should always be under or above par, I think – not sane and sober. I worked with my diseases quite successfully all these years. But if I am to become a perfectly healthy specimen I shall come to a full stop. Anyway, it's been good for me – a vacation.

Don't go haywire over that handsome yacht Hugo is offering you! It's too expensive to run. You'd need a crew. But the one in Amsterdam – slower, steadier, *Dutch* and probably handmade, sounds good. Buy an extra one for me.

I'll write you soon again, when I come out of my torpor.

I thought you were going on with the Book of the Dead? What's happened? Must you *suffer* some more first?

Did you see Joey's effort – *Aller Sans Retour?* Just read it. Like it immensely. What a guy he is! "A murderer on roller skates" (sic!).

Don't forget to give me list of books recommended by Bromage, will you? Love to Nancy.   Henry.

[P.S.] *Capricorn* due out May 10th – his latest dictum!

* 18 villa seurat paris XIVe   Saturday [20? May 1939]

Dear Larry –
Don't forget to bring the letter along from Bernard Bromage! If you can see him before leaving, do so, eh? His articles in *M.M.* were excellent. I am taking them with me to read & reread. Will do my Nijinsky in Corfu. Am worn to the bone now.

Write me soon as you can about question of mails & censorship in Greece. Do they open both incoming and outgoing mail? Do they lift checks & money orders? Are you allowed to *receive* money while there? I have written people for dough and some of it may only arrive after I leave. It's important to know. Because if they are going to open my mail I'll tell Kahane to hold letters or open them himself and extract things.

My itinerary is roughly as follows – with allowances for change, if climate etc. is no good for me: Corfu, Monaco, Athens, Istanbul, Dalmatia, Belgrade, Sofia, Bucharest, Vienna, Warsaw, Paris, London,

Devonshire, Cornwall, Wales, Dublin, Killarney, America via New Orleans (seeing Faulkner in Mississippi). America: Mobile, Charleston, Santa Fe, Las Vegas, Tucson, Miami, Galveston, Corpus Christi, San Francisco, Hollywood, Reno, Denver, Salt Lake City, North & South Dakota, Butte, Boston, Vermont, New Hampshire, Rhode Island. Then to Bagdad, Teheran, Jerusalem, Bethlehem, Egypt, Fez, Timbuctoo, Singapore, Java, Borneo, Bali, Easter Island, Siam, Indo-China, Rangoon, Ceylon, the whole Indian continent, Darjeeling, China, Tibet – *punkt!*

Enclose letter from guy in N.Y. who's been writing me about publishing venture if Laughlin falls down. For the archives.

Capricorn has had an advance sale of about 800 volumes!! "Not so bad for an unintelligent work," as Balzac said of his *Livre mystique.*

But my good friend Cendrars says only 1/3 of it is good – "*magnifique et sain*" – the sex & adventure, documentaire stuff – the rest bores the shit out of him. Ho ho!

So I have become the public "emmerdeur" no. 1. Hurrah!

      Henry.

*[Rocamadour]   *June 12*th [1939]

Sending you my notes on Balzac and Nijinsky's *Diary* to hold for my arrival. Too much luggage! Am at a wonderful town now – really medieval! Going to Toulouse to-morrow. Moving leisurely southward.

      Henry.

On the Edge

When Miller parts from Larry and Nancy Durrell at Tripolis in the Peloponnesus on a miserably wet afternoon the day after Christmas 1939, the separation is to prove far longer and more momentous than either expected. But they might have known: for one thing, it was an axiom with Miller, born on 26 December, that nothing good ever happened to him during the Yule season. In *The Colossus of Maroussi* Miller wrote that they had sat in a cold and damp café, facing 'abominable' food, and added, 'To me at least it was really beginning to look like Christmas – that is to say, sour, moth-eaten, bilious, crapulous, worm-eaten, mildewed, imbecilic, pusillanimous and completely gaga.'

In 1940, at the British Legation in Athens, Durrell holds the first of his various jobs with the British Council, and later with the Foreign Office, from which he will not escape permanently until 1956. While this employment will provide him with the material for later books, he is not to be again exclusively a man of letters until 1957. True, he keeps writing, but with his left hand, so to speak. Soon after his return to the USA, Miller launches himself on an eighteen-month tour of the country, which leads to his writing *The Air-Conditioned Nightmare* and then to residence at Big Sur.

Durrell's Greek friends, among them Katsimbalis, Seferis, and Stephanides, are all intensely involved with the war effort, first in the defeat of the Italians in the Albanian campaign, then in the desperate defence against the April 1941 German onslaught. Durrell is sent to Kalamata by the British Council to run a school. The correspondence suffers: as the conflict intensifies, letters become infrequent and the delivery time lengthens into, typically, five or six weeks. Miller, touring the USA in his 1932 Buick, may have missed or lost some of

Durrell's letters. Durrell, leaving Greece just three days ahead of the German armoured divisions, abandons possessions in the scramble for a caïque in which to escape. Precipitate and undesired though the flight from Greece was, it landed Durrell in the world of *The Alexandria Quartet*. No letters of 1940 from Miller survive, but Durrell's from this period are so vivid, so exciting, that they flash like mirrors, reflecting the concerns of the one man while they signal the adventures of the other.

*40 Anagnostopoulou, Athens   [after 6 February 1940]

Dear Henry: just a line to spell out congratulations for the belated celebrity; we went out to Katsimbalis last week where your postcard was being passed from hand to hand like a totem. It is about time they woke up and noticed you. Nancy went off yesterday with an Imperial Airways plane from Phaleron; she is flying all the way. For the last few weeks we have had strange spells of lovely spring weather, with branches of almond blossom being carried and sold in the streets; and today a sudden wild fall of snow which melted as it touched the ground. Can you imagine the Acropolis covered in snow? And in one stroke the hills drew themselves in against the sky; with a strange heather-coloured pointillism, like stubble appearing on a chin. Carnival began this week with clowns and harlequins (rather squalid as to clothes, but full of form) parading the streets singing, skipping, yelling, and beating heavy pig-skin drums to a peculiar rhythm. The shine is off the carnival this year because the government has forbidden masks, suspecting that seditious words would be said from behind them. Soon I get a week's holiday on full pay and am off to the islands with Tonio [Antoniou], the captain. I wish you were here to come on another trip with us. Max [Nimiec] gets back on March 1st from a rest cure and in the meantime I have his car. For the rest the same dull routine at the school and the general boredom, lack of international news, and rumours.

The "Reflections on Writing" has them gaping here; S[eferis] and K[atsimbalis] have put it into the Greek and printed it in *Nea Grammata* where it looks handsome. I say Can you wake Laughlin up about my poems. [. . .] I shall have nothing more to do with New Directions; he printed my piece from the BB without saying yes or no about the poems and has not written since though I've sent him postcard after postcard. I really think the American publishers and pseudo-men are much worse than the English for this kind of treatment; and I'm not going to have it from that cream cheese intelligence which edits half a million pages of pretentious balls a year, and can't even acknowledge a book of verse.

Is Anaïs still rotating on her axis coolly? Defying the enemy? Keeping ahead of the event? Thank her for the *Furiosos*, and tell her I hope she gets a letter I wrote her recently enclosing a little coin from the Mycenae ruins.

Henry if you get a chance to see *Troilus and Cressida* do so will you? It's all about the men of Tiryns and Argos. AND WILL YOU ASK LAUGHLIN WHAT THE HELL HE IS UP TO? Neither he nor Kahane can I get a word out of. What little rats these people are, running for the kudos always with their little tails up; and they'd suck your blood for a penny. Had long insane American letters from Simon and Schuster, and *Creative Writing* and a man called Symmes who invites me to walk in a wheat field and throw my excrement at the stars, while he will put a freshly killed lamb at the rectory. I don't know what to say to people who write you long poetical-lyrical letters, unless they are women. To indulge in this kind of metaphoric barn-dancing with men makes me feel rather dated, obscurely ridiculous, like a Morris Dancer who had entered a rotary club by mistake. The letter, of course, is a gem. I am sending it to Eliot to make him jealous. Well, dear Henry, all the best for your American adventure; may everything please you, customs, marvels, anomalies, chance meetings, meaningless fornications, meals and music. Do come back next year if we are any of us left next year to welcome you. Love to everyone.

L.

Miller had written the essay 'Reflections on Writing' around September 1939, during his stay in Greece.
James Laughlin edited and published four of Durrell's poems in *New Directions in Prose & Poetry 1940*.
Durrell was to publish two poems in the fourth number of *Furioso* (Summer 1941).

*[Athens]   [March? 1940]

Dear Henry: it was wonderful to receive your letter in the midst of this bad imitation of Bohemian life; it was a much needed corrective to hear you audibly suffering among the streamlined cuspidors west by west of us, mewed in Athens like kestrels' chicks. And I was getting so bored with the spurious provincialism of the town and the hard rubbery touch of the faithful virgins. Last night I ran into Katsimbalis, sitting huddled over an ouzo in a dirty little hole-in-the-wall kind of café which he at once pronounced the best bar in Greece and so on. We had an awful blind: or rather I did. Pouring drink into him is like pouring nitro-glycerine into a safe; he stands with his calves pressed out behind and his belly in front gently resting on the world, while his eyes race back and forth over the puzzling face of the universe like bats. After his thirtieth or so he will light up, a small blue bud of flame inside his waistcoat, and his eyes will become suave and kind and no longer frightened; then he will begin telling his Wagnerian cycle of stories. Last night we ended up after a lot of bad philosophy and boasting with some drab here, with Max complaining he couldn't sleep and K fucking in my bed like a Trojan horse. For a week after getting news of you or a letter from you he is quite unquenchably not himself. You seem to stand in the relation of a half-analyst because he develops this mock-colossus, like a mock-turtle out of nowhere. Then he begins to stagger and lurch and boast and swear; and every story he tells he says: "I forgot to tell Miller that one." Or "Miller would have enjoyed that one, eh?" Some of the stories are so manifestly neither funny, elevating or even commonly humane, that one winces for him and wonders why. But he goes on roaring and washing the air with his long flat dead-looking hands, trying to carve out this mythical personality for himself from the rubble of language. It's funny. He is the truest Greek I know, and a real Irishman to boot, not to mention a poet. The others are all lukewarm compared to old K. Last night he was in a dreadful state of unfulfilled suicide; he was going to blow up the hotel, set fire to Maroussi, going to drink poison, shoot himself, jump off a high-stool, strangle his wife, ring for the fire-engine. There was nothing that would really wake him up; he was running through his ideas like *mezedes* for a jaded palate; but whatever he does he cannot get his flemish body with its oriental curves to cooperate; it lies on top of him like the transpontine marsh, and he's sinking daily, while his little black eyes signal more and more frantically and his laughter comes out of the clouds. Now that he hears you are writing about him he is more unreal than ever; no more restless sitter ever sat and fidgeted in front of the photographer than George C Katsimbalis in his black transpontine business suit and his chain-mail underwear.

134

I think he visits Aram regularly, and he has already been to an analyst with what result I don't know. I haven't been myself as yet. My future doesn't bear dwelling upon. Nancy got bored with England and decided to return and have the brat here after all; and I have finally got Corfu, where we shall retire in May to lose the world I hope and be lost to it. Barring accidents I should be more or less OK. But I'm an exile now; my age has been called, and I can't go home for fear of being called out. I like the feeling; like Livy or Suetonius or one of those unfortunates exiled beside the Siberian lakes; only an inverse exile, northerner to a southern landscape. Whether I shall write ten books of histories remains to be seen. Last Sunday we went south again. It was like our selves becoming metamorphosed or something into swallows; after Corinth the cold scented spring air came out of the valleys, crushed scents of mint and thyme, and the whole Argive plain rose up like a green shield as we hit the rim of the pass. It was like something biblical and exilic, like the buckler of Jonathan or Gideon's valley of milk and honey. Mycenae, you should just see her now: gone all the Roman cruelty and ferocity of the stone walls against the winterscape; every little tump of ground was on a bias, softly goldened and greened by barley, and little wild anemones. The whole procession of medieval green hills fell away to a still dead blue gulf behind Nauplia. For me it goes too deep really for tears; such a matchless and impeccable land lying there, washed clean in the first spring rain, and hallowed, like a round soft Easter egg. I was afraid to go on to Epidaurus where he sits in his humane valleys eastward; we sat on the top floors of Tiryns and watched the sea for a trace of movement. The inner walls are quite infirm and abscessed like big molars, and even asphodels jut out from holes like discoloured tongues.

NIKH [Rhally] came to lunch yesterday and spoke of you and showed me *The Cosmological Eye*; what a bad putrid whining nonsense this man emits; and the whole book is jacked about to suit himself. She sends her love, I imagine separately as well. She said she wrote you now and again. I'm glad you rumbled to all my *réclames*: liking Greece, and after Greece the spirit of Greece in N and G[eorge] and S[eferis] and A[ntoniou] and all the funny painful men. I shall be back in Corfu by May; why not get an assignment from some imaginary paper and get permits to come back this summer. Probably it will be quiet; and certainly you can always dodge bricks as USA citizens. We could fix visas from this end I'm sure. WHY NOT? We could live like princes on my salary and bathe and cogitate and plan the new world. Perhaps we could run a little review from Corfu: just a little thing to tell the world, and give it away. Try and get back. Things look brighter in the Mediterranean. Probably no war. Love to A[naïs] and to you also, and to America.

[unsigned]

The Cosmological Eye was issued by New Directions in 1939 and Durrell may be accusing Laughlin of having 'jacked about' the contents, although the reference is not clear.

*40 anagnostopoulou, athens, greece   [*c*. March 1940]

Henry: just a swift line to thank you for everything and to ask you NOT to do any more. I won't have a U.S.A. edition [of *The Black Book*] and I refuse to submit to cuts. Listen, this isn't ingratitude to you, and your tireless boosting of me: no. But things have changed so much here since you left, new and more powerful enemies on the horizon, the system closing in, that I must use every ounce of anonymity to avoid being thrown out of the Council. Nothing is private any more: censors everywhere, letters being stopped and forwarded to the government etc. One breath of criticism and the apple-cart is overturned. That is why you must write what you want about me but not send MSS quotes of it: if you send a published thing it is o.k. It has a status as an utterance, a pronouncement: but manuscript can do harm. Therefore, dear H, be circumspect, because heaven only knows what you might say about me that could be wrongly construed by the official dog-catchers. It's purely a question of tact; as to the question of *fact*, that's another and literary business. [. . .]

The rest is purely personal: I seriously WANT to be quiet. I have no comment on the situation which could add to or subtract from it. Really. I have refused to contribute anything but poetry which is shorthand and too private to wash anyone's intellectual linen for them. The whole thing fills me with a calm devastating silence; I have no attitude. That is why I find *Horizon* and all the things like it just a little collection of dried vomit. Better silence until we have the golden word to say, than just words and whimpers and attitudes of this kind. That is why I want to be left alone and forgotten: a thing only too easy in England, since I was never noticed or remembered there: and, apart from your industry, should be easy in USA. Leave me to germinate. I am beginning to enjoy really the deep privacy – the communications all being slowly cut. The weather is cold and dark and yellow as Emily Brontë, and new things are coming over the rim of the world. I think the dignity and austerity of death closing round us all is a good feeling somewhere deep inside; it does no harm because life has been so extremely good to one. It makes one understand how responsible to death one is at every moment. Attack the reasons for which men die, if you like; they are the crust, the mere vessel in which this great impulse confines itself. The real miracle is that so many are willing and pleasant about it, and I am not among them; even to die with a good grace is something I have yet to learn from the others.

love to you all, larry

[P.S.] leaving for Cyprus in early June; possibly a good job: but the lion's den: ware the lion.

*NA28 16 CABLE RELAY VIA NR NY=ATHENS JUN 17–18 1940

NLT HENRY MILLER
    =GOTHAM BOOK MART=137 EAST 54ST NEW YORK=
URGENTLY NEED DOUGH CABLED=
    LAWRENCE DURRELL.

*40 anagnostopoulou, athens   [after 18 June 1940]

Dear Henry: I don't know whether you'll get this, but I wanted to thank you for the speed and size of the cheque. It saved our lives. All communications have broken down and I am busy trying to persuade my bank to telegraph money. I still don't know what the situation is; the school has stopped here, and with it my dough; and I'm supposed to get to Cyprus and start up there in September but at the moment there is no connection. Theodore passed through last week, with a commission in the army, heading for Cyprus via Turkey. I expect we will have to do the same. Beirut to Cyprus is only fishing boats they say: and difficult trailing a baby. O by the way: it's a girl! Penelope Berengaria Durrell. A voice like a siren, a nose like a Syren, and a skin like a saurian. I'm very pleased but don't know quite what to do with it: I mean in this world the domestic virtues seem rather an anachronism:

household gods at a discount. I may have to touch you once more perhaps: but I can pay back from the British Council work from September when I shall be a man of substance, so fear not, brother mole.

I wish I could give you a crumb of hope about Europe, but I can't. The situation is such a fatal ballsup, so fine a flower of our muttonheaded, craven-hearted policy, that one can only puke and look away.

Now I'm afraid it does mean war with a vengeance; there was always a hope that the damage of a year or two's war could be patched up: but this is going to be a war of famines. Already in Belgium . . . . It's such a pity we allowed sheep-ticks dressed in starched collars to lead us instead of men of tenderness and gristle; the material is so wonderful, you know, the english infantry man. I've been talking to some people who were mixed up in the Dunkirk affair; the guards can fight, he said, "with a ferocious tenderness: their fierceness comes from an obliterating shame at violence". Which is rather a subtle dissociation for a man who is not a poet: and for the guards themselves who are only a quarter human at the best of times. Enough of politics: I wonder when this chapter of treacheries is going to cease. Without the offensive spirit we are lost I feel: and I don't see a trace of it in the Mediterranean. Read *Troilus and Cressida* and you will see how we Balkan peoples feel. "Wars and lechery!" We still meet, Seferis and G.K., but it's like the meeting of ancients; we exchange silences rather and pipe smoke: and the weather is impervious to it all, smiling blue and green.

There is a wonderful photographer here, Herbert List: in the Brassaï class. I want you to see his photos of Greece which are becoming so famous: perhaps you can help him in USA. He is sending them to CURT VALENTIN, Bucholz Gallery, 32 East 57 Street, New York. Try and see them: you might like him to illustrate your Greek book: you know it's not just photoplay with List, it's really a creative work, his pictures: I was wanting to write about him, calling it "The camera as an extension of the eye". Also his agent BLACK STAR INC, Graybar Building, 420 Lexington Avenue, N.Y.C., is sending you a terrifying series of photos taken in the Capuchin crypt in Palermo, petrified bishops and things, like flowers under glass: perhaps you could persuade someone to print them, or they might do for a text of yours or Anaïs'. See what you think. He is only able to send so few, poor devil, and not large enough.

I do hope this letter gets through, but everything is so uncertain.

Anyway, my darlings, be as happy as you can on your peaceful continent, because no one knows how long it'll be.

We are cultivating the finer flower of a post-European resignation; after all, Minoa had to face it, and the Cyclades have lost all trace of it. I feel very Petronian about it; down with the silver age giants.

love larry

*C/o British Institute, Hermes Street 9, Athens,
Greece   [c. July 1940]

<Patchen – Read this about *The Tempest* & return, will you? HVM.>

Dear Henry: thank you so much for the letter. I hadn't written because I pictured you starting off across America on foot for Taos or somewhere and saw my letter taking months. Also there seemed to be little to tell you except that Greece is still here, still intact, still beautiful, only now orchestrated by cicadas and sea-cooled. We are living just outside Athens and I am waiting to be sent to Kalamata, where I am to open a school. It is right in the southern end of the Peloponnesus, and I am promised another district quite distinct in character, very unvisited and wild. Last Sunday we went down to Mycenae again to see it by sunlight; scorching day. And the big underground cistern was full of mosquitoes – but so full that we couldn't get down it. Argolis like the green plains of Eden.

I am sharing this house with Gordon whom you know and who entertains a great admiration for your books; things look fairly uniformly black, but the British are still stubborn. The truth is that being islanders they are the last romantics, quite unable to sacrifice principle to expediency: that is why they are permanently sucked in, and continue to beam with honourable pride. "Safe my honour, safe the world" to quote a poem of mine: it remains to see whether it works out as policy. Myself I doubt like Thomas; the gentleman carries his ball and chain of self-esteem about long after all ordinary men are fighting in their underclothes. Nothing remains, at this point, except an attention to personal honour. But how dreadfully wasteful and boring the whole thing is; no, I don't see the new world as yet: only an age of tyranny in which we must learn to be mute or invent an oral tradition.

By now you must have my last letter telling you that it is a girl; a big one full of quaint corners. So you have read *The Tempest*? Marvellous. I have been having long sessions with a young translator of it here. Don't listen to the nonsense that self-assured idiot wrote you. Nothing is "generally conceded" about S's epilogues. *The Tempest* one is certainly his. You know, you must translate always and transpose, because otherwise the true message behind *The Tempest* is apt to get lost in the purely dramatic cobwebs. See it, if you can, as an exercise in Astrology. Here is this outcast holy man in his cell on Corcyra; his retreat is really voluntary, because he is dealing with reality, his many inner selves. If you make Ariel an air sign, Caliban an earth sign, Miranda or whatever her name is Neptune you begin to see the edges of a kind of dramatic astrology peeping through. Now Prospero is rejected of the world, or has rejected it. The intrusion of the real world (the petty squabbles and human dealings of the castaways) has a real as well as dramatic value. It makes him realise that the artist who controls his Ariels and Calibans must sooner or later find his solution in the world of common people and affairs; and in the epilogue you have the clue to the whole artistic stance. The gesture of renunciation is pure wizardry; artist laying down his medicine, releasing his spirits, and putting himself AS A HUMAN BEING at their mercy. Prospero, who can control the winds by art, pleading with them to grant him favourable passage home.

It was the artist who came away to the island: it was Shakespeare who came home as a man. This last poignant verse is really a pure statement of the Hamlet-Prince theme: but with the problem resolved in Tao. "What strength I have's my own." That is to say human, fallible, subject to weather and gravity. It was the artist at last willing to become unconscious of his virtue; willing to release even his godly powers to the ebb and flow of his human and mutable life. You can look at the whole of Shakespeare's work through this final lens of the telescope, and you see the diminished figures of Hamlet and Lear and Macbeth, like in the wrong end of the telescope. In the new dimension which he found beside the Avon at Stratford the emphasis on the struggle was no longer important; it was better to smile and bless and enfold. So that the epilogue is a little benediction on a world which he at last allowed to *wound him to the quick*; in *Hamlet* and *Lear* he had been fighting against the death, like the neurotic fighting, with the cold wheels of his will-power. In *The Tempest* he finds that the wound itself is sweet, and that by giving up only can he continue his life. So Prospero falls upon his sword, blessing; not cringing like Hamlet or Macbeth. There is something in this for us I feel, now, this moment; a kind of lesson teaching us that the world counts apart from us, and that there is no positive solution to pain but to suffer and adore – and of course smile; *The Tempest* is like one long quiet smile. May we all renounce with the same grace and happiness. After Prospero you must turn up a text of Shakespeare's will and see how normally and calmly the final surrender was carried out; there is not a trace of the graven idol. I often think that Prospero was looking over his shoulder when he put his name to that human formula. We lesser people would have written a will in verse.

Anyway that is what I make of it, though it is written in great haste and reads rather muddled; my letter I mean, not the play. Now Henry, if you want to find another cryptic thing, look up Shakespeare's "Phoenix and Turtle". Buried in this polished ivory verse there is the most marvellous controlled pain about a woman; I think young Prospero wrote it. It might solace you in your grand chagrin. It feels contemporary with *The Tempest*, though it couldn't have been I suppose.

I hope you won't forget to look at Herbert List's photos when they arrive in New York; you will [see?] Greece again I promise you; no tricks; pure form and value like the cosmological eye at work.

Your manuscript has arrived and is being eagerly devoured; I haven't had a moment with it as yet. Everyone is so thrilled to be themselves etched out in print. I remember some excerpts you sent containing violences against the dear old British Empire of which I am now a paid servant. Really, Henry, you don't say if you are cutting them out from tact or because they don't seem good any longer. I liked the Englishman not being as good as the dirt between the Greek's toes; but thought that perhaps you should have said this specially of the idiots you met in Greece. Not in general perhaps; because it is not untrue so much as unsubtle. You must read *Forever Ulysses* by a Greek called C.P. RODOCANACHI, Viking Press. In this you will find the last five or six pages absolutely crammed with the most marvellous nationalistic generalisations by a poor Greek: anent English French and Italians. It is brilliant. I'm sure you will enjoy this telescoped life of Zaharof and Averof. It's in English. Try and get it. It shows the long-nosed triumphant adaptable Greek conquering the world – the modern world.

O and you said some hard things against Byron which I think you might retract if you read the poor man's letters. Also Gordon has got a little story which I have told him to send you about a man he met in the

American Express who wanted to be buried in the sacred soil of Greece; an American this time. A touching little story.

I think my job is more or less in the bag so you can let fly again by post with all the blue sedition you want.

Needless to say I am not writing a line. I can't. It's marvellous that you are keeping up to [the] line. I feel there's a new breath of revelation impending which will give me a subject more at peace with the heart, and less rending to the brain.

Am in the middle of *Moby Dick*; the strangest book ever written in America I think. Metaphysics side by side with frantic action: like a cowboy film with a running commentary prepared from the deeper parts of Augustine's confessions. Really something quite *new*. Have you read it. It's all about the great whale.

My love to Anaïs, unswerving ever, and to your daughter and to your publishers and patrons. And thank you so much for the dough. I will start paying it back in a couple of months or so. In the meantime bless you all, enjoy things. We are in a little oasis here of calm and form. Like Archimedes inside his problem while the infantry stormed the walls.

> Love from us all,
> larry
> nancy
> berengaria penelope nausicaa
> durrell

'The Cosmological Eye' is the title of Miller's essay about his painter friend Hans Reichel, whose works are notable for their 'pure form and value', but elsewhere Durrell has compared List to the photographer Brassaï, and this reference seems possible here.

Miller sent Durrell the manuscript of *The Colossus of Maroussi*, which features many of their Greek friends.

*s/s *Arntena*   10th August 1940

The peasants are lying everywhere on deck eating watermelons; the gutters are running with the juice. A huge crowd bound on a pilgrimage to the Virgin of Tinos. We are just precariously out of harbour, scouting the skyline for Eyetalian subs. What I really have to tell you is the story of the Cocks of Attica: it will frame your portrait of

Katsimbalis which I have not yet read but which sounds marvellous from all accounts. It is this. We all went up to the Acropolis the other evening very drunk and exalted by wine and poetry: it was a hot black night and our blood was roaring with cognac. We sat on the steps outside the big gate, passing the bottle, Katsimbalis reciting and Georgakis weeping a little, when all of a sudden he was seized with a kind of fit; leaping to his feet he yelled out, "Do you want to hear the cocks of Attica you damned moderns?" His voice had a hysterical edge to it. We didn't answer, and he wasn't waiting for one. He took a little run to the edge of the precipice, like a fairy queen, a heavy black fairy queen, in his black clothes: threw back his head, clapped the crook of his stick into his wounded arm, and sent out the most blood-curdling clarion I have ever heard. Cock a doodle doo. It echoed all over the city – a sort of dark bowl dotted with lights like cherries. It ricochetted from hillock to hillock and wheeled up under the walls of the Parthenon. Under the winged victory this horrible male cockcrow – worse than Emil Jannings. We were so shocked that we were struck dumb – and while we were still looking at each other in the darkness, lo, from the distance silvery clear in the darkness a cock drowsily answered – then another, then another. This drove K wild. Squaring himself, like a bird about to fly into space, and flapping his coattails he set up a terrific scream – and the echoes multiplied. He screamed until the veins stood out all over him, looking like a battered and ravaged rooster in profile, flapping on his own dunghill. He screamed himself hysterical and his audience in the valley increased until all over Athens like bugles they were calling and calling, answering him. Finally between laughter and hysteria we had to ask him to stop. The whole night was alive with cockcrows – all Athens, all Attica – all Greece it seemed until I almost imagined you being woken at your desk late in N.Y. to hear these terrific silver peals; Katsimbaline cockcrow in Attica.

This was epic – a great moment and purely Katsimbalis. If you could have heard those cocks, the frantic psaltery of the Attican cocks. I dreamt about it for two nights afterwards. Well, we are on our way to Mykonos resigned now that we have heard the cocks of Attica from the Acropolis. I wish you'd write it – it is part of the mosaic.

    Love to you all.
    Larry

    This letter was published almost verbatim as an Appendix to Miller's *Colossus of Maroussi*.

Kalamata, Greece   Nov. 10 [1940]

Dear Henry:
I hope you will get this some day; at the moment everything is upside
down and what with air raids and one thing and another I have hardly
time to think. We are submerged in the struggle; well, the Epirotes
have been having a picnic up there as I prophesied. Katsimbalis has
ridden off gigantically with the artillery; Tonio is away with the fleet –
just had a note from George S[eferis]. In the meantime I have been
trying to go up to Corfu with the navy or the air force with no result.
They say they are not operating at all in the sectors which I want to help
with; and the Greeks seem not to need help now. Everyone has been in
raptures over Greek successes: meanwhile the air-raid siren has entered
our lives three or four times a day: a most unpleasant experience.
However, we live and learn. We are in good fettle and so grateful to
you for helping us out. My mother is sending you back the dough
slowly from London.

I see no end to the business. It will go on for years because we are no
nearer to the individual solution – and the outer struggle is only a
reflection of it. Nothing remains really except one's personal honour
and one's love for the killers. We shall see.

Love to Anaïs and you and anyone over there who might be in need
of disinterested love! Ah Lao Tzu we need you here!

Larry.

*INSTITUTE OF ENGLISH STUDIES
[Kalamata]   [before 13 February 1941]

henry dear: I suppose you are on your travels because George sent you a
telegram when war broke out and had no reply: indeed the cable was
returned marked "address unknown". So far we have [been] living all
the time here in the suspense between air raids; so far no bombs, but
two days ago an Italian plane nearly flew into the dining-room window. It was a strange sensation to see this graceful grey thing sliding
out of the sky over the harbour. There was a good deal of shooting
from the only machine gun here, and it turned slowly and buzzed over
the mountain in the direction of Crete. I am not writing needless to say:

too much noise in the world to hear one's own voice. The old terra firma of the last year in neutral Athens which was such a musical comedy of spies and plots ended really with the death of Max – on the field of battle. To die in a Balkan cabaret surrounded by blondes! Max is a great loss: goodness and innocence were so deeply fused in him that from the surface he seemed vapid. There is a whole book about him and us and Athens – a kind of cell of quiet and suspense among the statues, which I must write one day. Stephan is off with the Infantry, Tonio with a destroyer, and the Colossus is learning anti-aircraft drill! I have sent up my name for the R.A.F. and am waiting to see what the Council have to say about it. Athens is blacked out and all the familiar faces missing from behind bars and kiosks and flower-shops. Sad world! but the Greeks are even more magnificent in war than in peace. Their humour! And they are clean fighters by tradition – scorn to burn villages, take hostages, or mutilate the enemy. You have probably read of the appearance of the Virgin of Tinos on the Albanian front; there is one other anecdote – less cheering. An advancing company of Greeks came to a silent valley, evacuated by the enemy. In the silence they heard a strong voice crying out in Greek. A captured *Evzone* had been hung up in a tree by his arms. He was complete in ballet skirt and pom-pom shoes, only the enemy had dug his eyes out and left him there to greet the advancing troops. Nice isn't it?

I sent my poems to Anaïs at the address she gave; perhaps she could let the Viking see them. Some are wonderful.

> "Well, of my 3 score years and ten
> 20 will not come again."

And so my good Henry, good evening to you. I feel like Sir Tophas, "an hundred hundred years old".

Love to USA.
Larry

Post Script Feb 13/1941
Before I post this let me add a temporary valediction, because it looks as if the Bulgars are coming and the Turks going. We are all in very good heart – no longer bothered much about dying or living or starving. Truly, the whole drama has gone into another dimension in which one is simply not *interested* in the deepest sense. But blessings upon your head for your kindness and support. Ironically enough yesterday afternoon

the cloud lifted and I saw the WHOLE BOOK OF THE DEAD lying below me like a forbidden superb city. I am ready to begin it now: it's a marvellous conception and complete – and I hope to live to complete it in your honour and Anaïs' – a monument to Villa Seurat and the dead cosmological past: the future is clear – so clear and calm that we cannot fail to reach it. In the meantime, with Sir Tophas "Love is a lord of misrule and keepeth Christmas in my corpse."

*EOLA HOTEL, NATCHEZ, MISS.
[i.e., from New York]   March 1st 1941

Dear Larry & Nancy –
Your letter of *Nov. 10th* from Kalamata just reached me the other day on my arrival in N.Y. (thanks to Leland Stone, I suppose). Where can you be now, I wonder – and will this ever reach you? They say no mail gets thru for Greece but I am taking a chance. Maybe the miracle will happen. You see from the above where I just came from. I had to fly back (ten hours) owing to my father's death. I arrived just 2 hours too late but understand he passed away peacefully in his sleep. Now I am returning to Natchez where I left the car (a 1932 Buick) and will resume the trip. I'm going by train via Pittsburgh, Cleveland, Detroit, Chicago, St. Louis, Kansas City, Memphis – stopping off at all these towns to give them the once over, as we say. With the whole world torn and confused and thinking of nothing but war, war, war, why it's like a journey in limbo. I am still detached – inwardly. Curse me, if you will, but I can't work up the necessary hatred. So I go on with my own plans and make what I can of my life until the madness is over.
You mentioned that your mother would repay me. Please stop her! I don't want anything back. It was the first time I ever really raised such a sum for anyone in years & years. I couldn't send a drop more, believe me. Nor now either should I want to. I just get by from town to town by the skin of my teeth. I have more confidence than ever in accomplishing anything I set out to do. It's as though now I had the gods on my side. I feel as if any desire will be met – provided I walk the line. And I'm doing just that. I have no doubt I will go from America to India – perhaps via Mexico – just as easily as I pass from my hotel to the railway station. What more can I tell you?
Do write me if you can. I am eager to know if letters do get through.

My love to everyone there, if you're still in Athens. And hereafter write me c/o Russell & Volkening, Inc. – 522 5th Ave., N.Y.C. (Though if you forget letters or messages to the Gotham Book Mart will always reach me.)

I cross the Mississippi soon for the Far West. God, if I could only have you with me now! It's strange how destiny decrees that we each go our own way! But I'm thinking of you always.

Henry

[P.S.] Listen, Larry – whether the U.S. enters the war or not, there will be a world-wide revolution to finish this off. *You* will yet see a wonderful period. Neither England nor Germany will win. We're in for the greatest change the earth has known. Mark my words.

*INSTITUTE OF ENGLISH STUDIES,
Kalamata, Greece,   March 13/1941

Dear Henry: Every time I start a letter to you some new quirk happens in the situation and I stop it, saying: "This'll never get through." Now, of course, we are sitting on the crater, expecting Yugoslavia to cave in any day, and of course the mails to crumple up. However, I am going through with this letter – if only to tell you that we are all well, and that so far we have not been bombed: one or two distant puffs and roars is all I have seen of the greater world war as yet, though plenty of planes come over and startle the life out of the townsfolk. Now spring is coming this valley is getting beautiful and serene, encircled by big snow caps, and raving with oranges. Last Sunday we walked up the dizziest mountain path to the snowline of our range, and saw the great white snout of Taïgetos in the valley beyond. Greece is so local and I know the Peloponnesus so well that I could shut my eyes and see it laid out like a relief-map – Sparta under the wing of Mistra, Tripolis in the great Pear-Campus, Argos and Nauplia thawing slowly in the haze with the first anemones and asphodels, and Epidaurus like some afterthought – an appendix to the old world with all the revisions and false starts and erasures put in their place in one superb act of thought. I still haven't had time to go there and write my dream diary: and it looks as if I'll have to wait now for some time. Last month all the schools closed and I sent up my name for the Air Force, but was told that we are being kept on temporarily by the Council. So in the interval I walk about like a free man and sniff the wind and relive my past incarnations as a goat, a tree, and a centaur. I have no more feelings about anything these days: which makes it impossible to write anything except bad poems.

The Greeks are in fine fettle: in the war they have discovered themselves and walk about in a dream: for the first time in her modern history there has emerged a public will – not a dissenting voice anywhere: so that they see themselves, darkly, like through a smoked glass and feel a great new form and shape descend upon them, without knowing what it is. Of course they are boasting and joyful.

I went up to Athens a while ago and found big changes: all blacked out and grim, with planes patrolling over the statues. I am so happy that England and Greece are in this together; with all their faults they both stand for something great. It is a cosmic trio really – Greece, China, England. We are the young one by comparison, and our great national Principle is still unstated and unrealised. I would like to do this in a book some time, because it should be done before we grow out of our young imperialist stage into the deep and shining dynastic age. Indeed unless the ENGLISH PRINCIPLE is stated we cannot grow into a deeper recognition of ourselves. Over there you can have no idea how moving and awakening is the effort and the love expended by the ordinary people caught in this great rat-trap of war; in England the children putting posies of wild-flowers on the graves of the German airmen who have smashed their towns to powder. In Greece the shop-girls who have been hastily enlisted as nurses weeping over two poor Italians who had to have their legs amputated for frost-bite; the beggars running beside the columns of prisoners giving them bits of bread or an orange – with that gay heart-breaking smile of generosity which is seen nowhere except in the faces of the very poor in Greece: the marvellous chivalry of the Greek air force – equal to anything in our own – who scorn to shoot down parachutists. And on the other side the lying crawling meanness of the Italians who bombed Larissa during the earthquake: who bomb villages from *30,000* feet for fear of the single defending machine gun as at Pylos: and who run before the wretchedly clad, poorly fed *Evzones* in their scarlet shoes. One thing is certain, that these rats are not the masters of Europe, and never can be: and of course, as we prophesied at the beginning of the war the arch-rat is France. You will see her declare for Germany before long: all she wants is an excuse.

All this, of course, has no connection with us in the ultimate sense:

only as T. E. Lawrence said once, "There are times when right living is cried down, and then only the sword can preach." I see the USA is being more and more rapidly implicated in the struggle.

I get an occasional line from Seferiades who is working like hell: Katsimbalis is the most impressive officer in Greece I hear: and the young are surging forward. Stephan the bearded magician of Mykonos is up in the line. Daperis and Xipollitos too. I feel like a sort of school-teaching Abelard – "her privates we" if you see the connection. In the meantime the child has grown enormously, has eight teeth, a vocabulary of two words, and a yell like a hungry starling. I haven't succeeded in teaching her to say "Uncle Henry" yet.

No news from you for a long time: I'm sure you are well, hope you are happy, and cannot believe that you have not written a dozen books since you landed. Love to Anaïs and Betty and Eduardo and Hugo and all whom it may concern; Nancy sends her love and says WHY don't you write and tell us about your daughter? Did you meet? Is she a beauty? Is she a writer? and so on.

I send you a leaf from a wild rose of Messenia picked beside the untamed and hero-loving gulf: and salute you in the name of Aphrodite the foam-born. love.

larry

Nightmares
Air-Conditioned and Alexandrian

Durrell leaves Greece on 25 April 1941 during the desperate evacuation ahead of the German advance. Larry, Nancy, and the year-old Penelope, aboard a caïque with a crowd of leaderless Greek soldiers, make a risky passage to Crete. They can travel only by night, when the small ship is supposedly harder for German Stuka pilots to spot, but the exhaust emits a comet's tail of fiery sparks. Finally they reach Cairo, where Durrell finds work as a press officer attached to the British Ministry of Information. Durrell's marriage does not survive – 'just the war I guess', he writes to Miller – but after this personal crisis he is transferred to Alexandria where he falls in love with the beautiful Eve 'Gipsy' Cohen.

Meanwhile, Miller is midway in his tour of the 'American nightmare', rushing about the USA as though the nations were not preparing for the most destructive war the world has known. Hating warfare in general and this war in particular, Miller defends himself by carrying on with his life and writing as if the only annoyances are the travel restrictions which keep him from returning to Europe – that, and his frequent visits to the dentist. By 1945 Miller is firmly settled in Big Sur with his young third wife, Janina Lepska.

This is to prove an enormously significant period for both men: Durrell finds the setting of his first major fiction in the overheated and fecund, sordid yet exotic ambience of wartime Egypt; Miller rediscovers that he is indelibly American, as American as the Walt Whitman he has always admired. With uncanny though perhaps unconscious foresight, Miller records the travel diary which is to form the basis for *The Air-Conditioned Nightmare* in a printer's dummy for *Leaves of Grass*. Egyptian themes and motifs – cabbalistic studies, gnosticism, desert oases – are never to leave Durrell, and recur in his fiction starting with

The Alexandria Quartet. Miller never again really sees himself as an *expatriate* artist, although he continues to look abroad for inspiration.

*N.Y. City   Dec. 28th 1941

Dear Larry –
The other day a typewritten excerpt from a book by Fraser (about my skull portrait) came – but no letter with it. I'm sure you addressed the envelope. Yesterday a post card from Seferis in Pretoria, S.A., saying I could reach you at the British Embassy, Cairo. I take it you never got any letters from me at that crazy address – *Luna Park Hotel!* Did you ever get *The Colossus*, sent to this latter address? Now I'm having New Directions send you *The Wisdom of the Heart* c/o British Embassy. One day I wrote a letter which a chap named Wayne Harriss promised to air mail for me – with a word from himself about his publishing plans. He and an Irish girl (from the Isle of Aran) are crazy not only about *The Black Book* but about your poems. So far no tangible results. Have had wonderful praise for you of the poems – likened you to Donne, Blake and others. The young & evil ones seem to know. My friend at Viking Press was *very* enthusiastic – but the firm couldn't see how they would sell more than 500. This, of course, is *America*. American attitude towards everything. They sell you the war in the same fashion. It must pay or no use. Et cetera.

You know, I'm back from the tour. Covered about 25,000 miles. A year wasted, I'd say. Am bringing the book to a close soon. Now well over 500 pages. But I doubt that it will ever be published. I may put it in the Library of Congress – for the archives. That means handing back the advances I received – about a thousand dollars. Will have to take a job soon – I owe much more, as a result of the trip.

I am still hoping to get to Mexico, India, China, Tibet. But how? Yet, I know I will. I am just cooling my heels. You know, I always have the feeling that I will bump into you and Nancy in India – either in Burma or Nepal. How *is* Nancy? And dear little Berengaria Penelope? I wonder how it is in Cairo. Interesting, no doubt. Here in N.Y. I have the feeling of being in the "Bardo". Absolutely. All that is needed to complete the picture are the bombs. And they will soon be here, no doubt. Nothing is changed here, on the surface. Plenty of neckties, silk bathrobes, etc. Business as usual. A complete air of unreality.

Anaïs sends her love to you both. Fred is now in Scotland "somewhere". Edgar is in Harlem – but I haven't looked him up yet. Betty Smart sends her warm greetings – saw her the other day. A blonde Viking type – Canadian. The other Betty I never hear from – don't even know her whereabouts. Listen, Larry, I will write oftener now. I feel you are *there*, in Cairo. Before I was dubious. If you get a chance look up a book called *Cosmic Consciousness* by Bucke. It's for *you*.

Henry.

*Hollywood   Sept. 15th, 1942

Address till further notice: c/o Satyr Book Shop – 1620 N. Vine St., Hollywood, Cal. [. . .]

Dear Larry,

I was overjoyed to get your letter of July 4th – the first I have received from you since you left Greece. If you wrote others they must have gone to the bottom. Once I got a queer letter from some young Englishman, giving his reaction to a portrait of me he saw in a book shop window in Paris. It was from Cairo and seemed to have been sent by you – but there was no word from you with it. Recently I had your letter to Fred, forwarded by him . . . . Well, so you are alive! That's marvellous. And Nancy and Berengaria in Palestine! That's incredible. How I envy you both! I wish I could be sent to Palestine or Syria or Timbuctoo – or Cairo. I swear I wouldn't mind the dirt, disease, or anything. It seems so rich to me, that world you are in. Even the crazy alphabet. Even the postage stamps look intriguing.

You see, I am in Hollywood – since three months nearly. Thought I might take a snap job in the movies – in order to get the money to go to Mexico and ultimately to India, etc. But I have made no effort to get myself a job. I loathe the work and the people who run the show. I meet them all socially and it is enough to make you vomit. I am living with a writer named Gilbert Neiman and his wife. That is, I eat with them. I sleep and work next door with the Jordans – from Czechoslovakia. A writer of detective stories – gruesome ones, for which he gets *$700.00 a month*! We live in a canyon about six miles out from Hollywood. Quite isolated. A wonderful climate and rather interesting scenery – mountain, sea and desert. A Lotus Land. The only bugaboo (for them!) is the gas rationing. Soon they may have to hoof it to and fro.

Now and then I go to a studio to watch them shoot a film. It's grotesque. Like work done under a microscope. The film advances about a millimetre a day – with tremendous clatter and clamour. In an atmosphere which is suffocating. The lights alone drive you nuts. Most of the people involved are technicians. The camera dominates every-thing. Millions of little screws to turn. Everything mechanical. The acting seems quite secondary. One wonders how the film ever gets produced finally. When I think of writing a script my hair stands on end. I have tried it in collaboration with a couple of fellows – I understand the technique – very simple – but, as Huxley told me in a letter recently (he's living nearby in the desert now), it's like fitting a jig-saw puzzle together. There is a type of young writer now who seems particularly adapted to this work – the new Soviet workers for whom art is a thing of the past . . . a Pleistocene luxury.

Just this morning I was offered a job as ghost writer to an old actor who is writing five books at once. (And getting them accepted too, by some N.Y. publisher.) I could have a luxurious place to myself, good food, use of a car, and all that. But I can't see myself writing those books – can you? I am asking a thousand dollars *a week* for my services – in order to hold them off. But I am afraid one day someone will actually offer me such a sum. Any price goes here. Though William Faulkner only gets three hundred a week at Warner Bros. Studios – where I had a sunstroke one day walking thru the artificial movie streets of Casablanca. (Temperature 120 in the shade.)

One day I met a beautiful Greek woman, called Madame Melpomene Niarchos. She gave me a royal banquet at her hotel in Pasadena (a millionaires' colony). It was one of the most wonderful evenings I have spent in a long while. She is now offering me the use of a cottage on Long Island (New York). Knew everybody in Athens apparently. Spoke warmly of Jeanne, Seferis' sister. (Is he in Cairo now, by the way? If so, give him my warm greetings.) [. . .]

The war! Every one is being drafted, shifted about, uprooted. They are talking of raising thirteen million men here shortly. Soon there will be nothing but women and old men left. I hope I shan't be too old – I mean for the women! I read the papers once a fortnight, roughly. Just the headlines. Wonder how many years it will be before one side or the other collapses. And will it be a bright new world, when it's over?

There is a Ramakrishna-Vivekananda Center (a sort of monastery) on the border of Nepal, where I am offered hospitality, if I can ever make it. I know a couple of Swamis representing this order. Meanwhile I am working on *The Rosy Crucifixion* (sequel to *Capricorn*). Have 700 pages done and must do about the same amount before I'm finished with volume 2. I really have no problems any more – except the petty one of food and board. I earn no money. ($450.00 last year, for royalties and magazine articles and everything. Handsome, what!)

No, Larry me lad, my serenity increases. I don't give a shit what the set-up is. I go my way. My health improves. I seem to be getting younger, instead of older.

Incidentally, if you ever read *Horizon* (Connolly's magazine from London), you may find soon some fragments from my American book therein. I've sent him over a dozen thus far. I am not having the book published. I withdrew it myself.

I do wish you would send photos of the child. What a beautiful name you have given it! Chinese, of course. I still have your little copy of Lao Tse – and the Nijinsky, of course.

And how is Nancy? Can't you send photos of all of you? I want to see if you have changed much. I always remember you as you looked that last day – in Tripolis – with the rain coming down, and me in that funny old fiacre. I'm sure you will survive everything. And maybe from Cairo you will go to India one day. Or Persia, or Arabia. Wherever it is I'll be meeting you. You can count on it. Somehow I don't think you'll see Corfu again for a very long time. I have the most terrible picture of Europe in my mind – after the war. The sort of thing I wrote about in *Black Spring*. I can't see it otherwise. I feel that Russia will dominate the whole continent. It may take till the end of this century to restore order. No more "balance of power" business. However, one man's guess is as good as another's.

I'm sending your letter on to Anaïs. She's been in Provincetown, Mass., all summer. I suppose you know all about her little press. Eduardo brought out a strange little book – astrologico-biographical sort of document. Printed it himself with Cooney at Cooney's farm. I met the latter, some months ago, in N.Y. He was quite a nice little chap – really harmless. Had the makings of a saint, I thought. We got along quite well. A bit boring, to be sure. He has a wonderful child called Deirdre – full of sex.

I'll write again, now that I know where to reach you and that you're still there to read my letters. I guess you'll be meeting lots of Americans in Cairo. The latest – about *Tropic of Cancer* – is this: that in Washington Madame Litvinov begged a friend of mine to let her read the book. *The Colossus* is now being translated into modern Greek by a young Greek professor in New Jersey – Homer Economos, of all names! Secker & Warburg are bringing out an English publication this Fall. Seems strange to me. Why would they want that book? Well, I never did understand the English. As Houghton says, they're fantastic – and always waiting for a miracle to deliver them. (And the miracle always happens!) You must read the *Julian Grant* book – it will bowl you over.

My love to Nancy and blessings on the little one. I must go in to Hollywood now to give an English lesson to a Russian refugee. There I shall meet Jean Renoir, the film director, and Vincent Korda, brother of the right honourable Alexander. Oh yes – did I tell you I am great pals with Marlene Dietrich's daughter – who is just turning eighteen? That deserves another letter. Cheerio, then, Larry me lad.

(If there are any American films in Cairo, be on the watch for Orson Welles' two films: *Citizen Kane* and *The Magnificent Ambersons*. I think you'd like *The Maltese Falcon* too – there is a marvellous English actor named Greenstreet in it. A colossus! I loved *Laburnum Grove*, the old English picture with Sir Cedric Hardwicke – what a guffer, that bird!)

Henry

Miller felt this was not a propitious moment for a book so critical of American society as *The Air-Conditioned Nightmare*, and so did not permit publication until 1945.

*Hollywood   Nov. 21st, 1942

Dear Larry,

It's Fred who suggested I write you via London, to expedite delivery. I'm hoping this may reach you in time to wish you a merry Christmas – you, Nancy and Berengaria the third. I'm pulling up stakes soon, to return to N.Y. Earned exactly a hundred dollars here (where diamonds grow in the street), doing an abstract of Wassermann's *The Maurizius Case*. The studios wouldn't have me, it seems. Unheard of. No screen credits. Too highbrow. And so forth. The only interesting thing that happened to me here was meeting Melpomene, the Greek woman. She is the apotheosis of all Greek womanhood. I hope to see her when I return to N.Y. It's cold here now, about like Athens was that month of December, when they turned the heat on an hour or two at a time, you remember?

Well, I'm thinking that soon the American troops will be landing in Athens. At this moment things are looking up a bit. The invasion has begun. I suppose Cairo is agog with expectations of one kind and another. At this writing the Germans still hold Bizerte and Tunis. But it's no longer a toe-hold, from all reports. I'm wondering what you will think when you get a glimpse of the Americans en masse. I suppose there's already a bit of rivalry afoot. Coincident with the turn of the tide, Churchill announces that he is not giving the Empire away (sic). That didn't meet with such a warm reception over here. We want the English to give their bloody Empire away, doesn't he know that, the old pfoof?

From the way you write I don't picture you doing any more reading. But if you do, take a glance at Frederic Prokosch's *The Seven Who Fled*. It's all about Central Asia – a real opium book. And tell me if you recognize any of the places, will you? Most of them I never heard of.

I just finished reading Céline's *Death on the Installment Plan*. It took me over two years, oddly enough. I gallivanted through the last two hundred pages. Magnificent. Ferocious. Still the best writer alive to-day, I do think. After they defeat the Axis powers they will have to lick Céline, it seems to me. He's got more dynamite in him than Hitler ever had. It's permanent hatred – for the whole human species. But what merry-making. He has a bloody corpse, towards the end, that provides more hysterical amusement than a band of comedians. Blood-curdling humor it is. Sometimes it turns your stomach. Do get hold of it, Larry – it will pep you up. You may enjoy it even more than I – the translator was English, and all the slang expressions, some of which are Greek to me, are in British English. That makes it quite droll. Imagine a Frenchman saying – "bugger off!" [. . .]

The movies have definitely entered the doldrums. No good pictures being made any [more] – not for the duration. All flub and foozle – with a $25,000.00 a year ceiling wage for the stars! Tough titty for them. How can they get along on a pittance like that? It's tragic. That's mere chicken feed to them. They need more than the President, more than the Pope at Rome, b'Jasus. I met one recently who was earning $1200.00 a week. A *week* mind you! All he has left, after paying taxes, alimony, state, federal, poll tax and Christ knows what else, is ninety dollars. How can a man get along on ninety dollars? He never heard of a coolie, I suppose. Nor did he ever see the Hindus sleeping naked in the streets of Bombay. Nor the child prostitutes in Shanghai. To believe our radio gents, we all need Vitamin B. A plain American meal lacks the necessary ingredients for health – that's what they tell you over the air. So buy vitamins – and Cuticura Soap and Electric Razor machines, and well . . . you know what. Yes, that fine, soft, tulle-like toilet paper. It will help win the war. The buying and selling goes on – right till the crack of doom. If people don't revolt at that stuff how will they revolt at anything? The way these bastards talk over the air you'd think the war was just a big football game with a dollar sign on it. [. . .]

Well, the next will be from New York, I guess. Remember that Xmas in Sparta – and the woman bringing the eggs back and forth? Who ever thought then that the year 1942 would see you in Cairo and me in Hollywood? And Fred in Scotland. Really, I think Fred got the best break of all, don't you? Must be a beautiful country up there. Right in the Highlands he is, the cute little bugger. Always did know how to pick himself a soft spot. And his woman is on the grain market – deals in rye and oats, I gather. Pretty soft, what? Tell me something about you and Nancy. How do things go these days – together, I mean? Are you still lambasting one another? I hope you haven't taken to beating up the child, have you? If it's a girl, as I take it she is, go easy on her. Don't let her become a neurotic or an epileptic. Remember, a soft word turneth away wrath. And use Nestle's milk, don't forget! Merry Xmas, Larry, and to you, Nancy, and to you, Berengaria!

Henry

*[Beverly Hills, California]   11/12/43

Dear Larry & Nancy
Just mailed you a wonderful little book I hope will reach you by Xmas or New Year's. How are you all? I think of you so often. Will the war soon be over, do you think? Will we see Corfu again?

Henry

[Alexandria]   [*c.* 25 December 1943]

dear henry – wonder where you are and what you are doing. Just been
rereading your Greek book and trying to write one myself. Strange
mad times – and how remote – last meeting in Tripolis in the falling
rain. I told Faber to send you my book of poems despite your dislike for
poetry. Maybe some images will recall Greece to you. I am in
Alexandria now and work in a little tower – very smart alec and quaint
– but we are all so wormeaten by the war that I do no work at all. I see
Seferis and have recent news of Katsimbalis who is alive still. Greece is
going right under this winter: heartbreaking situation, famine, disease,
and internal anarchy – walking murder abroad. Meanwhile *salut* for *The
Air-Conditioned Nightmare* – it is great stuff. For the rest we are dying
steadily inside and hoping for it all to end as soon as possible.

Nancy is in Jerusalem with the child. We have split up; just the war I
guess. After Greece, Crete and the Alamein evacuation we got to
understand what the word 'refugee' means. Will you write some time –
and disregard my bloody humours?

    Love to Anaïs and Hugo
    Larry

*Information Office, One Rue Toussoum,
Alexandria, Egypt   February 8. 44

Dearest Henry – it is so good always to have a postcard from you or a
little book with that characteristic joyful (euphoristic) handwriting.
Now today I get the notice of your show; I do hope it was a success –
even a financial success – for by now it must be over. I told Faber to be
sure and send you a copy of my poems and I hope they have done so. I
have been so long barren that I fear to tell you that I am *working* once
more: for fear I shall blow up and fall into an Alexandrian frenzy of
apathy. But lately I had a short holiday in Beirut and finished a long
poem called "Cities Plains and People" – a reader's digest view of my
own life – which becomes more and more an apology for itself in terms
of war-prostitution. I am a man of minor consequence now – an
Information Officer. As far as worldly affairs are concerned I have no
further ambition – like Lao Tse in his library.

Meanwhile Nancy and the child are well – in another climate; I get no direct news and it's nearly two years since I saw either of them so I've almost forgotten what they mean – symbolic appendices to walk around with. Here I am devilish gay and empty.

I have furnished myself a Tower *[◻]* where I have finished one book of verse, and am half-way through a book about Greek landscape – Corfu only. It's not a big book or even a book at all – but I feel I must wind up the old spring and tidy the 'time past' of the clock if I am to expect any 'time future' (*Burnt Norton*) from it.

I occasionally read y^r frenzied appeals to reason in the avant garde papers – sounding but *so* remote and *so* much like the voice of conscience as we reach into the fifth year of this sickening war – which mercifully some of us have escaped partially. Our feelings are those of the periphery; everyone going quietly bad and mad inside. *Me too.*

Xan Fielding sends his greetings. He has a terrifying tale to tell – which of course one may not repeat. But if you remember his particular languages and abilities you might have some idea of his sphere of action. As for me, I have just written an essay on you for a paper appearing here – more of a bulletin of information really than an essay – with an incomplete bibliography – will send it as soon as it appears.

There is little to add. The Alexandrian way of death is very Proustian and slow; a decomposition in greys and greens – by the hashish pipe or boys. But the women are splendid – like neglected gardens – rich, silk-and-olive complexions, slanting black eyes and soft adze-cut lips, and heavenly figures like line-drawings by a sexual Matisse. I am up to my ears in them – if I must be a little *literal*. But, as my friends remark, "Les femmes, comme les peintres d'Alexandrie, ont trop de technique mais peu de tempérament." But one has never had anything lovelier and emptier than an Alexandrian girl. Their very emptiness is a caress. Imagine making love to a vacuum – you must come here for a week after the war. After that you'll be so completely emptied of worldly goods that you'll be ripe for Tibet and all it means. Meanwhile we are crawling through the ever-narrowing conduit of this bloody war. Do write from time to time – you are like a voice from something very far but completely understood – while here one talks into the air round people – and words fly flatly off into space – sound and fury. Love to Anaïs and Edgar – where are they all?

Larry.

[P.S.] Now I think of the correct simile for the Alexandrians. When they make love it's like two people in a dark room slashing at each other with razors – to make each other feel _____?

*From Big Sur, California –
(Address R. & V. in N.Y. always a safe one!)   April 7th, 1944

My dear Larry,
I'm writing you to Cairo, though you say you're in Alexandria now. I hope you get this. It's so long since I heard from you last. Your brief message sounded rather sad. So you and Nancy have split up? And the child is with her, I suppose. In Jerusalem, of all places! How I envy you both. Who wouldn't prefer to be in Jerusalem now, or Alexandria, or Cairo? I am here at the very farthest rim of the Western world, right on the broad Pacific, and facing China. China is always in the back of my mind – also your now celebrated essay in *Delta* (or was it *The Booster*?) – "Hamlet, Prince of China". No one has equalled or even rivalled that yet. How that must get under the skin of George Orwell! A young poet named Nicholas Moore, whom you probably know, wrote a short monograph on me recently – did it get to Cairo yet? I'll mail you one, just on the chance [it] didn't. And then the other day I got a clipping from the London *Tribune*, containing a review of this little monograph (like cycles and epicycles, or changes of gear on those monolithic English bikes!) by our old friend Mulk Raj Anand. He sounds, in that review, very much like Orwell's chief satellite. I was touched, though, by his recollection of a visit to the Villa Seurat, his description of Anaïs and myself – me he portrays as Buddhist monk who just donned a lounging suit, sic! By this time you must have heard that I have found a friend and saviour in another Hindu in London (my publisher now, together with Secker & Warburg) – Tambimuttu. When I first heard from him I recalled your fantastic descriptions of the London meetings. I was for ignoring his letter altogether, thinking him a crack-pot. But in the next letter I discovered that he represented dear old Nicolson & Watson (the dear old baronets, I understand – reputation spotless, etc.). He says, so strike me dead: "we pay handsomely". And further on: "we will publish everything of yours that is printable". And he is making good his threat.

I shan't be able to send greetings to Anaïs & Hugo for you, unfortunately. Anaïs and I have also parted. That's the second big loss I've sustained on the Eastern front, so to speak. And since then a few more. The worst defeat I ever suffered was at the hands of the Greek girl in Hollywood. (Sevasty Koutsaftis.) You'll see some of her poems in Tambimuttu's magazine, and – hold your breath! – one of mine. That's to say, my first and only one, most likely. That's what Sevasty did for me. I wish you would tell me, if you ever see hers, what you think of them. They baffled me. But I think she is a potentially great poet. Sometimes, sleeping over at her home, she would retire to the kitchen after I had turned in (the mother and sister watching over us like hawks), write a "Quickie" for me and slip it under my pillow. I started to write about Sevasty before leaving Beverly Glen. Something on the order of Gérard de Nerval's *Dreams and Life*, but then a thousand things interfered. Anyway, she had hardly parted from me (for the last time), had hardly waved good-bye, when I got the opening line for what I thought was going to be another masterpiece. The whole thing had only lasted about six months. It was the first time in my life, I think, that I was ready to give myself entièrement. But I suppose there wasn't enough to give!

Anyway, after leaving Anaïs in N.Y. I followed the divine Laure to Hollywood. That flickered out even faster. Laure too was marvellous. Both she and Sevasty had sculpturesque heads. Laure had Polish, Basque and Peruvian blood in her veins. Some combination. Both a little too "strong", too willful, too tyrannical. When they melted it was almost unbearable – like a spring torrent. (Full of debris too.) Then, just as I'm leaving the Glen, the night before in fact, a young woman who had been doing some typing for me bursts in and declares herself passionately and shamelessly. All I could feel was pity. She had been seduced by the manuscripts. I eased out as best I could, thanking my stars that I had persuaded her not to run away from her husband and child and follow me. I tried to put my friend Dudley on to her, but it didn't work. He was too much the "movie type" for her. So there you are. Now I'm conducting a long distance mail order romance with probably the most lovely creature I've ever seen (judging from photos). Her name is June. I'm trying to get her to come out here and join me, but so far my efforts have been fruitless.

Yes, there we are, Larry me lad. A long way from the Villa Seurat days, and that smoldering café opposite the little église on the Avenue d'Orléans, corner rue d'Alésia. Reichel has probably been starved or beaten to death by now in some concentration camp. Edgar is somewhere in England, and a sergeant – do you see it? Still talking about his bloody Rudolf Steiner too. (By V-mail now.) Fred is crazy about the Scots, and says he's marrying some Ann up in Dumfries and I must come to live with them after the war. I wouldn't mind, either. God, if we could all reunite somewhere, what a time we would have! It would be like a reunion in Paradise. I don't believe any of us will die before the war is ended. Somehow I feel we are all "protected". I make up journeys in my head sometimes – for this after the war period. I see us all, you, Fred, Edgar and myself (perhaps Tambimuttu too, and if possible my new nigger friend, Beauford Delaney, a painter, and also Harry, Harry Herschkowitz!) visiting Claude Houghton in Bath. Having tea with dear old Mr. Symons. Only this time *I* am determined to serve *him*. I shall bring him tea and muffins in bed, stoke the fires, wash the dishes, read to him, dance for him, play the mime, anything he wishes. I shall even not mind too much meeting George Orwell. And then there's Reginald Moore, at Gelli Cottage, Llansantffraid, North Wales. He will surely take us to see that scallywag Dylan Thomas, who will be dead drunk and bursting with health. Do you see it clearly, Larry? And when we're ready to leave England we'll have my new Greek friend, Jean Varda of Monterey, make us a boat and we'll sail to Greece, eh what?

Must stop here. Lynda is taking me to town. Must mail all the letters. More again soon. Do write soon, won't you? I thought you had a grouch on. And be sure I will read the volume of poems Faber is sending. I've already seen some in print. I begin to cotton to them now. My last days I am giving up to painting and poetizing. That I've promised myself. That's the Chinese phase, which I reserve for the near-end. The last is Tibet, always. And about that, more in my next. I wish I could promise to bring June along!

Henry

Dear Henry –

Just read the open letter you sent me with emotion: you couldn't be more
in the right in what you say. It's the plight of all of us really – this bloody
compromise with security – and there's nothing to be done about it. At
least there's no hope that the state will want to support its artists; or if it
does it will select the palatable ones. Now if you had been a Dos Passos or
a Hemingway it would have been too easy: but to be a live immortal
walking about – a peer of Melville and Whitman – that automatically
disqualifies you for appreciation until 50 years after your death.

I have just written a little essay about you for a paper here, *Cahiers de
Limbes*; not 'critical' but a few facts about the sort of guy you are – with a
short bibliography. I will send it on. Henry, if you get to Europe after the
war, don't worry about anything; I'll keep you. Maybe even if you could
get OWI to send you out this way now you would be in a good position
for a return to Europe. Everything is smashed up beyond words –
internal economy, public services, currency; the conditions in Greece go
beyond all imagining and description; on top of the starvation now
Terror; young Andri Nomikos arrived yesterday with news of them all.
They were still alive last month – Katsimbalis and Co – but the killings
are getting everyone worked up to ferocity. At Omonia, in the Syn-
tagma Square – in open daylight – shootings every day. All the buildings
mined for the German departure; I think we will have a lot of practical
things to do after the war – living here on the edge of the crater, as it
were, and looking down into the gulf of all this small suffering – this
huge accumulation of personal tragedies – I feel that the time is not ripe to
reassert ourselves as artists and men yet. Anything we do is on the side
until this great bloody farce is played out. I am writing a bit these days –
very badly – like a man with a creeping paralysis – some poems of value –
some prose about Corfu – trying to tidy everything up, past and present,
to be ready to kick off if the daimon gets going after the war. I saw
Barclay Hudson in Beirut and we spoke about you.

Middle East is a dead centre – the outer ring of the whirlpool moving
slowly round and round – so we are all in Limbo and deader than the
really dead or the practically dying.

Love
Larry.

Durrell had just received Miller's 'Dear friends' letter of 'Easter Sunday', in which Henry wrote, 'It gripes me that in a year when seventeen books of mine are being published', he is not only broke but $24,000 in debt. He requested a 'loan' – not from Durrell – of $50 per week for a year, to permit him to complete *The Air-Conditioned Nightmare* and to write *The Rosy Crucifixion*.

OWI: Office of War Information.

*Big Sur, California   May 5th, 1944

Dear Larry,

I wrote you a couple of weeks ago on hearing from you. Now yesterday two letters at once, dated Alexandria where I write you henceforth. The other letter was addressed to Cairo – hope you get it.

Anyway, since that last letter I posted good news. Lots of news. First, I've found a patron – for a whole year – who is giving me fifty dollars a week and no strings to it. I am to pay back when, how, or if. No interest charges. This is a result of a round robin letter dated Easter Sunday, when I also answered the lovely cable I most unexpectedly received from Osbert Sitwell, Renishaw Hall, Renishaw (near Sheffield) England – bloody England!

When I get copies made of all these Open Letters I have been writing I will send them on to you. They will appear in book form anyway soon – see this letterhead. (Plight of . . . etc.) I am deluged with letters by all and sundry. It's colossal. And many contain little checks or just plain bills (cash), or promises. Some send packages of clothing, paper for writing or painting, tubes of paint, etc. etc. etc. I am like a receiving station.

The show in Hollywood was quite a success. I sold myself about twenty-four paintings before the show started. Got from $30 to 100 a piece. Some hang now in famous collections. At present Caresse Crosby is showing me in Wash. D.C. where she opened a gallery recently. I am turning over the proceeds of this to a poor Negro painter, Beauford Delaney, and a starving poet (who is also an invalid), Kenneth Patchen, author of *The Journal of Albion Moonlight*, remember? [. . .]

I also made up with my arch-enemy, James Laughlin, of New Directions. He made a profuse and profound apology to me in the presence of several people for all he had done to thwart me. Confessed everything. Alors, nothing to do but shake hands and start all over again. Now he can't do enough for me. Gives me fifty copies *free* of every book he publishes of mine – for my friends. He may bring out *Black Spring* in a couple of months. Is just producing now *Sunday After the War*, a collection again, on order of *Cos. Eye*. In short, Larry, there will be 17 books coming out this year here and in England. Every bloody thing I have is being printed. When I finish *The Rosy Crucifixion* I shall be able to take off for a while – by that time maybe the war will be over and I will join you somewhere, you and dear Alf in Scotland, and Edgar, who is now somewhere in England, a sergeant. In short, a year of complete fulfillment and realization. All except love. Blast me, but I have had more ill luck in that direction than I could ever imagine. I am just hors de combat, as it were. All ends disastrously. Just lost the latest one – by correspondence – June Lancaster.

So, when you write me about the Alexandrian vacuum with razor blades flashing and all that I am in a paroxysm. Let's get there! Christ, it's dead here. All this business flurry, books published, water color shows, means nothing to me. I'd give it all up to wander with you through those streets and see those sloe-gin fizz eyes, drown myself in that abattoir of love which you describe so eloquently.

No, Faber have not yet sent me your poems. They will come one day. Everything comes – eventually. Even Xmas. And so will peace come. And then it will be the merry whirl, and we will be planning the next war, bigger, better, more efficient, more ferocious. Listen ... I am just finishing a rather long excursus (in the *Nightmare*) called *Murder the Murderer*. About 65 to 75 pages long. I think I will send you a carbon of it; you may want to use it in that magazine – Cahiers de Limites, or de *Limbes* – which? Can't make it out. It's a marvellous piece – savage humor, wisdom, serenity, optimism-pessimism, satire, vaudeville, charley-horse and everything. Nobody has written about war this way. You'll love it, even if you don't agree. Remember, it will be from *The Air-Conditioned Nightmare*, which is due out before the end of the year. Doubleday Doran have option on it, but I expect them to reject it. In that case Laughlin (New Directions) promises he will take it. Tambimuttu also. I wish I could get an edition out in Switzerland (in German and French) and one in Spain. We'll see. Everything I touch works now – *except love*. However, I go on loving. I'm a born lover. And I still don't masturbate. I transform it. [. . .]

I wouldn't want an OWI job. I'll wait. It's just possible I may go to Guatemala for the duration. But I'll keep in touch with you. And the

N.Y. address is always good. Now I'll write Anaïs about you. Do you ever write Fred? I hope so. Fraenkel is still in Mexico City. Bored. I just sent him fifty dollars to clear an old debt from 1934. He's beside himself with joy. His tongue waters when you say MONEY.

Do give warm greetings to Seferis, if you still see or communicate with him. I do hope Katsimbalis comes through. I think he will. Also – I just heard from Sevasty, my Greek flame. She seems to want to start things up again. God, how I loved her! Now there's a Despina and a Helen and a Melpo – all Greek. What beautiful names! Well, as always, cheerio, Larry me lad! All's well that ends well. (Shakespeare & Co.) Listen – please send a copy of that magazine (*Cahiers*...) to June Lancaster – 113 West 49th St., New York (19) N.Y. – will you? And write her a personal letter about me, what a great guy I am – if you feel like it. June is almost a copy of the first June. I am crazy about her. She asked me to stop writing – because she's overwhelmed. She's in a panic. But you write her, Larry. From that vacuum where the razor blades flash and all go itchy-koo. Write Sitwell too. Write Alf. Write everybody, even Anaïs – 215 West 13th St., N.Y.C. Cheerio!

Henry

*British Information Office,
ONE RUE TOUSSOUM,
ALEXANDRIA, Egypt.   [mid-May, continued late May 1944]

Dear Henry: Yes I got the letters; I'm in touch with the embassy, representing them, so they pass them on. Your news sounds marvellous. Of course anything is less than what the world owes you for opening up the world with your own bright eye. Seventeen books sounds an awful lot to me; let me have any old duplicate proofs that come your way – I haven't read anything of yours since the marvellous Greek book. Here we are sweltering in an atmosphere that demands a toast – great passion, short lives. Everything is worn thin as an eggshell; it's the fifth year now and the nervous breakdown is coming into the open. Old women, ginger dons, nursing sisters begin to behave like bacchantes; they are moving in and out of nursing homes with a steady impetus. Meanwhile we are crippled here by an anemia and an apathy and a censorship which prevents the least trace of the human voice – of any calibre. We exist on a machine-made diet of gun bomb and tank – backed up by the slogan.

The atmosphere in this delta is crackling like a Leyden jar; you see, in normal times all the local inhabitants spend six months in Europe a year – so they are as stale and beaten thin as the poor white collar man. The poetry I exude these days is dark grey and streaky – like bad bacon. But the atmosphere of sex and death is staggering in its intensity. Meanwhile the big shots come and go, seeing nothing, feeling nothing, in a money daydream; there is still butter and whisky and café viennoise. A kind of diseased fat spreads over the faces and buttocks of the local populations, who have skimmed the grease off the war effort in contracts and profiteering. No, I don't think you would like it. First this steaming humid flatness – not a hill or mound anywhere – choked to bursting point with bones and the crummy deposits of wiped out cultures. Then this smashed up broken down shabby Neapolitan town, with its Levantine mounds of houses peeling in the sun. A sea flat dirty brown and waveless rubbing the port. Arabic, Coptic, Greek, Levant French; no music, no art, no real gaiety. A saturated middle european boredom laced with drink and Packards and beach-cabins. NO SUBJECT OF CONVERSATION EXCEPT MONEY. Even love is thought of in money terms; "You are getting on with her? She has ten thousand a year of her own." Six hundred greaseball millionaires sweating in their tarbushes and waiting for the next shot of root-hashish. And the shrieking personal unhappiness and loneliness showing in every face. No, if one could write a single line of anything that had a human smell to it here, one would be a genius. Add to all this a sort of maggot-dance of minor official place-hunting, a Florentine atmosphere of throat-slitting and distrust, and you will have some idea of what anyone with a voice or tongue is up against. I am hoping the war will be over soon so I can quit; I'm glad of this little death for all the material it's put in my way about people and affairs in general. But I'm worn thin with arse-licking and having my grammar corrected by sub-editors from the Bush Times in South America . . . Here in Alexandria though I have my own office and almost no interference; so I can run things in the way I like. You always used to laugh when I said I was an executive man – but I was right. My office hums like a top; and the people working for me LIKE it. The basic principle is that of the old blind pianist in Paris – remember? Edgar's friend Thibaud or some such name. "Anything that needs effort to do is being done from the wrong centres; it is not worth doing." Some time I'll tell you how I applied that to the running of an effortless speed organisation . . .

I've done about half of a little historical book about Corfu; tired anecdotal writing in the style of a diary – you know the French anecdotal novel type of thing. Poor stuff but I feel I must keep the machine running or I'll die.

No other news; the sloe-eyed people are still here. There's a lovely English wren and a girl with the hips of an acrobat. But it's all really quite meaningless. I want a long rest from this incessant plucking of little people with little minds at the root of one's reason and self-respect.

How about a year in Poros now – baked hard rock and glittering sea; followed by Autumn in Athens with Katsimbalis and George (both still alive and all right); and then Paris and Edgar and Anne of Dumfries? No more writing but lying about and taking a long myopic and unbiased view of the universe. Or do you prefer Savings Bonds, Maximum Employment, better plumbing, and a prefabricated spriritual life in tune with the Stock Exchange graphs?

It's so good to know that you're writing. Betsy and John Uldall send their love. I found *Tropic* the other day and read it again with such yearning for Paris and Villa Seurat; and Betty Ryan and Mr Chu, and Châteauneuf du Pape, and Denis Seurat, Nijinsky, *Booster*, *Delta* and the whole works. Maybe we have it all ahead of us and not behind? Write again soon. Larry. Writing Anaïs.

Since writing the last few lines I have been called to Cairo for a week or so, and have just returned, blind with heat and sweat and apathy. Have managed to sell another book of poems for the spring lists next year, and am on the last lap of the Corfu book. I have Theodore conveniently staying with me so I am picking his brains diligently. It was intended to be a book of atmospheres but it is terribly scrappy and ill-starred. If I had a little leisure and energy.

Four years is a long time to spend without ever once encountering a person who has an interest besides making a woman or making money; and I've forgotten almost how to express myself. But I am unjust to Gipsy Cohen – a strange, smashing, dark-eyed woman I found here last year, with every response right: every gesture; and the interior style of a real person – but completely at sea here in this morass of venality and money. The only person I have been able to talk to really; we share a kind of refugee life. She sits for hours on the bed and serves me up experience raw – sex life of Arabs, perversions, circumcision, hashish, sweetmeats, removal of the clitoris, cruelty, murder. As a barefoot child of Tunisian Jewish parents, mother Greek from Smyrna, father Jew from Carthage, she has seen the inside of Egypt to the last rotten dung-blown flap of obscenity. She is *Tropic of Capricorn* walking. Her experiences as a child here would make one's hair stand on end. And like all people with the Tibetan sensibility she felt that she was going mad – because nobody knew what she was talking about. It has been fun re-articulating her experience for her, and curing her panics, and finding her books to show her how great a part of the world of sense and creation is nonsense to Alexandria. It has been incredible to find a woman whose sex responses start upwards from the soles of the feet – without any corrupting romantic anglo-saxon nonsense. It has cured me for English women for good and all.

I think if I could get to some Greek island and live in real poverty with somebody like Gipsy Cohen I could work like a fiend; funny how one simplifies and pares away the inessentials. Sex now as a non-possessive form of friendship much more moving and infinitely more tender than the old anglo-saxon rout of ideas *about* everything, and experiences always intruding to throw one's little platonic systems out of gear. I have really grown up now and have plenty to say. I wonder how soon I can get free from the world of submen in order to say it.

We are publishing an anthology of our work in Egypt here, a few of us; it's called *Personal Landscape* and Tambimuttu is publishing this autumn so we will [be] alongside you once more, firing our pom-poms in support of your great booming broadsides.

The world has walls of dung really; and the human being a mind like a sponge. The next ten years should see us in full cry over the hills . . . Simple needs this time. A girl who really fucks with the heart and soul and buttocks; an olive tree, a typewriter, and a few great friends like you. What do you think?

Larry

Dear Henry: How wonderful to hear from you at length again; the old hard gayness which is like a lost world quality – shining over the rim. I have just posted off a little essay on you for an anthology of homage which some american woman wants to publish – I guess you know all about it. [. . .]

I am in charge of a goodish sized office of war-propaganda here, trying to usher in the new washboard world which our demented peoples are trying "to forge in blood and iron". It's tiring work. However it's an office full of beautiful girls, and Alexandria is, after Hollywood, fuller of beautiful women than any place else. Incomparably more beautiful than Athens or Paris; the mixture Coptic, Jewish, Syrian, Egyptian, Moroccan, Spanish gives you slant dark eyes, olive freckled skin, hawk-lips and noses, and a temperament like a bomb. Sexual provender of quality, but the atmosphere is damp, hysterical, sandy, with the wind off the desert fanning everything to mania. Love, hashish and boys is the obvious solution to anyone stuck here for more than a few years. I am sharing a big flat with some nice people, and atop it I have a tower of my own from which the romantics can see Pompey's Pillar, Hadra Prison, and the wet reedy wastes of Lake Mareotis stretching away into the distance and blotting the sky.

This is the world of the desert Fathers and the wandering jews; the country eaten away like the carious jawbone of a mummy. Alexandria is the only possible point in Egypt to live in because it has a harbour and opens on a flat turpentine sealine – a way of escape. At the moment I am in mid-stream fighting my way through the rapids of a love affair with Gipsy Cohen, a tormented jewish-greek. No news from nancy for over a year, but I believe she is working and is happy. I am sorry that you have split with anais; she was so much a complement to you – to us all. I haven't heard of her for a long long time. Yes, Tambimuttu will be as good as his word. He is a wonderful and crazy man. He is publishing our anthology from Egypt called PERSONAL LANDSCAPE, and I'll tell him to send you one. There is lots of amusing and exciting news I could give you about the Greeks, and about people like Fielding, but I'm afraid censorship wouldn't let it pass so I must content myself by asking you if you realise how close you are to Melville biographically? And will you read his biography and send me a copy of PIERRE? Books here have got a middle ages quality owing to their rareness; all the popular editions are out of print of EVERYTHING – I mean the classics like Dostoievsky and Proust and all those wonderful half-crown editions you could buy before the war. So we have a sort of hungry look when anyone gets a new book – even if it's only a detective story. Among recent discoveries is a copy of TROPIC which has knocked everyone silly here; when they read the Greek book they asked me what I was babbling about when I said Miller was the greatest contemporary writer? He was certainly good etc etc. Now they begin to see . . .

Apart from that I have got stuck about half-way thru a little book about Corfu – a guide to landscape. Hard going. I feel played out.

Wonder what sort of future there is in store – I see a gathering at Constantinople or Baalbec in Syria before we start off to the land of the book of the dead. My only consolation now is Lao Tzu of which Eliot kindly sent me a copy – funny patient crazy rectangular man that he is; this I have explained in detail to Gipsy Cohen who understands every word – but it doesn't prevent her from scratching my face open for infidelities which in this landscape and ambience are as meaningless as she, I, or Pompey's Pillar are. Feel we've come to the end of a spool, and I am trying to live as little as possible until the new film gets put in the camera.

It's funny the way you get woman after woman: and exactly what it adds up to I don't know: each more superficial than the last Gaby, Simone, Arlette, Dawn, Penelope . . . but only Gipsy Cohen burns black and fierce under her Tunisian eyebrows; the flavour is straight Shakespeare's Cleopatra; an ass from Algiers, lashes from Malta, nails and toes from Smyrna, hips from Beiruit, eyes from Athens, and nose from Andros, and a mouth that shrieks or purrs like the witching women of Homs or Samarkand. And breasts from Fiume. And what the hell?

But their sex here is interesting; it's madly violent but not WEAK or romantic or obscure, like anglo-saxon women, who are always searching for a tintype of their daddies. It is not preconceived but taken heavily and in a kind of war – not limp northern friendship – but fierce and glaring, vulture and eagle work with beak and claws.

Well, the last few days we've driven out through Bourg El Arab, and slipped down through the battlefields to a long beach where the real Mediterranean comes up in great green coasters and sky is smothered down to violet, all lambent and turning your body in water to a wonderful rose. The sea citron-green cold and pure with sandy floor; for the first time in four years I felt I was in Greece. Bathing naked. At our back the dunes running away to the deserted crusader fort, nibbled battlements misty and like a mirage. Thousands of empty rounds of ammunition, dirty bandages, twisted wreck of enemy tanks, lumber. Strange atmosphere this deserted battlefield with the sea inking in the edges of the sky and the old fortress glowing like a jewel. On the road an occasional Bedouin with his camel. And palms like old camel-flesh trees clicking stiffly in the wind. Strange transition to Cavafy's Alexandria, and a letter from George Seferis saying that he is feeling happier and happier now that he has dropped propaganda.

There is not much else to tell you that can be conveniently written; forgive the mad haste of this. I must see what the world-fronts are saying on the radio. Gipsy is coming for a drink at one. Life is long, art short, as Goethe did not say.

Wonder when it will all end? Do write again soon won't you?

Larry

'Some american woman': Durrell, under a misconception about the sex of Bern Porter, is referring to *The Happy Rock* (1945), a book about Miller compiled and published by Porter, with Durrell's piece as the title essay.

*British Information Office,
One Rue Toussoum, Alexandria, Egypt.   August 22. 44.

Dear Henry: It's wonderful really to be able to correspond at such a short remove – under a month each way. I had the illusion that it was impossible; an illusion perfectly matching my burnt-out state. Thank you for the essay. IT IS TERRIFIC. I haven't read anything of yours for so long that the impact of it came with something of the pristine clearness I first felt when I opened *Tropic* and heard those first gruff symphonic rumblings – as of a great orchestra tuning up in darkness. [. . .] Incidentally in England they are beginning to wake up to you – not to mention Egypt. I have given several talks on your books, chiefly to Jewish ATS here in Alexandria. Tremendous black-eyed big-bottomed girls, and all taking notes at terrific speed. They study literature as if it were more interesting than sex. Now the war seems to have taken a definite turn and we hope that it will be over in a month or so. I am written down for Greece. I terribly need to recover my sanity a bit – disoriented and bruised a bit still, and haven't seen anything but sand and palms for two years. I did not know before what Gaul meant to the exiled Roman poet or Siberia to the Russian. Now I know. Your heart shrivels in its case for lack of moisture. It has rained once since I've been in Egypt – for half an hour. A dirty brown exhausted rain which was tepid and unrefreshing. One could not continue to live here without practising a sort of death – hashish or boys or food. Yet it has the kind of fat deathly beauty of a caterpillar; the connection, by the way, is the one you mentioned in the Greek book, at Corinth. Fat red and sensuous – it was an Alexandrian atmosphere we were smelling that mad Christmas in Corinth. I have learned so much here that I'm bursting to start writing again. [. . .] I have a wonderful idea for a novel in Alexandria, a nexus for all news of Greece, side by side with a sort of spiritual butcher's shop with girls on slabs. But I can't make the big effort for a while until I am free – so I think I'll do a short anthropological study of the English tabus; like one would plot out the depth and shape of an anti-tank ditch before moving forward in force. I can't judge from your writing what sort of impression you have had of the war; it is detached and ex-cathedra beyond anything I could achieve for several months after it. But I think the issues you've stated in this essay are the biggest and wisest things written. In everything you do you are the great man of your age – even in your absurd begging letters – and the shy mad way you write to English gentry posing as artists (Sitwell) and praise their shitty little books about their governesses and aunts.

But what is so exciting Henry is that the structure of your prose has changed, to judge by this essay. It has become limpid and crystalline in structure without losing any of its fluency at all. The stream of images – often too cloying in their strength – has been incorporated into the formal *line* of the theme; no more digressions – but real *cadenzas*. I am dying to see some major book by you at this stage. It should blister and crackle and vomit without any sign of effort; you seem to know your own strength now and don't have to try – wonderful feeling.

Seferis has just returned from London after a short trip and I hope to see him here this evening; we shall have a real talk over some wine and I'll show him all these carbons and things you have been sending. It is curious that he is practically in the same state as I am – sort of exhaustion. In fact though he is my best friend in Egypt we almost never meet. It's as if meeting people who have real human demands to make of one is too tiring – or perhaps too guilt-making since we are both involved in this web of idiocy and panic – and I don't see what sort of political future waits for Greece. It only affects me inasmuch as I hope to live there and recover from this wave of world neurosis. What about you? You must I feel come back and see that landscape once more. Spend a quiet year going round and tasting it all. Then I think we could get in touch with Mulk Raj Anand and ask him to give us the names of friends so that we could move off slowly towards Tibet? It's more than ever clear that Tibet is winning the war – this war and the next half dozen. [. . .]

News of Katsimbalis: he is thin but talkative as ever. Gives public readings of his pet poets every week. Tsatsos, by the way, is out and arrived last week. Soon we shall be seeing them all.

And you too I hope – very soon –

Love and admiration   Larry

Durrell is apparently referring to the essay by Miller published as *Murder the Murderer: An Excursus on War* (1944), but Miller had also sent him 'Of Art and the Future', which had appeared in *Life and Letters Today* (March 1944).
ATS: Auxiliary Territorial Service.

*Alexandria, *Egypt*   [September 1944]

Dear Henry –   Grand to hear from you again so soon – yes, the books are getting through, sanctified no doubt by the Embassy address. As a matter of fact there is only *political* censorship, and as I am on the side of the angels I guess you can send me anything. *Pierre* I look forward to; I'm absolutely bowled over by Groddeck's *The Book of the It* – it's simply terrific. I have written England to send you a copy – I know you'll want to keep it like Nijinsky's diary. Sorry I made those errors in my piece on you; but I remember you being cross-examined in Villa Seurat by an intelligent Yankee who was amazed at the things you said you had never tried to read. Perhaps you were bullshitting him – "taking the lead" as Joe says. Anyway, annotate the damned piece and knock hell out of me in the asides. Just re-read the *Hamlet* Letters again. Wonderful things in them. I am coming alive slowly. The last three years has been a dull nightmare. I'm itching to write something; have just finished a little book on Greek landscape, and am about to start in with a straight narrative about some people who get lost in the womb. I feel stiff and out of practice and need the sheer fun of writing a couple of books – bad books too – before I can come back into focus on the Book of the Dead. Got some marvellous dialogues for it – and an iron-frame plot. Shifted the action to Alexandria and made the two central characters twins. But I haven't enough force to work on it even if I had the leisure. How painful it is to write from the nervous system. I shrink from it inside. I often feel that I sprained my soul on *The Black Book* and it will take some time to get strong again. Turkey, Palestine, Syria – *nothing* – an intellectual desert. The papers so bad you could not believe it: sheer waste of time to send you. But I am sending you a set of *Personal Landscape* (Cairo) our paper. And *Fountaine* (Algiers) which is very good. Met a grand Frenchman yesterday called Etiemble – great admirer of yours – teacher at Harvard – and is writing about you for South American papers. I'll get names and addresses from him for you.

What else? I am going to Greece sooner or later – most everyone is there already – must be wonderful walking in that blue light again, Seferis and Katsimbalis. I've sent the latter all kinds of messengers – some by parachute – with all the news about you and ourselves.

The air-conditioned MSS has just arrived. Haven't had time to do more than glance at it. But I enjoyed the Maldoror jest – but not the article on Fowlie, which seemed to me weak and dispirited as writing and didn't tell one very much about him. Never mind. The big things are important and I'm getting down to the *Nightmare* after lunch.

Hope that this bloody war will end soon now and we can start starving in our own dignified way – not behind *guichets*. Writing to Fred too – but have no answer yet. The weather is sour and damp and the doctors order me to a good climate. I hope it's Greece and soon. But keep writing me at the PUBLICITY SECTION, BRITISH EMBASSY, CAIRO and everything will be forwarded in the diplomatic bag I guess.

[signed only with sketch of a head with annotation:]
"Elephantiasis of Egg-Bag or Views of the Rockies"

[P.S.] I am going to send you some of *my* water-colours.

*Wash. D.C.   12/13/44

   Dear Larry –
Got more letters from you recently & will probably answer in full when
I get to Colorado – a few days hence. What happened is this – in New
York I ran across a 21 year old Polish girl (Lepska) and I'm taking her
back to Big Sur with me as my wife. Things have been hectic ever since
I left California. Have visited colleges in half a dozen states. Now en
route for the open spaces. Cheerio & look for a big letter very
soon.   Henry

*Big Sur   Feb. 18th '45

   Dear Larry,
I've been looking through your recent letters and pulling out all the
queries you raise. There's so little time to write a real letter any more,
what with the fan mail, the water colors, and the unfinished books.
First let me tell you of a letter I received from a soldier in Paris recently
– one of many similar ones – in which he speaks of seeing all the
Obelisk books in the Paris book store windows – rue de Rivoli and rue
de Castiglione particularly. Your *Black Book* was there and two of
Anaïs'. The exchange is low and the soldiers are buying them up like
mad, he says. I had a letter from Kahane's son, Maurice, some months
ago, too, saying he had continued business all through the war, was I
writing any more books for him, and could he do my books in French
now? He changed his name during the war to M. Girodias, and the
name of the firm is now Les Editions du Chêne – 16 Place Vendome, as
before. The Germans did not destroy the books, nor any of my private
possessions I left with him. I think you might get in touch with him –
maybe there are some royalties due us. And maybe too you could get
The Black Book published in French. At any rate, it's good to know
there are copies to be had. In England they tell me the censors don't
bother seizing importations now – too busy with military censorship.
So you could pass the word along to your friends who want to own
copies. I'm going to give him *The Rosy Crucifixion* to publish, when I
finish it – which won't be for a long time. [. . .]
   You know, the English take about everything I send them. It's
amazing. I've burst out there in the magazines and anthologies like a

                                                     177

sun flower. I think that's where I'm going to get my real royalties. The three books Laughlin printed here have all come to a second edition now, the *Colossus* too. How many copies of the *Cancer* were printed nobody knows – probably ten thousand or more. Now soon the *Capricorn* comes out, privately printed – also *Aller Retour N.Y.* (Imagine that since returning to America I have never seen a copy of the latter for sale anywhere. Not one copy!)

You ask if Anaïs has printed the whole diary. My God, no. She hasn't even done one. Abandoned the idea completely. I don't really understand it. Once I had enough money to get at least one volume printed, but she didn't rise to the bait. She's not going to be able to go to Europe either until next year – can't get a passport. Nobody can, except a favored few. You can see already what a rush there is going to be. All the refugees will be returning, that's certain. And all the expatriates whom the war drove back here. [. . .]

And do send me some of your water colors, yes! I wonder how you paint now. I'm painting more than ever, and quite seriously. Last year I made over three hundred, all of which I disposed of. I've had a half dozen shows in different cities. [. . .]

Just had word yesterday from my publisher, Bern Porter, that *The Happy Rock* has at last gone to press, and that your piece is the first in the book. Also from Patience Ross that she likes yours best and hopes to find an editor for it soon in one of the English magazines. [. . .]

In Washington, when there, I made eight records for the Library of Congress – for the archives, at their request. I read from *Capricorn* and *Black Spring*. Quite an experience.

I see that in an old issue of *Horizon* Alex Comfort speaks highly of your poems, in a blurb. I only lately read something of his – an anarchistic diatribe, which I enjoyed hugely. Is he a friend of yours? And whatever became of Dylan Thomas? And your brother Leslie, and your sister?

Going to bed now. End of a quiet Sunday at Big Sur. My Polish wife, Lepska, has just been telling me stories of Poland. I've only learned two words of that language so far – Good Morning: Sounds like Gin Dobrie. At this writing the Russians are only 30 miles from Berlin. Seems impossible that the war should last another three months even. Unless England and America suddenly take it into their heads to fight the Russians. Every day we take a sun bath. It's like Spring now. Amazing climate and gorgeous scenery. Something like Scotland, I imagine. It's one of the few regions in America you would like. I must describe it to you some day. One of the features of it are the vultures. The other is the fogs. And the third is the lupine which is like purple velvet over the mountain sides. There are also four crazy horses which I meet on my walks through the hills. They seem glued to the spot. And two of them are always in heat. I have a wonderful cabin, you know, dirt cheap – ten dollars a month. I have a young wife (21), a baby on the way probably, food in the larder, wine à discrétion, hot sulphur baths down the road, books galore, a phonograph coming, a radio also coming, good kerosene lamps, a wood stove, an open fireplace, a shower, and plenty of sun – and of course the Pacific Ocean, which is always empty. Alors, what more? This is the first good break I've had since I'm living in America. I open the door in the morning, look towards the sun rising over the mountains, and bless the whole world, birds, flowers and beasts included. After I have moved my bowels I take the hound for a walk. Then a stint of writing, then lunch, then a siesta, then water colors, then correspondence, then a book, then a fuck, then a nap, then dinner, and so to bed early and up early and all's well except when I visit the dentist now and then. So write soon again, and

cheerio! Henry

*BRITISH INFORMATION OFFICE,
1, RUE TOUSSOUM, ALEXANDRIA   [c. 1 March 1945]

Dearest Henry: I have just finished *Sunday After the War*. It contains some absolutely peak writing – the greatest of the age. Particularly the bits from *The Rosy Crucifixion* which lift one clear off one's feet. How purely integrated you are now with your own style; it comes like clear water from a well. And yet it hasn't lost an ounce of the power and glory. I sent you a complete file of PERSONAL LANDSCAPE about a week ago and a novel written by a young Egyptian which has points. Apart from this there is a horrid blank empty silence; the whole Middle East is a figurative and literal desert in which only the most awful literary blooms flower. This is due I think to the censorship, which under the guise of military secrets has now become an instrument which successfully blankets ANY AND EVERY FREEDOM OF EXPRESSION that might seem a trifle unorthodox. Operated as it is by nature's middle-men – the low-souled and the sneaking – it makes one's work as a writer and a thinker useless. Hence one doesn't write any more and tries hard not to think. I never explained my long silence to you because it would have involved discussing Greek politics in the Middle East, and I didn't want to accumulate a dossier of indiscretions. But as you can see from the present results, we have been behaving with an ignoble and stupid unimaginativeness – making my blood freeze slowly for years now. The result is now written so clearly that even the blind can read – we are defending the Acropolis caryatid by caryatid against the rest of Greece. Not that the EAM is any less totalitarian than Metaxas was; but it contains the best of the ancien Venezeli like Katsimbalis and Theodore; and the thought of British troops fighting them – you remember how much they were Europeans, how much they gave in the last war to join Venezelos and overturn the sneaking Bulgarophile régime – it makes one's blood run cold. But what an extraordinary piece of history, what a final curtain on the smallest country in Europe; withstanding Fascism in the field, nazidom in the home, and now the reaction on the part of the people they love and admire most. I will write a history of the last four years just as soon as I am free of this job.

Meanwhile I am waiting here to be posted to Rhodes, which will be a very calm backwater. "The Island of Roses"; I'm told it is as beautiful as Corfu but in a dry Aegean way. Shall I get you a little villa by the sea; you know, three cypresses all dusted with gold; a white wall with fishing nets drying on it; steps down to the sea; a little red boat with Aegean eyes painted on the prow; and a pergola of ice-green grapes where we can write our heads off and build the new world of The Overself? I'm sending you the new poems and the book on Corfu. Don't judge me by this rubbish. I have been like a prisoner writing on the wall with a rusty nail in order to keep sane. A little Aegean sunlight and freedom will give me the peace to undertake THE BOOK OF THE DEAD. It's all written in my head. They are liberating everyone everywhere. Soon it will be my turn. Then UNRRA will feed me and we'll all live happily ever after by monopoly capitalism. Love

Larry.

EAM: National Liberation Front.
UNRRA: United Nations Relief and Rehabilitation Administration.

[Postcard with Miller photograph; annotation:] From the Green House at Beverly Glen! (L.A.)

Dear Larry –
By all means reserve me that little villa by the sea on the Island of Roses – or any Mediterranean isle! No book, no poems received yet. Anxious to read the one on Corfu. Can I write direct to Greece soon – to Katsimbalis and the others? Where is Seferis these days? My warm greetings to him. Am hot to get more good Egyptian books, like Cossery's.

Henry

*BRITISH INFORMATION OFFICE,
1, RUE TOUSSOUM, ALEXANDRIA   June 22. 1945

Henry I wonder if this isn't the quickest way to reach you via London. I have just got back after ten days in Rhodes which is lovely rather in the Corfiot way, with Turkish mountains backing the skyline and the sea hushed and blue. The Italians have a great reputation as restorers and so on, but really they are super perverters of scenery. This tiny island is a mass of little nooks, artfully cornered off with walls and gardens, and splashed madly with purple bougainvillaea; a little too conscious. Meanwhile the imposing waterfront lacks a single taverna or fruit stall; dull faced public buildings, each on a huge scale, face the sky in a mock-medieval manner. Theatres too big to hold anything at all, modern cinemas and law-courts on a Roman scale. Here a superstructure of Italian officials live a heavily upholstered life in steam-heated apartments, converted from medieval buildings. Charming, charming, you repeat; but what a white elephant for a poor state to inherit. The poor Greek patters about in clogs or bare feet, and wonders what the hell it is all about; why, the lavatories actually work and the phone. There is a decorative order and prettiness which must drive him crazy. Of course all this will last about a week after the Greeks get in; then the pig-sties and confusion will begin.

I am not sure I'm going yet so when you write please do so to the above address. Our Egyptian anthology is out and I've asked Tambimuttu to send you on a copy, also Groddeck has been sent. Hope you

enjoy him; particularly his refusal to write professionally and his Hera-
clitean adaptation of Freud which makes organic sense of the discoveries
as a system, instead of a mechanistic attachment to Victorian physics.
Ach, I can hardly express myself any more; I've got a book brewing but it
will take time. Somehow I must escape from this nightmare of working
for a living. New books of poems coming; I sent you on the page proofs.
But it feels like the stubborn end of an epoch, and the new world refuses
to get born. I'm sick to death of uniforms and idiocy.

More soon.
Larry

*BIG SUR – CALIFORNIA   July 2, 1945
Dear Larry –
Yes, everything has come now, thank god! The only thing is to find time
to read. I take your poems to the woods now, when I go for my
constitutional. They read well there. I'll write you more of all this later.
Right now I'm like a mad man – writing my bloody head off. Just
finished my Rimbaud – one of my best, I think.
    Incidentally, I had a letter from Etiemble. He refers to my "explosive"
pieces which you showed him. Can't imagine what he refers to. (Unless
the *Murder* pamphlet.) But I *am* getting more explosive each day. I'll
blow myself up at this rate. Wish I could send you copies of every thing
as they come off the machine. Wish too I could send you some of the
recent Bern Porter publications – especially *Semblance* – but he doesn't
give me a *single* free copy, not even for myself – and these cost *me* $5⁵⁰
each! What publishers I dig up!
    (Girodias wrote that a French publisher is interested in doing *The Black
Book*. That's good news.) George [Leite] is waiting impatiently for word
to go ahead from your agents. True, he has no money. But he can *borrow*
it for this undertaking. There is a demand for the book. Anyway, he's
doing Cossery's. That's good too. I love Cossery's work. Very close to
myself, I find – or imagine. Now reading his second book – even better, I
think. What an Egypt he pictures! Frightful. Even worse than Gogol's or
Dostoievsky's creatures, don't you think?
    Valeurs (No. 1) came. I like it very much – what a different tone from
our Anglo-Saxon dribble! (Etiemble is the chief or sole reviewer, it
seems. A fire-eater.)

Fred is in Belgium – maybe now in Germany. I get cables & letters from one publisher after another in Europe. (See that Girodias places *The Black Book* in Italy – with *Mondadori*. The best publisher there.) Every thing is hay-wire over there. It must be even worse than we imagine. And where's the end? I think another war is brewing – within next three years or so.

Best to Seferis & Katsimbalis. I wrote Seferis.

How can I get published in Egypt? It sounds more alive to me than America. I don't mind if they rob me. What of your family – little Gerald? I hope they're all alive. And all the best to Gipsy Cohen. *Gewalt!*

Henry

This study of Rimbaud, 'When Do Angels Cease to Resemble Themselves?', appeared in two parts in the New Directions anthologies of 1946 and 1949.

New Loves
New Ventures

The autumn of 1945 promises marvellous rewards for Larry and Henry, the deserved harvests of many years of impatient labour. Although Durrell was to make generations of readers long for the exotic Alexandria of his *Quartet*, he himself is aching to get away, preferably to Greece. He secures the post of Public Information Officer on Rhodes, an assignment which comes with a staff, a printing plant, freedom to publish newspapers in as many languages as he can manage. Durrell is, as he claims, 'damn near' being the governor of the Dodecanese Islands. He is able to bring Eve Cohen along as secretary – even though it means the intercession of friends in the Embassy to outwit her disapproving father. It is as exciting as an abduction from a seraglio! Soon he and Eve are settled in the bougainvillaea-surrounded Villa Cleobolus; he is in the Greek world again; his work is exciting, and Eve, 'with her seven languages', is an able assistant. He has 'The Book of the Dead', *The Alexandria Quartet* in embryo, mapped out in his head and waiting to be born.

Miller's prospects seem almost as good. Late in 1944 he had met two Polish sisters in New York, and on 18 December of that year he had married the younger of the two, Janina Lepska, twenty years old and a Bryn Mawr graduate. At nearly the same time that Durrell is beginning his idyllic life on Rhodes with Eve, Miller is awaiting the birth of the first child of this marriage. (His only previous child, Barbara, was born to Beatrice Wickens Miller twenty-five years earlier.) Miller is going through a tremendously productive period; everything he submits for publication is being accepted, back titles are being reprinted and his water-colours are selling. American soldiers in Paris buy so many of his books that he finds himself briefly a millionaire – in francs, which he cannot take out of France, while the US Government is denying visas for 'non-essential' travel, preventing him from spending his fortune.

*Public Information Officer,
MOI BMA RHODES, DODECANESE.   [c. October 1945]

Not exactly Governor of these twelve islands, but damn near; I have just been up to Leros, Cos (a lovely Epidaurus kind of island) and Simi. Am living in quite a barrack of a hotel on the sea-front getting ready to enjoy my first Greek winter for six years; can't tell you what a feeling of a cloud lifting to get out of Egypt. I face everything equably now: even the burden of producing a couple of hundred quid to get the divorce cleared off. I've been working like a beaver. *Prospero* is out and a copy is coming to you. It will bring back many old memories I hope, with its portraits. Theodore and Spiro etc. Too bad you never met the great Zarian or old Dr Palatioano, a fine mythological old man on whom I modelled the count. He had the skull of his mistress on a velvet square before him on the writing desk; liked holding it up to the light and talking to it. Now my dear Henry I'm on the last lap of the race, finishing the labyrinth book – six people lost in the labyrinth of Crete which is still inhabited by the Minotaur. I have deliberately chosen a cheap novel formula and am trying to say urgent things in little squirts through the seven or so people involved. A rotten book but with some small lucid moments and one or two good lines. The new poems CITIES PLAINS AND PEOPLE are due for next Jan. They are really GOOD, for once I need not be ashamed, very good. Now, my dear Henry, I am sitting in this charming medieval building with the hum of linotypes; my office is very lovely, built round a medieval courtyard and draped in bougainvillaea. The Italian daily has been set up, the front page matrix of the Greek is finished, and the weekly Turkish is being censored. Cohen with her seven languages is busy upon them now looking charming black and smooth.

> Cohen à cheval
> Au bidet noire montée
> Discute en grand dame
> La vie chère
> La grand guerre
> Et nos âmes tourmentées.

I am beginning to write little things in French now, and in Greek. I feel a wonderful fluency. Just as soon as I finish this fucking little book I'm going into a retreat to sort out all the material for the BOTD (Tibetan way of spelling the book of the dead). By January this job ends and I shall be thrown on the mercies of the wide and welcome world. Propose to bum up to Athens in a caïque and get some little job to keep alive while I spend several years of really close work on a book. Young Kahane writes me nicely from Paris – would be interested in the BOTD. It's like a ray of light opening. I shall base myself on Paris, mother of all us torn and speaking creatures, and forget the British and US market until they choose to come on off their perch. Ah Henry Europe is so far upside down that it will take a few years to settle. I reckon we have five years before the atom war – can't we all meet and create a little of the warmth and fury of the Villa Seurat days; a glass of wine and pleasant soft furry murder of typewriters going; Anaïs in her cloak and pointed ears; the letter to Nijinsky; Fred and Madame Kalf; Betty Ryan and Reichel. It is all fixed now inside like a kind of formal tapestry – you with the skylight open, typing in your hat, and little Joe unwrapping the cheese with delicate fingers murmuring "Ja Ja das ist gut"; and do you remember Mr Chu? And the chiropodist whose legs you cut off before throwing her into the Seine in No 2 of *The Booster*; and Valaida Snow? Have you a set of *Boosters*? And Queneau and that hideous papal emissary Montgomery Belgion? And Herbert Read in the black muffin of a hat giving his young son an ice at the Deux Magots, and how you insisted on paying Chez Henriette to the acutely British discomfort of same? And how furious you were when you tried to sell *Booster* No 1 to some bastard in a bar and he was insulting about it? And those long icy walks by the Seine with Anaïs in her cloak through the garish sulphurous ruins of the Great Exhibition into the Latin Quarter to find the little street where Dante wrapped his feet in straw and where you found only the suicide MAX? And those strange evenings on *La Belle Aurore* with Moricand the astrologer? And walking in the Louvre like mad angels? And the sudden scream that Soutine gave one night? Had he discovered another painting? And Fred writing letters to himself in that little dog-leg room, starving to death; and Edgar talking talking talking talking, his noble pure face caught up in a tic of anguish like a curtain pulled back. And Buffie Johnson and the whores and that terrible .... It was a complete finished little epoch. I remember the particular smell of the *Tropic* typescript, and the early novel you showed me. And lovely black little Teresa Epstein at the Closerie de Lilas; hell, what are we going to put up against all that now that the war is over? I think Athens is a convenient mythopoeic centre with Paris coming up all the time. Do you plan to return to Europe now you are a father? By the way, boy or girl? You will make a charming crazy father. Now of course that you've got a basic salary and are a free man you could I suppose travel without panic and pain. I've just lost the tiny private income I had [. . .]. Never mind . . . .

Just got a letter from Curtis Brown about *The Black Book*; he says that Laughlin asked for first refusal two years ago and he's trying to clear him off the track in order to give Leite the OK. I've made it clear that I don't give a milk shake for Laughlin that shyster impresario of bad work.

Yesterday we went out in the big German office car; Romilly Summers, Eve and I, and walked right into the landscape carrying our food. Romilly is another old greekite and adores the Colossus. We sat under a tree and drank red wine and talked about friends past and present and watched the blue whipping sea bursting against Turkey in great muffled blows, and the sinking crusts of islands northward. We talked about Xan Fielding, who was a secret service agent in Crete for two years, and nearly died countless deaths. His last escape: in Gestapo prison in France, due to die at six a.m. A Polish girl, his accomplice, managed to get on to the RAF which BOMBED THE FRONT DOOR OF THE PRISON FROM LOW LEVEL AND KNOCKED THE WHOLE PLACE DOWN ABOUT HIS EARS, and he escaped. Ambushed in Crete many times on the end of a tommy gun. Finally his unit walked off with the German general in charge of Crete – fantastic piece of cloak and dagger like a bad novel. He writes from Kalimpong, Tibet, asked for news of you. I've given him your address. They were going to drop him in Tokio if the war hadn't ended. We talked of Seferis and Katsimbalis and the others. And we drank swingeing great draughts of wine and ate our bully and bread, and heard the slow clonk of sheep-bells and the wind in the olives. Something in this landscape talks to one – a sculptural utterance. Hush. Maillol is dead.

Well, Henry, that's all for now. Drop us a line when the wind blows our way. When shall we be meeting again? Soon I hope, in Greece or Paris, Tibet or Damascus. It's all one. I belong equally everywhere now. Am happy.

love larry

MOI: Ministry of Information; BMA British Military Authority

Durrell had written to Nijinsky during the Paris period; Madame Nijinsky replied in a kindly fashion, but stated that her husband's health would not permit the requested visit. Patrick Leigh Fermor and his group, not Fielding's unit, captured General Kreipe on Crete. The story is told by W. Stanley Moss in *Ill Met By Moonlight* (1950) and by Dilys Powell in *The Villa Ariadne* (1973).

*Big Sur, Calif.   Dec. 17th [1945]

Dear Larry,

I just realize how close Xmas is and what a slim chance this has of reaching you in time. For weeks I have been carrying an envelope around addressed to you but never had a chance to write. Have been back and forth to San Francisco several times. The baby was finally born – a month late – at Berkeley – Valentin Lepska Miller. She's a little beauty, an angel, and I'm madly in love with her. Gives no trouble at all. Sleeps perpetually and hardly ever cries. A real back-to-the-womber! Now in a few days we move to another cabin. A dump, by comparison – originally a convict's shack. Like one of those photos you will see in *Nightmare* when you get your copy. I take it Porter sent you a *Happy Rock*. Three more books coming out shortly. A flood of books this year. The Paris thing looms big, but I can't seem to connect with the money – no fault of Girodias, however. If it comes to the worst, I'll invest that money in a house and land in southern France. And another later in Greece. I'll build here in the spring. One must have a number of homes these days in case one is bombed out. (I enclose an article by Dorothy Thompson – she writes in this vein more and more.) Nowhere does one hear of hope or optimism. The whole thing is a shambles and a fiasco. It is getting to be precisely as Spengler predicted, with Germany the cancerous core. [. . .]

I've had a couple of wonderful letters from Giono recently. His *Jean le Bleu* is coming out here in English soon – I'll get you a copy. If you can get hold of Hanley's *No Directions*, do! It's a loulou of a book. I think the edition is exhausted – but someone in London might pick it up in a second hand store. [. . .]

Those post cards from Rhodes excite me enormously. You must indeed be happy now. And how does Gipsy Cohen like the change of scene? I wonder when in hell we will be able to travel. Still no hope. And the news of conditions abroad is appalling. No infant could survive the change of scene – and diet.

It's glorious to hear that you are on the last lap of the labyrinth book.

You seem to have a bag full up your sleeve. I haven't done a stitch of real writing in eight weeks. But with the move we now make everything is set for work. I have a little studio near the house, made from a horse shed – like one of Van Gogh's habitations. Am delighted with it. Made of driftwood and corrugated iron. Am going to start fishing soon from the back porch. Will send you photos shortly of the interiors of both places.

Have just been reading Krishnamurti – *Ten Talks*. Will try to get you a copy – think it will interest you. Expect to visit him very soon – he is about 150 miles away.

In the next few days I'll make you your Xmas present – a water color which I have long promised you. You will see if I have made any improvement. Probably not!

Well, cheerio and have a good Xmas if you can. I wonder how Claude Houghton and Osbert Sitwell will spend this Xmas. And Hans Reichel and David Edgar? Anaïs writes that when I give her the money I've promised she will start printing the first 20 volumes of her Diary. That's good news.

To think that I have over 3,000 pounds waiting for me in Paris and can't touch it – what irony! When I pay the mail man to-day for food, kerosene, laundry, etc. I will have left exactly six dollars and some cents. But I never worry about the money problem. It always comes when I need it. I could write a wonderful luminous essay on Desire. Desire versus Craving. Merry Xmas! And to you too, Tiny Tim!

    Henry

*MINISTRY OF INFORMATION,
DODECANESE ISLANDS
ADMINISTRATION, RHODES   JANUARY 1ST 1946

HENRY   HAPPY NEW YEAR FOR YOU THREE. Your latest letter is written while waiting for the baby. By now the little titan will be born. [. . .] I've just come back from PATMOS where Cohen and I spent Xmas with Father Porphirios. A little white island; crowned by the battlemented monastery with its white walls and strange turrets – like something built by Genghis Khan. Shattering whiteness and play of light. Like stepping into the silver of a mirror, or into the heart of a crystal. From the reception room you look out and everywhere islands in a glittering sea, like loaves of dark bread. While we were sitting talking to the Abbot and eating the fine lunch he had prepared for us, the sky slowly darkened, swelled, became bitumen grey and then black with clouds; the sea like a lake of pitch. It was like a chapter from the Apocalypse. Then the rain broke green from rents in the cloud, breaking open pencils of light which played on the darkness like the beam of searchlights in close focus. Strange moving pencils of green rain racing across the sea like fingers. And thunder struck out of the silence, like a huge metal gong, and the Abbot had his voice cut off – as though his tongue had been pulled out by the roots. A marvellous mysterious haunted island. You must visit it. You approach it along a dark waterway of broken rocks like teeth, and far, like the white breast of a sail, you see the sugar loaf mountain with its white crown. Can't tell you what an impression the visit made on us. Beyond words. Wonderful library of ancient MSS scrolled and illuminated with dragons and horned heads.

HURRAH JUST GOT YOUR LETTER. SO IT'S A GIRL!!! WHOOPEEE! Many many congratulations to you Henry. I see the glorious future opening like a peacock's studded tail. I guess you earned it with every breath you've drawn. I must design the child a porringer at the local pottery!!!

This job is going to fold up on us in a little while and heaven only knows what the future may bring!!!! I just signed contracts for the labyrinth book in USA and England. Finishing the fucking thing at top speed. What a life! My total takings will go down the hungry throats of the lawyers. Never mind! I feel the big happiness advancing with cat-like tread upon me – the superlative silent murdering panther in its spotted coat, crouching to spring! Skoal!

larry

*Big Sur, Calif.   1/22/46

Dear Larry,

Had no chance to write you last few weeks due to moving. (Address still the same, however.) Only now I am at the ocean, right over it, writing you from a little hut which is my studio – the first real isolated studio I ever knew. It's marvelous. Nothing but sky, ocean and cliffs and mountains. Waves pounding under my feet – like dynamite. [. . .]

I was showing your post cards the other day to Angelino Ravagli who now lives with Frieda Lawrence. They are spending the winter here at Big Sur – took over a sort of medieval castle by the sea with some other friends of ours. Frieda is a wonderful person. We get on famously. She said to me once, "If only Lawrence had known you when alive! You would have been the very friend he was looking for!" (I wonder.)

I am expecting any day now to get a 2 acre piece of land from a neighbor at a cheap price – magnificent site on a high hill, overlooking every one. Couldn't ask for a better home site. If I succeed, I will start building this spring. Then if you want to come to America, we can put you up. I will try to build a guest house too. But think long before you decide to come to America! The novelty will wear off soon. Creature comforts you can have, but nothing else. You will dry up here in no time. I feel that Europe or Africa or China or India – any of these is better than America with her creature comforts. But if you want to make a visit merely, fine, any time! How good I am as sponsor I don't know. I think one has to have money in the bank for that. But we could think up some people who have when you are ready for it. [. . .]

Alors, cheerio! Happy days are coming. [. . .]

Henry

[P.S.] Am now exchanging water colors for wonderful art books and music records. What luck! Am getting every thing the heart desires. How is little Gerald? Does he continue to write? And your sister Margaret?

*MOI BMA RHODES MEF.   [c. mid-February 1946]

Henry my dear: I have just spent a week in Athens and am still bewildered by the warmth of my reception there: both from those I knew, and from all those unlikely people whose existence I had forgotten: the Institute porter, a girl-student, the kiosk man from whom I bought the paper and a pack of cigarettes every day, Andrew in whose little bar we drank so often. For the first day I was in a whirlwind of embraces and tears and kisses. And most wonderful of all, most mysterious, was that Athens was under deep snow: purple and bistre shadows under the Acropolis, steamy breath of oxen and men. I walked beside the Colossus in a daze listening to his great voice filling in the span of years that had separated us with stories of all they had passed through. Neither Katsimbalis nor Seferis have changed – though the world has changed a good deal round them. Athens is unbelievably sad, crowded, ill-housed, with money practically worthless and prices soaring; and yet in some singular way what they have gone through has made them gentle and friendly and sympathetic to each other as they have never been before. Even in George, behind the tremendous effervescence, you feel a repose and resignation – as of someone who has faced death in his imagination for a long time, so that it has detached him from the ordinary life – which is only after all the joy of expectation. Yet the stories are more wonderful than ever. When I next write I will tell you the story of Palamas' funeral – at which George suddenly shouted insults at the German embassy representative who was laying a wreath on the tomb, and began to sing the national anthem, then forbidden under pain of death. "Like a man in a nightmare . . . yes . . . ten thousand people . . . no one would sing . . . my voice broke on the top notes . . . eyes bulged . . . finished the first verse alone amidst a terrified silence of the crowd . . . I was trembling all over . . . Aspasia trying to shut me up . . . Seferis' sister pulling my arm . . . I felt as if I had gone mad, quite mad . . . Terrific hush in the crowd and everywhere people whispering 'By God! It's Katsimbalis . . . It's Katsimbalis . . .' I started the second verse alone . . . not a voice raised to help me . . . German looking round angrily . . . felt like a drowning man in the middle of that huge crowd . . . Then over opposite me saw a fat Corfiot friend of mine . . . fat man but a big rich voice . . . He joined in and we finished the second verse together . . . Then suddenly as if you had thrown a switch the roar of the crowd took it up and we sang it with tears running down our faces . . ." Of course after this demonstration George was in danger of being shot and was terrified for some time! His description of hiding here and there is very funny. And of course there are other wonderful stories. But I feel that in some peculiar way Athens is very sad and exhausted at the moment. Write to George Katsimbalis, care of THE BRITISH COUNCIL, Kiphissia Road, Athens, and to SEFERIADES, POLITICAL ADVISER TO THE REGENT, THE REGENCY, KIPHISSIA ROAD, Athens. Send them books, any and every kind. And if you have a few pounds from time to time send it to George to use at his own discretion to help Greek poets: many of them are starving, Sekilianos among them. I saw the little captain Antoniou too – he has been through it though he is as silent and smiling as ever. I'm afraid you will have to give Athens a year or two to settle down politically etc before you can think of going there. But keep in touch and don't be worried if they don't write; they are working sixteen hours a day and meet only rarely. But the intellectual hunger is terrific. [. . .]

I see your reputation is riding higher and higher these days; glory in your well-deserved security, your studio, infant and secretary; hope the new books follow through. You have a tendency to splay rather these days, which is perhaps the influence of the US. But the *Sunday* book is a big gun; the sound follows the flash! I would like to see the latest two big books. Are they finished? No time for more / Must work.

Love to you three
Larry

*PIO MOI BMA RHODES MEF.   [28 February 1946]

Dear Henry: It sounds most impressive! A studio and a secretary of your own! What next? But I'm happy for you – you've earned a little space and light round yourself. We are still here. Just spent a week in Athens, fearfully moving and at the same time saddening; I know my letters sound pessimistic but you must not believe that the war has changed anything: rather it has made everything *worse*. If the war was brought about by the ego-will-power nexus of feelings in man, you would expect a bit of a let up through sheer exhaustion. Not a bit. The bigots of right and left are eager as ever to get killing again – not aggregates this time – France, Germany etc but their *sisters and brothers*. It is X across the road who is to be liquidated now, and Y because he is a royalist and B because he is a liberal. There is murder in the air and real starvation to help it rationalise itself. The final spasm is yet to come. And we are so tired – with this huge slice out of our lives. I was 34 yesterday: and there is no hope of a quiet connected life as yet. No foothold at all. The Middle East which has been sitting neutral, over-eating and masturbating for six years, is just about to break into flames. England I cannot live in. France is down the drain. Meanwhile the real power-will-ego boys – the Communists – are sharpening their hatchets. By God, you don't know how lucky we are in the type of civilization that bred us – Anglo-Saxons. If you could only see Europe! No, if I come to USA it will be to become a citizen. Land of the free! I know, I know, it's all rubbish. But there's not a *trace* of the world we think about on the horizon. Read what's coming out of Paris – the existentialistes! Pfui! It's all the same will-ego-action business; its logical end is in action not non-action – just as surrealist theory ends in the decoration of the Galeries Lafayette by Dali and the covers of *Vogue*. Believe me, there's something to be said for America; she buys out the artist, gelds him, and puts him on show. It's fair criticism, after all. It shows up the bad artists quicker!

I have been reading the second of Groddeck's books; just the world for it, this shining Greek light, with Hippocrates' Cos a blue blur on the horizon. I suppose you haven't had time to read the book yet. Don't be worried if at first it looks like a popularisation of Freud. That is the deception. It is the rearrangement of the Freudian concepts into a philosophic system in which the individual sees all round himself. The IT concept is TAO. "The sum total of an individual human being I conceive of as a self unknown and forever unknowable; and I call this the IT as the most indefinite term available, without either emotional or intellectual associations. The IT-hypothesis I regard not as a truth – but as a useful tool in work and life . . . I assume that man is animated by the IT, and that the assertion 'I live' expresses a small and superficial part of the total experience, 'I am lived by the IT'." In other words the mechanical view is replaced by a vitalist view. It is interesting in this book to read a long eulogy by Keyserling – whom Groddeck cured in a week of a relapsing phlebitis – in which he says that Groddeck of all men reminded him of Lao Tzu in his application of the Chinese idea of non-action. I do hope you take some afternoon off to really study the Groddeckian system. I can see what a tremendous effect it will have in the future – for the future belongs to Groddeck. Freud's part is the calculus. Groddeck's the attitude. Ah! if only we had known about him in Paris! *This* is all that we felt was missing from Howe and Rank and Jung! I am getting Eve to type out a wonderful bit about death from this book, which I think is not in the one I sent you. Do find out whether these books have ever hit the USA. They are quite unknown in England – though published by Daniel! Meanwhile Adler, Jung etc all have their fan clubs. Groddeck was asked to allow the formation of a fan club in every country! Refused! Hence this oblivion. Refused to have disciples! And indeed how could one have with a philosophy like that!

Wild March weather! Maddening south-wind! Would like something to read! Of course you would have done Lawrence a world of good: but do you think he would have been able to know his own master – for after all your work pulverises Lawrence's philosophy like an eggshell; I know, I know; he's a very great writer and no one can touch his *gifts* – but I'm talking about his abdominal philosophy. Been trying to write an essay on your work – "the critic's role is to save the work of art from the artist"! But I've torn up two attempts and am re-reading the *Hamlet* letters. You know, in some ways, you are really a wickedly careless writer! As if you can't afford to be! I'd give a bushel of split infinitives to write even "Reunion in Brooklyn" – a wonderfully moving, diamond-clear job. I am going up to Athens next week and will speak to Seferis about the little book. My trunks should have arrived from Kalamata by then and perhaps the books of yours and the little commonplace book will be safe! I hope so. Don't be surprised if you don't hear from them. They are simply hemmed in by their gloom. They never even answer my letters – and I'm only six islands south. I have to send messengers to ask for answers. I sent off a picture of Katsimbalis and myself which should please you. There's a good deal about you in the new *Valeurs* which they are sending you. Remorseless steady rise – like the rings in water from a boulder thrown in! No, don't worry about US entry. It would be easy on British quota. But I can't move until Xmas. Eve has no passport – another fruit of the Arabic world you think sounds so nice. I feel like a crusader when I think of Egypt. I'd gladly put an army corps into the country and slaughter the lot of those bigoted, filthy, leprous bastards! There! That's what taoism does for one in the XXth century.

There may be a chance of my getting a job in Athens some time. If so I'm going to take it and retain a little villa in Rhodes where I can store books, water colours etc. I sent Reichel a note. I'm so happy to hear that your fish-man is alive.

Just been writing a little diary to try and make some money and have launched a few darts in the direction of the English intelligentsia which is really quite intolerable now. These critics elegantly shooting dialectical piss-pots off each others' heads at twenty paces.

Koestler – seems to be interesting you these days. *The Yogi and the Commissar* is interesting I think, but the novels much of a muchness. I hear he is in Palestine and intends to live there – finds Jewish civilization wonderful! Rex Warner is in Athens – I think you'd like him; very solid, warm-hearted Welshman a bit slow and conscious as a writer, but a generous, fine person – no bloody affectation; and eager to learn more about his craft – a quality which few writers have! The middle ranks in England have a certain validity and balance; it's the social snob-culture levels that are so putrid – these Sitwells and Connollys (have you seen HIS latest). An imitation of you (and what an imitation). It will make you laugh yourself sick! *The Unquiet Grave* it's called, pseudonym Palinurus! Mea culpa, he shrieks on every page, I am fat, slothful, and snobbish – and then appalled by such a degree of self-knowledge quotes a page of Ste-Beuve! He also quotes *you* – because these days one is out of the swim if one hasn't at least HEARD of you! If I don't stop this will turn into a novel! Skoal to you by the blue Pacific! And the infant – how is her it! Tell Lepska to look out for her portrait in the BOOK OF THE IT.

Larry

Reichel characteristically included in his paintings a representation of himself as a fish.

*Big Sur, California   Easter Sunday [21 April 1946]

Dear Larry –

If I don't write you this minute I never will. Have been putting it off for weeks, because I had so much to tell you. So much to answer. Your letters are marvelous – the only decent messages I get. But my nose is kept to the grindstone – receiving unwelcome visitors, answering stupid bores. You'd think I was the Dalai Lama! I can find no rest, no peace. No hide-out. They track me down like sleuths. All wanting advice or encouragement – sometimes just to touch me. I feel as though I were on exhibition. I ought to be in a cage on permanent view. This is the result of writing in the __?__ aorist (1st person historical singular). It's become such a problem that I am growing desperate.

So you still look to America with loving eyes! Well then, come and see it! I'll give you six months to get a belly-full of it. Perhaps less. Perhaps six weeks. Here you will see how meaningless is the full larder, the full wardrobe. You have never seen the desert – wait till you see America. [. . .]

Girodias came across with a partial sum of 300,000 frs. Not bad. Buying land, me boy. Hope to build an anchorage here. Then get out & travel – by rocket plane only. We now have a plane which flies from

Los Angeles to Paris in 12 hours. $240.00 for a passage. Cheap, I'll say. China in about 18 hours, I believe. About the same price. Like this I'll be seeing India & Tibet after all. And coming home for breakfast, be Jasus! My warm greetings to Gipsy Cohen. So glad you were able to smuggle her out. Have you seen the ghost of John the Revelator? What do you know – of interest – about J.C.'s life between the Resurrection and the Ascension?

I hope to write again soon. Am with you always. Cheerio!

Henry

*MOI BMA RHODES DODECANESE MEF   Sept 25. 46

Dear Henry and Lepska: Just got your long letter – realise from it that being a public figure isn't all jam. You will have to take a rest from your admirers. Still it's better than being unknown I guess – though I wonder whether the *Booster* days were not FREER and HAPPIER all round. [. . .] Things have been marvellous here. One is only wondering how long it's going to last. Have moved into Villa Cleobolus at last; two rooms, studio and bed room, bathroom and kitchen. It is smothered in trees which curve over it, and as you enter the gate the gloom of dense oleander branches envelops you; I can't tell you what wonderful peace and quiet it is, having a house of your own after so many years living from suitcases in hotels, or sharing flats with awful people. We have breakfast under a sycamore tree off pottery which we cast and painted ourselves at the local pottery. Life at times begins to get its old prismatic hue. I am casting about in my mind for the form for a verse play about Sappho – dealing with the problem of action and non-action: taking war as simply one of the types of destructive action since the EGO was let loose on the world . . . The great "I will" . . .

Was in Cairo recently and happened upon the Wassermann trilogy which is being sent over soon; they need, however, concentration, and so I'm waiting for the gloomy winter days to start. I don't know what is to become of us. My job ends with the handing over of these islands; there will be a British Council here but I don't think they'll give it. One says glibly "starve"! It's hard to starve. Now the food situation has settled down bad again; the market is stripped of everything, and the people are beginning to look pinched again. [. . .]

Meanwhile we are all screwed down here waiting for the atom bomb

. . . How long do you give it? The results at Nagasaki, as published in the British White Paper, were fascinating. Complete sterility the most interesting. Now read Groddeck's chapters on all human creations symbolising unconscious desires; we are able to set a positive term to the life of the human race. It's a great relief! I was afraid they were going on like this forever.

I'm hoping to go to Athens with Eve next month – and show her round; but to judge by the present disorders it will be wiser to stay here.

Love to you both . . . Stay in USA another few
years . . . You don't know what it's like . . .
You can't . . . I didn't until I left Egypt which
must be rather like the US is, fat, well-off,
selfish, self-seeking etc.

Larry

*MOI BMA RHODES DODECANESE MEF   [c. October 1946]

Henry: I am inundated with them – books! You must be paying a fortune in postage! [. . .]

By the way THEODORE's book is out! It's called CLIMAX IN CRETE and is a diary of the Cretan campaign where he was caught with his pants down – and is really a marvellous mirror of his quaint temperament! Botany and parachutists go hand in hand – at the most critical moments, when all seems lost, the camp about to be rushed, bullets flying, he breaks off to observe, "I noticed with surprise a remarkable specimen of the flora tinctulitis growing by the road and took a specimen to press in my album. Flora tinctulosis better known as verbena gladiola is a low-growing mucilagenous musk-ox with little affinity to the flora of Crete . . . . etc etc." While I am on the subject of Crete, we have just had Xan Fielding through on his way to England – a lovely week. He was living in Crete for 3 years as a spy you know – disguised as a shepherd! His adventures are really hair-raising; later he was captured by the Gestapo in France and condemned to death, escaping 3 hours before the execution. I've told him to write you. He seems to be shaping into rather a good writer. With him came a wonderful mad Irishman called Leigh Fermor who was also in Crete and who captured the German general commanding there, took to the mountains with him, and dodged the German army for 18 days before he was able to get the general to Egypt on a submarine! Really fantastic adventures. The two of them reading Dostoievsky in caves! Being ambushed etc etc and reciting poetry all day long. Leigh Fermor is quite the most enchanting maniac I've ever met. Speaks five languages really well. We sat up in my churchyard till three every morning reading aloud. Can't tell you what a wonderful time I had talking books – first time for years. Xan is very keen on your work, and remembers vividly a meeting in Athens; together we printed a little booklet of his poems here on the army press and this he is sending you from London. [. . .]

Meanwhile CEFALU is almost out – shit: two good pages you might care to read / rest you can hang in the lavatory. Its chief virtue is that it paid for my divorce!

> Send me a picture of the baby.
> Love to you both
> Larry

*Rhodes.   January 20 '46 [i.e., 1947]

Dear Henry –

Just been re-reading your *Sunday After the War* and the rather deplorable *Happy Rock* – for which much thanks. It is extraordinary that so few people are aware of the way you have broken through and torn the whole frame of Anglo Saxon literature apart – simply devastating: there is nothing left for us young writers except to become ourselves! The *Rock* book, by the way, is a wretched affair – quite unworthy of its object. What a talent you have for attracting the immortality-hunters, the moral crooks, to you! How freely you let them feed on your own good flesh! It makes my blood boil! You really shouldn't do it. But the question of critical attention *must* be faced squarely. Just as soon as I am through with the beastly little job I have in hand I propose to do a decent book about you – it seems yr books are very hard to get still and I am probably the only person who has read all the Cancer ones as well as the 2 early bad novels and the original *Tropic* MSS – so perhaps I can draw a clearer bead on you than anyone else. Anyway I propose to do something which will contain enough attacks on that literary species of hermaphrodite – the Sitwells and their little crowd of flunkeys, their *salon*! And Connolly and his fucking school of pseudo-angst extension lecturers! Just flicked in passing, but with barbs.

Dear Henry, I am very happy; being married some time this month to Gipsy Cohen here in Rhodes. I hope it turns out all right but I find rather a lack of confidence in myself these days. Feel rather hysterical. Guess I haven't got over the loss of *my* small daughter yet – *that's* the real crux. However we compose ourselves slowly around our pains like the oyster round the grains of sand – and out of it come pearls, black pearls – in the case of the oyster at any rate. So far I have shed only pus and lymph these six years, but the pearl is forming. I feel it. I send you a book about Nietzsche's mental breakdown with some of the insane letters. I know it will interest you. I always remember the time I brought you back Nijinsky's letters from London – how you took the book, opened it, and walked out of the room (crowded with merry makers) into the street – *there* you absently leaned against a lamppost and read it from cover to cover – or almost. Joe found you ½ hour later still there!

I have written to Joe and Anaïs – and to Reichel – I want to feel the old bonds come back out of numbness and separation and war. Hopeless nostalgia for the forgotten Paris – like a buried culture. How clearly I see you, Villa Seurat, cap-à-pie, hammering that hellish old typewriter of y^{rs} as if you were being hunted down the streets of Brooklyn.

Love to you both
Larry.

*from the new home – the property!
Big Sur   2/9/47 – A Sunday A.M.

Dear Larry,
[. . .] I'm sitting in the new studio this morning and it's raining like hell here. It's an old garage, transformed. The house – one large room, with a little annex for the baby, is quite simple and beautiful – almost Japanese in its austerity. I have 2½ acres, not five, as I once thought. And it's mostly hillside – but no matter. I bought the view – sea, wind, air, sky, stars, not land. Have enough to grow all the vegetables for twenty people – and by God, maybe we will begin doing that soon. This next war, which every one expects, will see the demolition of all the big cities, all the arteries. We may have to be self-sustaining.

Do you really still think of coming to America? I can never understand that. Believe me, food and comforts is not all. There is absolutely no life here – except animal life. I am afraid you would go mad with boredom.

We are 45 miles from nearest town – Monterey – which is a shit hole. I hardly ever go in. Don't care any more whether I see a movie or not. (I did see *The Open City* recently in S.F. – Italian movie – excellent too.) The thing is there are no people of any stature here – no one with whom to hold good conversation. (Except for Varda, the Greek.)

Did you know I am now in communication again with Conrad Moricand, the astrologer? He's in Vevey (Voltaire??) Switzerland and worse off than ever. The only ones who came out well seem to be Fred and Reichel, who says he needs nothing – "ni l'argent, ni vivres, ni rien". (Mystery)

I should have written Xan Fielding more at length, but have no heart to write long letters any more. And I never muster the courage to write Katsimbalis or Seferis, why I don't know. I allowed too long a silence to intervene. Besides, what can I say to people who are desperate? Last night I picked up a book on Tibet again – and at once am stilled, serene, full of acceptance. Maybe they are the last unspoiled people in the whole world today. Do you ever dream of going back there? [. . .]

About water colors . . . through Ben Bufano, the sculptor, I sold over $1200 worth recently. In all I made over $2,000 on them this last year. Not too bad, what? But am always dead broke, always in debt. London is supposed to be showing me now – at Reid & Lefebre's, if I can believe that scallywag Tambimuttu, who is really a pest and a nuisance. And now I am sending some to France. Céline is in Copenhagen, in prison there, I believe, and has lost 70 pounds. The French want to try him – and execute him, I suppose – but the Danes are trying to preserve his life. He says – "How could I be called a Fascist or collaborator? I despise the whole lot of you, no matter on which side." These are not his exact words – but the gist of it. And I can damned well believe him. There was a wonderful review of his *Les Beaux draps* by a French Jew named Milton Hindus (not Maurice) in a recent issue of *Angry Penguins* – you should see it – quite wonderful!

Well, according to Man Ray, the Existentialists and the Surrealists are now about to join in battle. They are both ausgespielt, in my opinion. Two cadavers fighting a foolish fray, what! What the world wants, I find, is – coffee, sugar, grease and warm clothing. The ideological warfare is over. Russia and America are dividing the world between them. Where England comes in I don't know yet. She'll probably throw her weight on the stronger side. But if we do fight, I am not at all certain we will win this time – it looks like a bloody stalemate to me – the Bear versus the Eagle.

Well, my love to Gypsy Eva, yourself, Cefalu, Patmos, that whole beautiful desperate world, which I would love so much to see. I have cleared the decks now, and am about to buckle down to finishing *The Rosy Crucifixion*. And paint a few more water colors. God be with you – and if it grows too desperate for you, why come over, but at your own risk! I don't recommend it. (Except to fatten up.)

Sending a recent photo (sans lunettes) by separate mail – "surface" mail, as they call it. Gave me a jolt to hear that word – means definitely we are in a new age. Cheerio!

Henry

P.S. The baby is now walking. She's adorable. Jabbers away in her own tongue – has the gift of gab, I see . . . . Cyril Connolly paid me a flying visit recently. I suppose we'll read about it in *Horizon*. About Cyril – what he really came for, I think, was to see the last of the lost race of *otters*, which are off this coast. But he saw none – and showed his disappointment keenly.

Milton Hindus was an American academic and a loyal friend to Céline during and after the author's Danish incarceration.

*Rhodes   [*c.* February 1947]

Dear Henry:

Just got your note saying you were off to consult doctors. I am worried about you. You have scaled all the heights around you and now you owe it to yourself to take things easy a bit. Of course fame tears one to bits by degrees – the immortality hunters of the day are human vultures hovering everywhere; the non-creating, non-conducting, non-life-giving snatch at the chance of a word or a letter or a meeting to shore up against their empty nothingness. And not the least of these vultures are the "literary" men – the Sitwells, and the Connollys who have become first rate journeymen at the trade, and who try and drag everything within the orbit of their sickly little salon lives: to fatten on the distinction of those they know rather than what they themselves can ever be. If I thought you were not too tired to open a book I would send you the *Life of Blake* I have just been reading – how his visions were always being pounced on and capitalised and derided by the "genteel" Hayley and the crooked Cromek; and how, conscious of his real place in the world, he lived happily in two bare rooms with his wife Kate. Another marvellous life is that of Burns – who was also taken up by the gentry, never slow to batten on talent to fatten their dull dinner-tables! You should read *his* diary. These two great republican figures are the only sympathetic characters in our literature save perhaps Shakespeare who minded his profits and pleaded illness whenever invited to court to be petted. I have now finished *The Happy Rock* and must confess that I'm horrified at the banality, vulgarity, non-comprehension and vapid twaddle of most of this! So this is the best that Americans can do with their own great men; pissy little anecdotes about what he ate and drank – all unrevealing, uninspiring. With the exception of me, Fowlie and Fred and perhaps one or two others, what a banausic morass of glue and self-advertisement! I had no idea when Porter wrote me that such a book was intended! I thought some serious evaluating essays – a book in which mine would be the short-est and most unknown contribution; stuck up in front there as a title piece all the defects and scrappiness of the essay show up. I wish I had made it four times as large again, and risked giving a portrait of you which might be a little less meaningless than those downright stupid or clever-clever bits of rubbish and patronage. [. . .]

I must say Henry that as a dissipater of talent and profit you are hard to beat; I have had letters from every poet and writer under sixteen in England asking for poetry or prose: and all ending up, "Mr Henry Miller has allowed us to issue his book so and so. It will be off the press soon!" There go your first copyrights! I think sympathy with cranks and young writers an admirable trait but I don't think you can *do* it. Unless you start a correspondence agency. And think of the waste! It's worse than being a psychoanalyst. My youngest brother Gerry is emerging as a poet. He is rather an iconoclast at present – feels he has to assert his individuality – thinks you a bad writer and me *terribly* bad! At least that's preferable to writing us all day asking for contributions to papers which barely exist and to print works in 45 copies upside down!

Dear Henry, you need a manager! You also need a bodyguard, and a mechanical voice which Lepska can turn on from time to time to shout: "Henry Miller! Are you giving of your best?" Or are you too busy corresponding with the under Librarian of the University of

Baltimore? I know. I'll get you a parrot and Lepska can teach it to say anything she thinks appropriate. Apropos *The Happy Rock* – the one element in your character which was a puzzle was the clowning! I don't mean the banter and joking and so on but the prancing and cavorting! You will find Nietzsche doing that – a marvellous observation in the book I sent you a few days ago! Now wasn't there a famous American clown called Joe Miller? Did you ever identify yourself with him – because sometimes you were the most stupendous clown I have ever seen – as great as Grock! Do you remember when you tried to make Mr Chu "take the lead"? One of the most memorable scenes I have ever witnessed outside *The Brothers Karamazov*; Chu the colour of an unripe cucumber. And the Confucius you had been reading out of on the table! Wonderful! I felt quite cracked myself. [. . .]

But I liked your poem. So far the best poem you have done is the Inanimate Object one printed in *Sunday After the War*. Why don't you write a play in this kind of incantatory way? I am half way thru a book about Rhodes – literary pisspot style to épater that beautiful English public which can always recognise style – but which would be scared shitless if there was any content. Side by side with it, to soothe my vanity, I am writing a play about Sappho which is I think both good drama and very profound writing. It's a sort of mind-at-the-end-of-sex play! *Really* ancient Greek in its roughness of narrative line – and yet as crude in a way and used up as a Cocteau. But no guying of the theme – no telephones, cigarettes, jazz music – I hope to God it comes off. I was asked to write it by a man called Fryer who says he will put it on in New York when it is ready – he has an arts theatre at his disposal. By the way Henry, there is one great man in America who I am sure will understand you and you him. I have never met him. He is called Auden, and beside him and Eliot the rest of us poets are pygmies! If he ever comes your way do meet him.

Now: no further apologies for the shit I am writing these days. This year I've had to fight clear of all kinds of financial traps and it's the only way I have managed it. My big book is there all right – it hasn't gone. I looked into myself yesterday and it was sitting there, smoking a pipe and looking back at me. I made a sign to it and asked it to wait a bit, and it nodded and smiled as one who might say, "In your own good time, boy, I'm in no hurry. I can wait."

Today we sign the papers and about February 14 we take the high dive Cohen and I. I am very happy in my luck! But no more for fear the Hubris boys are listening, and you know what they are!

> Love to Lepska and You
> Larry

Joe Miller was a comedian whose *Joke Book* (1937) is an historical compilation of humorous quips and anecdotes.

*Rhodes.   27 [February] 1947

> Henry:

In great haste. This week leaving for Egypt en route for England! Owing to a balls up the job I wanted here hasn't materialised and I am attempting a transfer from the foreign office to the British Council. The idea is get sent to Italy or France – but it is possible that I shall fall between two stools and get stuck in England. In that case I am going to make a bid for it and strike out for USA with Yve. Might even get over to see you. It would be fun! I'll let you know the moment I am certain. Meanwhile address me C/o Faber and Faber. Got married yesterday so at least am free to move. Money restrictions are killing them in England. Only allowed to take 75 pounds out of the country! [. . .]

I find that journalism – even literary journalism – doesn't pay except in the USA! For England the best thing is books and more books. I am doing one on Rhodes. HOW didn't you get *Prospero*? I signed a voucher for it. Anyway I have sent Faber a telegram to send you one.

Too distracted to write more.

> Will write you fm england
> Larry

Creation in Big Sur
Lying Fallow in the Foreign Service

Durrell had hoped that his appointment in Rhodes could be used as a springboard to Athens, where he had already resumed the personal and literary friendships he enjoyed before the war. But he turns out to have an enemy in British service in Athens and is denied the post. This leads to a sojourn in a cottage in Dorset, and then, like some Roman proconsul in disgrace – so he feels – he is exiled to Córdoba, Argentina, as a lecturer for the British Council. While he makes good and loyal friends in South America, he finds the country, the dry distances, even the 'huge steaks – like loaves' oppressive, and returns to England after a year. He hopes that the Council will send him to Greece or France, but his fate turns out to be exile again: as Embassy press officer in Belgrade, which he terms 'this centre of barbarism comparable only to the darkest of the dark ages'. Despite official recognition – he meets Marshal Tito and plays a prominent part during Sir Anthony Eden's visit – and such replenishing of his spirits as is afforded by a month in Ischia with his friend from Corfu days, Zarian, Durrell finds he can no more write in beautiful but fear-oppressed Yugoslavia than he could on the arid plains of Córdoba. Only some poems, *A Key to Modern Poetry* (based on his lectures in Argentina) and the drama *Sappho* emerge from this period. In 1951 his daughter Sappho is born in Oxford, and by 1952 he is planning a final escape from the Foreign Office.

For Miller these are productive years. He revises *Sexus*, originally drafted in 1942 and destined to be the first part of *The Rosy Crucifixion*; then he writes *Plexus*, the second part. Following the suggestion of his friend Lawrence Clark Powell of the UCLA library, he pauses in the 'serious' creation of *The Rosy Crucifixion* to reminisce about his favourite reading, and *The Books in My Life* soon emerges. Although his chronic money difficulties continue, he buys land on Big Sur ridge and builds his first home. His only son Tony is born in 1948.

There is much talk of meetings, but Durrell and Miller do not see one another; the major crisis of these years comes when Durrell is 'bitterly disappointed' with *Sexus* and tells Miller so. Durrell's candour and Miller's response illustrate the calibre of both men and the depth of their friendship.

*FIFTY-TWO SAINT ALBAN'S AVENUE
BOURNEMOUTH ENGLAND   [June 1947]

Dear Henry:

Just this minute laid down the phone and here comes your card. It was little Joe telephoning from Scotland, asking me to come on up. We shall meet next week. I shall take the night train up to Inverness. God knows HOW he lives right in the heart of Scotland like that. It'll be wonderful to see him again – how I wish you were going to be there.

What a meeting it would be. But listen, next week I go up for an interview with the British Council. It looks as though they are going to send me to SOUTH AMERICA – I don't know where as yet but will certainly let you know pronto. Perhaps we could meet in RIO? Could you make that? Wouldn't it be wonderful? Jesus, I'd love to see you again.

Henry, I've mapped out the book on you, scribbled out little sections; it looks good, balanced and lucid as well as full of fireworks. But there's one thing missing from the picture. I haven't seen any of *The Rosy Crucifixion* volumes except the extracts published in the two collections by New Directions; are they available in typescript? Could you send me a flimsy – promise to return it. The essay on you is chiefly on the *Tropics* – that is your direct line of development: the Greek book, Rimbaud, the essays, *Hamlet*, are all peripheral really, though they give one clues and kicks in the pants, and some are terrific: notably "The Alcoholic Veteran" and "Reunion in Brooklyn" – which are masterpieces of the first order. But your prose – to judge by the excerpt from *Rosy Crucifixion* – has undergone a radical transformation, has got rarified and beaten out thin like gold – and unless I see a tidy chunk of this part of the saga I am in the position of someone trying to write about Proust who has seen only three of the seven volumes.

Apart from that one small thing needs to be done before I begin the book on you: I must walk through Paris again, along the Seine, the Rue Saint Jacques; I must revisit Villa Seurat and Zeyer's and the Closerie des Lilas, just once to recall it all and feel the current of Parisian life, which fed you, flowing again over the bridges.

Then another thing: could you give me permission to quote from your work and letters in writing? Not for me but for the publisher who will do the book – they demand all these kinds of safeguards against future complaints. I promise you that you shall see the book in MSS and delete anything you don't like, as well as comment.

I have been out of a job for a couple of months and using the time to try and make a little money from translations and various hack work. I send you a little essay from Rhodes which mentions you, and which seems to have been received here with some admiration and not a little irritation by the people I flicked over the rump.

England is really very pleasant, the easiest country in Europe to live in despite our groans; the Socialists have done a wonderful job on food distribution and price control. Tho' one is limited in everything, prices are lower than anywhere in Europe, and the distribution is equitable and just; people are hard up, but the old tag about the greatest benefit of the greatest number applies here more than anywhere else in the world – I am really very impressed and delighted: and civil liberties haven't suffered as in Dictator countries. England and France are the hope of the future I think – but haven't seen France yet. Kahane was in London for a day but I missed him. I saw Eliot, gentle, sweet, now older, more grey and worn looking, but very gentle and tired. He gives off a radiance now I didn't notice before – always felt he was like a senior civil servant. Dylan Thomas I missed – he is in Italy. [. . .]

By the way, Gerald, you remember my youngest brother, has turned out a zoologist as he wanted, and is leaving for Nigeria in September to collect wild animals and snakes for the English zoos; Margaret (who is married to an Airman) sends her love. At present I am sharing mother's house with her until I know for certain what my plans are.

Curtis Brown told me that his N.Y. office wrote saying that George Le·te was broke and couldn't raise the funds to do *The Black Book*, so they have contracted with New Directions instead. I am sorry. I knew of course that he'd overshot the contract mark by about a year, but I thought he'd make it. However, if New Directions will do it without loss to themselves so much the better. By the way, a correspondent from New York congratulates me on the production of "Zero" and

"Asylum" by Circle – does he mean book form, or in the Magazine? Have you seen a book around with the stories? If so I'd be glad of a copy. Haven't heard from Leite for several months though I wrote him from here.

Reynal and Hitchcock are bringing out all my stuff in the States including poems so at last I am fixed up; on principle and from long experience I avoid little presses and solo enthusiasts – and I'm always telling you to. They don't produce any *money* for one – and after one has had the fun of writing something, the next best thing is spend the money it brings on your girl.

Now Henry, don't feel obliged to write me: the occasional post card if you feel like it: I know how it is to be pestered to death by people: keep going on the big jobs and let us all go to hell.

Do you remember Spiro? Here is a picture of him cooking an eel with red sauce for Gerald, then aged about 12. The old car in the background. Just after this was taken the car was nearly carried away by the sea and we had to stand up to our waists in water and dig it out.

     Love   Larry.

Durrell's optimism proved ill-founded: nothing of his was published in the USA by Reynal and Hitchcock because the firm went bankrupt.

*ULLAPOOL   [Telegram, receipt stamped:] 1947 JUN 27

MILLER = BIGSUR (CALIF) =

IN VIEW PROBABLE DEVALUATION FRANC URGENTLY ADVISE INVEST-
ING PARIS CREDITS IN NONFLUCTUATING PROPERTY STOP WHY NOT
LET US BUY YOU VILLA IN SOUTH FRANCE WITH PART OF FRANC
ASSETS BEFORE MONEY BECOMES WORTHLESS =

DURRELL PERLES.

*52 St Alban's Avenue, Bournemouth, England.   July 9. [1947]

Henry:

For the first time in two months of business and travelling I've got a little spell of rest to tidy up my papers and write you a line. Seems that I shall be heading for Buenos Aires in August some time; rather looking forward to it. Propose to visit Paris for a month or so first, taking little Joe if I can. We have just parted after spending a week together in the wild highlands of Scotland, on the shores of a marvellous loch. We had our picture taken by the village photographer specially for you and sent it off pronto. Meanwhile I forgot to mention that the evening before we flew from Athens we had a little meeting, Katsimbalis, Giks [Ghika], and Seferis with Rex Warner, to listen to the marvellous reading on the disc you sent me. It was so strange in that quiet booklined room to hear your burring voice reading out those long ghostly sequences from *Cancer*, I remembered Paris and Corfu. Sef and Katsimbalis had tears in their eyes. Finally when it got time to say goodbye I gave them the disc and they thanked me as if I had given them a portion of you, a hand or an arm or a voice. I think of Seferis sitting there alone now listening to it and shaking his head with that sad smile as he repeats: "Ah Miller, Miller, what a fellow."

The next big thrill was seeing little Joe standing in the market place at Inverness, with his wrists up like a praying dormouse, bubbling and glugging like a child. It was a marvellous reunion; we set off for a sixty mile trip across the razor scarps of the Cairngorms or whatever the range is called to Ullapool, in a crazy little car, through a bleak bare countryside full of polished lakes and great trees. Needless to say we broke down near a place called Garve and were stranded. However we finally made the Picks' house and found a terrific supper. A lovely bungalow by the water's edge in a bay not unlike Kouloura in Corfu; great bare mountains all round and a still lagoon; some islands on the horizon. Sunlight – almost Greek in its bareness of line. All the trip I was remembering that other crazy trip we made to Sparta – through the great cloud that covered the mountain. Remember the green flashes of the Eurotas shining up through the cloud as we slithered down the mountainside?

Joe has changed – not in looks. And Henry, what an amazing change. He has become self-supporting, absolutely reliable, responsible, calm, unpanicky. A hundred times greater than the Fred we knew. Also (he

211

says it is old age and is rather worried about it) he has learned what his physique is, how to handle it, how to take things calmly and easily, with frequent naps. He has become almost a little saint. "On the Path" he says sardonically. When we got to London we made a crazy disc for you which perhaps you will have received by now – just to let you hear our voices – though God knows it sounded quite crazy on the playback. Meanwhile Fred is much exercised about some money you have in France and is worried that you might lose it in the devaluation; hence our cable from Ullapool.

Apropos the paintings: I have enlisted the services of Osbert Sitwell. Did you read the "Writer's Journal" fragments I sent you recently? Apparently O.S. considered that a mortally wounding attack and wrote me a silly letter – like a big fatuous baby. I answered it like a smaller but not less fatuous baby. God these English literary men make me sick with their prudish little mannerisms. Glad to be on my way.

Joe aims to hang on here until his British passport comes thru. Meanwhile he is okay for dough, and is writing a book about the *Booster* episode in Paris, panning us all. I hope in South America to do the Book of the Dead. I have about 200 pages of material and a mass of notes. By God, it'll knock their eyes out. I'm glad I've held off awhile; every day increases my control and technique in the actual medium. I calculate that I can now write with fifty per cent less waste of energy and concentration than I could five years ago. By the way, have you read *Billy Budd* – Melville's LAST SHORT STORY? Written just before he died after a silence of some forty years? You must. I am also hunting out copies of Rozanov et alia for you. I am starting a stir to get *The Book of the It* <Groddeck> reprinted in England – would awfully like to hear your opinion of it. No doubt you haven't had time to read it, or you might have flipped it casually and mistaken it for a popular rewrite of Freud. Soon some very dear friends of mine are calling on you, David and Mary Abercrombie, she is a Yankee and he British. They are going to stay with their folks for a month in the hills somewhere near you. Jesus how I wish I could come for awhile. Joe says that next year we must both come over and visit you in your Japanese grand lodge. But I'm wondering whether I couldn't fly up from Buenos Aires for a week or so and see you before.

All the best to Lepska and the babe.
Larry.

[P.S.] I've found a whole bale of your letters in an old trunk which I thought lost. Marvellous reading. Have spent the whole morning rereading them.

Durrell had written that 'England is flooded with gentry-art' and 'masses of Sitwelliana' in 'From a Writer's Journal', *The Windmill* (1947).

*Big Sur   July 12th [1947]

Dear Larry:

A hasty scrawl in answer to yours from Bournemouth about article on me. Am in one hell of a mess, trotting back and forth, calling up people, writing begging letters, etc. Money situation almost impossible at this moment – completely distraught. But am getting some influence to bear now on authorities in France. (I'm even writing Osbert Sitwell to exert his influence – so you can imagine my straits.)

But about my style, etc . . . . I don't want to ship you the ms. of *Rosy Crucifixion* for the reason that as it stands it is in the first writing, with not a correction and I may delete whole pages or sections when I get down to it. You are wrong, I think, to judge from excerpts you saw: there is every sort of style and treatment in the 750 pages I have written, and a good bit is diffuse, opaque, rambling, hugger-mugger. When it comes to the autobiographical narrative I really don't change much. Also wrong of you, I think, to consider Rimbaud, *Hamlet*, etc. as "peripheral". It's all one. If one lived long enough the whole man would come through in the work – ideas, sensations, experience, philosophy, aesthetic, and everything. Those *Tropics* warped the readers' minds. "Cannibalistic" I notice was used somewhere. Only the Anglo-Saxon would use such a word where frankness is concerned. Certainly you may quote from books and letters – but I do want to see the passages and approve, of course. You must also get permissions from the publishers for quotations from books – but that's almost automatic. I'll try to remember to send you a story of 30 pages I wrote expressly for the book Léger is to illustrate – about a clown named Auguste. Called *The Smile at the Foot of the Ladder*. Just had letter from Léger begging me to write something different, something in the vein of *Black Spring* or the *Tropics*. This is really different from anything I wrote. But doesn't indicate a new trend. All these "new trends and directions" which the critics discern with each new work – all this sort

213

of apperception is false. Who will publish this book, do you know yet? Remember France – you should get it accepted there even before England or America. (Call on Girodias to aid you – or I'll give you other clues later.) You should meet some of the critics who wrote about me in the papers and revues – remind me later and I'll give you names. Good men, I think, and *their* slant is leagues above ours.

I'm writing Leite to send you *Zero and Asylum* – yes, beautifully done – amazed he didn't send you them. Did you get my note about the water colors with Tambimuttu? If you go to Paris see the silk screen book – *Into the Night Life* – at André Breton's (or at the Surrealist Exposition); Breton lives at 42 rue Fontaine, Paris (9). See his friend Pierre Mabille, author of *Le Miroir du merveilleux*. Man Ray is there now too. It should be a good moment to go.

I can't leave this place yet – too many entanglements of all kinds. It's all I can do to get to town (Monterey – 45 miles distant) when I have to. Always without a sou. And pressed on all sides. And now have to raise passage for Moricand to come here – he has his visa to travel. I do no work, nothing . . . just sit and plot how to beg or borrow. Frightful. Been going on for months – was never worse off, not even in those bad days in Paris.

I think of you and Eva and wonder how it goes. I hope well. Best to Gerald, Margaret and every one. And more soon. This on the wing. Writing Joey to-morrow. Are you still in Scotland, I wonder? Things will have to take a radical change soon – this situation is impossible. Saw Anaïs fleetingly – she's going to Mexico now – Hugo to Paris. Alors, what by the clock?

Henry

---

*52 Saint Alban's Avenue, Bournemouth, England.   [mid-July 1947]

Henry Dear:
No. Don't ship me the MSS. I was not clear about it. I thought it was all finally proofed and tidied up. I guess the bits I've seen give the clear line through. Fred showed me a delightful section about him and Villa Seurat – and my horrible laugh. It brought tears to our eyes. No: when I said "peripheral" I didn't mean to denigrate from the other works; but if one must study the demolition you have performed on the XXth century literary set-up, one can I think see its line and implications

more clearly in your direct autobiography than in your essays: in the latter you reveal more about your soul and your beliefs: but in the others you are tied to the more objective grid of action and its results; in other words one can attack your really major contribution more faithfully this way; because though it is just as autobiographical the action-sensibility polarity creates round it an OBJECTIVITY of form which makes it malleable in the hands of a critic. Also, do remember that while you are famous here, no-one has had a chance of reading more than the excerpts. They are very highly thought of: but to all your admirers I keep having to say: "Yes, but have you seen him in full flight, unhampered by cuts and puritanism?" Hardly anyone has read the *Tropic* here. Don't you think this line of approach is a fertile one? After all how would you go about lining up Rousseau for people who haven't read him in the whole? The man is more clearly there in the letters and the novelettes, but the *Confessions* are the key somehow.

Damn. It looks like South America in September. I rang up the bank today about sending you some money – I've got a little; but these currency regulations are maddening. Have airmailed New York to see if a friend there will cable you some against a London bank draft. This is illegal but it might work. I thought you were on easy street now. Joe says you have plenty in France; why not sail over with Lepska? How much do you need? Is it just day to day expenses or have you some income tax troubles? Ah Lepska, this improvident Henry of yours – he hands his money away to all and sundry when he gets it and then finds he has none for himself; I am telephoning Tambimuttu also to see if he can't get some sort of export draft. But from the tone of your letter it sounds as if you need a lot of money – not a little. How about Laughlin? [. . .]

Love
Larry

[P.S.] Going to London tomorrow and will see Joe. <Henry – has your patron stopped giving you the stipend?>

Dear Larry,

What with the bombardment of cables, photos, post cards, and finally
that incomparable disc (just played it last night), I couldn't sleep all
night. Was up at daybreak – 4.45 A.M. this morning, and out over the
hills surveying the broad Pacific. Wish I could afford a cable to send
you all my blessings. It was so wonderful to hear your voices, as
though you were in the next room. (I never realized how foreign Fred's
English accent was till now. Living with him I never noticed it. And
that bloody French he threw in – *extraordinaire!*) Sure, you know I
would have come a-running if I could. But it seems each one of us is
being made to play his own part, go his own way, just at this moment.
But the time for reunion is soon, I feel it – and even Edgar will be with
us, then, and perhaps Reichel too. Perhaps even Anaïs. And of course
Moricand. I just heard from him too yesterday, telling me all about that
malevolent Pluto. He says this coming month of August will see some
sort of diabolical conjunction, very similar to the set-ups in August
1914 and September 1939. He can't be hinting at another war, can he?
Maybe just a "crise" or a "craque"! Anyhow, and this will comfort
Fred – it's his idea too – when it gets bad for the world (as it will next
year, he promises), it will go good with me. And probably with you,
and surely with Fred, who lives the miraculous life of the cockroach
and the bedbug combined.

Listen, something will happen about that money in Paris. I've got
people working for me now. Influential ones, I mean. Will have definite
news in about two weeks. And come the worst, I will have Man Ray
invest all that I can squeeze out of Girodias in paintings and bring them
to me. (Picassos, Braques, etc.) You may have been joking, but I think
too that the franc is due for another squeeze. I predicted that money
would be worthless soon after this war. We'll see.

Along the road this morning I was thinking that in order to suffer
one must be in good trim – strange idea. I mean by that that I never
realized how much more I could stand until just this morning. Physically I am O.K. Never finer, maybe. When I pull thru the present
ordeals (all vague to you, I realize) I will be at the peak and ready for the
kill – as to writing, I mean. I'm going to tackle that *Rosy Crucifixion*
with the meat axe – pole-axe it, as you'd say. [. . .]

Well . . . so you may be going to South America! Or to Paris? Either way fine, I'd say. And if you can't, come to Big Sur. When I heard your voices I couldn't believe it was eight years since we last met. I remember vividly how I parted from you – in the rain up there in the mountains. Or how I parted with Katsimbalis. Partings, partings. Enough of them. More reunions, I say.

Wrote George Leite to send you copies of your book – what a bastard! More soon. Must catch a car now to go to town. Love to Eva and give Joey the good news. Will write him separately. [. . .]

Cheerio and Toodle-oo!
Henry

*52 St Alban's Avenue.   20 August [1947]

Henry – How infuriating! Just got your letter on my return here *from* Paris. I meant the 25th of *last* month – but you will be glad to know that Kahane-Girodias is working on the Moricand problem for you. We spoke of it while I was there. He was cabling some francs to Moricand – I forget exactly the transaction but he said you would be losing by it – but then you didn't seem to mind! I am sorry things aren't so good between you and Lepska – I had hoped that you were all set for a fattish domestic life: but can't judge whether it's really the kind of life for you or not. I am sorry though – and what about the kid? Kids take some looking after these days. You can't fly around the world with one of them in your pocket.

Paris was heaven – I'm writing you at length about it – but utterly impossible to live in. A meal costs about £3. Eve and I spent five pounds a day while we were there.

Apropos Sitwell – I enclose correspondence. These English literary gents! Besides, now you're famous they want to collect you for y^r talents – for their social drawing-rooms and letter files. I shudder to think what O.S. would have said in '37 when I brought *Tropic* across here. Remember Bernard Shaw's reaction to it. Now it's all smooth water. By the way the passage at arms all started from those notes I wrote in *The Windmill* about 'gentry-art' and the patron turning artist. <I sent them to you – a while back.> Then I wrote to him about y^r paintings – very polite and business-like. I enclose his answer and mine. No – It's amusing in an exasperating fat-arsed way.

I leave for S. America in September sometime. Not a moment too soon. You should *see* the literary men here. If you do come to London you'll find me at 10 Orme Square, Bayswater, for the week or two before I leave.

I was amused by y^r article on Cossery! Dostoievsky? Eh? Wait till you meet him! The book I sent you is grand and deserves praise – but I wonder if you'll like him or think so highly of him when you hear him talk. Anyway your praise came at the right time and put him over in Paris – for which he is deathlessly grateful.

Send us a cable if you're coming this way. Joe has nearly finished his book about us all.

Skoal!

L

*C:o BRITISH COUNCIL,
LAVALLE 190, BUENOS AYRES.   [*c*. end November 1947]

Dear Henry:
I had a note from Lepska saying you were back at work, and wrote her an account of our arrival in the Americas but can't remember whether I airmailed it or not, so this is just to let you know we've arrived and that the address is OKAY. This is a perfectly fantastic country: but then so is the whole continent. The interesting thing is the queer lightness of the spiritual atmosphere: one feels buoyant, irresponsible, like a hydrogen balloon. One realises too that the personal sort of European man is out of place here: one cannot suffer from angst here, only cafard. So much is explained here about the American struggle, the struggle not to get de-personalised. Because this is a communal continent; the individual soul has no dimensions. In architecture, in art, religion, it is all community – skyscrapers, jitterbugging, hyperboles – it is all of a piece. I understand now why the American artist has no sense of form – because his soul is continually being siphoned off into the communal soda water fountain, and his struggle is to concretise it enough to suffer. In other words everybody is happy in a mathematical sort of way, and the huge skyscrapers of Rio when the jungle swallows them will be not unlike the fantastic Inca remains, the temples and altars they keep finding. The fury, the destructive fury which you inveigh against so much comes from the European soul trying to gain a slippery footing in this oxygenated air and getting panicky because nothing –

nothing has any value here: break it, break it. All this is quite under-standable the moment you hit Rio. But what sort of white ant's dream is the art of this continent? The Maya, the Inca, you can see the sort of thing which is possible: the rest is European panic, European guilt: but there is something quite new and strange about the atmosphere here. It is a spiritual vacuum flask: I am not sure Tao is not like that. Maybe the Indians can tell us? Have they said anything yet? Have they spoken? Human faces, clouds, the Andes, the pampas – it is all somehow unqualifiable in European terms ... damn it, I'd better stop before I write a book about it.

Yes, Kahane was very nice, we borrowed fifty pounds or so off him, and had a whale of a time. He claimed that once the franc fell printing costs would become normal and he would put us all back into print again – but he is sadly like his father, tight, wolfish, and queer: at the moment he has the charm of youth, but I'm afraid the future is black.

I left Joe in rather a bad state of mind: his book had just been turned down, and he was rather worried as he is living on his writing. If you can send food parcels, coffee tea sugar chocolate etc, send him one. Also if you have a carbon of your projected *Black Book* introduction send it on because I am thinking of doing an English edition here later this year. We leave for Cordova tomorrow night for a two month spell in the hills. Mails will be forwarded.

> Love to you three
> Larry

*Big Sur   12/19/47

> Dear Larry –
Just got your first letter from under the Equator. Have written Nancy Leite to send you a copy of my Preface to B.B. (have none here). Will keep after it!

Am just reading Joey's MS. now and laughing my head off. Didn't know it was turned down in England – too bad. Still some hopes here however. Will brush it up best I can. There are some wonderful sections in it – and some weak ones too.

I hope this reaches you during the holidays. A Merry Xmas to you and Eve! Expecting Moricand any day now. Maybe next spring you all & Joey & Edgar will get here for a reunion. If not, I may go to Paris.

Waiting to see what this winter will do to Europe. Things couldn't be worse apparently . . . Nearing page 1,000 now of *Rosy Crucifixion*. And going strong. More soon. Cordova-in-the-hills sounds wonderful. Liked your article on Rhodes – and all the lost Colossi. What a traveler you are!

Henry

[P.S.] Had a strange warm letter from Somerset Maugham.

See Miller's *A Devil in Paradise* (1956) for a forthright account of Moricand's visit.

*[Córdoba] THE BRITISH COUNCIL,
190 LAVALLE, BUENOS AYRES,
ARGENTINA.   [December? 1947]

Dear Henry:
It was delightful to get your book as we arrived in Córdoba where I am due to start up my work. The *Remember to Remember* episodes are some of the most moving things you have ever done: also you capture little Joe perfectly. I think you still write better about France than about anything else; and it seems to me that you are doing too much intimate portraiture of the Rattner style. It comes easily to you, but it is also getting a little bit repetitive . . . you will see that you have said almost the same things and in almost the same way of Anaïs, of Benno, of Reichel etc . . . The tone of voice is familiar, and I feel that this type of portraiture corresponds in you to what would be, in a lesser sized man, journalism. It comes easy, too easy, and though it's delightful and breath-taking to read if you are new to it, if you are an old Miller fan of the 38 vintage as I am, you long for more of the new Miller (*Remember to Remember* and the "Washboard Veteran") where the integration is flawless and smooth, and where you don't have to reach for an out of the way image, it lies inherent in the matter . . . But I've no doubt that the new *Capricorn* is already finished and that THAT sets the seal on the other books. I'm particularly happy to get the book because this time I left all my Miller in England: those red Corfu bindings with their gay inscriptions. I felt that I must not risk losing them: I must have something to hand on to my kids. So I packed them all carefully and left them with Alan Thomas, though it broke my heart not to have them in

my book-box. I have just had a long letter from little Joe, who has learned how to make the Royal Society keep him alive: he is heading in your direction I believe, though how the devil you are going to keep him *and* Moricand I don't know. I would have come and visited you sooner only I did so want to be solvent when I did and not to throw Lepska into a flap about the next meal . . . I've got three books coming out in the States but owing to the new laws I can't get dollars for them . . . Ah, you complain about the timidity of the young and you are right: but you do not seem to see how in Europe the economic foundations of POVERTY have been swept away. What did you pay for Villa Seurat in rent? 10 pounds perhaps: it would now cost sixty or seventy. Studios are impossible to find in Paris and fetch millionaires' prices. When we stayed in a little hotel in Rue Notre Dame des Champs for three weeks we spent £5 a DAY on food: £35 a week: £420 a year . . . There is no starvation line now: and there is no-one to beg from because the rich are living on the last shreds of their capital. England is far better off for the artist today, but life has got even drabber there . . . Meanwhile here we are stuck in a hideous South American town as poor teachers . . . This winter I must knock out another book . . . Each book makes me freer: soon I shall be free of this organisation, free perhaps to visit you even: how we look forward to that day when it comes . . . Of course I am really free, free to walk out now: but I am not, under the same terms, free to have a wife or a child or a place to live in: there's the rub . . .

Meanwhile onwards, onwards: I want to do a book about Rhodes where we spent the last two years which were marvellous happy: collecting peasant legends, and travelling about those clear blue seas: it is characteristic too that two protesting Latin American specialists have been posted to Athens while I, no less protesting, find myself here . . . It is part of the new logic which is going to lead to the new war in 5 years' time.

Meanwhile everyone writes from Athens congratulating me on my luck and telling me to count my blessings . . . I must try to. Your letters and books are among the greatest of them.

Will write you at greater length when we are settled down more in this inferno.

Love,
Larry

[P.S.) Perhaps little Joe will have reached you by the time you get this: give him my love and tell him I'm sure that in *two* more novels he will hit the jackpot – but he must learn *construction*. How?

(1) Never read anything by Henry Miller.
(2) Study Stendhal.

Love to Lepska and the Babe –
Larry.

[P.P.S.] Sold a new book of poems to Faber. Good I think: title: *On Seeming to Presume*!

*Argentina, The British Council,
Lavalle 190, *Buenos Ayres* [i.e., Córdoba]   [March? 1948]

Dear Henry: Just a brief note to hope you are managing to keep on working despite the world situation which looks more like war every day: by the time we get back to Europe it will be about as interesting as the deserts in Texas. I think a very short war – say six months – could account for all the major cities of Europe: which means, of course, that Man is tired of city life as such. What sort of civilization can follow? I don't know – but the answer lies with the USA, strange and hideous as such a thing may sound to you! Wyndham Lewis is writing a book called *America and Cosmic Man* which sounds interesting: sounds heretical to you perhaps – but then everyone loathes his own country and countrymen if he is any sort of artist – and this doesn't mean to say that I disagree with what you have written in the *Nightmare* book – au contraire. But I am thinking of the future. The other day I sent you off a plan for a Miller anthology – hope the idea appeals to you. It is better than nothing – and you are publishing in such a fragmentary way that your great genius is not as widely accepted as it might be. You are considered a superlative 'performer' merely. We have settled into a flat in Córdoba – very dull town. Would you consent to visit Argentina as a travelling lecturer if I could get you invited? Three or four lectures only? It would be such fun to see you again. I haven't *talked* to a real person for so long I feel my speech-organs are in a state of atrophy almost. Has little Joe arrived? What a noble beautiful monument to our life in Paris *Remember to Remember* is – one of your finest works. I've read it so often that I know it almost by heart. It's a gem! And how well

I remember Joe coming out with that phrase! How we laughed! I have a new book of poems coming out and have done a *real* translation of *Pope Joan*.

Love to Lepska & the kid—Larry.

The Communist takeover in Czechoslovakia in February 1948, coincident with rising Soviet–US tensions over the occupation of Germany, increased fears of a world war.

*[Córdoba] Argentina   [end March? 1948]

Henry:

Just a swift spot answer. [. . .] Apropos Moricand, I was afraid that you would find it rather cramping: glad to hear there's a second kid on the way. Not much of a world to get it born into though . . . Six months before the next war it looks like. Argentina for Moricand? I think it would be a disaster. Argentina is exactly like USA in 1890 – full of tough go-getting tycoons fighting over the undeveloped riches. The weak are driven to the wall. The only menial jobs might be a job on an estancia – but you need physique and energy; and if M. speaks no English it would be a great handicap. Argentines know only Spanish and English. Surely there are a hundred astrological societies in and around Hollywood that would look after him. Theosophical society? Why doesn't he try and become Paris correspondent of the *Astrologer*? You see, from the impression I had of him he is quite helpless – as a baby. And his only subjects are astrology and literature, which as you know don't pay. It's an awful fix to be in. I do wish you calculated a bit before saddling yourself with learned but helpless people . . . What about French lessons? I'm afraid he would find B.A. worse. Climatically an inferno, and morally the final circle of hell. I honestly think that he'd be better off in London than anywhere else in the world. I will ask if there is anyone willing to offer him a lecture-trip on astrology . . . but nobody knows French here. It's not taught in the schools. If he were young and energetic he might do something here, but otherwise he would be driven to the wall I'm afraid. Everyone with any sensibility is trying to get out of this place, including me. I think I would rather risk the atom bomb than stay on. It's so dead . . .

Love Larry

Henry – Congratulations on the boy-child! Bravo Lepska! How lucky you are to be settled enough to enjoy children. We are on the move again! I've resigned my post here and propose to reach London by Xmas – probably an atomic Xmas! What fun if we could meet. But I shall be on the bread-line I guess. There are so few jobs going and I can't earn enough by writing. We propose to make a bid for Greece. Rather starve in Athens than anywhere else. The climate is so magnificent, one feels so well. Here it's awful.

A few days ago I sent you & Laughlin a sort of ground-plan for the Omnibus after doing a thorough rereading. Think it shd. make a fine book. Like all great men you have nothing to fear from selection: and like all American geniuses you have no sense of form whatsoever. So that helps. I've been studying your changing prose style. Your American as against your European style. It has gained vastly in power and flight, but you have lost a great deal of the critical control over it. Maybe the USA undermines values in a subtle way. I thought for example that quite half of "Murder the Murderer" could have been blue-pencilled out. It seemed repetitive and platitudinous. Could have been cleaned up a bit. Also the later portraiture – compare "Rattner" to "Reichel" – the latter so compact, the former so loose and wandering. But the *best* of the new style is far and away greater and wilder than the old – "Rimbaud", "Balzac" and "Remember to Remember" are terrific – as the two late stories ("Reunion in Brooklyn" and "The Washboard Veteran") are. The difference is perhaps in the use of the blue pencil. These observations may sound a bit impertinent, Henry, but I'm thinking of the books to come – to get the best out of your new powers it seems necessary to frame and trim them up like a water colour – or else the book becomes a Bergsonian rampage and its positive qualities get lost because they are not contrasted – the clear hard limestone-formation of the *thought* gets muddled. Looking forward eagerly to see what new work you are doing. Hope to have the Omnibus ready for inspection by Jan. or February. It's a great honour for me – I couldn't have had a nicer compliment paid me by Laughlin. Will you come to England if you "go abroad" or shall we meet in Greece? I know just the island to spend the next summer in – Patmos! Bare as a sculpture, a few orchards, a white stream, blue sea, and the

Apocalypse—Love
Larry.

Dear Larry –

Max Dickmann of "Santiago Rueda", publishers in B.A., is trying to
contact you about various things.
Just preparing Vol. I (*Sexus*) of *The Rosy Crucifixion* for Girodias to
publish, in English, then French. A great work!!! Have read it thru
several times & am still making revisions. No order – yes and no! I see
now what is *my* order – at least in this work. It is the picture of
"germination" in all its phases. That other, *imposed*, order – by the
brain or will – will never be mine. Goethe said: "The very inability to
finish with a work is the mark of greatness." (Sic!) There are two types
always – one working with & in Chaos, the other with law, form, etc.
No use comparing them or putting one above another – systole &
diastole: Apollonian & Dionysian, what! I *love* Cendrars, for example –
"le torrent enraciné" – but I also love Giono – *and* Gérard de Nerval.
Yes, the latter so much – *Le Rêve et la vie*. And Novalis and Nietzsche
and Faure. Do try to get *Magicians, Seers, & Mystics* by Maurice Magre
(French writer). Pub. in London (in the '30's as *Return of the Magi*).
Plan to go to Paris next Spring, if no war or revolution first. Via
Ireland & England and Scotland. *Ireland above all!* Sure – go to Greece –
Patmos, yes! Not *England!* Had visit from *Angelos* Seferiades, who is
teaching Greek in "The Presidio" (military school) in Monterey near
by. And Seferis' book of poems, with your translation. All's well here –
baby fine. Only always broke. Hope you write soon again. What about
Eve? Cheerio, amigo.

Henry

*British Council, Buenos Ayres
190 Lavalle [i.e., Córdoba]   [*c.* November 1948]

Dear Henry:
Sure, and we wouldn't be afther asking you to impose a Form of the
outer, the reasoned, the Willed – sorry if I gave such a silly impression.
No, I meant that we had a right to expect work of a certain horse-
power from you now, and that here and there you allow some lesser
jobs to creep in. For example the essay on American bread in the last
book, and the story about astrology. The *writing* ain't tight enough . . .
Of course I know 100 years from now we'll be treasuring the smallest

fragments – but that don't excuse you not making them as powerful as only you know how to. And sometimes you do run on and worry an unrefreshing theme to death – *Murder the M.* contains much that [you] might excise, thinketh the heretic who has just completed a course on you . . . I am in touch with Dickmann who must be living in a dream. Does he not know that the Government has just issued a Catholic censorship ban on about a hundred books ranging from *Forever Amber* and *Gone with the Wind* to *Ulysses*. Things are getting mighty tight here. I shall see Dickmann when I return to Buenos Ayres on my way out to England . . . I can perhaps bequeath him *Black Spring* . . . No *Hamlet* here, in England . . . But I've started something of a vogue for you in high society in BA. People are reading *Capricorn* in French which has just come in, and you have some stout fans. So far no ban on you. But translation into Spanish would bring that pronto I think. Will talk to Dickmann about it. Dying to see the new work: will take a trip to Paris to see Girodias and get it. I propose to get busy now on the next successor to *The Black Book* – must wipe out a few small items first. Is there really a hope of meeting next spring . . . How magnificent! I'm dying to see you again and hear the saga unrolling from your lips over a glass of wine . . . I have so much to tell you about America. It is much blacker, much darker than I ever imagined possible. Every stricture you make is dead true . . . but seems to me that people are at the mercy of the influences on this continent . . . They are not to blame . . . The soil and climate are talking the whole time – saying ugly swinish things . . . More when I cross the River Plate on my way home . . .

Have written rather a good play in verse about some ancient Greeks: will send you a carbon this week.

Love to you all. I have resigned here, by the way, got ill this winter, Larry

*Santos, Brazil   [December 1948]

Loading in a tropical port which might well illustrate Rimbaud – the later phase. Silence, haze, huge mountains. All this is very different from what we've just left – Rio built like a great dazzling pipe-organ – the pipes the Organ Mountains – the town with skyscrapers running up beside sugar-loaf ant-hill formation mountains. The main street is one of those empty-ended streets that bisect a Chirico painting. Think you would like

Rio! Sitting in cafés drinking the milk from green coconuts through a straw.
Myself I am sitting on deck reading Laforgue's *Hamlet* which couldn't
be more appropriate to what we all feel in our shrinking European souls
at this vastness and luxuriance. Brazil is bigger than Europe, wilder than
Africa, and weirder than Baffin Land.

    Larry

* 52 St Alban's Avenue, Bournemouth, Hants, England   Jan 22 [1949]

    Dearest Henry –

Sorry for my long neglect. I haven't been awfully well this past six
months – bad nerves – due to Latin America as much as anything I think.
Felt too fed up to answer letters or think even – I'm resting up at home for
a month or two. It's hard, you know, to reconcile the conflicting claims
of jobs and writing. Perhaps one shouldn't try. But I don't like starving
and I feel under obligation to be an ordinary human being too, paying for
a wife and child etc. . . . Consequently these periods of gloom and
exhaustion . . . England is wonderful after Argentina – the damp particularly & the cold. I resigned from my last job and am trying for
another soon which might take me to the Mediterranean. I have yet to see
a country as fine in every way as Greece – and we are still aimed in that
direction. I haven't got beyond the ground-plan of your omnibus book.
Tambimuttu is in financial straits – he is a hopeless devil – and unless he
cooperates Laughlin thinks the book will be too big. What about a *Viking*
portable Miller? Have you suggested it? At the moment I am simply
loafing about waiting for this frightful melancholia to pass. I'm planning
a long essay on you for *Horizon*. Connolly is d'accord. [. . .]
    People are reading you a great deal, you know. England is fatuous and
apathetic as usual – the sweaty Christians are out in force – publishers
demand a strong pietistic note. As if we weren't *religious* writers!
    I haven't seen Joe as yet. God knows where he's hiding. Are you
coming over this way? Pl. let me know if you are. It would be such fun to
meet again. I don't feel any older – only much wiser and a bit exhausted
with things. Waiting for the spring!

    Love to Lepska and the bairns.
    Larry.

Durrell's 'Studies in Genius VIII: Henry Miller' appeared in *Horizon*, volume 20 (July
1949).

227

Dear Larry – Wrote you a tremendous letter (in my head) two days ago at the sulphur baths here. Felt something was wrong – and with Joey too. No word in ages from him! Take a good rest. Don't worry about literature. I often think the Consular Service must be the ideal solution for a writer. But evidently it doesn't pay enough to keep two wives and a kid. Writing books & articles *to make money* is what essentially destroys one, I believe. Do anything else, if you can, rather than that. Nothing is going to sell well any more – as I see it. It will take twenty, maybe 50 years, to get a new and better (?) world order. Get some fun out of life and reconcile yourself to receiving no due reward for your labors.

I get tired, very tired, of pushing editors and publishers around. Make a hundred suggestions – but no action. Financially, things are at their worst now. I am bartering for the necessities of life. But go right on working. Made the 6th and final revision of Vol. I – *R.C.* Waiting to see how I will get paid before mailing to Girodias. Hope to get you either a carbon copy of it or proofs – if not too late. In the middle of Vol. 2 now. I enjoy every bit of it. Write with a smile, even when it's horrible or tragic. *That's progress*, I think!

Will get a real letter off very soon now. So much to tell you. Think of you constantly. And Eve – how is she? Hope you are getting on well together.

Anyway, as I said – there's nothing like a good loaf period. Fuck a duck! Rest is just as essential (for the soul) as work. "God wants us all to be happy!" Yes, even in the midst of anguish and chaos. Cheerio!

Henry

Dear Larry,
Just reread your long critical essay for *Horizon*. Superb piece of writing! Merlin, you say somewhere. Mais, c'est vous! If anyone can seduce, drug, exalt the English, it is you. I wonder what the response will be ... Wondering if this copy is for me to keep or to be returned with suggestions? Holding it temporarily, till I hear from you. Meanwhile a few observations which may or may not be of interest to you. (Too bad

you haven't read *R.C.* script. Sending you *The Smile* to-day – this is probably utterly different from anything I've done before.)

Here are some more or less "considered" reflections on your brilliant study.

To begin with, I feel you might have taken advantage of the occasion to belabor your compatriots for not having published the autobiographical books. Whose fault is it but theirs if they are reading only fragments of my work? Had you thought of that, cher ami? Toynbee (the nephew) in reviewing a recent work bemoans the lack of the virulent *Tropics* material – but would he lift a finger (as did the French writers en masse recently) to fight the government? More of their bloody hypocrisy, you see. Just as here in America. You almost kowtow to the bastards. I see your point – you want to win them over. O.K., but you should rub it in, too. Never miss a chance, Larry me lad.

Freud . . . You've made these statements about my absorption of him, and the influence, several times. True, I've read him well, but as for "influence", I'd rather say that of Rank and Jung, if any. Bergson belongs to my "youth" (tailor shop days). How much he influenced me is imponderable. The great influences were Nietzsche, Spengler, yes, Emerson, Herbert Spencer (!), Thoreau, Whitman – and Elie Faure. You can't stress the last-named enough. More and more he stands out like a giant, to me.

And about "the artist" . . . It's not that I put the sage or saint above the artist. It's rather that I want to see established the "artist of life". (The Christ *resurrected* would be such, for example. Milarepa was another.)

This ties up with the progression, as you put it, from Bergson-Spengler to Chinese-Hindus. I think I've passed that too now. The key-word is Reality (few have put it better than Gutkind in *The Absolute Collective*). The nearest philosophy to my heart and temperament is Zen, as you probably know. I find individuals here and there, all over the world, who belong to no cult, creed or metaphysic, who are expressing what I mean, each in his own way. As near as I can put my finger on it it always comes back to reality here and now, nothing else, nothing before or beyond. Emphasis is on vision. Adjust your vision and there is nothing to do. "All has been given." The world is – and it's good, right, perfect. The vulgar think this self-hypnosis. It's not. It's Samadhi all the time. It's God everywhere – and nothing but. Or Spirit, if you prefer. But no duality. Whatever is negative, vicious, evil, etc. is due to poor vision, poor understanding. You don't seek immortality because you are in the midst of eternity. Und so weiter. You're not concerned with good and bad, moralities, because you don't set up as "judge".

Orwell – Pfui! That man lacks nearly everything, in my opinion. He hasn't even a good horizontal view. You should read, by comparison, what the French critics write of my work – even those who are "hostile" to me. Miles above your Orwells.

You have one line, among many, which I dote on: "Its weird tracts of half-explored vegetation running along the snow-lines of metaphysics". Bravo!

"Poor literary sense" . . . It seems to me you have an ambivalent attitude here. You make a good defense of my "formlessness", etc. Yes. But then you make these concessions to the dead-heads. Picasso said once – "Must one always turn out a *masterpiece?*" Where does creation lie – in the thing done or in the effect? What and how a man does, acts, thinks, talks, every day is what counts, no? If you have this criterion of "literature" you nullify the other important points you make. You are talking of something altogether "illusory". The makers of literature are not the masters of art. Great books are – literature isn't.

"Lord of Misrule" – I like that! Where does it come from, if anywhere?

"Literary *clochard*". Yes, I see the point. But perhaps simply "*voyou*" would have been better, no? Voyou is most expressive and untranslatable.

"No *characters*"??? Perhaps. But I think with *The Rosy Crucifixion* you might speak differently. Certainly they are not characters in the novelistic sense – but they are full-drawn, ample, rounded. Some of them have already made their debut in the earlier works. I keep a list of them on my wall, so as not to forget – i.e., who they really were – their real names. Quite a collection of them now.

Lastly, you may not like *R.C.* at all. In some ways it is a reversion to pre-*Tropic* writing. Much more conversation, direct and indirect. Many episodes, dreams, fantasies, throw-backs of all sorts. But a steady forward progression chronologically, because I am following my notes (written in 1927!). *Capricorn*, as you know, took about two and a half pages of these notes, only. This first volume was written in N.Y., in about six months – first half of 1942. Hence all the bloody revision. Though no drastic changes. But I've labored to make the expression more perfect – more effective. One day you will see the revised script. It's a beauty. Anyway, in writing Vol. 2 – half done now – I began to get real joy out of the writing. Laughed and chuckled a great deal. *And*, there is a perceptible change from Vol. 1 to 2. Inevitable after 6 or 7 years. Good too, I feel. When I finish Vol. 3 I intend to do the little book, *Draco and the Ecliptic*, like putting a cap on a milk bottle, to seal it hermetically. Haven't the least idea what it will be like – just know it must be done – and masterfully. Then I am off into the blue . . . Joy through work hereafter. No more compulsion. I will be emptied. Maybe I'll just whistle, like a peanut stand. But I want to try sheer nonsense. Do you remember that Mozartian laughter in *Steppenwolf*? I hope by this time you've read Cossery's latest – *Les Fainéants dans la valle fertile*. Remarkable! And try to get the little book *Blaise Cendrars* by Louis Parrot (Edition Seghers, Paris). I will send you anything you can't get.

And now this . . . you don't mention Eve in your letters. Fred said he met her – adored her. How is she? What is she doing? Are you happy?

So glad to hear of your daughter. Eight now. I wish I could meet her. Send me a photo of her as she is to-day if you can. . . . Don't think I'm not trying to get over. It becomes more and more probable every day. (I must see Ireland – and Edinburgh!) My ideal trip would be to these three cities, by plane – no in-between stops: Timbuctoo, Mecca, Lhasa. I dream of it often.

Hope you don't take my observations as carping criticism. I think you did a superb job of it. Too damned good for *Horizon*. Ask Connolly to lend you the issue in which Hermann Hesse wrote about himself – it will please you enormously. Too a loo!

Henry

P.S. Penguin books, England, have contracted for the *Colossus* – first of 1950.
P.P.S. Are there still copies of *The Black Book* available in Paris?

*The British Embassy, Belgrade, Yugoslavia   [*c.* June 1949]

    Dear Henry –
A brief line to tell you that we have arrived and that conditions here are far from pleasant though much better than Latin America. The diplomatic circle is completely ostracised by the people who will not meet you

and dare not be seen talking to you. Consequently the life we lead is a chain-gang existence. Communism is something so much more horrible than you can imagine: systematic moral and spiritual corruption by every means at hand. "The perversion of truth in the interests of expediency" – but when you see it at close quarters it makes your hair stand up on end. And the smug cooperation of the intellectuals is also terrifying! They are paid to shut up – and they have. The terrible *deadness* of everything is fantastic! It really is a menace, an intellectual disease. How to combat it is another problem. At any rate England and the USA are havens of tremendous calm compared to this place – and the only hope for the future – if any. Sounds odd perhaps, but it's true. This brief line is just to tell you to use the diplomatic bag in writing me. It's safer and quicker. [. . .]

> Yours with love
> *Larry*

*BRITISH LEGATION, BELGRADE.   Sept 5 1949

Dear Henry:
Just a brief line: frightfully busy. Received *Sexus* from Paris and am mid-way through volume II. I must confess I'm bitterly disappointed in it, despite the fact that it contains some of your very best writing to date. But my dear Henry, the moral vulgarity of so much of it is *artistically* painful. These silly, meaningless scenes which have no raison d'être, no humour, just childish explosions of obscenity – what a pity, what a terrible pity for a major artist not to have critical sense enough to husband his forces, to keep his talent aimed at the target. What on earth possessed you to leave so much twaddle in? I understand that with your great sweeping flights you occasionally have to plough through an unrewarding tract of prose. But the strange thing is that the book gives very little feeling of real passion. The best parts burn with a new cold luminous ardour – mysticism; and you have interlarded this with chunks of puerile narrative. You won't mind my saying this, because you know that I consider you one of the greatest living masters. But really this book needs taking apart and regluing. The obscenity in it is really unworthy of you. It is just plain silly to murder the good parts of the book with this silly kind of vituperation – written so badly. The anecdote on page 24 of volume I is the kind of thing I mean. It's just

painful – nothing else, and contributes nothing to what you are trying to do. I'm fearfully depressed to have to sound impertinent to a genius I admire so much – but Henry, Henry, Henry . . . Ten minutes' thought would have saved the book. As it is it gives the air of being written by Jekyll and Hyde (and the Hyde is not really monstrous and frightening, but just painfully disgusting) . . . You will probably blow me out of the water for writing this, but I think it's better to be candid about it. All the wild resonance of *Cancer* and *Black Spring* has gone – and you have failed to develop what is really new in your prose, and what should set a crown on your work – the new mystical outlines are all there; but they are lost, lost damn it in this shower of lavatory filth which no longer seems tonic and bracing, but just excrementitious and sad. One winces and averts the face. What on earth has made you slip back on a simple matter of *taste* – artistic taste?

No time for more, we are in the middle of a lively crisis and much work on hand. It's a joy to read you nevertheless you bastard – even though I'm angry becoz I think you've failed yourself on this one. Love. Larry.

*BEOGRAD   [Telegram, receipt stamped:] 1949 SEP 10 AM 6 45

LC MILLER BIGSUR=
        CALIF=

SEXUS DISGRACEFULLY BAD WILL COMPLETELY RUIN REPUTATION
UNLESS WITHDRAWN REVISED LARRY=

*Big Sur   Sept. 28th, 1949
        Dear Larry,
To-day I got another letter from you about *Sexus* together with your carbon to Girodias, which was really "the works". I know you'd feel better if I did get angry with you, but I can't. I laugh and shake my head bewilderedly, that's all. Naturally I can't take an objective, detached view of my work. If I could perhaps I could see what you're driving at. To judge one's own work is impossible. Maybe you are right – maybe I'm finished. But I don't feel that way, not even if the whole world condemns the book.

The other day I finished Book 2, which I am now correcting. About the same length as the first. Not much sex in it at all. But it will probably have other faults – in your eyes. What I want to tell you is this – I said it before and I repeat it solemnly: I am writing exactly what I want to write and the way I want to do it. Perhaps it's twaddle, perhaps not. The fact that I put in everything under the sun may be, as you think, because I have lost all sense of values. Again, it may not. I am trying to reproduce in words a block of my life which to me has the utmost significance – every bit of it. Not because I am infatuated with my own ego! You should be able to perceive that only a man without ego could write thus about himself. (Or else I am really crazy! In which case, pray for me!) Since 1927 I have carried inside me the material of this book. Do you suppose it's possible that I could have a miscarriage after such a period of gestation? Perhaps it's a monster I'm giving birth to. But really, I don't care. The paramount thing is for me to get it out of my system – and in doing so to reveal what I was and am. I made a herculean effort to represent myself for what I then was. The only artistry I endeavored to employ was the capturing of that other self, those other days. I've been as sincere as I possibly could, maybe too sincere, because it certainly is not a lovely picture I made of myself. In justice, however, I think you, you particularly, should be able to read between the lines, to reconcile truth seeker with artist, liar, playboy and what not.

It was not my idea to bring these volumes out separately. I had wanted to hold them until I had reached the very last page. But Girodias implored and I gave in. I keep telling you to wait until you have read to the end. Not that I think there will come a change of style which will appeal to you, but simply that everything will then fall into place. Even trivial things take on a different light when viewed from the proper perspective. "Life's traces", wrote Goethe, speaking of *Wilhelm Meister*, I think. I read that in my teens – that phrase – and it sank deep. I want this book to contain "life's traces". Whether it is in good taste, moral or immoral, literature or document, a creation or a fiasco, doesn't matter.

I am trying to give you my honest thoughts, not to coerce you into changing your mind. One of the hardest things to accept is the divorce of a loyal admirer. You are more than that to me, of course. But aren't you trying to protect what you have always hoped I would be? Those defects you always spoke of blushingly, now they have come to a head, apparently. Soon I shall be just "a bundle of defects". That's classic. Inevitable, did I persist in going my own sweet way, which I have, you see.

Did I ever tell you, by the way, that *Sexus* was written from the end of 1941 (after the *Nightmare* trip) to the middle of 1942? I read it over since about four times, making revisions each time. The last time I read it over – correcting proofs – I was dazzled by it. In short, it seemed better to me each time I read it. If proof were needed to show how far gone I am, there you are! Of course, I ought to implement the foregoing by explaining that each time I read those incidents of my life I relived them – and quite presumably (as authors will) read into them all that I might have left out in cold print. On the other hand, it's usual to feel a growing disgust with a work on each rereading. Especially when it comes to the proof-reading. Faute de mieux, that was my sole criterion.

Book 2 was written these last two to three years, and under rather harrowing circumstances. Yet I like it even more than Book One. And as I make ready to tackle Book 3 I have a feeling of regret that I am coming to the end of this priceless material. My autobiographical life will then be done for. What's to follow God alone knows. Maybe I shall retire – defeated. But Larry, I can never go back on what I've written. If it was not good, it was true; if it was not artistic, it was sincere; if it was in bad taste, it was on the side of life. If I were a braggart and an egotist I might have written more gloriously. There is a poverty and sterility I tried to capture which few men have known. Far better to have been a gallows-bird! But I had only this one life to record. That passion you sense to be lacking has been put into the minus side. That life of "senseless activity", which the sages have ever condemned as death – that was what I set out to record. But as I say towards the end of Book 2 – I suffered out of ignorance – and thus was highly instructed. Perhaps in the summing up, my life will be seen to be a huge pyramid erected over a minus sign. Still, nevertheless, a pyramid. Perhaps better understood when placed upside down.

Thinking of your "defection" – if I may use that word without harshness, because I feel none towards you – I am suddenly reminded of a curious fact about myself, that when I like a writer profoundly I can read anything he writes and enjoy it – and I mean literally "anything". In a recent work Cendrars writes that he is the sort of reader who when he takes to an author not only reads him all the way through – and in the original language – but reads everything that was ever written about him. That I can't do. But again, what I am trying to say is – and this is undoubtedly my unconscious "plaidoirie" – what one looks for is the man, and the man is always there if you will examine the fibre of his creation.   . . .But men deteriorate sometimes. Yes, Larry, they do. When I come to realize that I am deteriorating I shall hide away and never be heard from again. I promise.

But you should be here, we should be talking face to face. Then we could meet heart to heart. Anyway, it's not arrogance or conceit that dictates this response. I don't have those thoughts about myself, my relation to others, to the world, which you impute to me. I have no thoughts about myself. I know what I am. It doesn't make me proud. I am . . . you are . . . he is. What does it amount to? That we are all one and the same. The important thing is that God is. And that we know ourselves to be part of HIM.

The "considered opinion" about this letter is that you are to feel at liberty to baste hell out of me to all and sundry. I will understand that you are doing it out of love for me. I would be a fool if I thought otherwise.

You know, when I laugh or weep over my own words, as I do on rereading the R.C., I think sometimes that I hear the whole world laughing and weeping. As a veteran (though perhaps still a "sentimentalist"), you must admit it is not so easy for me to do this. But if I am laughing and weeping alone – ah, then there's something wrong! "Quick, Watson, the needle!"

So far I have heard about the book only from you and two other readers. Haven't received a copy of it yet. Maybe somebody else wrote it and signed my name to it. (!!!)

Ever yours,
Henry

P.S. In the August issue of *La Nef* (Paris) you will find a fragment – in French – from Book 2 – *R.C.* Called *"Mon ami Stanley"*. Get a whiff of it!

*[Big Sur]   *Same day!* [28 September 1949]

Dear Larry –
Forgot to enclose this photo – or did I send you one before? If so, send it
on to Fred!

But anyway, here is a glimpse of my unknown brother from Pekin.
Is he not wonderful? No one is here to guide my hand or overlook my
work – true. Alas and alack! But this glorious Sage is ever at my elbow
– and in Book 2 (*toujours* "R.C.") – I take a riff and tell about him, what
I think he is and what he means to me. And the thrilling thought (to
me) is that he is not "unique" – that there are thousands like him in the
world – only most of us overlook them. They appear as paupers, not
princes.

How far all this from the preoccupations of Tito, Truman, Stalin et
Cie! If it's Belgrade there it's Big Sur here.

What by the clock?

Just yours –
Henry

*BEOGRAD   [Telegram, receipt stamped:] 1949 SEP 29 PM I 12

HENRY MILLER=
    BIGSUR CALIF=

DEEPEST APOLOGIES UNJUST CRITICISM WRITING NOTHING SAID
QUALIFIES ADMIRATION YOUR GENIUS HOPING FRIENDSHIP UN-
AFFECTED=
    DURRELL=

*[Big Sur]   *10/3/49*

Dear Larry –
I had just mailed you a long letter when your cable arrived. You will see
that I did not get angry. How could I? It is your privilege to attack me if
you feel I have written a bad book. I understand too that it must be
rankling – especially coming on the heels of your *Horizon* panegyric,
about which I am still getting enthusiastic letters. Why don't you ask
Connolly to give you space again – and blast hell out of me? Barkis is

willin'! In these matters friendship can only be asserted and maintained by the strictest probity. I have long ceased to defend myself against criticism or judgments. The work has to stand by itself. This doesn't mean that I am "immune" to criticism. Any good effects therefrom will have to be revealed in subsequent works. Argument and dispute is time wasted. I am not "the master". [. . .]

"Fratres Semper" (see Book 2). À vous toujours.

Henry

*Belgrade   [early October? 1949]

Dear Henry: I knew you would be wounded and of course it upset me bitterly to write to you. I shouldn't have done it really – little Joe is right. I enclose his letter [with] every word of which I heartily agree. But knowing how robust you are and how much yourself I felt I could take the risk of telling you how deeply horrified and disappointed I was by the book. But you say it is just the book you want, the way you want . . . And that is enough for me. Who knows really? You see far into the mists of the future and are probably a better judge [than] I of what will be what. But if I had seen the book in MSS I would have pleaded with you not to publish. I think you know I love you more than any man I have ever met; I owe you a lot. I felt I also owed you a truth or two about my feelings; it was no use pretending that I liked the new work. What I did not realise until I got Joe's letter was that my own criticism was ill-tempered waspish and liable to injure an old friend. Perhaps it is due to the fact that I found myself in a frightful dilemma; after the *Horizon* article I accepted three invitations to review your new book in three good papers. I tried to think what the hell to do. The book I thought really frightfully bad. Was I to do the usual murmuring trick that critics do? You wouldn't like me to do that. Yet you wouldn't want me to do what fashionable critics do – i.e. praise something because a friend had written it. I drew a deep breath and decided to come out in the open with it. I didn't realise that the tone might wound you – little Joe is right, I should have written differently. I was so god-damned hopping mad with you however, and so god-damned anxious to try and boost English interest in you that I nearly died of blood pressure. I took my annoyance out on you and I'm deeply sorry; and if you were a lesser sized man you would punish me by breaking contact. I did a review (I did eight reviews <in all> in fact) for *Horizon*. It is what I feel; it is terribly unkind.

Meanwhile from another angle the *Herald Tribune* was running a banner blurb for the book quoting me, and in this service we are supposed not to get our name in the papers; all published stuff has to pass the filter. <foreign office: some of my colleagues were wondering about it –> The essay was okay. But if *Sexus* had been the sort of book I hoped for I would have skipped that; as it was I felt so bad about it that I asked Kahane to take my name off the blurb. If it had been *Tropic* (which in some ways is much fiercer) nothing would have budged me. But Henry I simply couldn't defend *Sexus* to myself, let alone anyone else. It was a ghastly dilemma; believe me if I wounded you it was not in any spirit of wanton idle silly malice. You stand as high as ever you did for me. No one can take away what you are and what you say. But where I disagree with Joe is here: he thinks that you should be lulled and indulged. I DON'T THINK YOU ARE WRITTEN OUT. I THINK YOU AT THE EDGE OF THE MOST FERTILE PERIOD OF YOUR LIFE. A PERIOD WHEN THE SCALE OF THE MAJOR WORK MAY TIRE YOU, BUT WHERE THE LUCIDITY IS BRIGHTER AND SHARPER THAN IT EVER WAS. When I read the good 20 pages of *Sexus* in an anthology I thought it purer and greater than anything yet. But buried in the body of the book nobody will ever find it. I also knew that in USA you would not find friend or critic worth facing you on the issue. What a wilderness of cross-purposes. How sorry I am. I know that criticism doesn't really teach; but what is one to do in a case like this? Now I get your letter and I'm heartily sorry for my smallness. Please forgive me and ask Lepska to forgive me, and let's forget the whole business if you still care to. I don't think detailed criticism is much use with your work. It is only shape and density of structure that you could alter with a blue pencil. How I wish I could talk to you for a moment, could reach across the gulf. I know that you would see that in my heart I revere and honour you as a great genius of the XXth century. The rest doesn't matter really. But I must be true to the real you which I didn't feel was fairly represented in *Sexus*. Ask Lepska to write me a line: ask her to forgive my bloodiness and believe that really, far from being your bitterest critic, I am still 100 per cent for you and with you. Forgive me, will you?

     love   Larry

[P.S.] Henry dear, be the man you are, and forgive an old 'lover' <in the Elizabethan sense> and friend – I shan't be happy until I hear that you have. Only then will I say another word about the book.

*BRITISH LEGATION, BELGRADE.   12 October [1949]

Dear Henry:

Just a brief flash – I'm madly busy at the moment as you can probably guess; I hope you got my great packet of apologies and embarrassments. Furthermore I hope you swallowed your most justifiable rage and accepted some of them. Meanwhile I have been away on a long trip and have been reading you in Sarajevo, reading you again. I know what's wrong with the book now – its subject matter is no longer of any interest to you fundamentally; so you deal with it in a conscientious enough way but without the mad poignance etc of your other books. Now if you had written the same thing *from your present position* you would have integrated it properly with the new style (the last chapter is the new style for me – refined down to a point; the agent-provocateur is a marvellous creation). But all the tracts of Greenwich Village stuff come about because you try to throw yourself back into – and treat it as – suffering actuality. From your present peak in Darien there is only one attitude true and possible to you – emotion recollected in tranquillity. That gives range and detachment and a new kind of purity to the stuff. But these Ulrics and Maras belong to the *House of Incest* genre and simply cannot support a huge structure of 1000 pages. As to technique again I think the writing is laboured – stammer and stutter and trust in the blue pencil. But some of the longueurs are well below your average cruising standard; and the obscenity bites like an acid bath this time. It don't revive one. It's too much, one feels, too bloody much. But of course this is very unjust I see because you are always working towards something *through* something else . . . Mea culpa. We critics don't have half the patience and humility that goes with our station in these things. So pl. forgive.

Sarajevo is a strange place – a narrow gorge full of rushing waters; granite-red mountains and the town perched up on a cliff in a series of coloured bubbles of minaret and mosque; veiled women. Narrow streets full of mountaineers and mules. Wild crying of eagles in the air above it and all around a petrified ocean of rock with roads bulging round mountains, coiling and recoiling on themselves. I had a poem for the road which wouldn't get any further than

> Ideal because their coils were apt
> To these long sad self-communings
> Among alien peoples . . .

So I threw it in a gorge and took the flat road over the plain to this dreary white city on its dirty rivers. Life is an awful bore; looks like plenty trouble by the spring.

> Love to you all
> Larry

Big Sur   October 15, 1949

Dear Larry and dear Fred –

I wrote you, Larry, a longish letter about ten days ago, assuring you that I was not offended and urging you to get permission from Connolly to blast hell out of me – about *Sexus*. Now comes your letter with Joey's marginalia and his letter. I want you boys to stop worrying about me. You don't suppose that after all I've been through I would fold up because a dear friend happened not to like what I wrote, do you? I see you are concerned about my eventual, or immediate, sterility. Joey looks forward to my going gaga soon. Hold your horses, lads! True, I am approaching the grave, but I don't feel finished yet. J'ai encore quelque chose à dire. . . .

I wish, Joey, you were here sometimes to help me with my French. I'm now correcting Roger Cornaz' translation of my Rimbaud opuscule. I know what is wrong with his phrases but I can't tell him how to say it, in French. I want to recommend to both of you Giono's *Pour saluer Melville* (Gallimard 1945 or 46). This was written after spending three years on the translation of *Moby Dick*, which has just come out, I hear.

Only the other day I received a copy of *Sexus* for myself. Haven't had a chance to reread it yet. Busy revising Book 2 (*Plexus*).

I think the one word which sticks in my crop, after all the jeremiads launched at me, is "vulgarity". Such as it is, it is deliberate. And I begin to wonder if this ingredient will not also have to be reappraised, as was "obscenity" previously. Always remember that "I am just a Brooklyn boy." Recently I tried to reread my great favorite, Petronius – the father of the novel. Couldn't stick it. But there are analogies and reverberations there – to *Sexus*, I do believe. Sometimes I think that you, Larry, never really knew what it was to live in our modern age – of asphalt and chemicals. To grow up in the street, to speak the language of the Voyou. In Cendrars' recent autobiographical trilogy – and how I wonder if either of you could read through these! – there is an immense difference, in tone, between his backward looking and mine. (With Giono – *Blue Boy* – still greater – and Giono's I love best, I think!) But I was not born in the same milieu or tradition. Yet I not only appreciate their works, I adore them. I love what is different, as you know.

More and more, as I think of your words, Larry, I smile to myself, especially when you refer to the inane or inept or trifling conversational passages, some of them quite long too. I was rather proud of myself for having caught these so well. It is as if I took a few steps backward – towards an outmoded realism – but not really. I don't know how to explain what it is which, to my mind, saves this work from being "realistic" (in the crude, vulgar sense). But I am sure of it. Perhaps you have to examine more closely the work of certain painters who, though masters, were able to deal with "trifles". I think that the "trifle" was very important in my life – if you get what I mean.

Joey, I enclose a letter from *European Affairs* with this which you may make use of. Perhaps you can persuade them to accept something from your pen – on Paris, Vienna, Frankfort or London. I haven't decided yet what I shall do. I turn most requests down automatically.

Still planning to come over with the family next Spring! Soon even the small nations will have their atom bombs. Why worry?

Good cheer to you both – and no more apologies. Dying to read the blast! You know, I've always said, what I need is a good enemy. In this case "a friendly enemy". (Ennemi-frère, as the French say.) But remember about that "law of reflection"! As St. Exupéry says – On va où l'on pèse. . . .

Henry

[P.S.] Did Lepska write you? Don't pay attention to her remarks. She doesn't know what goes on in my head.

Giono's book on Melville appeared in 1941.

*BRITISH LEGATION, BELGRADE.   Oct 27 [1949]

Dear Henry: just a brief line on the Eve of leaving for Salonika by jeep where we hope to spend a week – I am on duty but it will be pure pleasure to get out of this filthy echoing rambling town, full of sodden Serbs, and strike out for the Macedonian hills again. Our crisis grows steadily uglier like a screw tightening, a little bit every day. Nobody can see the outcome – and the funny thing is that people loathe the Tito regime so much that they are completely apathetic about the outcome. Many would like to see the Russians come just in order to watch the block knocked off these communist gauleiters with their neat little theories; of course they realise with their rational faculty that the Soviet would be much worse. But they are simply desperate with the present police conditions. In this context I can assure you, having had a close look at Communism, that the USA witch-hunting and all is taking a far more sensible line than anyone else. We are still rotten with woolly liberal socialism and industrial guilt and are playing into the hands of these swine with every word we utter. There is simply no issue for us along Marxist–Leninist lines; it means the destruction of every value we stand for – as writers I mean. I know that our own culture was rotten – but compared to this it is flourishing in its decay, it is hopeful. This is sheer death. I am sending George Katsimbalis a telegram to ask if he can meet us in Salonika – it would be fun to see him again and talk over old times. You have immortalised him so successfully in the Greek book that he is now a famous Raimuesque character in Athens, and everyone calls on him just to say they have really met him. More news when I get back – if there is any that is not in the headlines.

I've sent Joey SEXUS in the dip bag: I hope to Christ it gets through all right to him. I'm curious to see what he makes of it; whether he is as enraged as I was . . . Forgive my stupidity cher maître.

Love to you all from your devoted Larry Durrell

*[Big Sur]   11/11/49

Dear Larry – Just got yours of October 12ᵗʰ – also review (Chesley Saroyan) in *Points*. Don't worry. Time will decide all issues. *Sarajevo!* How I envy you. Love to Eve and yourself. Cheerio! "L'ami, ni ardent, ni faible – L'AMI." (Rimbaud)

Henry

Dearest Henry and Lepska – a belated line from a snow-bound capital. We've been on the move again, hence my silence: this time we went north, through Croatia and Slovenia to Trieste, a strange treaty-port encircled by communists on the edge of the sea. Here at least we could see shops with something in them, and people who did not look whey-faced with starvation and fear. Cafés to sit in, and smiling faces. But the town for all its Italian population has a curious sedateness – a lack of southern brio. I discovered why – 60,000 Slovenes and 6000 Croats. The character of these Middle Europeans is dull, self-pitying and Slav – like the Poles; heavy as gunmetal. Far far from the Mediterranean lightness and sensuality. It was good however to see Trieste and understand why Stendhal reacted against it so strongly. After Italy he tasted the first harsh notes of Central European landscape and character – it smells of the great Hungarian plain and the steppes beyond – like a wise man he turned back to the warmth. I wish I had the same luck or good sense, or both. I have been reading a deal of Stendhal these days, more and more convinced that in his two big novels he has demonstrated a rationale for fiction which is the one most germane to the writers of the next fifty years. The power of creating an n-dimensional character in a single phrase: then letting the action develop the character without further interruption. As an autobiographer too he is delightful – struggling with a sensibility too charged with femininity and a shy pudicity – anticipating Freud, by the way, in a remark which follows a phrase describing the death of his mother, "Là commence la vie morale"! This view of character, by the way, emerges also in your agent-provocateur, in the latest novel, so ably defended by little Joe ——

Friday

Just got your card mentioning a belated Xmas present. We are a clearing-house for parcels for Yugoslavs, and often we get things we think are intended for us only to receive a following letter asking us to pass the parcel on! Latest and most mysterious parcel is three pairs of superb snow-boots, with nothing to indicate where they are from. I've telephoned everyone in this town to ask if they are expecting boots. Nobody appears to be: I'm wondering if they are your present. But if they are – how the devil could you get to Bond Street and buy us boots which are a *perfect* fit! When you write next pl. disillusion us about these boots. They are not being worn until we're sure they are not intended for someone else. Eve can hardly take her eyes off them they are so lovely. Perfect for Belgrade, too, where the winter is as heavy as Russia. We are way below zero with heavy snow and ice. I won't begin to tell you what the Slavs are suffering – no coal, not a scrap of warmth or decent clothing for any but Communist officials. And the government frantically depressing the standard of living in order to buy capital equipment which is broken as soon as they try to use it. What a madhouse Communism is. And how grateful we are to the USA for taking it seriously. Europe is a sheepfold full of bleating woolly Socialists who simply *cannot* see that Socialism prepares the ground for these fanatics. I wish you could come here and see it for yourself.

Needless to say this foetid atmosphere is not conducive to thinking or writing; and this political set-up gives me an awful lot of work to do. Nobody can tell how it will end – but there is a brief détente while the snow and ice hold out. I don't know how the Russians see things at all; but this Protestant movement is having an effect in surrounding countries as it is in England. It offers the psychological chance for Socialists who have begun to doubt to get off the band wagon and still save face. But what an unhappy country this is! Thank God we held Greece. I'm afraid, though I hate to admit it, that Churchill's view of things was the right one. But if *I* had to come to a communist country to understand that you can well imagine how muddled everyone is who has not seen this in action. Let's hope the old boy gets back into office – though we always let the mess become irretrievable before we invite him to clear it up for us. What a world.

Are you writing anything? Your piano looks swell. I saw a movie which would appeal to you – *The Fallen Idol* by *Carol Reed*. I'm still trying to persuade Friedman to do a Henry Miller anthology. What a book it would be!

Love to you all from a snow-bound
Larry and Eve

Miller's piano, featured on a postcard he sent, was painted in bright yellows, oranges and blues by the artist Zev, *nom de peinture* of Daniel Harris.

Dear Larry –

Always put off writing you because I seem only to send you notes. So difficult to find time to write a letter. I have been working *feverishly*, since January 17th, on a new book – about books – my experience with them. Fascinating! Have done 165 pages thus far. Now halting for breath and revising. God knows where or when it will end. But what a subject! Suggested to me by Larry Powell, the librarian. (Bless his name!) When I finish I'll tackle Book 3 (*Nexus*). Paris police seized French version (unexpurgated) of *Sexus*. Girodias put out also an expurgated one – for the public – both without my knowledge or consent (sic). More fat for the fire. No tears.

Don't worry about imminent war! If you knew this government's plans & projects (as I don't! but surmise), you'd rest easy. Do you know what? "We" are not worrying about Russia so much as about invaders from other planets. In 50 years "we" (our "*space men*") expect to reach the planet of a distant star *Wulf No. 6523* (?), to have a girdle of space ramps outside the gravitational field, *et cetera*. *Seriously!* Something's afoot – very, very mysterious. I think myself, that the inhabitants of other planets are worrying about damage we may do, unwittingly, with our new bombs and other diabolical inventions. Laugh, if you will! Communism will be knocked out not by an *opposing* ideology but by force of circumstance. Our "inventions" will upset the present order – of permanent conflict. Not superior views, better government, more humanity! You'll see.

Rest in peace! Working for the political hounds you lose perspective. Change the "frog" perspective for the "bird's". The age is so far ahead of its seeming problems. There's a knocking at the door. No one hears it. Too busy bickering, worrying, straightening things out.

I've made wonderful discoveries about my early reading – the deeper meaning of books for boys. You'll see when I finish. Discovering more about myself as I write of books. Childhood is *the* great period. Am trying to reread some very old ones. Just reread *She* (Rider Haggard). Have a look at it sometime. May surprise you.

No, we didn't send the boots! We could have, had we known your need. Filch them anyway! What *do* you need now *vitally*? Tell me.

More in a few days. This is a prologue. Best to Eve always. Wish you could get free of "work". You need to be on your own. Is it so impossible? You'll always be working for someone, if you think it's "necessary". Take a good think some day. Map out your life as you'd like to live it. Then jump! You are a "protected" individual. Life will take care of you, never fear. Because you *give* life!

Henry

P.S. That photo-card from Salonika – with the "fathers" – superb! You look very fit too. And Eve always beautiful. She has real human dignity, that wife of yours!

*BRITISH LEGATION, BELGRADE.   [early March? 1950]

Dear Henry: Just a line between trips to tell you that everything is okay – by that I mean everything is as hellish as ever here: and I'm afraid my letters must have the same lack of variety and newsiness as the letters from a prison: for that is what this is – on a scale impossible to understand until you've been here. Unluckily too the climate of this dust-blown capital is awful too, though the rest of the country is really beautiful. The people are like moles, frightened to death, shifty, uneasy. Meanwhile American and British left wingers arrive in this centre of barbarism comparable only to the darkest of the dark ages to inform these stinking communists how decadent we are and how we are about to collapse. Hitler was baby play compared to this. If capitalism isn't pretty it's at least one hundred thousand times prettier, more noble, freer, than this. But basta ... you will think I am raving until you come to [a] place that has fallen under the Marxist spell. ...

The prospectus about the discs sounded most exciting. Did you send me a set through the diplomatic bag? I'm sure they will arrive okay if you have; looking forward so much to hearing your voice again rolling out the sea-swelling periods of the books which "belong now to world literature" as someone says. I see there was some trouble in Paris about *The Rosy Crucifixion*. Hope it blew over in the usual way. You seem destined to rouse people: true mark of genius one supposes. Little Joe is at me for daring to criticise the master; Goddammit, the master isn't made of putty. He is suffering from post-war exhaustion and doesn't realise you've climbed right up beyond us into effortless period of pure play: where angustia is quiet. Reminds me I saw a picture of little Picasso at seventy – looking like a thirteen year old tomboy. He must be absurdly proud of his good figure as he won't be pictured unless he's in a bathing costume. I was reminded of that peculiar lightness and youthfulness of you in walking or swimming – eternal children. Eliot just sent me his *Cocktail Party* which is really a little masterpiece: effortless and wry and beautifully put together with every symbol working overtime – including the cocktail party and all it stands for in this age. To be profound *playfully* is new for him: he's become a Chinaman. And I can't tell you how sweet as a human being – vastly unlike the grave and composed man you met in our flat in 1938. His gentleness and humour and lovability have come to the fore. I send you a Groddeck prospectus: a good deal due to my efforts that he's reissued by a new publisher. I'm proud of my work. Hope they do the novels now which are supposed to be magnificently funny – so says Joe. I'm sending you the proofs of a new essay (in the real sense): it's a play called SAPPHO or THE TENTH MUSE which is due out in April. Wonder what you will think of it. A bit turgid but there are good things in it. Planning to spend June in Ischia with Zarian: wonder if there is any chance of you coming to Europe then? Love to you all.

Larry

For Durrell's view of the 'Chinese' Eliot see 'Tse-lio-t', which appeared in *Preuves* (April 1965) and *The Atlantic* (May 1965).

*[Belgrade]   [March–April 1950]

Henry –

Just off to Zagreb and the coast – I write you in haste to commend to your notice a most remarkable book I have just read by a man called Francis J. Mott, whose books are published by the McKay Co. of Philadelphia Pa. *The Grand Design* is an extension of the birth trauma idea – and gives a hair-raising and circumstantial account of the intra-uterine experience. *Please* make sure to read him. I think his books are as big a step forward from Freud as Freud's Dream Analysis was from the psychology of the Victorians. He is, in fact, a man of your own size – an American I gather. He is very modest, not a good writer, but his worth breathes the "liberation and harmony" of a great man. He speaks touchingly of neglect and isolation in his prefaces. Unknown in England.

But he knocks Rank, Jung and Groddeck cold by the breadth of his vision and the simple outlines of his new psychology which he calls "biosynthesis" – one of those uncomfortable U.S. neologisms like "mortician" and "cuspidor"! He's a great man. Please read him. He runs some sort of centre of integration or something I gather from his preface. *The Universal Design of the Oedipus Complex* will delight you by its sweep, and its tie-up with Eastern & ancient religions. I wish I could send it to you to make sure you got it and read it.

Love
Larry

There is no record of a book by Mott entitled 'The Grand Design', but his *The Universal Design of Birth* (1948), vol. 2 of his *Trilogy of Biosynthesis*, discusses the birth trauma at some length.
The 'Dream Analysis' Durrell is referring to may be Freud's *Dream Mechanism and Its Analysis*.

*[Big Sur]   6/26/50

Dear Larry –
Don't know if you've heard from S.F. attorney (for the Civil Liberties Union, N.Y.) – George C. Olshausen. He's defending importation of the two *Tropics* shortly. Seeking testimonials from noted critics, authors, professors as to "the *literary* merits" of the books. If he writes you I hope you can respond. I've told him of your article in *Horizon*, of course.

Funny thing – until I got a letter recently from Chesley Saroyan – cousin of Bill Saroyan – I thought *you* had written the article on *Sexus* in the Paris bi-lingual revue *Points*. Didn't believe there could be any but *Bill* Saroyan. Forgive me!

Deep in the new book. Nothing new of any consequence. But feel *quite* certain now we will get over there next Spring. Did you ever get the recordings I sent you – with the famous "Letter from London" (Perlès & Durrell) included? Sent you some worn-out Jugoslavian slippers bought here for $2.50. Wondered if you see these over there and could send me another pair same size – my expense? Larry Powell was here & sends warmest greetings. He dotes on you. Goes abroad in September on a fellowship (Guggenheim). You must meet him. He will make headquarters in London but fly to Continent now & then.

Je t'embrasse, tous les deux.
Henry

[P.S.] Have been getting wonderful letters from dear old John Cowper Powys in North Wales – one of my early "influences".

*Belgrade   [July 1950]

Dear Henry: Just got back to this hellhole from Ischia where we had a delightful month with old Zarian – who incidentally suggests that you should spend a year in Ischia with him discussing the fundamental problems of life, art, sex, death ... On arriving back I'm up to my waist in papers; tomorrow I leave by car and cross the mountains to Sarajevo and Dubrovnik, and thence north along the coast to Split and inland to Zagreb ... a tiring journey through an impoverished if magnificent landscape. Back here all being well in 8 days I hope and will write you another letter on arrival; so much to tell you but literally no time. Situation is as ever blackish with few patches of light about: god knows how long it will be before the whole bag of tricks goes up. I'm anxious not to get captured by the Russians either and spend the rest of my life in a salt mine. I guess I've got enough material about men and affairs to furnish a dozen big novels. Next step is to buy a small house with the acre of land. Believe me, I know that every word of your letter is true; but our money set-up prevents me at the moment from buying a place anywhere but England. I haven't adopted this profession for love but because it's a useful means of getting into position to buy a house in a country I like; a Greek or Italian posting would decide the matter pronto for me ... I'm unlike you: I plan things as carefully as possible, trying to curb my Irish impulses as much as possible! I am trying to find the owner of a house on Ischia who wants to sell for pounds; if I buy then we shall cut the traces and see what fortune has in store for a writer pure and simple.

No, the discs never arrived. Did you address them properly? Perhaps they violated some customs regulations, but it is odd that the Foreign Office did not notify me of the arrival of anything from the States; if you send me a set of anything like that, that might seem dutiable to the idiots in the customs, please mark the package COMPLIMENTARY FREE SAMPLE, and it might get through. Books seem to arrive okay.

As for the Yugoslav slippers ... my dear Henry you are crazy. You cannot have the faintest idea what a communist country is *like*. It is quite impossible. I remember that I could never quite understand what it was all about until I struck one . . . I won't try and tell you. Your old shoes would fetch twelve dollars here on any street. There are no new ones of any kind to be had. You can sell needles at a dollar a piece. A ten cent pocket comb at the moment fetches four dollars . . . No, but you won't understand even now. BUT IF YOU CAME HERE FOR A WEEK, you'd realise that even a great war would be justified to prevent THIS, and liberate the millions under the yoke of this tyranny, this moral prison. That is why my heart leaps when I see that the USA has really tumbled to Communism, and has bounded into Korea. Hurrah. While our milk and water liberal cryptos are havering, and while the European artist is disgracing himself irretrievably by his support for something 100 times worse than Caligula at the least, the god-damned old Yankees have woken up with a start to what this really means . . . But you will disapprove. You should see this place.

Much love to you both and the kids
Larry

*BIG SUR: CALIFORNIA   9/2/50

Dear Larry –
The carpet slippers from Slovenia just came – and just fit. A great surprise! Thank you! Lepska bought last pair obtainable – for herself – recently, for 98 cents. Just had good letter from an old literary favorite of mine, a Croatian – Prof. Janko Lavrin of the University, Nottingham. Hear frequently now from John Cowper Powys, living in Wales. Dylan Thomas was here a month or two ago. Much fatter – very soft, tender, lovable – and wiser!
Just finishing Vol. I of my new book about books, for Laughlin to publish next Spring. It will run to several volumes. Then I go back to R.C. to write Book 3. Girodias hasn't called for script of Book 2 (Plexus) yet. Brought out a new, one volume, paper edition – cheaper – of Sexus.
Hear from Fred you have a new book out. Good!
George Dibbern, author of Quest (first world citizen) won 10,000 pounds in a lottery & bought an island off Tasmania. All my friends welcome, he says. Remember, in case you need a quick refuge. Address – Kettering, Tasmania. Permanent mail address – 2, Corry Avenue, Napier, New Zealand.
Every one loath to believe war will spread. See only suicide for all

concerned. But nobody *knows* anything. All goes forward, as usual, with secrecy and complacency.

At last I see what your job is, *your office*. Hoop-la! You'll be "pro-consul" next.

Love to you both meanwhile.

Henry

The United Nations police action in Korea was causing concern that eventually China and the USSR would become actively engaged. On 26 November 1950 Chinese forces crossed the Yalu River into North Korea.

*[Big Sur]   11/4/50

Dear Larry –

Sappho came at last. Superb work! Enjoyed it thoroughly and marveled at your steel-like grip of subject matter. Phaon and Pittakos – splendid portraitures. Your language always under command – how could you do it, living the life you have these past few years? I see now the "poet" is unscathed. The dramatist in you most promising. You keep remind-ing me, in this, of Shakespeare. I must say that, in spite of yourself, you put the case for Pittakos, tyrant, victim of life's will, most convinc-ingly. Phaon, talking to Sappho of his island life, touches the heights. I'll write you more soon, on a second reading. Sappho in a new guise, most enchanting and very much *you*. (With a tincture of Eliot's gray foreboding wisdom.) But somehow Shakespeare comes out in this – the flavor of him, his essence, his magic of language. Yet it's Greek – and of no time, or all time. "We" are not deceived by tyrant-and-mob business. What wots here is the poet – his fate. It's secure. There are passages on the role and effect (of poet) which are revelatory & per-sonal. It's very alive, your play – and the drama itself thrilling. I'd like to see another book in another medium on just Sappho and Phaon. In them you have terrific symbolism to play with. But this is all sketchy, too rapid, unthinking. I'll write again soon. Just wanted you to know quick! I feel somehow that this work will launch you. Don't *cut* as suggested in back of book – cut down on some of the sometimes too florid, vague, too beautiful (precious) speeches. But it's your *poetic* utterance I like – and the poetic feeling. Do more plays, yes! Hallelujah!

Henry

P.S. Got a wonderful walking stick from John Cowper Powys. He's a darlint of a man.

Have you gotten in touch with Larry Powell – Amer. Exp. London? He's dying to see you, I believe. He's one of your keenest, staunchest admirers.

*Belgrade   December 1. 1950

Dearest Henry – what a pleasure to get one of your generous ringing letters about *Sappho*. I'm glad you liked her. She's been most extraordinarily lucky ever since she was born. First Eliot liked her so much that he insisted on publishing her – at a dead loss to Fabers I'm afraid. Now Margaret Rawlings has bought her and intends to act her in London (she is, so to speak, the Catherine Cornell of the English stage). Also Knopf have decided to produce her in the States in a fine edition. One can't complain, can one – and now you praise what I would have [been] gladdest to hear praised – the symbolism! And particularly the warrior! Hurrah! Our literature is so full of either-or's; peace or war; mystic or warrior. It would have been easy to load the scales *for* contemplation against action, for peace against war. But recently I've become less and [less] sure of generalised judgements and more and more sure of what's true for me. To attempt to impose my Me as a judgement falsifies it. And the shape of the world – such a dream really! – is beyond our wildest cognitive efforts. So my warrior is also growing on another part of the wheel in his own measure. Who knows whether one god's dung isn't another god's perfume? We have suffered too much from a limited Pantheon. The Greeks were right to *crowd* theirs in praise of all contradictories!

Meanwhile terrible amount of bloody work – and the gathering clouds. We're in a sort of trap here, a killing-box! I'm so tired of being chased out of countries, too.

Have you ever read *Walden*? What a lovely fruitful book – all about the Chinese too. *How* did Thoreau ever find them to read in the USA of his time? His references however are unmistakable – and of course he's an ironist after Lao Tse's own heart.

Love to you all – keep writing and smiling. The live spirits know what your value is – never mind the neglect of the dead. I see the Russian radio

is attacking you, bracketing you with Kafka, Sartre and D.H.
Lawrence!

Larry

The proposed Knopf edition of *Sappho* was never published.

*[Big Sur]   1/16/51

Dear Larry –
Thoreau is one of the (4) American writers I respect and was influenced
by – you know the others: Emerson, Whitman – the 4th I can't remember (!). (Probably Dreiser)
    Just read Henry Adams' *Mont St. Michel and Chartres* – what a
beautiful profound book! Do read it! It's for *now*.

Henry

*Belgrade   [early September 1951]

Henry, dear, it was a great disapp[t] to miss you in England. We had both
so much looked forward to seeing you. It seems such an age since we
said goodbye in Sparta in the mist – and it doesn't look as if we are
going to meet in Tibet does it? We got back here yesterday after a
boiling trip in the Simplon Orient with our new baby Sappho, who is
charming and very dark like Eve: and shows signs of being good-
tempered and pretty. We saw something of little Joe and his wife (who
is lovely and very charming) in England and were hoping for a grand
reunion, specially as George Seferis is at present in London and very
keen to see you after so long. There is also a young man called Ackroyd
who proposes to edit a book of y[r] letters. I felt rather strongly about
this, perhaps Joe wrote you. Your reputation is v. low in England and it
is time somebody did a serious study of y[r] work. I see no purpose in
letting somebody, who seems not to want to do any of the work, climb
onto your shoulder into the public view. I very much fear another
disastrous *Happy Rock* will be the outcome. I'm only anxious about
your sales – I know where you stand as a writer. But it seems to me that
you are no longer in the position where you have to grab at every
straw, at every unknown admirer. I wrote and pleaded with Ackroyd

254

to do a serious critical study of y^r work which we would all be glad to help with; but all he seems to want is for us all to write his book for him. I really don't see *what* his part in the affair is; nor for that matter who will accept the sort of book he envisages. People are a bit shaken by the *promiscuity* with which you've lent your name around for inferior people to use – and if a book composed of letters, a sketch of you by Alf in his Central European vein, and a portion of Ackroyd's writing itself, comes before the public, it will not help you at all. A serious study would at least force your merits and/or demerits upon the reviewing press. It would have to be discussed at length: and there are enough people who admire y^r work to begin the task of re-instating you with the general public – which you badly need. It hurts me very much that after so many years devoted to your art, and with such a great bulk of immortal writing behind you, you don't rank higher in the esteem of your fellow writers – who after all were the first to draw attention to you and to signal your appearance. If I were your publisher I would try and get a serious book written about you – and then to press forward with an anthology of your best work on the lines of the ground-plan I sent Laughlin two years ago. Meanwhile I would persuade you *not* to appear in any more little mags free of charge – but to demand good prices for your work and only print it in well-founded quarterlies. I think within three years you would shed the reputation for hopeless *irresponsibility* and take on the mantle of the greatest American writer of the day – which of course you really are. As I say, it is only y^r sales which concern me in this respect. I think they would begin to pick up. I put all this to Joey with some force and I think he half-agreed with me, but meanwhile I think Ackroyd is going ahead with his idea – a hopelessly misconceived one I think, though of course the writing will be good and the book possibly interesting, and Mr Ackroyd will get his name before the public in good company with the minimum of personal effort. O Dear! I wonder if you see what I mean? At any rate, before sending Ackroyd the letters of yours which I possess I thought I would tell you what I feel about this project. It is no good. Though perhaps I am wrong about it. Let me have a brief line telling me what you think.

I feel that a visit to Europe is *essential* to you for y^r work this year. I think the feeling of a vacuum (critical) around you and the lack of competition at your level is bad for your work. In Europe you would feel surrounded by a fruitful medium which would be like a compass-bearing for future books. And with you one always feels that some perfectly astonishing work is just around the corner. I don't feel that you've passed meridian – but that your greatest work lies ahead of you: where the personae of your books can be gathered up and rewoven at a higher *symbolic* level. I foresee a sort of prose *Faust*. Ah! if you could only lie fallow for a year, not writing, not thinking, by the Mediterranean, it would come, this book full of the innocence, amorality and ripeness of old age. Have you read Petronius? Your books are still middle-aged books. You are now moving into old age with all the ripeness of practice and the terrific equipment of a prose-gift unique in this age. To rehash the subject matter of *Cancer* à la Vol 1 of *The Rosy Crucifixion* is *not you*. It represents a fixation about an attitude to life which you can no longer support and *act* from: but even here the traces of the *other book* are clear. I wish we could drown the project in good wine on some Greek island, and walk among the Delian statues to talk you into your new-old self. The fulcrum is repose.

But *come* to *Europe* – poor ravaged Europe. You will still find the conversations, the spirits and the food you need for this next step. Eliot sends his greetings to you. And we send our homage and our love.

    Larry

*Big Sur   10/22/51

    Dear Larry –
Haven't been able to write you because I've just been thru another crisis – Lepska has decamped. I am to keep the children. Have Val with me now and Tony as soon as I find a woman to help me keep house. As for Ackroyd and that book, I leave it to the gods. I do appreciate though your concern about it. What does it really matter however? I am irresponsible, yes, in a healthy way. *I* can't take measures to preserve my reputation. Me and my reputation will always be separate things.

    I'm delighted the girl is called Sappho, and not named after some new British man-of-war!

    You know, perhaps when things straighten out here, I may come over – with the two kids. I long to see Europe again – and you and all the old true friends. I pray every day now that Providence will send me the woman I need for my children – that is all I ask. Otherwise I am safe, sound, hearty, even growing merry again now that the storm is over. But it was an ordeal. Ça travaille dedans. Like Ramakrishna, I must now wear skirts as well as pants. Ça fait du bien. Greetings to Eve, to Seferis too. All will be well.

Henry

*The British Embassy   Belgrade   [November? 1951]

Dear Henry – just got your letter about Lepska. I'm in the dark – you sound pleased about it so I don't know whether to condole congratulate or commiserate. But whatever the set-up is it seems obvious that it's a bad look-out for the kids – you simply can't look after them by yourself – if you are the same Henry we once knew. What are you going to do? My dear Henry – I was hoping that by now you were a settled family man and were going to sit down and give us the great fireside books of your later period. You can't start all over again – I mean the travelling bohemian life – roving and suffering and starving – can you? I've no idea what came between you but is it really permanent, irremediable? And a bust family for the children is like a solar system without a moon. But of course you know all this and have been through it all before – so what is there to say? What about Lepska herself? What is she like? She looked a sweetie from the only picture you sent, and the kids marvellous. What is to happen to you all now? I just had a letter from little Joe saying that he had no news from you and feared something was wrong. He is proposing a joint book about you. I would do a critical study and he would do the portrait side of it. I wonder if we could make such a book seem homogeneous – connected. As soon as I finish the Rhodes book which I hope to do by the end of the year I must face the idea seriously. I doubt that collections of letters etc will advance your fame in England. I would like to put up a serious challenge to the critics to assess your status. But at the moment I work like a nigger – and this country is unpropitious for thinking –

Write soon and tell us your plans.
Larry.

Dear Larry –

No, I am no longer the same Henry you knew – not quite, at least. I am taking care of the kids. I adore them. Have no time for anything else. Nothing else matters now. I must wait until I find another woman – a new "mother". It is very difficult – perhaps the hardest job in the world. And I am now 60! What a turn!

Don't worry about "my reputation" and all that. That belongs to posterity – and destiny. Doesn't interest me in the least. I know I shall yet write *Nexus* and perhaps "Draco and the Ecliptic" too. After that I am ready for the next world. Ready any time, in fact. If this life was good, as it was, the next should be even better.

I will come to Europe in the Spring, with or without the kids, if I can possibly manage it.

All the best to you & Eve and the little one. The little ones! They are *our* protection.

[unsigned]

My dear Henry – my heart goes out to you. You are at least lucky to be left with your daughter: it would have been much worse if she had been stolen as mine was. I *do* hope you solve the problem of looking after her satisfactorily, and still manage to do your work. We are having enormous fun with Sappho-Jane, who is a great comedienne and most intelligent.

I am asking her godfather John Mott (a man after your own heart) to send you a copy of his latest publication which is, so to speak, the sign-manual for a new group he has founded which I am joining. It is so refreshing to find a philosopher who wants to organise and activate, rather than just to weave hypotheses. So much that he has to say applies to us – great amateurs that we are of all religions and philosophies – but to which we refuse full allegiance: Mott is against "all the idle chatter of the fore-brain" as he calls it, and yet he insists on a bare and scientific approach to mysticism which reminds me of the ancient Greeks – for whom the *noumenon* was not a vague and shadowy territory but a clear factual chthonic reality. I've already sent you Mott's books which deal with the psychology of the individual. Now you will see his attempt to apply it to a group. I must confess that he is one of the most remarkable men I've come across, and the absolute silence which has greeted the appearance of his work – complete neglect – confirms the view. No publisher will touch him, no critic examine him seriously. He is exactly in the position that you were in when we first started agitating about *Tropic of Cancer*. In many ways he reminds me of you – physically I mean – and he has the same puckish sense of humour. I don't know whether you will find him easy to read: the beauty of his work lies in his thought rather than in literary charm of expression. But I think his idea once grasped cannot help but make one gasp – and the new theory of consciousness, of Mind [?], he puts forward is really something we cannot afford to miss. Will you have a look at this book, carefully?

Our intellectual position in the West is so sterile – a mere onanistic flirtation with ideas which lack the basic discipline of a creed – Tibet, China, Steiner, Ouspensky, Catholicism etc. I think Mott has come nearest to satisfying the claims of both reason and illumination, and that in a sense the future will belong to some such formulation as his, "affect engineering" as he so beautifully calls it. At any rate here is an organisation whose structure is determined by a voluntary belief in cosmic form operating on the human level – a chance both to belong (who doesn't need to today) and to continue one's self-exploration fruitfully as a contribution to a pattern, and not an irritant sand-grain in the oyster-flesh of the world – yielding the black pearl of a poem perhaps for whom the public remains unborn —— Basta ——

>Love from us both
>Larry.

The book by Mott that Durrell is referring to here is apparently *The Universal Design of the Oedipus Complex* (1950), in which Mott describes the development of the consciousness through a 'configurational sympathy' between 'the human organism in its various stages and organs' and the cosmos.

*Big Sur   3/10/52

>Dear Larry –
No, that Mott book is not for me, sorry. I must say however that that "Constitution" is without precedent. But there just can't be a Society of

Life. Also, I think it's time to stop worrying about the destruction of life. Life is inextinguishable and eternal.

The man who really gives the quietus to "the forebrain", who explains the basic split, etc. is an unknown Jew named S. Greiner. *That* I've never read the like of. Now Erich Gutkind has come out with a new book – *Choose Life: The Biblical Call to Revolt.* It's just up my street – and I am only a Goy, as you know. But still ——. No, Larry, for me there simply are no English writers or thinkers. They are all terribly "corrugated" – like the folds of the brain itself. You know, I suppose, that it is from the brain surgeons themselves – not the Christian Scientists – that we are learning how little the brain has to do with mind. You can now cut away about 7/8 of the bloody brain and still function. Remember Joey saying (à la Steiner) "food is the enemy of man"? Ditto the brain.

No, you'll never organize the "new group" (The Ark) – or whatever – with a Constitution and set of rules such as friend Mott outlines. It defeats itself. I believe all you say about the man and I wish him well.

Now both children are with the mother – temporarily at least. I couldn't cope with the situation single-handed. My friend gave up, the young woman quit after 48 hours of it, and there I was – and locked in, too, by a ten day rain. *Formidable.* I was utterly exhausted.

For a new mate maybe I'll have to come to Europe. A Belgian next, or an Italian, I hope. Not an *Anglo-Saxon.*

Did I tell you Hachette has taken over Girodias' firm, will publish *Plexus in English* by end of this year, and promise full, regular payments? Just paid off my last personal debt. Getting on my feet, slowly. Am a good housekeeper, gardener, etc. But I am not happy. Too much to ask, maybe. Love

Henry

P.S. Even in French I think you will like *Plexus,* due out this Spring (Corrêa, Paris). *The Books in My Life* due out in England & U.S.A. simultaneously this Spring too. A honey.

Dear Larry –
Just a word to tell you things have altered radically for me – for the
better. In the first place, I've found an "Eve". She's been here since ten
days now, and it was a thorough go from the first. Every day I congratulate myself on my great good fortune. I tell you, I feel like a new
man – and about 30 years younger! Moreover, I look it. It's just
unbelievable what a change she has wrought in me. Naturally, she's the
complete opposite of Lepska. It's like living on velour, to be with her.
And so capable she is – so gracious, tender, full of understanding.
Reminds me in many ways of Anaïs. Strange thing is that she is the
sister of my friend Schatz's wife. I'll send you a photo of her one day.
To compare with your Eve. She's Scotch-Irish-French with a drop of
Jewish blood in her – a fine leaven. I haven't lost my temper once, nor
been grouchy or irritated or depressed – which I was constantly during
the seven years with Lepska. The children will be here with us for the
Summer. Then I hope we (Eve and I) can take off for Europe, for a few
months' visit at least. Like Anaïs again, she brings with her the feeling
of ease and abundance. So, wherever you are, rejoice for your miserable
friend who was for many months in the throes of despair. Soon you
should be receiving my Rimbaud, *Plexus*, and *The World of Sex* – all in
French. Alraune (my *Scenario*) was given a tremendous & successful
broadcast from Paris recently.

Henry

[P.S.] You should also have by now *My Life with Books* from the
English publisher, Peter Owen.

'Alraune' was the title of an unpublished novella by Anaïs Nin that became the basis for
her *House of Incest* (1937, but written as early as November 1932), which in turn inspired
Miller's surrealist piece, *Scenario* (1937).

*Belgrade   [May 1952]

My dear Henry – I am so happy for you! It is wonderful to feel the
sudden lift and curve of happiness come through even in your handwriting! And if you come to Europe can you make Athens? Listen, we
leave on the 1ˢᵗ of June by car for Salonika and Athens. We have

complete camping equipment to make us independent and the idea is to find a small fishing village about 40 miles from Athens and to settle down for 6 weeks' leave there. We've got our tiny daughter Sappho-Jane with us who must be baptised in the Mediterranean and I want to find a peasant house with a kitchen so that the routine of her feeding and sleeping is easy to fix and doesn't cost Eve too much effort. Myself I only want a couple of days in Athens to hunt for a possible job but if there was any chance of seeing you and carrying you both off to my hideout I would, of course, jump at it. Cable me will you if there is any chance of us being in Greece at the same time. Failing that I am planning to spend August camped by the lake of *Bled* in northern Yugoslavia. Very beautiful place. Where will you be then?

> Best love to you both and
> Hurrah!
> Larry

*BIG SUR – CALIFORNIA   9/21/52

Dear Larry –

Returning herewith the c/s with Mott, except for Alf's letter, dated London March 1952. This I'll copy & return, if you wish it.

Your letter to Alf I read with great interest. I would say, Larry, keep at it if it means this much to you. As a defender, upholder, champion, referee and expositor extraordinary you are without equal. Anything you are passionate about must have significance and what's more, be of vital concern to *you*. The getting of adherents (to any cause, principle, doctrine, idea) is always a dismal affair. The problem doesn't concern me, though I recognize its existence. In the closing pages of *Siddhartha* (Hermann Hesse) you have my thoughts on the subject expressed incomparably. Wonder if you ever read it?

Also wonder if you got a copy of my book on books – Peter Owen, London, was to send you one, and Alf too. But they are constipated, these bloody English publishers, and so vague! What ails them? *Dead ducks.* [. . .]

Now getting a divorce. Children being shared – one yr. with mother, one with Eve and me. They're with mother now. My life goes along like a song with Eve. The first real mate I've had.

Did you know *Plexus* was out – in French only thus far? About ten

262

books in translation now – the (2) *Tropics* coming out both in German & Danish. And *Black Spring* in Swedish.

Not much chance of going to Europe yet. No money. Need lots of cash for such a trip. But I still hope to make it. Expect a Russian invasion and occupation of all Europe in next 3 months.

Have started *Nexus*. Am painting too. And gardening. Well, all the best to you, Eve, Sappho and the Life Society. Why don't you retire to a Greek island soon? Don't see how you stand that life of turmoil. England is definitely finished as a nation, you know that. But the Italians will live on, and the Greeks and the Spaniards. Before your death you'll probably see a *Chinese* invasion of Europe.

Good cheer, Larry me lad. And where's Gerald now?
Henry

*Belgrade [c. October 1952]

Dear Henry – Marvellous to hear from you. [. . .]

A thousand thanks for the *Books* book which has just arrived and is full of marvellous things. I'm mid-way in it, and it brings back so many memories to hear your tone of voice again. Last week in Trieste I happened upon a pile of *Cancers* and *Capricorns* in a bookshop. The new edition with Anaïs' preface. Riffling them through I suddenly remembered you standing at the table talking in Villa Seurat, the sun shining, a bottle of Volnay on the table, Betty cooking and Joe repeating "Ja Ja Ja". Such a pang for those good Paris days with *The Booster!* Wonder when we'll meet again. How good it would be to hear your voice.

By the way I'm quitting the service in December and we are setting off to Cyprus I think. No money. No prospects. A tent. A small car. I feel twenty years younger. Heaven knows how we'll keep alive but I'm so excited I can hardly wait to begin starving.

I'll take you on the Russian invasion – Chinese? Well, let's get through the first to begin with. Hope to Christ we get out in time. 2 hours from the border here.

Love to you both
Larry

Larry Frustrated
Henry Fêted

Durrell plans carefully for 1953: it is to be his big year; he resigns from his highly paid position as press secretary in Belgrade, calculating that he has enough money saved to buy a small house on Cyprus and have a 'golden year' free to write his long-planned 'Book of the Dead'. Around Christmas 1952 he is scheduled to leave Yugoslavia, but Eve has a nervous breakdown and is flown back to England. Durrell and the baby, Sappho, go to Cyprus after the doctors assure him that his presence will not help Eve's condition. He buys his 'Turkish house' near Bellapaix Abbey, and the purchase and remodelling of his dwelling are to form one of the dramatic currents of *Bitter Lemons*. The expense of maintaining Eve in England, and an army of masons and plumbers locally, drains his finances, and soon Durrell is teaching a class of sixth-form girls in Nicosia.

Durrell never shows anything but joy at Miller's good fortune during these years, yet Henry's triumphant progress across Europe with *his* Eve – Eve McClure, sister-in-law of his good friend the painter Bezalel Schatz – must have led to wry comparisons. For seven months Miller is courted by his French publishers and visited by his old friends: Georges Belmont, Brassaï, Hans Reichel. He tours Spain with the Delteils. Back in Big Sur he receives Katsimbalis and Van Wyck Brooks; Perlès appears to complete *My Friend Henry Miller* and to re-create their usual good times together. Barbara, his first daughter, whom he had come to consider lost to him, arrives and they get along famously. His joy during these years is darkened in the spring of 1956, when he returns to Brooklyn to sit at his dying mother's bedside for three months, but he also resumes writing this year, making some progress on *Nexus* and completing *Big Sur and the Oranges of Hieronymous Bosch*.

Durrell's position in contrast is bad – he has an ill wife, an endangered marriage, a low-paid job, a child to look after – but he does, eventually, have an attractive house, made over to suit his need for space and an artistically satisfying environment. Then he makes a fatal mistake: he asks Alan Thomas to send out the books stored in the loft above the bookstore. By that act, as Thomas has noted, Durrell seals his fate: an international catastrophe is bound to ensue. When Thomas sent Durrell's library to him on Corfu, the Second World War broke out. Within months of the shipment to Cyprus EOKA bombs begin going off as the Greek Cypriots agitate for ENOSIS, union with Greece. Durrell is invited to return to Foreign Office service, as press officer in Nicosia. He finds it necessary to abandon his Bellapaix home, both for personal safety (he is nearly shot one evening in a local taverna) and to shield his neighbours, who might be killed merely for associating with an Englishman. However, through his work during these chaotic times he meets Claude Vincendon, the woman most nearly able to sustain his demanding daemon; and during this time he completes *Justine*.

*from Vienne (Isère)   3/16/53

Dear Larry –
Fred just forwarded your card (to him) of recent date. Am overwhelmed. What rotten luck! Can't believe, yet, that all's over between you and Eve. I know so well what you must be going through. But surely you can find some one to take care of the baby in Cyprus – or have you both children there?
    Here we are, Eve and I, knocking about in France. Expect to stay another 2 months, then back to Big Sur. [. . .]
    Don't come back to Europe to stay! I am convinced there will be war before the Summer is out – it seems absolutely inevitable. England & France will again have a rough time of it. Pick a good spot – remote, peaceful – to weather the storm. And remember what Kate said when her husband asked "What do we do in such a case?" "Why we get down on our knees and pray, Mr. Blake." Yes, Larry, pray – even if you don't know whom to address your prayers to. Remember too, we are never alone. I have been through it time and again, and each time emerged purified. Try to imagine that you are now *180* years old, instead of 40. You may even begin to laugh. Your laugh I can never forget. It was tonic, Gargantuan, healing, saving.

Anyway, don't relapse! You quit the job and it was a right move. Now comes the supreme test. Stick to your guns. Believe me, to be naked before the world is not the horrible thing people imagine. It is then you begin to live. [...]

Here, chez Maillet, I have found a kindred spirit. A sort of Christ – the real one, not of the Church.

Zen is usual life.

March on!

Hallelujah!

Damn you, laugh! You're not "the man of sorrows".

Henry

*Ionian Bank   Kyrenia   Cyprus   25 March [1953]

Dearest Henry – wonderful to hear from you. I was a bit shocked when I wrote Fred because we had planned this move months ahead and worked it out to the nearest penny. I was to have a whole golden year off to work! We were going to buy a small house etc etc – and this comes right on top of my resigning and burning all the bridges behind me. Of course Eve is not quite right in the head yet – but it has put me in a hell of a spot. There is nothing one can do with a small child round one's neck. Nevertheless I have stuck to the main plan. I've bought a small Turkish house on a hillside in a village near here; it will be fixed by the end of May. It should be very nice. But of course keeping two establishments and living here is eating into the capital we'd saved for the house – and as yet I don't know where the income to keep us here is coming from. I'm not in immediate need or anything – thanks for offers to help. I don't need help as yet and may not if my gamble comes off. What a pity you can't come and camp with me for a while. You can get here from Marseille for about £21 on quite nice line. Meanwhile Seferiades is Greek Minister in Beirut – you could call on him. Then Suarès in Alexandria – he is very rich and hospitable. Cyprus is comparatively cheap and I reckon that by about early June I could find you a corner in the house. Think about it, will you? I'm aiming to settle here. It's a big coarse-grained island with lovely spots in it. People nice, good roads and you can buy *anything* English or American. Palm trees. It's a piece of Asia Minor washed out to sea – not Greece. It's Middle East – taste of Turkey and Egypt.

I'm trying to write a book about Alexandria at night – but I'm dead beat usually after handling the baby. She's such an angel. No I haven't forgotten how to laugh – but there hasn't been a fit subject for the last few months. Eve has been frightfully ill – and now I'm engaged in a desperate gamble, spending capital, waiting for some baby solution which will enable me to work.

I've been watching the tremendous and deserved accolade the French Press have been giving you. Your reputation is at meridian, hurrah. Think about a visit – you should see where Aphrodite was born and her baths. There are masses of cars on the island and good roads – good wine too. Pick up Katsimbalis at Piraeus and bring him along.

> Love
> Larry

*Paris   May 3rd '53

Dear Larry –

We just got back from Belgium – Bruges particularly – and in a few days plan to leave for Montpellier (south of France) to join Delteil, the French Surrealist writer, & his wife, and go with them by car to Spain for a few weeks. We have with us Eve's sister and her husband, Lillik Schatz, who live in Jerusalem. Lillik is my best friend from America – did the *Night Life* book with me. A painter. Warm, open human being. Well – if all goes well, we thought the four of us might go from Spain to Cyprus, stay a few weeks with you, and then to Jerusalem, whence we leave for Big Sur – by middle August the very latest. Eve & I will have the children with us for a year, beginning this September. [. . .]

All depends, too – our moves – on the war situation. I am following events like a hound. Can't see how another blow-up can be avoided. These days seem so similar to "Munich" days – and worse in all implications. The white race will have to get out of Asia and Africa. We have nothing to offer these peoples. Neither has Russia, I fear, but her projects sound more attractive to the hungry and desperate. How right I was about China and India, what! How small, how feeble, the Western world now seems! Europe is out of the race, you know that, I guess. Not the slightest chance of forming a solid defense front here. The whole American policy is based on mirage and illusion. We lose whether we fight or remain at peace. Time is with the Asiatics.

So – I only mention this to tell you that if the wind blows unfavourably I am beating it back to the States at once. My fear is that we have at best only 2 or 3 months ahead of us – before the storm breaks. You may have picked a good snug place there. I pray it be so. [. . .]

May this bring a happy turn of the tide for you. Cheerio!

Henry

*The Ionian Bank   Kyrenia   Cyprus   [May? 1953]

Dear Henry – since last I wrote things have taken a turn for the better. Eve is okay and has been ordered six months rest. She's going to Devonshire to do a job and my mother is due to arrive towards the end of this month with my youngest brother and his wife. Meanwhile the house is going too slowly and will literally have to be built around us. I was aiming to find you a clean room in a peasant house. The village of Bellapaix is about 4 miles from the sea in the foothills under Buffavento – rather like Kouloura only not so nice. Kyrenia, where I am living at present, is a little sea-port and holiday place on the N. coast. It tends to get v. crowded and expensive so give me good warning of your arrival and I'll decide, according to what your plans are, what to do about you. If we are here I'll try and scout you rooms in a small house; if we are moving to Bellapaix I'll try and find you something up there. I am not very clear about the set-up as with a baby I've been unable to really prospect. But the village is a pretty one. I'm also worried whether the house will be habitable in time as I've got to leave my present lodgings in mid-June. Cyprus, like most places, is expensive – but it has two scales of living, the English and the Greek, and one can live modestly if not cheaply if one knows how. A room in a tiny pension or hotel is about 10/– a day – 1 dollar forty. There are of course luxury hotels at 3 dollars a day etc. But I think it is a weird and rather malefic sort of island – not at all like Greek islands. Palm trees, camels, the smell of Syria. It is really a piece of Anatolia lopped off. Much hotter than Greece. But it has some really spectacular places and is so big that you don't get much island feeling. Massive mountain ranges etc. I'm still trying to puzzle out why Aphrodite was born here as the climate is not at all sexy and the inhabitants have a listless Outer Mongolian look. But it has something quite strange of its own – and after feeling disposed to hate it when I first arrived I am now slowly feeling my way into its landscape – weird sort of place really.

Handling children is hell – how you managed *two* I don't know at all. It would be so lovely to meet after so long and to hear you *talk* again. There is no good talk any more, have you noticed. And why not kidnap Katsimbalis and bring him along?

You have a name here among the Greek intellectuals already for the Greek book – happened I was reading it when your letter arrived. No, Cyprus is *oriental*. I'm trying to write a really good book now about Alexandria – at night when the chores are done. Feeling awfully old these days. Wish to Christ I could stop getting married and roam about with a pack on my back through the Near East. Keep me posted with you – and give me plenty of warning, and I'll do the best I can. But it may be both primitive and chaotic so beware.

    All the best –
    Larry

*Toledo, Spain   5/5/53 [i.e., 5 June 1953]

    Dear Larry –

We've been motoring thru Spain last 3 weeks and a bit fagged out now. Returning to Montpellier, France, next week, via Andorra and will probably rest a week there and decide what next. Money low now. Below par. And the heat – in Andalusia – just floored us. I can imagine now what it's like in Cyprus and Jerusalem. Pretty certain we will *not* be able to make either place – for several reasons.

We met Fred and Anne in Barcelona and had 2 full days with them. Fred was just as always – even more so. Hasn't aged or changed a bit. Remarkable. We laughed from the time we met – which was by accident at the American Express. Haven't laughed that way in many a year. And naturally we spoke of you – how much more we would have laughed had you been with us.

This trip to Europe – hectic – has given me confidence in my ability to come over again and perhaps frequently. Now I am so used to Europe. I shall miss it once back in America. But I feel a need to return soon and establish my own rhythm. Traveling does not permit of work – at least for me. I go blank, my mind goes to sleep. Spain is a remarkable country. I don't think I'd want to *live* here, but it is certainly worth knowing. The landscape (always wonderful) often reminded me of Greece. But in no country have I ever been stared at so much! They have the curiosity of primitives. Andalusia is all it's reputed to be. The impress of the Moors is tremendous – and always *good*. Seeing the Alhambra, the Alcazar, the Mezquita (Mosque), I feel I have seen three of the seven wonders of the world. Catholic Spain is dark, morose, sinister, brutal. [. . .]

Keep your pecker up! Our address always c/o Hoffman, Paris. Haven't had mail for 3 weeks – nor seen a newspaper. Wonder what's happened.

Cheerio!

Henry

*[Big Sur]   8/15/53

Dear Larry –

We're home almost two weeks now but scarcely adjusted to our "New World" which I find is even emptier and more poisonous than ever. I keep wondering how you are getting along. How fares the infant? *We* (Eve & I) are exhausted by nightfall – just looking after our two healthy youngsters – 5 & 8 yrs. old.

It was a great misfortune not to get to Cyprus. We really wanted to. But it was just too much this trip. If World War III doesn't break out in a few weeks, as I firmly expect, we plan to leave next September, '54, for Jerusalem and from there come to see you in Cyprus or wherever you are. [. . .]

We saw Joey in Wells, did I tell you? It was more than good to be with him. He's improved and grown *younger* and wiser. And what a clown – still! How we laughed! Here nobody can make me laugh. We'll have to get back to the Old World soon – and remain there. But not England, eh? England is really *weird* – no other word for it. Yet you can't hate or despise the English. I had a glimpse of Wales – much better. Saw old John Cowper Powys at Corwen. What a joyous old codger! A lively mage.

Well, blessings, me lad. More soon.

Henry

Dearest Henry – I am so sorry to have neglected to write you – but for the last two months we have been building my little Turkish house into something really beautiful. I haven't even had a table to write on. In addition I've started an arduous job as a teacher which involves getting up at 5 every morning and working till two – with a 30 mile drive thrown in. We should be all set in another ten days. In addition I have been working at a new MSS "Justine" which is something really good I think – a novel about Alexandria – *4-dimensional*. I'm struggling to keep it taut and *very short*, like some strange animal suspended in a solution. I never felt in better writing form, free of angoisse etc. And never have I worked under such adverse conditions. Meanwhile my enchanting daughter Sappho is well and my mother is staying with me to help look after her. She is adorable. Eve says she is coming out soon – when I don't know exactly. I can think of nothing but my book – though several strange lovelies have provided distraction from time to time – human poultices. [. . .]

Glad you got the Rhodes book – it is all right – but cheese cake really to what I am going to *try* to do now. God! how I wish I could have visited Stratford with you! It must have been a wonderful pilgrimage. You'll find Martin Buber in Jerusalem. If you are going to Cairo or Alexandria let me know in advance and I'll give you some contacts there – Georges Henein et alia – who will show you Egypt. If you have any old books you don't want send me a parcel from time to time – any old galleys or presentation copies of shit from admirers. I'd be glad. I can't afford to buy books at present – too poor. This island has only been discovered in the last year – or else it's me arriving – but lots of writers and artists are beginning to settle here. It's not as lovely as Greece but very exotic – a voluptuary's island, *Aphrodite*. Did you know that it is the only place where there are a lot – literally several dozens or more – true hermaphrodites? See Plato's Symposium. *Today*, I mean.

Love – Larry.

1 Durrell and Miller in Corfu, 1939 [Durrell collection]

2 Durrell with family and friends in Corfu, 1930s. Nancy second from right, next to mother (seated) [Alan Thomas]

3 Miller, *c.* 1940 [New Directions]

4 Eve Durrell in Turkish costume, Rhodes, 1946 [Mary Mollo]

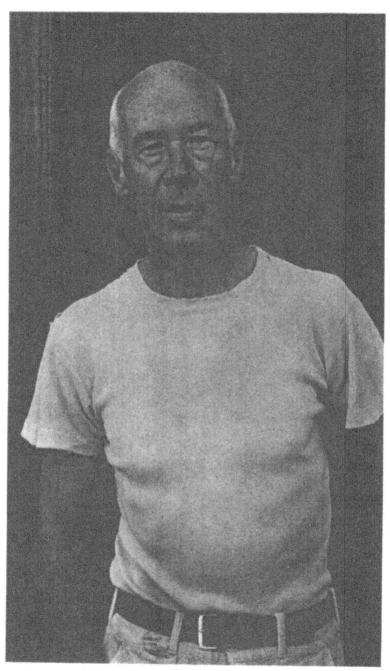

5 Miller in the mid-1950s, Big Sur [Bernard Stone]

6 Durrell and Claude, early 1960s [Durrell collection]

7 Reunion at Sommières [Durrell collection]

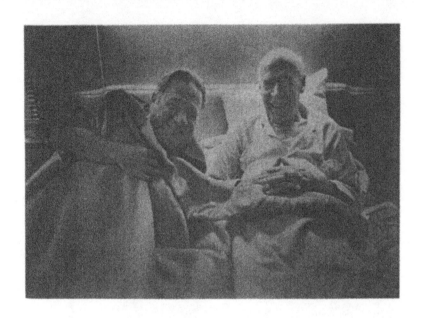

8 In bed [Jill Krementz]

Dear Larry –

Just noticed new address. Sent big bundle of books & mags. etc. to your old address a few days ago. Will send more soon again. Delighted you're getting on with house – *and* the writing. We, of course, can't budge from here till next September. Then, if I get break from my japanese publishers (they've taken 5 or 6 books already) – we may go via Japan, India, Jerusalem to Cyprus. I hope Eve rejoins you soon. What calamities you have gone thru these last ten years! Zen is more and more the only thing which makes sense to me.

No, Stratford gave me no thrill, I must say. J.C. Powys – in Wales – did. And the homes of Rabelais and El Greco. [. . .]

I never read Buber. But have heard much about him. Will look into it. I love Berdyaev. It's like my "alter ego" writing.

Keep your pecker up. So glad you have your mother with you. All's well, believe me. Even in hell. Love to Seferis, Katsimbalis & Ghika when you write them again. We are both living in extraordinary places. Let's live up to the places!

Henry

Dear Henry – how good to hear from you again and thank you for sending papers etc. Reading matter always welcome even though there is no time to read. My job is unbelievably arduous but I think when I have no house problems I shall manage to do it and also live. At present I'm up at 4:30 bathe and dress, check the car and write the odd letter. (This for example by candlelight.) I motor to Kyrenia and thence into Nicosia where I begin work at 7. It is really thrilling – the dark dawns, tip-toeing down the village street with the first yellow flush rising behind the gaunt stone spars of the ruined abbey of Bellapaix. My mother is keeping the house and child going while I work. There is no news more of Eve, and if [it] were not for Sapphy I would not bother any more; it is so wonderful to possess yourself when you are working on a book. All my waking hours I am writing in my head: but as yet I have not fixed up my little study so I have nowhere to write. Women are merely a tiresome interruption: they are convinced that they are personalities whereas they are simply the collective illustration of a biological need or a universal principle. Best enjoyed when least cared about, say I. Nicosia is the weirdest mixture of village and bazaar – very oriental and crammed with English goods. The inhabitants are also strange: like *babus*, deracinated and full of indolence and whim. But 30 hours teaching is too much. Nevertheless I am in good heart and if once the house is finished I have any energy left I shall be able to make *Justine* a worthy successor to *The Black Book*. I'm keeping my fingers crossed of course. Mary [Mollo] has sent me *Plexus* from Paris – but owing to some fault in the make up Vol I and Vol II (with different covers) have identical contents. I've told her to notify Kahane about this. The island is very beautiful now in the first snows. Opposite us, over the sea, the Atlas Mountains are snow-tipped.

Night before last there was a bang on the front door and a shout and Seferiades walked in; you can imagine how warmly we embraced each other. He had not altered by a day – still the graceful and lovely humour-man and poet. He had never been to Cyprus before and is ravished by it. The mixture of temples and Crusader forts – Stratford and Knossos – is indeed quite strange. My village is built round a Lusignan ruined abbey like Christchurch Cathedral. Gothic windows and olive-trees! Sef. has gone off to Famagusta on a walking trip with Loizus whom you may remember.

Owning one's own house is a wonderful thing: I want Sapphy to have a peaceful village childhood here before she kicks off into the world. The beauty of the Mediterranean – one can't have enough of it. I insist on dying somewhere along this holy and pre-Xian shore. And of course we are lucky because all the time friends are coming through – I have a thousand friends from my travels and they never come within 500 miles without calling. Patrick Leigh Fermor touched here last week, Zarian is coming here to live – all sorts of writers and painters are settling here, driven by the exchange. And it is becoming an international air and sea centre now that Egypt and Persia are trouble-spots. All the wives of the British army are here bored to tears. If only I took my vocation seriously I would set up a little bureau for them. But I am so enjoying being an artist again that I only occasionally and purely medicinally nibble at the fresh fruit lying about – just to sleep better. I don't sleep too good – or perhaps just not enough.

Best love to you both
Larry

[November? 1953]

Dear Henry – a brief line to thank you for the two great parcels of books which arrived, followed rapidly by two more. It was wonderfully generous of you, and it's good to have something to read in this fragmented life. It was nice to see the little Belloc essays which I loved so much as a school boy and despite their heavily whimsical manner they stand up pretty well. I'm pushing my book about Alexandria along literally sentence by sentence; I'm dog-tired by the time I get home in the evening but every waking moment is possessed by it so that by the week-end when I type out my scribbles I usually have about 1500 words. I feel like one of those machines for distilled water – it is coming drop by drop running contrary to physical fatigue etc. This is really writing one's way upstream with a vengeance! Never mind. I remember your struggles and blush to think of my own. If you haven't left USA for Japan *please* bring with you Isak Dinesen's *7 Gothic Tales*. She is a marvellous writer I think and would please you – particularly her *Winter Tales* which I have.

I'm writing this at 4:50 a.m. A faint lilac dawn breaking accompanied by *bright moonlight* – weird. Nightingales singing intoxicated by the first rains. Everything damp. In a little while I take the car and sneak down the dark road towards a dawn coming up from Asia Minor like Paradise Lost.

Love.
Larry

*Bellapaix, Cyprus   Jan 5 [1954]

Dear Henry – a letter for New Year to wish you all good things for the coming year and to hope that we shall see you this year. My little house is more or less finished now except for details and we have successfully put up one guest for Christmas. It was so lovely too to see Seferis again after so many years, as gentle and as humorous as ever. I teach you know at the Greek Gymnasium and he was brought down as a distinguished poet and given an ovation, so I was able to be present as a master. He made a touching address to the boys, full of thoughtful things very gently said. His hair is going white and his voice has tiny crackles at the edges, of old age – though otherwise he does not seem a day over fifty. He has promised to come back incognito this summer specially to meet up with you. How are your plans shaping? Don't try to do too much; stop off in places for a few months at a time and laze about. I think you will like Cyprus in spite of it being so un-Greek – it has the lazy moist sensuality of the Eastern Levant, of Egypt and Syria – the mindless sensuality which made the Sybarites. It is dimmed out, autumnal, sleep-impregnated. It would not have suited me as a young man but now in my old age (42!) I think it is a good enough place to settle for a few years to let Sappho get a good grip on life and learn two or three barbaric languages. Of course I have to work pretty hard at present which is a bore as it makes me too tired to get on with my novel – which I think and pray is going to be good – better than anything since *The Black Book* anyway. My youngest brother Gerry has scored a tremendous success with his first book and is making a deal of money. He collects wild animals for zoos and writes up his adventures after-wards. The one pays for the other; how marvellous to have one's career fixed at 25 or so and to be able to pay one's way. The perpetual nibbling of money-worry is the worst of curses when one has children or can't bear squalor; and the lack makes it so hard to see and enjoy one's friends properly.

Zarian is supposed to be coming over soon to start a giant inter-national paper in French and English. He would amuse you. Cyprus is becoming quite a literary centre and hordes of artists and writers are moving in and trying to settle here. There's a little Italian boat which goes from here to Rhodes, Smyrna, Piraeus, Kalamata, Venice – which would please you as a trip. Write a line when you have time and tell me what you *are writing*. Can you send me your eassay on Rimbaud; I'm just reading his letters; he worked here – of course you know – and built the Governor's house on Mt. Troodos. There is no mystery about the man. How hard and sane and unselfpitying his letters are. I'd never seen them before.

Love   Larry

*Bellapaix Abbey   Cyprus   [*c.* April 1954]

Dearest Henry – no news of you for some considerable time. I do hope you are well and happy and working – and no further woman-trouble has engulfed you. I'm sorry I have become such a rotten correspondent these days. I'm simply hoarding physical energy for my book which moves like a snail, paragraph by paragraph. I've only written post cards for ages, never letters. Perhaps you too are preparing a polite bomb for the beer sodden anglo-saxon publics. Eve has just arrived back from England, v. pretty and gay. She is enchanted by this crazy house and the child who is three now and very pretty and wise. Everyone had the impression that she left me because of my bad treatment of her but in fact she simply had a bout of Judeo mystical schizophrenia. The Jews are extraordinary people – the extraordinary shallow hysteria and the enormous sexual charges given by race-continence and intermarrying. I am so glad I belong to the equivocal, sluttish uxorious Irish and not the Jews. We are looking forward so much to seeing you this summer. Please write me a post card and tell me your plans. You would love this island I think – and might even consider staying through the autumn which is lovely. Lots of writers and painters are coming through – it is the port of call before Syria, Egypt etc. So that one has good company perpetually renewing itself which is indispensible when you live on an island. I am hoping during the course of this year to find something congenial to do to make just enough money to live on. The English book-trade is so bad that one can't hope for any money from books any more and the advances offered one by English publishers are ludicrous. As for the American publishing scene it is farcical. The kind of letter U.S. publishers write makes the hair rise on the scalp. I've had a card or two from Seferis. He is terribly overworked in Beirut; and he is counting on me to let him know when you are coming so he can get some leave and join us. Please dear Henry don't fail us. Just send a p.c. in good time so we can let him know. He for his part is planning to coax Katsimbalis over. A reunion in Cyprus! How wonderful it would be.

Best love from us all   Larry

*[Big Sur]   5/7/54

Dear Larry –
Forgive silence. Nothing wrong. Just lots to do and lots of interruptions. So glad to hear your Eve is back with you – et l'enfant beaux et heureux. Yes, Katsimbalis was here, for just two days. I sat and listened all the time. Found him more wonderful than ever, and younger and

healthier too. As a result, I've just read Rex Warner's translation of the *Anabasis* – found it very exciting. Could still be improved on – the translation! Am writing Seferis now for his book on the troglodytes of Cappadocia – Xenophon's stamping grounds.

Our projects are still tentative. Everything depends on proceeds from Japan and France. And whether or not war III this Fall, which I fear. Wouldn't leave here before September anyway, as children would still be with us till end of August.

Mailed you book on Flying Saucers. And – the *Big Sur Guide*.

Writing more soon. Off to San Francisco now. [. . .]

Bookman in dep't store in town spoke of "your book" on Greece with fervor. Odd how books get around, to remotest places. Keep well, stay in love, and blessings on you all.

Henry

*Information Department,
GOVERNMENT OF CYPRUS,
Nicosia, Cyprus   [*c.* November 1955]

My dear Henry – how wonderful to get a long letter from you after so long – and at such a time. We are in the middle of a very nasty little revolution here with bombs and murders on the Palestine pattern so that daily life is sharp as a bite into a sour apple. It is so long since I've written that I can't remember at which point in my crowded and disorderly life to take up this correspondence – Eve and my daughter are in England. My little Turkish house I've had to lock up; but there is a deserted mosque (The Seven Sleepers) on the sea-coast where I go for the week-end to cool my mind. The sea-line is bare, barren, stark – not unlike some of the pictures of Big Sur – a savage lime-green sea, and the little white mosque built sheer upon it. One's loneliness increases gradually – I suppose it to be the only real capital I have. Of course there are plenty of women and adventures still but inside I've reached a new stage – a very small advance upon my own true nature whatever *that* may be. I'm deep in Zen Buddhist treatises these days – Suzuki! What a marvellous *speechless* religion. Now that travel is dangerous and life getting more enclosed I treasure the sea and the mosque as people treasure jewels of price. I have nearly finished my *second* novel. You'll remember when I did *The Black Book* I planned 3 *real* novels, youth, maturity, and old age. Well, in the midst of all this noise and slaughter I'm half way through a book called *Justine* which is about Eve and Alexandria before the war. I believe it is very good. We'll have to wait and see. I think probably I shall divorce Eve this year and go and live in the mosque for a while. It is on a barren spit of land by the sea. There is a shy old Hodja in charge who never stirs out of his room. Seven tombs of unknown Turkish soldiers sleep a stony sleep under green awnings. Happiness is really within reach – only this job is killing me. I shall have to leave it soon and starve my novel out of my system. Henry do send me a few of your books. I'm out of date on your new work. Didn't care for *Sexus* but I still hear the surf-thunder of your prose in memory as the biggest experience of my inner man. Is Joey with you still?

    Love Larry

*Public Relations, P.I.O., Nicosia, Cyprus   [*c.* January? 1956]

dear Henry – I am just reading – with what nostalgia I cannot tell you – little Joe's account of you which was sent to me from England last week, presumably by little Joe himself. I am rationing myself in order to spin it out, so wonderful is it to read about Paris in this curfew-ridden town. My goodness, how alive and free one felt in those days! What has happened to the world since then? I have just finished a book about Alexandria called *Justine* – the first *serious* book since *The Black Book*; much clearer and better organised I think. I will send you a set of galleys when they come in. It's a sort of prose poem to one of the great capitals of the heart, the Capital of Memory, and it carries a series of sharp cartoons of the women of Alexandria, certainly the loveliest and most world-weary women in the world. I had fallen into a bad patch of distress and apathy after Eve left for England in the middle of August with the child, which I miss, and by a stroke of luck (by the way Eve & I are washed up) a lovely young Alexandrian tumbled into my arms and gave me enough spark to settle down and demolish the book. (She is French, Claude, a writer with something oddly her own.) Night after night we've been working on our books, typewriters at each end of the dining-room table; sitting up over a scale map of Alexandria before a log fire tracing and re-tracing the streets with our fingers, recapturing much that I had lost, the brothels and the parks, the dawns over Lake Mareotis etc. Outside the dull desultory noise of occasional bombs

going off, or a few pistol shots, or a call from the operations people to
say that there's been another ambush in the mountains. A very queer
and thrilling period, sad, weighed down with futility and disgust, but
marvellous to be able to live in one's book while everything is going up
inchmeal around one and the curfews settle on the dead towns. Must
write about it one day. Wish we could meet. I may be in England in
August.

> Best love to you
> Larry

[P.S.] Send me any old thing to read will you?

*GOVERNMENT OF CYPRUS   9 August [1956]

Dear Henry –
Am leaving Cyprus on the 26th for London where I'll spend a fortnight
and thence over to France where Claude hopes to borrow a place to
live. We have enough money to last us 3 months in which we'll finish
our current books. After that what? I don't know. For the first time in
my life I shall be prospectless and dead broke – and doubtless on the
streets quite literally. Will you write me c/o Faber and Faber 24 Russell
Sq. London. I'll write you from France.

> All the best
> Larry

*STONE COTTAGE, MILKWELL,
NEAR DONHEAD ST. ANDREW,
SHAFTESBURY, DORSET   [October? 1956]

My Dear Henry:
Devil take it, I am so sorry not to have written you and Joe; specially
after your good letter giving me the names of so many good contacts in
Paris. My plans went suddenly awry and dammit here I am for a few
months in the heart of the Hardy country, where the people talk in the
identical tiresome moralising way they do in Hardy. The accommodation Claude found just outside Paris fell through at the last minute, and
this coincided with Eve beginning a new job in London – also unable to

280

find a flat; so that I was left stranded with Sapphy on my hands and nowhere to go. Meanwhile I have promised Faber the MSS of the blasted Cyprus book by Xmas and so I was forced to try and set up a temporary headquarters until the mist lifted a bit. Fortunately Diana Ladas rented me this tiny cottage where at present Claude and I are installed, both working like maniacs on our books. Saph goes to the village school – her accent daily getting broader and broader – but seems to enjoy it. I had a card from Joe giving me his address but as yet have had not a chance to see him. He's in Reuter he says; I loved his book about us all. And incidentally your study of Moricand is devastatingly good. I remember him so vividly – the heavy personal odour of the baby powder and the lotions – and I can't see a late portrait of Wilde – scented and curled hair, high collar, pearl pin and polished cuffs like cerements – without thinking of Moricand. Only the other day I was going through some papers in a friend's loft and stumbled across my horoscope by him! I am sending you my *Selected Poems* which have just come out; and my young brother has just scored a big success with a crazy book about Corfu which I've asked him to send you. He's off on another expedition next month. A best seller now – but only interested in animals. Last evening, as a change, Diana drove me over to the next county where I met James Stern for the first time – you used often to mention him in the Villa Seurat days; I found him anxious for news of you. He seemed a pleasant shy person with a good set of humours. Told me strange stories of Joyce, Hemingway, Bob McAlmon etc. Also Djuna Barnes – wonder if you've come across her yet.

In a little while I'll be sending you the first volume of JUSTINE, a novel about Alexandria which I hope and pray will make you smile and perhaps just faintly cheer. Second vol follows as soon as I have this Cyprus book off my hands, pray God by Xmas. By then of course we'll all be starving and have to find a job – perhaps in France. Claude has two huge children to support and I one. But meanwhile we are living warmly and economically and working all day, from around eight when all the housework is done and the child off to school. Our only recreation is to visit the local pub where the accent is so fantastic as to be better than the movies. Have no radio, no television, and not even daily newspapers. In fact the best holiday I've had in years. I don't know what's happening in Cyprus – maybe they've burnt my house down by now. I left a young English poet in it called Penelope Tremayne (marvellous name). All her ancestors were beheaded for treason being Cornish, so she has turned rebel and become a nurse. Cyprus is so tragic it doesn't bear talking about. Clearly we can't go on being a great power if our political grasp of things is so elementary; Russia can do it because she shoots to kill. But we can neither shoot nor think it seems. Never mind. I'm well out of that lot.

Meanwhile October is all sunshine and green grass and smoke from cottage chimneys. Nothing has changed. The Englishman still laughs without removing his pipe; his wife wears a hat and carries a lap dog. Everything is serene and bland as suet. I'm a bit exhuasted by travel and women and divorces and alimony – but I've got something in hand for poetry. If only I could make a little bit of honourable dough . . .

Best love to you both
Larry (Durrell)

Durrell's 'Cyprus book' was published as *Bitter Lemons* in 1957.

Climax in Sommières

Durrell writes about places with a verve and brilliance which has led many to compare his 'foreign residence' books to Lawrence's on Mexico, Italy and Sardinia. But the truth is that he has always hated travelling, and has repeatedly tried to put down roots wherever he finds a place to his liking. He added a second storey to his landlord's house at Kalami in 1938, and would have stayed in Greece to write 'The Book of the Dead' had not the Second World War intervened. During the early 1950s he planned to live indefinitely at Bellapaix, Cyprus, in his Turkish house. His mood is desperate when he moves into the Villa Louis in February of 1957, just up the hill from the railway tracks on the edge of the small medieval town of Sommières. For twenty years he has carried inside himself and on the flyleaves of one or two notebooks the idea for an ambitious work which he hopes will be of the same class but greater in kind than *The Black Book*. By Durrell's standards of industry, he does not have much to show in print for the past twenty years of creative life: *The Black Book*, a novel unpublishable in England or America; another novel, *Cefalû* (*The Dark Labyrinth* in later editions), which he dismisses as a potboiler; four volumes of verse; and *Sappho*, an unperformed poetic drama. Then suddenly Miller's faith in Durrell, and Durrell's own promises, are fulfilled in a year of terrific accomplishment. He publishes books in four genres, all successful to a greater or lesser degree: *Justine*, *Bitter Lemons*, *Esprit de Corps*, and *White Eagles Over Serbia*, the last a thriller based on his Yugoslav experience and aimed at teenage readers.

Miller's praise is now chorused by the critics, and suddenly Durrell finds himself in the position Miller has long warned him against: he is a sought-after public figure, besieged by editors offering commissions, by interviewers and television crews, by curious tourists. Durrell continues to work at a feverish pace, writing reviews, articles for *Holiday* magazine, and two more volumes of *The Alexandria Quartet*. Durrell and Perlès initiate a correspondence about Miller intended to clarify his intentions and explain him to the public: Miller cannot bear to sit on the sidelines and soon derails the correspondence with an eight-page letter about himself. These exchanges, including Miller's epistolary *tour de force*, are eventually published as *Art and Outrage*. In the midst of being forced out of the Villa Louis by the owner, who needs the house for his family, Durrell undertakes the vast task of selecting a representative sample of his friend's œuvre for *The Henry Miller Reader*, a labour of love and gratitude. Miller is delighted, and weighs in with a long list of titles and many paragraphs of advice. Although he is bedevilled by visitors, correspondence, and petty tasks, Miller publishes *Big Sur and the Oranges of Hieronymous Bosch* and pushes *Nexus* along slowly.

*[Big Sur]   2/13/57

Dear Larry – Just got your *Justine* and have almost finished it, in one sitting. Fascinating! And what writing! Nobody can wield the English language like you. Hair-raising sometimes. What a picture of Alexandria! Justine sounds somewhat like I imagine your Eve to have been – only magnified, what?

I will write at length in a day or two. Have more to say about it. (Je crois bien.) This is just to felicitate you. Luck to have Book Society recommend it. You should be able now to sell it to an American publisher. If not already contracted for, tell Faber to send copy to Mr M. Lincoln Schuster of Simon & Schuster, N.Y. He's fond of me, because of my spiel on Powys. May well take it. It's a good, live house. (Also tell Faber to send me 3 copies of book with bill.) And can you dig up your *Pope Joan* book for me – lost my copy. Will pay.

Still trying to do something with your *Sappho*. This is a great work, I think. You are certainly not falling behind. Your troubles have done you good. How is Joey? Ever see him?

I've just been elected a member of The Institute of Arts & Letters – which is our apology for a French Academy. [. . .]

Are you still in the dumps – still broke? Write soon.

Henry

284

My dear Henry – we have finally fetched up here in the Raimu country – a medieval town asleep on its feet – a castle whose history nobody knows. It just happened. And all built v. insecurely on the arm of a river which floods the whole place every other year, carrying away people and houses. Nobody seems to care. Life is a good deal cheaper than in Paris and the people I think much nicer. They do not behave like Logical Positivists with a high temperature. We want if we can to try and settle in France – Claude is French by nationality. Her first novel has just been accepted in England and the U.S. agents are enthusiastic. Somewhat to my surprise Dutton have bought *Justine* in the U.S.A. and offered quite a handsome advance on it. All this of course doesn't mean much – but it's a ray of light under the door. If I could earn the smallest steady money . . . There are lovely little – no, big, *huge* – village houses for sale all along this coast for about £400 – 1000 dollars isn't it? If we could get one! They are all built round large courtyards, stone, well-tiled. Over a period one could make a lovely house out of any of them. Idle dreams! I'm glad *Justine* interested you – première ébauche merely – 1st stage of an etching I hope will carry three more cuttings – hence the apparent obscurities in the 1st book! My book on Cyprus comes in Sept and will rustle a few dovecots I hope. I tried hard to reach Fred but was only in London on single days and his line was dead. Arranged to spend Xmas with him down at the cottage but he had to go to Gloucestershire to see his wife – sounds funny that! I thought she lived in Wells. Anyway I tactfully didn't enquire! Everyone is marrying and divorcing – even Eliot was overcome by Spring Fever and eloped with his secretary. This has set the key for the year. What are your prospects of visiting France this year? Do keep in touch if you get on the move – it would be so wonderful to meet again after all these years and gros rouge is still only one shilling a bottle in France!

If I can only find a way of settling here I shall be a happy man. Cyprus is out as long as we go on being foolish.

Have you come across *Zen in the Art of Archery*? Watkins published it last year. Tremendous! Yes, I know about Blyth but haven't read his book on Zen. Travelling so *fast*!

Love,
Larry

Raimu country: Jules Raimu was a famous film and stage comedian from Provence.

Happy Easter, O Master of the Heraldic Line! Have just read first
chapter of Cyprus book and am already enchanted. How you are
writing these days! Not that it is a sudden change of style, but now all
the work of the past years shows in every line. I don't see how
intelligible English prose can be pushed any farther. And now I recall
how you looked on the balcony in that little house at Corfu, with a
pencil and pad, scribbling, scribbling, polishing your style, rewriting,
writing some more, bathing, drinking, singing, laughing, but always
coming back to the pad and pencil. One can see how you have
struggled to master the medium, and not just the medium, but the
language itself, the English, the King's English. Now I read you
enviously. Why didn't I say that? What a marvelous adjective! What an
image! (That whole duck shoot in *Justine* – something out of this world
. . . like Louis Armstrong with his trumpet. Turgenev would have died
happily to write this way.) [. . .]

And now tell me, has this book been sold yet to an American
publisher? Dangle it before New Directions, if not, but only use them
as bait. Sell to highest bidder. All our old big publishers, like Dutton,
Harper, Putnam, etc. are doubling up with other firms. The paper
backs have won the day. And why not think of Penguin for a pocket
edition right now – on Cyprus book, I mean? [. . .]

Yes, and what are you doing toward getting your other books
published here in America? Now is your time. I feel it in my bones.
These things come in waves. If I knew your horoscope I could tell you
better. Now it is just a hunch. But if you know your hour, date and
place of birth, send it to me again. I know a woman who has been most
accurate. She's Danish.

Enuf! I'm drunk with ideas for you.
Henry

My dear Henry
I'm terribly ashamed at all the time you spend writing about me
instead of yourself! Surely for an autobiographer this is a terrible waste
of energy. I don't know how to thank you, or what I can do in return to

show my gratitude. The foreign rights of *Justine* have gone to French, Swedes and Germans; but best of all is a really interested U.S. publisher – Duttons. This has encouraged me to grapple with the second book which I finished yesterday, and which I think will amuse you more than the first. The ground plan, if I can do it, is four books of which the first two fit into each other – different but the same book – Giordano Bruno! The next which I shall start after tea today is a big orthodox novella interpenetrating the two previous ones at many points! Anyway, to hell with it all, we shall see. *Justine* has had a tremendous press in England – rather a worried plaintive note from the dovecots where our literary men drowse – but enthusiastic withal. I'm curious to see what the second one does!

[. . .] In France the moral atmosphere, even down here in the provinces, is just *right*: one has a sense of life being in agrément, all les valeurs de la civilisation bien conservées – in the smallest thing. And they are wise and witty – and do not bother you like the Italians and Greeks, who are as sentimental as spaniels: want to sit in your lap all day and feed you sweets. In short living in the southern Mediterranean has its trials. People won't leave you *alone*. It is like living in an Italian movie – great fun if you have nothing to do as they never seem to have. But just try to read or work! Now these people have marvellous reserve as well as being really friendly; they read. On the buses you will see the conductor at a stop fish out *Figaro Littéraire*! And the mania for artists is so endearing – they never ask if you make any dough! At Nîmes, the Inspector General of Taxes when he found I was un écrivain, stood up at once and shook my hand with real congratulation which meant "By God, I envy you, I wish I was." Yesterday I had lunch with Richard Aldington in Montpellier. He told me that last week he was sent a summons by the Vice Squad to appear; a puzzling thing – he has no vices! It turned out that the head of the police Vice Squad was a writer who admired him and wanted him to check over an essay about his own work which the cop had written for the *Police Quarterly*: about Aldington's work. Can you beat it! And well written, too. He showed me a copy. Of course I've always known and loved this about France, but it is good to see that it hasn't perished under the successive waves of Anglo American dollar-itis. Ordinary life still has the passionate cool authenticity of a line by Molière; and here in the south the *heartlessness* which you always criticised in the Parisian – but which is only a big town, as opposed to village, phenomenon – is missing. They are generous to a fault – Provençal as well as French. Of course there are bastards here too, like our Chef de Gare, but the *frame* which protects the individual life is marvellous – though so venerable and so slow a growth it is modern, modern as tomorrow! Ach but you know all this! We've cut the marvellous picture of you out of that French mag – with the caption "Freedom – is it French?" It looks good on the wall. Of course it's French. You never spoke a truer word O Master!

Bless you Henry
Larry

*VILLA LOUIS   SOMMIÈRES
GARD   FRANCE   [end April 1957]

Dear Henry: just got back from Nîmes where we went with Richard Aldington and his lovely daughter. A good lunch and a touch of mistral but the vines doing well – stretching away to the horizon in every corner of the sky. I think I must still be rather a baby because it is such a big thrill to talk to a writer who knew Lawrence for years and was with him when he died; and the span of whose literary life started around 1910! Imagine, as a young man he was corresponding with de Gourmont and Proust. He is now sixty-five and in poor health and has recently fallen into disfavour for attacking some of our more notable buggers; but in good heart otherwise. It is fun to let his memories run on . . . Middleton Murry Katherine Mansfield Eliot Ouspensky etc. . . .

This week Roy Campbell was killed in a motor crash; I don't know whether you know his work, the finest and most flamboyant poetry of the day. He was a bullfighter here in the arènes of Provence. Aldington is very cast down about it; but Roy the old devil with so many unforgivable satires to his credit couldn't have died in bed; I'm sure he has already lampooned St Peter and been put in irons.

I mustn't forget to tell you of a rare stroke of luck I've had; someone must have been dozing in the committee. The Book Society have chosen (not just a recommendation – which is like connecting with a passing paintbrush) but chosen the Cyprus book. Of course this doesn't mean very much as it does in the USA where the book clubs run into hundreds of thousands; it means about ten thousand copies. But as a kick away and publicity for the others it's a good thing to happen. Meanwhile of course I am so glad to feel that I don't have to find another job until at least next year that I have finished *Justine II*. I'll route the MSS via you to Dutton; tell me if it stinks. It is only the second of four. The next one is totally different in style – a naturalistic job; then I hope to add the 4th dimension Time in the last volume. Claude is starting to type the old nightmare out this week. Her own novel comes out from Faber in Sept.

The more I see of France the more convinced I am it is the only place to live despite its expense today; in the country it is not bad and the income tax set up is so good I am declaring for it – registering from England as an "emigrant"!

I think in a year or so we shall have a chance to really see Provence – Aldington says there are ravishing, completely overlooked and forgotten medieval towns tucked away north of us, more remote than Spain, where one could find a house like we have and a river or lake to swim in. I am going to investigate all this most carefully before thinking of buying. But even here it's lovely on this gracious river; something Stratford plus Canterbury – if you know them. When the devil are you coming to Europe again? Couldn't you manage some time over here now you are so famous? A lecture or two perhaps?

> Love as always
> Larry

*Villa Louis   Sommières   Gard   France   [early June 1957]

My dear Henry: yes, Duttons have taken *Bitter Lemons* and *Justine*, and the second volume of *Justine* is being typed. I hope it will amuse you. It's strong stuff I think. Yes, Roy Campbell was killed coming back from Toledo; front tyre burst with his wife driving. They smashed into a tree. He died on the way to hospital. Sad. Aldington was in close touch throughout and copied letters to me from Rob Lyle who flew out at once to take over; he is a rich friend and admirer of Roy's. They buried him near Cintra. The family are okay, finances in good order. The *Collected Poems* had just been proofed and tidied for press. It's a great sadness. He was a marvellous antelope of a man, bullfighter and runner and drinker; and an angel-tongued poet of a good order – Mistral, Camoens. I got to know him quite well when we were both marooned in London – he for two years. He believed in punching his critics on the nose when they annoyed him and often did. I want to try and write a piece about him but am waiting to get over the heavy feeling of sadness at his loss. So few real gallants left in poetry and life these days.

Hey! this Tullah girl sounds a honey – you don't say. I'll send her *Justine*; but I don't think colour pics of me in a bathing suit will do anything to help.

Horrible weather: floods etc.

But soon the sun must come out. I'm taking a month off before starting the third book of this four-dimensional job.

Love   Larry

*Villa Louis   Sommières   Gard   France   [June 1957]

My dear Henry: some lovely sunny days after a lot of storms and it is beginning to seem worthwhile to live in Provence again; today an advance from Dutton on the Cyprus book – and as I have just finished the second *Justine* I shall float till Xmas at least without having to become a bloody diplomat. Many thanks for *Homecoming* – which arrived just before the rain so that we both read it twice while locked up. Splendidly constructed book and certainly one of the queerest I've read about an oriental country. Did you notice how queer: all the intellectual Moeurs are European – the old-fashioned Weltschmerz of a European German movie; sighs for the Impressionists, the cathedrals, Paris . . . At times I tried mentally changing the names to Schmit and Schmatt and found myself without any jar in post-war Berlin – the same wrecked shooting gallery feeling with Coka Cola and tarts and GI's smoking cigars with ringed fingers. Of *Japan* as such I got little feel – perhaps we have imagined a Japan which never existed, or which has been wiped out. Once or twice there is a mention of a Zen temple – like a reference to the Albert Memorial in a British novel, seen on a rainy day from the back of a bus. But when the evocative note is struck it is always Europe, cathedrals, Paris, etc. Funny to think of these little handmade Japs running round with their skulls full of Gauguin, drinking Martell and fornicating à la us . . . I have never been more amazed in my life. Even the criteria which Saeko (mata hari?) establishes in order to show how soignée she is are pure *Vogue*, pure Helena Rubenstein, face pack and all. Yet the book is masterly, oeuvre magistral, but with Japan completely missing. Now when you read a Kazantzakis you feel the peculiarly Greek difference in the people; they share our emotions but starting from different premises somehow. They certainly aren't Greeks pining for the post-Impressionists; they think French painting is something to eat. Are the modern Japs just deracinated Europeans with a shadowy schmerz – finis? Another thing about the book gave me a queer feel – the height and size of people; "he was a tall graceful man". My Japs have always been five foot one. "The man's florid face was pink with the heat" . . . Utterly mysterious. I thought they were tiny and yellow like tree-frogs . . . You must tell me your impressions of this book. It looks strange on the shelf with the three volumes of Suzuki which were the only books I brought with me. Also tell me if you got the ZEN IN THE ART OF ARCHERY I sent you – another Japan altogether this: seen through German eyes. I think you will be thrilled by it. The postman has just called with a huge book about Bernard Shaw, full of loving inscriptions from an Egyptian who encloses two nude colour pictures of herself – at your behest she says; she looks a good lay – though I shall have difficulty in reading about Shaw's love-life: about as nourishing as a barium meal. However I shall respond asking her to come up and see me some time . . . Is she nice? Tell me when you next write; or is she a bore? As for poor Shaw, what I saw of Marxism in action makes me cheerfully want to dance on his grave, the dry old half articulated skeleton. How does a belly dancer choose such a piece of ship's biscuit as a subject for a fat book? Mysteries . . .

I am going to send you the MSS of *Justine II* in a few weeks. Claude is just typing it out; I'm curious to hear what you think of it – the pattern of the story is beginning to fan away from the centre now, from subjective to objective . . . Anyway . . .

I'm expecting my daughter and Claude's two kids out here for a month's holiday from school and we are frantically trying to install a lavatory and a primitive shower; we've been shitting in the garden and washing in the front porch from a bucket and watering can up to now; somewhat cold but okay. I send you a couple of pictures of us.

    Love to you both
    Larry

Homecoming (1955) is by Kiyohiko Nojiri (pseudonym of Jiro Osaragi).

Dear Larry, Your letters are piling up and I've had no chance to reply
lately. [. . .] I am getting really wacky over the Japs. Everything they do
they do very very well. I am going there first chance I get. And from
there to Burma, surely, then Java, which I much long to see. Then
Europe again, on way back. When? Right now I'm sunk with work,
responsibilities, all sorts of things. [. . .] Now my two children are here,
and they may possibly stay on indefinitely with Eve and myself. Big job.
Tony is near nine, Val near 12. Wonderful kids, but high-strung, active
as dynamite, undisciplined, etc. etc. etc. I love them.

Richard Aldington, a neighbor. How strange. A man of sixty, you
say. Why, I am now 65, don't you know? However, I'm hardly different
than at forty. Get ired quicker, for one thing. I mean "hopping mad".
And less patience with bores and nit-wits. And fighting like a demon
(wrong thing) to achieve more "peace and solitude". Impossible here.
Simply invaded continually. [. . .]

Lectures! I get offers every day, from $200 to $1000 per lecture. Never
accept. Hate public meetings. Loathe gatherings. Detest readings.
Especially poetry readings. Do you have a phonograph that will play
long-playing records? If so I'll send you the two recordings I made in
New York with Ben Grauer. Just out. [. . .]

Wonderful about Aldington and the police. Reminds me of my run-in
with Fernand Rude, préfet of Vienne – see *Big Sur* book. There was a
scholar! Also, Franic Raoul of the Paris Préfecture! If I had not had good
French friends like these men I would still be getting my visa O.K.'d!
That Paris Préfecture is a veritable nightmarish labyrinth. Positively
frightening. But there I sat with M. Raoul, talking literature, cool as a
cucumber, and everything I had done or said (in my papers) was wrong.
And the meeting with the Paris Juge d'Instruction. Marvelous. I felt like
Baudelaire after that meeting. A real honor and privilege to be hailed to
court there.

To close – have you seen any Japanese movies yet? Do let me know. I am
wild about them. Every one of them. The last I saw was *The Magnificent
Seven* (*Seven Samurai*). Just out of this world. Puts me in ecstasy. And
Fred, poor dope, couldn't stand it. Thought I liked them because they
were "foreign". He's weird sometimes. "Unadventurous", what! When
you see this film you will tear your hair. Same for *Ugetsu*, in which there
is a marvelous mad woman. But I could rave on forever . . . .

Enclose a thousand dollar bill to see the circus.

I remember standing with my bike and looking at that Pont du Gard in 1928. I remember the Nîmes amphitheatre – first bullfight I ever saw. And Arles. But have you been to Montserrat where the last of the Albigensians were walled up? Or to Sète, to visit Valéry's grave – very simple and inconspicuous.

Time's up. All morning answering letters. What a life! If I don't get a secretary soon I'll die of congestion. [. . .]

Carry on, and send me pages of *Justine II* any time. Then I'll reread *Justine* (1) again. I wish I could read your horoscope. I'll bet there are great things ahead for you, right quick. Don't laugh! You've had your years of martyrdom. I think your path is clearing up. I sense it. I pray for it. You deserve it. Be gentle with the women. God, what *women* these Japanese characters are! They fill me with awe, love, devotion. There are none such elsewhere – unless in old China. Wait till you meet "Golden Orchid". [. . .]

Avance Toujours!
"Ma main amie" (Cendrars)
Henry

[P.S.] Cendrars is now paralyzed on one side, his good side.

Miller apparently confused Montserrat (in Spain) with Montségur, where the Albigensians made their last stand in 1244.
Cendrars had lost his right arm in the First World War.

*Sommières   [mid-July 1957]

THIS LETTER REQUIRES NO ANSWER!

My dear Henry: Marvellous! Just finished first reading of your *Oranges*. You achieve real Japanese hokku effects in the prologue, and the centre panel had the great pug-marks of genius one always finds when you become airborne. I found you perhaps too indulgent to your neighbours who don't sound a wildly thrilling lot – but then indulgence and affection in you never ceases. Look how indulgent you have been to your juniors not the least of whom is yours truly! And living together casts a powerful spell over one and roots out egoistic dispathies (Rolfe's wonderful word). I couldn't help being amused by your groans about correspondence; why you devil you adore writing letters. I must have held you up for weeks on *Capricorn* with my letters from Corfu which you answered at such length. Self-indulgence. I had hoped by now you could afford a bodyguard to expel visitors and sift your mail of all trivia because I know that the sight of a Chinese stamp would make you answer a perfectly pointless letter from a student written in pigeon: pidgin. Anyway, I don't write to bother you just to salute you. Thanks to your efforts *Justine* goes into four languages and thanks to Rowohlt's contract Faber has come across with a contract which, if I can honour it with two books a year, should enable me to drop everything and *write*. Wonderful. A new avenue opening up I hope. At any rate I needn't try for a job until next summer now so I hope to get *Justine III* off my chest pronto. Fabers seem very excited by II so far and are setting it up. Germany has bought *Sappho* too and promises a production next year. With a bit of a shove I shall push the barn doors down I hope. [. . .]

Claude just back from London having sold her second novel to Faber. I think you'd adore her; she is an Alexandrian Becky Sharp, gay resourceful and good tempered. Luck! How I hope you manage to get to Europe this year, even via Cambodia. For me Europe from now on and the true heart and pulse of it (France) if humanly possible. Always wanted to live here. Now it looks possible – thanks largely to you.

Love to you both   Larry

*Big Sur   July 31st, 1957

Dear Larry:

I finished reading the second book of *Justine* yesterday and am sending it off to Curtis Brown now. It's fabulous. Every bit as good as the first volume and full of the most amazing incidents and events. The carnival scenes are out of this world – hair raising. I like the Interlinear too. I can't make criticism. I am too spell-bound. Will only say that the two letters at the end seemed a trifle unnecessary and a bit of a let-down possibly. But don't take me too seriously. I read it with great difficulty over a period of ten days, interrupted each day, several times a day, so that sometimes I was able to read only a few paragraphs in a day. But even under that disadvantage I was enthralled. I really don't see how you can improve on this writing. You are at the top of your form. And, strange to say, in some ways you remind me of Paul Valéry. Those aesthetico–religious–metaphysical speculations especially. I'll say this, there is nothing like this *Justine* in all English literature – what I know of it, at any rate.

I've already received the American edition of Book One, and it looks good. I meant to tell you that you received a marvelous tribute over the air by the American writer, Kenneth Rexroth, who wrote the preface to one of my pocket books (*Nights of L.&L.*). [...]

Before I go East I hope to visit the Hopi Indians in Arizona. Everything I read about them, about their way of life and vision of life, intrigues me. And makes me sad, too, for here, it seems, is *the* way, real communal life, and a great cosmic understanding. And no hope for us whites ever to profit by it. We are killing them off – and with it our one chance of finding a way out. The oldest city in America –Oraibi – dates back to 1200 and was their first city. Continuously inhabited since that date! Now only about 36 people living in it, I hear.

Never have I been subjected to more intrusions, more invasions. I am going nuts. I can't even find time to answer my letters regularly. If it continues I am going to quit Big Sur. Cheerio!

H.M.

*[Sommières]   [mid-October 1957]

My dear Henry: Just back from a three day visit to Aix where David Gascoyne is staying with a painter – a big rambling Provençal house full of animals. It made a welcome change, as I was getting stale on this bloody book around page 100; but doubly because we could talk of *you*. I was surprised and touched by the devotion with which David spoke of you; we punished the bottle, sitting up late of nights, recreating the Villa Seurat and Fred. [...] (David reminds me very much of Christopher Smart – have you ever read the long poems he wrote when he was mad called THE SONG OF DAVID? It is the first truly surrealist work in English. *Nadja* looks like a peepshow beside it. The only comparable things are Gérard de Nerval's trances – the lovely prose woman. I'll see if I can get you a copy. I think New Directions did it.) Well, David has emerged as a splendid harsh mystical poet though he's only done one book since the war; and he is the same vague, wistful endearing person – doesn't look older by a day. How we talked. Then we came back to find scads of mail, including the brochure about the *Sexus* business in Norway with your excellent letter, Claude's bloody old novel, and an overlooked bottle of Château Neuf. In the same mail came a letter from Fabers of some interest; I wrote some time back saying it was a scandal that there wasn't something apart from Joe's book about you in England. The situation is really mad. Here you are regarded as the peer of Tolstoy in Europe and hardly known in England by the young, except vaguely. I had somewhere an old essay on you which Connolly printed and I thought tentatively that it might make a good point of departure for a short study of your work – I mean nothing pretentious; just an introductory volume about as long as Stephen Potter's little first study of DHL, thirty thousand or so; an outline merely, with no attitudes or cleverness or sparks. The sort of thing a poor writer in Glasgow might welcome. I remember with what eagerness I bought Potter's book. It was *cheap*. Well Fabers seemed interested, so the next thing I banged off a letter to Girodias with a *mandat* ordering the books of the second trilogy. They should arrive next week and I shall start making notes for a brief essay. I think Fabers will play this time; they are beginning to pay attention to me at last. Why? I don't know. I thought in the intervals of MOUNTOLIVE to mock-up what might be a guide to your books, with a brief outline of their pattern, AS FAR AS POSSIBLE EXPLAINED IN YOUR OWN WORDS. On the pattern of the Giono booklet you sent me, though of course with not quite such extensive quotes. Anyway, you shall have a look at the thing in typescript and see what you think. Joe has done the *man* very well; I'd like to do the writer. We'll see what comes of it . . .

What else? Things are moving slowly; I can now see my way clear into next autumn, largely thanks to you. My first FRENCH translation comes NOV 25. I'll send you a copy for old time's sake.

The new contract looks tremendously good, and the Book Society windfall on *Bitter Lemons* paves the way for an all-out onslaught on this fucking relativity novel. After that I have a plan for a comic-grotesque set in Greece, about the building of a perfect town – a true story . . . Too good to jumble on to paper. I'll keep it to tell you over a bottle. WHY the hell are you not in Europe? France! Leave all those teeming Asian spots and come here! By God, how splendid *The World of Sex* is! You've hit a nerve there. The balance, and the fugues are perfectly timed – like a close dialectical argument which keeps turning into dancing. You really are a damned poet. What now? One never knows what the hell you are hatching. Ach but really it is sad that you never settled here; I nearly wept at that bit in Big Sur about the dough! "It's not for me" you cry; why you perishing angel you could have flown over here and bought a house within 150 kilometres of Paris for 1000 dollars! Have put yourself on a salary for 15 years ahead; taken your time, relaxed, had a look round . . . But there, these things are in our fate. I probably wouldn't be here had it not been for the cunning and resourceful Claude. But I have a feeling I'm here to stay; nothing except child trouble could shift me now. I'm divorced too! Marvellous. Never Again! And never another bloody Leo! They've had us both by the balls. Try Taurus next time – the gay practical, warm simple one . . .

We spoke of Moricand too, David and I. He knew him well and praised your wonderful portrait; and as if coincidences mean something – two days before David had had lunch with Delteil among the vines outside Montpellier and they had drunk a glass in honour of you! It's harvest now and the lanes are crowded with carts bulging with wine, with grapes. Just like that marvellous passage in Delteil describing a Provençal harvest . . . But until you have seen a Provençal bullfight, cockade snatching, you have seen nothing. The day Roy Campbell died I was at one, thinking of him as the men in white moved in, softly as Cretans on the Minotaur . . . God what a thrilling sport. You *must* come down here, Henry.

Rather incoherent; this is a bottle of 1952 Château Neuf du Pape. It is like drinking gold on fire, and then a woman's skin immediately after, and then a long space of candle-light. Today the mistral has been howling, the first winter rains coming, huge grape-black clouds. But we have a warm stove going – a garlic *brandade* preparing and a bottle of Tavel. Celebrating the sale of Claude's third novel. It would be perfect if you and Joe were here. Glasses raised to you, Henry, in the good wines of the south. Don't be long. This is where the good life is.

Love to you both.   Larry.

[P.S.] Don't for godsake feel you have to answer this!

*[Big Sur]   12/6/57

Dear Larry and Claude:
Haven't written for a good week or more – too many chores. Must tell you how much I enjoyed those last photos. You look good, the two of

you, and Claude just delicious – reminds me strongly of some one I know, but can't think whom. Anyway, very feminine. Treat her well!

[. . .] Did you ever read the French version of *Aller Retour New York* (Guilde du Livre book)? I added a final letter, about our reunion in Spain. Very revelatory piece, this, and tells you how much (in retrospect) I do owe Fred, bless him!

In your letters you give the impression of not being sure of the chronological order of my books. These are given in the Appendix of Fred's book. I've about twenty more to add now, mostly translations, of course. Theoretically I am now working on *Nexus*, last of the trilogy. Actually I haven't done a stroke of work on it in months. Started it three times in last four years and abandoned it. But think to tackle it in earnest after first of year. I must. Until I get this book off my chest I won't feel free to write anything. And I want this to be the end of the autobiographical series. After that the blue . . . .

You seem to want to write something about me. I don't mean to dissuade you, but only to urge you to hold off till you're through with all you wish to write. To finish the Justine quartet is a feat in itself. I can wait – and so can the world. The longer I live the less important everything seems. Once through with *Nexus* I don't care if I ever write another line. The hack work which it entails – answering fool letters, all sorts of demands, slays me. I spend half my day wading through this crap. I'd rather paint, by God.

It's quite useless, too, to think you'll make any impression on the English. Americans at least get abroad frequently and buy the banned books. Not the English. Not any more. And now that half a million people have read me, what does it mean? About two dozen people are all I really count as understanding admirers. It is worth winning them perhaps. Perhaps.

It gets more and more difficult to do any continuous work here. Living on the land, two children, endless visitors, endless chores, no recreation except ping-pong and a half hour's reading a day – no more! – no contact with vital people, no interest in the cultural, or less and less, desirous only of learning how to live easy and relaxed and in the world but not of it, the urge to write recedes. I do want to travel, yes. But it's a great problem. Right now, for example, I am a thousand dollars in debt, and begging my publisher in N.Y. (New Directions) to advance me 500 dollars to tide over. I need quite a few thousands to pick up and travel with a wife and two kids. I want to see Japan,

Burma, Java, China, if possible, and India. Then Israel, Italy, Jugoslavia and France again. But it all seems far off just now.

However, as I often tell you, my life is one of unexpected breaks. I can't seem to work for anything – it has to happen of its own. And it does, time and again. Right after writing T.S. Eliot, when Fred was here, asking if he would lend me a thousand (and getting a No, polite, to be sure), I received a few thousand from France – back payments due me which I didn't even know about. So it goes. Trust in Providence. Or as George Dibbern put it: "Serve life and life will take care of you." Which I do. Sometimes I think I am nothing but a servant – of any one who comes along. "A votre service, monsieur." Oui. I rarely say No to anything or anybody.

Of course if you saw this place you would understand much better. It is virtually ideal. And I have just sunk about ten thousand dollars into renovations – mostly a studio for myself, and a place for the kids. We moved into a one-room house originally. I drive a Cadillac, 1941 vintage, for which I paid $300. Very cheap. We have an old broken-down station wagon too. I spend a day a week in town, seeing my feeble-minded sister and shopping. I play with the kids. I walk the hills. I play ping-pong with any one who happens along, and if not, with the kids, who are very good. Tony's nine now and Val, the girl, 12. She has a horse of her own. Stabled eight miles away. Must go fetch her three times a week. All costs. Food here horrendously high. Costs us $200 a month, *at least*. In fact, right now I am spending almost a thousand dollars a month – on everything. Good reason for being broke, what! [. . .]

And dear old Somerset Maugham. How tired he must be of receiving letters! I wrote him a few years ago, after lapse of 20 years, to thank him for what he had tried to do when the *Cancer* came out – remember? But he's so over-rated, as writer. Like Hemingway, whom I can't read. Nor Steinbeck, nor Dos Passos, nor even Faulkner.

Ouf! Sounds like a lament, all this. Don't feel rotten. Just getting it off my chest – to re-orient you. When in doubt or despair I can turn to *Zen Bones, Zen Flesh* – adorable. Or to Kikou Yamata's works. Or to Hermann Hesse. Have you read his *Journey to the East*? If not, I can send you a copy. Love it.

All now. The toilet's out of order. Must drive miles to find a plumber. This winter (here) will be a terrible one, it is predicted. We may be marooned by heavy rains for several weeks. Laying in food supplies now. So if you don't hear much after X'mas you'll know it's the weather.

You were so right about that village of yours! I did eat that letter up!

Cheerio, you two!
Henry

*SOMMIÈRES   [mid-December 1957]

Dear Henry: just got back from London after an exhausting trip to collect the Duff Cooper prize, which enabled me to have a long evening session with little Joe, a marvellous long evening of reminiscence and good talk. I've been trying to help him tailor a new MSS a very uneven book he has written. Got back to find your good letter and the French *Justine* which I have sent off to you under separate cover – the translation is marvellous and your preface a terrific accolade. I can't thank you enough for it. I am just finishing the third book in the series so that I shall have two fat novels for next year; *Balthazar* comes in April – I should have copies soon. Dutton seems at last to be getting worked up about me, and I may unload some back titles on the US market! Anyway we eat this year for certain; Claude has just sold her third novel to Faber and a US publisher is interested, so we are feeling quite optimistic. I am in the holy state of alimony again. I brought back the old disc of you and yesterday we had an orgy. Played the lot twice over. It is marvellous to hear you actually reminiscing in the house! Yes, I have been re-reading you from the start, as if I didn't know your work at all, making notes. I found somewhat to my surprise that SEXUS which I once was so shocked and disgusted by is really as great as *Tropic* – only it is very unpruned. (Have you by the way ever thought of publishing the Original Tropic – the huge MSS you once let me read, and from which you chopped out *Tropic*?) I was very much struck on the disc by what you had to say about Phagomania, and Claude who is reading *Plexus* suddenly pointed out how closely the food and fucking references march together; in some places you actually describe the act in terms of food. A great deal of Rabelais in you – the great meal and the great fuck march together and there are even strange connections – as in that wonderfully hypomanic scene after your marriage to June where you get drunk on water and *eat* a painting. I have never really thought about you as a psychology, but there are wonderful things to

300

be discovered here because of the truth of the narrative line. [...] I learned much about Big Sur and how you live from Joe, and I must say it sounds wonderful; but the lack of people to talk to must be a bore. Incidentally, you *can't*, simply can't travel around the world with the children. Not only is travel upsetting itself – but the Orient is a pretty dirty place. What would you do when they get (as they will) amoebic dysentery in India or run the risk of typhoid in Burma? Believe me these places can't be trifled with and you would have to exercise great caution trotting round with two kids. It would ruin the journey I think. Why not put them into school since they are both quite big now? Otherwise it sounds murder to me. Remember I was a child in the tropics and I remember how my parents had to slave to keep me fit; unless you moved from one great air conditioned hotel to another you would certainly run into trouble – not necessarily mortal trouble. But a sick kid on your hands for a month in Bombay ... Expense and terror and Indian doctors! Ouf! Do think most carefully about it won't you? From what Joe says Eve sounds a wonderful ménagère – let her advise you; as a woman she will know all these things. And besides, on such a trip you must be free to feel, and not full of anxieties! Go alone with Eve! I was struck in your letter by the great amount of money you are spending. Jesus! For that amount you could live en prince in France even today. But I suppose the scale of everything in USA is larger than life and the cost of living twice anywhere else. Anaïs has just sent me the incomparable Keyserling *Travel Diary* – so I am travelling too while sitting still. What marvellous observation! Do re-read him if he is to hand. It will put you in the groove for travel. Myself I am so happy in this exquisite Roman walled town with its quiet river and vines, and the whole dramatis personae of Clochemerle to talk to that I wouldn't move out of France for anything. By the way, I am going to pay French Income Tax this year and become a resident – do you know that it is one third of U.S. tax or English tax? Why not try an exploratory year in France? Come over alone, rent a place and have the kids over here? If you lived in the country you could rent very cheaply; places just as remote as Big Sur. But you wouldn't need a car. If you ever think about it I could get Claude to cost it all out carefully for you ... I am still trying to sell my house in Cyprus.

Languedoc is primitive and dusty, but wonderful wine country; they have never heard of a toilet and we have imported a couple of camp ones from England which they regard with awe. They shit outdoors with the mistral blowing up their assholes. Our rent is only £100 a year for a decent size villa with lovely rooms, part furnished. We eat for about £40 a month when we are extravagant, but can cut down to about thirty without eating badly when the need arises and money pinches.

Joe seemed in great heart, but somehow the addle brained English outlook seems to have got into his bones and his new book is an uneasy mixture of styles which I don't know how to alter. His real tone of voice – the wicked sly Viennese voice – is submerged under a sort of doctrinaire Puritan canting tone – Bishop of London! However, we talked far into the night and I think he is going to cut the MSS down hard.

Yes, I have the order of your books right; and there are no gaps. But I've started again at the beginning and have just got to *Plexus* now. I'm not going to hurry over it. I thought of a book about Art and Obscenity worked around your importance and the meaning of your work. We shall see. Meanwhile now you are getting an English edition out PLEASE consider rearranging the material. I would be inclined to keep stories together and essays ditto. When Tambi printed you he was taking the stuff as it poured out; but I think a volume of your short stories in one lump would show your greatness better than a miscellany and your claims as a thinker would be better supported by a complete selection of essays (two volumes if necessary). *Because* your great books cannot be issued there is every reason for you to study your line of attack with the books that can; and every reason to rearrange the stuff to achieve maximum impact. What do you think? I may be wrong.

Must go down to town and buy some brandade for lunch. Every good wish to you all – and for Christsake don't feel you have to answer me at length. I just post off to you whatever I think might amuse you and write when I feel like it. But even when I hear nothing I have the feeling that you are always there, like Blake.

Love
Larry

*Villa Louis, Sommières, Gard, France   18th December 1957

[Letter from Claude Durrell]

Dear Henry Miller,
This is primarily a description of the Solemn Investiture of Larry at the hands of the Queen Mum and secondly an effusion. If you haven't time now, put it aside and read later. No urgency.
I don't know whether he told you about the Duff Cooper prize? It is awarded annually by a select committee at something-or-other college at Oxford, and this year he received a nice little letter telling him that his Cyprus book had copped it. Nothing loth, he replies, "splendid – accept with pleasure" imagining that it would be paid into his bank in due course. Then suddenly a flood of telegrams from publishers, etc., to the effect that his presence is urgently required in London in order that the Queen Mum may hand him the treasure with her own fair hands. Larry jumps around the kitchen, clad in dressing-gown and deerstalker, shouting "I won't! I won't go and shake hands with the Queen Mum!" A little careful interrogation, and the thing is clear. "Oh, yes you will! Think of your two daughters! They will never forgive you if you don't!" Also family, friends, etc. To be honest I felt that after finishing the first draft of MOUNTOLIVE and having worked so hard this year, the change, no matter how much he loathes London, was justified. Also, constant dripping wears away a stone. We went. We, because if I wouldn't go, he was going by air, which would have cost as much. And he insisted, and I wanted to see my children. So we went. Wonderful journey. French couchettes are "mixte" – which I being short-sighted don't notice, but Larry does, and commercial travellers getting unrobed in top bunks and into "crumpled blue pyjamas" (I quote Larry) "in a complicated simian way with their balls swinging around in mid-air". If you should awake around 3 a.m., the fug is unbearable – six people in two cubic metres of space! Plus "le chauffage" which is intense though well-meant. London as usual – no time to enjoy any of the few enjoyable things it has to offer: press, publishers, banks, income tax, a hostess with her insides carved out two days before to be waited on, and the lethargy that goes with pork pies and Bass. We rang Joey up at once and had a wonderful evening with him, during which the wine we had thoughtfully ordered "en avance" did its stuff, and Joey on his hands and knees was explaining how wonderful I was. Finally Larry said "If you want to sleep with

Joey, do . . ." and swept him off. I only wanted to sleep with myself –
preferably for ever. It was murder but isn't Joey nice? We talked about
you all the time. With tears in eyes. Monday was devoted to publishers
and such-like minor irritations, culminating in the arrival of Pinky
[Penelope] on the scene. She had been briefed the day before, and was
pale but composed. An ice-maiden, ravishing. All blonde and
"effarouchée", tall, slim, seventeen, timid and yet bold. On meeting
me: "Where exactly do you fit in?" Larry explains! Off they went,
Larry creaking with starch, Pinky pale but determined. Diana L. – with
whom we were staying – and I trying hard to cheer them up. Larry: "I
shall be sick in the Queen Mum's lap, I know." A dozen people invited
to pat him on the back after the performance, so Diana and I left
behind. Much preparation. They return, light-hearted. "When I went
in, I was astonished to see some Giles cartoons with gardening hats
waving ham sandwiches at me from the middle of the room. Then, by
God, I thought 'That's Aunt Prue – and that's Aunt Mamaie – and
that's Aunt . . . .' " All his aunts had obtained tickets for this private
thing, and had been urging his mother to come up to London for it. But
she said she had nothing to wear but a shawl, and the chimpanzee
couldn't spare her. "Bring him with you" said the aunts firmly.
"Thank God she didn't!" he breathed. "Can you imagine!" As it was,
Pinky stood in a most dignified way throughout the ceremony, but
when the handsomely-bound volume was handed over, she couldn't
resist whispering "How much is the cheque for?" Only a life-time of
Foreign Service stood between him and disaster. "I can't look now!" he
hissed back. And the speeches went on. After the whole thing had run
its course, the Queen Mum slipped her detectives and courtiers and
crossed the room again to Larry and Pinky and said "Mr. Durrell, I just
wanted to tell you once more how very much I enjoyed your book, and
how truly excellent it is." Well – she may not be a literary critic, but
these things are valid in Pudding Island!

I enclose the short speech which L. wrote out in very large letters in
order not to use his spectacles (vanity, thy name is man). <L. says no!
Que faire?> He read it, according to Atticus of the *Times*, in a most
moving way. Anyway, it was all very good. And the cheque covered
the trip and a little over. Paddy Leigh Fermor lent us his suite in Paris
when we returned (paid for by Fox Movietone – 10,000 francs a day!)
and we saw only my father for a brief evening and no-one else. We
wandered around Paris on our own, which is the best of all, and didn't

call on a single "contact". We bought discs! We visited the Villa Seurat, and there is an estate agent living in your studio. We ate châteaubriands, because the beef down here is lousy. We thumbed through books on the Quai Voltaire. We sat in the Closerie, the Dôme, the Deux Magots, the Flore. We spent money like water. It was lovely. We washed three times a day by courtesy of Fox Movietone. We are cleaner, still, than we have been for a year! Then we came home, and put on your older discs, and the new ones. A fine slice of Henry Miller! He bought some Bartok, and I had tears because I can't register in a twelve-tone scale. We bought some Mozart too, and rubbed our stomachs. Menuhin. Wonderful. It's blissfully quiet again and sober and provincial. I mean Sommières, not Menuhin. You would love this place. [. . .] All the very best to you and Eve and Val and Tony for Xmas (that wonderful hangover) and la nouvelle année.

> Claude.

The presentation of the Duff Cooper Memorial Award took place on 9 December at a private ceremony at Hyde Park Gate. Durrell was given a copy of *Old Men Forget* by Lord Norwich (formerly Sir Alfred Duff Cooper) and a cheque for £200.

*SOMMIÈRES GARD FRANCE   [before 20? January 1958]

Dear Henry: [. . .] Just sent off the huge MOUNTOLIVE mss; they want to set it up now so I should have a proof in a while which I'll route via you as a curiosity. I wanted you to read *Balthazar* as it was counter-sprung and have a clue as to the form. This big novel is as tame and naturalistic in *form* as a Hardy; yet it is the fulcrum of the quartet and the rationale of the thing. With the fourth I can plunge back into the time-stream again as per *Justine*. You may yawn your head off over *Mountolive* and whisper "Shucks"; we'll see. Meanwhile I have had a small optional contract for bit writing from the *Sunday Times* which not only leaves me free as [a] bird, asking only six articles a year on anything I like, but amounts to a tiny steady income – about half what a plumber would get. But by God it is steady. It is a basic wage. I always was a timid bugger about that basic wage. Never understand where you got the courage to walk out on it! [. . .]

Had a good letter from Eve which I must answer – I think Claude put out an interim answer; she (Cl) has just sold her third novel to Faber. By the way her married name is Mrs C.M. Forde but she gets a lot of mail addressed just Claude as it's her pseudonym. We've just bought a beautiful Canadian birch bark canoe for the river. The children are going to be crazy about it. I'm nearly through *Plexus*, taking notes. Soon I shall poop off at Joe. What a huge rich cataract of treasures in these books – and the lapses are as great as the conquests like in all the great. Tolstoy Melville and co . . . One despairs really (for oneself I mean).

Well, we have had quite a run of luck; and quite a raft of help on the foreign rights side from henry miller. *Balthazar* comes out in April. I didn't send you *Esprit de Corps*; thought you mightn't find it funny. I had to pay for the baby's shoes somehow and wrote it in a very short time. To my surprise *Harper's, Atlantic* etc bought bits so perhaps it is not too British after all – or perhaps Americans sometimes enjoy sodden British jokes. Anyway I'm sending it along for you to see. Six thousand copies in a month! And the *Times* is mad about Antrobus and offers to run one a month at forty guineas! They take me twenty minutes to write. Only 1000 words. All this is very perplexing to my fans who don't know whether I am PG Wodehouse or James Joyce or what the hell.

I am "resting" this way for a month or two before I start on *Clea* – the last volume of the quartet. The weather has been pretty bad this last month but today at last we get a halcyon spring day, real Provence blue. Almost warm enough to plunge in among the water lilies. Your kids look lovely, both of them. Lucky man to have come to anchor in such a place! I sympathise with you not wishing to voyage around. One's own house is such a step; alas I shall never get back to mine thanks to our fatuity and Turkish imbecility – and Greek pottiness. But maybe if I can put some dough aside slowly I can buy something right here. This would suit me very well indeed I think.

The Mediterranean for me. You'd have got along swell with the queen mother. She is very attractive and has a mischievous eye – a merry widow look which doesn't appear in her pictures. And the pink warm complexion of Eleanor Rumminge (Skelton's ale-wife). Certes, une vrai femme.

> love to you all
> larry

I think I told you that Duttons have finally taken the plunge and are moving into steady production to try and hit me up a readership, *Bitter Lemons* in March *Balthazar* in August; and so on at a steady plug until they have the *whole* of me (even the island books) in print! What stupendous luck. They are going along with Faber on *The Black Book* also which will follow up the *Justine* quartet! I think that TSE is really responsible; made the original decision and sold it to the firm. I think his backing would neutralise high level interference . . . Funny how things turn out. He has been a very good friend to us despite our leg-pulls and bastinadoing; and yet he has never pulled a critical punch or boosted me when he thought me bad. A good man in the good sense of the word. It is a great pity Faber isn't doing you in England. They have a little more courage than the others. Mind you Heinemann is a big commercial house of splendid repute; but Faber is a family affair, old Sir Geoffrey is sweet and his daughter Ann is a good novelist herself. They've waited twenty years for the new Djuna Barnes play; and who else would publish such a thing? Anyway . . . I've just delivered MOUNTOLIVE and they all seem quite excited; this time it's a novel à la Stendhal believe it or not! I'll route you a galley for fun when they set the brute up. These two have turned the end of the bloody sock. Now for a bit of a rest for a while; want to lock horns with Joe on an exchange of letters . . . [. . .] Have you ever thought of doing a child's picture book with that three bears piece in *Sexus*; big illustrated book? Ditto "Picodiribibi" illustrated by Picasso? You ought to think about it. A Henry Miller story for children from one of the outlawed books would raise the most tremendous interest and laughter; with good illustrations etc. Consider, *cher maître*, as a practical gambit. It would be piquant in the extreme. Make Heinemann do it; or let's try Faber . . .

Things are beginning to look up; I won't be driven back across the channel this year at any rate. Brother Gerry has become a television star owing to a clever little ape he brought back from the Congo which does everything but vote apparently; my daughter Penelope (Nancy's) is starting in as a dancer; she's very pretty, blonde, 17, and quite a "highbrow" in taste. Saph the baby is seven, black as a sloe and sly as a mascot, and full of anti-social drives! At 46 I feel about 406 with such shooting up offspring. No, I've never to my shame *heard* of Reich – who is he? Ought I? [. . .]

Rowohlt is unhappy about the German translation of J. and is having it done over again; means the book won't appear until the autumn now. But he's bought *Balthazar* Snap like that. I have got your "It's not for me" feeling about all these strokes of luck.

Larr.

sommières   [*c.* 27 February 1958]

dearest henry: [. . .] We are in the process of being evicted these days; and the feeling that we may find ourselves on the road again without a settled habitat is unsettling. But I am going to loose off at Joe one day this week. I'll send a carbon along to you so you can see how the correspondence rides ... My plan was to deal with you only as an illustration of the naked work of art ... the outrage on the established sensibility. And by the way, Duttons *are* going to do *The Black Book* with Faber sheets; and I suddenly remembered that you (poor you, always prefaces and boosts) had already written a BOOST for the BB in *The Booster.* I couldn't remember it but wondered whether it wouldn't reproduce and so give you a moment's peace and quiet, free from your importunate juniors! But I have no copy. Perhaps Joe has! [. . .]

I'm with you about the Jap forms; the trouble is with us lack of a metaphysical resonance in proper nouns. Their impact in terms of affect is nearly always personal, or traditional. That is why Valéry flew to mathematics and chiselled out his stuff as fine as a cobweb, to achieve the *heraldic ideogram.* When a Jap writes "cherry" "moon" "grass" the ideogram has a mystical-metaphysical ring quite different from the set of associations we stir by using them; hence the image making that we have to put into it; I work hot to cold like a painter. Hot noun, cold adjective ("mathematical cherry" rather than "sweet cherry"). Or on a sour abstract word like "armature" a warm and sweetish one like "melodious" . . . The Chinese ideogram carries the "given verb"; our syntax dictates a subject verb object copula in order to create a complex of affective sounds. Tough on us, isn't it? Ach! Mallarmé and Valéry hacked away at the problem. Ever read *Igitur*?

No other news; bad weather! Claude is writing a book about France in the form of letters. FRENCH LETTERS. If Fabers run true to form they will make her change it to GALLIC MISSIVES without moving a muscle.

love
larry

*Big Sur   4/1/58

Dear Larry,
Your two letters to Fred, of which you so thoughtfully sent me carbons, excite me no end. Not because it's about *me*, but because of the
nature of the project. What a task! Of course, you won't really get
anywhere, you know. Take that for granted immediately – and you'll
travel far and enjoy it.
There are many, many things come to my mind at the outset.
Helpful hints and clues, for the most part. Though I trust you understand that I too have difficulty putting my finger on "it", making the
right, eternal statement. But I can offer some correctives and some new
tacks, perhaps.
One of the first things that hits me between the eyes is this effort you
are making to discover the "intention". You speak of the difficulty of
explaining or placing me with the younger generation. And with it you
couple this business of morality and iconoclasm. As the recipient of
thousands of letters, most of them from young people, I get such a
different picture. (Could it be that there is this difference in comprehen-
sion between the British and the American youth?) At any rate, the
young who write me do "get" me to an amazing extent. Naturally,
they "identify" with me, particularly those who are trying to express
themselves. But how interesting it is that the same situations are at
work eternally and eternally molding new artists. One could almost
sum it up, like Lawrence, and say our troubles are largely, almost
exclusively, societal. The social pattern remains the same, fundamentally, despite all the dazzling changes we have witnessed. It gets
more thwarting all the time – for the born individualist. And, as you
know, I am interested – like God – only in the individual.
One of the things which irks me most, with the critics, is the
statement you throw out – about being unlike myself. This is simply
impossible. I don't care who the artist is, if you study him deeply,
sincerely, detachedly, you will find that he and his work are one. If it
were otherwise the planets would be capable of leaving their orbits. I

think your trouble may lie here, that the part of me you don't know from direct experience – I mean the me of youth, of long before we met – you tend to idealize. The man you met in the Villa Seurat was a kind of monster, in a way, in that he was in the process of transformation. He had become partially civilized, so to speak. The tensions had eased up, he could be himself, and his own, natural self was, at the risk of being immodest, what you always sense and respect in me. (To myself I always think I was born "ultra-civilized". Another way of saying it, a more invidious way, would of course be to say that I was over-sensitive.) And I suppose it is always the over-sensitive creatures who, if they are bent on surviving, grow the toughest hides. This tough hide revealed itself in my case more in what I passively permitted to be done for me and to me than by what I did of my own volition – vindictively, outrageously, and so on. The coward in me always concealed himself in that thick armor of dull passivity. I only grew truly sensitive again when I had attained a certain measure of liberation.

I don't want to embark on another autobiographical fragment! Stop me, for God's sake. If I let myself go it is only because with the years I get new visions of myself, new vistas, and their one value to me is that they are more inclusive pictures of the parts that go to make the whole – the enigmatic whole.

Here I digress a moment to mention a noticeable difference in the reactions of Europeans to my work. Seldom do they, for instance, speak of these "discrepancies". Perhaps they have had too much contact with discordant authors all their lives. They seem to realize, without mentioning it, that all the contrarieties of make-up and attitude are the leaven necessary to the making of the bread. When they are shocked, to take another example, it is because of the language itself, what has been done to it and with it by the author, not by the moral or immoral impli-cations of this language. There is a difference, do you see? And when I say shocked, I mean in a healthy, agreeable way. It is an aesthetic shock, if you like, but one which vibrates throughout their whole being.

And here, all the young, and often the old too, are unanimous in writing of the therapeutic value of my work. They were altered. They thank me, bless me, bless me for "just being", as they often say.

But to come back to "intentions". It is almost classic, what I have to say on this score. I know it all by heart, and when you read again, if you read with this in mind, you too will see it very clearly.

(Oh, yes, but before I forget – one important thing! Remember always that, with the exception of *Cancer*, I am writing counter-clockwise. My starting-point will be my end point – the arrival in Paris – or, in another way of speaking, the break-through. So what I am telling about is the story of a man you never met, never knew; he is mostly of a definite period, from the time he met June (Mona-Mara) until he leaves for Paris. Naturally, some of what he is at the time of writing comes to the fore. Inevitable. But the attempt is – I am talking only of the auto-novels, of course – to be and act the man I was during this seven-year period. From this segment of time I am able to look backward and forward. Very much as our own time is described – the Janus period, the turning-point, where both avenues become clear and recognizable – at least to those who see and think. Oof!)

I wanted so much, so much, to be a writer. (Maybe not to write so much, as to *be* a writer.) And I doubt that I ever would have become one had it not been for the tragedy with June. Even then, even when I knew I would and could, my intention was to do nothing more than tell the story of those years with her, what it had done to me, to my soul, if you like. Because it was the damage to the soul, I must tell you, that was the all. (And I doubt if I have made that at all clear in my writings!) And so, on the fateful day, in the Park Department of Queens County, N.Y., I mapped out the whole autobiographical romance – in one sitting. And I have stuck to it amazingly well, considering the pressures this way and that. (The hardest part is coming – *Nexus* – where I must reveal myself for what I was – something less than zero, something worse than the lowest knave.)

With June I could not begin this magnum opus which, as you know, I thought would be just one enormous, endless tome – perhaps bigger than the Bible. My suffering was so great – and my ego too, no doubt – that I imagined it needed a canvas of that scope.

Note: *My* suffering I say. For *then* I was concerned with what had been done *to me*. As I wrote, of course, I began to perceive that what I had done to others was far more heinous. Whoever greatly suffers must be, I suppose, a sublime combination of sadist and masochist. Fred easily perceived the masochist that I was. But neither you nor he see so easily the sadist. Fred has touched on it in a subtly diabolical way – really too exalted to suit my case, I think. It was plainer, coarser than that. (But here you are up against the dilemma of not being privy to the facts of my life; it is my word as a man and a writer, against the apperceptions of readers and critics and psychologists. I admit that I have the power to warp what I honestly think may be the truth about my thoughts and actions. But I do believe I am nearer the mark than the outsider.)

So, as you hint, I coined this word Truth. The key to my whole work was to be the utter truth. And, as you realize, I found it easier to give the truth about the ugly side of my nature than the good. The good in me I only know as it is reflected back to me in the eyes and voices of those I talk to.

Whether I *then* knew what later I have come to know absolutely is a question, namely – the words of Jesus, that the truth shall set ye free. If I had only set myself to tell the truth about myself, that would have been fine. But I also wanted to tell the truth about others, about the world. And that's the greatest snare of all: it sets you above the others if not precisely above the world. Time and again I try to cut myself down. You all know how I rant and rave. There's always some truth in these outbursts, to be sure, but how caricatural!

Yet I do feel that truth is linked to violence. Truth is the naked sword; it cuts clean through. And what is it we are fighting, who love truth so much? The lie of the world. A perpetual lie. But I'm going off again . . .

Let me tell you something more simple and yet revealing. I said I wanted nothing more of God than the power to write. Yes, this began in my late teens, I imagine. In my early twenties, confined to my father's shop, a slave to the most idiotic kind of routine imaginable, I broke out – inside. Inwardly I was a perpetual volcano. I will never forget the walks to and from my father's shop every day: the tremendous dialogues I had with my "characters", the scenes I portrayed, and so on. And never a line of any of this ever put to paper. Where would you begin if you were a smothered volcano?

And then, after the first attempt at a book – when with the Western Union and married to that woman B——, my first wife – I dream of making my entry into the lists – by the back door. To write something that will sell, that people will read, that will permit me to say, "There is my name signed to it, you see." Proof.

And then the break, thanks to June, the plunge. And I am free, spoon-fed, have leisure, paper, everything, but can't do it. Oh yes, I do write, but how painfully, and how poorly, how imitatively. And then when June left for France with her friend Jean Kronski, then I broke, then I mapped out my whole career. And even then, think of it, even after leaving for France, three years later, I still do not begin that great work. I write *Tropic of Cancer*, which was not in the schema – but of the moment. I suppose one could liken it to the volcano's eruption, to the breaking of the crust. (Only, let me say it as knows, it was such a feeble eruption compared to those imaginary street-walking ones I had every day, inwardly, walking to and from my father's shop!)

How well I know the tremendous décalage between what one wishes to do and what one does! Nowhere in my work have I come anywhere near to expressing what I meant to express. Now, if you can believe this, and I am sure you must because you must also suffer it, then imagine what sort of beast it is that a woman, any woman, has to live with who marries a writer. Imagine what happens to one who never says all, never does all, who smiles and nods his head in that civilized way and is all the while a raging bull. Well, what happens is that either the writer gains the upper hand eventually, or the man. One or the other must take the lead. My effort has been to give the lead to the man in me. (With what success others know best.) But there is no war involved, you must understand. It is rather a matter of leaning more this way than that, of shifting the emphasis, and so forth.

And I do not want to be a saint! Morality, in fact, drops out of the picture. Maybe the writer will drop out too. Or the man. Never the ego, rest assured. Nor do I give a damn about that.

I certainly do not hope to alter the world. Perhaps I can put it best by saying that I hope to alter my own vision of the world. I want to be more and more myself, ridiculous as that may sound.

Where the writing is concerned, I did nothing consciously. I followed my nose. I blew with every wind. I accepted every influence, good or bad. My intention was therefore, as I said, merely to write. Or, *to be a writer*, more justly. Well, I've been it. Now I just want – to be. Remember, I beg you, that this infinitive is "transitive" in Chinese. And I am nothing if not Chinese.

Does this help? If not, walk on – and over me.

  Henry.

             Next day – April 2nd.

It's pouring and I feel like saying a bit more . . . . Those fan letters I spoke of. If someone had the courage to publish these, volume after volume, what a broadside that would be. And how revealing! Here are the books which readers say have influenced them, enlarged their outlook on life, altered their being: *The Colossus, Capricorn, Cancer, Wisdom of the Heart* – primarily. [. . .]

What I can never write enough about are the "influences" – both men, haphazard meetings, books, places. Places have affected me as much or more than people, I think. (I find it the same with you here.) Think of my repeated journeys to Toulouse, or of the returns to the old neighborhood (the 14th Ward), or to the places where as a boy I spent my summer vacations, or to the regions in America where I dreamed things my own way, only to find them so otherwise. Strange that I never think of the afterlife this way! Dear old Devachan, which Fred and Edgar and I spoke of so often. All I see there is a breathing spell, another "open" womb, so to speak, where all the senses and the intellect are intensified, clarified, unobstructed – and one learns just by looking, looking back at one's meagre, pitiable self in action.

But this business of youth – rebellion, longing for freedom – and the business of vision – are two very cardinal points in my orientation. At sixty-six I am more rebellious than I was at 16. Now I *know* the whole structure must topple, must be razed. Now I am positive that youth is right – or the child in its innocence. Nothing less will do, will satisfy. The only purpose of knowledge must be certitude, and this certitude must be established through purity, through innocence. Fred can tell you of the unknown man from Pekin who hangs above my doorway here. When I look at him I know he knows and is all that I expect a human being to be. (The photo of him is on the back of the Penguin edition of *The Colossus*. Study it. That is the person or being I would like to be, if I wanted to be someone else than I am.)

Influences . . . It should have been an eye-opener for you to read that chapter in *The Books in My Life*. At various times you have credited me with a live interest in certain writers and thinkers, who to tell the truth were only passing fancies. My loyalty and adoration have been constant – for the same men, all throughout my life: Whitman, Emerson, Thoreau, Rabelais, above all. I still think that no one has ever had a larger, freer, healthier view of man and his universe than Walt Whitman. And the passage from one of his prose works which I cited in my essay on him (originally published in some French anthology, now in English in the *Colorado Review*) comes close to expressing my own view of how man may live and function in this world with joy and meaning and purpose. (Look it up!)

And there was always Lao-tse, even before I had read him. He stands there, at the back of one's head, like the great Ancestor. Old Adam Cadmus. ("What's all the fuss about? Take it easy! Sit down, get quiet, don't think . . . . *think!*") And from him the line of Zen masters, which I only got wise to from Villa Seurat days on. "When you walk, walk; when you sit, sit; but don't wobble!"

But no one, it seems to me, can honestly put his finger on the real and vital influences which affected his course. That's why I mentioned, along with books and people, trivial things as well – things, happenings (little events), dreams, reveries, places.

In a book, for example – I say in a book and not *the* book, of a certain book – there are lines, just lines, page so and so, top left, that stand out like mountain peaks – and they made you what you have become. No one else but you could respond to those lines. They were written *for* you. Just as everything else which happens to you was intended *for* you, and never mistake it. Particularly the bad things.

(And this reminds me to say again that perhaps one reason why I have stressed so much the immoral, the wicked, the ugly, the cruel in my work is because I wanted others to know how valuable these things are, how equally if not more important than the good things. Always underneath, you see, this idea of "acceptance" – which is Whitman's great theme, his contribution.)

And then there is this curious business about Knut Hamsun. The one writer I started out to write like, to be like. How much time and thought I have given to that man's work – in the past. How I struggled to phrase my thoughts as he did. And without the least success. No one has ever remarked on it, after reading me. How do you explain that? When you look at early Picassos, early Gauguins, early Van Goghs, you can very easily trace their influences, their idols. They did not begin as Picasso, as Gauguin, as Van Gogh. I sometimes think of those two novels I wrote before going to Paris: what was I, who was I then? I have borrowed these scripts from the Library, time and again, but I am never able to read them.

And then I must say another thing – perhaps it bears on the foregoing, perhaps not . . . The other day I began reading *A Glastonbury Romance* by John Cowper Powys. My head began bursting as I read. No, I said to myself, it is impossible that any man can put all this – so much! – down on paper. It is super-human. And what was it stirred me so? A description of a man and a woman in a boat floating downstream. (I thought of that marvellous Japanese expression employed, I believe, to describe a certain genre of painting: "This floating world".) Old John had caught the world by the throat. And lovingly and surely he squeezed every bit of beauty, of meaning, of purposeless purpose out of it in a few pages. Utterly phenomenal.

And old Friar John, as he calls himself, was one of my first living idols. I a lad then of about 25 and he in his forties. The first man I beheld who was possessed by his daemon. Talk such as I have never heard again in my life. Inspired talk. And now at 80 he is still inspired, still writing masterpieces, still filled with the joie de vivre, the élan vital. You mentioned Chuang-Tzu. He was old John's great favorite. I too loved him better than Lao-tse, I must admit.

You mentioned Otto Rank. Yes, dear Otto too. But then, you know, after a time it palled. *What*? This seeking for meaning in everything. So Germanic! This urge to make everything profound. What nonsense! If only they could also make everything unimportant at the same time!

Ah yes, only a few years ago it was that I stumbled on Hesse's *Siddhartha*. Nothing since the *Tao Teh Ching* meant so much to me. A short book, a simple book, profound perhaps, but carrying with it the smile of that old man from Pekin over my doorway. The smile of "above the battle". Overcoming the world. And thus finding it. For we must not only be in it and above it, but of it too. To love it for what it is – how difficult! And yet it's the first, the only task. Evade it, and you are lost. Lose yourself in it and you are free.

How I love the dying words of St. Thomas Aquinas: "All that I have written now seems like so much straw!" Finally he saw. At the very last minute. He knew – and he was wordless. If it takes ninety-nine years to attain such a moment, fine! We are all bound up with the Creator in the process. The ninety-eight years are so much sticks of wood to kindle the fire. It's the fire that counts.

To come back . . . The child is alive with this fire, and we, the adults, smother it as best we can. When we cease throwing the wood of ignorance on the fire, it bursts forth again. Experience is an unlearning, an undoing. We must start from the beginning, not on the backs of dinosaurs – culture, that is, in all its guises. "Lime twigs and treachery" – that will be the title of a forthcoming book if I can ever get down to it. The title is borrowed from one of Brahms' "Waltz Songs", so help me God. [. . .]

Allez voir Joseph Delteil à Montpellier un de ces jours. Ça vous fera, vous et Claude, du bien. Il peut vous parler des Albigeois – et mille autres choses, comme St. François, par exemple, ou le cimetière à Sète et l'esprit qui y trouve son sommeil tranquille, Paul Valéry. Salut à Frédéric Temple et au Pont du Gard. Je l'ai vu pour la première fois en 1928 quand June et moi avons fait un tour de France avec bicyclettes. Je n'oublierai jamais ma première vue du Méditerranée, des oliviers, des vignes, de tout un pays ensoleillé et sec et brillant comme une gemme. Ta-ta! Assez pour une séance.

Henry

Miller's letter was published in *Art and Outrage* (1959), the book which started as an exchange of letters between Durrell and Perlès discussing Miller. It contains four letters by Durrell, three each by Miller and Perlès.
Miller's projected 'Lime Twigs and Treachery' was never completed.

*[Big Sur]   April 3rd 1958

Dear Larry –

Just a word about *The Black Book*. Don't compromise! Make 'em print as is – or give it to Girodias. In the long run you'll find he'll do as well with it as the Americans or British. It will *stay in print*, if banned. Whereas with the others, it will get raves and then die a quick death – possibly. Besides, you are powerful enough now to have things your own way for a change.

Don't buy any more shoes for the baby! Believe me, they are better off without.

Must you go on paying out alimon*ies* for the rest of your life? I hope not!

I'm dying to see your progeny – and Claude's. If we *all* went to see you – what a time! You always mention the expense – they are worth it all and more. Sometimes I lie abed watching my two eat breakfast. It does me good just to look at them. I love *them* – what does it matter whether they love me or not? Eve just got the bidet-toilet-book-flower article from Claude.

Love to you all.
Henry

317

Henry – what a stupendous letter! You have stepped in and banged our fat heads together! Makes us look like a couple of punch drunk hacks cutting paper dolls. But this important statement must be published – either separately or as a postscriptum to our book if it ever shapes up. We are still, as you see, circling warily round each other. I don't know yet what will come of the project, but if we overwrite and then cut down we may have what, in effect, could be a brief introduction to H.M. for the British, blast them! The question of intention! Anglo Saxons tend to view art as didactic. If you want to write Merde they at once think you are inciting people to mess the sidewalk; you have been poorly served by lack of detailed criticism and unavailability in UK and several of your younger admirers have a distorted view of you in one sense; they don't realise the central nature of your search, and that the books are a sort of spiritual by-product of the search. In other words they don't get the rationale behind what they call your "deliberate obscenity" – without realising the true meaning of its "deliberateness". Meanwhile of course I don't know which way Joe will see things and how he'll respond. Easy does it.

But meanwhile HAVE YOU A COPY OF YOUR LETTER? HAVE YOU SENT A CARBON TO JOE? YOU MUST SERIOUSLY CONSIDER PUBLISHING. I WILL HAVE IT COPIED BACK TO YOU IF YOU HAVEN'T KEPT IT. IT IS SO MARVELLOUS. ACTUALLY IT WOULD MAKE THE PERFECT POINT DE DÉPART FOR THE THIRD VOLUME? FOR *NEXUS*. IT IS LIKE THE PLAY WITHIN THE PLAY IN *HAMLET*.

No, they are not going to bowdlerise *The Black Book* at all; and the few cuts they want in *Mountolive* are so laughable that I let them do it. The French will do it now <in toto> – I am at ease. One, by the way, is the *Latin* word *fellatio*. I don't think anyone in england would understand it except Marie Stopes! It is too absurd.

Baby's shoes! I am in the process of learning to write by a process [of] progressive unselfimportance and my experience of *forms* is paying off; I can write in several different modes without strain by suddenly realising how unimportant it is to write at all! Learning to relax at last. At least I hope so. And if I can eat for six months at the cost of an 800 word feature – I do it before breakfast. I am resting now awhile before beginning the fourth book. "It rests by changing" (Heraclitus).

love to you both
Larry

*Sommières.   [April 1958]

My dear Henry:
Our letters will have crossed – I copied your own back to you realising
that you were improvident enough not to have kept a copy of this small
chef d'oeuvre; wonderful thing it is to be sure. In the interval comes your
next with *The Sergeant* which I found an excellent pull away from the
shore – drive and shape and purpose; if a neighbour of yours as the blurb
says give him an extra hug from me. It's a touch down and no mistake!
Of course I would love to do a Henry Miller reader or even help to do
one; I sold the idea to Peter Owen in London remember, and worked out
a rough scheme for them which I copied to you. And I think it excellent
to get someone respectable for the preface – particularly as you like and
respect Herbert Read (I find him unreadable, hush, but honest kind and
thorough). [. . .]
Yes, doubtless you do find me a bit prosy and tiresome with my
chattering about intentions – but do you realise that I (your oldest and
most devoted fan) had no clue as to the anti clockwise pattern you
outlined in your letter – it is NOWHERE stated? Similarly I had no means
of telling that in *Sexus* you were enacting the life of the pre-*Cancer* Miller
– before the divine afflatus hit him; that is what I meant by the siting, the
intention. So much of this book is quite gratuitously hair raising, and one
deduces from it a different author to *Tropic*; though (maddeningly
enough) the writing is very much greater in huge tracts of it. The
persona, the I, baffles one; he's less mature, less ripe and less selective
than the I of *Tropic*. But once one understands your firing-site it becomes
clear – this letter is a small corner stone to the second big trilogy. Because
you are, in effect, going back and enacting the human Henry
geologically, one stage below surface so to speak. And if I fuss and fume
it's because I want the english reading young to get as much lift and
laughter out of you as I've had – and a pointing finger into the bargain!
Thirty blows with your slipper to dumb durrell,

        more soon   Larry

[P.S.] YOU MUST TRY AND MARKET THAT IDEA OF THE CHILDREN'S
STORY FROM *SEXUS* AS A BOOK? LAUGHLIN MUST BE MAD NOT TO SEE
IT'S THE BEST PUBLISHING IDEA OF THE CENTURY.

The Sergeant (1958): novel by Miller's friend Dennis Murphy.

Dear Henry – books all arrived and I've started in; it is quite frightening, the magnitude of your achievement – all stacked up here on my desk. One's brain spins wondering how the hell you've done it all and kept sane. I'm in direct touch with Laughlin and won't bother you until we have a complete typescript for you to see and approve. While I want the thing to give a good account of your protean genius I am also keeping a wary eye on reduplication of material which has already been made available in other forms. This should be both "representative" and as "new" as possible. Laughlin presses for an introduction – but hell one does not "introduce" one's reverend seniors! Even if one heads the clever-but-so-what list of young novelists! We shall see. First the work. I'm trying to use your letter to Joe and me.

Gerald Sykes will be posting you on the proofs of *Mountolive* soon; keep them for a rainy day and don't swear at the pedestrian "naturalistic" form. It's only the 3rd movement (rondo) of a symphonic poem. When one has all four they will I hope all swim in solution like clockwork fish and the whole job "float" like a Calder "mobile"! Esperons!

I have found a desolate little "mazet" on the garrigue north of Nîmes, direction Uzès–Avignon. Seventy square miles of heath, moorland, sage, holm-oak. Dry rocky soil, sunburnt. Like an abandoned corner of Attika. We move there around September 15th when the children fly back to school. The new address will be

MAZET MICHEL
ENGANCES
PRÈS NÎMES. GARD. FRANCE.

Guard it with your life! Don't send me any curiosity-pokers! With any luck I shall be in the clear next year and can finish *Clea* easily without writing rubbish for the *Times*. Whoopee! Things are moving my way now – wind is changing quite perceptibly. (*Holiday* magazine want me to go up the Nile!) What next? I bet *you'd* love it; but I loathed Egypt! (Not a word.)

Yes, I liked some of A.S. Neill's books but I gather that "Summerhills" is a sort of bear-pit – and my suspicions are aroused by the fact that Bertrand Russell is on the board and has all his children there. It must be crank! Russell has spent sixty years trying to rinse the intuition out of mathematics! But I realise your concern, having American children to think about. I think "junior" is one of the most horrible creations on earth, far worse than superman, and I'm a bit astonished that you seem to hold a brief for the undisciplined child – for that is what "junior" is. I think kids need a sense of direction as well as the configurational development by a loving *family* – but mostly *mother*. She is the key – and she should devise the suitable disciplinary pattern for them; without her they topple inside. Every sweet pea needs a stick to grow up; and discipline that is purposeful and moral – *not* physical (i.e. the cane) gives them self-confidence. I must say our own three are marvellous all things considered; Claude has a knack of joining forces with them and leading them from the inside, so to speak. But we're fucked if we'll have bad manners or stupidity – and we seldom get it. They respect us, keep quiet while we're working – and we play as fair as we can by taking them all over the place and *really* working at awakening the little buggers up. I paused several times reading the *Oranges* to wonder (from your hair-raising description of the *behavior* of the kids) whether you were not doing for children what Jean-Jacques did for the imaginary Noble Savage – a sort of idealised belief in their world. I'm glad you are doing a book about them. I'm genuinely interested. I know what pain and delight they give, of course, but in my case have decided that we use them as objects of self-gratification emotionally. Only an effort of will prevented me from behaving like Beethoven in that book you couldn't read. It wasn't the psychoanalysis, incidentally, but the *story* that struck me. No man can be a mother! Enuf!

Joe's new novel is sheer hell: so bad, so tired. I had to tell him the truth, since I can't think where to "place" it for him. Claude's book about the French is shaping awfully well – now this you *will* read with keen interest I know when it comes out.

Anaïs is coming next week for a flying visit and so is Rowohlt from Hamburg. Ouf! it's late; I'm tired. Both my daughters dance wonderfully – particularly the baby. We've been a-swimming for two whole days at the Saintes-Maries – the headquarters of all the Gipsies in Christendom. Why the hell don't you take a year off in Europe! Joe is planning to make the jump soon, and so is *Anaïs*. Why not a French lycée for your kids?

Love.
Larry

[P.S.] Do you know Eiluned Lewis's marvellous aphorism – "Children are only grown-ups with their eyes open"! Goodnight!

Dear Larry,

A post card by way of answer will do. Since you have just read "all and
everything", could you tell me if you recall seeing a passage of one or
two pages, perhaps, wherein I meet a fairy in an Italian restaurant,
allow him to take me home, hoping he will give me passage money for
Paris to join June there, get up in the night, read Molly Bloom's
soliloquy, then rifle his pockets and beat it?

I've just written this now in *Nexus* but have an uneasy feeling I might
have done it before, either in *Capricorn* or *Sexus*. Too lazy to reread
whole books gunning for such things. Just say if you recall such an
episode, then I'll get Emil White to track it down for me.

Also this episode – several weeks' stay in Vienna at home of June's
uncle – playing chess, war stories, no seeing Vienna, locked in room all
the time?

The trouble is, you see, that I have held so many things in back of my
head for so long, and probably written them out in my head dozens of
times, that I get confused. Also, now and then I jump forwards or
backwards, chronologically speaking. I've kept a rough synopsis of
incidents and events already written out in autobiographical
"romances", still . . . .

Am coming soon to the European trip with June – 1928 – when we
toured France by bike, then Vienna, Budapest, Prague, etc. Always
remember our first sight of the Pont du Gard . . . also Les Baux. And
how often have I dreamed that I was back in Orange on one sunny day,
sitting outside a bistro, hot as hell, the awning flapping, looking at the
Arch, dreaming . . . . (Or was it a mingled remembrance of my own
experience and that of Jean Gabin in one of his early pictures there?)

Anyway, I'm at page 300 <only 1/4th through, in short!> now and
going fine. Indulging myself. Lots of conversation, often idle, but so
natural. Trying out all sorts of things in this final tome. Why should I
the author not have a good fling too, eh?

It's so hot to-day, at 9.30 A.M., that I have to quit. First dreary fog,
now heat. (Around 90 to 100 and over all day from sun up on.)

One more query: would you remember where I might have quoted a
passage from Gogol on Russia? A sort of peroration like this . . .
"Russia, Russia, where are you leading us – or dragging us?" It goes on
about the horses, their manes flying . . . all prophetic. May be from

Dead Souls but can't find it where I thought it was. Don't let any of this disturb you. Just a yes or no will do – by post card. "Mazet" is not in my Larousse. Imagine it to be an adobe house with thick walls. "Garrigue" is a beautiful word. So is "pralaya". When you finish Tome IV take a good holiday! You owe it to yourself! No man could have done more. You're king of the road now. Call these four your cornerstone. Want to write but am dripping with sweat. Enuf! Love to Claude. She has an almost lacy expression sometimes . . . so feminine. Don't let her destroy her beauty writing books!

Ta-ta!
Henry

Pralaya is a yoga term denoting the achievement of stability.

*SOMMIÈRES

Dear Henry: sent you off a ground plan a couple of days ago; had a long, good letter from Shapiro (a good poet by the way). I declined a long generalised correspondence about your work on the grounds of being chock a bloc (true); but I made it clear that I have no parti pris in the matter, my name won't appear on it etc. I sent him a carbon of the ground plan and suggested that he, Cowley, Laughlin and whoever else felt about you strongly should constitute a sort of friendly committee to advise on the final book. It is very much quicker that way, and less hampering for me. I won't quarrel about changes; we must each of us have favourite passages, and I can't explain to everyone why I dropped one and chose another; but they can and should advise *you* that my selection here or there has been weak, and propose solutions, other choices etc. So that you have the benefit of all our brains on the job. Don't you think? And then you can weigh the pro's and con's and decide. It's much more honest this way, and leaves my sword arm free as it were to build the maquette of the book. Yes, I'll watch about libel but . . . there isn't an invented character in you, is there? And I think we can put some fiery passages in here and there, though not the ones crammed with fruitcake! After all, it's an introduction, a sample, a cross section . . .

I'll be sending you some pics of Joe's visit soon; I must say you've ploughed a hole in our famous correspondence – where to go from here? Did anais find me so subdued? Well, in 18 months I've written three full size books and two little ones apart from a mass of miscellaneous stuff to keep wolf from the door . . . A bit exhausted I guess; but in good heart underneath. Besides I have a very special attentiveness towards anais which prevents me from shouting and screaming in my normal way; our rapport is pin point, and she's so very fine that I feel clumsy and heavy as a water buffalo. You don't shout at Dresden china do you? I think she always found me a bit of a puzzle: strong watchful brain perhaps? I see someone very young in her always, unmarked by experience, and feel like Uncle. This is probably fantasy. She has just arrived back in Paris, by the way, and another visit impends; we have all had chicken pox except me this last week which may account for my being rather subdued . . . male nurse to a prostrate household, brain buzzing with projects but no chance to work. Hence grey hair. God just wait till I'm rich!

> more soon,
> love to you both
> Larry

*Big Sur   Aug. 29, 1958

Dear Larry:
I've just received a copy of Laughlin's recent letter to you about the *HM Reader* and as he is obviously eager to speed up production of the book I thought to give you some further ideas *now* (while hot) before the plan is frozen. Some of the texts I am suggesting for inclusion you may already have selected, some you may wish to reject, but I'd like you to know what I myself would like to see appear in the book. A few I will star, as being especially dear to my heart. I am looking at your original ground-plan, with its five divisions – implementing it.

Short Stories:
  *"Astrological Fricassee" (which was reprinted in a pocket book: a killer-diller for general public).
  *"My Friend Stanley" (from *Sexus*); reprinted in one of New Directions' Year Books. (A piece of writing that *I* like.) Not exactly a "short story".

Essays:
  *"Balzac and His Double " (from *Wisdom of the Heart*).

324

"The Diary of Anaïs Nin" (same book, I think).

"Shadowy Monomania" (on DHL); from *Sunday After the War*. (This and "Creative Death" – also on Lawrence – are among my best essays, I think.)

The chapter "Rider Haggard" from *Books in My Life* expresses my views on youth vs. adults and ties in with the Rimbaud book.

"Creative Writing" (reprinted in Mentor pocket book) – a favorite with my readers.

"The Staff of Life" (from *Remember*): great favorite with readers . . . humorous, satirical.

"The Angel Is My Watermark" (from *Black Spring*).

My "Preface" to *The Astrology of H.M.* by Sydney Omarr.

An excerpt or two from *Maurizius Forever* (possibly).

Excerpts from *The Time of the Assassins* (Rimbaud).

Excerpt from *Nexus* – to appear in *The Prairie Schooner*, ed. by Shapiro, shortly.

"Walt Whitman" – from *The Colorado Review*. Short but good.

Portraits:

"A Boddhisattva Artist" (Abe Rattner) – from *Remember*.

Chapter on Blaise Cendrars – from *Books in My Life*.

Chapter called "Remember to Remember" – for portraits of Durrell and Perlès. (I'm fond of this.)

Postface (revised) to *Aller Retour N.Y.* Revelatory text concerning "influences" in one's life.

Excerpt from "Patchen, Man of Anger . . . Light" (possibly).

Perhaps chapters called "Influences" and "Living Books" from *Books in My Life* – especially the *former*.

And where have I written about my good friend Emil Schnellock? He ought to be among the "portraits". I called him Ulrich in the banned books – but I mean aside from these.

And what about Katsimbalis and Seferis – from *Colossus*?

What also about an excerpt or two from *Semblance of a Devoted Past* – written as letters to Emil S. Do you have it?

About Section Five, the "Aphorisms" – that's your job exclusively! [. . .]

I hope by this time all the books and brochures you asked for have arrived.

In Laughlin's letter he urges you to write an Introduction. Evidently you were thinking not to. Out of modesty? Or what? You would be the one, no mistake about it. I often think of that gem you wrote for *Horizon* and of the one in *Booster*, "Hamlet, Prince of China", remember? Rather prophetic, what! What I'm thinking is, Larry, that in a preface from your pen, and as coming from a *friend*, you could say all those things I think you ought and want to say – about my weaknesses, my limitations, my bad writing, my obsessions, my lack of self-criticism, etc. etc. etc. I've had plenty of laudatory comments and lots of picayune criticism from little shits, but you could really blast me – it would be fun. And it would also teach the "critics" how to fire with two guns at once – and remain a friend and a loyal reader. That Thomas Parkinson text (from BBC) in *The Listener* recently was bad in that he didn't know where he stood or what he was aiming at. You could also make mention of lots of things the average reader does not know about me or my work, for ex. – the many prefaces I've written (and the many more I refuse to write!), the many texts for foreign reviews, for which I seldom receive any payment; the book reviews I've done, the correspondence I wage with all and sundry (to my utter detriment, to be sure – but one of my "weaknesses" – *of character*, perhaps). And how this vice has happily made me the kind of writer I am and not a literary figure. And – quite important – as I hinted before somewhere – how in one and the same period I am writing in quite different veins – sexual travesties, metaphysical pish-posh, analyses of books, pen portraits, landscapes, fantasies and so on. Or how (or why) the sexual is so often larded with humor, and, though often verging on (sic) the pornographic, never perverse. At the worst, I'm a "voyeur" – and of course a filthy "voyou". And, or, how difficult it is to predict the coming direction or trend in my work, seeing as how I don't know myself. (In the oven lies a sort of infantile Céline-like blast against "adults" called "Lime Twigs and Treachery" – from Brahms' Love Waltzes (sic).) Or that the only revolution which means anything to me is in the field of Education. That I've given up the adults as hopeless, now and forever . . . that all I care about are children. (And a few adults who come near being children – "the happy lunatics", as the Zen master might say.)

And here's another thought for you . . . did I ever broach it? As time goes on I care less and less (and how!) for literature, especially "good literature", recognized literature, yet . . . now when I do find a good book – *good for me*! – I am enthusiastic, less critical, more completely taken in, mystified, reverent, than ever before in my life. In short, completely vulnerable. This I must regard as one of God's great gifts to an erring soul. How thankful I am that it took me twenty, thirty, sometimes more, years to come upon certain books. Because now, only now, am I ready for them . . . ready to *enjoy* them, I mean. And I must stress it again, though it's boring, that from the so-called bad books I got as much as from the good ones. "One man's meat is another man's poison." To this day I haven't the slightest idea how a book gets written. It remains for me in the realm of the miraculous. I know less now, in other words, than when I began. I do know this, if it means anything, that a book, like a life, is the result of what you are every day, including the bad days and the lazy days and the infertile days. No estimable critic can evaluate the sublime leaven of idleness – for a writer and for a liver of life! As I said to Joey in the "Postface" – do less and less! Being is all.

Larry, I feel sorry for you. I'm just adding to your worries. Take what's useful out of all this and throw the rest in the garbage can.

And do take a bit of royalties, won't you? Don't stand on pride or honor. Remember those starvelings of yours – a whole brood of them . . . and your ex-wives . . . and your future travels. There's more than enough to go round. I wouldn't miss it, even though broke, I can tell you. Every day I continue to live in this frightful country I have less and less respect or understanding of money. It means nothing here . . . absolutely nothing. The harder I work the less I have. If I had nothing I imagine I would be supremely happy. I was checking up in my mind, just the other day, the invitations I have had in the last few years from "fans" and friends all over the world. If I gathered the family together and took off, I could keep traveling from place to place for the next ten years – rent free, good food, good talk, no worries, seeing the world. Why in hell don't I do it? I belong out there. I could also not budge. Drôle de con, quoi!

Well, enough! Love to Claude and all the little ones!

"Other Rooms, other voices!"
Henry

Reunion in France

Miller remained fixed, except for a few trips, at Big Sur from 1944 to 1962. During this period Durrell lived, except for short periods in England, in Alexandria, Rhodes, Córdoba, Belgrade, Bellapaix, Nicosia, Sommières and, finally, the Mazet Michel, a peasant farmhouse just outside Nîmes. Although Miller was to live for nearly seventeen years at his last home in Pacific Palisades, it was Big Sur along with 18 Villa Seurat that left their mark on his life and work. While Alexandria clearly had an enormous effect on Durrell's work, he was far happier at three other places, each associated with a different wife: Corfu with Nancy, Rhodes with Eve, and the Mazet Michel with Claude.

The Mazet Michel sits on a gently sloping hillside amid frost-stunted olives, wild thyme and scrub timber. An ungraded road, unpaved when Durrell moved in, winds for a mile to the Engances thoroughfare, and Nîmes is only another mile distant. Durrell and Claude work and spend royalties to turn the 'mas' into 'an ideal hideout for a couple of boozy writers'.

This is a good time for both men. Miller has in *his* Eve a woman who is a good household manager and a talented painter. He completes *Nexus*, which is published in French by Corrêa in 1960. Durrell's Claude seems to be his first wife to keep pace with his enormous energy: she cooks gourmet meals, controls the children during holidays, writes her own books. Together, they go to Hamburg for the triumphant première of *Sappho*, directed by Gustaf Gründgens and starring Elisabeth Flickenschildt, at the Deutsches Schauspielhaus. Durrell finishes *Clea*, completing *The Alexandria Quartet*. And in the summer of 1959 comes the reunion Durrell and Miller have planned, looked forward to, and been repeatedly denied over the past twenty years.

Dear Henry

I dotted you off a preface to the anthology yesterday which you must look at; and tell me if you like or not. By the way when sending books don't forget to put

SERVICE D'AUTEUR

good and large on them as from time to time they make me pay customs on them which I don't need to if they are marked plain!

We are still in a hellova mess, tidying up; soon I must get down to this blasted fourth volume. A complimentary of *Mountolive* is on its way to you. You'll probably find it stinks if you like Kerouac; I have only seen one sent me by Anaïs. Found it unreadable; no, I admire it in a way, as I admire *Catcher in the Rye*. It is social realism as the Russians understand it. But ouf the emptiness really of this generation of self-pitying cry-babies. We have our own group in England. And how can you not see that God or Zen is simply catchword, as Freud was in our time . . .? It doesn't really mean anything.

It is only here that I think America is really harming you, making you critically soft; beware of cowboy evangelism and Loving Every-thing and Everybody Everywhere! Or you'll be doing a Carl Sandburg with a portable harp! Sharpen up the Miller harpoon! Batten down on the soft, the lax, the self-pitying, the self-indulgent. Have you seen the excellent article on the "beat" boys in the new mag HORIZON? It is really good. Pin points them. But I guess I am perhaps too vieux jeu to mistake lumberjack's manners for art. And it don't really touch me at any place. They are turning the novel into a skating rink; I am trying to make it a spiral staircase.

Here's a quote from de Rougemont to ponder and perhaps pin up somewhere: "When under the pretence of destroying whatever is artifi-cial – idealizing rhetoric,the mystical ethics of 'perfection' – people seek to swamp themselves in the primitive flood of instinct, in whatever is primeval, formless and foul, they may imagine they are recapturing real life but actually they are being swept away by a torrent of waste-matter pouring from the disintegration of the ancient culture and its myths."

Ouch. Watch that large hearted self; keep the hand loom turning at full pressure!

Bless you,
larry

Dear Larry,

Just got the Preface to the *H.M. Reader* and I do like it! And why not,
since you flatter the shit out of me, as Joey would say. One thing
surprised me – the reference to message from Keyserling. Did I really get
that message or did you make it up? Since then, of course, I've had
hundreds of extraordinary messages from extraordinary people, not the
least of them coming from an Indian guru via a physician in Ismalia who
had cured him of some illness. That and the one from Tagore, via our
mutual firebrand Hindu-Communist friend (in London – forget his
name now) are outstanding in my memory.

There's just one sentence I want to comment on, for your benefit. It
needn't be altered, however. It's where you say that I am "reconciled (to
judge by his latest book)" to my native land. That's dead wrong. I am not
even reconciled to Big Sur, though I have accepted it and made the most
of it. But America . . .! I loathe everything about it more and more. It's
the land of doom. I will yet escape, I feel. How, I don't see yet.

And this leads me to Kerouac, that book I sent you. No matter what
you may have read or tried to read of his before, don't pass this up! I say
it's good, very good, surpassingly good. The *writing* especially. He's a
poet. His prose is poetry. Or, shall I say, the kind of poetry I can
recognize. How representative he is of the Beat generation I can't say. I
know little of these boys, I avoid them, I don't read them. As for
growing soft – in criticism – never fear. Whom have I praised among
American writers – contemporaries? None of the celebrities do I read or
can I read. The publishers send me their dreck and I chuck the books over
the cliff. I can't even bother to pass them on to some poor bastard who
can't afford to buy a book. I wouldn't waste his time.

Aside from yourself, Céline, Cendrars, Giono – and good Friar John –
what a book, I repeat, is *A Glastonbury Romance* – I see none. Wasteland.
No Moses trekking across it – and no Sinai to reach. Rubbish. Drivel.
"Social realism", you say? Worse.

All this for the record . . . .

A good note. Just got Rowohlt's handsome German edition of the *Big
Sur* book. A honey of a book. Beautiful jacket, good paper, good print,
good format. Why, oh why, can't the English and Americans bring out
such productions? And did you see Ernst Rowohlt's touching encomium
to you (*Justine*) in a recent issue of *Das Schönste*? You're a success already,

in Germany. With this revue came a copy of *Du* from Zurich – issue devoted entirely to Hermann Hesse. How tender! And what wonderful photos of him at all ages. Especially the one with a beard and black rimmed glasses: there he is the poet, painter, musician and magician all in one. I'm going to frame it. To put beside that strange looking guy Gurdjieff! Does *he* look like a master, wow! Well, enough. Hope the mistral blowing through the garrigue doesn't destroy the mazet.

Henry

Miller's comments refer to Kerouac's *The Dharma Bums* (1958).

*le mazet michel   engances   près nimes.   gard.
france.   [*c.* 6 November 1958]

Dear Henry: Keyserling! I saw you get the telegram and exclaim; afterwards we were lunching with Joe at L'Escargot and he told me what was in it, and you had the grace to blush as you admitted the soft impeachment! You were quite shy, and deeply delighted – as who would not be? It stuck in my mind; and an accolade from a philosopher somehow seemed to give point to your reputation not as a mere novelist etc but as a thinker, visionary etc . . .

Anyway; let us see what Laughlin has to say. About Kerouac, whose new book has arrived, what am I to say? Question de goût I suppose; I can't go along with you. I found it really corny, and deeply embarrassing. (Read pages 30–33 aloud in a strong american voice); and worst of all pretentious. All these nincompoops crawling up hills with their food in polythene bags and attitudinising about religion like Oxford Groupers. You have done the most devastating satires on this kind of savin' and keepin' line in *Black Spring*; and I remember once dragging you to a movie where Bing Crosby, in a dog collar, sang a little jazz about Jesus from a pulpit in a penitentiary; and you were so god damned mad you wanted to throw rocks at the screen. No, this really seems campus stuff. And all those cute little fucks stolen in the name of Zen (just substitute the word Jesus and see what you make of the *content*). It is hick stuff. Remember the nursery odyssey?

> ma's out, pa's out,
> LET'S TALK DIRT!
> Pee, po, bum, bottom, drawers!

332

Sorry if you think I'm unjust but it seems to [be] about Errol Flynn level; and gee when they open their little peepers to drink in the universe, gee how alloverish they come! No, No! As for the writing, yes it's fluent with good key changes but it has that breathless wondering lisp, the prattling tone which seems to have been handed down to american writers by Anita Loos. "So I went down to the hotel, grabbed me a cornplaster, docked my luggage, and I says to myself if God don't know (with the mountains so lovely) why I don't know either, and if I don't know who the hell does? So I went and had a slug of rye and God . . ."

Saroyan has killed himself as a writer in this genre, the breathless lisp of a sweet little boy who is granted all the wonderful, wonderful treasures of God's own landscape! It is fundamentally pretentious-sentimental, and goes along with being tough as hell and hep and yet "so quiet, saintly and Christ-like, just another bum like Krishna was, and maybe even Jesus out there on Galilee . . ."

I'm trying to isolate a *tone* of voice which irks me! God knows, Kerouac may yet turn into a writer. He's young and hard working. But what a devastating picture of what young intellectuals are saying and doing over there; they need a week at a French lycée to be taught to think and construct!

Anyway, what the hell! Don't be angry with me for not going along on this book; maybe it has fine things in it which are not on my wavelength. But that other boy, *The Sergeant*, why he's a real writer, not a splurger, and his prose has melody as well as bite.

(You'll think I'm suffering from enlarged spleen!) By the way, the counterpart of this tone of voice in english prose is (I owe this observation to Claude) *Little Women*! No, old fogey that I am I thank goodness that our Henry Miller ain't this kind of writer, even in his worst bouts of sentimental fantasy! Love to you both. (*Mountolive* is a book of the month choice. No idea as yet what this means in dough!)

Love. Larry

According to Durrell, the telegram Miller received *c.* 1938 from Count Keyserling read: 'I salute a great free spirit.'

Dear Henry: just a swift line. I'm glad that the preface seemed okay, and hope that the book goes forward now if and when you approve. About being "reconciled" I quite understand; I originally wrote "reconciled to friend and foe alike" and it seemed silly, reconciled to friend. Also you have managed in Big Sur to sound "at home in the world you was borned in", and even managed to capture a touch of Paradise in it; it would be a pity to spoil the impression now, specially as Americans like the British seem to be as touchy as Argentines these days about the home base. It never used to be true of us before the war; but now the slightest criticism and people flare up. When there is so much of great value we must try and get across it would be a pity to unscramble some Home Truths in a preface! Let be unless it maddens you.

Yes, I don't think a prolonged siege in USA could do anything but dehydrate one; I think it is wonderful you've stuck it out the way you have. I mean without very frequent visits abroad. Mind you, I don't think it is the people: I really believe that places have their own rhythm and compulsion and some are hostile to artists. But I think the American scene is enriching in another way; a big spiritual potential which isn't being capitalised due to our beastly puritan culture. In England the landscape is good, nourishing; one can work there. There isn't any hostility to the artist. What is killing is the spineless and revolting life they have built up around themselves, the habits, the boredom, the lack of la bonne chère. No belly worship!

Here we are at the centre of an axis: Avignon, Nîmes, Arles; Pont du Gard is twenty kilometres. It's a real hub; and up here on the wild garrigue it is . . . curiously like Greece. The typics of the place are all out of Rabelais, huge mutton-headed, pink-cheeked, potatoe-nosed belly-worshippers with laughter like a force three gale. There is only one topic of conversation – food, past and to come. Never money. Often lavatories. Seldom sex. But always food. Just suit you down to the ground!

I am trying to sell our correspondence; Faber doesn't think it adds up to a book; rather a fausse couche, as Joe says somewhere. Also they think the only really good things are your letters; they say mine are lousy and Joe they think too reverent. Anyway we'll see what we can do.

Anaïs wants me to preface her first novel to appear in England. Lord. I must be getting quite important with all these prefaces to the work of my elders and betters; well, it's a toe-hold in immortality I suppose.

Okay about Kerouac; I expect you'll have me eating mud and apologising again. Wonder if you have ever read *Green Mansions* by Hudson? I think you'd find a lot of the same unconscious symbolic stuff you dug out of Haggard.

every good thing to you all
larry

Durrell's unpublished preface to Nin's *Children of the Albatross* was to lead to considerable misunderstanding and some bitterness, when Nin resented having the words 'feminine-subjective' and 'iridescent' applied to her writing.

*from this joint→ Berkeley Travel Lodge,
Berkeley, California   Nov. 11th 1958

Dear Larry –

Came up here to see a proctologist – hope you know that word! – and brought *Mountolive* with me to read. Am half-way through now and write to tell you how very very good it is – in every respect. Am always amazed by the way you digest the countries you've lived in. A vast, penetrative knowledge rendered in poetic fashion, even the mud, the sores, the flies! (The slaughter of the camels, which I read a while ago, is simply tremendous.) All the characters are exciting. You seem to know your subject intimately. How little I know of your life! I could listen to you for weeks on end! And as I read you, then get up and walk the streets of Berkeley, I almost feel like weeping. This is a completely sterile and sterilized world over here. I had to kill three days – alone. Didn't care to see a soul. You can't imagine what it's like, a place like this.

Well, to-morrow back to Big Sur – a long journey. Back to *Nexus*. I guess if I didn't have my books to write I'd jump in the river.

My arse has been fixed up, for another few years. No cancer-schmanser. In other respects I'm A–1, I believe.

Returning to *Mountolive*. Sorry it isn't 3 times the size!

More about it when through.

Cheers for Claude.
Henry

P.S. They even have the *Mormon* Bible in every room here – furnished by the Gideon Society.

Dear Larry:

Don't feel you have to reply to all my letters! Let me write you – I can afford to waste time, what! Writing again to-day because the whole day has gone answering queries from this one and that, and other chores of similar nature. So, I'm wound up. No use tackling *Nexus* with only half hour to go. (I need at least an hour clear.) Just got your last about receipt of American dollars, lavatory, Enfants de la Terre – *and*, this is why I write – your deprecatory remarks about *Mountolive*. My dear man, don't say such things, ever, not to any one! That book is a perfect gem. I am thirty-five pages from the end now; I have read it like a Yeshiva Bocher would read his Psalms. (I wrote you, surface mail, when up in Frisco – but it was just a brief note; I had been reading in bed.)

Some day we're going to have a long talk – tête à tête – about Egypt, Rhodes, Jerusalem, Greece, Jugoslavia, Armenia, Turkestan, Argentina, and so on – where haven't you been? And Cos! My God, when I see you call up these places, how deeply you have absorbed them, how magnificently you have given us their spirit and essence – even down to the flies – I am dismayed. Who is this man I have been corresponding with over the years? What do I know about him? He was almost a cherub when we parted – in Arcady. Yes, I knew he had genius, but not such genius! And now he is in his forties, and I know him only through his books and letters. What a great pity! I long to know all, the whole man, the whole life – especially all the setbacks, disasters, frustrations, bedevilments, detours, ennuis, alimonies, etc. without which no one could have written such magnificent books. (And what a darlint of a writer you are to have kept all this nasty personal dreck out of your books!) Hourrah for the Durrells of this world! Hourrah!

No, *Mountolive* is not to me a naturalistic novel, nor indeed any classifiable novel. It fits into the tetralogy like the key in the lock; gives one a thrill to get behind previous scenes, in and under certain characters encountered before. (Also to see again these words – "gras, delgat et gen".) No, it's masterful, the scaffolding, the armature, the plan or whatever. And the writing never lags, never palls. Same Durrellian

336

level – gem-like, incandescent. What you call the "cinerama" parts – good expression – sure, we look for them, all of us. But do we deserve them? And whence come they – out of what depths, what experience (actualities)? But I find descriptions, characters, conversations, reveries, literary and historical allusions – what a savant you are! You seem to have forgotten nothing you ever saw or heard. No, I read you with a powerful magnifying glass. Nothing escapes me. (Even that questionable "boustrophedon" passage – aren't you wrong there?) No matter! It's vast, vast, this work – the whole tetralogy. A vast pool from which one can gather what he likes. There's no one alive writing like this. I said before – you're king now. I mean it. You say you got a windfall from America. A thousand only? Man, they'll be paying you in diamonds yet.

Larry Powell (librarian – your greatest admirer in U.S. aside from me) was here the other day. He spoke with reverence of you, as always. He's come into his own, he said. Yes, I said, it's like watching some great tropical flower open up. (Like that moon flower I once saw in Los Angeles, which opens at five minutes before sundown, on the dot, every day. The swans, again!)

Tell Claude to serve you an extra good meal this evening. I'm nominating you for the Nobel Prize soon. You'll get it, Larry, believe me!

Budd Schulberg. Yes, I read the book. Good in its way. Exciting, sort of. But can't say more. I met him too, just once. Disliked him.

I see "Cossery" in bracks. Do you know, I still think that his *Lazy Ones* is one of the unique books of our time. Not great writing, but great story – or "out of this world" story. He writes well but tight. Efficient. And my friend Dennis (Murphy) whom you like, he too is tight in his writing. But he's a comer. He'll blow yet. When you hear him talk you hear what he might write – someday. Great possibilities. Kerouac, you see, is just up my street, as far as American writing goes. He swings. Doesn't worry. Good, bad, indifferent – cancer-schmanser. What difference, so long as you're healthy? Something comes through, writing this way. Something that never happens with the usual "good" writers, I mean. We all can learn from this effortless effort. We need to learn to enjoy what we do while doing it. I'm dog-goned if I believe one must squirm in labor doing it. (Especially not after the fifth book, what!) Theory is, if *you* enjoyed doing it, chances are the other fellow will too. I talk enjoyment. Forgive me. That's all I have learned from the books I've pored over.

337

Do you laugh sometimes while writing? It makes fun, as Reichel would say.

I'm going down now for my apértif. Here's a new one I'm trying: equal parts of gin, Dubonnet and Cinzano. It clicks. Two and I'm swacked. Just got case, thru friend, wholesale, of an excellent year of Châteauneuf-du-Pape. If I could, here's how I'd do it each night, every night: Nuits St. Georges, Gevrey-Chambertin, Château Rothschild, Clos-Vougeot, Vosne-Romanée, Aloxe-Corton, Pommard, Medoc, Beaujolais. Then in reverse. Do you ever taste Verveine (liqueur) there? Almost as good, I think, as Chartreuse Verte. Shit! Wish I were there to talk to your neighbors. Food! What better topic for conversation?

Signing off now: just had crazy letter from hotel clerk in Monterey, saying he heard a long distance telephone conversation to N.Y. Times, from a nut, claiming he had proof that I (!) am the real author of Lolita. I haven't been able to read that book yet – opened it, didn't like style. May be prejudiced. Usually am. As Reichel says of paintings – "a book should smile back at you when you open it, nicht wahr?"

Oh, that German song you introduced was really something. Wondered where you dug that up. I have a beauty, in Yiddish, for when I come to my Rumanian episode – Nexus. "Rumania, Rumania, Rumania. . . ." By Aaron Lebedeff – a cheder boy.

Henry

*Nîmes etc.   [mid-February 1959]

Dear Henry: Claude is writing Eve direct about the tiny flat in Sommières; we haven't yet heard from the St Maries, so there may be something there. I had held off a little because I believed that someone with lots of room like Delteil might come across and invite you to stay or rent you something, but it doesn't seem likely at present so we are going on with the job ourselves; I think France like England is suffering from the lack of servants, and consequently the old type of large hospitality is fading away.

It is terribly hard to decide things for other people, and we've argued the whole Sommières project back and forth for two nights! Trying to get into your skins and see what you would find good or bad about it. Myself I think you'd love it and Eve too; but when one is a travelling family unit all kinds of strains and stresses come up which always do when one isn't chez soi. My own hope is that this three months will finally decide you to stick and settle here; my only terror is that having done so you will write a *Big Sur* about the Languedoc and start a landslide! I've just turned down two handsome offers to do a travel book about this part; having fouled my own nest in the same way in Greece I'm not taking any chances, no sir! I sign my books 'Ascona'! But . . . I believe that IF you take the Sommières flat and IF it works as it may well you will experience an entirely new reunion with France – a different France; that is why I am so anxious that you should be the ONLY foreigners in the little town, which is quite unencumbered. You would wake up every morning in the *Middle Ages*; and every Saturday morning your balcony would hang above a sea of coloured tents – Market Day; the forains pour into the little square, spread out their huge coloured marquees and set up their stalls; and the Provençals from the surrounding villages come in to buy boots and aprons and pitchforks and tractor spare parts; and the cafés fill up with hundreds of Raimus in berets. All day you hear the click of *boules*. Such a variety of character, too; placed in such an intimate contact with the town the characters of people come up clear, and within ten days you will be simply delighted by your talks with Lopez the mason, and Serafim the hairdresser (he paints horribly), and the butcher baker etc. When I think of the terrible poverty of the human material you describe in the Big Sur (despite your marvellous writing *about* them their lack of shape and interestingness came thru, reminding me of Joe's grim description of you sitting surrounded by genial morons) – when I think of them thar, and the people you will meet in the Languedoc I can see you simply hop with joy! As for the children, they are anglo-saxons, and like ours will hate the smells, the sanitation, and the fact that movies and comics are in French; but love the river (*fishing* for your boy), the old fort, the market, the Glacier ice cream, the cake shop, etc etc. Moreover this particular situation is the best of getting a real bird's eye view with a view to settling; a forty mile radius gives you a bewildering variety of landscapes and altitudes, from the foothills of Cevenne (skiing at Esperou, one hour away) or the marshy flea-bitten Camargue; you have first class micheline services to Nîmes and Montpellier four times a day; you can reach me without a car in three quarters of an hour, half an hour train and [then] taxi from Nîmes; the same for Temple-Delteil. It is near, and at the same time quite quite off the beaten track; you will own the only flush lavatory in the place; the two hotels have turkish loos, one per landing, and nobody has ever heard of a bath. In short you can revisit medieval France, quite unchanged quite untouched; notaries out of Balzac. But I told Claude to tell Eve to read *Clochemerle*!

Phew! signing off now; as soon as we have a peep from the St Maries we'll signal you. Mum's the word and I duck under.

Larry

*mazet michel   engances   Nîmes   Gard   France   25 Feb [1959]

Dear Henry:

No news; time wearing on. I've just had a card from the head of bureau in Saintes Maries. No go after June for livable accommodation so if I don't hear from you by tomorrow I'll motor over to Sommières and book that little flat with a downpayment. Shit, even if you *loathe* it (and I'm sure you won't) it will be a safe pied à terre, to leave your finds; and a good axis to radiate from, near sea and mountain; and if you can give yourself a few months of quiet unpublicised prospecting I'm sure we can unearth you a house to buy and make over, for about 800 to 1000 pounds; less in the country. No idea how your income rides but am sure you could do fine here, run a tiny car and educate the children either in Paris or England. I laughed when Eve said "somewhere right there in Engances", because our well is busy drying up and it looks as if we'll have to rebore the bloody thing. *Water!* since the Romans left nobody has done a stroke on water; you won't find a lavatory in beautiful villas with every modern contrivance, even central heating. It is mad! Women wash clothes in public troughs, and draw buckets from wells for the cookhouse; later the same bucket is popped under the bed as a pot de chambre. Privately I think it's the secret of French psychic health but . . . toujours anglais I do love baths and shitting pleasantly.

Still wrestling with this bloody book to try and get it finished before you arrive at least in draft; I've got two commissions for *Holiday* this summer which may mean some decent dough! Viva Amerika! Old Rowohlt is a treasure. Buffie Johnson and novelist husband [Gerald Sykes] arriving briefly soon. Putnam are going to make a nice picture book of the letters to Joe. They might coincide with your

Nobel! I'm really beginning to break thru the sound barrier on three fronts now; if *only* I can get this bloody book the way I want!

Love to you all   Larry.

P.S. Buchet is ecstatic about your return. I told him you will summer in Toulon or Aix with Sagan!

*[Big Sur]   3/8/59

Dear Larry, dear Claude –

Yes, all's set – passports, visas, tickets. All *I* need to do is relax. Working feverishly to finish re-write of *Nexus* before leaving. (Just had letter from Fanchette. He's using the text I wrote expressly.) Think we have a place in Paris – at a hundred (dollars) a month. Sommières is cheap – these days. Hope it's livable. If not, I'll forfeit the rent and find a good hotel somewhere. Can't abide medieval conditions any more. America spoils one. And my ideal (now) is Japan. Why live like dogs in the age of the atom? Isn't it ridiculous? But don't worry – we want to be near you. For me it will be a tonic! Incidentally, don't be frightened either – that we will eat into your working day. I am most sensitive about that, living as we do at the mercy of any Tom, Dick or Harry who takes a notion to visit us. Before we go south – while in Paris – I may go to Copenhagen, Brussels, Amsterdam, Stockholm, Hamburg. Maybe I'll take the kids with me. Eve wants to stay in Paris. For me it means nothing any more. Ghostly.

I got the German ed. of *Justine* and Dutton's of *Mountolive*. Both look good. With that Book of Month biz. here in U.S. you should soon be sitting pretty. And in Germany Ledig says you are doing well. I don't think you'll ever be poor again – certainly not after you win the Nobel Prize!

About keeping my whereabouts secret. I'll certainly try. I'm curious to see how successful you will be in warding off visitors. They find you out, you know, eventually. Are you coming to Paris for the launching of your book – chez Corrêa? I told Buchet I wanted none of it – for *my* book. Well, those 12 little cafés au bord de la Vidourle sound wonderful. Maybe I'll find a ping-pong table there! It's great fun – ping-pong. To-day I'm walking like a cripple – after strenuous rounds of p.p. with Tony who is awfully good at it. The kids love to swim. Val rides (an old nag). I just hope to Christ the mosquitoes are not there! I'm also trying to estimate (from map) distances from S. to Engances, to sea-shore (Aigues-Mortes), to Die (Drôme) and that beautiful stretch of *great* wine country from a little south of Beaune up to Dijon. (Et puis – le Puy – ever been there? Et *L'Aveyron?*)

We made plane reservations to return from Paris about 20th August, I think. However, if the kids liked it, if we put Val in that "École d'Humanité" in Switzerland (it sounds great – Tagore wrote about it!) and Tony somewhere else – who knows? But there's their mother to reckon with. And I am not quitting Big Sur for good – not yet. It's a real haven. Besides, I do want to see Japan, China, Java, Burma – *etc.* And stop writing! Maybe after that Nobel Prize, eh?

I hope Fred joins us somewhere. He hints at it. It's a must.

And to see your dear Claude. I'm sure we're going to like her! And all those kids of yours and hers! Ho ho! You know, I'm at that senile stage now where I enjoy better talking & playing with kids than with adults. I'm really death on "*adults*". Unless they've grown child-like.

I'm laughing already.

Cheerio!
Henry

P.S. Don't you people get hot water by sun from roof? Very simple.

Wines: Clos-Veugeot, Gevrey-Chambertin, Nuits St. Georges, Romanée-Conti, Beaune, etc.

---

*chez A. Maillet, 1, Place de l'Hôtel de Ville – Die (Drôme)   6/9/59

Dear Larry and Claude –

Expect Eve to arrive with Joey latter part of this week – so we should be coming along your way perhaps Tuesday. Will let you know in advance definitely. Wondering if we pass near Engances (in the car) on our way to Sommières. I'm just about getting over the rotten cold I caught in Paris – *indoors.* Have been weak as a cat and coughing like a lost one.

(Did you know that Hannibal passed this way – supposedly – when he came from Carthage? I love to think it's so.)

Often, gazing at the landscape, I think of Caesar and his legions – and how they must have rejoiced seeing this smiling land, then peopled with savage Gauls. This was a Roman town (Dea – goddess) once – and old ramparts of solid masonry still exist – and on the walls here where we are living (an ancient "évêché") there are Gallo-Roman bas-reliefs and scripts of bulls, etc. Close by a house in which Diane de Poitiers once lived.

Must see Salon (Nostradamus) and environs – a little plateau some kilometres distant where, M. le Juge tells me (this is a Tribunal now, this house), there is such a sad, classic, nostalgic view to be had. I wish I could see the house where N. wrote his *Centuries*! Must also go to Lacoste (Vaucluse) one day to see an old painter friend – Bernard Pfriem – who inhabits, I believe, a château of the Marquis de Sade.

But where are the ancient demesnes de Gilles de Rais, je me demande? Especially one place called Tiffauges? That's the country I'm curious about. And about Montségur (Albigeois) which I saw from the road coming down from Pyrenees (Spain).

It seems that Schatz (Lilik) may join us in Sommières later. You will like him, I'm sure. (Fred writes somewhere that he never cared for *any* of my friends – except Giles Healey of Big Sur.)

Eve writes that she is bringing something for you, Larry, from Girodias. I met the publisher (Rosset) of Grove Press in Paris, lunch with Girodias. They began with a pigeon paté that cost about 1,000 frs. – the price killed my appetite. I expect to eat very well – a whole meal! – at that price. (Déjeuner gastronomique à un prix astronomique.) Decided nothing so far about *Cancer*.

My friend Maillet lent me *Sentimental Journey* (L. Sterne) to read. Édition bilingue. I find it about the most stupid, detestable, dull, flatulent book I ever looked at. (The French version is a trifle better. That vile English language of that period – reminds me of horrid horsehair furniture, for some reason.) And to think I was compared to Sterne – by Herbert Read! Oi Yoi!

Does anyone down your way have an American typewriter, I wonder? Not too important. Sometimes, when bored, I feel I may write. ("Lime Twigs and Treachery")

Always, when traveling, I notice, I grow despondent about the state of the world. Seems absolutely hopeless now to me. Being detached, and in the midst of it all, I see as if from the planet Venus. The first thing needs correcting is – education. How any one can become a genuine adult under present educational system is beyond me. Doomed in the womb!

Well, we'll have a good laugh on it, eh? If those bistros along the banks of the Vidourle are anything like you describe I'll be content. (Pourvu qu'il n'y a pas des moustiques!) I may even learn to play billiards. Swimming, for me, is out – because of the holes in my ear drums. But I can paddle about like a child, eh? And the canoe! Ah, like a dream. (Reminds me of Shakespeare's country – the bloody Avon and picnic on the grass.)

No telephone here. None chez vous. Good. Telegrams will do, if needed.

À la garrigue! Avanti! ("Mais, je les ai vu!" – Rimbaud. Vu *quoi?*) Rereading him and Nietzsche here – parallelisms of expression. Remarkable! Wish I could settle down to doing a free translation of *Une Saison.* His words always ring in my ears. Enuf!

Henry

*from Le Chambon   9/7 [i.e., 9 July] 59

Dear Larry –

Finished *Clea* yesterday with a feeling that it was a huge tome. Came away as one does sometimes after attending a bullfight – battered and dazed. Particularly devastating is that under water scene – Clea's hand nailed to the boat. And then the dervish dance. *And then* – the *Hand!!* And ending à la da Vinci. A note of sublime (and delicate) horror. But from the beginning there is the incessant flood of poetic imagery. One drowns in it – willingly, voluptuously.

What I missed, by obtusity, no doubt, was what you told me to look for. Unless it was in those notes of Pursewarden. This part – like an interpolation – seemed weakest to me, though containing much profound observation on art and life. But, for me, it had a sort of surgical quality, a sort of desperate last minute opening up and sewing back again. The humor didn't always come off, for me. To be frank, of all the characters in the quartet Pursewarden is the least interesting to me. Darley and he seem to be the two halves of a coin – like Lawrence in *Aaron's Rod.* I never get the conviction that he was the "great writer" you wish him to seem. I think he'd come off better – forgive me! – if you sliced down his remarks or observations. They get sententious and tedious and feeble sometimes. Too much persiflage. (By the way, doesn't something of the sort occur in *The Black Book* too?) What I mean, more precisely, is that one is not sure at times whether the author is taking his double-faced protagonist seriously or ironically.

Keats you handled wonderfully, I thought, and in the few pages devoted to him, in *Clea*, you gave a picture of war with its multiple aspects that was tonic. Keats we feel *will* become a writer. As for Darley, one feels sometimes that the self-deprecation he employs is unwarranted, exaggerated – false modesty. The man who recounts and observes, whether the author in disguise or not, can not be this crippled writer!

Forget all this trivial criticism. I don't know why I pass it on to you, except that I feel I *owe* you such frankness. What *is* important for you to know is that all four books have the same specific gravity. Throughout the quartet there is a repetition (of technique) which reminds me of the divisions in a bullfight. Always, à la fin, the mise à mort. The cape work always remarkable, thrilling, *dangerous*. I like too the way you handle the lesser figures – they remain unforgettable. But Scobie again seems to have received undue weight and importance. (From the *reader's* standpoint. I can understand an author's infatuation for a minor character.)

Oh, by the way, the bit about the homunculi – so marvelous! But, I wonder if you knew that in one of his books Cendrars has a very similar situation? (Forget which one now.) One ought to do a whole fantastic hair-raising book on this theme. It gets under one's skin, what! And I liked your preparatory explanations – da Capo's. You have a *book* there!

To come back to Pursewarden. Maybe I should reread – all four books and see afresh. No doubt I've missed the boat somewhere!

Another lesser point . . . . Because of the condensed aspect – lack of new paragraphs, conversations set apart – know what I mean? – *Clea* takes on a heaviness not just. Too packed. It's a book of 500 pages really – not 200. (I do like the way you will end a long paragraph with a single line in quotes – a remark. It does something.)

And, oh yes! no doubt whatever that the city itself, Alexandria, is the real hero. You've made it immortal. It communicates always by and through the senses. It also gives the impression of being inexhaustible – like a god. Bravo! (How different, in essence and in your handling of it, from my Brooklyn and New York!)

One curious question to put you. This propensity of yours for making characters speak through exchange of letters. Has it some special value, in your eyes? Each time it happens I have a feeling you are about to lose your grip – you don't, of course. But it gives the effect of heavy breathing (whilst sitting on a rock) after violent exertion. Your last letter to Clea, for example – isn't it a bit like slackening a taut rope? And, at the end, to give that much space to Darley's new job, new residence, future plans, France, and all that – it weakens the book, all four books, it seems to me. Clea's response, of course, is a shocker. One will never forget that steel Hand, never! Or the wonderful "lesson" imparted by implication – to wit (as you have stated explicitly or implicitly thru one person or another throughout) that the hand, or whatever the implement, resides in the psyche. Yes, you have said many many wonderful things (even thru Pursewarden) about the nature and purpose and aim of art. Bravo! I repeat. And I see you re-introduced "the heraldic universe". Let us clap our hands.

It all needs rereading, careful, scrupulous rereading. Not the intoxicated draughts such as I indulged in.

You know with whom, in some ways, you have a kinship? Malaparte! Because of the "horrors" employed. I think of so many episodes – the chopping up of the live camel, Leila's disfigurement, Narouz himself – a magnificent horror – Liza's blindness – cruel and disturbing always – only to mention a few – and the *lovely* horror of the drowned Greeks standing under water in their canvas jackets – and that most excellent touch of growing familiar, even playful, with them whilst swimming below! And, but this no horror! the perfectly marvelous touch of swimming in a phosphorescent sea, after the storm! Je te salue! All this wonderful sun-and-sea period with Clea (I always transpose Claude for Clea) is better, far better, in my poor opinion, than the vaunted beauty of Homer. Yours is the distilled essence of the Greek world. Homer reminds me so often of the clotted, catalogued passages in the Old Testament, every thing dragged in by the hair and at the wrong moment. (Was *that* Greek, I ask you?)

And then over all and above all, I must say that you seem to have harpooned once and for all – *morality*. The moralities, better said. Alexandria < – *your* Alexandria – > is the whole pantheon of Homer's bloody, senseless gods – doing what they will, but *conscious* of what is done. The Homeric gods are more like blind forces, components of the now exposed psyche – atomic, in other words. Whereas Alexandria – thru and by her inhabitants, climate, odors, temperament, diversity, freaks, crimes, monstrous dreams and hallucinations (*but why imitate you?*) – gives the impression of living herself (her panthe*onic* self) out, of washing herself clean through complete enactment. Alexandria *enacts* (for us) – that's it. The act and the actor, the dream, or vision, and the drama – all in one. Do I make myself clear?

And your Nessim, to switch a moment. Do you know that he has the qualities of a great and gentle monarch? A royal personage, truly. I feel towards him as towards a great brother – not spiritual so much as an enlarged human. He moves with the dignity and felicity of a panther. His (recovered) happiness makes one's heart swell. He, Narouz, the mother – what a world you created – to say nothing of the décor in which they swim!

No, by God, if I let myself go, try to review it all in memory, even patchily, it's overwhelming. And to know that it was done so swiftly! No, it's incredible.

What matter, then, if the ground plan escapes me. I become just another reader, avid for more, unquestioning, glutted yet insatiable, crying as he reads – "Hosanna! *Hosanna in the Highest!*"

We'll probably see you chez vous demain, or whatever Eve said by post-card. Prepare the fatted calf. Must drink to your health, your arrival (like a nova) on the firmament of creation.

Apologies for handing you these reflections in such shoddy fashion. When I travel I'm dispersed. I ingest only – but like a bivalve.

Just begun reading *Bernanos par lui-même* (Albert Béguin – you must know his *L'Âme romantique*, no?) Anyway, entranced by Bernanos' obsession avec le sujet de l'enfance. He says all the time what I have struggled so hard to say. Have you ever noticed that chez vous l'en-fance, *votre* enfance, est absent?

More à vive voix!   Henry

P.S. Yes, Claude, I know you are there. How are you? It will be good to see you again.

*Big Sur   9/2/59

Dear Larry,
If I remember right to-day is the day you sail for England. We are back home about ten days now, after a spectacular jet flight from N.Y. to Frisco – 5 3/4 hours at a height of 30,000 feet and all smooth as oil. I had

a real vision of the future during that flight. Of our immediate future, I might say. One thought kept hammering itself home all the time – that we are now, already, definitely in the era of the Mind. It won't be long, I think, before the whole mechanical age will crumble, and with it the fuel and power business. When they build rockets which will take you from Los Angeles to Paris in forty minutes – and they plan just such by 1975 – won't they see the absurdity of power-speed and find out what motion (or real power) is and just harness it? You can't bust atoms still farther. The next step is mind, or imagination. Anyway, in the plane, I could see it all clearly – what would come to pass. Inevitable. We are like men of the Old Stone Age with one foot in the Atomic Age. But the atomic age will be even more short-lived than any of the preceding ages. The clock speeds up with each change. No, all that we now see is doomed. We're having a last look. There *will* be space travel, but it will be a space such as we have only dimly imagined. And the planets will be quite other too, believe me. We are being compelled to realize that imagination is all. We won't be able to live with anything less.

I'm going through some sort of crisis. Never felt more desolate. Yet underneath very hopeful. Two nights ago I got up in the middle of the night with the firm intent of destroying everything – but it was too big a job. So I'll hang on and finish *Nexus* (Vol. 2), then see. Writing seems so foolish, so unnecessary now. (Not yours, of course, but mine.) As for you, I feel such a glorious future for you. You've just opened the vein. And with what a salvo! Go on, you bring joy everywhere. As for me, I seem to feel that all I have done is to create a booby-hatch. Now I can throw the letters away without replying. It's easy. The next step is to throw myself away. That's harder. One thing seems certain – that I've built on sand. Nothing I've done has any value or meaning for me any longer. I'm not an utter failure, but close to it. Time to take a new tack. Years of struggle, labor, patience, perseverance have yielded nothing solid. I'm just where I was at the beginning –which is nowhere. And perhaps that's good, real good. Perhaps I'm getting to that stage of utter doubt which will dissolve all doubt.

I think of our talks in Engances, Sommières, Stes. Maries, Nîmes, Paris. They meant much to me. I would love so much to be near you, talk to you when I felt like it. I like the underneath gravity which you have acquired over the years, without loss of effervescence, enthusiasm, spontaneity, joy. I must have been a sorry sight most of the time. A dud. Too bad. But I shan't forget those evenings under the tent, over a vieux marc, stepping out under the stars, the road to Uzès hard by, the ride through Nîmes and the villages between, all so unlike anything here. And dear Claude. Such wonderful dishes she cooked up, such wonderful talks, such good, honest friendship, such regal hospitality. Now it's all like a dream.

Our kids will be going to live with their mother in a few days – perhaps for the whole school term. And Eve will be staying with her mother in Berkeley till she dies. I will be alone, as I was when I first came here, but a different aloneness now, harder to bear, considering all that has happened here since I first came. Maybe it will be good for the "work" – ha ha. If only the "work" seemed more important, more urgent.

Stop! When I think of all you have endured these past fifteen years or more and of how discreetly, tactfully silent you have been, I grow ashamed of myself.

I do hope you'll have some good innings with Joey there in London. Haven't heard much from him since Sommières. Give him a good hug for me. Be good to yourselves, as he always says.

Cheerio!
Henry

Dear Larry and Claude –
Claude's letter with Bournemouth address came only a few days ago. Presume you leave for *Engances* soon! Not going to Hamburg for the play? [. . .]

I was on the point of taking off for Japan, Siam, Burma, when my astrologer gave me the Stop! signal. Must wait till after end of this year. (That bloody Saturn again!)

I sure miss seeing you both. If we only had you here, under a tent, a little Chambertin, un vieux marc, a bit o' talk, a laugh or two – Ho ho! Ha-ha! – it would be grand.

Well, I guess I'll just have to get down to work – *Nexus 2*. No rest for the weary, no peace for the soul.

Saturn *is* a hard task-master, believe me. Can say it as knows it. Oof!

But better days lie ahead. All passes, with time. And one day we will pass too.

Good cheer! Je vous embrasse fortement.

Henry

Dear Larry –
I miss hearing from you. Are you back at the Mazet? Are you working?

After those depressing messages I sent I'm happy to report that I've got a new lease of life, am happy as a lark, feel fit, and look better than I have in ten years! I'm even thinking of writing again. Just laid out schema for *Nexus 2*.

We live and die a thousand times, it seems. And we never die of heart-break.

When is *Sappho*'s première? I'm sure it will be a success.

And how is our darling Claude these days?

Here it's divine weather. So warm, so clear, so transparent. It's how I feel inside now. Grand, what?

I'd give anything to be with you both now. I feel as if I were giving off magic rays.

Blessings on you!

Henry

*Big Sur   10/31/59

Dear Larry,
How good to get your letter at last! And to hear that our darling Claude is well again. I hope they only removed the cyst, not the ovary. Hold on to the ovaries – they're precious! You say the garrigue is lovely now; so it is here. Divine days, and threatening to continue on into the New Year. Somehow I'm full of expectancy. Sometimes I'm up before dawn, filling the bird bath or watching Venus fade out. (She's at full candle power now and becoming more and more beneficent.) [. . .]

This morning, after three hours of cleaning up around here, I took a seat on the bench under the oak tree (it's a pew my sister got for me

350

from a Baptist Church), and I began reading the page proofs of Delteil's St. Francis. I read only the Preface (20 pages) and I was delirious. You know, I've written you from time to time about Delteil, that you ought to get to know him better. He *is* a saint, a modern one, who knows how to wield the pen. (Writes in bed, with a quill, I believe, before having breakfast. And Caroline beside him, writing her mad book.) Reminds me of Anaïs writing her Diary right under Hugo's nose, then hiding it under the mattress. (Delete this!)

But do you know what Joseph is talking about in his Preface? He wants us to start all over again, from the beginning. Back to Paradise, no less. I thought I was the only fool who talked this way. One can never go back? Nonsense, he cries. Why change the world? *Change worlds!* (St. Francis) He talks of poverty, of Francis electing for it. Liberty in poverty. Not the miserable suffering kind of poverty, but the privilege of being poor, the privilege, in short, of rejecting all that we do not need, did not ask for, do not want, cannot use, etc. In short the kit and boodle. For Francis, he says, it was a matter of throwing overboard, of rejecting completely 30,000 years of civilization. What he railed against, in praising holy ignorance, was our bookish culture, our crazy, deadly sciences.

Familiar? All too, perhaps. I recall your disdainful laughter when you handed me back Maillet's book. The true Christ! How naif! you said. Did Jesus really live? Which Jesus? Etc. As if it mattered whether a man named Jesus lived or not. He lives. And we live in him, or live not. Socrates, Gautama, Milarepa, le Comte de St. Germain – did they live? Astound me, if you can! I believe. I know. Don't talk about God – be it! Find the place, the formula. (Rimbaud) Écrasez l'infame! Or, as Lord Buckley renders it – "Stamp out the terror!"

Ah, Larry, it isn't that life is so short, it's that it's everlasting. Often, talking with you under the tent at Engances – especially over a vieux Marc – I wanted to say, "Stop talking . . . let's *talk!*" For twenty years I waited to see you again. For twenty years your voice rang in my ears. And your laughter. And there, at the Mazet, time running out (never the vieux Marc), I had an almost frantic desire to pin you down, to have it out, to get to the bottom. (*What is the stars?* Remember?) And there we were on the poop deck, so to speak, the stars drenching us with light, and what are we saying? Truth is, you said so many marvelous things I never did know what we were talking about. I listened to the Master's Voice, just like that puppy on the old Victor gramophone.

Whether you were expounding, describing, depicting, deflowering or delineating, it was all one to me. I heard you writing aloud. I said to myself – "He's arrived. He made it. He knows how to say it. Say it! Continue!" Oui, c'est toi, le cher maître. You have the vocabulary, the armature, the Vulcanic fire in your bowels. You've even found "the place and the formula". Give us a new world! Give us grace and fortitude!

All I was trying to say, bedazzled as I was, and it was like trying to put a knife into a crevice, was: "What's it all about?" After the last line, *what*? After the television appearances, after the Academie, after the Nobel Prize, *what*? Remember my visit to Valéry's tomb with Rowohlt? What a day! Such a view from the cemetery! And later, along the river bank, the curving line of façades like a Guardi, the puffing launches, the masts bobbing up and down, the nets spread out to dry, oysters, prawns, crabs, eels glittering on the ice, and Rowohlt thirsty, his eyes moist with friendship, thinking back, the two of us, along the ancestral stream – Walther von der Vogelweide, the Hohenstauffens, Friedrich Barbarossa, Parsifal, the Minnesingers – oh yes, I would come to Hamburg, to Bremerhaven, to Hanover-Minden, we would go here, there, everywhere – but it was so good just to sit, just to watch the river flowing, the boats passing, the façades changing color. Just to look into Rowohlt's eyes was something. Such an honest man, such a tender, loving soul. A brother. A blood brother. (Did you ever remark how different he looked when he removed his spectacles? Two brown eyes. I used to play it on the piano for my dear Tante Melia before she went mad. A special from Hamburg, it was.)

It was always a sort of thick talk we had, Rowohlt and I. Guttural, soupy, sentimentalisch, quoi. Sometimes we merely grunted. The waiter always filling the glasses. And Jane, that pale odalisque with the most beautiful feet I've ever seen, sitting serenely drinking it in, interrupting only to add more flavor, more celery salt, more brotherly-sisterly love ... what a woman, what lazy delicatesse! A sort of Germanic geisha whose pleasure it was to please because she was too lazy to do anything else. A divine slothfulness. He really loves her, I believe. And she loves being loved. I always see her, as they're going to bed, saying in her delicious, indolent way: "What position would you like me to take?" Giving him at the same time a gentle push with her alabaster foot, as though to say – "I like men with ambition."

Where was I? The knife in the crevice. Or the chink in the armor.

More and more I'm intrigued by simplicity – simplicity of act, work, thought. Reading plays, for example, I'm fascinated by all that's left out. The bare bones – how wonderful! Looking back over my more tumultuous writings I began to wonder if perhaps I was not trying to hide something? Or perhaps I was hiding from myself. You know, for example, that when you are "emotional" you're not really feeling. You're pumping it up. You put something outside that should be inside. Right? Now I would like to be able to make the reader laugh and weep by a few well placed words, a phrase, a short sentence – or an exclamation. Fuck the hammerklavier and the well-tempered clavichord.

Having done battle for so many centuries, I feel now more expert in the use of the rapier, the stiletto – or the axe. I love the Japanese sword play with the grunts, the heavy breathing, the slow, steady footwork, the shift of stance, and then presto – cloven through the middle – one swift, clean stroke. Just one. (The opposite is Alexandre Dumas via Douglas Fairbanks, get me?)

But I can't change horses in mid-stream. For *Nexus*, vol. 2, I've got to stick to the last. I wonder, though, if you, you especially, ever realized that from the very beginning of the trilogy I was trying to be more simple, more straightforward. I didn't succeed, of course. But the intent was there. What I feel like saying sometimes – when the whole bloody *Crucifixion* comes to an end, is – "Ladies and Gentlemen, don't believe a word of it, it was all a hoax. Let me tell you in a few words the story of my tragedy; I can do it in twenty pages."

And what would be the story? That, wanting desperately to become a writer, I became a writer. In the process I sinned. I became so involved with the Holy Ghost that I betrayed my wife, my child, my friends, my country. I fell in love with the medium. I thought – if one makes a stroke on the blackboard that was the thing in itself, the reality. I almost fell in love with myself, horrible thought. I recorded what I saw and felt, not what was. To explain . . . it's a bit like what happened to the Jews. In the beginning there were men who talked with God. As the power or faculty dried up men began talking *about* God. A world of difference. I would like to talk to men or with men in a different way now. Like Parsifal, not Pagliacci. My heart was never broken. I'm intact, comme dit Rimbaud. I held on by a thread, no doubt.

Two or three days later. . . . Just had a letter from Fanchette telling me of his visit with you recently. Says he saw that dummy which I wrote for you – where? Corfu, was it, or Paris? How does it sound now? Only a few months ago I got a photostatic copy of the one I wrote for Reichel. I fell in love with it. Never will I be able to say things as I did then. It was hallucinating, especially the bit about Madame Ginsbourg, our landlady at the Villa Seurat. Do you remember her, the old harridan? I had pasted a photo in the dummy, at this section, showing a freak from a sideshow with an extra pair of legs, useless ones, to be sure. That was Madame Ginsbourg. I'll never forget the day that Fred, overcome with remorse for smashing the window panes, went downstairs and sat on her lap and billed and cooed, called her his darling mother, etc. etc., while fondling her big cabbagey breasts, and she loved it – and we never had to pay for the repairs.

Excuse me for running on. This is a warming up exercise. Sooner or later I've got to get down to work. I left off, at page 3, vol. 2, where Mona and I have registered at the Grand Hotel de la France, rue Bonaparte. I'm standing on the balcony listening to the bells of St. Germain. It's May and Spring has come to Paris. But here's the point. I don't fall for Paris immediately. I had thought it would be more exotic. Soon I will buy bicycles and Mona will take lessons in that narrow little street, the rue Visconti, where Balzac had his publishing house and failed heavily. Not far away, a parallel street, Oscar Wilde had lived – in a modest hotel, I see it clearly still. We will be leaving for Fontainbleau by train, there to start our cycle tour. I don't know then that the great Milosz lives there, with his birds, his poems, his Lithuanian memories – and "the key to the Apocalypse". Maybe I didn't even know that Gurdjieff had his sana there, or whatever he called it. And that Katherine Mansfield would be one of his patient-disciples. Or that, much later, I would be weeping in the Noctambules whilst listening to Francis Carco (born same place as Mansfield – New Hebrides, New Caledonia?) recite his poems. In the lobby outside his books are on sale. Piles and piles of them. He must have already written 50. Think of it. I wept for all the poètes maudits that night, myself included. It was glorious. In the morning the birds sang as usual, and as usual I took my constitutional (before breakfast) along the exterior boulevards, arriving always breathlessly at the Place des Peupliers, where there was a sort of scaffold, it seemed to me, though I never heard of anyone being executed there. Blissful days, those. Time for everything then. Once a week I'd visit Moricand in his attic and study horoscopes. Thus I acquired a cane belonging to Kisling – or perhaps it was Modigliani. I lost it in Rocamadour, in a fit of ecstasy one night. Just before visiting the Gouffres du Padirac.

Listen, if you and Claude ever travel up the Rhone again, take the left bank and stop at La Voulte. It's absolutely insane – people and architecture. Also a good hotel there with excellent food – near the bridge. *But*, it was somewhere near there, between Vienne, I imagine, and La Voulte, that on that bicycle trip with Mona – Paris to Marseille – we stopped at a café one hot day and while in a trance, a blissful one, the spot so fixed itself in my memory that it was more real than reality. Like a spot you recognize – the *déjà vu* business – from another reincarnation. Maybe I sat there, at that very spot, in Roman times, my chariot parked nearby, and I knew the Vandals were coming, knew that all was changing (forever), and I was having a last look. I do wish I could find that place again!

You see what my task is. I have to write about a Paris I haven't yet become acquainted with. I must walk certain streets I later regard as brothers or sisters of mercy as if I hardly noticed them. The rue St. Dominique, the rue Mouffetard are not yet discovered. The Rotonde is a café where every afternoon a German girl, Magda, I think it was, used to meet us by accident. That is, meet Mona, whom she was in love with and hoped to mulct for a few hundred francs. She loved her hats, her gowns, her cape. They would always excuse themselves to run off and do a few errands. Errands! What kind of errands? And I'm too much in love (with my wife) to give heed to the vultures who surround me. Besides, I had no French. About all I could muster was a "Oui ou non, Monsieur" and "L'addition, s'il vous plait!" Oh yes, I could also ask how to get to the lavabo.

Oh yes. . . . Then one day, when I'm by my lonesome, sitting again at the Rotonde, a woman gets up from the terrasse of the Dôme and starts crossing the street. What a creature! Only twice have I met the like. (Once with Fred, on the grand boulevards, when a magnificent cocotte with violet eyes – but *violet*, I tell you! – passed us, and like automatons we wheeled around and passed her again – just to see those eyes.) But this one at the Dôme was a bit like your Nancy, tall, willowy, with auburn hair which fell down her back like a waterfall. She had the walk of a queen – something out of the Arthurian legends. Definitely English. Irish-English, I'd say. So stunning that I trembled from head to foot. Then I was up and following her. No thought of accosting her. Ah no! Just to follow and gaze and feast my eyes. A long walk, up and down side streets. Finally she ducked into a dress-shop. I walked over to the opposite side of the street, went as far as the corner and turned back. Imagine my astonishment when, just as I pass the shop, I find her lifting her skirt over her magnificent fall of auburn hair. She stands there in her slip, more willowy now than ever, more ravishing. And she is totally oblivious of anything outside. Innocent as a dove . . . . That's all. I never saw her again. I was happy. I had seen her. Maybe she was an actress from the Gate Theatre. Maybe it was Lady Gregory. Maybe she was a pawnbroker's mistress. For me, it was as if I had seen Guinevere. And I knew (later) why the good, the glorious Arthur had to be betrayed by his friend Launcelot. He had taken Beauty (Rimbaud) but had forgotten to sit her on his knee. It was too noble a betrothal. Guinevere's infidelity always moves me deeply. It makes her a woman. She had to step down or be lost in legend. And as she sinks Arthur rises. How wonderful is Arthur with Launcelot. Stop! I may grow maudlin.

[. . .] The wonderful thing – this ties up with what I mentioned earlier – is the sloughing off of the built-in man (the man of society, tradition, education, background, etc.) and the emergence of the new man relying upon his intuition, knowing that whatever it is he is practicing is "magic". The certitude that grows and grows, until, like a Christ, one can say: "Get up and walk!" And the man walks. So, many times, when I am sorely baffled, I will say to myself – "Write it, put it down! What difference whether it makes sense or not." And then it's as if some panel inside one slid open, the musicians are there, the note is sounded, the walls give way, the images beckon – and you find yourself saying it without knowing it. Fatal to pause and reflect. On! On! Until the strength gives out. Then, in quiet, after a prayer of thanks, you read – and you see the traces of another's hand, God's maybe, or maybe your own, your concealed, your suppressed self. All one. God needs us as much as we need Him. Dixit.

And so I say to you, or ask you rather – imagine us still under the tent at Engances – when we arrive at this stage, even if only once, must we not question this power, must we not feel chastened, must we not blush when signing our own names? If, whenever we sat down to write we could summon the spirit, would we want to go on writing? How often have I told you that the books I wrote in my head were the best, that nothing manifested in print ever approaches them? What we put down on paper is but a pale imitation, a faint and faded remembrance of these sessions with the silent spirit. What are we doing, I sometimes think, is to trace the outline of our irrepressible ego. Instead of the act we give a performance. The author is in the wings, the writer is dazzled by the footlights. Rimbaud leans out of the wings. His shadow, at least, is visible to all.

Interruption again . . . A fan, all the way from N.Y., sans sou and famished. And I had had such a marvelous dream, during my brief nap. I was going to insert it for you – gratis. Then this lad whom Eve should have shooed off but didn't because – guess why! – because he resembled our beau-frère de Jerusalem when he was 19. I was riled. And sometimes when I'm riled I recommend Maxim Gorki or Meister Eckhart. I told him it was good to be a slave, to crawl like a worm, to bark now and then, to stand on one's hind legs, etc. He was slightly bewildered. (What he really wanted was food, but he didn't have the courage to ask for a crust of bread.)

Anyhow, that was yestereve. Now it's 7:30 A.M. next day and I've already bathed, shaved, eaten, walked the dog and cleared the crumbs off the table. Brought Eve home last night drunk as a pope. And not on that delicious vieux Marc either, more's the pity. She's lucky though – no hangovers. So I had a few hours' sleep while the dog licked my hand as if to commiserate with me. All in all life ain't too bad. We might have both been drunk and gone over the cliff, what.

Whenever I rise at dawn I put the gramophone on real loud – usually Monteverdi's Madrigals. Or else Gaspard de la Nuit. Or the fifth piano sonata of Scriabin. So doing I fill the bird bath and place a few bread crumbs around the edge of it. Dante, whose plaster head is cemented to the bowl, is always gazing at his reflection in the water. Thinking of Beatrice, no doubt. If the fog has rolled in I wait for the nimbus, i.e., the magnification of my image with halo and all, cast on the iridescent soap suds below by the sun which has just come over the mountain in the rear. Then I think of the Lord Buddha – "I obtained not the least thing from unexcelled, complete awakening, and for this very reason it is called unexcelled, complete awakening." Could anything be clearer?

When I rise before dawn I feel horsey. Think of Nijinsky trying to climb out of the orchestra pit like a horse. Think of Gogol – what horses! *Russia, where are you leading us?* Etc. The day begins with the sign of the pit, the chasm, the gouffre. Means I will tumble into my own pitfalls. *Attention!* Méfiez-vous des femmes! On one side of the chasm the dodo, on the other the totohotsu or whatever the bugger is called. (He appears only in phantasmal landscapes.) I may start for the hot baths and end up in the forest. I will have written ninety letters, three plays and a half and started a romance. Night will find me at Nepenthe ordering a gin and tonic. There, while shaking hands and saying "Happy to meet you," "Yes, thank you, I'll have another," I plan the next water color move. Something allegretto, something very subtle and delicate. In the midst of it I suddenly remember: "Darling, where are you?" That's a tentative title for a play rolling around in my noodle. You can't imagine what I can put into that *darling!* And so with Eric Barker on one side of me and Ephraim Doner on the other, both talking rubbish by now – and the owner staring me in the face like a majolica hand-painted pisspot – I weave into the opening. The scene is always two in the morning, time same as always. Always begins in the middle of a sentence. For decor, a table, a coffee pot and a half-finished bottle of some ratgut or other. The talk began hours ago. Just getting to the boil as the curtain rises. Comes the familiar phrase, like a gong – "You want the truth, do you?" Here I get fuzzy, because the truth is like a tapeworm – you never get rid of it.

In this house, or rather in this play, truth is served up at all hours. Always on tap, so to speak. You can have it cold or hot, scrambled or fried, varnished and unvarnished. Usually it's predigested. Sometimes given in powder form. Always soothing and conducive to nightmares. The house is divided into sixteen marriages, forty peccadillos and a few amourettes. The slats between the walls thrum like loose banjo strings. The alarm never goes off. Flanking the bedrooms are the slave quarters where the Master plies his varying vocations . . . .

But enough of this. To come back to Scriabin, a first love and a lasting one. I started a long extravaganza about him in *Nexus*, vol. 1, but cut it down to a cadenza because I had already run off the trolley too many times. I felt I had to stick to the leitmotif announced in *Capricorn*: "On the Ovarian Trolley". [. . .]

I was twenty-five when I first heard Scriabin. It began about nine o'clock one evening, in a Russian café on Second Avenue, and lasted till dawn. It was like an inoculation – I never got over it. They talk of jam sessions. But what's a jam session to a night of nothing but Scriabin – played by a mad Russian who will hang himself a few days later? Before the year is out two other friends have hanged themselves. (One of them made a living writing jokes for the newspapers.) I never liked the feel of the rope else I might have tried it myself.

358

Now, some ninety-five years later, it's pleasant, as Virgil would say, to remember these things. Then I had to wake people up in the middle of the night to tell them of this new discovery or that. Now I send it out over the waves – to the birds and fishes, to the snails and the sow-bugs. If nobody gets it, tant pis. Nothing's lost, not even yesterday's garbage. "Good morning, Mr. President. How do you like your new home?" (meaning the White House).

Reminds me of Fred after a night's debauch. Saying: "We sacrificed to the elementals last night, didn't we Joey? How do you feel?" And I would answer: "I feel fine. And you?" And then he would put me in stitches, saying how his gal had the curse or a short leg or something unromantic but he did his best. Followed by "When do we eat, Joey?" And then a grand cockalorum about the 20 page letter he was writing to his inamorata in Dalmatia. Maybe I could add a few lines, he was running dry. The evening after a night like that would be a poetic one for me. A long walk alone, preferably in a drizzle, and always in an unfamiliar neighborhood. Thoughts would ooze out like pus. Perhaps I'd recall incidents or characters I meant to elaborate on, things I had forgotten, things I had skipped in the rush of spilling it out. Or I'd think of rhythms, think of the book as a symphony. (There was a whole period when I knew a man from Hong Kong who lent me his Chinese records. Got to love stone music and the faint sound of gongs dropping their aspirates.) Coming home I'd be ready to write. Sometimes it was too good, I couldn't write it down. I would just flop on the bed, clothes and all, and enjoy the writing that went on in my head. Next morning I'd be up bright and early; again the constitutional, the Place des Peupliers, maybe a chat with the children on the bench near the scaffold. Swinging into the Villa Seurat I'd be singing to myself. And like that, one morning, just as I've struck the right rhythm, who walks in on me but Tihanyi, the deaf painter, remember? He tells me in his cluck-cluck language (which he always supposed we understood, but no one did, not even his Hungarian friends) that I should go right on writing, he would talk to me as I wrote. And by God, I did! And it was amazing that I wrote as well as I did – nothing lost, as I said before. He talked for twenty minutes while I polished off two or three pages – of "The Wild Park", I believe it was now. All he had come for was to tell me he had fixed a goulash for me. When I got there that evening he was lying beside the telephone, dead.

To be continued.

Henry

359

The song Miller played was 'Two Brown Eyes' (originally 'Zwei braune Augen'), set to music by Edvard Grieg.

*The mazet. (Rainy weather but by the fire)   [early November 1959]

Dear Henry:

Our letters will have nodded to each other in mid-air; today comes your hundred watt shout of joy. But my dear chap . . . having once met Eve I have, like *everyone* else, *stopped worrying* about you. It is quite impossible to take a few storm clouds seriously while she's at the rudder; what luck some artists have. I told you we got back pretty tired and found a bloody mess here; the mason had run the well dry, drunk all our wine, fired off all my shells, disamorced the fucking electric pump . . . everything; so it's taken us about a fortnight to bring order out of chaos. Luckily *Sappho* has been postponed by a few weeks; I was really dreading more travel. In fact I've come to hate travel entoirely, and would gladly sit here on my arse and not move. Old age? All countries seem the same, less interesting than France! Though in justice I must say that England was *marvellous* this time; you really would have been startled to see what three months of solid sun (first time in 200 years) can do to my compatriots; such humour, kindness, serviceability, exquisite manners, rugged laughter. It was uncanny! It was like a real move forward. People were sparkly, alive, forthcoming devil may care; and all as brown as berries. Food's improved too – or else my fame is rating me higher class meals! But the day we left the rain closed in again, that heartbreaking steady drizzle! Claude has surmounted her operation nobly; like all tiresome multiple diagnostic jobs (four possibilities) it led to a big scar, but instead of a feared hysterectomy it turned out to be a cyst on an ovary which was extirpated okay. We dragged a whole load of books and papers back here and I'm sorting out stuff I haven't seen for years and years, and mostly your letters; they are going to be a job to microfilm as the earlier ones were written north south, and then south north, and then side ways, and many not dated at all; but I think I have almost every scrap. Unlike Joe who tears everything up. I felt they'd come in useful sometime, maybe pay Tony's gambling debts! Anyway they'll make a fine book even on their own; but I won't bother with scraps like postcards etc etc. I'll keep those to give away as presents to your fans when they call. Among other things I've found the little Jupiter diary which you wrote for me in 39; do you know there are about 30 Zen quotations in the book? You had the impression you only heard of Zen postwar, but it ain't so. There's also a reference in the *Hamlet* book. I think you must have read Sinnett coz there's no reference to Suzuki, and you once mentioned *Esoteric Buddhism* in an essay. Anyway. I also have some amusing scribbles – your first Greek lesson (transliterated), and a few pages of impressions of Athens. All this I will hoard for my daughters on condition that if ever Val or Tony are in need they will turn them over! We are waiting for a telegram from Hamburg about the play, and another about a film team coming to photograph the master in his natural surroundings. What absurdity! But the three little rooms Giraud is building are going on apace and will be done by Christmas. Big fire. Pot au feu. Claude is correcting the French and Italian translations of *Mountolive* by it. I fired a broadside into my agent Hoffman and Corrêa with the result that I have really got them weaving now, and no more bloody nonsense. French publishers are devils really; but I am not a Mediterranean for nothing; with publishers and agents I believe in stuffing them up each others' backsides. Hence I have sold *The Black Book* to Gallimard, using Girodias as agent; and stuck Corrêa for a hair-raising advance on *Clea* to which they have agreed, moaning about the huge sacrifice etc. Well! I think I've got the French end sealed up now with people really weaving. Next week I have to meet the Italians in round table debate and try to firm them up equally. Then Hamburg I suppose. Ouf! I really want to sit by this fire indefinitely, that's all.

Clea is to bed in UK and USA. Don't know how things will turn out. We must wait upon the event. So much depends on luck; so far the French and German critics who've seen it in proof are thrilled. But I fear that it is too explicit, too simple to please our domestic highbrows. They suspect the easy; if it don't bore a little they feel cheated. However we'll see. *Mountolive* really does sound magistral in French, better than English and much more exotic! The saxon shock-points don't shock here, and many saxon commonplaces seem wildly rare and exotic to French people.

Anyway, what the hell; don't drive over that bloody cliff till you've done another dozen at least. [. . .] You'll be the home-grown doyen of Yankee litcheratewer yet, mark my word.

Love
Larry

Dear Larry:

Why this Marathon I don't know. There must be something I want to
unburden myself of – and you are "the witness". Soyez à l'aise donc!
Pas besoin de répondre. Écoute seulement!

Just finished the second chapter of Delteil's *St. François*. The meeting
with the leper. Decisive. Like the Buddha's first encounter with the
world outside . . . But what a style, what a rhythm to Delteil's prose!
He writes on horseback, as alive and aware, as free and as joyous, as the
animal itself. Every now and then interpolations – a phrase, a sentence,
from this writer and that. Like giving the spur to the beast. Many from
Rimbaud. One often repeated: "La vraie vie est absent." Will come
soon a chapter called "La Vraie Vie". We know it will be the true life –
not only of St. Francis but of every one. And after la vraie vie – pure
love. And it will be pure love. We don't want to come on it too quick.
So I put the book down. To-morrow or the next day another chapter.

[. . .] I am going through a crisis of some sort. Can't name it. Don't
want to. Have been through the agony already. Had a faint illumination
too. Now in a state of *attente*. Great expectations. "Dead, your majesty.
Dead, my lords and gentlemen. Dead, Right Reverends and Wrong
Reverends of every kind. Dead, men and women, born with Heavenly
compassion in your hearts. And dying thus around us every day."
(Dickens on the death of Jo, the crossing sweeper.)

In this state everything acquires added significance. Books and
pamphlets, even the fan letters, all bring something touching on . . . I
was going to say "the malady", but it isn't a malady at all. It's more like
a death and resurrection. Each day, it seems, I'm faced with new
drama. And all the while there is a perpetual drama going on inside me.
A drama which refuses to come to an end. History will come to an end,
man will come to an end, but not the drama. I don't know precisely
what I mean by this, but it's so.

I can wake up of a morning pure as a bird, and by night it will befall
me to live through some cruel, some heart-rending experience. It's as
if, having stabbed yourself twenty times over, you wait each day for
that monster to appear with knife in hand and say: "Again! Deeper!
Through the heart this time!"

As I said once: "When a man menstruates he bleeds from every
pore."

It's nothing to weep about, of course. In fact, it's all rather jolly. Rejuvenating – that's the word for it. A pity that so many great tragedies end with a corpse – or five or six. If the playwright only knew, he could start afresh, with the same corpse or corpses, and make even greater tragedy. What's tragic is not the end, but the set-up. The real theatre is dehors, where nothing comes to an end. Life is just an ante-room, a vestibule. You keep waiting for your turn. If you knew what you were about you'd get up and walk out. The one exit leads to Hell, the other to Heaven. Avoid either. Rise up and take wing! Life and death are illusions of the mind. Reality is when you kiss the leper full on the mouth.

Interruption .... A bitch of a mail to-day. Terrific. All good. Including an invitation from a Japanese editor to make use of his home while in Tokyo. Also a free trip to Norway, to talk to students there, which I must decline. (Third time I've been invited to Norway, all expenses paid.) But here's what. Just had a letter from Brassaï, together with ms. of his new book on *Graffiti Parisiennes*, to be published in Stuttgart. Says he is now compiling book of his 100 or more conversations (and photos never seen before) with Picasso. He will let Picasso talk (sic). And then he asks if I would intercede with you to permit him to come see you and do a portrait (I don't know whether drawing or photo) of you for *Harper's Bazaar*. I wish you'd do it. Primarily to get better acquainted with Brassaï. I adore him. He's truly mellow. He will amuse you too. If you have the time, take him to St. Remy and get a photo of Nostradamus' birthplace, with yourself standing in the door-way. I'll use it one day in "Draco and the Ecliptic". Anyway, you write him yes or not, will you? His address is 81, rue du Faubourg Saint-Jacques, Paris (14). Pity you never visited his studio. You would see there, in file after file, every aspect of Paris life, from the slaughterhouse at la Villette to the lovely little whorehouse rue St. Gregoire-la-tour. As for the graffiti ... well, wait, the book will be out soon. You'll dance. The bugger has unearthed graffiti even in the Fortress of Carlisle, England, to say nothing of the Château d'If (Marseilles) where the Count of Monte Cristo passed a pleasant sojourn, in the mind of Dumas, at least.

Your rainy day letter by the fire has just come. You mention Zen, my earlier acquaintance with it. Don't you know that the book you mention – *Esoteric Buddhism* – I asked for when I was a kid of eighteen at the Brooklyn Public Library and the librarian said yes we have it, but do you know what you're asking for? Alongside this I range *The Letters from the Mahatmas*, written presumably by Blavatsky herself. But it was you, my dear fellow, who put Alan Watts' book on Zen in my hands, circa 1935 or '36. It was then I went overboard. I remember so well standing in the bedroom, Villa Seurat, after midnight always, and instead of jumping in bed with whomever it was, as I was supposed to do, I would say, "Wait a moment, won't you . . . listen to this!" And I'd quote. Then came Suzuki, more Blavatsky, Nijinsky, Dane Rudhyar, Paracelsus, Jacob Boehme, Meister Eckhart – and finally R.H. Blyth, bless the name. (And let's not forget dear Erich Gutkind: *The Absolute Collective*, which Eliot could make nothing of. That is the book I underlined and annotated more than any other book I have read. I can still pick it up, turn at random to any page, and do a back somersault.)

How I chortled when you said that you had ceased to worry about me. What's better is that I have ceased to worry about myself. It seems inevitable that when I start sinking I sink to the bottom, only to rise like a cork. Two rudders, Moricand once said I was equipped with. It's true. When the one gives out the other goes into operation. Should I fall into the orchestra pit someone is sure to hoist me up and fling me back on stage. And then it begins, like with Nijinsky. "I love Russia. I love Poland too, and Germany, and Roumania." Etc. Finally – "I love everybody." And you secretly wish the enemy would appear, so that you could say – "I love you too!"

And now to Monterey for the day. Hourrah! La vraie vie n'est pas absente, as Rimbaud said, mais *ailleurs*. The play is fomenting – in my noddle. Every day I think up a new title at least. To-day it's: "Merdre, Foutre et Deirdre". Curious thing is I am full of French at the moment. Could almost do it in French. All the crazy things I want to say I can say much better in French. (Without the use of the subjunctive, bien entendu.) Yesterday came *La Revue des Voyages* (put out by the Wagons-lit, Paris) and in it is an article on Uzès, with a good double page photo of the town. And last night, at Nepenthe, of all places, I was talking to an American from Vermont who had spent six years in southern France, and what does he begin to talk about but Les Baux. Said that those crazy Baux brothers (murderers, traitors, etc.) had given asylum to all in need always, that they controlled several kingdoms, including Naples (sic).

Anyway, he asked me if I had ever walked around and through the ruins on a night of full moon. I can imagine that on such a night the rocks speak volumes. If you go to Les Baux – I recommend it! – take time off and stop at La Coste (Vaucluse) and see the ruined Château of the Marquis de Sade. Ask my friend Bernard Pfriem there to show you the statues left by the crazy man who deflowered all the young girls of the village. They are far better than Picasso's, I assure you. Some of them look Etruscan. He buried himself in a cistern, with an air hole which he concealed, in order to work . . . unmolested. À partir d'un certain jour he never went into the village; his wife had to do everything, even make caca for him. So they say. He has a sculpture of a captain of the horse guards in full uniform, which he did in two days, epaulettes and all. Formidable! After a while he began hiding his work. So now some of them are deep in the earth, covered with moss and lichen, hard to get out, even with a team of horses. Nearby is a marble quarry, and in cutting the marble, they made portals which look like entrances to Egyptian tombs. All this says nothing of the view, the panorama. Sublime. And on a hill opposite in a wind-swept town lives that young man who wrote *Paris insolite*; he is compiling a history, or has already, of the queer characters throughout Provence. Y compris notre sculpteur.

But if you go to Uzès one day, please send me some big colored postcards of the place, will you? I want to show them to someone. I am even thinking of tackling Racine now. Why not? If I could finally read that 18th century English writer who infuriates me so – I never remember his name! – you know! the one I am supposed to write like – I can read Racine or Corneille.

Ah, but get this . . . . Reading Brassaï's script sur les graffitis, I discovered (what I already knew) that Restif de la Bretonne used to write on the walls of the parapets along the quai d'Anjou; recorded his whole agony, his amours, his failures and triumphs, his epitaphs même – but his enemies erased it all in the 19th century. It gave him greater comfort to read what he had inscribed in stone than to read his memoirs. How I understand! Was I not in Pekin (in another incarnation) touching the engraved calligraphy that runs for a mile or so along the palace walls? Nor was it boustrophedonous writing either. I'm going to do some graffiti myself, here on the premises.

As I leave I will throw some mags and books on the bench-pew under the oak and see what happens. See whether people will steal them or hand them to me. Now and then I put a dull book in a neighbor's mail box. Better than finding a dead rat, what!

(to be continued)

Henry

One of the texts Miller is referring to in this letter is Alfred Percy Sinnett's *Esoteric Buddhism* (1883). The documents attributed here to Madame Blavatsky are apparently the *Mahatma Letters to A.P. Sinnett from the Mahatmas M. & K.H.*, transcribed; compiled and with an introduction by A.T. Barker (1924).

*Paris   [early December? 1959]

[carbon copy sent by Durrell to Miller]

Dear

A brief note to keep you abreast of Europe. First about the books. The first three of the *Quartet* appeared on the 25th in Copenhagen, separately but together; rather risky publishing but the editor said that he was sure of unloading first editions of 12,000. On the same day *Justine* appeared in Italy and *Mountolive* in France. I was in Hamburg for the first night of *Sappho* which went like a bomb; the poor author got six curtains and the company about 36. The play is sold out. It has now been put into orbit as part of classical repertory in Germany, and is orbiting happily between Schiller Goethe and *Woyzeck*. Four other theatres have taken it, including the Zürich Spielhaus; five radio nets are broadcasting it, Rowohlt is issuing the whole text in pocket book with pictures of the first production. Margaret Rawlings flew in and out again in a rage and promises an English production in Spring. I tried to get a little publicity for this English triumph on the Continong through the *Sunday Times* and sent them pictures. Nothing. However by the time I reached Paris the huge German press had hit them and notices of the success were beginning to appear. My dear chap, what am I to do with my compatriots except sigh. I had a telephone call from the British Council rep in Hamburg offering me terrific congratulations and trying to cadge a seat "as he would have to send in a report"! He added, this charming representative of our culture, that he did not know my work at all and found the books impossible to obtain. I had just come from a personal appearance act [at] the biggest bookshop in Hamburg where I smirked and signed copies of the *Quartet* – at least a third of them the Faber English edition! Later at a cocktail party the loutish so-called press officer of the consulate said he thought "all this adulation must be bad for me" – a remark so gratuitously offensive that I felt constrained to reply . . . but I won't trouble you with my thrust through the soft white underbelly of the F.O. [. . .] In France I was given a terrifying lunch with twenty-five critics and was interviewed at the table; what with my French being bad and my mouth full it can't have been much of a success. I also did a fifteen minute television interview in which I fouled up all my subjunctives and nearly fell off my chair trying to illustrate a continuum with my fingers. [. . .] What I really need is a part time press attaché or a double as there is hardly time to write what with having to explain my genius as well as demonstrate it. Now for a fortnight of rough shooting and stone walling.

yours
Larry

Gustaf Gründgens's production of *Sappho* opened on 22 November and starred Elisabeth Flickenschildt, Maximilian Schell (Phaon) and Ullrich Haupt (Pittakos). *Sappho* shared the Deutsches Schauspielhaus season with Georg Büchner's *Woyzeck*, Shaw's *Cäsar und Cleopatra*, and Schiller's *Maria Stuart* and *Die Verschwörung des Fiesko zu Genua*.

Love Affairs with the Theatre
and Just Plain Love

In 1960 Miller is coming to the end of yet another seven-year cycle – in wives: beginning with his marriage to June Mansfield, that was about the usual term. Seven years with Lepska, and now his marriage to Eve is coming apart. He accepts an invitation to be a judge at the Cannes Film Festival and on the way meets Renate Gerhardt, a beautiful widow and the English-language editor with his German publisher, Rowohlt. Soon they are talking about marriage and a European home for their respective children. Henry sets out to find the ideal place and, of course, fails. Christmas brings the obligatory depression; he has just turned sixty-nine and he feels used up. To raise his spirits he writes his first play, the hilarious *Just Wild About Harry*, in three days. Soon he is making arrangements to have it staged in Germany.

Durrell in contrast had long been interested in drama, and had drafted a play entitled 'The Hangman' during his Elizabethan-struck period in the 1930s. *Sappho* was published in 1950, and in 1952 he had written a farcical anti-Communist 'pantomime', *Little Red Riding Hood*, to be performed by his colleagues at Her Majesty's Embassy in Belgrade. However, there had been no financial rewards, and novels seemed a surer way towards securing his independence. With the success of *The Alexandria Quartet*, he can return to the theatre: by the end of 1961 he sees *Acte* performed at Hamburg under the direction of Gustaf Gründgens, who had produced *Sappho* in 1959. Friendship grows between them, and in 1963 Durrell writes *An Irish Faustus* so that Gründgens, who affected a satanic mien, can play Mephisto. Gründgens dies before the production can take place. Durrell writes no further drama, but he tries a second screenplay: *Judith*, a role he creates for Sophia Loren. (In 1960 and 1961 he had written several film scripts for Mamoulian's *Cleopatra*, but little if any of Durrell's material was used in the final version.) He spends weeks on location with Miss Loren in Israel, and is so impressed by her intelligence and sensitivity that he rewrites his entire scenario to suit her conception of the title character.

Miller and Durrell meet a number of times during these years, but finally Henry buys an imposing house in staid Pacific Palisades, where he comes to be seen as a model neighbour. The likelihood that the old allies will again share Europe between them on a permanent basis fades.

*mazet michel, Engances,
NIMES, GARD, FRANCE   [early March 1960]

DEAR HENRY.

Sorry I am such a lousy correspondent these last weeks; I felt so damned exhausted that after pushing CLEA out into the wide world I got typewriter sickness and have just been mooning around wall building and reflecting on how Japan is going to hit you. I hope it hits you right; is Eve going along or staying behind? But I'm overjoyed that really you have a notion about coming to Europe again for a real long stay. I don't want you to be sick of your own USA; just to feel calm and happy about it, take it or leave it; but I think the cosmic rays out of the ground over here are really more of a help to work. And while the slowness and relative inefficiency is maddening I can really see you happy and working in a village. Even if the Midi were too far, somewhere around Blois, say, or Cher. And I can see (goes without saying) Eve's radiant face.

I've just written Girodias to try and get a *Nexus* out of him and see what the hell type headache you've brewed us there. The anthology goes well, despite a frosty press (for me) in one or two places. What the hell. It will *stick*. They like it a lot, those who've read it. I got a relatively good press in London on *Clea*, better than I hoped, as I thought that bloody man Pursewarden would earn me stripes. Now . . . I'm free wheeling for a little while, doing a few small articles just to keep the pipeline open. I wish I had your insouciance. I think up every damn eventuality to save money against, and then piss it away on something silly like a wall. Pissing away is okay, if I didn't waste the energy on the first operation. However, give me a bit of time. I'm reading Patanjali now. I think you would like him a lot; translation by Yeats. Also Eliphas Levi whom I enjoy very much. Very French, very flambé method of exposition; an honest fellow. I like him and believe in his blasted Lucifer. To such an extent I forget all the psychoanalysis I know when I confront the picture of the Old Goat. What else? The almonds are in bloom. It raineth every day. But Spring is nearly here. My forty-eighth year has struck with a dull boom and gone. Soon I shall be fifty and ready to start on a big cycle of something . . . perhaps comic? We'll see. How is your play? Mine is stuck half way, but I'll be starting on its tail in a while.

The children are coming out for Easter for the holidays. I hope to Christ their rooms are finished or they will be sleeping all over my workroom. Have you read Saul Bellow's new novel? Now there's a *writer*. And the new Michigan Press Petronius (unexpurgated) is a treasure. Look at it and see what you done, you and Lawrence.

> love to you both from us both
> Larry

*[Big Sur, California]   3/4/60

Dear Larry, dear Claude –

Once in a while I get a break too. Guess what! I've been asked to be one of the 11 members of the jury for the Film Festival at Cannes – May 3rd to 20th. And I've accepted. I plan to leave here about first week in April and, if weather is O.K. spend a few days with Rowohlt in Hamburg. Then go to Die (perhaps to pick up the Fiat), and see you two – if you're not all tied up in knots with new projects, interviews, T.V. etc. After the Festival I would go to Italy for a month or so – I have 3 publishers there – they ought to be able to show me around! Then Greece possibly – some of the islands – and Crete – to see my dear Alexandros. Home by mid-summer, to see the kids – then off to Japan for the Fall. The Film people pay transportation aller retour Cannes and all expenses while in Cannes. Chic, quoi!

I'm coming alone. Don't know if I'll remain alone. But anyway I'm in a different mood now, and in much better shape than when you last saw me. (I must have seemed *decrepit!*) Lots was happening I didn't tell about. Lots can still happen. But I don't give a fuck any more. So, good cheer – maybe I'll see you soon. Can one get a really warm (heated) room in Nîmes? I don't mind the price now!

> Ta ta! Henry

Dear Larry and Claude,

Been here about five days now and promptly laid up with a heavy cold from which I'm just recovering. It's like living on another planet down here. TV is the principal pursuit. You glue yourself to it. If you want to take a walk you get into your car. To go to the grocer or the liquor store you must have a car, though you *could* walk it in twenty minutes. Must confess one thing about the American – he's awfully kind and courteous behind the counter. Amazing what you can ask of them and have them do for you with a genuine smile. (Even to cashing a check.) "The client is always right." Every house for miles around is a good one, costing from 20,000 to 100,000 dollars each. Nothing lacks, not even the garbage disposal in the sink, which makes a noise like giants being strangled under a hood. Frightening – but efficient.

Watching TV I caught up on the ball games. Takes about 2½ hours for a game to unroll. Last night two leagues were playing at night in a heavy fog up in San Francisco. Spectacular. When the batter hit a high fly it was lost in the clouds. Add to that that the field was muddy, and every one slipping and sliding like mad. Had to halt the game for a half hour till the worst of the fog passed. The players were chilled through and through. Huddled in overcoats while waiting their turn at bat, imagine. To me an interesting item was that nowadays about half the players are Negroes, and good. Maybe soon we will have Negro senators at the White House.

Listened for six hours while the Democratic Convention nominated Kennedy and Johnson. Same old pattern. Same old ballyhoo. And the public loves it. How clean a dictatorship like de Gaulle's seems. If Kennedy is our next president, our "boy president", something will happen. His being a Catholic isn't going to cut much ice, as some used to fear. It's his hair cut, his Harvard accent, his wealth, his cocksureness. They keep emphasizing youth. No one talks of wisdom. And if Kennedy dies in office we'll have Johnson from Texas, about the narrowest-minded group of people in America, Texans. He's rich too, and proud of having been a school teacher. Can you beat that? The best man, Stevenson, came in last – only natural. They'll probably make him Secretary of State, or something like that.

More and more it looks like I'll be back in Europe in two months – or else Japan. And Vincent Birge with me, as secretary and general facto-tum. I must look sharp this time for general headquarters, especially for the winter months. Then, if I hang on longer, I can arrange to have the kids come over for big vacations. If it's Europe I may hop back to America for Christmas holidays. Eve will stay on at Big Sur and hold down the fort. Trying hard to collect herself. Needs for me to be away. Guess I'll be better off too away – at least for a while. Coming back this time I felt more of a stranger than ever. All I noticed was the jungle which had grown up in my absence. I find I can cook all right, but don't get much fun out of it. Seems like a waste of time now. And all that dishwashing and making of beds and sweeping and watering and weeding, ugh! I'd rather meditate.

While in bed with the cold the last two days I got an idea of how to tackle the last tome of *Nexus*. All I need now is a map of the world and the key list of my characters. Then a huge omelette, backwards and forwards. I saw it all very clearly. Hope I can hold to it. If I can, I should be able to write it in 3 or 4 months, rapid fire. And "Lime Twigs and Treachery" grows in my head too. Guess I really need to get down to work. Not in ten years or more have I been able to write a book under serene, happy auspices. I'd love to have a free stretch ahead to do it in one lick, the last volume. I feel I could do something like Beethoven in that last quartet without form. After that I'll cede to the young-and-evil. [. . .]

My Cadillac runs like a top; wish I could take it with me when I come over. It takes about eight hours to get here from Big Sur. One long stretch of utterly uninteresting landscape except for patches here and there. Patches where nobody lives – just big rolling mountains all brown now or gold. We could accommodate half of China here with ease, I feel – and feed them well too. But the motels – they're just ducky. Beats any of the deluxe hotels I know of. Complete privacy, no tipping, car at your door, every comfort, including TV, wash cloths as well as superabundant towels and soap, everything sterilized, etc. But nowhere to walk once you're registered. Just an endless nowhere all around you. Incredible, really. And every little town gleams at night with Neon lights, like [a] miniature Las Vegas or Reno. Behind the lights vacuity. This is America, and whether we have a young president or a decrepit one, it won't change. It's the land itself speaking; or the ghost of the Indians who've put a hex on us. America is loneliness in the midst of hubbub and confusion. One has all the comforts and luxuries and nothing whatever of what is essential. Maddening. And every one so nice, so amiable, so civil, so helping, so sympathetic (in the wrong way). The bars are the worst: a Stygian gloom, with mirrors reflecting drunken soliloquizers. How people can spend what they do over the bar amazes me; seems to cost a fortune. Anyway . . . [. . .]

Lepska has been telling me about the problems of the machine man – the robots they now create. Trying to convince me they can solve problems with independent minds, or something like that. Talks about the area of the brain called the hippocampus, which sounds like a subsidiary of the autonomic system to me. For ex: how when driving over familiar ground you may remember nothing at all until you get home – don't remember how you got home because thinking of other things. But "it" (hippocampus) remembered, get me? I asked her if they can create, these robots. She thought yes. If they can do that, we might as well demission, what! I'm willing to believe they can think better, faster, more accurately, than we, but create (even a minor masterpiece) no. I asked if they had illogic as well – she said yes, to a degree. They get emotional, she said. But that's not illogicality, what. But here's the most interesting part . . . via her friends, the psychos and the robot-makers. Man is now concentrating on matter, what it is, etc. He doesn't want matter to resist him. He wants to get friendly with it, find its ways of behaving. So . . . instead of making faster rockets, etc., he hopes to learn soon how to transfer his body, which is matter largely, to whatever place he wishes instantaneously. Or go through a wall without hurting himself. And so on. It's not so fantastic either. I came to similar conclusions not long ago when I wrote about my first jet ride and the conquest of speed or time – the impasse that will put mechanical-minded man into. I mean when the time of arrival equals starting time – no lapsed time, in other words. All this business is part of ancient man's accomplishments, which we get now through dream, myth and legend. We are finding the way back maybe – back to the source, as Alf wrote somewhere. From psychosomatic to Mind alone, all Mind, is but a step. Can you make it? Just close your eyes. It's a cinch. And so truly logical and plausible. So simple, really. Too simple, that's the trouble. [. . .]

They've got a TV program now called "The Twilight Zone". All weeirdie stuff, via science-fiction pseudo knowledge. One about a baseball player who's a dream of a pitcher, invincible, until it's discovered by accident that he is a robot. To make him "legit" they operate and give him a mechanical heart. Result what you may well guess. He gets happy and compassionate – can't strike men out because he doesn't want to humiliate them. Marvelous stuff in this area for TV or films. Much better than the mystery dope we've been fed up with over the years. I imagine you could do us a real stunner. Imagine a diplomat who had the brains of a robot, when it came to solving international problems. An idea – for our next president a robot! [. . .] I'm now going to play ping-pong. Poor Tony, he can't win a game; I have the damndest luck. I really ought to do ping-pong the Zen way – just for my own improvement. No need to become a champ. Easy does it – now almost Zen-like, that expression. [. . .] Three strikes and out! The Dodgers are in the lead. Willie Mays leads in home runs. All the players have marvelous names – like painters.

Henry

[P.S.] Love to the gang from Val & Tony. And from me too.   HM.

*Nîmes   [late July 1960]
    Dear Henry;
just a swiftie to acknowledge your good letter; now the children are here we are so busy that we can hardly think, as you can imagine. Bathing all day at the Saintes. I've located a room we can use as a camp site with camp beds . . . I'm glad you are ironing yourself out satisfactorily, but on the practical front there is nothing you can do until you decide between Europe and Japan as a habitat. Wonder how this will fall out? Perhaps the best thing would be just to abandon the children, float about, and revisit them from time to time? Of course it also depends on dough; I don't see you doing your own cooking for long, though if you lived in the country in France you could probably find a femme de ménage . . . I don't know. Probably a good long journey round the world for a whole year would answer best. [. . .] The correspondence, critiques etc from the *Quartet*, is pouring in still unabated, and sometimes I feel that I shall never escape from these mountains of paper. I hope this year it will all die down and give me a chance to think. I now have enough money in hand for two years on a book if I wish – but I am being nibbled to pieces by people wanting to meet, congratulate etc. All this is dispersing and annoying, and I must find a way of folding myself up to attack something on a decent scale soon. Started to feel my way into oil painting and have done one or two quite respectable daubs this last month.

The children ask after Tony and Val; particularly last week as we went to a spirited 'encierro' in Sommières which we watched from your balcony; eight bulls let loose in the square in the midst of a huge screaming holiday crowd. How nobody was killed is a miracle; people were thrown around like ninepins. It was really something. Afterwards there was a good course libre; we wound up at the glacier drinking marc in the company of the good Mr Bevalo. They all send their love, and say you should really revisit them! The children bathed in the millpond, and so on . . . We plan to spend as much time on the beach as we can, as the summer this year hasn't been very good; big thunderstorms all over the Gard.

Best love to Eve; she is the one who should be coming to Europe to give her first show . . . why doesn't she?

    love from us all,
    Larry

*Big Sur   August 12th [1960]

    Dear Larry,
Know you're busy vacationing and all that. This is for later – when the rains set in. Do read Karl Shapiro's In Defense of Ignorance (Random House, N.Y.). Especially note these essays in it –: "What Is Not Poetry?", "The Critic in Spite of Himself" and the Dylan Thomas one. Reading him I feel as though I were writing it myself, through him. Right up my street. Specially as regards his views on poetry. I feel better now – I mean, about poetry and all that. Up Hölderlin! Up Pindar! Up Nerval! Up Hopkins! Still reading Women of Cairo. By God, if it ain't you a hundred years ago. And Egypt Egypt. Here and there remarkable glimpses of his Germanic understanding (he translated Faust, you remember) and a certain occult knowledge. Some of it amazing – transmuted through tales in mouths of others. How have they missed this book? It's a gem. <Allah akbar!>

When I come again we must make a tape together, so that it can be made into a platter. Agreed? We could have a rollicking time doing it, and you could cut whatever made you blush – afterwards. I want to get you on record – unbuttoned. I'll play the fool and you can choose your own instrument. And wouldn't it be dandy if, on the reverse of each disque, we had Claude's running translation and commentary-exegesis à la Claude – *in French*? Though you of course could talk French to me now and then and me answer in Urdu or Tamil. [. . .]

Yesterday I got back from a friend to whom I had loaned it (and who claims he doesn't understand it – a most intelligent man too) Gutkind's *Absolute Collective*. I am going to read it again, slowly, for the nth time. Just riffling the pages makes me dance. Few books I can think of are packed with such wisdom, such beauty, such really penetrating insight as this one. I see that I made voluminous notes about the book; I am going to copy them out, perhaps elaborate on them. And to think that this is straight Judaism! But a Judaism that only a few Jews have ever known or understood, I imagine. What is beautifully strange, as you grow older, is to find that you can accept with equal love and admiration the most diverse views – if they are well expressed. Here am I, always ready to rave about any one of the following, and where is the connection? Ramakrishna, Krishnamurti, Swami Vivekenanda, R.H. Blyth, Erich Gutkind, Berdyaev, Lao-tse, Nietzsche, others too – but not Plato, not Aristotle, not Descartes, not Socrates, not Spinoza, not St. Thomas Aquinas. Meister Eckhart, yes. Brother Lawrence, yes. St. Francis, yes. [. . .]

The other night I had a very close shave. Came home from Nepenthe slightly lit up – my head lucid as a bell – and in the deep fog and the white line erased and the speed I'm driving at, I missed the curve on a bridge, hit the bridge and bounced from side to side, damaging my beautiful Cadillac considerably (it's still in the garage), but stepped out unhurt, laughing (still drunk, I suppose), got picked up and slept on a mountain top. But never again – never drink and fog together. No sir! Reminds me of that story of Plato whom someone found in the middle of a room with his arm upraised to strike. Seems he was about to strike a slave who had angered him, caught himself in time, then decided to hold his arm in that same position for a while in order to let the lesson sink in. [. . .]

Enough! The fog has been here off and on for ten weeks now. Phenomenal. Played ping-pong yesterday with five youngsters, all fairly good players too, and came out ahead – as usual. But am I lame this morning! This went on for three hours, and I hadn't played since France. No, correction. Since the Feltrinelli château at Lake Garda. I'm making water colors again. Now I hit on a good idea – I paint over the writing – on the torn pages of the *Night Life* book – have several hundred such pages. Effects are wonderful. Try it! Ta ta! Love to the Forde-Durrell progeny. They must be whooping it up in grand style.

Henry

*Nîmes   [after 7 November 1960]

Henry dear; think you are very wise to be leery about the *Tropics* in England, as I have been about *The Black Book* despite Girodias' yells and screams. *Chatterley* decision means nothing; the very next one they fall upon will get ten years. Richard [Aldington] incidentally points out that the case represents a £10,000 fine for Penguins in costs, a sum they would never recover from any paperback. On the other hand *The Black Book* has got through in the States with nary a murmur to my intense surprise and I believe that with a wise political handling you might get the *Tropics* through there; but you are in the hands of people who will do anything for dirt publicity, and are mighty dangerous. In spite of your sweet words about publishers I think the exceptions are rare – a Ledig, a Feltrinelli, an Alan Pringle. But those who are honest have no taste and no intelligence – Ledig will bite his nails when he sees the come back in store for Groddeck: it took him a year to say no! As for the others: are you happy to keep Girodias in overheads for a night club with what your books earn? They are quite mad I think. And they will buy anything if it is mentioned in LIFE. I knew Nabokov was a great writer in 1938 when I reviewed *Sebastian Knight*; I said so. Twenty years later they catch up purely on a scandalmongering case about a book, and quite forget his others. *The Black Book*, praised by you and Eliot, has lain dead since 1938. ANY publisher worth the name would have realised that I was worth a few hundred subsidy in order not to have to waste my time . . . But . . . Finally Girodias and Dutton had a terrific battle; the sum of money paid in advance and in royalties was really cruel. They have so little mercy on each other that I draw my own conclusions!

I'm glad if you are planning a hook up because I think despite your roving eye you need a firm support on the practical side to keep you free to write; it's hard on the women I know, but the debt can be paid back in other ways.

Just going to Maussane to have lunch with Richard.

much love from us both
Larry

*Hotel "Am Rosenplatz", Reinbek bei Hamburg   29 November 1960

Dear Larry –

Got your letter to-day and from Big Sur the clipping from *Life*. Hoch soll er leben – drei mal hoch! What was a pleasant surprise was to see your oldest daughter in that Degas pose. What stout limbs, eh? And Claude looked absolutely stunning. [. . .]

I may hang on here another 2 or 3 weeks. Will write you again definitely, soon as my plans take shape. Now I am enjoying a love and a happiness such as I haven't known for years. So why move on? But I must, eventually. I must find that spot to settle down in. And begin all over again. I know you can't keep this under your hat but at least don't blow it up. This time it's a real woman. God grant me the strength to stand up to it.

(I am now doing a Preface for the new Gallimard edition of Elie Faure's *History of Art*. Oof!)

Ping-pong as usual. Hold my own with the local champion.

Ta ta now. A bientôt quelque part!

Bless you all!
Henry

*Nîmes   3rd December [1960]

Dear Henry; glad about your good news; you can count on our discretion. Whenever we write Eve we don't mention you at all in any context which might be thorny: fear not. [. . .]

We have just done a five day trip in Gascony for HOLIDAY. Heavens, what scenery and what food; how I wished you were with us. I held the trip as long as I could but the weather started to break and I was afraid of ice conditions on the N 117. One of the most beautiful trips I think I have ever made, starting at Perpignan and going direct north to Pau. And food! Jesus, it is all goose country, with livers the size of plates. An ideal place to settle, somewhere round Foix I should say; must see it on your way down to Spain. For godsake don't get married again!

much love from us both
Larry

Dear Larry, Just got yours of 3rd December and have slipped Ledig a note (he's in the adjoining office) about *Acte*. His father, Ernst Rowohlt, died three days ago; the funeral ceremonies take place tomorrow. He's busy, nervous, depressed a bit. But will bounce back again after the funeral, I imagine. I have a wonderful time with him – love him more and more.

[. . .] Believe I will spend X'mas here – with my dear Renate. She will have a 3-week vacation starting near X'mas and we hope to spend it together. We may go to Berlin together for a week or ten days; she comes from there originally – left it as a teenager – in ruins. I've never been there and am anxious to see it, having heard how lively it is, unlike most of Germany. And we will see Hildegard Knef, the stage and film actress, with whom I have had some correspondence. She sounds wonderful – talked to her over the phone from Berlin a few weeks ago.

So, there it is. Don't get married, you say. Well, marriage or not, I intend to hook up with Renate – soon as I find that second home in Europe, France preferably. You don't have to be on guard with Eve when you write. I tell her everything. After all, we're getting divorced and on good terms. And even the kids want me to be happy, find a place over here where they can spend the summers . . . even Lepska, their mother, is all in favor of it. My life there in Big Sur is about over, though I don't want to give it up altogether. And at present I don't quite see how I can bring Renate and her two boys there – not the place to live permanently – too American, isolated, etc. She's a great worker, Renate. Knows French and English quite well, has done lots of translations, knows many writers and artists I know – our paths have crossed in many curious ways over these last seven years. And – most important – we get on famously, on every level. It seems solid and real – and I haven't known this kind of happiness in ages. She loves France too. Well, there's much to do and think about in all this. Qui vivra verra, as Fred always says.

When I think of Chaplin with his seven children and Simenon and his family – both well adjusted, happy, working – with marvelous wives, mind you – I don't see why some time or other I shouldn't get a break too. I have nothing to lose any more but my life, and that's almost gone anyway. [. . .]

Anyway, don't worry about me. I'm in good hands. Oh yes, have met another fabulous astrologer here in Hamburg. A Dr. Wulff, very celebrated. More than an astrologer. On the wall of his sanctum the first thing I espied was a photograph of one of those two "Masters" whom you will find in Blavatsky's book – *Letters from the Mahatmas*. He is in touch with them – on the "astral" plane, I imagine.

Every day some interesting person walks into my private office. It's not dull here, even if only a village. I'm more in touch with the outside world here than in Big Sur. But I couldn't live here, of course.

Well, a good X'mas, if you can do it . . . I never can. And best to dear Claude who I hope is well and happy and working like a beaver. I miss you both very much. But will definitely see you sometime in January.

Oh, this . . . letter yesterday saying Heinemann would like to consider doing the two *Tropics*, now that *Chatterley* got by. But they are crazy, in my opinion. *Chatterley* is no precedent for any book of current importance. It was like opening a grave. However, shows you how the wind is blowing. . . .

Ta ta, sleep well, keep the fires roaring. And have that vieux Marc handy when I come. Here it's "Steinhäger", which I find vile. But the French red wines here are, or taste better, than in France, believe it or not. The climate here improves them – a fact.

Henry

[P.S.] That *Life* article was something. Should sell you 50,000 more copies of everything. Everybody worries about you getting a swell head. Not me. Moi, je reste un croyant. Je crois en vous. Alors, démerde-toi!

HM.

*Nîmes.   [mid-December 1960]

Wow! We are under deep snow; frozen roads, frozen water and light cut off. I write this by candlelight. But when you get it is another matter for the PTT is on strike! I've been lighting fires with sodden wood. The countryman's winter joys!

I know your views about publishers, but they are stark mad – scusi. You have been ditched, swindled and sucked dry by them from the very start. What a rosary you could make of their names starting with Kahane! And your friends and admirers on New Directions! Someone said to me the other day that two fifths of your time has been spent writing begging letters because you refused to be practical! Exaggeration, of course, but there is some truth in it . . . I should quote another victim. Byron's version of St Luke he said would begin with the words, "And Barabbas was a publisher"! No. It ain't philanthropy, it's business. Even with the best. I don't hold it against them; they have a right to get the best price they can, just as I have to ask the best price I can. It's barter. And any publisher has the right to shove a bad contract under your nose if you are fool enough to sign it. [. . .] I hope by now you have received the excellent English press on the anthology; it occupied pride of place in both weeklies so you should sell quite a few over there. I see that George Seferis' *Collected Poems* has just come out and received a v. good press too which must please him. He is still Greek Ambassador in London I think. [. . .]

Wrap up warm when you trek south; and remember that January and February are the worst months in the Midi for mistral rain and snow. But maybe at this rate we shall have used up our ration of bad weather by the time you arrive. I have no idea *what* would really suit you best; I think you'd be lonely down south and ideally should live in the country fifty miles from Paris, the Cher, say. But then the children want to swim and ride etc. I wonder if somewhere near Marseille? I don't know.

I am supposed to appear on television tomorrow; the boys from Marseille are coming up here (in the snow?) to make me talk bad French onto the tape and presumably photograph my blue nose. What the hell!

much love and a happy Xmas to you both.
Larry

*Reinbek/Hamburg   Feb. 7th 1961

Dear Larry:

[. . .] I just got back two days ago from Berlin – it was good, especially having Renate along. Saw East Berlin too. My first smell or glimpse of the Communist world. Pretty sad, dismal, morne, triste – worse! And this is the show-window, they say, of the Russian front. What imbeciles these leaders of the world are! If I were Stalin (or any other idiot) I would have spent a fortune making that Russian Berlin look like something. (I talk as an American business man now.) How can they make any one believe that this sector is better than the other? Are they mad? I saw one little shop there, a woman's "mode" shop – with nary a skirt in it – only some paper skirts, very poor, like in a dime store, and pieces of wadding on a broken limb of a tree – to make it look cheerful. About the most dismal picture of la haute couture, or any fucking couture, I have ever seen. The ruins are wonderful. Just as fresh as the day after the war. (It's fifteen years since now, and they haven't done anything. Incredible. But for a photographer, it's a magnificent study of war and peace.) I'm almost tempted to write a piece called "Ruins East and West". In the West sectors they look polished, cleaned up, as if they were toys not ruins.

Well, another two–three weeks here and then to Paris. I've got, thanks to Vincent, the most complete picture (meteorological) of Europe one could ask for. Ecumenical! I know now how to fly – like the carrier pigeon. Menton is the best in all France, apparently. I want to see Prades, where that cellist lives. Know it? And the Engadine (Suisse) – all Tessin-Ticino, in fact. The play is simmering. Got a hundred different jobs to do in between. But it'll come – and I think it will make everybody happy. [. . .] Still in love and all going beautifully in this respect. Ta ta now!

Henry

*Hotel Regina = Locarno (Ticino) (*Suisse*),   3/15/61

Dear Larry –

When you did that article for *Holiday* on Gascony you wrote me that there were some wonderful spots there. Can you remember any particular villages off-hand? (I never saw your text.) I doubt that I want any of this Ticino region. It's extraordinarily beautiful but not my piece of cake. I'm already getting fed up wandering around like a lost soul (of a millionaire) looking for the "ideal place". Have ruled out Spain and Portugal for various reasons. Greece too. Little left. France still appeals most to me. If I find that spot I may swallow the bad climate (winter). I could take the Hamburg winter I found. Really mild – like England. But Germany is out of the question.

It's almost as if, in quitting Big Sur, I walked out of my true Paradise – and now, like the hero in *Lost Horizon*, I am fucked! Certainly I never felt so completely lost and out of the world. (And I have money to choose – what good *is* money?)

I may go from here thru Italy – Venice and Milan and up the Italian Riviera to France. So write me c/o Hoffman, Paris – or better yet, if you do think of a place in Gascony, wire Frau Renate Gerhardt – c/o Rowohlt – Reinbek to tell Henry thus & so. (She will know where to reach me quickest.) She did a lot of work on your *Clea* incidentally (the translation – corrections).

Vincent is with me. We have the Fiat. It's in good shape. Should be seeing you when you get home. Will write again later – to wherever you say.

Feel lousy – constant belly-ache, nervous, ragged, dispirited – *and* disoriented. Say a good prayer for me when you have time. Cheers to you and dear Claude.

Henry

Durrell's 'The Gascon Touch' did not appear in *Holiday* until January 1963.

*[Montpellier?]   Monday Afternoon [24 April 1961]

Dear Larry and Claude:
We're clearing out for Switzerland in the morning early. The situation looks too damned bad to me. Only woke up to the gravity of it all when I glanced at the papers about two o'clock this afternoon. Sorry I won't have a chance to embrace you before leaving. I'll leave the Rao book with Jacques [Temple], unless I decide to take it along with me, and mail it to you later. Also the manuscripts you left with me. Don't know what to say about Joey's bit. The writing is terribly uneven, but one feels he meant well by you – and that's important.

Even if it doesn't come to open civil war and bloodshed here in metropolitan France I feel it's risky and the atmosphere too tense. Especially having the children in mind. Anyway, I'll write you from Lausanne. Write me there – not Hoffman, Paris – as mail to Paris may not get through. Address me care of American Express, 7, Avenue Benjamin Constant, P.O. Box 1653, Lausanne.

Give my thanks to M. Brusart; what a pity we had to break off like this. Was going to the Roussillon day after next. What about you two – will you hang on and see it through? I suppose you will – you're used to these things. But think about your francs – they may go down to nothing if trouble gets more serious. I'm trying to get all mine out immediately.

Alors, ta ta, cheers and God save the Queen!

Henry

[P.S.] Your piece on Gascony was a treat. Made my mouth water. Must get a real "Arquebuse" – tried one at café here – tasted like Anisette.

De Gaulle had won support in a January referendum conducted in France for his plan of granting self-determination to Algeria. Then on 22 April French Army troops revolted under retired General Maurice Challe and seized the major Algerian cities, hoping to thwart the independence movement. Many feared the rebellion would spread to France and lead to a civil war, but de Gaulle reacted effectively and the threat was over in four days.

Perlès's 'bit' is evidently *My Friend Lawrence Durrell* (1961).

*Lisbon   May 24th [1961]

Dear Larry, dear Claude –

Once again we're on the move. Portugal no go – particularly for the kids. Though it's a very beautiful country. (With terrible cuisine – like Greece.) We go thru northern Spain – Salamanca, Burgos – to Biarritz (with our Fiat, which still runs). Will look around near St. Jean de Luz – and interior – a couple of towns near Pau Brassaï recommended and one that Belmont goes to every year. Then on to Paris to meet the children who arrive June 10th. We may be in Paris June 7th or earlier. C/o Hoffman, as always.

In Biarritz (May 30th) address c/o Thos. Cook & Sons – 3, rue Gardères. Cable "Sleeping" – Biarritz. Just in case you have a brilliant idea. We're both just about exhausted – on all levels. The only next thing to do would be to return to U.S. (But I'm a marked man there now – what with the launching of *Cancer* some ten days ago.) It's possible we may go to Die (Drôme) where Maillet lives. The kids have been there and feel at home with his family. This as last resort. Say a prayer for us!

Henry

*Reinbek – chez Rowohlt   20/6/61

Dear Larry and Claude
Sorry I couldn't make it chez vous. Got here Saturday. Ledig just back
from holidays – looks great. Lots of activity here. *And cold.* Your books
are just everywhere – even in tiny villages!! *Cancer* permitted now to go
thru mails in U.S. Great quick victory.

Cheers! Henry

*Reinbek   22/7/61

[note written on margins of letter from *Holiday* magazine inviting
contribution]

Dear Larry – I told them I doubted I could do it. Don't have the talent to
dash their slop off with my left hand. Even *Life* is after me now – for a
good interview. Disgusting. Ass-lickers!
   Just back from Berlin, after week chez Hildegard Knef – a 9 day
wonder. Going to Denmark in day or two. Then Milan to get head
sculpted by Mario Marini. May spend Fred's vacation with him, late
August–Sept. in Cornwall, Devon. Maybe see Ireland too.

Toot a loo!
Henry

*Cork (of all places!)   8/31/61

[postcard by several hands]

Dear Larry, dear Claude – don't know what to make of it yet. Strange
country. Henry

Lovely country, Ireland; am living on Ex-Lax & Irish whisky – delicious!
Love to both of you. Fred

Neither has any need to kiss the Blarney Stone, nevertheless we go to
Killarney tomorrow. Anne

386

Dear Larry – May be passing your way again very soon. Where to I don't know yet. Am in a complete funk – canceled children's trip. Think my destination is either the bughouse or Père Lachaise. C'est déplorable! Henry

*Current address (chez Lepska), 661 Las Lomas,
Pacific Palisades, California 10/30/61

Dear Larry –

A quick word, knowing you go to Hamburg soon, to be sure and see ma chère Renate (Gerhardt) at Rowohlt's. Her home address is – Schaumanns Kamp 28 – Reinbek/Hamburg. Telephone: 72–55–29. Try to have lunch or tea with her – alone. That is, not with Ledig and Jane. It won't be difficult, I promise you.

I don't know yet when my play goes on in Berlin. Now it's opted for by Denmark and Sweden. The Royal Court Theatre (London) turned it down – "too sentimental".

I'm living near the children, have dinner with them daily. Get on swell with Lepska now – since there's nothing to fight about any longer. Strange world here, as you can imagine. Have a hermit's cell – cheap, furnished room. Do my stint regularly. Yesterday I went to see Aldous Huxley, who is leaving for India. Met Colin Wilson and Isherwood – what a jamboree. Soon I meet Harpo Marx – and Jerry Lewis – more up my street!

Haven't been to Big Sur yet – and don't know when or if I will. I'm no longer harried, strange to say. Just float. Wait for directions, so to speak. [. . .]

Did I tell you Fred and I made a broadcast (chez Fred) for the Canadian T.V.? Talked at random, he and I, for about 2½ hours. Great! No butting in of interviewer. Fred surprised me – perfectly at ease, nonchalant. Like an actor, b'Jesus! I hope you see it one day. Must be a little like Grock and Fratellini. [. . .]

I met Alexander Neill (Summerhill School) in London. Wonderful chap. Up Summerhill! Up Shantiniketan! Up Yasnaya Polyana!

Love and kisses all around. Better days are coming – with H bombs, fall out, and super-satellites. I must stick around to see what happens, eh?

Cheers!
Henry

P.S. I've made a new friend of an ex-pugilist (middle weight) who works in the films as a stunt man. Has marvelous jive language – about 2500 words. Reads Rimbaud, Proust, Ramakrishna, et cetera – and asks tough questions. I "underplay" it with him.

Joe Gray, the ex-boxer, remained Miller's friend for many years.

*Nîmes   Dec 1. [1961]

Dear Henry;
just a swift line to signal our return back to this rain swept cottage from Hamburg; both with splendid colds brought on by the central heating in Paris I imagine. Hamburg was hard work but gave me masses of information about playmaking; and *Actis* was quite a loud success which was a relief for all concerned. But hotel-life is a bore really. Ledig was away most of the time and we couldn't arrange effectively enough between transport and times to see much of Renate; met us for a while at a publishing party. Very nice and inordinately pretty. Hamburg was full of the rumours of your imminent return; and someone else said that you were going to start up publishing on your own in Berlin which sounded fun if a bit chancy these days . . . I could neither say yea nor nay, so I wore my special mumchance look and said "Really?" with a British accent. Scads of work has come in in our absence and we've decided to spend Xmas here, coughing our little souls out, instead of going to see the family in Jersey which we'd intended. We both feel terribly travel stained. I still get anxious letters about your welfare and mood – out of date by now I imagine, from Brassaï (most anxious) and Charles Haldeman in Athens (ditto). I have replied reassuring them that you are back at work and seeing the children, and sound to me relatively heartwhole. There was a good piece in *Esquire* which sounded as if you had struck your old chord again in the middle; splendid stuff, and must have set the ears back on the average *Esquire* reader. It proves that you are now repeating your international success on the home front at long last. What else? Ledig says that Andrić and I were the two runners for the Nobel this year and I just missed it by a couple of votes. All this is rubbish – it's a game of roulette. But now Christmas stares us in the face with presents and cards for the children etc. A lot of staff work for a couple of influenza cases. A long piece in the *Atlantic* about the *Quartet* which strikes the right note of grave reserve coupled with lots of good

388

praise. The German press still goes pounding on as does the French. The British keep their lukewarm eyebrows glued to the mast. Altogether everything much better than I probably deserve.

Are you coming to Europe in the spring? It might be amusing to revisit Greece briefly and see George K. I don't know. Apparently it's crammed with tourists now and is very expensive. I'm afraid I've just about forgotten my Greek; tried to do a tape interview with *Akropolis* in Hamburg but got stuck . . . terrible my memory has got.

Much love to you and to the kids when you see them; tell Tony he still owes me ten francs for a window pane he punched out once!

Drop a card when you feel like it.

    love
    Larry

Durrell wote a satirical rejoinder, entitled 'Ode to a Lukewarm Eyebrow', to a statement in *The Times Literary Supplement* to the effect that 'Mr Durrell and Miss Compton-Burnett meet with such praise in France as to raise many a lukewarm English eyebrow.'

*Paris   4/24/62

    Dear Larry, dear Claude –

I'm on my way to Formentor (Mallorca) this Friday – by plane. After that I don't know what my plans will be as yet. Maybe Berlin for a few weeks. May have to return to U.S. end of May. Will return to Paris May 5th and stay 3 days certainly.

So – maybe I won't get to Engances at all this time. [. . .]

It's a record heat here now! Had lunch with Ionesco and his wife Sunday – at Le Vésinet. Right up my street. Suppose you detest his plays (?). Here (in France) it's best not to have more than 3 or 4 characters – otherwise too expensive.

I'm in excellent shape now. Don't kill yourself with work. And get Claude out of her sick bed soon!

    Cheerio!
    Henry

[P.S.] Laughed my guts out listening to Brassaï on Dali the other night – chez Rattner – where I met James Jones, Bill Styron, Mr. Schuster (publisher) et tant d'autres. Waiting for Renate (like Godot) now!

*Berlin   29/5/62

Dear Larry – I've been reading what I consider a darn good (fine) British author lately – in Penguin books: H.E. Bates. His war novel is one of the very best. And that jolly family (*A Breath of French Air*) and now some novelettes – all tender, beautiful, sensitive, alive. Hurrah – for *me* finding a good Britisher other than you! Leaving here Thursday – more from America. Henry

*Rochester, Minnesota   10/5/62 [i.e., 10 June]

Dear Larry – Haven't heard any further from Edinburgh people. Will go if my physical condition permits. Now on way to see friend in Missouri Penitentiary – then home (Pacific Palisades).

Cheerio!
Henry

For several years Miller corresponded with Bill Witherspoon, and supported his attempts to win parole.

*Pacific Palisades   6/26/62

Dear Larry – To-day at the grocer's here I saw your *Black Book* on the rack. See it everywhere now. How you get around – in all the far corners of the earth! Prospects for Edinburgh trip look OK thus far. Heart is not damaged – just a bit weary (now looking into the prostate condition). Aside from that I feel just lovely. Best to Claude and all the kiddoes. Henry

*Nîmes   July 1. [1962]

Dear Henry;
I had a hunch that the physical shape was okay and that you were simply tired by travel – too much and too fast. But I'm glad to think that we shall meet up in Edinburgh; I believe you'll like Scotland land-scapewise, and of course we having nothing to do will be able to see quite a lot. I've refused to give an address but will answer questions if I can. We might of course do a telly act together, and discuss our

respective 'infrastructures', peace be to the soul of Cau. I see he's won the Goncourt, much power to his arm. The children arrive in fifteen days' time and Clo is rushing madly to try and finish the big translation she undertook on Tutankhamen – seems we will never escape from Egypt one way or another. I'm doing nothing except bigger and bigger paintings in oils. Acromegaly setting in. How the hell to control a large area is a mystery to me. Unluckily all my best ideas seem to have been Soutine's; but instead of action painting with a drip can tied to a bicycle I have patented a method of 'asperging' which is quite fun and gives the genuine 'maculé' effect; but Jesus what a waste of paint, which is expensive. In October I want to visit Greece briefly to make a few notes for a novel; how about coming along now you are rich. Katsimbalis will be delighted to see us I know; and a drink of Greek air is always invigorating. Last week Austen Harrison came thru and I gather from his description that we won't recognise a thing; but October is out of tourist season so it might be okay. I've got rather a good idea for a book; been mulling it longtime. [. . .] Much love to you all

Larry

*[Montparnasse, Paris]   8/29/62

Dear Larry – I sure let you down, didn't I? Slept till 4 o'clock. Forgot you wanted to take a bath chez moi. Never called Girodias either. But it was a good last night, what!

Henry

*[Israel]   Friday the 12th [October 1962]

Dear Henry we have had two strenuous but very interesting weeks in Israel investigating it from various angles, including the borders – all three. I still don't know if there is a novella in it, but there is certainly a novel for anyone who cares to mop up the colours. The south is pure Arabia, camels Bedouins and all; the north, Tiberius Galilee etc is green verdant and beautiful. Two separates – geologically and ethnologically. Met quite [a] lot of people some of great interest and stayed the odd night on one of the collectives they call 'kibbutz'. This I believe would interest you very much and is, I think, unique to the country. Every

shade of opinion is shown in the structure of these little collectives from
fanatical religious bigotry to straight atheism – from collective farms to
co-operatives. And 38 nations represented! It's really something to
see. [. . .]

We reach Athens on the 16th for 10 days. Any chance of coming?
Hotel Xenias Melathron, Bucharest St, Athens.

love Lar&Clo

*F3179 PACIFICPALISADES CALIF 21 5 900P<   [6 January 1963]

URGENTLY NEED AT LEAST DOLLARS 5000 CABLE WHATEVER YOU
CAN AFFORD LETTER FOLLOWS< HENRY MILLER<

*[Pacific Palisades]   Jan. 6, 1963

Dear Larry:
Hope my terse brutal cablegram didn't upset you – had to send out four
or five at once, no time for refinements. Here I am, richer than ever, in
one way, and poorer than ever in another. It's a temporary condition,
otherwise I wouldn't have dared wire you for help. I *had* to buy a house
– renting one would cost almost as much and not deductible from
income tax. Besides, Lepska had already sold hers and we were obliged
to get out – this Feb. 1st. Then I miscalculated on my income tax –
forgot that I would be regarded as unmarried for the whole of 1962,
though divorced only the latter half. That more than doubled what I
must shell out this year, and I had to fork out – in advance – the
difference between one year's estimate and another – a staggering sum.
I made other mistakes too – learned a bitter lesson this past year. Since
dealing with lawyers and tax consultants – my affairs are horribly
complicated – I've learned a lot. One burns first, though.

If I shouldn't be able to pay you back before, I most certainly can and
will when I get to Paris and begin receiving the extra monies allotted
me in the film contract, as consultant. Something like a thousand a
week, plus fifty dollars a day for hotel etc., plus plane trip – for 17
weeks.

What monies I receive from producers goes into the corporation I
had to set up (in order to secure lower taxes); then I draw myself a

392

salary, a thousand a month, if I choose. But the big advance they will pay will only come about 60 days hence. They have paid two lesser sums in so far, but I can't touch this yet.

I tell you all this just to let you know I am not bankrupt or going out of business, so to speak. In fact, things look better than ever for this year, as far as income goes. But right now I am strangled – and it's quite desperate. No doubt you've got your money safely tied up in various ways. I just pray to God you can find a way to unloosen some of it. Meanwhile I am asking in other directions – and I may get a bigger sum than I count on from Hoffman. If it flows in freely I'll repay you quickly.

You can imagine that I must have been hard put to it to bother you. Forgive me. Do what you can.

> This in haste.
> Henry

[P.S.] Love to Claude – suppose you are all back from Jersey by now. What a winter you are having! Brrr! Here it's like Spring.

The film referred to is *Tropic of Cancer* (1970), in which Miller made a cameo appearance.

*Nîmes   Sunday 13th [January] '63

> Dear Henry;

no, of course I wasn't and would gladly have complied by return but your cable caught me with my pants down; we had just done income tax and then on top of that I had cleaned myself out by making a five year downpayment for schooling – our biggest headache is always school fees. Such money as we had planted in bank loans could have been unwound but the process was not one which one could do in 24 hours as they ask for notice. I had the brainwave of ringing Hoffman to concert action and he told me that a very large sum, larger at any rate than the one you mentioned, was on its way to you from Calder in London; and he added that even if that were not enough he would find a way to dépan you okay; and that I was not to worry. So I hope by now that you have crested the wave safely. But are you settling in Los Angeles? Seems strange. I am tentatively planning a Greek visit for May or June; perhaps by then you might snatch a planned week-end to look up your colossus. Everything is frozen and the entire plumberie of the mazet was buckled to death when we arrived. Even down here we had twelve below zero –

the whole department is full of bust pipes and bust car radiators (people too mean to use anti-freeze!). The pump people had over fifty bust pumps in one day. Now it's started to freeze again and we are wondering if we are in for another coup de gel; can't you stop these atomic tests – they are fucking up the weather. My scenario is nearly finished and soon I shall be able to pay out the line and plan something really good for this year – at least a sketch of same. My brother is also having serious money trouble with his zoo and is in danger of having to shut up shop. O dear. Love from us all to you all; and don't spend too much on your house; you might want to buy one in venice or athens.

Larry

The 'scenario' is the first draft of Durrell's film script for *Judith* (1966), which he completely rewrote after meeting Sophia Loren.

*Nîmes   Monday March 4 '63

Dear Henry – delighted you have a swimming pool at last! That puts you slap in the Hollywood bracket! I imagined you were busy moving and signing leases etc hence the silence. Yes, I know the excellent Prevelakis essay on Kaz. It was sent to me by Kimon Friar an old acquaintance who translated the epic – very well I thought and also the ASKITIKI which I gave you a copy of at Sommières. That bears a close look at if you have the time – a marvellous little book. We are off to Geneva for ten days for Claude to have a medical look over: nothing serious, fibroids! Late April we plan to take the car and hop down to Greece. I wish you could come too. I believe that to revisit all your friends and the place would make you all oxygenated. It is so *tonic* the place – and of course K and S are there. It's as if they had never moved! Think it over. We plan about 1½ months. I want to show Claude an island or two. Also *Sappho* is being turned into an opera there for San Francisco next season. Can you beat it? If you get a chance to see the film *Electra* please try. The old story is filmed without any props or trucage in the ruins of Mycenae! It is stupendous and very moving. The text is in peasant demotic modern Greek and is harrowingly beautiful. As for Irene Pappas – what a terrible and wonderful player – pure Greek. Knocks Magnani into a cocked hat!

I've finished my bloody script and now can take a couple of months off to loaf. It got me so excited, the very thought, that today I wrote a rather good poem! I'm as usual awash with ideas and don't know what to start

394

on next. *Faustus* has been accepted for Hamburg this autumn! What luck I have had so far. Fabers are producing the correspondence in May to chime with *Cancer*. I think you'll have trouble in England myself – or rather Calder will. I hope he can pay!

We'll be back in ten days at the longest.

> Love to everyone – the kids!

> *Larry*

Peggy Glanville-Hicks adapted and scored *Sappho* as an opera, financed by a Ford Foundation grant, but her version was never produced.

Lawrence Durrell – Henry Miller: A Private Correspondence (edited by George Wickes) was published by Faber and Faber in Britain and by E.P. Dutton in the USA during 1963.

*HOTEL TOURING-BALANCE,
Place Longemalle, GENÈVE   May 1st [1963]

Dear Henry – we are here because Claude had to have an operation on her insides. She has got over it very fast and will be out of bed in 3 days' time. But she must spend a convalescent period of about 10 days within arrow-shot of the doc for check-ups, so I suppose we'll be here for the nonce and not get back to Nîmes much before the 12–15th. Our tentatively planned Greek trip should start around 25th.

More soon. Went to Madrid last week and met Loren who is a sweet creature, great dignity and style. By no means a "mere actress". Roughing out a story for her.

> Love
> Larry

*Nîmes.   2nd Oct. 1963

> cher maître,

this week we share the front page of *Figaro* which will doubtless reach you as soon as this letter does; sinister picture of me looking beatnik and dazed pouring wine from a bottle . . . All else goes well except the climate. Winter has started. The children flew away in a rainstorm and today we have enthusiastic letters about how nice they find school. They mean it! I am plugging along with this script for another fortnight and then digging in for the winter. My notebook is nearly full and I have now a firm shape for a new novel – very St Augustine and I hope a little Petronius too. My new play comes on December 10 in Hamburg where I shall I suppose go; I think it is not bad and will send you the published version this month. I think you will approve the idea whatever you feel about the form and treatment. Meanwhile Haas, who has seen a text, has written something v. good about it, and since he is the top drama critic in Germany it's a fine sendaway. What luck! I enclose a grimy photofax of it.

I saw a cutting from Edinburgh saying the Cambridge Players ran into trouble with your piece. I don't doubt it. You are writing for full orchestra there and it must be done with all the fluency, speed etc of a big musical to get by; someone who saw it properly dressed up at Spoleto said it went very well indeed. But I trembled for the poor Cambridge Players in their little village hall – no room to turn round, and no scenery. In such circumstances the only hope would be if the Dublin Gate or Habbema did it – professionals could get away with it without props, but not amateurs. Anyway what fun writing a new form of thing is! Only the people in films fill me with creeping horror – what a crowd of boorish ignorami lolling about up to the waist in gold.

I have just had a note from the Colossus. We are planning a trip to Greece by car about April, dawdling through Italy and fetching up perhaps at Rhodes. If we find a cheap to rent house we might consider taking it for six months and flying the children out for their next summer holiday there. We shall see. Everyone in Athens asked tenderly after you and I really think you would be most surprised if you visited it again. Nothing really seems to have changed in the radical sense. Paris, London, Cairo – everywhere one is conscious that time has passed, buildings have fallen, people have moved into new houses . . . Strangely enough nobody in Athens has done that; even Seferis' new little house is filled with the familiar treasures we would recognise from his little flat in the Plaka. All the old mixture is the same – the english bugger scholars, the tremendous eccentrics, and a lot of new young people of good address like Charles H[aldeman] who is living in Crete with John Craxton, painter, an old friend of mine. If you want to come in April let's drive slowly down Italy and embark for Corfu as if it were still 1939. Theodore has just spent three months botanising there and says that really nothing has vitally changed; the tourists have flattened the grass along a simple safari route like they have in France but two kilometres from any road one would never find a foreign face. As for

Corfu the whole north is still without roads as it was in my time. He wants to buy a house somewhere. O dear, I wish I was younger, as I would like to buy a house too; just to enjoy April May and June, and October November. But perhaps we can rent one for a hundred years on some island like Patmos and use it when we feel like it. I don't feel I am going to abandon France as an HQ now after such a struggle to get established here. No. No.

There is some talk of interviewing us both live on telly, you in the USA and me here; they will marry the film in Paris they say . . . Well, don't forget to discuss your 'infrastructure' seriously will you?

love from us both
Larry and Cl.

Durrell's *An Irish Faustus* was produced by Oscar Fritz Schuh at the Deutsches Schauspielhaus.

*[Pacific Palisades, California]   10/30/63

Dear Larry –
Your letter of Oct. 2nd only reached me yesterday. Carrier pigeons would be faster! Delighted to hear your play will be given in Hamburg. How that city has figured in our lives, eh?

I sent Seferis a cablegram on reading news of Nobel Prize award. How wonderful! I started a one act (curtain raiser) play some weeks ago. Hilarious! Pure burlesque. (An author in court answering charge of obscenity.) The Spoleto prod. of *Harry* was a slaughter. Now there's a chance for a B'way or off B'way performance. Also – Rome, Berlin, Oslo, Stockholm, Copenhagen. Maybe even London – with the Lord Chamberlain's permission. (What an ass, *he*!)

Meanwhile I am working like mad, doing water colors. Must get about 35 done in next 3 weeks (!). (All to reduce gross income by $20,000^{00} – or I'm sunk.) Have made 155 W.C's to date this year, but gave almost half away, unfortunately. I'm really getting good at it now – very bold, strong color, direct. Better, honestly, than a lot of accepted water colorists.

Where I go this Spring depends on the film project. At present all concerned in it are suing one another. I stand back and watch – with chance to lose $75,000^{00} (!).

I'd love to see Rhodes – and Cos *and* Patmos, if only for dear John the Divine's sake. Trying to urge Fred to try Rhodes. He's leaving soon – for Athens – you know. (And is studying Greek – seriously.)

Am having a passionate romance at moment with a stunning Israeli actress who is here. [. . .] (Will send you a photo of the two of us soon – don't give it to the newspapers, *please!*)

I swim in the heated pool (84°) every day and ride my bike – and get (2) marvelous therapeutic massages a week. Look at least 10 years younger – and of course my spirit is high. (What a change from my morale in Sommières – or even last time I saw you. Another resurrection, b'Jesus! How many more can I take?)

You say of "work in progress" – St. Augustine and Petronius. How do you manage to fuse the two? You must be using the ancient Egyptian welding technique! Anyway – hurrah! ("Love God and do as you please!" – St. Augustine.) Was it from him that Rabelais got the motto over the portal of the Abbé Thélème?

Charles H. says Claude has taken on weight and looks wonderful. Good news! (Does she still remember her Hebrew? I am learning some stock phrases now – like "Ani oheve otach", for ex. *Or* "Yakara shelly!")

Enough! Back to the water colors. I price them at from $250⁰⁰ to $350⁰⁰ – and get it. Can you beat that? Doing some etching too – and silk screens, with the nuns at the Immaculate Heart College in Hollywood. They – the "nuns" – adore me. Et moi, je les trouve séduisantes surtout les jeunes. My ex-pugilist friend, Joe Gray, is reading life of Keats. I find wonderful lines in it.

Alors – je vous embrasse, tous les deux.
Henry

P.S. Just read Gerald's article in latest *Holiday*. That boy really gets around, what what!

Ani oheve otach: I love you. *Yakara shelly*: You are my beloved.

1964–6

Serenity

After the tremendous success of the *Quartet* and the excitement of seeing his plays well performed by actresses of the calibre of Margaret Rawlings, Elisabeth Flickenschildt, and Maria Gorvin, Durrell seems content to bask in his popularity. With the help of artist Nadia Blokh and photographer Mary Mollo, an old friend from his time in Rhodes, on 6 March 1964 Durrell launches his gouache paintings with a one-man show at the Galerie Connaître in Paris. Roguishly, he hides his identity under the *nom de peinture* Oscar Epfs. He has been painting since the 1930s and, in dialogue with Marc Alyn, cheerfully acknowledges his mentor: 'Miller taught me how to paint masterpieces. His technique went like this: you paint a horse or a woman or any old crap; then you make for the bathroom and run it under the tap; and you've got a masterpiece!' He indulges himself in other ways as well: he buys a Volkswagen Microbus, a Zodiac inflatable, and a powerful outboard, and with these toys he crosses to Greece from Brindisi. He writes a number of travel pieces for *Holiday*, including 'Oil for the Saint; Return to Corfu'. He keeps writing seriously, however, and fills notebooks and a stock of typed sheets with material for a 'comic novel' to be called 'The Placebo'. In fact, he has been struggling with this project since 1961. It is not to be completed to his satisfaction and published, although some sections eventually emerge in *Tunc*. During the summer of 1966 he and Claude move from the beloved but rustic and somewhat cramped Mazet Michel into the largest house in Sommières, set amid tall chestnuts and palms, a rather sinister *fin de siècle* three-storey mansion with a mansard roof and the name 'Mme Tartes' over the door.

Miller too is not very productive over this period. His hip, operated on for the first time in 1960, continues to give him problems, but he recovers well enough to resume playing table tennis, at which he usually wins, even against his son Tony. His major efforts seem to go into painting – he donates countless works to museums in an effort to reduce his taxes – and to the courting of film stars and nightclub singers.

*Nîmes   [early] Feb. [1964]

Dear Henry;
I was wondering how you were getting along. I've just got back from England, and the dacent burying of my mother; she had an obsession about "being a trouble to people" and this time she performed her ploy to such good purpose that she almost slipped away before anyone knew where they were. Anyway . . . Yes, from every corner of the globe people are quoting that absurd *Time* report, activated either by malice or misreporting I know not. The funny thing is that while there were a few kids hooting back centre we got more calls than for either of my other two 'successes'. Isn't it strange? And the play is booked out for the whole season which I suppose is the test. I'm very puzzled; the play was both critically praised and panned but in that huge theatre of 2500 places there wasn't one empty one at the end . . . And by one of those odd reversals of things the much feared critics like old Willy Haas who had grim things to say about the others liked this one, and vice versa. I'm also having trouble with film people though not as serious as yours seems; they owe me a couple of months' salary. I must be patient. I've written them rather a good Israeli story; they said Carol Reed would direct and I was able to be serious for a while. Now I don't know what they are doing, but my part is through anyway; their IQ is so steeply oriented towards the nadir of things that one despairs of them. I have got two smashing scenarios in mind; but I'm not having anything more to do with the silver screen. Basta. We plan to slip down into Greece in a while, camping out mostly; just to see if we can't rent an old box for this year's children's holiday. Everything points towards a meeting in Athens of us all around May June; why not? Joe Seferis K etc are all there; you'd be surprised how little has really changed. I'll send you a swift one when we touch down. Claude has nearly finished a new novel, and I am having a small show of oils . . . Ahem! We are still solvent and with a bit in hand to spend on retzina (I hope). It is strongly rumoured that you are just about to arrive *incognito* with a ravishing

twenty year old. A source digne de foi; a television interviewer told me
this not a week agone. Ho! Ho!

> much love to you from us both;
> bloody cold here, mistral, but we
> are working while we swear.
> Larry

Time wrote about the Hamburg performance of *An Irish Faustus*, 'Durrell himself was
hooted from the stage at the end.' But the *New York Times* reviewer, while acknow-
ledging that 'some dissent was audible from the upper regions of the theater', asserted,
'The cast, the director and the Irish poet who stuck his neck out by adapting the old
Germanic legend for a new Germanic public were cheered for 20 minutes.'

---

*Nîmes   15th February [1964]

Dear Henry;

I get the most confusing picture of your private life these days; so
Lepska has also married again? Well. Yes, of course I would think that
if you aren't enbosomed in domestic felicity and enjoying home cooking you'd be better off in a small hotel in Paris or Athens, with all the va
et vient of your friends and acquaintances. But that is up to you; but
with Tony and Val launched what holds you to Calif?

We are going up to Paris early March and then back here; originally
poised for a leap towards Greece on April 1, I am now holding back
until I see which way the Cyprus situation develops; it could lead to a
Balkan war which would be nasty. On the other hand if the case for
partition (the Turkish wish) were supported by USA and England at
UNO, our name would be mud in Greece, and tempers would be
ruffled for at least a year – with every peasant asking why we didn't
love Greece any more etc etc. You know how it is; but we should see a
pattern by the end of March.

For the rest, things roll well with us; my little painting show will take
place soon and then I shall seriously consider carving out the prelims to
a new novel. I am seriously tempted to go on writing and not to publish
until, say, I'm sixty or something like that; at the moment we don't
need money, so why? I also think the feeling that one was playing about
for one's own amusement entirely would give a pretty freehand style.
Audience reaction is the very devil. [. . .]

No other news except that Claude's cooking, always good, has become superb. Result: I must lose weight or pay double on aircraft.

much love from us both
Larry

Gout! You must have worked to achieve that.

Larry – I can't go *anywhere* until extradition proceedings (by Brooklyn authorities) are settled one way or another. Had to swear an affidavit to this effect. But still hoping I will get to Crete in May for the Reunion.

In haste,
Henry

Miller was named in litigation over the finances of the *Tropic of Cancer* film.

*C/o Ionian Bank Corfu Greece   [*c.* May 1964]

<Telegrams to Tourist Pavilion
Paleocastrizza Corfu>

Dear Henry
Held up here on our way south by a silly accident – Claude broke a couple of ribs in a fall and has to go easy for a month. Tedious rather than anything else and well on the mend already. But the delay has enabled us to find a house by the sea for the children's summer holiday – we will defer our trip to Athens until July when they fly out. Meanwhile I am going to work a little and swim a lot. Are you coming, and when: a universal question? George K. has been ill with shingles I hear but sounds in good heart from a recent letter. I hope you are well. Greece is marvellous as ever. Went back to Kouloura – everyone asked after you, and said "Tell him to come. We are waiting"! More of this anon. This is only way to establish contact.

Love from us both
Larry

*Mazet Michel   Nîmes   Gard   France   October 6 [1964]

    dear henry;

long time no news, and I must confess that I deserve it. Corfu induced a fantastic laziness, a real envoûtement which paralysed every desire to write . . . and of course the traditional hopeless post office troubles didn't induce one to lose pounds sweating in order to send off an airmail letter to the US. But all in all it has been a wonderful long holiday and the children's first encounter with Greek scenery was well beyond expectation; they received that first terrific kick in the pants which we all felt the first time we hit Greece – or Greece hit us. Amazingly little has changed; we went up to Kouloura and spent a night in the old white house, now become a sort of shrine which tourists visit in caïque loads! It was strange to sleep in the old room with the sea sighing outside. Totsa is wrestling against a succession of strokes but is quite compos mentis and little Kerkyra is in great form. All their children are married; of course numberless questions about you, when were you coming etc etc. Nico the schoolmaster and Totsa and I jogged down to the shrine of Saint Arsenius together one brilliant morning; I had brought some olive oil from the trees here (we had a bumper crop last year and made kegs of our own oil: you should taste it). Well, I had brought some for the lamp of Saint Arsenius and with due ceremony we lit his lamp. The two men were delighted. "Now you are drinking French, you old dog," they told the saint. The lamp lit clear. Everything smelt of dry thyme and oreganum; the water was like a mirror in the little cove. The cave is there but our statue has been licked away by the winter sea – like a tongue cleaning out a hollow tooth. We sat in the dazing sun on the bluff by the cypress and smoked a cigarette and talked idly, voluptuously about old times. Remembered so vividly the days we spent there swimming and eating and arguing. It all seems in another world, another planet. Among other honourable survivals is Heleni Theotocki, the countess, of whom we saw a lot. She is in tremendous form, full of energy and humorous wickednesses directed against the dull society of the island. Longing of course to see you again. She will be in Paris this winter. We found a tiny but marvellous little house on the sea at Paleocastrizza; dramatic and beautiful site. And here the children dug their teeth into the summer with a vengeance. Couldn't get them out of the water. Well, such tears when they had to come back! We found our way back here through Italy and are now snugging down for the winter; apart from a few days in Paris to check my poems with Bosquet for Gallimard I plan to stay put and do some work this winter. What of you? Are you coming into France? How goes the health and the writing? A post card will do.

> love from us both
> Larry

p.s. Xan Fielding is living quite near us, other side of Uzès; he has sold up in Portugal and plans to buy somewhere here.

> Dear Larry –

I was wondering *where* to write you. Wonderful to hear about Paleocastrizza – and that little shrine (Corfu) where I had my first fuck with that English girl visiting you.

Yes, I expect definitely now to be in Paris in the Spring – while they shoot the film of *Cancer*. Must also be in Hamburg in April for the première of the Opera (*The Smile*) for which Miró is doing the décor.

My life here grows more and more hectic – reminds me of the Paris days – except that I get hardly any work done. But I am enjoying life. Health excellent – except for irremediable bad hip. But I swim and ride my bike every day. I ought to be over there for 2–3 months when I come – and will surely see you and Claude. (I wish I could make a quick hop to Japan first!)

Am painting on and off and really improving – in my own queer fashion. I wish I could give up writing altogether and paint. Such fun! *And* something to look at and enjoy when the day is done. I *donate* most of my work to institutions – in order to reduce my tax payments, which are "terrific". Now and then I keep one for myself. If I sell I only add to my income tax! What irony, eh?

Give my best to Xan Fielding. He had such a lovely place in Portugal. How did he ever give it up?

I am now reading a biography of my *beloved* writer (and inspirer) – Elie Faure. What a man he was! I wrote a preface too for Prevelakis' novel, *The Sun of Death* – which I loved. His book on *Kazantzakis and His Odyssey* is a real gem. Wonder if you ever read it? More soon,

Larry me lad. I think of you always – with tears of joy. (Joey reads &
writes Greek now, he says. Quel homme!)

> Love to dear Claude,
> Henry

*masmichel, engances par NIMES, Gard France   February 6 [1965]

Dear Henry;
the silence is as much my fault as yours; we have been passing through
rather a gloomy time for the last few months; Claude's parents took it
into their heads to die rather painfully of cancer. Various other small
pepins, too, came to swell the general gloom and made us rather
disinclined to write. But we've been working along doggedly and
having a number of delightful times on this tumble down property. I've
brought myself to the point of buying an American tronçonneuse
which cuts wood like butter, and has halved our fuel bills. It is much
admired in the quartier and I can loan it out whenever politically useful
– in exchange for a helping hand at stacking logs. What else? Xan and
Daphne Fielding have abandoned Portugal and have bought a huge mas
quite near which they are upfixing. Also seen a good deal of Cath
Aldington and Temple.

Your leg operation sounds worrying; can you fiddle with bones at
this stage? But I suppose you have the best advice, and I hope that you
will at least enjoy a painless time afterwards. Listen; about our plans.
We have kept a lien on the Corfu villa for this year and plan to go there
end Mayish, either by car or by sea with car. We'd spend some time in
Athens, and possibly Crete before going to get it fixed before the
children descend on us. How about a Spring meeting in the Plaka? A
sea journey could be quite leisurely; no need to stress that the Colossus
and I and Joe and . . . god knows half Athens would be down at Piraeus
to meet you. Greece is so tonic if you come early and get safely to an
island before the summer heat sets in. Why not think about it – in terms
of a leisurely tempo? I believe it would do you good; and of course
warm all cockles by arriving back after so long. Reflect upon it cher
maître.

I have started a novel of sorts; but I don't know where it's going as
yet and feel rather in doubt about the whole project. However we'll see
what comes up. It's terrible to have a success; everyone wants you to

repeat it by writing the same thing over again. I want to risk failure for a change by a new ploy. I have just been writing a piece about Eliot and recalling that long ago evening in Notting Hill Gate when you were both so relieved to find that the other was a human being! Also I have started to try and learn to DRAW. It's so hard but so exciting when one has total failure of exact vision. I can't even draw a cube right without a ruler. Later I'm going to have a bash at some new paintings. How slowly one learns, and how little time there seems. Brassaï said that the fifties are the worst period for both health and morale; turning sixty, he says, opens a huge perspective and one has all the time in the world and all the guts. His description of Picasso at 82 is mouth watering; bursting with new ideas and at the sparkling top of his form with the selective delicacy of attack that only ripe experience brings. Well.

Sappho sent me a marvellous Xmas present; a little book containing the thirty-foot scroll of the Japanese Sesshu's last painting. Line and wash. Of course it's only a tiny reproduction but very faithful, and the book rolls up like those tourist postcards (eight views of Athens), so that one can unroll it and study it in the whole as well as the parts. It's ravishing. It's published by Tuttle (Rutland, Vermont). Quick, order a copy to read while you are in bed! It was done in 1486. At the end the artist writes, "Painted by the aged Toyo Sesshu, who formerly held the First Seat at the Tendo Temple, on a peaceful day in his sixty-seventh year." He was a Zen master, by the way. The original is fifty feet long and a metre wide. It's a whole summary of his world. Well, enough; you have probably seen it half a century ago.

> much love from us both, dear
> Henry; keep at it and write soon
> Larry

*[Pacific Palisades]   2/22/65

Dear Larry – Just remembered you have a birthday on the 27th. How wonderful to be only at the half century mark. Congratulations – *Leb' wohl! Shalom! Peace!* I am still in bed and have to postpone hip operation some weeks. Otherwise fine and dandy!!!

> Henry

Dear Henry;

It was a happy birthday present, your card; how the hell did you remember my birthday? It's very flattering and very touching. The children come up and remind me from time to time, but I guess they have inherited my Groddeckian amnesia about times of birth. Claude wisely reminds me when hers is coming up so that I can do something honourable about it. Well, what the hell: 53. I'm sure it's worse than 63 or even 83; it's the bloody old menopause period when one has to start refurbishing everything in the attic and more or less starting anew. The period when one feels one has said all one can, and that it's wiser to shut up ... But is it? We are having our usual Provençal winter with all its good things, like duck on the broche, but also with the mistral howling like a wolf around the doors. And the rain! I've been wrestling with a new book which is no good though the idea isn't too bad; just recalled it and started again from the beginning. I'm suffering from too much to say and a dislike of the novel form as a way of saying it; alas autobiography won't do either, nor poems. Well, so I must plod along like a pregnant washerwoman with a changeling inside her.

About this leg of yours; is the operation really necessary? I mean there are now such handsome pain killers for localised conditions that unless it is continual agony instead of a rheumatic ache ... I agree that mobility is essential but even if at the worst you walked with a limp and with a stick would it matter? Damn it you can't be expected to do the nine day bicycle act any longer; but if you can swim a bit? At any rate you can count on your marvellous athlete's physique for everything even if they want to shave a millionth of a millimetre off your thighbone. Thing is to see what you really feel about it. But check these medical boys. They are always anxious to do their stuff and show how clever they are. And of course they are and we owe them a great debt. Nevertheless it's always wiser to see what one can make do with ...

No other news except that you are much missed by everyone and in every letter I get from France comes the question as to when you are going to reappear on the scene of your major triumphs. I think there will always be a big drum and a dozen majorettes waiting at Orly for your arrival. We are working hard, the children are well. Almost every day people write or cable me for news of you. I say you are on the way. I hope this is true.

much love from us both, from us all.
Larry.

[P.S.] Long good letter from little Joe in – Crete – he can now use the aorist in Greek! The devil has beaten us all – I can't!

*[Pacific Palisades]   7/5/65

Dear Larry –
Guess I never did get your note with Corfu address. I'll bet it *is* lovely there – if you are at Paleocastrizza. Are you? Betty Ryan is now somewhere in Greece, hoping to stay. She's going to visit Fred at Chania. Apparently she's a sculptress now. Still the same timid, gentle soul.

I'm back at water colors again, after a three weeks' lay off. I love it. Writing is now a bore to me. But I hope to tackle the one act play soon – I left off, after an interruption almost a year ago.

Imagine this – recently Grove Press brought out the complete *Rosy Crucifixion* and *World of Sex* and *Quiet Days in Clichy* – all in paper backs, and cheap as dirt. They were forced to do it because a pirate publisher got to it first. No copyright (for U.S.) on any of these titles. Result – the R.C. is No. 1. on the "best seller" list. What a joke! And so far no court cases, no threats. But I guess that will come soon enough.

Joe Levine has postponed *Cancer* film shooting in Paris for one year. Now Carroll Baker is suing him for $2,000,000^{00} – because he left her out! (She was going to play (4) different roles in it. Sic!) I just pray it never gets done . . . What about your *Quartet*? Did Fox Films shelve it? I doubt I'll get over to Europe this summer. I visit three doctors each week. Still no hip operation – and still bloody painful. I use a cane to walk a block or so. Most I can do at a time. But when I ride the bike there is no pain – feels good. I wish now I were an angel – I could fly places with ease and comfort. <Or, if not an angel, a "mezuza" hanging from my loved one's neck! The latest flame is a Polish film actress (and painter & pianist – *Sofia*!) from Warsaw.>

Have you seen the Israeli comic film – *Sallah*? Everyone says it's great.

408

Are *you* still painting? One day I must send you a water color – of recent vintage.

Here's a line I got from a friend in Japan . . . (It's from the Portuguese.) "When shit becomes as important (*valable*) as money, the poor will be born without ass-holes." Good, what? That really shatters the Marxian dialectic!

Give my love to Claude. And a warm Hello to all the kids. I envy them. What a wonderful organized, regulated, productive, happy life you lead. Bravo! And a 21-gun salute – from America, the lost kingdom. Be good to yourself. Carry on. Take it easy. Work hard. Play harder.

Salut!

Henry

Import Books published an unauthorized edition of *The Rosy Crucifixion* (*Sexus, Plexus,* and *Nexus*) in June 1965, and Grove Press followed almost immediately with the titles Miller mentions. Because Miller had first published the trilogy outside the USA and did not take steps to secure American rights, he was not protected by US copyright law.

Miller subsequently had stationery printed with the Portuguese saying, 'CUANDO MERDA TIVER VALOR POBRE NASCE SEM CU', at the foot of the page.

*Masmichel, Engances, Nîmes. Gard. France   October sixth [1965]

Dear Henry; as you will see we are back at last. Ouf, these voyages! Now I hope we can snug down for winter and get on with a little bit of work. The Corfu trip was exhausting, but the little boat we took (an inflatable Zodiac with motor) paid off handsomely, enabling us to visit remote beaches and islets and swim for the most part naked. We often wished you were there. While there we shot a long colour sequence for a television movie by CBS called *The Search for Ulysses* which seems to have turned out very well. Watch for it (CBS production) as it will show you not only our house etc but also the local village dancing and drinking. Will revive old memories I hope. I had finished one third of a new novel before leaving; a rag bag novel, this time, disorderly – not a formal trial. And this I want to work at slowly this winter among other things. It may take ages to do, but I am not going to hurry – it's a pure self-indulgence this time, to please myself and I'm indifferent to its success. Some other projects coming up which are of interest. Mai Zetterling who has recently stopped being a film star and started an independent unit to direct – her first movie has made quite a hit – has fallen for an idea to make a feature movie of *The Tempest* and shoot it in Corfu spring after next. I am going to rough in the scenario this winter; there is also a chance I might do Oedipus in Greece for television movie . . . this tentative as yet. But both these should be great fun to do seriously. The Sophia Loren film opens in New York in a month or two, but this isn't my work really. I wrote a short story and they've altered it around – probably for the better, I don't know yet, not having seen it. I hope it is successful for Loren's sake – she's a treasure that girl. What else? Some travel essays on France, a book of poems. I'm polishing up a few items in case we are dead broke next year.

Claude found and bought a rambling, ugly house just outside Sommières, with a lovely parc, tall trees. Not a château you understand but a large comfortable solid vicarage type of thing – maison de maître in fact – such as a prosperous notaire or country doctor might own. We are knocking it about this winter; but it will takes ages to furnish etc. Slowly slowly . . . we are okay here and want if possible to keep this property as it is now giving us marvellous olive oil, salads, truffles and god knows what. I've been a lousy correspondent this year. Sorry; it wasn't a very good year for me, I don't know why. Work piling up and a general paralysis setting in! Full of ideas but incapable of action. And far far too many visitors, too much talk talk talk. What a curse it is, for the strays exhaust one and prevent one enjoying one's real friends. By the way, the Fieldings have settled quite near at Uzès – your preferred town. Paddy is building a house in the Mani. I saw Theodore in London a week ago, in great form, among other people . . . And now at last we are snugging down for winter. Weather calm and sunny, Provence looking most séduisant. I've done a few features to pay off our expensive holiday trip, and am beginning to smell freedom – freedom I mean to be serious a bit. Everyone in Corfu sent you love and asked when the hell you were coming back to Greece – needless to say the Colossus in the van with tremendous oaths and roars and flourishes of the massive stick. Damn fellow Miller, where the hell was he? Looking at me as if I might have brought you after all in a suitcase. George S. is also being hunted like a stag by admirers after his Nobel; keeps disappearing to remote islands to hide himself. Much love from us both dear Henry

Larry

*Nîmes   26ᵗʰ Oct. [1965]

Dear Henry – George K arrives in France today or tomorrow and is coming down to spend a few days amongst us. This is to warn you that we'll be toasting you in your absence, all six of us – The Fieldings are settling nearby. What a pity you can't seize one of the jets you like so much and buzz right over to dinner. We'd spit you a wild boar with mustard and melon. Much love – hope all goes well

    Larry

*444 ocampo drive pacific palisades california   11/3/65

    Dear Larry –
Salute to the Colossus! What an adventure for you all! Give him a great big hug from me. People write me every week to ask – is he a real person or an invention? He's both, non? He "invented" himself, cane and all. May he live forever!
    And Xan Fielding too? Hurrah! I used to think he was Ian *Fleming* (?) of the James Bond biz. (I loathe the Bond stories and films.) Give him my best. Wild boar! Did you know that there is an invasion of wild boar in Big Sur now?
    The Revenue people are threatening to rob me of an unexpected huge sum – if they win I'm wiped out. Hurrah again!
    Writing from bed – down with a cold after excessive 10 days' heat – near 100° every day – too many draughts! Aside from that feeling great.
    Have to make about *40* W.C's now to reduce my income tax. What a life!
    Take good care of yourself *repeatedly*, as the Japs say. Claude too. "Love all around", as Eve says.

    Henry

*masmichel engances par Nîmes
Gard   France   21st December [1965]

Dear Henry; four days to Xmas and we just got your card together with one from the Colossus who has now safely arrived back with Spatch after a really triumphant tournée in the Midi. The only thing it lacked was your presence. By extraordinary luck too the weather took a hand – one of the most memorable golden sunny autumns I ever remember; never has the landscape looked lovelier, never did the food seem deliciouser; and the Colossus, who has these past months been in fretty and somewhat bearish mood, at once reverted to the Essential Colossus; rose to the weather and food and the company (Xan and Daphne were always with us) and positively shone like a beacon. All the great stories rolled out like the magic carpet; and several of our contemporary adventures were so mad and piquant that I could see that great Johnsonian mind mulling them over as a potential source of other stories to come; crunch crunch like an olive press. Then he would take a trial flight with a short piece of the ridiculous encounter in Montpellier and give it a trial flight, just a small piece, to see if it were airworthy so to speak. Altogether it was one of [the] most successful trips he has ever made; by great luck everything fell out as it should. And I see from his tone that it was really a rest and that it has had a real restorative effect. Spatch says he has been sad and grumpy and angoisse this last year and this trip has thrown him back into his old copious and frolicky self. We visited Delteil together and had a most amusing evening being televised around the big self-portrait of you. I think Jacques is sending you some pics of this event. Meanwhile please send me a small water colour for the new house in Sommières; it won't be ready yet awhile but I'd like to have a small spot of colour from you among the lares and penates thereof. It is rather elegant ugly – a sort of Balzacian house in a small parc with tall trees. It's across the bridge on the way to Saussines. An old solid bulldog of a maison de maître. George loved it. Comfortable and roomy and without pomp. I expect by now Moore will have sent you the tribute to Richard book which has a pic of us all on the bridge at Sommières – it seems a century ago already. [. . .]

Are you writing anything? Some aphorisms I hope at least – guided missiles!

my dear Henry, have a good Xmas and
remember that we are constantly thinking
of you and raising a glass.

Larry

[P.S., in red:] Don't forget about the pic however small.

Richard Aldington: An Intimate Portrait (1965), edited by Alister Kershaw and Frédéric-Jacques Temple, includes a contribution by Miller and a photograph of Aldington, Durrell, Miller and Temple, taken in 1959 on the old Roman bridge over the Vidourle.

Dear Larry –

Someone sent me the enclosed. Maybe you've seen it already. Everything I hear and read about London sounds fabulous. What a city it has become overnight. Really swinging, eh?

Betty Ryan just sent me a copy of my *Colossus* in Greek. A surprise to me, since I don't recall signing a contract with any Greek publisher. May be a pirated edition. I can't make out the publisher's name and address either, but have asked Fred to ask Betty. *She* gave me her address in Greek letters – somewhere in *Euboea* (?).

Am now dating a Japanese singer & piano player – former film actress in Japan. "The Shirley MacLaine" of Japan they call her. Met Elke Sommer (German actress) lately – good talk with her. Also Inger Stevens, Swedish actress (very good). Must have quite a list now.

My water color show here was a huge success. Still painting, you know. My pool is heated to 86 degrees now like a wonderful bird bath.

Our "Colossus" looks great in the photos Temple sent recently. How are you all these days? I'm almost a champ at ping-pong now. Very seldom beaten, except by pro's. And this with a game arthritic hip! Comme disait Rimbaud – "je suis intact." Cheers!

Henry

[P.S.] Best to Penelope Berengaria when you write her again. Lucky she's not a boy and available for military service. *Vietnam* – how it stinks!

The 'Japanese singer' is Hiroko (Hoki) Tokuda, who became Miller's fifth wife.

*Sommières   [postmarked 12 December 1966]

[on printed greeting card "From a design by Lawrence Durrell for the Jupiter Record 'Contemporary Poets Set in Jazz'".]

Cher Maître – another year has passed and we haven't seen you this side of the water. I think I shall have to come next year to visit *you* –
Our best love

Larry

Love and Death

This year finds Miller, aged seventy-five, in ardent pursuit of the Japanese film actress and nightclub singer Hiroko Tokuda, aged twenty-eight, whom he had met at a party in 1966. Though he sees himself as a septuagenarian Goethe in love with teenage Ulrike von Levetzow, his behaviour is eternal youth: soulful gazing upon 'Hoki' at the piano, midnight telephone calls; he even writes a set of lyrics for her – only the third poem he has ever penned. An image that comes to mind is the Chaplinesque clown who always lands on his feet, no matter what the threatening situation. It is fitting that Miller and Chaplin became great friends and, with Georges Simenon, formed a trio in search of hilarity.

Nineteen sixty-seven begins for Durrell with the death of Claude on New Year's Day in a Zurich hospital. He is stunned: until the last few days, the doctors had been talking optimistically about a curable bacterial infection. Claude's illness turns out to be cancer. As if to underscore the disruption in Durrell's life, the correspondence lapses, and Miller's reply, if any, to Durrell's terse note announcing Claude's death, has been lost. Like Miller, Durrell is very resilient – a less tough man could hardly have kept his emotional equilibrium, let alone continued to create, during the upheavals he has faced – war, professional setbacks, divorces, the mental breakdown of one wife, the sudden death of another, and so on – but in Durrell the disasters point to tragic conclusions, and so inform his art.

Miller's *Rosy Crucifixion* is, finally, Rabelaisian and comic, as befits his egocentric personality. The direction of Durrell's life and fiction, while presenting continuation rather than tragic finality, points to his ego-fleeing nature. He strives to overcome hurt and loss through deflection rather than confession, disguise rather than self-portraiture;

death, from wry Death Gregory in *The Black Book* to the gnostic death cult in *The Avignon Quintet*, is Durrell's great subject. With *The Alexandria Quartet*, and particularly in the works written after Claude's death, the shadow of mortality lends his work a serious tone which belies the laughter.

*Sommières   17 January [1967]

Dear Henry –

A very brief line to tell you that Claude died in Geneva Jan 1ˢᵗ of pulmonary cancer. It sounds so improbable that I can hardly believe what I write: yet it *is* so. I was there all the time so I know. We are back here now, sorting and tidying in the house she made so very much her own: wandering about in a tremendous vagueness. One wonders what she is thinking about if anything: one listens, tries to overhear perhaps.

Well, dammit, there we are.

love to you
Larry

*30 – Sommières – France   13 Feb [1967]

Dear Henry;

just a brief line to tell you my movements, as I shall be going to London on the 22nd for about ten days; staying with Alan Thomas in Chelsea [. . .] thence to Paris very briefly to spend a week with the Blokhs [. . .]. This is just in case you spread your wings and fly over for any reason. In a general sense my plans are all in a muddle; I am still clearing up, sorting, doing paperwork. Ideally, if I could get all my affairs straight I'd like to go to Greece around April for the summer; but I must see what the money position is first. There is nothing very agreeable to recount from this end; Clo has of course left a huge hole in the pavement. I must finish this book. Ouf.

every good thing
Larry

Eve's death has added immeasurably to the general gloom caused by

Claude's disappearance; among all those who knew and loved her here dans la région

The Eve referred to is Eve McClure Miller, who had just died.

*30 – Sommières – France   April 19. 1967.

Dear Henry;

Synthéses came today and I've been reading it with pleasure, thinking how much appreciation of your work has deepened – people unerringly give the right reasons for admiring you, these days! Also the professor's book, which is typical of its type but isn't all that bad. I confess that I am glad to see you canonised in this disagreeable field, not for any critical values that might emerge, but simply for the sake of the young, who will have the blessing of the profs to read you. Apart from all that it always gives pleasure to read about *The Booster*, Alf etc, and the past. But how marvellous was the anonymity of being unknowns, friends; now one seems to belong to the journalists. Katsimbalis gets raging mad at all the prying and says we have become a set of international clowns . . .

Apart from all that I have been slowly and steadily consolidating morale here, which was badly shaken by Clo's so sudden and so unexpected death; she's left me with a huge house on my hands, and since the children are hardly at all here now I wonder what the devil I am going to do with it. Vaguely I am thinking to get a small caravan (motorised) and to spend my summers footloose in Greece and Italy and firm up the mazet (already pretty well wired for comfort) just for the winter months in France. It was what I always urged on Clo, but she hated travelling and wanted to sit tight with monthly vacations here or there. But I think it might suit me as a life: to rove about. When one is alone it is easier to imagine. We shall see, there's much to be done here before I can think of it. I may visit the States next spring for some lectures, and if I do I'll try and get across and see you – if you don't turn up here before that, that is. For the rest I am enfin on the last leg of a new novel which has cost me a very great deal of trouble and annoyance to plant and tend these last few years; not big in bulk I suppose but with a different kind of hitting power. But these things one can't tell until the proof stage. What the hell?

Anaïs has come into her own in Europe with a vengeance, but seems

417

to think there is something wrong with me, about my attitude to her – which hasn't changed a jot in affection and admiration since Villa Seurat; she seems to have become very touchy, and I don't really know what is expected of me in order to appease her concern. Well, what the hell, I've done what I can.

At the moment I have Saph and Barry here, and Diana who works in Geneva comes down for week ends; great pleasure, but they eat so much. However, next week they are off again and I shall be on my own regretting my meanness over the household accounts. I hear George K hasn't been at all well recently. Spatch wrote me. If only I could get away this summer I could cheer him up – it's only company he lacks. I see the Fieldings quite a bit, but nobody else. Hope everything goes well with you. We were all terribly saddened by Eve's death – Pocahontas. She had won all hearts, that girl; one can't think of her without a deep pang of regret. And I didn't write for such ages.

never mind, she was a forgiving soul.

much love henry from all of us – barry
and saph too.

[P.S. by Sappho:] Much luv & hope you are thriving – Saph. XXX
XX
X

*[Pacific Palisades]   7/9/67

Dear Larry –
I got your card some days ago but don't have your address in Athens, nor Katsimbalis' either. Hope this reaches you!

As for a reunion this September, I can't say yet if it's possible or not. I'm due in Paris, for my show, Sept. 20th and will stay about 10 days, then go to Sweden for another show, and after that to Tokyo. I don't see my time schedule clear yet. On verra. [. . .]

Are you still painting? I have to do about 35 W.C's in next (6) weeks. Oof!

Japan will be my oyster, I believe. More soon as I know better about schedules. Give my love to K and Seferis and all the others – your sister too. Have a good time – be good to yourself! Cheerio!

Henry

Dear Henry;

I shall be back in France to meet you, I hope by Sept 1st all things being equal; I have spent the last few weeks mapping out a television film about Athens seen through the eyes of Katsimbalis. He is going to play the lead in the film – Raimu to the life! – while all the others will also support. It is being made by a brilliant and pretty BBC woman producer, and will be shot next spring. I will do scripting narration and general provocation to keep the frames moving. But as it's not possible to think about our *parea* without thinking about you who first introduced them to the world I think we must impose on your good nature and ask for a tiny chapeau to the film; if I could interview you for three minutes in some Paris garden it would offer a fine point de départ for all we will have to say about K, Sef., Ghika, Tonio etc etc, not to mention Athens itself. I have told Margaret McCall to get in touch with Hoffman this week and spy on your movements; I am coming back overland around the twentieth and will do likewise. All the detail will be done via Hoffman and through the BBC. But I hope you won't be too busy to fall in with the little plan – about half an hour in the Luxembourg it will cost you – and if the film comes the way it should it should be gay, amusing and with an intellectual backbone.

There's not much news otherwise of this rather ghostly summer; some small chagrins and much vague wandering in L'Escargot my little Volkswagen, which is a dream to travel in.

much love to you
Larry

Dear Larry –

Hope this finds you in Sommières! Rushing, rushing ... Getting married *to-day* in about 3 hours from now – to Hoki Tokuda. Bringing her along, of course.

About your "K" film – 25th would be good. Perhaps even 24th, tho' I can't tell too much ahead of time.

Would love Joey to be there, but this time I can't afford to send for him and put him up in Paris. (Am draining my bank a/c already. Is it possible expenses for him could be wangled thru the BBC or any other way? Will *you* try to think about it, *please?*) I'm up to my neck in problems of all sorts – not just the marriage biz. Incredible what all can happen at once.

See you at my Hotel Montalembert – soon. Arrive the 19th. Georges Belmont is au courant to all. 3, Place du Panthéon – Paris (5). And in next room to ours will be my secretary & buffer, Gerald Robitaille, whom you may know of. All telephone calls for me go thru him! Otherwise I'd never have a moment's peace.

"Peace! How wonderful!" Cheerio! Henry

Gerald Robitaille's book, *Le Père Miller: Essai indiscret sur Henry Miller* (1971), gives his somewhat critical view of Miller.

*[Paris]   Thursday 10/19/67

Dear Larry –

Sorry Diane [Robitaille] didn't put me on the phone when you called yesterday. Paris is on the cold side now – clear and brisk. But the flat is well heated and the hot water is hot! The toilet broke down but is being fixed now.

We did thoroly enjoy ourselves chez vous. What a treat it was. I really hated to return. I can't get over your beautiful house – and everything working so smoothly. Only the Rothschilds could surpass it. I hope I can get back there again one day. [. . .]

Hoki sends warmest greetings – and to Marcelle too. (Found two gifts from her in our luggage. What a gal!)

Must go out to film now. Will keep in touch. Take good care of yourself. Better days are in store for you, I feel it strongly.

Cheerio!
Henry–San

*Pacific Palisades   11/15/67

Dear Larry –

Home again, after a grueling 24 hour trip [on] Air France from Paris. Feel I never want to take a plane again. Next day appeared at Immigration Bureau. Monday we go to Las Vegas to get remarried. And even

420

after that it will be 3-4 months before Hoki can get a permanent resident visa. It's nightmarish. I'm dead tired but OK. Hoki seems happy in her new home. Got our dinky piano tuned for her immediately. She's virtually all to rights already. My kids, on the other hand, are in the midst of new problems – Tony with his draft board (military – he dropped out of school) and Val, freed on marijuana charge, at loose ends – where to live, what to work at, etc.

I'm ready to sit down and paint and write soon as we're back from Nevada. Am sure Marcelle is right – that I will work like a beaver whether I want to or not.

Paid a visit to doctor today – got an injection for my hip and found out that with relatively harmless medication and an injection once a month I will not have to be in perpetual pain, as I have been these last four years. This may work wonders for me, psychologically.

And now I'll tell you what Joey and I were thinking of when Diane read your cards. It was that you would soon find the right woman and get married again, and enjoy that wonderful home you created in Sommières. It's coming to you. I also feel there is a good possibility of a sudden long voyage – because of a woman, which one, I don't know.

You seemed in fine fettle the last days in Paris. I hope it lasts. You were not made to live like a hermit.

I was surprised and delighted to see how well you and Miriam Cendrars got on together. She's a wonderful creature, I think. I'm trying to read the MS. she gave me, but find it tough. (Don't tell her yet, please. I'll give it my best attention.) The guru may be wonderful to be with, but the writing is another thing.

All in all the trip did me good, I believe. I feel more confident now that it won't be the last time I see you. And, I must repeat, you certainly are one of the most considerate persons I ever knew. You always were, but this time it struck a deep chord. I hope we didn't bore the shit out of you in Sommières!! You seemed like a caged lion at times. Give Marcelle a good hug – from Hoki and myself. "Triomphe sur tout!" Je ne l'oublie jamais cette phrase.

All the best now, my dear Larry, and don't let anything let you down. Your best years are ahead of you. "God wants us to be happy!" (Nijinsky) Oh yes, trying to get embalming book for you. More on that soon. Henry

My dear Henry;

Delighted you are safely back, and that everything begins to fall into place once more; I don't think it's age that makes one more casanier, I think every creative person needs a basket, like a kitten, and returns to it with relief and pleasure. I spent a few days in Paris after you left with the dear Blokhs, and dined twice with Miriam. Yes, sure I know her – I regard her as one of my closest and dearest friends; we exchange books, ideas and much fond thought whenever we meet, always with the Jap-slant. Despite my very lazy Western cast of mind she enjoys testing ideas on me. She left for India two days ago to have another drag at the dugs of her swami – who sounds marvellous by all accounts. But of course, as you say, writing is another thing. She regards you as quite as important in the Western spectrum and revels in your irreverent impudence! Well, as usual you have left a lot of friends behind; Marcelle when she brings the mail every morn says "Dites c'est pas l'écriture de Monsieur Miller?" or "Rien de Madame Hoki ou Monsieur Henri?"; and if there is I get no peace until I've read it to her. (A long voyage still for Hoki, a small chagrin resolved for you: this week's cards. Main picture very very fruitful for both.) Meanwhile I have arrived back with a small oyster-poisoning in the form of a rash and three kilos over weight. I must attend to this pronto. I shall soon have proofs of TUNC for you to read. I don't think it's too bad, as I feared. Some new poems coming, and I am starting to paint with the new cement Nadia got me – giving big thicknesses over which one paints. Simone Perier as well as the Temples ring up every few days and always ask how you are doing, full of the medieval Mediterranean *concern* which makes me laugh but is very touching. I'm so sorry I didn't arrange for you to meet another writer, a rather beautiful woman called Paula Wislenef, she was so downcast to hear you had been here. Only wanted to SEE you from afar. "C'est si quelqu'un m'avait dit que Dostoievski était de passage à Nîmes." She sent me the horrible big plaster mould of Bigot against which we were photographed – so I sent her a copy to pacify her. I'm delighted about the leg; the thought of that operation alarmed me no end. I am sure that your excellent physical condition should keep up, and that at the most you might get slight rheumatism which massage would dispel. Well but ... I'm grateful for the thought but I think another marriage would be disastrous, and isn't necessary; I've been married since 23 and paying alimony since 27 and have passed through stupidity schizophrenia and death on a sort of ascending scale. Enough I think. I need four tedious mistresses and a good typist, that is all and I rather like the empty house echoing around me to the noise of a typewriter. You should join forces in PREVENTING me from making any more fool mistakes like that; a quarter of an hour's mental concentration each day might prevent disaster – for the likes of us marriage is madness, though I have enjoyed mine, particularly the last. But no more, please.

Love   Larry

*Sommières.   December 2nd. [1967]

Dear Henry; just got back from a little trip to find mountains of proofs to correct; soon you shall have a page proof to read. It's not bad, this bloody book: a bit too cerebralised perhaps, but then I have another volume to go – you don't open the stops till the end. Despite Marcelle's vision she didn't see her mother falling under a cupboard, so today she has stayed at home to nurse her. Funny thing about her cards; she often tells me something is going to happen when it just *has* happened; always something she didn't know about. This reminds me of the man in the Rhine telepathy experiments who could never guess the next card right – but to their surprise they found he was always guessing the next but three quite accurately. In other words his divining sense was okay but his chronology was out by two units. Marcelle has about twenty percent of things which have already taken place as ABOUT to take place. What else? I am fixing up Xmas and expecting the children; but I have come to loathe Xmas. The children are too big and the event too trumpery, a piece of tinsel mummery now. It will be nice to see Saph again, though. I have started vol two, am proofing a new *Collected Poems*, and playing with various ideas; Dutton wants me to come to New York end of March for the book. I suppose it is a hell of a way across to the other side to call on you? We shall see. Sometime I must visit the USA. I'm getting so damn lazy, there's so much to do here. And so little time does there seem ... I've started painting again, thanks to your watercolouring; and tell Hoki I'm writing a musical called Smoke which she must score, and possibly sing in, for me ...

I asked Nadia to find me an embalmer's guide in Geneva, and all she

423

sends is this crazy twenties ad. which she found in a library. My face got finished in the end – it looks horrid (sculpture). Like the chairman of a bucket shop.

And so, dear H, let us have some more of this new vein of pure poetry – the antique land piece of yours; it's wonderful. The newly framed watercolour looks fine too. Tell Hoki my stomach is as admirable as ever – never have I been admired for what we consider a serious blemish on our otherwise perfect beauty. I study it a lot and polish it with floor polish till it gleams in the sunset.

    love to you both
    Larry

Nadia's enclosure was advertising copy for Clarke's Fluid, an embalming agent: 'EVERY TIME YOU SEE A PRETTY GIRL THINK OF "CINTIO" & "DE CAGE" / The chemical that preserves the beauty.'

424

A Time of Reunions

Durrell comes to the USA for the first time in 1968, stays with Miller and his Oriental coterie in Pacific Palisades. Hoki and her cousin take Larry to Disneyland – which he loves. His Sommières home is expertly burgled: 'They took only my best Elizabethan books and the paintings given me by famous artists – but left all my own art,' he complains. This causes Durrell to seek a safe home for his correspondence and manuscripts, and his personal archive, including many of the Miller letters printed in this volume, is sold to Southern Illinois University at Carbondale.

The next year, 1969, *The Alexandria Quartet* is filmed as *Justine*. Durrell studies the gnostics and writes the first volume of *The Avignon Quintet*. He begins a cycle of frequent visits to Geneva and Paris, and returns to America in 1970, 1972, 1973 and 1974, the last time to teach for three months at the California Institute of Technology. During 1972 Durrell and Perlès celebrate a reunion in Paris.

Miller is enraged by the film *Bonnie and Clyde* and writes an article on it; he is deeply moved by the suicide of Yukio Mishima and composes a long essay. He falls in love with Lisa Lu, a celebrated Chinese actress, and concentrates his still-prodigious letter-writing powers on her. He makes a list of thirty of his oldest pals and begins writing his *Book of Friends*.

Just before leaving for the Caltech teaching stint, Durrell marries for the fourth time. His choice is Ghislaine de Boysson, a lovely model born to an old French family. Ghislaine and Larry are given the use of a house on the beach at Malibu, within easy driving distance of both Henry and Anaïs: the trio of the Villa Seurat Series is together once more.

Dear Larry –

[. . .] I'm glad you were here to witness the riots, the fires, the looting. So American! You can see what savages we still are – and I don't mean the Negroes. The country is splitting more and more – like in pre-Civil War days, I feel. If we don't get that man Johnson out of the White House soon it'll be bloody hell. (I wonder if you got to Chicago, or if the visit had to be cancelled. That is one of the worst cities in America.)

Got two small reviews of the B.B.C. showing of ½ hour of our documentary film. In one they said that in the pool I looked like "an early Primate but later in the studio, dressed, like a Tibetan lama". How's that?

Well, I feel like that old 'un in *Lost Horizon* – remember, the Belgian with one leg off, who was supposed to be 140 years old? Was laid up a few days from food poisoning (or over-eating, in Italian restaurant). I thought I was going to die – the pains were so bad. And I never call a doctor till I'm better – exactly what I did this time. Anyway, the thought of death becomes more and more appealing to me. How long must I hang on, and for what good? I smile when you write me about opportunities to travel, to do this and that. Man, I don't have that vitality any more, nor the desire to move about in the world. I can feel my powers diminishing week by week. Soon I'll be in my dotage, if I haven't already entered it. (However, when Hoki returns I'll see if I can't work out some music with her. I doubt she'll let me – has to do things her own way.) Tonight, while the commercials were given over T.V., I started playing Tony's drum – and was surprised how well I did at first try. Instead of storming Heaven I may drum my way in. Then I went to the piano, and you know, even though I disregarded laws of harmony (to say nothing of counterpoint) it sounded like music to me. The idea is to play *as if* you were really playing. Try it some time!

What's getting me down is insomnia. I'm quite sure I don't have the gout, but there's something gnawing at my little toe. I get up at 3⁰⁰ or 4⁰⁰ A.M. and take a sleeping pill. That don't do nobody no good, as the folks say. I'm sick of pills. Maybe I ought to just get up and stay up (at 3 or 4) like you do – stay up till I fall down.

To change the tune . . . . . . if the peace parley is held in *Paris* we'll really be shown up for what we are – plus riots, marches, window smashing, etc.

Now I'm getting drowsy – only 1³⁰ A.M. Will hop into bed and see if

I can do a good sleep. Last night I had one of the most wonderful and terrible nightmares ever. It was so vivid that even after I was up a few minutes I was still in it. Maybe I can get back into it again tonight. Now the magic formula – "Nam myoho renge kyo!"

Cheers, salut, long life!
Henry

Nam myoho . . .: Reverence to the sûtra of the Lotus of the Good Law, a mantra expressing the unity of mind and body, the mysteries of life, the law of cause and effect, and the sounds of the universe.

---

*Sommières Gard France   May sixth [1968]

Dear Henry;
just got your letters, and brief card from Hoke saying your show was a great success; what a pity you didn't go instead of staying home to watch that abominable telly with its moronic ten-second commercials. I felt quite ill in New York after two evenings of it. Anyway everything went off very well and I have got back here footsore and weary; am settling down to a mountain of correspondence. Amusing your reaction to *Bonnie and Clyde* – namely violence against violence; it's not on a sufficiently high scale of values to be worth anatomising, but what I found so interesting (as a contrast to the Dillinger type film where you wait for the police to get him) was precisely that the two lovers were asses, not really thugs. I read it like a US version of the Babes in the Wood. They knew not what the hell they were doing, this is what was frightening on the moral *plan*; its application to young America (or young England for that matter – for England has become a sub-culture of the US now) was not only accurate but terrifying. To do ill without having any value in mind which the act represents – that is what flatters the young by the accuracy of its portrayal, that's why they like it. It excuses them, because they feel they are like that – not bad, but just *lost*. I wish you'd come with us, and we had spent the evening talking about it. On another *plan* as a foreigner I liked the reconstruction of the old far west mythology of the twenties, the cars and the clothes – it had great appeal. Anyway, as I say, it ain't a great work of art; but it did interest me. I am besieged by requests to do a travel book about the USA and would really like to. I saw your haunts in N York, by the way; much much cleaner and sprucer than corresponding places in London and

427

Paris. I thought NY a beautiful homey town, and met some marvellous characters there. Yes, as soon as I finish the next book I'll plan a long ragged ride through the States in my little caravan and winkle up a book. Seen a lot of Miriam and Diane Deriaz – both coming down for a week. The Fielding bunch send love, as do we all. Marcelle made a hit on my last television programme (Paris) and is now the belle of the town.

more soon, much love; keep off the pills. Do some elementary Yoga (seriously) and use hot water for sleep inducing.

Larry

*[Pacific Palisades]   May 13, 1968

Dear Larry,

I had just written Hoki two days ago that you were probably in Greece by now and here comes your letter from Sommières. But I take it you *will* be leaving soon for Greece, non? I mention it because Hoki now has a chance to go to Paris to interview the Japanese wife of Sukarno for some Japanese magazine. And I have been warning her to think twice before going to Paris now – because of the riots – five days of it now – which I think will continue all during the Peace talks. By now over a thousand policemen have been injured, not to speak of the students. That's quite something, much more than occurred in any of our bloody riots in the Negro quarters. Much much more! [. . .]

So you're still thinking of coming over in the Spring and touring the States, are you? Not me, my lad. I've had it. What I wrote in the *Nightmare* is duck soup compared to what has to be said today about America. If ever a revolution were possible in this country, which I strongly doubt, then we are on the verge of one now. The Blacks are not going to be put down, they're not going to wait indefinitely. And, it's not only the Blacks – the poor white trash is just as bad off. You'll see, if ever you travel through the south. Tomorrow begins the Poor People's sitdown in Washington, D.C. I hope you'll be able to watch it on TV. It will be an eye-opener. It is admitted now that we have about 15,000,000 people in this country who are starving, which means not even one decent meal a day. We used to have plenty of money for guns, but even that no longer holds. We are bankrupt, physically as well as morally. The Viet Cong hold the trump card at the Peace Conference. They can go on indefinitely, but not us.

I just knocked out about nine pages on *Bonnie & Clyde*. A diatribe, of course. Am sending it out to a dozen different countries. You'll say I'm ranting, making too much of it, but do you know, whenever I think of this bloody film I am furious, still furious. You have a wonderful, broad threshold of tolerance. Somehow violence is one of the things I can't stand. Which reminds me . . . last night, 1:00 A.M., while taking a walk around the block, suddenly a car stops short beside me and two teenagers, evidently on dope, begin to bully me, threaten me, curse me. I wasn't far from the house, so I just kept walking, they following. I thought at one point they would jump out and tackle me, but fortunately they didn't. And I who talk about violence, do you know what was in my mind then? To let them follow me right to the house, let them follow in after me, and then I'd go get my razor sharp machete, which I keep handy, and cut them to ribbons. This sort of slaughter, you see, I regard as "justifiable". Afterwards I began trembling. Not because of what they might have done to me, but what I might have done to them! Beware of the peace lovers, I always say. Beware of the just man! Do you know what it is to dance with rage? That's what I do inwardly again and again. Fortunately I always wear my Buddha-like mask.

Well, enough of this . . . . If you see Joey in Greece give him a good hug for me. I'm eager too to see what old Katsimbalis looks like on the screen. Oh yes, I saw David Frost on the telly recently, here in U.S., but must say I didn't like him, not at all. Good thing we never locked horns. Give me Cassius Clay any day. Best to Marcelle, the dear trollop, and tell her her predictions seem to be doubly true. Especially for Hoki. Alors, hoki-doki and une bonne pétarade pour tout le monde.

> Henry-San
> Alias Val or Harry
> Cheers!
> Henry

*SOMMIÈRES – (Gard) 30 – France   June 22 [1968]

Dear Henry. I hope all is well, hasn't Hoke touched down as yet the gallivanting creature? I've just taken Marcelle de toute urgence to the hospital: a mixture of fulminating appendix and fibroids they say: so she will be away for at least two weeks which is an awful bore. I had all the period of the strike alone in this house. On the other hand I am waiting with impatience for the visit of my acrobat of the high trapeze Diane Deriaz. Her story is a singular one, can't remember if I told you about her: a star of the trapeze at the Tabarin she became friends with the whole Picasso Eluard Audiberti circle; I think this could only happen in France – that a trapeze performer born and bred to the circus could become a deeply cultivated and intelligent (and beautiful) woman and be the close friend of writers and painters. Well, I was on an Air France plane for London when a very pretty hostess saw I was reading Eluard's poems and said she was a friend of his. The plane was empty, she found some champagne and sat by me to talk about Picasso's early days, Montmartre etc. Clever, warm-hearted, spontaneous, candid. I was completely charmed by her, asked her to dinner in Paris. We spent up to four in the morning in the Closerie and then did a walk across Paris like students. Her life story is absolutely fascinating. But her career came to an end with a crash; she had invented a new fall which she missed and cracked her skull. No good for the high wire she simply couldn't stay on the ground, took a job as a hostess; visited Eliot in London, has a mountain of adoring letters from John Hayward. THEN she fell for Japan, learned Japanese and was loaned to Japanese Airlines by Air France and spent years doing the Tokio run. We had no love affair alas but an immense sympathie, and kept in cheerful and loving touch with postcards and Xmas cards. She is so shy and virginal that the whole of the artist set nicknamed her the pucelle, and Audiberti dedicated his play about Joan of Arc to her under that title. Much beloved and a real woman she is really quite irresistible and I have asked her to come and be my secretary – she is just forty and has been retired from Air France. She has much of the shy virginal side of Anaïs, but accompanied by tremendous drive and warmth. Well, truthfully, it's a mix of Anaïs and Claude. Anyway, I won't bore you with more; she's coming on the tenth. She's infected me with her goddamn shyness too, and I simply wouldn't begin to imagine how to set about making love to her, I mean if she wanted, which one day she might. She's only had one lifelong lover and he died the same week as Claude. At the moment she's mooching about Paris translating Japanese children's books. O dear, I must be an awful fool; but it isn't possible not to like this woman quite hard. No other news. I have three smashing songs for a musical about Ulysses which I'm writing from sheer boredom. There are other small adventures, some touching and strange; but nothing that shifts the epicentre. We shall see what Diana has to tell.

O there is something else – I met an agent who told me that the Maugham estate is bankrupt because of the tremendous U.S. death duties. *Despite* the fact that he wasn't domiciled there ever. You had better have your accountant take a rain check on this aspect; it may pay you to spread the money away now in packets instead of just losing it to the state. I think you can do this over three years . . . anyway have a think. I am getting Curtis Brown to get me a lawyer's report on my U.S. dollars so I can devise a way of sidestepping such an eventuality.

> love to everyone
> Larry

*444 ocampo drive – pacific palisades california   July 9th, 1968

[margins decorated with stamped word 'CUNT'. Printed card attached: 'FUCK somebody TODAY!!']

> Dear Larry,
Hoki's been back about two weeks now – did a number of extra things for herself – like 12 songs for Sony and perhaps a good part in a Japanese film, when she returns in September. She came home via Hong Kong, Bangkok, Rome, where she was to interview Sukarno's Japanese wife – but it fell through. Anyway, she got my *Bonnie & Clyde* piece published in the first number of a new Japanese mag called *My Way* and when she goes back they may have her do a monthly column on America regularly. Here it seems impossible to get together to do any song writing. At least so far. I heard the Japanese version of my song – from tape she made – and also a version by my friend Gimpel, the concert pianist. Both sound catchy – and of course utterly different. I note what you say about lyrics. I tried deliberately for a sentimental, romantic effect in that first one; if I could get Hoki to sit down with me I might do them in different style – more zany or Surrealistic like – a mulligatawny of words and phrases from outer space. The trouble is I am not versatile like you. You can turn your hands in any direction.

Great news, say I, about Diane Deriaz. Maybe she's with you now. Too bad she wasn't there when Hoki and I were visiting you. When I finish a rough translation of Madame Nogi's letter to her niece "on marriage", I may send it to you to show her. I want to write it out in

431

my best handwriting, frame it, and put it over my bed. It's the only recipe for a successful marriage, but no one wants to believe it any more. The woman has to act like a queen and the man, to be sure, like a king. Where do we find such like today. The suchness of it all is lost, buried, forgotten. [. . .]

To come back to Diane Deriaz whom I would love to meet – remember in Paris at our apartment, before cards were read, I said I had a hunch about you? (And didn't Marcelle also tell you something similar when we were at your place?) Well, I feel it's coming. Like it or not you're hooked, me lad. And it will be good for you. I don't know why you should feel discouraged about another mate in your life. It's the spice of life, even when it goes wrong. I felt bad seeing you tramp about that big house of yours alone at all hours of the day and night. It wasn't natural.

I enclose a note for Marcelle. Love from Hoki-San.

Ta ta now!
Henry

*444 ocampo drive – pacific palisades california   Nov. 7th 1968

Dear Larry – Just a few words from bed – down with flu which Puko brought me from Capri! Today, Mai Zetterling called but Gerald answered phone. I'll talk to her tomorrow. Hope she's all her films promise! (I liked Anouk Aimée when we met – very sincere.) The ménage here – yes, always exciting with 3 Japanese "Omankos" (Honorable Cunts). They laugh all the time – and I really have wonderful conversations with them, especially Michiyo (my former teacher) and Puko, who is really a wonderful soul. Hoki due back this weekend. What about that wonderful "acrobat" you met on the plane? Dying to know what came of it. I hope you keep experimenting. No matter how many times it fails, a new romance is always worth while.

Strick is back – was fired! Will see him in a few days.

That *Playman* mag. (*Bonnie & Clyde*) was authorized by me. I thought you meant it appeared in a French revue. (Do you ever see *Executive* – Italian revue? Like *Playboy* or *Esquire* but with better *nudes*.)

Joey writes he may have to leave Greece. Gov't wont' let foreigners have perpetual residence. However, he's appealing. Wants to hang on to perfect his *subjunctives*!!

432

Give warm greetings to the lady from Nîmes. Give her enclosed card – with translation. (Why don't you marry her? *I* would at the drop of the hat.) (Barkis always willin'.) Listen, if a guy named Elman writes you ever for help with a book about me, don't answer. He's a bore. So are they all. And now we have a clod like Nixon for President. What's new? A warm hug.

Henry

*Sommières, Gard – 30 – France   Feb 16. 1969

Dear Henry; a quick line to hope that you are well, all of you; my most recent news of you is very encouraging. I saw Mai Zetterling two days ago and she gave me an account of a call she paid on you with David her husband; found you in wonderful form apparently. She adores you – and is herself rather an adorable woman I think. Also Simone Perier rang me the other day and said she'd had a pleasant note from you – made her very proud as she is *the* Fan of Fans as far as you are concerned. Picture in her room and all that – long *before* she knew I knew you, I mean. I have been busy and travelling – spent nearly a month in London helping Margaret McCall tidy up the film we shot in Paris, which is really a series of interviews with people like Brassaï and Eleonore [Hirt]. It makes a really very interesting one hour film and my Parisians come up with tremendous punch and éclat fully justifying the reputation of the capital for wit and intelligence. Then I came back here, caught a pretty nice Asiatic flu, and at last locked myself up for a whole month, seeing not a soul. I've managed to push the second volume of *Tunc* to within about fifty pages of the end and if I can keep the heat on like this should be through in April some time. Ouf. Giroux has just finished the translation of *Tunc* and somewhat to my surprise tells me that the French who've read it are bowled over by it – an unusual thing seeing how allusive and elliptical it is. Anyway it comes from Gallimard in May. But meanwhile a book of essays on places comes from Dutton and Faber in April; may have some small things you like, or places you could compare with your own memories of . . . I'll send it anyway. I haven't yet fixed up any plans for this summer but we were going to film Katsimbalis' Athens in June – but he says that he is bedridden with rheumatoid arthritis so I don't know what the hell is going to happen as yet. Failing that I shall just stay here I guess, perhaps with a short flip to Italy which I would like to know a lot better than I do.

We had planned a trip to the USA this year but Gerry hasn't been at all well and feels unequal to a long trip; thinks he will rest up in Corfu where they are filming his crazy book about the Durrells. Meanwhile *Justine* is moving forward, and now there is some talk of filming my translation of the Royidis *Pope Joan* which should be fun enough. Nothing else much; I am beginning to feel my age – don't laugh. Click click go the bones when I do my Yoga. Never mind. I am getting used to living alone, and think that it is probably the nicest way to live after forty – if one can de mother fixate enough not to feel the need for mother substitutes around all the time. The ideal is just to have them to dinner and to stay an occasional night when one doesn't feel too old, no?

> much love to you all
> keep the brushes flying
> Larry

Besides 'essays', mainly on travel, *Spirit of Place*, edited by Alan G. Thomas, contains among other items a selection of letters, plus generous excerpts from Durrell's first two novels, *Pied Piper of Lovers* and *Panic Spring*.

*Ritz-Carlton, Montreal   Sept. 3rd 1969

Dear Larry –

I've just come from seeing *Justine* here in Montreal. Am somewhat bewildered, largely because I couldn't catch all the dialogue. Also because things seemed to have been juggled about a bit. I must say I liked the scenes, brief though they were, of – where? Egypt, Algeria, Tunisia? Made me wish I had seen Alexandria and Cairo, the desert, the sea, the temples and mosques. Lots of color. Lots of drunken carnival scenes. Melissa seemed badly cast. Anouk Aimée rather good, I thought. But Pursewarden and Darley bothered me – the latter too young, too naif. (In a physical way, though, he reminded me of you at 22 or '3 or '4.) Was it Michael York? and what part did Dirk Bogarde play? I think the ones who came off best were the homos and transvestites! Hollywood had fun with them, I take it. That opening with the sailors giving the girl a dose of Spanish Fly seemed awful to me. Narouz did quite well but Nessim no. Oh well, these are only *my*

434

reactions ... I think Shamroy did well with the photography. One really good touch was the variety of interesting masks used during the carnival. Reminded me of Marcel Marceau's collection of masks – and his antics as he tried each one on. (Coming down the staircase.) I wonder if you have seen the film yourself yet? Naturally you'll squirm. It could hardly be otherwise. No film can ever live up to a good book. I remember recently walking out during the intermission of *War & Peace*. Bored to death. [. . .]

If you think *Justine* puzzling, go see Bresson's *Une Femme douce*. Couldn't make head nor tail of it, even when it was explained to me. Soon comes my turn – with *Cancer* and *Quiet Days*. Ouf! Did I tell you that the guy who plays me in *Quiet Days* is a homo? That makes my hair curl. But I like the black & white quality – especially for Paris street scenes. I left without phoning you – forgive me!

A good hug and say hello to Marcelle for me,
Henry

In the *Justine* film, Michael York played Darley, Dirk Bogarde Pursewarden, Anouk Aimée the title role, and Anna Karina was Melissa.

---

*Sommières, Gard – 30 – France   12 September. 1969

Dear Henry; It was good to get your long letter from Montreal and see that you were in fine fettle – though disconcerting to think of you sitting through Hollywood's *Justine*. By comment from friends I gather it's the worst film ever made of a decent book; but the press has been so damned charitable that I began seriously to wonder if perhaps it had been bribed by XXth Century. It would seem logical with such vast expenditure, such overheads, and such shoddy work. Perhaps you too will receive such anodyne guff for the dreadful *Tropic* they are embalming. Well ... I have half written my musical and at last found a musician eager to collaborate on it; who knows, we might get it on! It would make me laugh. I tried my best to interest Hoki on the idea of collaborating but she seems to have turned against the piano and the writing of music in favour of singing it. Well, she does this well, and she brought me a fine disc, but I regretted that he [Southam?] couldn't raise interest in my Ulysses libretto. However, tomorrow we'll see what Anthony Hopkins makes of it. For the rest I have the whole BBC in my hair with colour cameras; Margaret McCall is making a film, supposedly about me but in fact mostly about the landscape hereabouts, and more particularly about tramps – l'homme sans attaches; they are quite a feature of this land, in a way more typical than bulls and horses and the blasted folklore which is kept going for tourists from Belgium. I don't yet know what we can make of it all but the scenery should stand up all right.

I've finished and delivered the second volume of *Tunc*, and to my surprise and relief it seems really quite good – at least worthy as a successor to the *Quartet*. Now what? I don't know. This winter I shall make some cartoons. (I've started painting again for a show in Paris.) Think I shall be in New York in March, and if I can snatch a week end I'll fly over and say Hullo. Or vice versa if chance brings you the other way. Marcelle has good things to say about you being in fine working mood this spring, and she usually knows. She also threatens me with another blonde woman . . . ouf. I hope not. I'm beginning to get that faded feeling.

For the rest peace and silence and the swimming pool, though unheated, is a delight and a relaxation; we hope to keep swimming until October.

Everyone here sends love; now that I know you are coming down to Paris for Xmas I feel that the distance isn't so vast and that I might even get you down here for a rest. See how it plays. I finish this film October 15; then Paris and Geneva for a very few days, then back here to lock myself up.

> every good thing
> Larry

Durrell's *Ulysses Come Back* (Turret Records, 1970), better described as notes for a musical than as a complete work, was produced by Wallace Southam and performed by Durrell with Belle Gonzales (soprano), Pat Smythe (piano) and Jeff Clyne (bass).

*[Pacific Palisades]   1/4/69 [i.e. 1970]

> Dear Larry –

Forgive tardiness in replying to your last two letters. Much doing here and I have neglected the c/s. I won't be coming to Paris till the warm weather arrives. I just can't take a Paris winter any more. Tony seems to be doing quite well on his own.

Besides the *Cancer* film *Quiet Days* will also be coming out about the same time – March of this year. Barney Rosset will distribute the latter here in the States, which virtually insures it being a box office success.

I am going thru inner upheavals, partly because of age, partly as a result of foolish behavior. I think this year will see me doing new, strange things. Don't be surprised at any thing.

Will we be seeing your documentary film here in the States? Let me know a bit in advance if or when you're likely to come to L.A. It's just possible I won't be here then. I'm sort of taking the bit in my teeth, if you get what I mean.

It's about 2⁰⁰ A.M. At four I'll take a sleeping pill. At noon I'll rise from the dead. St. Augustine said – "Love God and do as you please!" I'm taking the hint.

Cheers now!
All the best for 1970.
Henry

*Sommières, Gard – 30 – France   FEBRUARY TENTH 1970

DEAR HENRY

Your last letter was full of dark thoughts and stranger insinuations, and I couldn't tell what the hell you was up to, if anything at all; but I hear from spies that you have struck oil again and are watercolouringaway like mad. This is only a brief note to give you my various landfalls which might by luck coincide with yours. I arrive in New York, appropriately enough, on St Patrick's Day. I haven't yet had an itinerary from Dutton and don't know whether I'll be flying about the States at all or staying put in New York (at the Algonquin again, my little dreamboat). I shall be in London March one to stay with Alan Thomas for ten days and kick the book off there before coming to USA. I only tell you this because rumour has it that you are coming to Paris in April to see Tony – a French television star says that you have agreed to do a programme on you in which I am supposed to help you off with your coat and gloves and ask you dazzling questions about Jesus. I don't know how much truth there is in all this, but I am aiming to get back to France at the tail end of April on my way back here. I have to make a disc of my musical in London before I do – Wallace Southam came down for a week and has put it all on paper. I think it's

437

funny and good in parts. I'm just finishing a sort of poetic diary called the Vampire Notebook which I hope to read in New York. Not much else to record. Some crazy adventures of no importance; they can keep for gossip over a drink in a speakeasy. A ground map for a new book just sketching itself. Some good new poems.

> Much love to you all;
> if I can I'll come to tea.
> cheers
> Larry

The Red Limbo Lingo: A Poetry Notebook was published by Dutton in 1971.

*444 Ocampo Drive, Pacific Palisades, California   2/27/70

Dear Larry –

Tony is now in Montreal. If I do anything, I'll go to Japan with Hoki about end of April. That's all nonsense about my doing T.V. with you in Paris. Don't think I'll get to Paris this year – but then one never knows. If I go East I'd love to see *Penang* – ever hear of it?

So you'll be in N.Y. on St. Patrick's Day! *Erin go bragh!* Try and make it out here, if you can. Room to spare upstairs. Hoki and I are living apart at present but on very good terms – better than ever.

Cancer film opened in N.Y. at the Paris Cinema on 58th & 5th Ave. last week. Mixed reviews by critics. Waiting for release of *Quiet Days* – maybe in May. May be a real "shocker", I hear.

I wish I knew how to parcel out my time, like you. I hardly get anything done – except letters. All crazy about my W.C. fiesta! Wish it were true.

Anaïs is in N.Y. getting medical treatment. Think she'll be back here before you arrive in N.Y.

Getting exciting letters from French women fans recently – result of *Sexus* by Buchet, I suppose.

Met Isaac Bashevis Singer, the Yiddish writer – my favorite – recently. We talked about Knut Hamsun – his *Mysteries* especially. Strange, but if I could, I would still like to write like Hamsun. ("Good morning, Fröken, is it permitted to touch your *puff* today?" Remember?) Did you get copies of *The Booster* – *Delta* yet? Sells for $25^{oo} a copy – ordinary edition. The signed copies at $50^{oo}. Who'd have thunk it back in the '30's?

438

Alors, c'est tout pour le moment. Tout va bien à présent. A part l'arthrite, le coeur, le cou et d'autres choses. On ne vit qu'une fois. Et c'est bien assez!

Cheers! Henry

*444 OCAMPO DRIVE, PACIFIC PALISADES,
CALIFORNIA   May 4ᵗʰ 1970

Dear Larry –
Last night (at half-past midnight or "Totsi Vahetzi" in Hebrew) I tuned in on your conversation with a Mr. Neuman on our T.V. What a wonderful performance you gave! I was going to send you a cable then & there but the telegraph office was closed. I enjoyed (and was instructed(!)) by your elucidation of Groddeck's theories. Remember you putting me onto him years ago. Also the bit on time-space continuum – excellent. What a mind, what a memory you have! You know, you're just made for T.V. You answer so easily, so readily, so "pungently" questions that would floor me. [. . .]
Alors – I didn't go to Tokyo, Q.E.D. Decided I'm not ever going to travel any where if I can help it. It's a bore. I am absent when traveling. I need too many comforts and conveniences. Much easier traveling in the head, what! Hoki of course went – had to, for work. She's sore, naturally, that I disappointed her. But I'm tremendously relieved. Am at peace, feel healthy, no dearth of females here, "happy days are here again", etc. etc. This is a big year for me, apparently – in many ways. I'm getting on the Path again, slippery though it be. Soon I'll join up with the "Ein Sof". Give my best to Simone Perier and to Marcelle. Treat yourself well. You seem in fine shape. And you're still a "charmer". Never say die!

Cheers! Henry

*30 – Sommières – France   May 12 [1970]

Dear Henry; my only regret about the Jap trip is selfish; you hinted that you were coming back via France, and this would have given me the chance to see you either in Paris or here. In fact, this is what reconciled me to being turned back by snow in Chicago; I figured that I would see you in a month or so, so I didn't worry unduly. Damn. But travel is

439

tiring I know, and you tend to make it an expedition each time. Should just arrive and not let anyone know; it is still possible in Paris if you choose a way out quartier or a big right bank hotel, or even Sommières where your balcony has become much looked at as a "spot" in history. I am just back and resting up; I had the most tremendous bit of luck. Suddenly Fiddle Viracola rang me from London, having arrived unexpectedly; I invited her down and we spent a week together here, all solitary, with wood fires and walks across the garrigues in the rain, and visits to the old mazet to pick lilacs and so on. A wonderful spell. I put her on the New York plane yesterday with love and kisses; she was sad and so was I. But I have got too old to regret anything – and indeed regrets at such a perfect experience would be unworthy of it. Now I am back in harness, walking three hours a day and sleeping calm. Last night the Temples came to dinner. [. . .] They behave as if they had never seen food before; and I reproach Eliane for having made me disrespectful to Flaubert. I thought he had *invented* Mme Bovary. But no. He just copied Eliane or some other wearisome provincial like her – sad fag end of the precieuse of the dix-huitième with a mentality planted in her by *Elle*; the modern programmed middle class woman. O dear. After Fiddle with her gay nonsense and her frequent Wows and Superwows and New York slang it was all flat and funless. [. . .] I am still waiting for the California television project (two months on a yacht in Greece) to firm up. No other plans; cleaning the pool out for summer.

    Every good thing.
    Larry

*Sommières, Gard – 30 – France   FOURTH OCT 1970

Dear Henry; when one hasn't written for a month or two one has the feeling that an eternity has gone by and that one will never make up the leeway – let me see, where do I start . . . Strangely enough though I have been moving about it has all been in little flashes to Paris or London etc. The summer, after I got back fron N.Y., was fairly static. I was holding everything for the Greek trip promised by the Californian TV, but they left it too late and perhaps have forgotten altogether as film people tend to do. I made a comic disc of Ulysses and his girls in London which you'll be getting soon. Then I came back here to make a longish telefilm in French for Michèle Arnaud – I think you rather liked her songs awhile ago. My brother turned up as well with his entourage of females, he travels with a permanent seraglio like a Turkish potentate (or do I mean imbroglio? It often amounts to the same thing). We fooled about and made an amusing film, all rather Pagnol, with Marcelle in great fettle acting the fool in a Midi accent. Wrote a couple of pop tunes in French for Annie la Mome. For a while the house was full of cinema people (Miriam came down to interview me). It was not unlike one of your rodeo shows out there on the coast. Then everything went quiet for awhile; McCall came through on her way through to Italy to film. And then came a call from London – Fiddle Viracola on the line. So I had the adorable monster sweetheart down to stay for a week or two and tried to repay a little of her kindness and sweetness to me in New York and Chicago (Rush Street blues). She adored it here, the calm and quiet, the long walks and good food, and music and NO television. Meanwhile I was preparing my expo of paintings for November 4 (under the name of Oscar Epfs) and we had to somehow take them up to Paris in my little battle wagon, which we duly did: delivering them safely to the gallery in Rue de Seine. Fiddle had a few days in Paris doing the sights, and meeting up with quite a lot of her compatriots, and I think she was rather sad to fly back to London at the end of it. Anyway several WOW letters since then. At present she is singing selections from Hullo Dolly to 50000 card holding Pure Land Buddhists in Japan in a temple the size of Grand Central – or do I mean Central Park? She is meeting the Prime Minister and all the top brass – if she doesn't come back with the shinbone of Sakyamuni on a velvet cushion she's not the girl I think she is. Paris was slow and full of petrol fumes; and of course everyone wanted news of you, and when were you coming and so on . . . The desire to please overcame me (I couldn't say NEVER) and so I said next spring. As a matter of fact both Fiddle's seer and Marcelle think you will see Europe again quite soon, for what such prophecies are worth. All this distracting twaddle has enabled me to mark time and start trying to firm up the outlines of a new novel – I hope to row it away from the shore some time this winter. After the jamboree with the paintings I'll come back here and clear all the decks for a winter of work. The pool makes a huge difference to this house; haven't seen the sea this year, nor missed it a bit. Saw the Fieldings yesterday with Jimmie Stern and Mai Zetterling and they all send love and hugs. I hope things are going swimmingly with you – you sounded gay and confident in your last line. Keep it up.

Simone Perier rings me up to talk about you – you've made a killing there! And of course the Temples. My daughter Saph is just going up to University of York. Barry, Claude's boy with whom you played chess, is a naval radio officer, very handsome and kind.

> Every good thing from us all
> Larry

The exhibition of paintings was held at Marthe Nochy's bookstore and art gallery, Librairie de Seine.

Marcel Pagnol: prolific Provençal film director and playwright whose favourite character actor was Raimu.

*444 ocampo drive – pacific palisades california   Oct. 5th 1970

Dear Larry – wherever you may be now!
A thousand pardons for not writing sooner. It's getting more and more difficult each day to do what I have to do or ought to do or hope to do. My life seems to be one of utter disorder and procrastination. It's also full of problems and they get tougher as I get older and more foolish. I won't bore you with details but believe me they are staggering sometimes, and of course all of my own making. Yet, strangely enough I am not unhappy.

And, listening to that delightful recording you sent me – to say nothing of Fiddle's messages – I gather that you too are rolling beautifully with the punches.

This frightful, senseless "activity" (is it?) in which every one seems involved really gets me down. It's like an invasion of locusts. I don't know how many times I say No, no, no! but just one little Yes brings about an avalanche of the futile and absurd.

Recently I had a letter from a new Zen group in Paris asking me to be an honorary member and so on. This because of what I said about Zen on some T.V. program (French). I quickly informed them that I am far from being their (supposed) man. A reader I am, yes, but a be-er, no!

Well, the recording. You know, I began laughing when I heard your opening. Somehow you reminded me strongly of good old Noel Coward, whom I used to put down, but whom I have come to admire, even adore (sic) after seeing him on T.V. several times – in long interviews. It's a jolly good attempt, this sketch, as you call it. Must have been fun to do. What's remarkable (to me) is that you manage to find the time to do the things you like to do. Bravo! When people ask that idiotic

442

question – "And what are you working on now, Mr. Miller?" – I can and always do truthfully answer – "Nothing!" But it's not the "nothing" that I believe in. It's an *involuntary* nothing, if you know what I mean.

And how and where is Fiddle these days? Will you tell her I think of her when you see or write her again, please.

I'm sending you separately an announcement about (2) lithos. Read the text that goes with the lithos – *in the circular*.

I hear that my play (*Harry*) will go on at the Olympia, Paris, in French in late November. Ho ho! Take it nice and easy now.

Cheers! Henry

*Le Royal, 212, BOULEVARD RASPAIL, PARIS-XIVᵉ,   28 Jan. 71.

Dear Henry – I am sitting at the Dôme waiting for Michèle and I thought to send you a wee signal. Our famous correspondence has rather lapsed. It's my fault. Whenever I think about starting a new book I get into depression and become quite incommunicando. I'm here in Paris for a couple of days but already pining for the quiet of Sommières. Had my two beautiful daughters down for Christmas. Saph the baby is simply dazzling for beauty and brains and is going to be a poet I think – she already writes well at 18. I had a wonderful time with them. Had plum puddings sent down from Paris. Now the house feels rather lonely. I try to cheer myself up with a whole daisy-chain of love affairs – but it doesn't really work, and the more indifferent one gets the more people seem to fall for you. Paris is particularly annoying – it puts you in a 'mauvaise posture' – you feel you ought to be in love and since you can't make it any more you feel frustrated and become cruel – 'les caresses brutales' – and so forth. Perhaps this spring – I shall be 59 in February – everything will change and some magnetic female will emerge from the jungle!

I have started a queer sort of novel about the gnostic heresies, the Templars etc etc. It's still all very fragile and may well jolt to a stop before I finish it. I don't suppose you are bothering to write any more. My painting expo. in Paris was a great success and I sold awfully well considering everything. Well, that's all the news for 1970. I'm still alive, single, and living in the gaunt old house and trying to keep working – it's the only lifeline I think.

Every good thing for 71, old friend. Love to everyone.

Larry △ .

Dear Larry –

Am slow in responding. Seem to be in and out of bed a lot lately.
Nothing serious – just frail and vulnerable – and awfully tired. Too many
projects in hand all the time. Can never seem to find free time to do what
I want to do. Intend to write rather fulsomely about Mishima's suicide.
Seems to have some strange meaning for me. Makes me do what the
French call "un examen de conscience". Or, a revaluation of values –
personal values.

One of my beloveds is now in Tokyo, another in Hong Kong. Gives
me the chance to write more love letters. While I don't wish to marry
again, I am not averse to falling in love over and over again. In fact, I am
dead unless I am in love. You sounded so disillusioned in your last – I
mean, about love, women, marriage. And you are still so young. You
shouldn't worry about making another mistake. Mistakes are healthy
too, don't forget. Just so long as you can forget yourself, any thing goes.

Did I ever send you the big "Broadside" about the *Insomnia* book/
portfolio? I sent Simone Perier a set of the W.C. reproductions which
go with the text of the book.

We had an earthquake here, as you probably heard, but no damage
done in this neighborhood. However, the quake was strong and rather
terrifying. I only reacted to it some eight hours later – typical of me.
One day this whole coast is going to slip into the sea.

Tony hopes to get a dishonorable discharge as a deserter (2 years a
deserter!) and soon as he is free will write a book about his experiences.

Give my love to Marcelle. She sent me a lovely Valentine Day's
greeting . . . . I got Gerald Sykes's book and have been reading here and
there. (Not too bad on "music".) Cheers now; wassail, gung-ho!

Henry

*Sommières, Gard – 30 – France   19 February 1971.

Dear Henry; it was a pleasant surprise to get your letter this fine sunny
morning; still traces of snow among the vines, left over from a short
but fierce winter spell which has only just ended; and as if totally
unaware of temperatures the almond blossom has come out. I am

letting the mazet to my brother this summer; he wants to make an insect film based on Fabre. [...] No, I'm peevish and spoiled I guess; don't seem to be able, precisely, to get close to anyone any more. Of course lots of adventures, but I have a feeling that I'm cheating a bit by not being really committed. Menopause, I guess, but so far most of the women this last year have more irritated than turned me on. It will pass. Justement, last evening I went to Montpellier to meet a little girl full of sparks, and dined with the Temples; he spoke of you at length and was just sending you the Cabeza de Vaca. I think he has done a marvellous job on it – worthy of Giroux for insight and feel. You will see. I wrote Curtis Brown asking them to obtain me a copy of your HOKIBUKI, but then this postal strike closed in and now for the last six weeks there has been no movement of mail allowed. Alan Thomas is beside himself – his whole business is postal, sending out books. I am going up to Geneva this week to have a small check up, to see whether this persistent asthma-eczema complex I've been taking round the world this last year (making a mess of my temper and my love making alike) isn't perhaps a fish allergy caught by eating too much scrod in Grand Central Station Oyster Bar – a favourite haunt of mine. I'll send you something foolish from the town, probably jointly with Denis de Rougemont whom I shall see when there for long good talks. He missed the Nobel this year by very little; he's had a heart trouble which he looks after in the finest malt whiskey style. Myself I am laboriously starting on a new novel again, perhaps a bit prematurely; but I have found a theme which is congenial as well as real. I have always been intrigued by the catastrophic overnight collapse of the Templars, and the charges of heresy brought against them: also the mystery of WHY this order, so renowned for holiness, frugality – a huge army of 15,000 men, trained and armed and in perfect battle shape, and located in a chain of unbreachable fortresses stretching from France to Syria – why they should have allowed themselves to be disarmed, imprisoned, tortured and burnt at the stake, without uttering a word? They would have been capable of overturning France and Italy at a blow and taking charge. What happened? What was their sin? What turned them into rabbits? Everyone has their own view – mine is Syrian gnosticism with its roots in Alexandria or Oxyrhyncus. When I was idly reading about them I suddenly realised that in my travels I had unwittingly been posted always to one of their strong points, one of the places outremer where the so-called heresies were contracted. Taking Avignon as my apex, then, perhaps a modern novel with the sense of enchainment, of the complicity of Templar destiny? I don't know. I've only just started and it's all very fragile; like the second month after pregnancy, haven't decided whether to keep the foetus or to have an abortion. We shall see. Anyway the material is rich and sinister – and gnosticism is very contemporary, very hippy if you like, and the Cathars are coming back to haunt.

> Love to you all, keep happy and in love
> Larry

The reference here is to Haniel Long, *La Merveilleuse aventure de Cabeza de Vaca* (1970), translated from the English by F.-J. Temple.
The 'HOKIBUKI' is Miller's *Insomnia; or, The Devil at Large* (1971), inspired by his love for Hiroko Tokuda.

*444 ocampo drive – pacific palisades california   2/27/71

> Dear Larry –
> Got your good letter *of Feb. 19th* – this is just a quickie – more later. You mentioned the Gnostics. Curious, but just this morning I got a book called *La Cendre et les étoiles* par Jacques Lacarrière, Editions André Balland. It looks exciting – all about the great Gnostics. You say Gnosticism is very "contemporary"? The moment I opened the book (above) I felt as one does on hearing opening bars of a favorite symphony. I'm marking it up. [. . .] Henry

*Sommières, Gard – 30 – France   March 5. '71

> Dear Henry; just back from Geneva to find your letter; delighted you were so keen on the Lacarrière essay – I knew you would be.
I had Marthe Nochy send you one by air mail and a second to Denis; but the author had already sent him one. I was struck by the fact that this little essay could be a preface to the *Quartet* which is impregnated through and through with all I read and adopted philosophically chez the gnostics in Egypt. I had all the scattered texts – Mead, the Hermetica, Poemandres etc as well as the run of the Patriarchal Library, and the pre socratic philosophers. I added, of course, a wing to the building on the scientific side; Alexandria was the source of our science, and if the great library hadn't been burned down we'd surely find that

Niels Bohr and Heisenberg had been anticipated by them. Even the prose of the *Quartet* was intended to have the intermittency of quanta movements, non-deterministic that is – NON ASSOCIATIVE in the joyce sense which is a dead end. French writing is at such a low ebb, a real sargasso of pretentiousness and boredom that they are only just coming round to this notion – a rough analogy is what is called jump-cutting in cinema. The Tel Quel boys have a glimpse of the matter. But I did it ten years ago using the Pistïs Sophia and the Oxyrhyncus fragments as a point de départ. Anyway I had a very good evening with Denis who was equally abreast of all this stuff. But my goodness how few we are. I can only think of Michaux and Yves Bonnefoy perhaps who would value this sort of thing. Every one wants to talk Mao, nobody wants to talk Tao. What a BORE the world has become. I had my first medical check ever, nothing radical; alcohol gorged heart and ditto liver which means cutting down on the booze for a while, but nothing much else; mind you the doctors who examined would not have been capable of doing the double lotus on their heads which I now do for three minutes . . .

What else. I am taking a carbon of this letter con permesso for Michèle Arnaud who joined me in Geneva to meet Denis, was present with us, is reading the essay in question, and entertains the idea of doing a short film on you if you accept. She knows her stuff, has done a good job on me, and of course being French might not cut across your arrangements with that piece of inertia Snyder. I don't know about this but if she approaches you remember she is a friend and someone rather special. You may remember her work – she was and is still a very famous popular singer – now gradually changing into film producer. A girl for you really. Anyway so it goes.

For the rest I am slowly opening up my masked batteries to take this same subject from the rear, so to speak; after looking at Europe through the Alexandrian telescope, I have turned it round and am looking at Alex from here. Lacarrière's doesn't carry on the story of the dispersion of the gnostics with their great *refus* and their scattered broken remnants you can still meet in the heart of Bosnia. In Languedoc – O many places. I wonder if I can pull off an exciting and readable book once again? Let us suppose a sort of Rider Haggard written by Valéry.

Much love to Hoke; keep them fires alight. Mishima? But the Japanese are not sodden suicides like the Swedes; they can die because something is too beautiful, like a flower petal. Beauty as a grave danger, an aesthetic thrill brings on vertigo and death. Ask Hoki, she told me this when you were in Sommières.

cheers LARRY

*Sommières, Gard – 30 – France   FIFTH MAY SEVENTY ONE

Dear Henry;

No news for a little while which I hope is good news; mine is all much of a sameness, but a good deal of travel and some nice wildtrack adventures with delightful women == but alas I don't think the valiant Claude is easily replaceable so I have stopped trying to dig out a compagne from the surrounding vistas of personable young things which range from mere fluff to phantom matrons. They get altogether too encombrant, so they go the way of all flesh – grass words. I am firming up a version of what may well be my best novel if only I can get it the way I want it; and I have been casing up Avignon as well under the aegis of a lunch club which gives me greater amusement than anything Mr Pickwick thought up. Imagine lunching twice a fortnight outdoors under a tree with Raimu, Fernandel and company . . . and playing boules afterwards in a beret. It has been of the greatest help to me on the local history side – I have met a number of small savants – you know, the essential kind: schoolmasters who have written a monograph, a mayor with an interest in ghosts and buried treasure . . . All the people one can never find because one doesn't hear of them until years later. And the inevitable dark eyed Susan who forces one to dance the paso doble with imaginary castanets. So I am okay that way; in fact spoiled. This month Gerry my brother has taken the mazet for a year and is moving in this week. I have had rotten health (strange for me) this year – eczema acute, which has only just departed, I hope for good. On the other hand after two years of yoga smoking has just left me. (No act of will involved, which is so odd: like everyone else I have gone through the agony of willfully trying to stop it.) I say yoga because I haven't done or taken anything else which might account for the sudden indifference to tobacco. I have now stepped up my asanas to about an hour a day and can re-do things I never thought I would ever do again – like the lotus in the headstand, and the breathing lotus etc etc. Well, I shall be sixty next year; probably celebrate by a headstand lotus if I can still manage it. [. . .]

I have a new book of poems coming next month and will send you one from London town. It's all about Jesus and vampires and the blood of the lamb etc. A summer of visits and films faces me, and I don't know where to fly as yet. Perhaps Greece? The Fieldings are going and some other people too. Shall I in my little caravan? And who shall I take along?

much love,
keep things threshing about
Larry

*444 OCAMPO DRIVE, PACIFIC PALISADES, CALIFORNIA June 26, '71

Dear Larry –
That was a bitch of a deal at the hospital. First operation failed – had to undergo a second one in 24 hours. Put artificial artery in me from base of neck to groin, to have blood circulate in right leg. I still don't know if it is going to work. The foot is always half asleep (pins & needles) and the little toe burns like fury. Otherwise I'm OK. Slowly regaining lost strength. Don't dare smoke – and that's hard to bear sometimes. [. . .]
   I'm supposed to do a review of Hamsun's *Mysteries* (my favorite novel) for *N.Y. Times*. So far I haven't enough spirit to tackle it. But I'm delighted that this particular book is being republished. Don't suppose you ever read it. Dear Herr Nagel, dear Marthe Gude, dear old Minuten – and dear, lovely Dagny – Fröken Dagny! "Good morning, Fröken, is it permitted to touch your puff today?" (Ain't that delicious?)
   Was it you who sent me the French book on the *Gnostics*? I marked almost every page of it. Right up my street – and how! Before going to hospital I finished a 33 page article on Mishima, the Japanese author who committed hara-kiri. The Japanese mag. paid me $10,000⁰⁰ promptly for it. I couldn't believe it. Can you? Give my best to Simone, yes? A good hug,

   Henry

Dear Larry –

Just saw a British film (on T.V.) called *Term of Trial*, with Olivier and Simone Signoret. I was amazed how much alike you and Olivier look; have people told you that many times? Sometimes the resemblance was so strong I had to shake myself to assure myself it wasn't *you* I was looking at. Incidentally, I like him much better in these ordinary roles (he's a school teacher in this) than in the heroic ones. [. . .]

By the way, the operation was not *on* my leg, but *for* it. The artery leading to the foot was obstructed. *So* – they inserted an artificial one, running from the base of my neck to my groin. It sticks out under the skin like a drain pipe. The feel of the foot (and little toe) is not right yet, but I have hopes it will be normal in a month or two more. I now look better than before the operation – 'cause I take it nice and easy, eat well, get the sun, swim a bit, and so on. The strangest of all is that ever since entering the hospital I quit smoking and have had no struggle over it. Seems incredible – after 50 to 60 years of steady smoking. I don't have much desire to drink (alcohol) either – wine at dinner satisfies me. I suppose I'll soon be ready for the monastery – or the grave.

So you are plagued with visitors. It's the penalty for living in the country.

Naturally, if I were to put you and Olivier side by side the resemblance would suffer. But apart – well, I just can't get over it. The resemblance is greatest when you act very modest – a little sheepish, in fact. Even the tone of voice, the delivery . . . . well enuf! Look him over carefully next time you see him. And give him my love.

Cheers now!
Henry

*Sommières, Gard – 30 – France   August eleven, seventy one

Dear Henry;

Delighted and relieved to see from your handwriting how very much you have recovered your form after that nasty operation; you have climbed up and over the post operational shock which is almost more to be feared than the op itself. Good. Very good. I saw the programme about you last night and it wasn't too bad. It was called "Les Amis de H M en France", and we each of us did a piece of about five minutes, each spiel being interspersed with stills and montages from various parts of your life. Brassaï and Belmont were both very good, but the funniest and the one you would have loved best of all was Marcelle, who launched herself into the higher criticism with lots of meridional bravura. All about how she read *Sexus* and dreamed she slept with you and it was very nice; then when she heard you were coming she expected some huge satyr and was astonished to find how reticent and quiet and well mannered le monsieur was. At the end she got mixed up and when asked which book of yours was her favourite tried to say Big Sur, but in fact said Ben Hur! It was a fine contrast to all the heavy thinkpieces we had been dishing out. I tell you this because it seems that Arnaud has shot her bolt, has used up what she collected, and won't want to go no further. So I doubt if you will be bothered. But by the same token I had a call from Snyder who is showing your film at Avignon Festival. I am afraid he is trying to prepare a fête for you behind your back, and it is very difficult to know what to do about it unless you expressly forbid *him* to do it. But he says you are too much alone, that your birthday is an international event etc etc. And as far as the film goes I know that you are sharing costs and would do what little I could to get them back, though I fear that you have a festival film if not an archive film on your hands, and that you will always have distribution difficulties with this type of film. However, as I say there is little to be done unless you yourself tell him to shut up; but it seems to everyone that he is operating with your sanction and as everyone is a fan or a well wisher . . . and so on.

I am going to Geneva shortly for a sort of International jamboree, the kind of thing I hate, but paid for and will enable me to see a girl I have a passing weakness for, and to say Hullo to Denis de Rougemont. Margaret McCall, whom you may remember filming you and Ghika in Paris for the BBC, has spent a month here, and just gone back. Eleonore Hirt has just arrived for ten days. The Midi is hot dusty and smelly and crowded with tourists; what are we going to do with all these people? More and more every day. I am glad I am as old as I am, and have no desire to probe the glorious future described by the Fullers of our time – poets of Mobego.

You know now with the recul in time I believe you would actually be amused and interested in my spenglerised novel, *Tunc/Nunquam*, if you have never done the whole thing. Your query about Olivier and the television thing is strange; only once have I been compared to him, by the *Paris Review*, and I took it to be a kindness. But *often*, both in the States and in England, I have been compared to W C Fields by reviewers of television interviews. More, by daughter Saph who had never seen Fields, went to a Fields festival of four films and came away saying she would have recognised her father's nose anywhere! You can't beat the ball it seems. But I was compared to Richard Burton by the *NY Times*.

    Cheerio LARRY

*Lake Orta [Switzerland]   Thursday. Evening. [23 September 1971]

What a beautiful place – small and quite condensed like Les Baux – but with a plate glass lake: all life is boat life. NO first class hotels – *all* 3rd class albergos – marvellous. My motives were mixed in coming – I accepted a commission to write up the lakes – I'll be going to Como and the Borromean Isles next week. But it was also to meet a blonde dakini from Périgord who is walled into an ice block in Geneva, and who is coming down tomorrow to meet me by train. The small Wagnerian overtone is appropriate as it was *here* at Orta that Nietzsche first told Lou about his plans for Zarathustra – the girl is partly coming for me, partly for the Sacro Monte where this huge momentous intellectual love story took place. Tomorrow we will climb it together with appropriate reverence and a little (no, a lot) of our personal passion thrown in. I have, alas, no Zarathustra to confess to. But early this morning, by soft lake mist and wobbling waddling reflections I dozed into this little port – found a tavern for coffee – and when the newsman came by picked up a *N.Y. Times* with a long obit. on George Seferis. It was a cruel piece of jump–cutting. I had read of his illness and cabled my concern to Marika ages ago. I pictured him among the roses in Paros, convalescing. People have no right to do this to their friends.

    In the meantime I've accepted to come in January and wrap a laurel wreath round your head on behalf of the world. Better me than some damned don, no? I hope all goes well – with your book which I received just before taking off in my little camping car.

    Much love
    Larry

Sunday 23rd January [1972]

Dear Henry – my bread-and-butter letter, to thank you for all your
princely hospitality in Los A., comes to you from this enchanting town
where I have been a week now with Margaret McCall (who bids me
thank you warmly for the dedicace in the *Playboy* book, which she
treasures). Yes, we are having a marvellous time in the frail winter
sunshine – the town buffeted by great gusts of wind fresh from the sea:
and alive all night to the whewing of seagulls which ride high above the
hotel in packets of snowflake. As might be expected we have been
sucked into the world of the pubs with all their booze-folklore and the
black black beer and tangy whiskeys of local fame. And such conversation! Well, so much of this has been so harped on that I was prepared to
feel a reaction and to be bored or irritated. Not so. The Dublin charm is
all-seducing and the people, while not specially beautiful, have eyes of
such heart-stopping blue candour that one is continually jolted into
smiles of sheer welcome. This afternoon we visited Joyce's tower
together – it was under the most brilliant rainbow I've ever seen – a
grey rolling sea, soft clouds and skirls of rain far out chasing their tails
like puppies. Now we are waiting for the pubs to open, rather later
because of the Sabbath. They hardly speak of the troubles in the north
here, at least not to me. I have [had] a fine paper read on my work at
Trinity College and spoke myself for a while. Good bright kids, very
innocent, very idealistic.

Much love to you all – to Tony and Val and sweet little Connie so
pretty and heart-winningly kind – and you!

   Larry

*444 ocampo drive – pacific palisades california   Jan. 29th 1972

   Dear Larry –
I've been holding the enclosed for days, wondering where to send it.
Had a letter from your Claude, she, too wondering where to write you.
It's *she* who told me to mail the enclosed to Sommières.

   I was delighted to read of your reaction to Dublin and the Dubliners.
I don't picture you drinking champagne in the ould country – it must be
whiskey now, no? (*Rye?*)

   Today my cook told me she had heard you and Bob [Snyder] on the air earlier today. I haven't heard any of your now famous addresses or what have you yet.

My hip has been giving me frightful trouble since you left – as if it were falling apart. I have to get the doctor to come here and give me an injection – can't make it to his office. Am stumped to know what next to try, if injections fail to help. (Maybe acupuncture.)

Cynthia Sears gave me a recording she made of Isaac Singer reading from his own work. The accent (Yiddish) is so thick it's unbelievable. The story itself very funny, with the accent it's just incredible. (Bob on hearing it reminds me that my accent "for Gentile audiences" is also pretty bad, pretty thick – he means Brooklynese. And I always imagine I lost it in France!) Ho ho ho!

Mrs. Levinson (the cook) found *your* accent delightful – understood you perfectly, she said. (That meant – in spite of your British accent!) Hoho!

Your Claude writes a beautiful French. She must indeed be something. (I'll *never* forget that Friday night after the U.C.L.A. reception.)

Speaking of accents, Anaïs' is pretty strong too, the worst is that she doesn't know where to put the stress when she reads – not the case when she talks, however.

Now I've got to write prefaces for new, thoroly revised translations (by Belmont) of *Capricorn* and the *Colossus* (in French). Apparently, a major operation, his part of it. When I hear the word "Preface" I reach for my revolver.

Let me hear more about Ireland *later*.

Cheers! Henry

P.S. Everyone hereabouts talks of you in hyperboles. (Don't forget "boulimie" (aboulia) – I got it from you, I believe, as I did so many jewels.) The pain is letting up a trifle – I begin to feel human again.

The Claude mentioned here is Durrell's friend and muse for *Vega* (1973), his collection of poems.

*Sommières, Gard – 30 – France   Saturday   twelve Feb   1972

Dear Henry; here I am at long last, battered and bitched and travel-stained, but home to silence – except the mistral howling and the noise of the rain: home in this old vampire house. I write to convey the thanks of two women for your kindness – Claude and Margaret both of them kiss your shadow. [. . .] But hardly had I got back than the floods came, the Vidourle jumped its bed: no lights, no phone, no heat and two foot of water in the cellar. I spent a morning in darkness dragging out floating treasures like my outboard motor, the washing machine, etc. And being hit by floating wood from time to time. The town was cut in half; and just at that moment a Telex call from Arnaud to say she was arriving at six in the morning in Nîmes. I rushed through the flooded roads in my gallant little escargot and just found her, lost and disoriented on the long long Nîmes station, looking pale and small and tired and like a lost partridge – she is actually a superior demon and never at a loss; but she looks pigeonsoft and shy. Well, because of the floods we couldn't get back to this town – the army was repairing the barrages etc. So I lodged her in Nîmes where we spent the day. It's astonishing how we get on – like a couple of pirates. I saw her off to Béziers where she has had an ear operation. Then back to wrestle with the water in the cellar by lightning flashes and impromptu candles; caught a bad cold – what with Dublin on my heart and the cold in my belly. But grace was at hand, for Claude came down from Geneva to comfort and sustain me – like a great gold and grey imperial Siamese cat; soft and calm and uxorious and sleek. An ointment of a woman. And as I couldn't get nothing to work in the house I locked it up and took her to Avignon, the only unflooded part of this fucking province, where we lay in tender exhaustion in the Europe Hotel, and I told her all the works and she was appropriately (but so softly) jealous and tender that I realised that I was a very superior sort of shit. However, to compensate her for this divine tenderness ('cloud soft hand of woman' writes Auden, who must have been thinking of her) I took her to Vaucluse to have a week end with Petrarch – ah these long long conversations while making love or just sitting by the jade green water – which in this season swells ripe as a boil from the mountain, flush with trout which one eats by the water. But now she's gone, everyone's gone, and here I am with harsh barren Languedoc under deep cloud and rain which bounces up off the roads to the height of a man. And solitude and a wood fire and damned fucking sadness – mixed with a kind of volupté, being so alone. I lock up the whole house, lock myself into one room, and dance or recite or tell people what I think of them. (Schizophrenic withdrawal, you will mutter.) Anyway that is how it goes for the moment. In ten days I shall be sixty and am praying the gods to send me a little good sense as a birth day present and a feeling for the so-called golden mean which I have never managed to achieve.

I am still getting fine letters from Los A. Apparently we all did a fine job for your birthday. It was a moving experience for me – tho I try to hide these things as much as possible. Thanks for the imperial welcome and the fine fine hospitality.

> every good thing cher maître
> Larry

*444 ocampo drive – pacific palisades california   March 31, 1972

Dear Larry –

Have been trying to write you for days now. Am delighted with your *Entretiens*. The moment I opened it I was electrified, really. There's magic in everything you say – and all is on a beautiful high plateau. One thing concerns me – your several references to possible suicide. This I just can't believe. I have "suicided" myself so often it becomes a matter of course now. Supposing you do lie fallow for a while – even for several years – what matter? You'll never stop writing. At 80, like Hardy, you may be writing the kind of poetry you always wanted to.

I got a beautiful big book about Strindberg recently. Was interested in his daily program, when in his prime. From 6–10 P.M. was his agony. Alone, what to do? (He played the piano to amuse himself – the classics, no less. Sic!) Anyway, he talks of drink – what a god-send it was. If he hadn't had the booze he would have killed himself. He says he was never an alcoholic – just a "hard drinker".

I go to hospital in about 3 weeks. Am feeling great – the pain has left off for last two weeks. Everything should turn out well; I'll be a new man when I get this new hip.

Incidentally, you say in the book that I wrote *The Colossus* while in Greece. Not so. I wrote it in N.Y. (back of a synagogue, listening to the music) and a brief bit in Virginia. (No importance.)

I must confess I am still the kind of rat who deserts the ship when it's sinking. I mean by that, still a-political.

Give my best to Cynthia. I think Fiddle may soon look you up too. How is *Claude*?

The "Ambassadress" [Lisa Lu], as you call her, is in N.Y. at the moment. The Chinese film she starred in – *The Arch* – is opening at a cinema there in a few days.

Am more and more in love every day. It's better even than champagne!

Henry

Miller is referring to *Le Grand suppositoire: Entretiens avec Marc Alyn* (1972), published in English as *The Big Supposer: A Dialogue with Marc Alyn* (1973).

*Sommières, Gard – 30 – France   Tuesday April 1972

DEAR HENRY. Thanks for the good letter which shows you in good spirits; I hope the new leg works out. I shall think of you on the 23rd, and not alone, as Cynthia Sears will be here for a night or two on her way through to Spain to see her brother. [...]

Yes, a miracle. There is an esoteric gentleman called LUDO from Arles who exhibits dried herbs here in the place du marché every month. Well, he issues a grotesque prospectus promising snake oil cures for every known disease through herbs. In despair after four years' misery with this eczema I asked him for his eczema cure. Three packages of dried herbs arrived with instructions written in a cuneiform handwriting. The maid made me a decoction. It is supposed to last three months the cure BUT AFTER TEN DAYS THE ECZEMA HAS COM-PLETELY VANISHED. IT'S A BLOODY MIRACLE. I am now going to interview Ludo, and if he will deliver the secret composition of his cures I will do a pamphlet on the subject. I am slowly preparing for my Italian trip; I aim to strike Orta on the first or second of May. Ravishing scenery. Lake mists. Nietzsche etc. I must really try and knock out this damned novel this year. [...]

Good luck. Keep the Moët et Chandon flowing (brut)

Larry

Ludo Chardenon is the subject of Durrell's booklet *The Plant-Magic Man* (1973) and the author of *In Praise of Wild Herbs* (1984), which contains a Foreword by Lawrence and a Preface by Gerald Durrell.

Dear Larry –

It's 2^{oo} A.M. – near bedtime for me. Just got your letter about Paris and Joey. [. . .] Remarkable, however, that in spite of everything, Fred holds up and never looks a day older. He has a way of protecting himself, which, disgraceful though it may appear, reminds me only too vividly of my own shameful behavior in the past. Don't feel sorry for him – it's not eating him away. And don't be too concerned about his not writing more. More and more I think less and less about one's achievements as artist, poet, or whatever. More and more I feel a profound pity for those who are *blessed* (?) with genius. What martyrs, most of them. What a grueling struggle – and for what ultimately? More and more everything seems to be of equal value – *to me.* We do what we must, not what we can. Don't you feel a bit silly sometimes when you read your fan mail and realize what conflicting (and largely trivial) reactions your work inspires? How very very few understand what you (or others) have done or tried to do. Each one takes his little slice of cake and thinks he has consumed the whole cake. Joey is naturally lazy, naturally a bon viveur. He wrote only to save face, as it were. One has to do something – so he wrote. I don't mean to belittle him, I hope you understand. But Joey's role in life was more to make it pleasant for those around him, to clown it rather than fight or assert himself. I always loved his lack of ambition. With him it's an art. He makes us look like drudges, non? When you think of him you smile. Anaïs has never forgiven him for his "capers". How sad that is! It hurts her when I say that the best, or some of the best years of my life, I owe to him – his light-heartedness, his fickleness, his pranks, his treachery – whatever. She, by the way, lacks a sense of humor very often.

Seems to me I received several gifts from you recently, all unacknowledged. So much keeps pouring in on me all the time. (Should one complain of receiving too much?)

Did you know I wrote Miriam Cendrars when I learned you both would be in Paris? I tried to find out where you were staying so that I could write you there. But perhaps she was away on vacation or no longer at the old address in Passy. Anyway, I'm delighted to hear that you had a few good rollicking days together. If I ever have this bloody hip operation and can walk nimbly again on my own two feet, I'll see you over there, I hope, before I die. I keep postponing the operation, not because I fear it will be unsuccessful, but because I don't want my heart to give out under the anaesthetic. I am not ready to die yet. Two years ago, three years ago, it wouldn't have mattered much. But now that I am deeply in love, and with this wonderful "Ambassadress", as you called her, I would love to linger on just a few more years. Even if I were in for another grand disappointment, another heart ache, I don't want it cut short. It should be just long enough to avoid utter decrepitude. For all the pain and misery, the discomfit this hip causes, I remain quite cheerful, enthusiastic and still capable of doing a little writing. Nothing to boast of, to be sure. Even my ping-pong holds up, painful as it is to play. I'm only a semi-invalid thus far.

And what has happened with la femme Suisse? Or have there been a half-dozen others meantime? Like myself, I don't think you should ever marry again. We must have bad aspects in the House of Marriage. But the House of Love – there are the two, you know – seems reasonably free of malefic influences.

I just read a little piece you wrote for *Life Style* magazine. I never realized the winters were that bad in Greece! The proposed sale of the islands is fantastic. Buying one of them would be like making yourself a voluntary "banishee" – exile for life. I always remember your account of your stay on the Island of Rhodes. It sticks with me like the pungent fragrance of Turkish tobacco. And then you mention Patmos! I have a small photo of the monastery there (maybe you sent it) on my bathroom wall. It looks like all rock – and not too happy rock either. But that John the Divine was there (and still is) redeems everything. You know, you have been most fortunate in having visited or lived for a while in so many outlandish places. I envy you that. And especially do I envy you your birthplace. The Himalayas! My dream world.

By the way, Bob Snyder is making a documentary – to be an hour long – on Anaïs. There are passages in which she comes off sublimely – just sitting at an empty table, for instance, and talking about herself freely, poetically, and, so to speak, "with authority". I was really moved. It's strange, don't you think, to think of Anaïs meeting the world face to face, lecturing, autographing, answering questions, and with it all seemingly very much at ease. Who'd have thunk it!

Well, enough for the moment. I'm beginning to rival Balzac in the daily letter to the beloved. Hardly a day passes, even though I have seen her, spent the day with her, that I don't write the "inamorata". Big fat letters often, and usually at 3^{00} or 4^{00} A.M. Among my best, I think, in this genre. In a way, I'm coming full circle. I mean, I began my "literary career" by writing letters "to all and sundry". And now I'm at it again, but to the one and only now. If they are ever discovered by the wrong person I won't be alive to tell you about it. Every one is pure dynamite. On top of this, not a midnight passes but we don't talk over the phone for an hour or more. Quelle vie! *Délicieuse!*

Cheers! Henry

*Sommières, Gard – 30 – France   ELEVENTH DECEMBER 1972

Cher Maître;

A quick line which, I calculate, with all the strikes and go-slows in the post office, will hit you round about Xmas. I had some good news of you etching etc from Connie this week. In spite of Bob's kindly solicitations (and machinations) I couldn't make an early visit to LA but I have just sent off a letter to Caltech in Pasadena to accept an invitation for January–March next year. I thought to come a bit early and see something of you over Xmas if you are not too swamped by admirers, while I settle into my job. What am I saying? With typical American munificence the job consists in residing there poetically on the campus for two months, occasionally reaching out a languid hand to pick a peach. I hope by that time to have finished this exasperating book which keeps trying to dictate to me like a bloody schoolmistress – and I have to keep shutting it up and cutting it back. I have no notion about how long it will be or how preposterous the theme. We shall see later on, I am only 125 pages into it as yet and it doesn't feel as if it has started yet. My yoga has progressed quite well now and I have had two good remissions from drink – it's now over three years since I had any tobacco, and quite painless it has been but now I have a faint hope that I shall, not abolish, but at least limit and control my alcohol intake which would really be marvellous because drinking heavy is wasteful moneywise as well as healthwise and after sixty one comes to so much value healthy walking and easy muscles. I stand on my head for 5 minutes every morn now! It looks foolish but is so good. Yesterday Menuhin came through and we compared yogas etc. He can play the fiddle standing on his head! I can't write poems yet in this position but there is no reason why in the long run I shouldn't manage to. Not much other news. Our winter has started with brilliant icy dawns, and my olive oil is in. This week I take the olives to the mill and watch them draw the first pression – the green oil they call *vierge*. The old house is ugly and gloomy but very warm and my dracula owls are so tame that when I come back after dark they sail down into the garden and whistle at me and do a figure or two in and out of the light like figure skaters. I'm going to Paris for Xmas as no children this year, they are all scattered and with boy friends. Just been proofing *The Black Book* and it brought back many old memories of that astonishing period in Paris, Greece etc. Heleni Theotocki writes from Zürich that she lunched with K recently who was damning and cursing in traditional style. His legs have given out – the wounded knee – and his chauffeur often has to shift him about. Naturally he hates it, and everyone for good measure. Seferis' death was a blow too, they were close friends. Just had Claude down from Geneva for a marvellous visit – log fires, champagne, roast chestnuts, music, candles, quietness, and long silent sleeps just waking and falling asleep like the deep sea breathing. We'll meet again in the new year.

Well, Henry, keep going with the etching; and with the ambassa-dress. She's clearly good for you the angelic creature.

Love, LARRY

*444 ocampo drive – pacific palisades california   1/3/73

Dear Larry –
Cheers! Happy New Year and all that! I hope you're content, if not slap happy. I'm OK. Operation postponed another few weeks. But love goes on and on.

I have begun a big book – "The Book of Friends", I am calling it tentatively. It's going easy, to my liking. Simple, nostalgic, perhaps even sentimental at times. Began with my first friend, Stanley Bor-owski ("Stasiu") whom I met at the age of five! The past is like an open book – rather, a cinerama spectacle. Nothing is ever lost, what! Have 30 friends listed. Hope I can finish it before I croak.

Happy to know you too are deep in yours – the book, I mean. I have to smile when you talk about 1974. So far off! Who knows if we (or I, at least) will still be alive. Caltech sounds like a cinch. You can handle it easily.

I sent you a book by Kurt Vonnegut, Jr. – a name familiar to youngsters. Tony persuaded me to read it. I enjoyed it. Wonder if you will simply chuck it in the can.

Did I tell you I'm doing a film with young Tom Schiller – in and about my bathroom. It's fun. (Bob Snyder not connected with this project.)

Am in writing mood. Feels great. Also made some etchings and lithographs for my Japanese art collector. Hope to do some water colors now. This love of the "Ambassadress", as you call her, is doing wonders for me. It's better than Casanova's last years, eh? Incidentally, I bought the 12-Vol. set for Tony for X'mas. I never read him. Should I? I read only an hour a day, before falling to sleep. Can read quite a deal that way. Well, I'll knock off. Keep your pecker up! Have fun and don't become a *total* teetotaler!!!

Cheers! Henry

*Sommières, Gard – 30 – France   12 January '73!

Dear Henry – Marvellous to have your New Year letter and to know you are in working fettle again. I'm forced to reply by hand as I was burgled on New Year's Eve and all three typewriters have gone. The new one has a 'continental' clavier. I'll try and be as legible as I can. Today it is marvellous, heavy ground frost, bright sun, and snow in the air. All through the valleys the patient snop-snop of sécateurs trimming the vines, a reminder that the earth is a full time job. I have primed up the car and soon I am making a jump across to Avignon where I shall wait for the night-train from Geneva to bring me Claude, all blonde and weary and bursting as much to talk as to make love. We will stay tonight in my little hotel – some flowers and a tiny bottle of champagne and an assiette of something. It will be snowing outside by then. Perhaps a hot-water bottle for a weary lady? We shall see. Tomorrow we come back here for the week-end – if this winter sun keeps up I'll take her into Camargue on Sunday. All this is very wise loving-passion and respect and friendship all in one! Ah, you talk about time, but it is endless. I shall be dropping in on you for Xmas – going into training this summer, determined *for once* to beat you at ping-pong! We'll see if I can realise this dream. Tonight we'll talk about you in Avignon, in the big double bed with the eiderdown. Claude much amused by Joe's book about you. I'm shaping up a goodish novel, I think – but it is

462

getting too long like every thing I do. Never mind. My yoga is improving me very much – no, I never intended to cut out drink, just to control it a bit – Si on est dieu pourquoi cochonner? Much love to you all, and bless the Ambassadress – and keep on loving and writing.

– Happy '73 Larry.

Joe's book: Perlès's *My Friend Henry Miller* (1955).

*Sommières, Gard – 30 – France   FEBRUARY TWENTY FIVE, SEVENTY THREE.

DEAR HENRY

I AM SAFELY BACK IN SOMMIÈRES AGAIN AND HASTEN TO THANK YOU FOR your great generosity; and to express my amazement at the wonderful athletic stamina you show in everything. You are even in better fighting form this year than last, and nobody knows how you do it. But it's a fact; and the way you stood up to the tedium and disturbance of film making was a lesson to us all. The camera man is sure that it will be the best thing the ORTF has done and so was Michèle, so I felt great relief and joy that our disturbance had been worth while.

It is an astonishing trip, coming to see you, in a jumbo – a sort of flying cathedral; going north into Canada first and then across the frozen wastes of Greenland with a weird moon among the icebergs. Then Scotland and London. But here we ran into a French air strike which grounded us so I had myself rerouted through Belgium to Geneva where a sleepy Claude was astonished to hear my voice speaking, she thought at first, from Los Angeles. She rushed down in a taxi and we spent the day together in the bookshops and pubs and walking by the frozen lake in a stiff bise which blew my cold away. The next day I picked up the old Catalan, the Barcelona express, and wobbled down to Nîmes. I had rung the maid from Geneva so I found a warm house and something to eat in the fridge. It's relatively warm here compared to the ice and snow of Geneva but there is lots of mistral. I lie in the bed and listen to it howling and screaming – as if one were in the frozen north. This morning I celebrated with a full yoga and a long walk in the garrigues. This coming week-end Claude is coming to spend here. Good.

463

My only misadventure, and not serious, is the mislaying of a light mackintosh with a mustard coloured lining – maybe in the house somewhere, or maybe at Michèle's; we shall see. Ask Connie to cast an eye, and give her a squeeze from Old Sitting Moose. [. . .] Anyway I was astonishingly reassured about your health this year and sincerely hope that you can do without the operation which carries a certain risk like all things of the kind; but perhaps you were in greater pain than your pride permitted you to show . . . And yet . . . those tremendous games of ping-pong! I had to admit to the village that once more I had been thrashed, and so we couldn't ring the church bells as they had promised.

Thanks once again for the marvellous hospitality. See you soon.

Larry

[P.S.] George Katsimbalis' wife Spatch has just died of cancer, in case you want to write him a line. I shall be 61 in two days' time – catching you up! Theodore is 77.

ORTF: Office de Radiodiffusion et Télévision Françaises.

*444 ocampo drive – pacific palisades california   March 31 '73

Dear Larry –

Tom just brought me an interview with you in some English weekly – written by a woman – photo of you preparing a snack.

Jesus, it's out of the world, this piece. Best on you I've ever seen. What a "Master" you are! A super Noel Coward with a super tongue-in-cheek. I howled with laughter all the way through. I would give my right arm to pull off a stunt like that. Stunt, not "stint", what!

I never knew you were such an adept cuisinier. That touched me. I always thought of you as helpless, starving if no one were around to feed you.

Behind all the drôlerie of your poses, maxims, axioms, metaphors and pyrotechnics the real you emerges. You have a right to think highly of yourself – seriously, don't worry if you can't pull off another "Quartet" now. You can lie fallow for a while – no harm done. In fact, it might do you good – unless you feel defeated and guilty. We are at the mercy of the gods always. "We" don't create a bloody thing, as you well know. (Voir Rimbaud) All we can do is to see that our antennae are properly hooked up and that we are in a condition to receive the emanations. Right? When you really understand that, nothing will disturb you. It's a terrible mistake to think one *has* to keep writing – *or working*, which is even worse. Dans le néant on s'épanouient (*my own*, sic!). (I wonder now how my fucking French came off on the T.V.) Michèle says everything turned out beautifully. I hope to Christ that, after all these sessions, she doesn't cut it down to *one* hour. We gave her plenty, non? And maybe never again.

Don't "take care", as they say. Take it easy. Enjoy the bliss of doing nothing, if you can. The itch will pass, and the drink too. But don't become a teetotaler! I'm in fine fettle and pass it on to you. I miss you!

Henry

P.S. Say hello to Claude for me. I still haven't had a chance to reply to her letter. I'm *flooded* with c/s, chores, rewrites, etc. etc. Fuck it all!
P.P.S. Tom brought me a bottle of Armagnac last night and we all drank to Gurdjieff's memory. Result – I slept 14 hours!

Dans le néant . . .: 'In nothingness, one opens up.'

*Sommières, Gard – 30 – France   5th April 73

Dear Henry – just got your fine letter this sunny morn – high wind and sunshine. Amused you saw the *Observer* article – I spoofed that lady and she got so squiffed she drove into a ditch. I thought she contained an innate malice very well; I really was abominable and got off lightly I think. By now you will have received *Entretiens* with its various articles – nice one from Diana Menuhin! No, I have another big book some-where in me – all this neo-hysteric-alcoholic-period of the last three years has been due to this fearful skin thing, the eczema. I really have been through the Book of Job – sometimes just peeling off inside my clothes and sticking to them like secondary burns. I have disguised it all – but the state of my shirts and trousers would have startled you! Now a blessed remission for a while – and of course *instantly* I have plans for something really big – à longue haleine – which, if this holds up, should not take too long! I would of course be vastly helped if I could find a girl to help me, but so far, no luck. Claude is a darling (she comes tomorrow for the week-end) but *must* not desert her own beautifully

465

made happy family. I shall pick her up at Avignon at midnight tomorrow. It really is perfect this way, with separations of a couple of months, and the whole Orta-Nietzsche-Lou episode behind us which was so poetic and really structured our great attachment for each other – thanks to Lou and Nietzsche and Rilke!

By the way, Anaïs just sent me a biography of Lou by Peters which is marvellous: it was Lou who started off this whole thing in Geneva – her wicked sexy spirit – the spirit of the Great Instigators, like that of Anaïs herself! "Les colombes inspiratrices." Anyway it's wonderful for me! And it *has* grown Claude up a good deal – you know she is a friend of Dali who is mad about her head and runs it into his crowd scenes – she is the girl of the dolphin, for example.

At the moment I am answering (outrageously) a questionnaire from Cannes – where I am following in your footsteps as Film Judge for the Festival in May. But first London for a week – *The Black Book* is coming out for the *first* time with all its history – involving of course your heroic sponsoring of it. The usual crazy round of television, interviews etc.

No, Michèle has rung me *twice* about how excellent your film is, profound and simple and light à la fois. Be sure she won't cut a frame that's good. Apparently we did 50% in French and the same in English, almost as if it had been prearranged! An ideal *mise* for the seven language distribution! I think it will be cut and edited this month. She may turn up chez vous – as she is spending the night in Los A. on the 16 – thence New York. *Make her cook!* I must rush out and post this as the secretary is ill and I am all alone. Music, sunshine, loneliness – how *Marvellous!*

love   Larry.

H.F. Peters wrote *Rainer Maria Rilke: Masks and the Man* (1963).
Entretiens: Lawrence Durrell (1973), edited by F.-J. Temple, is a collection of memoirs and essays published as vol. 32 of the Éditions Subervie series.

*Sommières, Gard – 30 – France   5 April '73

Michèle rang me from Paris and read me your letter so full of fireworks! How bright the flame shines! Hurrah! I quite agree with you and she is flying to you now with the intention of getting a little more conversation – don't quail! Though television is boring and fatiguing it is really made for the great *discursive* talkers and writers, of whom you are among the greatest. You do it so easily and with such enjoyment – never showing off like me, the crazy actor: and the things you say drop like ripe fruit. I am so looking forward to seeing you around Christmas when I come to Pasadena. I think your new rhythm suits you v. well. You were breathing from a different *centre* – the long-distance-runner one which is what all athletes envy, and all yoga boys too. Spreading the oxygen nicely through the whole nervous system. Michèle has promised to cook you some French food if nothing else, and to ring me from time to time. [. . .] Much love to you all – tell Connie I dream of her and I'm expecting great things of her in the fall!

    love Larry.

*[Pacific Palisades, California]   Oct. 2, 1973

    Dear Larry –

Got your letter today. Here is the latest from the sick room. Progress, slow but steady. Yes, I made a remarkable recovery. Must have unusual vitality. But I'm still confined to the bed most of the time.

The worst thing is the loss of vision in my right eye. They are not sure if I will regain my sight or not. There's a blood clot somewhere near the optic nerve.

During or after operation I had a glorious euphoric experience. I was back on the Island of Crete and so happy to be there. I could speak Greek fluently. Everything was beautiful. The doctors thought I had lost my mind. Why should they be alarmed if one is happy, eh?

Today, sitting by the big window looking out on the pool, I saw a bird suddenly swoop down looking for some crumbs. I felt grateful I could see that bird with half vision.

I try to write and read. I even have my paints laid out in case I can do a water color.

So you finished a book in this brief intereval. How wonderful! You don't let the grass grow under your feet.

Everybody who goes to London tells me how beautiful Kwintner's Village Book Shop is. He's a strange good fellow.

Tom's film may be up for an Academy Award. Man in charge of awards wants to help him get it. Lisa [Lu] is on the Board of Judges. But he has to blow it up to 35mm, which will cost him about

$3000⁰⁰. He really did a wonderful job in revamping it. Hard to explain.

I keep waiting for news about the girl you found. Hope you haven't driven her away already.

Everything goes blissfully with Lisa and myself. What a lucky discovery for me in my declining years. What a euphemism – *declining years!* I'm not nearly as good as Casals at 96. I'm more like a boxer who knows how to take punishment. But just being in love means everything. Not a day passes but I think how lucky I am.

Well, for one long spate this is enough. I can hardly see the letters you know – I just feel my way along.

I look forward to seeing you this winter. I hope I don't bore you to death.

Cheers now!
Henry

[P.S.] Are you still with the champagne?

Miller had a second artificial artery implanted about 1 September.

* *Sommières*   8ᵗʰ October [1973]

Henry – Your wonderful letter full of calm optimism and gaiety came today and delighted us all. I was a little uneasy about the lack of news for a moment and wrote Connie a line – I didn't want to bother Lisa. Have full confidence in her thoughtful and deliberate efficacy – however. I believe the eye will cure itself with rest – besides, a temporary black patch will add to your allure! I am trying to find a ship to get me to Frisco or Los A. about 20 December. Thought we might blow in around Xmas and say hullo to you. I'm bringing Ghislaine [de Boysson] with me – if she hasn't left me by then. She's nice, rather sulky looking – a French aristo who knows everyone in films and once upon a time nearly married Bing Crosby. It sounds most distressing, but a gentleman of my age learns to overlook mistakes. I start at Pasadena on January one for two months of seminars, and I suppose boredom – but it will be a change of ideas. I'll get my second wind and perhaps launch out into a big book again. I've done nothing very original since the *Quartet*. This is one about the Templars is OK, I think, but I ache to run *wild* with a huge cancerous book. This is just an interim note to say how happy I was to get your line. I'm copying it to Joe. Michèle rang today and was delighted – sends love.

Cheers   Larry.

Miller in Love (again)
Durrell at the Typewriter

In 1974 Durrell teaches for one term at the California Institute of Technology; he publishes *Vega*, a volume of poetry, which delights Miller; then out comes *Monsieur: or, The Prince of Darkness*, which puzzles Miller. Just as before, artistic disagreements and doubts in no way impair the friendship. For Miller, 1976 opens auspiciously with a telegram from France announcing that he has been named 'Chevalier de l'Ordre National de la Légion d'Honneur'. During the year the first volume of his *Book of Friends* appears, to be followed soon by *My Bike & Other Friends* and *Joey*. Both men divorce their wives during 1977 and, while Durrell professes to enjoy living alone, Miller discovers the last of his great loves, the dancer and actress Brenda Venus, 'an Ariel to his Prospero', Durrell writes in his Preface to the book of Miller's letters to Brenda. Anaïs Nin dies the same year after a long and gallant battle against cancer, and so is severed one of the strongest ties to the Villa Seurat period. She is followed in 1978 by Katsimbalis, the figure who represented for Miller so much of the fascination of Greece. Durrell writes *Sicilian Carousel* and wins Miller's praise; then he completes *Livia*, 'sibling' to *Monsieur*, and struggles with *Constance*. He also writes the text for *The Greek Islands*, a lavishly illustrated celebration of Greece. In 1980 Henry, dying and almost blind, dictates a cheerful last letter to Larry.

*[Pacific Palisades]   3/6/74

Dear Larry –
Am reading slowly and thoughtfully your poems in *Vega* and am overwhelmed by the use of language you permit yourself. It's almost frightening. How safe and stale now seems most prose! My own

included. For me it's like jumping suddenly from ordinary arithmetic to integral calculus.

Whether intentional or not, you make it seem that anyone can do it, that no intermediate steps are necessary.

And thinking thus I got out the pad and penned the enclosed to you, which is the nearest I have ever come to writing a poem. (Except for that one – "O Lake of Light" – I wrote for Sevasty Koutsaftis [. . .]. Remember?)

Anyway, reading you once again reminds me of those days in Corfu when you sat on the balcony, "doing your exercises".

They paid off, begorra!

Henry

P.S. I like those French lines you inserted occasionally.
P.P.S. I think the whole bloody book is a tour de force. Vive le poète!

[Enclosed:]

For Larry

All my life I thought that to
be a poet was the most difficult
(or the easiest) thing in the world.
I never knew, until I read
you

That a poem is a renunciation of
language, at least as most of
us understand the term.
I never realized that words could
exist separately and brutally

That the way a flower, crushed or
uncrushed, lies upon the paving,
has meaning and beyond that
makes music, albeit for assassins,
monsters, idiots.

I did not understand that
you could call your shots, disregard all rules, ethics, metaphysics.

Roll in your own smoking dung
and enjoy it, piss in your beer
and think it ambrosia
or –
Completely deny all reason, all
intelligence, all kindness and consideration and babble like a lost
baboon.

*Sommières, Gard – 30 – France   EASTER SUNDAY. [14 April 1974]

Dear Henry   What an overwhelming Easter egg of a gift your
two letters were – so unexpected and so reassuring about your
fine *tonus*: the poem is a great honour for the poet who was not
only touched but also bowled over by the easy mastery of it, its cool
putting down of primary colours – laying out the sentences like a Tarot
pack of cards upon which the reader can 'scan' or divine. Hurrah. I am
so delighted. Yesterday we went to Lunel with your painting to have it
framed. It looked gorgeous as we unwrapped it, bright as a peacock in
the dingy little shop, and it brought back good memories of the whales
dancing cheek to cheek at Malibu and the sun pouring into the Wyler
house. I hope Mrs Wyler will lend it to you one day to help on your
work with the sound of the ocean. It was wonderful to lie awake and
hear it slapping and slumbering on the beach outside. I am so glad also
to have finished *Monsieur* there and I shall send along the first proof I
can lay hands on because I think you will like it and get a laugh or two
out of it. Faber has just produced *Tunc–Nunquam* in a single fat volume
called *The Revolt of Aphrodite*. It is easier to judge it now as a one
volume job and I think it is better than it seemed and will get a decent
critical press.

My translation of *Pope Joan* in French (my version of it, that is) is
coming out next week in Paris and I am going up for the inevitable time
wasting cocktail party. I shall see Michèle and also the film which
everyone finds excellent. She says she was simply too fatigued by the
summer's work to face America but will come later. Meanwhile she is
editing a version for the Cannes Festival in May which should make a
good trailer for its general television release later in the month. Did I
look so serious in Cal Tech? You know one has to look ridiculously and

hypocritically solemn in universities. It's part of the job.

And how glad I am that it is over. There have been so many propositions awaiting me here that I think I shall have to put off my scheme to take winter students to pay the fuel bills, at least for this year. I have written to Bob's friend in this sense and hope he won't take it amiss. Also that man Epfs the painter; though he is somewhat travel stained after the USA he has started painting again and hopes to have another show in Paris perhaps in September when everyone comes back from the holidays. The text of *Monsieur* should be along in a month or so. It's got lots of Egyptian colour and a gnostic theme which (since the Lacarrière book pleased you) may also intrigue. I am developing a new kind of gnomic prose now which resembles jump cutting – no doubt a bit risky but the bright bits of broken glass stick out and, I hope, cut the reader's fingers as he reads. What a bore all this obsessional writing is. I look at my huge bibliography and sigh. But then. . . . To be able to be free, to make a living by it and stay home . . . that is a miracle which keeps me forever amazed. Every morning when I wake I say "no more office to go to" and I breathe a prayer for all poor trapped spirits enmeshed in tasteless insipid routine work just to make ends meet. How lucky we are. Keep weaving at that book cher maître and when Connie types it tell her to send me the fifth carbon. There is *nothing* at all being written today of any density. Happy Easter

Love to you all
Larry

Dear Larry –

I finished the book last night. Now I am somewhat puzzled, bewildered. Somewhere after the marvelous episode in the tent with Akkad and Ophis the book seemed to fall apart, forgive me for saying so. I can see how the succeeding chapters had purpose and meaning – for you. But, for us? As I look back it seems that these chapters only added complications *and* more *un*intentional mystery. Toby and his Templars, while interesting in their way, add nothing to the central theme. The Gnostics are lost for a while.

All the time, however, the beauty and the magic of your prose continues. Only somewhere about the middle it becomes a sort of three-ring circus. *Anything* may happen. And indeed strange, unexpected and seemingly meaningless things do happen. You are always "the Master". But one wonders sometimes – where to, what next? And then there is the book or books within a book. And here, at times, I get lost. I don't know any more who precisely is talking, who is the *author*. You write on several levels and in different guises, but it is always *you*, Lawrence Durrell, the *adept*, if you like. Brilliant, overwhelming, stupefying – yet, not quite what we expect.

I kept wondering as I read if you had an American publisher for it. (I can't see more than a few hundred Americans capable of reading a book like this.)

I hope you'll forgive me for being so blunt, but I felt you wanted my criticism and not just my approval.

Good luck! Love to Ghislaine.
Henry

P.S. I suspect you could give us still another book dealing with the Gnostics. *They* are grand! I wallow in their thoughts.

*SOMMIÈRES – (Gard) 30 –
France   [postmarked 23 September 1974]

Dear Henry   am delighted by your letter and not cast down by your feelings of disappointment about the shape of the book; but you know the book is the first of five – and my main stream is going to gradually expand through the lives of the 'real' creator and his puppets. Of course the rate of acceleration is calculated over a large canvas. By the way, I had this problem with *Tunc* and *Nunquam*, and was badly manhandled on the first vol by the critics. Only now when the two volumes have been united am I getting a serious discussion of a single volume.

I have just done the first fifty pages of the successor to *Monsieur* called LIVIA or BURIED ALIVE. I will send you the MSS if you can bear to look at it – it exposes this strange form I have decided to try. Of course if things don't come off they don't and there is no need to weep. BUT THE REACTIONS TO THIS VOLUME HAVE BEEN ASTONISHING SO FAR FROM JUST THE PEOPLE ONE MIGHT THINK WOULD FIND IT A BORE AND

OBSCURE. VIKING FOR EXAMPLE RUSHED IN WITH FIFTY THOUSAND DOLLARS ADVANCE AND ARE RAVING, AND SO IS FABER AS WELL AS THE AGENTS. ALSO THE FRENCH – THE RIGHTS ARE ALREADY SOLD IN EIGHT LANGUAGES ... So you see it does not seem so obscure really; Gallimard usually wait a year or so, but they've rushed at it.

Perhaps when I finish *Livia*, which will also have its Egyptian section, you might recover confidence in the PROJECT – I fully accept what you say. Let me see what I can do to recapture my only real reader.

every good thing from us both, and I hope your own book is sailing onwards. If you don't feel like reading the fifty pages of LIVIA don't bother, tell Connie to post it back. I feel kind of optimistic though I think your feeling of dismay may be shared by many other readers. I still have to win out. You know I had this trouble with the quartet over the 2nd volume which was greeted as a great let down, but in the end I redeemed the project.

I will see if I can do this and won't abandon the ship until vol three ... God what a bore.

I would much rather write your books, but what would you, I can't

Love

Await that quincunx O master

Larry

*444 ocampo drive – pacific palisades california   Sunday – 9/29/74

Dear Larry –

Just finished *Livia* – d'un seul trait. Easy reading, this one. *Marvelous* description of trip down the Rhone. What memories it evoked for me! Especially Vienne, where Eve, I, and the children spent a few weeks chez that eccentric school master, *Maillet*. (Remember him?) They (Maillets) hated the place, but I liked it very much, probably because full of Roman ruins. (I never knew that Pontius Pilate spent his last days there.) By the way, I've often noticed the facility with which you drag in facts of this sort. Does it mean you keep notebooks full of such data from your prodigious reading? Funny, before I was properly launched, I kept notebooks, often with quotations from books I read, but later I guess I disdained to use this material. Anyway, now I read so much (and with one eye) that the notebooks couldn't keep up with all that I'd like to remember. I loved too your description of Avignon, where I have sat many times, wondering why it was so celebrated. It is an ugly mausoleum of a place, as you say.

Where *Livia* fits into your scheme I don't yet perceive, but I am intrigued. Of course, I can never get over the idea that you are such an architect, civil engineer, city planner, etc. (Must be inherited from your father, the engineer!)

The dialogue between Sutcliffe and Blanford very amusing and witty *and* mysterious. Just when we think we know, we don't know at all. That character Cade is a card. <And that negress *Trash* and that word "quaire"!!> Where do you pick them up? Don't tell me these are all creatures of your imagination! If so, then I am *not* a writer, but some sort of crazy reporter.

I almost fell over when you told me of the advance you are receiving from the American publisher. I don't think I ever received more than a thousand dollars until (and never again) Grove paid just that for the advance on *Cancer*. (I had refused it two or three times.) [. . .]

[unsigned]

*Sommières, Gard – 30 – France   28 MARCH 1975

Dear Henry

How marvellous you are taking time out to write – what a spanking article for the women. I have ordered the books you review; and [feel?] concern for Anaïs who was in very fine form when she was in Paris in November. I was showing at the same time and only managed to exchange emissaries and presents but at last had a long phone talk with her. Yes, Hugo was rumoured to be there but in another hotel.

I was most acidly ticked off by Anaïs for mentioning him as her husband in an article and had to do a public repentance with sackcloth and ashes. Now she has forgiven me but not until I "apologised formally for my mistaken views". I wonder what Rupert [Pole] makes of all this mystery and whether she doesn't feel that the diaries will in the long run lose spontaneity – for obviously one day all will be revealed by an industrious sage from Garbo College? Or someone's memoirs, perhaps Hugo's? I don't know. But it is quite wonderful to see the way she deliberately skates where the ice is thinnest! No wonder the MLF is proud of her!

477

I have done 100 pages of the new book and have begun 'merging'. My 'real' characters are beginning to interfere in the lives of my 'imagined' ones. One should soon begin to get a marvellous sense of vertigo – stereoscopic vertigo. We shall see. The pilot book had a bloody press in USA, good in London. But I am beginning to get marvellous fan letters – which is just the way it was with *Justine* which was roughly handled at first. There is always this delay.

I am only just getting considered articles on *Tunc* and *Nunquam* now reissued as *The Revolt of Aphrodite*; they also got chewed by the press; now they are starting to kick in the womb of futurity.

Nothing much else to report except days of walking and working. Ghislaine is here for a few months more! No need to hurry or worry at my age. She has several film offers and now it looks as if I shall film for Michèle in September in Greece.

Marcelle rang yesterday and said she had done your cards all this week; gives you another five years at least with more work ahead. Says you will be embeté by your physical mishaps but in very good fettle moralment and eager for work. She has done some bad divining but in your case she did announce the second operation before even the first . . . what does Langmann say?

Much love from us both. We are getting on really very well.

> love to all over there
> Larry

[P.S.] Have you seen Noel Young's *Blue Thirst*?

MLF: Mouvement de Liberation de la Femme.

*444 ocampo drive – pacific palisades california   4/9/75

Dear Larry and Ghislaine –

Bonjour and bless you both! I wish, instead of five years more of work, Marcelle could read cessation of physical pain, etc. (Ever notice how one's fans keep encouraging one to go on working? What foolishness! Go on *living*, yes! Not rotting in bed.)

I'm a little puzzled by your first sentence about the article on women. (Or did I send you a copy of the article "The Mystery of the Japanese Woman"?) Somehow I manage to continue writing – all manner of

478

things – even tho' I am half blind and feel that way.

Yes, A.N. is indeed a puzzle! She's still recovering from the operation – but her voice sounds strong. Why she "denies" Hugo, who treated her so wonderfully, I can't make out. But talk of "deceivers"! She takes the cake. We are lucky to be spared, eh?

Yes, Larry, I did read *Blue Thirst* and was enchanted with it. I had intended writing you immediately but got swamped with "schlock" (good Yiddish word, non?).

Did I tell you I have been trying to read *The Flame of Life* by D'Annunzio? Did you ever read it? What magnificent rococo language! I wanted to know more about that devastating relationship with the Duse.

By the way, Lisa Lu is due back from Hong Kong next week – the 15th. From the photos she sends me she looks younger and more beautiful than ever. It's been a long wait – 9 months. Never again! I wrote her exactly 224 letters in that time. Almost as good as Balzac, what? So both you and Ghislaine will be filming shortly! What will Ghislaine appear in? Geneviève Bujold was here to dinner recently. Reminds me a bit of Bardot!

Did you know that Fred and Anne returned to Cyprus? I am waiting for an address from him. (He had been living for a while in the Thomas Hardy country (sic).)

Well, I must stop. My eye won't permit more. Love to you both!

Henry

P.S. I also don't understand what you mean about the books I "review"!?? Sometimes Tony writes these reviews under my name!
[P.P.S.] Give Marcelle a good hug for me! Delighted to hear you and Ghislaine are getting along very well. You ought to, you bugger. She struck us all as a gem.

*Sommières, Gard – 30 – France   NOVEMBER THIRD 1975

Dear Henry

As usual your cheerful letter was a welcome tonic. I have just got back rather exhausted from Greece after a scamper around the islands with some farcical and some tiring interludes including a terrific sea passage off Hydra which pinned everyone's ears back. But cinemasts are no fun really. I don't know why this should be but the presence of a camera makes everyone hysterical. Anyway I profited by spending two evenings with the Colossus who as I told you is in bad shape. But his huge physique is still what it was and there is a grave *danger* that he may live to 100 but in a semi paralysis. The notion is intolerable for him and he is roaring and thrashing about like a stranded whale. I think from what he tells me it is that old untreated clap which he had many centuries ago and refused to treat. Once it transforms into arthritis etc it is not really possible to treat except with heat and mud – Palliatives merely. But the REAL problem at the moment is acute prostate which he is too scared to have operated upon. He needs to pee every five minutes. This has ruined his literary life. For example, every night he sat like a king at ZONAR to meet people, to receive the young poets etc. But as he explained the lavatories there are a kilometre away and down two flights of stairs. He can only walk fifty yards . . . So the result is that he lies up in total seclusion. Spends most days loafing in bed or being massaged. Gets up in the evening to eat and drink heartily – still a bit of ouzo and whisky. But nobody ever comes because he discourages them, saying that he is ill, dead, done for, fucked etc. Even those who would love to come and spend a moment with him (he is DYING for company) feel they dare not intrude . . . It's ridiculous. I thought perhaps a telephone call from you might help morale. You know how deeply the Greeks value old friends? It's childish really, but it's also good and naïve and warm. Anyway I have given him a good talking to and left him a beautiful American girl with a tape recorder with instructions to stand no nonsense, to make him start to record his stories on tape. It might make a wonderful book if he could be got back into full voice once more. And there is plenty of sulphur left. <He has started to walk 100 metres every day which is something.> Only one gets panicky and infantile and hopeless when one is ill; and Spatch died last year which did not help. We shall see what happens.

The autumn is calm and lovely now; light rain and cloud but sunny days following. Leaves falling. The vines have turned blood red, the sunsets are fabulous. Yes, Ghislaine has gone to Paris but we are on very good terms and there is nothing earth shaking about the matter. She may come for next week end if she is free.

Well, after all these adventures I needed a little spell alone with some wine and some music; I do an hour of yoga every day and walk in the lonely beautiful garrigues for two hours each afternoon. What more can one need? But I am planning a WINTER in Greece, probably in Rhodes. I was re-seduced by the island again and after October there is nobody there.

every good thing, keep swinging
[unsigned]

*[Pacific Palisades]   Saturday 12/20/75

Tomorrow is the shortest day of the year. Hurrah, that means Spring will be icomen in, eh?

Dear Larry – Forgive me for being so remiss! (By the way, those envelopes you use for your letters are wonderful. I also admire your Epfs letter head. Funny, I tend to use words, phrases on mine. For my next one I would love to use this from the Buddha: "I obtained not the least thing from complete, unexcelled awakening, and it is for this very reason it is called complete, unexcelled awakening.")

Last year on my birthday I invited all the beautiful women I know to banquet with me at the Imperial Gardens (Japanese restaurant where I met & fell in love with Hoki). As a toast I rose and repeated the above. Funny, what? Wisdom and cunt. Together. Hoki sat on my left and on my right a Persian woman (a new one, not Minoo Javan!) who as she removed her fur coat, bent over me languidly and, à la Greta Garbo, said: "Kiss me!" Very theatrical mais, quand-même à quatre-vingt-trois, bien agréable, quoi!

This reminds me to tell you I finished a little book in French which Gallimard was begging me for. I doubt he will publish it – it made only 32 typed pages. I had written it in longhand in a printer's dummy, and practically filled the dummy. Was aghast when I saw it shrink to 32 pages. Anyway, I learned one thing. Never try to write in a second language. You, yes! You could do it superbly, I imagine. Not me. Mme Arnaud and I were praising your French the other day – she was in L.A. four days.

I'm terribly sorry to hear about Ghislaine. You know, not only I but everyone to whom she was introduced adored her. The faults you speak of didn't show, naturally. It always hurts to see love die. I can't imagine that ever happening between Lisa and myself. It's the first time

(I should say "since A.N.") that I feel on solid ground. She grows more wonderful as time goes on. It's about ten years now that we know one another. She is in Taiwan for a few months, doing a TV series (in Chinese) in which she plays the role of Kwan-yin, the Goddess of Mercy. How it fits her, that role! She is, to me at least, very much like a goddess.

By the way, Anaïs had or may still have cancer. I think she is hanging on by her teeth. Very courageous. [. . .]

I seem to be in excellent health. I say "I *seem* to be". (Fred used to use the German word *Schein*tot (seeming death) often.) By the way, I had a letter from him today. He's in the same place, only now it's Turkish. Even Kyrenia has a Turkish name. Mail goes to Turkey first. He sounds pretty depressed and you know he doesn't "depress" easily.

I'm surprised you find Brassaï's book so good. For me it's full of factual errors, full of suppositions, rumors, documents he filched which are largely false or give a false impression. It has the fault of all biographies – it's padded. These fucking biographers are like leeches. They invent, imagine, suppose, "no doubt", etc. ad infinitum. Also, he's too glib and a bit too "snickering". Fred and I used to steer shy of him – he bored us. As photog. OK, excellent. As writer, a swashbuckler. Excuse me, if I seem a little hard on him.

Nobody could do a biography of me that would satisfy me. I am still reading the book, slowly, as my eye (the only one) bothers me. It's tough. I write a while, then go to bed to rest my eye. Then up again. Letters to write. Flocks of letters, flock of women. More women in my life now than when I was a young man of fifty or sixty. Listen, if I survive the eighties I may really live to be a hundred. In a sense I feel better now, despite my hundred and one infirmities, than at any time in my life. I drink only wine at dinner, never smoke. And sleep plenty. Maybe it's a prescription for living to a ripe age (?). I suppose you are spending X'mas in Sommières. Was that young girl you mentioned the one you brought to Paris several times – lives not too far from you? She was quite thrilling. Give her my best, when you see her again. [. . .]

Merry X'mas and all that!
Henry

Dear Henry;

A quick line to hope that all goes well with you – I just got your damning anti Brassaï letter (copy); it will hurt him deeply I think and specially as he considers you his friend. But it was silly to risk this sort of situation in not showing you the book in MSS – the least of things to avoid misunderstandings. Anyway, it's done now and appears to be selling well. As you say, there will be plenty of others. There was an amusing thing about your Légion d'Honneur which I don't know if it was carried extensively in the press or not. I was told it by Temple by telephone. Apparently the league of prostitutes who are taking themselves mighty seriously were very much wounded when the news of your decoration was announced as they felt you had treated them all too lightly in your books and so they sent a large deputation of filles de joie down to picket the Elysées and express their disapproval to Giscard! Can you beat it? The wheel has come full circle with a vengeance . . . The women are on the war path, poor disoriented little amazons. I wish them good luck and better fuck, but it is really straining at the leash of biological good sense. It's a very amusing situation; haven't yet received your book but just the cover and I see a blurb . . . there which should sell you out! Did you ever get Jolan Chang's letter about Taoist immortality? He says that if people mastered the orgasm they could live to an easy 150 with greater joys than one gets by letting fly . . . He will send you his book when it comes out. He has returned to Stockholm where he lives with seven Swedes, he claims to make love ten times a day with full aesthetic pleasure but one orgasm per 100 actions. I must say with Swedes anything is conceivable they are so inert and limp and sexless; I can't judge the seriousness of his ideas but he is some sort of saint and cooks beautifully. He has also helped me master the drink and consequently lose weight. Well! I am alone now, Ghislaine has gone; it is very unpleasant. It is stupid to believe in the couple and enjoy marriage as a state of things which enables me to be happy and work. But this time I picked an impossible proposition; but the charm got me, and she is very nice in an unwifely way;

       all good things
       Larry

*Sommières, Gard – 30 – France   APRIL 28 1977

DEAR HENRY.

I haven't written recently – at least since the death of Anaïs – not because there was no news but Michèle gave me a bad report on your eye fatigue and said that STILL you had not found someone to read aloud for you and handle your mail. ENFIN. I can't understand why. I was saddened by the departure of Anaïs, though I half-expected it for quite a while; her tenacity was extraordinary and her Roman dignity in the face of death. Actually this year has been singled out for a number of deaths – people more or less precious to me for the fact of association in writing ventures, or just that [I] like[d], as friends. Patrick Kinross is one; and now recently Robin Fedden who got mortally sick crossing a high pass into Tibet. He and Paddy Leigh Fermor and Xan Fielding set off to climb the Himalayas. Robin appeared to recover and then relapsed again. You may remember him as a person you very much disliked, but who organised a dinner in your honour in the Plaka at Athens just before your departure from Greece, one night. You hated his stammer and his effete way of talking and have framed a sharply satirical portrait of him in the *Colossus*. By the way both George K. and Seferis were there I think and dear old Theotakas; also Dimaras whose asthma you brought on by describing your attack of hysteria at Phaestos – remember the evening at Maroussi with George and Theodore and Sef? Well, what a long time ago it seems, and how fragile memory is; it is difficult to remember details already. As for Anaïs, I suppose the fur will start flying now as they search for the real girl among the four or five masks she left lying about with false clues attached to them. I have already had a word from her "official biographer" while the egregious M Martin is still in the field with wild and probably true stories. It's rather humiliating to have been her friend and yet not to be able to referee the battle – in truth she was so secretive and pudique that I know nothing about her and could not answer the smallest biographical question. In a sense though it is better that way than my having to sit upon uncomfortable secrets and tell half-truths to prevent Hugo being fussed. As things are the official statue of Anaïs will be carved by the two men who knew her best, Rupert and Hugo – and this is quite as it should be.

I am finishing my huge TREASURY OF GREEK ISLANDS which I hope to deliver before August; then I would like to go to Greece for a rest and to start up LIVIA again, part of which has appeared in the *Malahat Review*; but it needs more pondering and fleshing out. [. . .]

Love
Larry

Anaïs Nin died on 14 January 1977.

*Sommières, Gard – 30 – France   FIRST JUNE 1977

Dear Henry

Sorry I have been off the air recently because I was trying to shape up this blunderbuss book about Greek islands which will I hope fix my next year's expenses, though with the sort of inflation we have here the dream may be an illusion. At any rate it is nearly done and will be delivered this month thus leaving me free to work on *Livia* a bit which I would like to clear before Xmas. But I am going through a restless period – old age I guess – and may yet take my caravan and rush off to Corfu for the rest of the summer. I am supposed to make a BBC film in Egypt end of October. How I wish you could come on the trip with me and see all those places you dreamed so much about. But that will be the last thing I do for television. I am now closing up shop and going to concentrate on turning my quincunx of novels into a masterpiece if I can – what insolence! I am currently reading the latest Anaïs journal with relish as it recounts her visit to Sommières which was wonderful and rather strange. She found me wounded and withdrawn, the old romantic. I was actually exhausted after working so fast on the *Quartet* and was likely to fall asleep at table! There are good things about Paris in this issue which brought back old memories. It seems centuries ago now, and Paris is horrible, full of diesel fumes and frenzy. They come down here the Parisians like convalescents panting for air. London is much less strain, less polluted and noisy. I have found a tiny flat by the sea for a month in order to sort out my *Livia* notes. My long legged Lestoquard the sand-leopard has got gravely ill poor child with cancer just like Anaïs and has retired from the world. I am making do with a rather fine blonde woman who looks like Marlene Dietrich did in *The Blue Angel*. But she is not so young alas. A handsome matrona. What the hell. I think end of this year my yoga is going to quietly become pre-eminent and probably I shall become indifferent to love affairs,

485

which would be a suitable sentiment for an old buffer like me. No complaints either, I have much to look back on with delight and thanks to the 'chemin' created by the yoga and the zen pathway, much to look forward to as well. My brother arrives this week and wants to buy the mazet off me as well as rent the flat above stairs here so that I won't be alone all the time. Ghislaine is here at the moment for a spell and we are expecting our German lodgers for a month on the 25. I suppose you are not in shape for a European journey? With you one never knows, it depends largely on the company you have. I will keep you posted about my movements, just in case

every good thing   More SOON   Larry

*444 ocampo drive – pacific palisades california   June 16, 1977

Dear Larry –

I got your letter of June 1st some days ago, but have just been too lazy to sit down and answer. You make me laugh when you talk of approaching age, the austere life – no more love affairs, etc. I have truly entered the period of old age and do just as little as possible. (Tony has taken Connie's place, as she now has a child – and he does damn well, I must say. A good business head, for one thing.) I am now in love with a 30 year old beauty (mixed blood), who is a movie actress, and somewhat of an athlete. Gets up at 5 AM, runs 5 miles, then horseback for an hour, then teaches ballet to children for the rest of the morning. A French TV crew is coming here end of this month "for just a few minutes", as they always say.

The other day I finished rereading one of Claude Houghton's novels – *Julian Grant Loses His Way*. I don't know if you ever bothered to read any of Houghton's books. Anyway, for 3 days, whilst reading it, I was thoroly intoxicated. He handles the period after death superbly, I think. And that's one of my favorite themes. Val and Twinka are going to Mexico for 5 days tomorrow. I let go of 2 Persian women who claimed to be madly in love with me. The funny thing is that nowadays the women pursue you, even when you are old and decrepit.

I am having eye trouble now, seeing a specialist Sunday – one of my fans. [. . .]

Oh yes, I finished Vol II of *Book of Friends* (five Jews, one Gentile and

486

the last chapter – "My Best Friend" – about my racing wheel!). So I'm dead-alive, as it were. And plagued more than ever by every god-damned son of a bitch who reads me, it seems. Give my best to Ghislaine, won't you?

Cheers again!
Henry

P.S. I must say you are a demon for work! Incredible, all that you get done. I'm just snow-balling. Stick to Zen. Fuck the work. But then you write only masterpieces, so I shouldn't chide you.

HM.

Miller entitled his second *Friends* volume *My Bike & Other Friends* (1978).

*Sommières, Gard – 30 – France   AUGUST SEVENTH 1977

DEAR HENRY.

I have been rather neglectful for a moment – for which you were probably very glad because of your eye and the need to rest it. However: I have just spent a month and a half in a little workman's flat au Grau du Roi, next Aigues Mortes, on the étangs, with no telephone but with all modern conveniences and the sea quite near. A wonderful moment. It enabled me to finish the huge Rainbird book called Treasury of the Greek Islands, which is a romp I am sure you will enjoy, if only because it invokes your name so often. Then I have pushed LIVIA to within 40 pages of the end ... wow, it is getting delicate as the so-called "real" characters are getting infiltrated and changed by the "imagined" characters of their own creation ... O dear, the third volume is going to be hell. I don't know if I can bring off this cats-cradle, roman-gigogne ... The main issues it raises are those to which we know the answers but most people don't; namely is the "ego" a stable entity, and is time something to jump out of or to get strangled in? Anyway we shall see, I hate the roman à thèse, and this won't be one if I can help it.

Apart from all that nothing. I think very gently and in friendly fashion we shall push our divorce into action at the end of this month, though it will take a few months to mature. I have no other candidates for the sceptre and throne. I made a fearful and costly mistake here, though G is all right and full of charm – and will have no nasty deal from me cos I really like her. But what a terrible misjudgement I showed. It is all my fault. She has really nothing with which to reproach herself – I am the fool and the clown. In October I go to London and thence to EGYPT for two months to make a colour film for the BBC like my Greek one, which has kicked the tombstones off books 30 years old and provoked new editions all over Europe. I hope that the EGYPT of Lawrence D will do the same for the flagging quartet and the novels. It will tide me while I complete THE QUINX, this quincunx of books of which *Livia* is NO 2. The Chinese say "The mixture of five colours makes people blind . . ." I am trying for a fruitful synaesthesia . . .

> always thinking of you; am sending on a marvellous fan letter from Australia which should really have been sent to you and not me.

> love from us both
> Larry

Durrell's travel book is titled *The Greek Islands* (1978).

---

*[Chelsea, London]   [postmarked 14 October 1977]

am heading for Egypt Monday to film. Going right up river to Luxor, Abu Simbel etc. Rather dreading the heat and the fatigue. If I shoot a crocodile I'll send you the skin! London full of sunshine and autumn leaves. Hope all is well with you. love.

> Larry

---

*[Alexandria]   [late October? 1977]

Here, as a lucky charm, is a line written on the very desk where Kavafis wrote "The Barbarians" and "The City". Alexandria is still full of luciferian charm and magic.

> love   Larry

My dear, dear Larry –
What a master you are! Salut! Hail! I finished the Sicilian Travel Book
this morning, feeling sad that it had come to an end. I read slowly now,
as you know. Must have spent a week or ten days reading your book.
The slow pace made it all the more exciting. Listen, this isn't another
travel book. This is *it*! One of your very best efforts. I was profoundly
moved throughout; in ecstasy, in fact. You have covered so much
ground – not in mileage alone, but in every realm of art. (The poems
were ancient, I take it, or were they *yours*? Anyway, I enjoyed them
immensely.)

   You know, for days and nights, I have lain in bed, pondering your
words and wondering how to convey my love and admiration. For
with the actual Sicily you have given us such remarkable slices of
antiquity, one wonders *how* you did it. Pure magic.

   Of course, your beloved Greece was there ever as a sort of spiritual
compass. You make us realize *why* this lost ancient world is even now
more alive, in its ruins, than ours ever will be. To apprehend it one has
to have a keen imagination, and that you have, mon cher. You mention
your favorite writers of ancient times – poets, historians, reporters,
dramatists – but I feel you are in the van, one of them, and definitely
not the least. You make this lost world come alive. You appreciate it
thoroly. Bravo! What a life of dedication you have lived! And you are
still going strong, still traveling, still peering over the edge of the
horizon.

   It seemed to me you reached your peak in the chapter on Agrigento.
There you give us a little of everything, a sort of *ratatouille*. But
sublime! And when you discourse of the great figures (men & women)
of the past you fill me with envy. What your head contains is just
unimaginable. Bravissimo!!! You did it! And don't pretend you just
dashed it off.

   Yesterday afternoon I gave my last talk at an Actors' Laboratory run
by a friend of mine. The 4th Saturday of Questions and Answers. I
never thought I was capable of standing before an audience of a hundred or so and keeping them on the qui vive. I had them delirious. They
wanted me to continue doing this once a month, but I refused. And you
know why? For fear it would turn my head!

   Several times I was asked if I would say a few words about you and I responded warmly. When asked about Anaïs, on the other hand, I found to my surprise that I was rather negative.

Well, I wonder just where you are now. I am OK except for the things which ail me. The sight is the hardest to support. I am more than half blind.

I am waiting for a young woman named Minoo Phillips to show up. She was here a few months ago, sent by Maggi Lidchi who wrote that extraordinary book – *Earthman*. Is now running the Aurobindo Ashram in Pondicherry! I think Minoo lived in Auroville, which still lacks sufficient inhabitants.

And this reminds me – will you ever go back one day to visit the place of your birth? What a book you could give us about that! (This book – above – by Maggi Lidchi I most heartily recommend to you. It was published by Gollancz in London about 8 years ago. Try to find a copy!)

Where is Fred now, do you know? Back in England?

Well, enough for the present. Has your divorce gone thru yet? I am in the "throes" of one with Hoki right now. Money, always *money*. Q.E.D.

That woman Martine must have been wonderful. I don't recall your ever mentioning her name before. Who will the next one be, eh?

> Cheers!
> Henry

P.S. You are better than Norman Douglas and his *South Wind*!

The narrator's mentor in *Sicilian Carousel* is a supposedly deceased friend named Martine. It is no mere coincidence that Marie Millington-Drake, mentioned by first name only in *Bitter Lemons*, had moved to Sicily and had often urged Durrell to visit her there, but had died shortly before his trip around the island.

*Sommières, Gard – 30 – France   25 November 1977

DEAR HENRY   YES I am back after a very tiring but I think success-ful trip – from the film point of view for our pictures are stunning; but the reality I had almost forgotten. I had been so often accused of overwriting it that I expected it to be paler than my reflections of it. But . . . the flamboyance and extravagance of Egypt cannot be exaggerated and beside the reality my versions read like washed out and twice sucked jujubes. Of course one must except poor dusty down at heel Alexandria – which however had the grace to put me up one young Justine, just to prove that the old rose tree is not dead. But where the Arabs go they take the dirt and the dust and fanaticism of the desert. Cairo is one horrible sweat of mankind and cars. ALL the world is being devoured by the petrol engine – what can we do? But once upriver the feluccas take over and their grave manoeuvres colour everything. The Nile is not all that broad, and in some places very narrow and calm like a village river. All life flows down it: the artery attached to this narrow line of green and ending in the umbel, the lotus of the Delta. Down below there on the sea all is sophistication, but once upriver gravity sets in; the statues become enormous and grave and they sit pondering in deserted valleys bathed in a gold pharaonic light and framed by the whistling desert with its winds and odours. One walks in time and space as if in a thick solution of something opaque, a jelly. The mind goes numb and people have to repeat questions twice because you don't hear the first time. We picnicked and filmed on little islands which, come the Nile flood, can disappear to reappear in other places. Saw a cobra or two at Kom Ombo – marvellous desolate palace full of engraved lovers in the middle of a mangrove (sugar beet) swamp. Saw only stuffed crocodiles, but they were there upriver. Abu Simbel was too big for comfort, as if it had been drawn on rubber and inflated; the sheer mass impresses but the aesthetic sense is poor. It is institutional art – the kind of thing that Banks commission, as also at Luxor; but the massive weight and volume of stone strikes a chord. But there is a cheat about the whole matter – time confers aesthetic value on things, other-wise how admire a medieval fortress aesthetically when it was purely functional in origin, to repel foes? Two hundred years from now we will be sighing romantically over tanks in museums and the remains of Banks, declared monuments classées . . .

[. . .] Now I must see what I want to do this year. Perhaps sell this unheatable house and buy something smaller? Perhaps return to Greece about which I still dream, tho it seems far and the winters are bitter? I am going to let things roll as they will and see what happens. More soon, Henry, every good thing to you for 78.

love   Larry

[P.S.] Thanks for writing so warmly about the *Carousel*: I was so relieved. It is selling too well to be good! Ghislaine departing sends her love to you!

*Sommières, Gard – 30 – France   [postmarked 3 January 1978]

Well, here's to you, dear Henry, on the sill of a new year 1978 – my goodness how time gathers speed after 40. Old Moschorias in Alexandria, the Patriarchal Secretary (whom I found as sprightly as ever at *84*) cried out "what – *only* sixty-six? How wonderful my dear Durrell to be so young!" And he clapped his hands and chuckled with joy. He, like you, is a "Ripeness is all" man and knows the value of things. I am learning, I suppose, but not fast enough. At any rate voilà! a new year to pass without so many friends who decided to abscond last year – Anaïs was only one of about five fellow writers! Never mind, in a way, because life itself is simply an illusion – blown up like a piece of Venetian glass for a few breaths – and then crack! Of those you may remember in *London* Alan Pringle, John Gawsworth, Robin Fedden, Patrick Kinross died last year. Meanwhile thanks to yoga largely I have finished two books – one on the Greek islands, a big picture book, and then *Livia* with which I am frankly pleased – it presages the form of my quintet of short novels – the Q novels – a Quincunx which is the magic pentacle etc etc! All things being equal, as they say in geometry, the divorce will come through in early February and free me to . . . enter a monastery. It's about all I feel good for. Women have become such a bore, wailing about their freedom and their alimony in the same breath. Never again this stupid adventure. I am however in good heart – the Egyptian trip did me real good, and I ran into a new Justine in Alexandria who set my poor old heartstrings twangling.

I may go down to Athens in March. I hear that K. has been – enfin – quite ill with a heart attack. With his physique it is amazing – psycho-somatic I'm sure. Theodore, at 84 in London, is as chipper as anything: walks for hours every day and writes lots of poetry which he gets actually published by a U.S. University. Just received from Noel Young the Larry Powell novel, which is a delightfully nostalgic little book – good portrait of "our" France which alas no longer exists – Paris smells like New York now, and the people are yellow, exhausted, cadaverique. I can't bear it any more. Happier down here – though one gets lonely for lack of lively company – I know so few people who are not terrible bores! Well, I'm lucky in good health. How is yours, by the bye? Have you solved the reading aloud question? And a secretary to whom you could dictate? I hope now we have a new year on us you will give these matters attention! I hate to bother your eyes with my scrawl, for example, and it gives me a complex about writing too often.

Happy New Year
Larry

Lawrence Clark Powell's novel *The Blue Train* (1977) has as an Afterword a letter of 26 May 1943 from Miller.

*Sommières, Gard – 30 – France   TWELVE MAY 1978

Cher Maître

[. . .] *Livia* is not bad it clears up all the queries in *Monsieur* and opens the way forward for Constance in Love, the next bloody book. But much more congenial for me and more exciting is the fact that Fabers are going to do my *Collected Poems* – a real collected at last. After this I can die happy. "Kiss me Faber and I die happy." My verse has been plunged into shadow by the novels. Perhaps I can give it air. Anyway for better or for worse it means that all my work to date is quite definitively gathered and placed between covers. It's a wonderful finalised feeling. I will turn myself out to grass now and waste a couple of years fooling about the rest of the Avignon quintette "the quinx" as I call it. Without hurry or fuss. I am very mighty old and grey at sixty-six and all systems are slowed down or on the blink? as they say. I still stand on my head a good deal and have mastered every vice except red wine. [. . .] My brother Gerry is buying the mazet and is busy knocking it about. He plans to marry a nice American girl this year and spend the summers there. He is rich and famous as a zoo man now and has very happily shed his last wife who gave him a lot of trouble. My sister Margaret spent a few days at the mazet this spring. She is supposed to be writing a book. If it's autobiographical it should be full of sweet peppers. I have learned to cook extremely well. It is a great relief as I am now quite independent of women? No longer helpless? And it will strengthen my resolve to live alone until if ever I find someone livable . . . [. . .] Shall I give your

493

love to London? Old memories are there – Dylan Thomas and you setting off for the Holborn Empire. Eliot rather startled to find that you didn't use bad language. Dear me, the years roll away so fast.

keep weaving and doing the old one two

> your old friend (chela I guess)
> Larry

*444 ocampo drive – pacific palisades california   May 30, 78

Dear Larry –

Got your good letter the other day. You know, I read both those BBC bulletins about your trip up the Nile and was in ecstasy. Another wonderful voyage and experience for you. (Now you can finish your Hermetic novels!) You know, the book on Sicily was wonderful – not a travelogue but a spiritual experience. My eye specialist just read it and felt the same way. (He's a book collector.)

Well, by me things are not too bad. I won first prize in an International Art Show in Tel Aviv recently. (I who can't draw a horse, dog, cat or mouse!) Got a kick out of it. (No sales, however. Israelis too poor buying weapons and ammunition, I guess.)

Am still going with Brenda Venus, my flame since a year or so ago. A most harmonious relationship. She's a beauty too – with Sicilian, Spanish, French and American Indian blood. Comes from a little town in Mississippi – not far from New Orleans.

I think it's Brenda who keeps me looking so well. Nuff said . . .

I was so happy to read you had fallen in love with Egypt again. Who can describe it better than you! You know, more and more people are going to Greece each year – as a result of our writings about the country. And they write that it is just as we said, despite all the turmoil and confusion.

I am now writing a lengthy chapter about Fred to round out a book about women I did *not* sleep with. Writing about him makes me feel good. Isn't it just like him to wind up in a village called Cerne Abbas (Dorset)? Do you ever write him or think of him? My son Tony may visit him in a few months. He "digs" Joey.

Well, Larry, I trust you are now in the pink of condition and following the Chinese Master's advice. You have so much still to give the world – and it all comes out of you like pure gold (only it's mercury, *what?*) You remind me more and more of one of the arcane Masters. You are *there*, wherever that is.

I wonder if you will go to Alexandria to stay a while.

Oh yes, I suppose you heard of Delteil's death. What a beautiful man he was! I shall never forget him. (Best to Temple.) Assez pour le moment.

Henry

*Sommières, Gard – 30 – France   JUNE FOURTH 1978

DEAR HENRY. WHAT A DELIGHTFUL SURPRISE TO GET YOUR CHEER-FUL LETTER. I have just got back from London where I spent ten days firming up a couple of books which will surface around September. The novel *Livia* is the second in my huge roman gigogne THE QUINX. Things won't however become crystal clear until the next which I hope to begin quite soon. But I must see that you get the first copy of GREEK ISLANDS because of the illustrations. I know they will bring back many an old memory of your travels in Greece – it has always been rather mysterious to me that you never had the wish to poke your nose into it a second time and revive old times. It has changed of course as every-where has, but I think the vibration down the spinal column is still there. Myself I feel rather stale with Provence and would welcome a chance to spend some time in Greece; perhaps this autumn I shall try. France has become so crowded and diesel-dirty and Paris is full of skyscrapers like Manhattan – an inconceivable ugliness is spreading everywhere. One is reminded that this wretched land spawned the worst architect in the world, Corbusier – and his blighted influence hangs on. Paris has become a vast RABBINAT of Jewish intellectuals chewing their own blankets and puffing each other. Between LOVE STORY and Barthes there is hardly a seam showing . . . It's terribly depressing, it's lost its magnetism and is imitating America more and more each day while professing to hate and despise it. Of England . . . there is nothing to say; it's in a mess, and financially bankrupt as well as intellectually. The poor young are trying desperately to find something worth saying or doing, but as in all places where le peuple is on top and has all the pocket money, there is nothing much to do except drug and demonstrate and fiddle money. It is depressing beyond words. O dear, I wish I could feel happier about things; but the future seems charmless

495

really after what we have seen and known. More and more I realise that I have led a charmed life, discovering Greece at twenty-one, knowing Paris and its fauna in 34 35 . . . Then having 15 good years in Provence. It's sinful to complain after that! But of course Provence has now been discovered as a subsidised tourist playground – all the little seaside towns are shot to hell with jerry-building. A hamlet like the Grau for example which has a population of 4000 souls is now surrounded by terrifying dingy skyscrapers cheaply constructed and already half falling apart, which house 60,000 people for four summer months. The winter desolation of these places is quite terrifying! It has taken barely six years to ruin all the towns with huge suburbs, Nîmes, Avignon, Montpellier – the whole lot; immense skyscraper graveyards now surround them. With all this too comes crime, drugs, murders, and people afraid to go out after dark just like Los Angeles downtown. I am coming to the end of my rope now and this big novel will be the last; also THE GREAT NEWS is that my *Collected Poems* comes out next spring! After that I shall turn myself out to grass and shut up. Hurrah. Maybe I will find some little pension in Corfu or Mentone or Orta and dodder myself into the grave . . . Yes, poor Delteil, but he had many happy years behind him in the south and he was tired. No, I haven't heard from Joe at all since they took on Cerne Abbas to mind. But I have redirected some Canadian mail to him and given some dope and his address to a Canadian don who says he is editing the correspondence between *you* and him . . . and then asks if Joey is still alive! I presume you know all about this. I told him yes and forwarded his letter to Joe. What a lucky man you are and what a good life – so long as one has a girl! I wish to hell I had. There is a beautiful young Alexandrian coming to meet me – writing a thesis on me – who might swap a heartbeat with me, but one gets hard to please with age; it may just turn into pleasant target practice. Keep happy, Henry; will

write again soon.
Love   Larry

496

DEAR HENRY; JUST GOT YOUR COPY OF *PEOPLE*. WHAT A CHARMING
NEW GIRL YOU HAVE – TENDER AS A FOAL. I HOPE YOU FEED HER ON
SUGAR LUMPS AND CLEAR SPRING WATER. YOU ARE A LUCKY MAN. I
HEAR FROM MATHIEU THAT YOU ARE BETTER LOOKED AFTER THAN
EVER YOU WERE AND THAT YOU ARE EVEN COAXING SOME WORK
OUT OF YOUR TIRED EYE. GOOD. I MEAN BY THIS THAT I DIDN'T MEAN
YOU TO READ THE GREEK ISLAND BOOK BUT TO LOOK AT THE PRETTY
PICS AND RECALL THAT FARAWAY JOURNEY. DID YOU SEE THAT THE
OLD COLOSSUS DIED RECENTLY IN ATHENS? I SAW THEODORE IN
LONDON LAST WEEK AND OF COURSE HE WAS SAD – THEIR STRANGE
COLLABORATION ENDED ON THE PALAMAS POEMS. (Katsimbalis tele-
phoned every night and they worked for an hour or two on the text
using a scrambler telephone. He simply could not find ways of spending the huge fortune which that house in Platea Syntagmatos brought
him. It is now the First National Bank. How ironic at LAST to be a
millionaire and become ill, bedridden and unable to walk fifty yards.
Just the income from capital brought him in, so he told me, a "Nobel
Prize every year . . . ." But you can't win agin your karma.) Well, we
all dutifully wrote off about *your* Nobel Prize but of course they gave it
to the man whom you have been praising the shit out of for the last two
years . . . It presages ill! I fear that your indiscretions will result in Miss
De Johngh and Normal Mailer being the next. I met a man on the
committee in Hamburg years ago and asked why they had not the
courage to give it to you. He said something like "One must wait for
Miller to become *respectable*." Surely that is now the case, no? I think to
get that sort of prize one must be a sort of UNESCO wire puller and
president of PEN – like Mario Praz (Premier Prix Zagreb, Prix d'Honneur Kiev etc etc).

Yes, I am living alone. IT'S WONDERFUL. I have to answer to
nobody; sometimes a nymph strays into my net – I keep all the twigs
limed, mind you, and then I break stride for a moment. But I have at
last got on top of that terrible hippogriff – "unable to be alone"; in the
course of this whole evolution I have learned to cook for myself and
clean for myself. No sailor can match me now, and with an hour of
yoga at dawn I feel in good physical shape as well. LIVIA has had a good
press and I am shortly going to move into the centre-pin novel of the
group – Constance in Love. It's like trying to sew the fleece round the

infant Heracles – very coarse stitches with a sailmaker's needle. Or a surgical repair on the belly of a whale; pray for me, but to the God of abstract entities, that they should take on flesh and coherence . . . I should soon be getting the book on Anaïs from friend Mathieu. It should be good, he sure knows his stuff. [. . .] What was [Jay Martin's] book like finally? Or didn't you read it? Or perhaps it never came out?

The autumn is big and heavy and the wine is safely in; the days boom like an empty barrel and all the insects fly slowly about, half dead with ripeness. I have just taken a sideswipe at the Italian lakes to refresh my mind – I have written a long essay on Taoism which will I think make you laugh a great deal if you get it read to you. But not for a month or so yet. Otherwise everything is moving steadily forward.

yours in the frenzy and the fun
Larry

Theodore Stephanides and Katsimbalis translated three volumes of Kostes Palamas's verse, *The Twelve Words of the Gipsy* (1974), *A Hundred Voices* (1976) and *The King's Flute* (1982), over the London/Athens telephone lines.

Durrell's book on Taoism, *A Smile in the Mind's Eye* (1980), was inspired in part by his friendship with Jolan Chang.

*[Pacific Palisades, California]   Sunday – 23rd [October 1978]

Dear Larry –

Great to get your letter. No, I wasn't robbed of Prize by Singer – my applications are for 1979. Of course, as you hint, I may not get it – and maybe Norman Mailer will. *Respectable!* What shit! Just like these Swedes of the Academy.

You're right about Jay Martin. He *has* written the book – comes out very soon. I turned him out of house when he came four years ago – told him flatly I detested him, and would not trust him to do a biography of me. Nor anyone else for that matter. Yet he went ahead – telling people I wanted him to do it. The book will say on the title page – "An unauthorized biography". The best I could do. Anyone has the right to do a book, as you know.

Yes, my Brenda is the best ever. No tiffs or arguments. Perfect harmony. It's unbelievable. *And* – she is from our Midi – *Mississippi!* Near New Orleans. Has conquered her southern accent – for film work and theatre.

Also got my divorce a month or so ago from Hoki – easy settlement. Larry, I don't want Nobel Prize for fame or glory. Shit, I have more than enuf of that now. I want it to give to children, as my assets at death won't pay inheritance taxes, I am told. (Of course I don't publicize that. May seem hard to believe but true.) On the other hand, with my lucky Jupiter, who knows? Maybe a huge sum will fall into my hands just before death.

Think a lot about death recently. Am on good terms with her. (Like St. Francis of Assisi, if I may be so bold.)

Just wrote short Preface for book by Fritz Peters (new edition) called *Boyhood with Gurdjieff.* What a guy, G—. Fabulous.

Yes, I didn't read your *Greek Islands* book, as Japanese would say. Can barely see to write this. But did enjoy photos. Edith Sorel of *Le Monde* sent me a book – letter from Castellorizo – very tiny island. You may know it. It's not even on the maps.

Good to hear about living alone. One is really never alone. "At worst with God." (H.M.) My daughter Val lives alone in Big Sur and it has improved her character immensely. But then, as I tell her, she is not really alone – she has the ocean, mountains, sky, stars, plants, trees, flowers, fruits, God knows what all. Much better than being with people. So Larry, enjoy it to the full. Time you made it.

A cunt now and then won't do you any harm. Like a drop of Schnapps!

I paint more than I write. Am about written out now. What matter? *Must* we write forever? Je ne crois pas. Yes, every night I have a different cook – some young gal, usually a fan, not bad. Also now have wonderful super-intelligent secretary. So, all in all, not doing bad. Except for sight. One day I awoke totally blind – but only for seven minutes, an awful sensation. But enuf. Carry on – you have *tomes* still inside you. *You* will undoubtedly receive Nobel Prize one day – even if it's just a lot of horse shit to you. Cheerio!

Henry

*444 ocampo drive – pacifics palisade california   X'mas 1978

Dear Larry –

Tomorrow I'll be 87. Yet all this past year I told everyone I was 87. My memory plays strange tricks on me. At the moment I am seemingly

OK – health wise. (But who knows what germs or viruses lurk beneath the shell unobserved by the medicos.) Primarily, I feel OK, probably because I'm still madly in love – and beloved – with my Brenda Venus. I'll have to send you a special photo of the two of us soon. She has a character and temperament that suits mine wonderfully. She's a scorpio again. But a *different* one this time.

Shit, forgive me for running on about my self. How are *you* these days. Reports have it you're in a better frame of mind. Awfully glad to hear that. Because I just can't see or believe you to be a victim of melancholia. (Though I am what you might call "disgruntled" – with everything.) Yet I would say – *joyous*. Or better – serene. It's strange to be so near death and not to be worried or fearful. Someone recently gave me a line from a poem by Wallace Stevens (an American poet I can't read). It goes like this:

"Death is the mother of Beauty."

Do you make anything out of it? I don't.

By the way, Singer didn't nose me out of Nobel Prize. I am and was trying for the 1979 award. After what you wrote me – "not respectable yet" I doubt I will ever get it. Those blasted Swedes. They ate up *Quiet Days in Clichy*. But – I must tell you some other time how I offended Artur Lundkvist, Swedish poet and translator. <Head of Lit. Committee there!> Good story but no time for it now. (Let me only say this – there are no greater, no more *colossal* bores than most Scandinavians, with Swedes in the lead.)

Joey sent a recent photo other day. Christ, but he looks *young*. But he had the right philosophy, non? He was Zen without knowing it. He too is in his 80's. And *you*, you're just a *spring chicken*!!!

Hallelujah! Don't work too hard. Fool around a bit. Be lazy. Don't worry, Life is – *forever*. (Shades of Marie Corelli.) Larry, *if possible*, try to read her *The Life Everlasting*. I can promise you, it's not shit!

P.S. Some one sent me a few records of Brel – who died recently. He was one of your favorites, wasn't he? Eyesight still *bad*.

Love and kisses!!!
Henry

[Printed at foot of page:] "I PISS ON IT ALL FROM A CONSIDERABLE HEIGHT." L. F. Céline

Dear Henry; what a marvellous New Year present to get a letter from
you – and a gay one! No, you have plenty of time for the Nobel as I had
a deck of cards laid down for you by a soothsayer I consulted recently.
She guessed your real age right and said you would live until 93 or 94 at
your present rate! I didn't know Lundkvist was on the Committee – he
is a Com and received the Prix Lenin; it explains why I lost it that year
to Steinbeck with his "preoccupation with the fate of the people" . . .
What the hell. You will certainly get it and quite soon.

I am writing this gazing out over Provence under deep snow, the
vines covered up to their throats, with more snow falling but in
brilliant sunshine. It is both really cold and really hot, and this afternoon I am going to take a long and lonely walk along the white
garrigues. All animal life now prints itself in the snow – can't escape –
so you can follow it like a movie – footsteps of fieldmice and ferrets, of
badgers and the slither of foxprints; or the large warm 'form' where a
partridge has snuggled!

I spent Xmas in Jersey at my brother's zoo; lots of snow of course but
the sound-track was pure tropical, which was surrealist. Lions roaring
in the night and the sudden screech of wild birds at dawn or the *hugh
hugh hugh* of the chimps. It is a strange island really, claustrophobic in
some ways. But I elected to spend the New Year alone at the Coupole
in the old bar seats where we so often sat long years ago, drinking a
good champagne, glass after glass. Ghislaine came and had a drink –
indeed got so tipsy that she lost her papers and money and cheques in a
taxi afterwards, just like you did once. [. . .] I was glad to replace her
with that little demon Buttons who turned up for a New Year TRINC
and stayed the night with me finally, in my eternal little Room 13 at the
Royal – so much impregnated with memories which date back to 1937.
My youthful catapult Arab Canadian has been hauled back by the hair
to her musician's arms – with some regrets I think. She promises a
further escape next month. But these girls from the new world are all
brutalised and for the most part anaesthetic because of the vulgarity and
brutality of their men. They are so pathetically happy with some simple
tenderness and consideration for the importance of their feminine role
that they melt like ice creams and simply won't get out of bed, not to
mention out of town . . . What a filthy brutal dirty culture you have in
North America – with of course its obverse *sentimentality*. Ugh! Flavour

for flavour – French for American – the difference in soul (I am thinking of a night with Buttons compared to a night with X) is really extraordinary. I couldn't live with such robots I think.

But the old Paris quartier is much the same, the old eccentrics the same; we had twenty minutes of rather drunken Dixieland jazz – a very old tradition – by the American artists of the quartier, dressed in Max Sennet fashion with bowler hats and striped jerseys; some of the music was a bit off – hard to play tubas and slide trombones (in negro jazz the tuba is called a grunt-iron) if you are awash with champagne. However, the old tradition was affectionately applauded. Then midnight with its riots of actors in masks and drunks and ruined ladies riding on the backs of waiters, Yugoslavs being expelled for the wrong reasons and sleeping cinéastes . . .

No need to go on – you know the scene as well as I do! Then a lonely little walk to the Closerie where I was picked up by a couple of poets who made my head reel with all their abstractions. I had left Buttons on her doorstep as she had had an attack of morality, and I was too tired to bother with "Les Sentiments"; so I went home and was just in bed when the door burst open, and in the bar of light there she was; she came in without a word and shut the door and said, "Life is too short to act entirely from principles. Il faut réfléchir." Then she tumbled into bed with her clothes on and undressed in this awkward fashion like an oyster out of season. I said "How long have we known each other?" and like a gunshot she replied "dix ans". In the morning when I woke she had gone to look after her child.

In fact Paris, though grubbier and more expensive, has not changed at all and if you arrived one afternoon in a balloon you would find everything in place to supply a meal starting with oysters and ending with a prime Roquefort. I don't know about the night life – the Jockey is still there but seems slow. I am so lucky at the moment in love that I positively welcome week ends like this one – quite alone for a change. In fact this year has been a bad one – the death of many friends has made a few big holes in the décor which I feel. There is now NOBODY in Athens, and ditto for the Cairo of my war years. But meanwhile if I can get this big intractable metaphor of a novel done it will (if it works) stabilise and justify the new series – the QUINX as I call it, and as it will later call itself, unless this one is a fuck-up and I abandon the series. What matter? Next year my *Collected Poems* come out – this marks a halt in things.

I am at the moment under fire from a twenty year old concert pianist from Angers – this promises well, except for the difference in ages! She came all the way down and bust into the house with a load of questions and was so happy to be treated right and listened to with patience that I now can do no wrong and we are meeting in Paris this month with quite unpredictable results. Ouf!

I did not know that CAPRA is doing the Jay Martin book nor that Larry Powell initiated and supports it; was I wrong then about Martin and his furtive candid-camera methods? We shall see. I shall read it this week end with the old rambling Brassaï. Yes, send me a nice pic of Brenda Venus, Mathieu says she is an angel of a soft footed stag of a godsend . . . just what you need in fact! I gather that PARIS MATCH has done a thing about you and her. Several people rang me up and told me and have agreed to keep a copy for me. But I'd prefer a decent one if you have time.

> every good thing Henry
> warmest embraces for the coming year
> Larry

*SOMMIERES   TEN JANUARY 1979

Dear Henry; here is another line to tire your eye since you won't get things read aloud to you! The JAY MARTIN book arrived in the same mail as your last letter and I have just finished it. It is rather tame and pedestrian but I think there is nothing set down in malice and on the whole it's thorough and accurate. Of course the absolute impossibility of writing up *your own* writing shines throughout . . . The trouble with the book it is clear is that you have done it all yourself and better . . . Or perhaps I am the wrong reader for I can flesh out the scenes and the people from memory – I can add the colour which is missing. But even then the fellow is no writer – I mean Lamb's TALES FROM SHAKE-SPEARE does not pretend to be Shakespeare, but it is perfectly valid Lamb and will remain so. But this . . . The tone in the last chapter suggests that it was written with the idea of rushing it out immediately after your death – to cash in in Academe! Have you noticed? There would only be one sentence missing, namely the date of your death! It's the sort of consideration which would spark a Mailer . . . This poor bugger will have to wait ten years now with his book gathering dust!

Serve him right! There is only one small point which might cause him ennui – mention it to Noel [Young] when next you talk. It is the statement that BRASSAI peddled porny pictures in which you posed in the nude . . . There is a reference in *Tropic* which gives some reason to think this was so but you did not name the photographer precisely. Anyway, what the hell? It's the kind of small thing that people pick on and he is all shot up over his contretemps with you. Brassaï I mean.

I have just come back bleeding like a sucking pig from having a couple of deep cysts carved out of my back; curious, I went to the same surgeon as the one who last operated on Claude ten years ago, and the whole thing took place on the same table à froid – I mean with only a local. It was eerie to listen to the chat of the surgeon as he went to work slowly and patiently like a gardener. And the noise of the scissors and the scalpel, snip snip; he was talking about the transplanting of roses, snip by snip, so to speak, so that finally I had the illusion that he was tailoring a rather unruly rose tree which was growing out of my back and setting it to rights. I remembered too that Claude wanted to drown the mazet in roses and oleander and indeed she went all over France for her cuttings. The amazing thing is that though untended these ten years they are still active and flower each year; and now that my brother is buying the place he intends to revive them on a big scale. They were planted in pure stony land. Well, snip snip, I thought of your life and Martin's book and Claude's roses and Eve's laughter, and your last visit to the stony old garrigue where we drank so much . . . It's amazing to have participated in the creation of a legend. It will please you to know that the new Cacharel scent named after Anaïs ('Anais-anais') is a great success and when last I had the luck to take a youngling to bed in Paris that was what she smelt of. I lay there in the dark smelling it and thinking and saying never a word.

all good things to you and your antelope.
LARRY

*444 ocampo drive – pacific palisades california 3/29/79

Dear Larry –
Delayed writing you because of poor eye sight. Still dim. However, I reread your last two letters and was inspired to answer instanter. Am very glad you are at last "friends" with Ghislaine. I always thought

highly of her. As for the "cunts" – amazed that you are still keen about them, still testing your strength or your manhood, is it? (When will you begin looking for LOVE?) It's the only thing. Sounds trite, but true. Sorry to hear about your operation for cysts. Nasty things, cysts. But interspersed with roses from the old manse it sounded beautiful. My pet ou *bête noir* is the mail. Can't accommodate to it. Ruins the day, so many idiots to answer. Get less and less work done.

How's this? I am (slowly) rereading one of my favorite books 80 years ago. Called *The Heart of a Boy* by Edmondo de Amicis, an Italian. Did you ever read it, by chance? So wonderful. What a different world that was in our childhood. I never adapt to the "modern" age. Seems like nothing but crass ignorance, violence, wars and revolutions. Have to stop, Larry.

My Brenda thinks you are something very special – and you are! Is the liver improving? You're too young to be old yet!

Henry

P.S. Fred has moved to Wells, did he tell you? He seems fit as a fiddle.

*444 OCAMPO DRIVE, PACIFIC PALISADES,
CALIFORNIA,   June 9, 1979

My dear, dear Larry –
What a surprise to learn you went to Vienna – and detested it. To me it resembled Brooklyn somewhat, worn, sad, decrepit, past glories. You mention Joey, I was just reading proof on my *Joey* book, the 3rd of the *Friends* series. Proofs all messed up. Waiting for a second run. It's a queer book with ten stories about women-in-my-life tacked on, together with an Epilogue about Anaïs and her unfair treatment of Joey – telling him all the latest about her – how she herself gave permission to three women friends to tell the truth about her life, revamp the diaries, etc. etc. What a scandal is brewing! Ho ho! You'll enjoy this part, I'm sure. I call her somewhere the greatest liar and at the same time the most truthful person . . . .

Larry, you're all fouled up on my arterial condition. About 7 or 8 years ago I had the whole artery – from neck to foot on my right side – removed and an artificial one installed. This lasted only a month or so and then another operation to remove *it*. So, I am completely without an artery on my right side. I can hobble about with a cane but usually use a wheel chair which I push around. The worst is a burning sensation in my little toe of right foot. On my left side I have a hip dislocation, which impedes walking. But you should see me with my "antelope" Brenda. Quite a different picture. If you can bring yourself to believe it, she loves me. I feel certain and secure – in bliss – nary a bitter word between us. Always like a visit to Paradise – and it's going on 3 years now. I *look* good and am full of spirit and still talk people's heads off. (How right you are about the dolts and the duds. There is no "conversation" here – you call it "talk". Whatever it is it is sadly lacking.) My worst affliction is my poor sight. When I was on the operating table (16 hours) the optic nerve in my right eye died. I am also totally deaf in left ear and wear a hearing aid in the right one.

But all these things – afflictions or whatever – are as nothing when love exists. Larry, it's just too wonderful to believe. [. . .]

Whew! This is a lot for me to write all in one breath. Glad your spirit is brightening. Spring is here. Can Summer be far away? Death to visitors, fans, reporters! Cheerio!

Henry

[P.S.] Did you ever hear of Mohammed Mrabet from Tangier? A young writer – *illiterate!*

---

*444 ocampo drive – pacific palisades california   Aug. 9, 1979

Dear Larry –

[. . .] I have been given a book called *The Colossus of One* by a Kenneth Dick, I believe, published in English in Holland. It is divided into 3 chapters – one on me, one on Anaïs and one on June. I only had a glance at *one* chapter, on June. Purportedly an interview, in which he compares what I wrote with what she *says*. Scurrilous and full of lies. (She even beats Anaïs at it.)

I finished correcting 2nd proofs on the *Joey* book. Wait till you read my Epilogue – on Anaïs and Joey's book about her. His falling into unredeemable disfavor. You more lucky. I suppose you've heard that her Diaries are coming out soon in their *original* form. And she has given Evelyn Hinz permission to write her biography. Telling the whole truth about her. I know one of her late-in-life friends, Barbara

Kraft, a wonderful friend to us both. And I am seeing Evelyn Hinz next Wednesday to do a video tape interview for the anniversary of Lawrence's death 50 years ago. My discarded book on him has become the king-pin! *Sic*!

Glad you got the photo of Brenda and me, plus the colored litho which I did the original of in 1955! Have two more – same period.

Three days ago I made four WC's – which I think are the best I ever did. And I am so blind! Strange, but my favorite painter now is Shiko Munakata, dead a couple of years. He is wilder, more exciting than any European painter I know of throughout the ages. And he was so near-sighted his nose almost touched the paper when he worked.

Still, I'd rather be less able and see better. It's a tribulation. A good friend of mine has just discovered the beauty, depth and magic of my great favorite, J.C. Powys. Remember his *A Glastonbury Romance*? Or did you miss it?

Am now slowly reading a biography of Marie Corelli, my female favorite. Resemblances to Anaïs again. But Corelli more pure, more strong, even if a favorite of Queen Victoria, Shaw and Oscar Wilde among others. Enuf, eh what?

> Blessings on you, m'lad!
> Henry

P.S. Got this off while waiting for my masseuse. She's working on my feet to improve eyesight! Hope *you* are in fine fettle these days. Bert [Mathieu] & his Geri due here midnight for 3 days. On way to Greece!

The full title of Kenneth Dick's book is *Henry Miller: A Colossus of One* (1967).

---

*GARD 30250 SOMMIERES FRANCE   14 december 1979

Dear Henry – A line to wish you all good things for your birthday at Noël. Not sure where I'll be but will send you a cable to 'marquer le coup'. From your side a prayer for the well being of my 'pivotal' novel *Constance* would be in order. I am just starting the 'feedback', i.e. feeding back the 'imaginary' characters into the furnace of the actuality, the action. It is rather an alchemical stunt and I feel like a physicist cautiously playing with some atomic process. Up to now the feedback idea has been purely temporal as a notion; but I am trying to feed back second-degree fictions into field inhabited by first-degree ones. Will the result be over-contradiction and chaos – ('reality over-determined'!)? Or will they marry and settle down happily ever after like nouns and verbs in the same poem? I'm curious to see. It felt that if somebody didn't do *something* the novel was going to be about as modern as morris-dancing to flageolet & drum soon! If the bloody thing works however it will give a new flavour to fictional reality – with luck.

I'm waiting for my daughter –

> love to you all
> Larry

*GARD 30250   FRIDAY BEFORE NEW YEAR 1980
SOMMIERES FRANCE   [i.e. 28 December 1979]

Dear Henry;

I have just got back from a week in Paris – change of plans, propose to see the new year in here, ouf! I went up actually to meet a girl, a new girl, a young doctor whom I collected during the summer music festival here, and thought interesting because she is thymus-dominated and has great haunted eyes like wet eyelashes; well anyway I also had to oversee the slowcoach translator of the novel and Claudine [Brelet] the firebrand translator of *Acte*. This is to explain that I did not initiate but participated in the 'tartine' which appeared in LE MATIN, a copy of which is on its way to you with all the affection that Paris can bestow for your birthday, Xmas day, which I spent virtuously abed with my private doctor. I could get extremely fond of this girl if she were free for fondness, and less a slave to black psychiatry (the throwing of intellectual custard pies). Never mind, love is blind, kindly pat on the behind. But I am really quite smitten in an aged way. <Nicole! She beautiful and timid and resolute – only 31. Fully fledged MD.>

When *Le Matin* contacted me I agreed to help with the 'tartine', though I am not responsible for sending you to bed with Brendan Behan . . . The thought that your antelope was in town made everyone sit up and hope for an interview with her about your current plans and general state of health etc. I told them to try Hoffman in order to try and find Brenda. I thought it would amuse her to be the guest of a paper, taken all over Paris, interviewed at Xmas etc. Alas they could not find her – so had to be content with B: the egregious and myself; they did not even flush Belmont. I later met Michonze for a drink at the

Dôme and he showed me his new drawing, which is for crying out with effective dulness. He sits all day in Bourbourg *copying* the cartoons of Leonardo and Goya if you please – but this means translating these lightning flashes of insight into sloppy scribble, flaccid and insipid copies . . . One should never copy unless one can improve! But he is a nice old he-bear now, with three studios and a way of life which is of unredeemable boredom.

And Paris now smells not of piss and garlic but of diesel fumes. It is now an entrepôt for business meetings like the Waldorf; but no one lives there. Everyone inhabits the remote countryside and spends one day or two a week in Paris.

I am sending a short book to bed which will amuse you; about Tibet and France. I thought Joe was great fun, the book I mean; I wish you could have brought the portrait up to date. He is the original coq en paté.

> I am having such trouble with this novel; it is already written in my head, but just won't move on paper. <Constipation.>
> every good thing
> LARRY

P.S. Now they say that 1980 is your Nobel year! And damn it all, what about mine? My *Collected Poems* are coming this spring – after that I can turn myself out to grass happily!

Tartine: tiresome article.

Bourbourg, i.e., the Beaubourg, popular name for the Georges Pompidou Centre of Art and Culture.

Durrell was finishing *A Smile in the Mind's Eye* (1980) – French title: *Le Sourire du Tao* (1982) at – this time.

---

* 444 ocampo drive – pacific palisades california   Jan. 9th 1980

Dear Larry –

The enclosed was returned to me today. What a fool mistake of mine! That's due to too much mail to handle.

Listen, Brenda arrived yesterday looking spic and span and fit as a fiddle. Wants you to know how grateful she is (me too) for all the help you gave her. She had a good meeting with Truffaut whom she seems to revere. I met him once here in L.A. in an Italian restaurant with a wonderful French-English actress (forget her name now). He struck me as a rather stuffy fellow and not a conversationalist – rather glum. The person I want Brenda to meet is Lina Wertmuller – her Giancarlo is just made for my Auguste role, I believe.

That article you wrote about me in *Le Matin* – sorry, my dear Larry, but you got my message to you a bit twisted. Shit! You must know I am never going to become a "*pasteur*". I merely wanted to point out (probably I'm all wrong) that you are always in trouble when in love – and who isn't? But I suspect it's the failure to realize *true love* that is the reason. Love means giving and taking – not chiding, criticizing, slapping around. (Does this strike a bell?) For 3 years or more now – and for first time in a long life – I have had an absolutely harmonious relationship – deep love – with Brenda. Forgive me for putting it to you this way. I'm sure you can take it.

Apparently Brenda was interviewed by editor of *Le Matin* and also by Edith Sorel, a correspondent-reporter for *Le Monde* who has been here to interview me 3 or 4 times. We hit it off very well. (She is a Sabra, by the way, yet more French than the French. Maybe you know her?)

Anyway, I want to repeat – Great thanks for all the trouble Brenda put you to. She came nigh visiting you in Sommières. How she got along as well as she did with no or very little French amazes me.

By the way, Jacqueline Langmann was a guest of mine recently for about two weeks. Made a wonderful impression on everyone she met. Fell in love with Brenda and predicted great things for her in next couple of years. On verra.

Well, Larry m'lad, I hope this year 1980 will be a good, rich, happy year for you. Forgive my remarks about your writing, please. There are days I can't even read *Alice in Wonderland*.

But I have read, or reread, *The Heart of a Boy* by Edmondo de Amicis. After 80 years found it to be a marvelous work – for adults as well as boys. Also (to your horror, I imagine) have reread Loti's *Disenchanted* and wept at end. *And* a biography of my great favorite – kick me, if you wish – Marie Corelli. Bet you never even touched a book of hers. If you ever try, try first her *Sorrows of Satan*. And take a pill afterwards.

Alors, assez pour aujourd'hui. Love from both of us. Nous ne *vivons* pas ensemble, dommage. Mais j'étais very glad to read that elle vous écrit des lettres merveilleuses. I take it *Joey* didn't mean very much to you.

Henry

The 'Auguste role' is the clown-protagonist's in Miller's *Smile at the Foot of the Ladder* (1948).

*444 ocampo drive –
pacific palisades california   5.8.80 [postmarked 15 May 1980]

Dear Larry,
I'm having my friend Bill Pickerill take this down for me.

Georges Hoffman and his camera crew were here for a few days despite the fact that I'm half gaga. What they did was to interview me with my dying breath, as it were, and it damn near was though I'm still alive and able to give this message. I think you said something that they may call you to be the voice over. Well, that would be in French or English. O.K. with me. Most tender regards interim.

Hold up yet another twenty years!

Cheerio
Henry.

P.S. Larry old boy. This is a reply to an earlier letter which must have escaped me. It's appropriate as I am truly dying now – or at least I think I am. Yes, Anaïs more than partly wrote the preface – she did the whole job. With the cutting I don't think she had very much to do. It was Fred, there, who helped. I can't tell you how much this last letter impresses me by its spirit, its tenacity. My friend Bill Pickerill who is taking this by dictation was just saying how lucky you are to be going back to Greece; and I was saying how unlucky you are with the rental situation. Even with that you are still lucky – they can't shut off the light. I had a rather interesting prologue to death, live on T.V., arranged by Georges Hoffman. Oddly enough it came out very well. Now I can't reproduce much of it. I have just put in a full two or three hours' correspondence in this way by the kindness of my good friend, Bill Pickerill. He thinks enormously of you, and though not a littérateur he is very highly interested in books, but more particularly in painting. He may find a way of showing you the last watercolors I did which he photographed in color. I hope so – they're the works of a dying man.

That's about it, Larry. All the best.
Henry

This is the last letter Durrell was to receive from Miller, who died on 7 June 1980.

511

Acknowledgements

The editor thanks Lawrence Durrell and Tony Miller for their patient cooperation in the preparation of this volume. I appreciate also the assistance of Henry Miller's daughters, Barbara Sylvas Miller and Valentin Lepska Miller. I am most grateful to Alan G. Thomas for his enormous service in the preservation of much of this correspondence and for making available letters from Henry Miller now in his keeping, and to Shirley Thomas for her charming hospitality and advice during the editing process. The help given by Robert Hatch, Gerry Tirrell and Renate Zeiher of the Crocker National Bank, Los Angeles, in locating the later correspondence of Lawrence Durrell has been indispensable. Lilace Hatayama of the University Research Library at the University of California, Los Angeles, has given me superb professional assistance in my examination of the Miller Collection and of uncatalogued Miller documents stored in the Manuscripts Division. Brooke Whiting, now retired from the UCLA library staff, drew upon his immense knowledge of Durrell and Miller bibliography to guide me to rare material. I am deeply indebted to David V. Koch and Shelley Cox of the Morris Library at Southern Illinois University at Carbondale for placing at my disposal the unparalleled Durrell Collection in their keeping. To all those mentioned above go my profound thanks for their help in locating and editing the primary texts.

I appreciate the help of Curtis Brown Ltd of London, principally that of Lawrence Durrell's agent, Anthea Morton-Saner. Many friends of Durrell and Miller have assisted me, and among them I particularly wish to thank Catherine Aldington, Ludo Chardenon, Jean Fanchette, Claude Kiefer, Simone Perier, Heinz Ledig Rowohlt, F.-J. Temple and Fiddle Viracola. A grant of sabbatical leave by the State University of New York Maritime College and the generous support of Joel Jay

Belson, Chairman of the Humanities Department, have been invaluable in facilitating my research. The staff of the Luce Library at Maritime College has been most helpful, notably Cheryl Bloom, Alvina Mary Kalsh, John Jong Jin Lee, Filomena J. Magavero, Kathleen Pyzynski, Tereze Rancans and Anita Zutis. Among the friends and colleagues whose assistance has been especially valuable are Billie and Bill Cadwallader, Christine de Lailhacar, Beatrice Moore and Robert B. Sennish. I have been greatly aided in the preparation of this volume by the fine text and careful annotations of George Wickes, editor of the 1963 edition of the early part of this correspondence. The very real and essential support given me by Susan S. MacNiven includes all the commonplaces of editors' wives – indexing, proofreading – and extends beyond recounting. Finally, I wish to thank the kind people, too many to name individually, who have helped me with this text.

Ian S. MacNiven
Bronx, New York, 1988

Letters and verse drafts by Lawrence Durrell and reprinted or published here for the first time with the permission of the author and of Curtis Brown Ltd are Copyright © 1988 by Lawrence Durrell.

Letters and a verse draft by Henry Miller and reprinted or published here for the first time with the permission of Agence Georges Hoffman are Copyright © 1988 by Barbara Sylvas Miller, Tony Miller and Valentin Lepska Miller.

This material appears here with the kind permission of the Research Library of the University of California, Los Angeles, and of Special Collections at Morris Library, Southern Illinois University at Carbondale, owners of a major portion of the correspondence.

Portions of this text appeared previously in the following publications, herein gratefully acknowledged:

Art and Outrage (Putnam, 1959; Dutton, 1961)

Delta (Christmas 1938)

Lawrence Durrell/Henry Miller: A Private Correspondence (Faber and Faber and Dutton, 1963)

Mademoiselle (January 1963)

Twentieth Century Literature (Fall 1987)

Index

516

522

Made in the USA
Monee, IL
22 January 2023

25890970R00329